Sport Psychology

Concepts and Applications

sixth edition

Richard H. Cox
University of Missouri–Columbia

١٧٩

Boston   Burr Ridge, IL   Dubuque, IA   Madison, WI   New York
San Francisco   St. Louis   Bangkok   Bogotá   Caracas   Kuala Lumpur
Lisbon   London   Madrid   Mexico City   Milan   Montreal   New Delhi
Santiago   Seoul   Singapore   Sydney   Taipei   Toronto

The McGraw-Hill Companies

 Higher Education

SPORT PSYCHOLOGY: CONCEPTS AND APPLICATIONS
Published by McGraw-Hill, a business unit of The McGraw-Hill Companies, Inc., 1221 Avenue of the Americas, New York,
NY, 10020. Copyright © 2007, 2002, 1998, 1994, 1990, 1985 by The McGraw-Hill Companies, Inc. All rights reserved. No part of
this publication may be reproduced or distributed in any form or by any means, or stored in a database or retrieval system, without
the prior written consent of The McGraw-Hill Companies, Inc., including, but not limited to, in any network or other electronic
storage or transmission, or broadcast for distance learning.

Some ancillaries, including electronic and print components, may not be available to customers outside the United States.

This book is printed on acid-free paper.

1 2 3 4 5 6 7 8 9 0 FGR/FGR 0 9 8 7 6

ISBN-13: 978-0-07-110642-9
ISBN-10:　　0-07-110642-1

www.mhhe.com

Contents

In recent years, interest in applied sport and exercise psychology has soared. *Sport Psychology: Concepts and Applications* is written for students who are interested in learning about sport and exercise psychology as an academic discipline *and* in using that knowledge in applied settings. The book is designed primarily for undergraduate students, but instructors can readily adapt the book as a foundation text for graduate students by supplementing the text with current articles from research journals.

The focus of the book is reflected both in the subtitle and in the "Concept and Application" boxes that appear throughout the chapters. The concepts presented are all supported by scientific research, and the danger of applying unsupported concepts is emphasized. Where research has led to inconsistent or contradictory conclusions, concepts and applications have been derived based on the preponderance of evidence.

As in the fifth edition, the title *Sport Psychology* has been retained even though many chapters are devoted to issues that can be considered topics in exercise psychology and in the social psychology of sport issues. For much of the world, *sport psychology* is an umbrella term that includes these areas. Similarly, the terms *sport psychology* and *sport psychologist* are used throughout the text as shortened versions of *sport and exercise psychology* and *sport and exercise psychologist*. This usage reflects the view that *sport psychology* is a broad and readily recognized term used by educators and psychologists worldwide.

New to the Sixth Edition

For this edition of *Sport Psychology,* the organization of the book has been revised and streamlined for easier use in a 15-week semester. In response to requests from reviewers, chapters with related material have been merged and the total number of chapters has been reduced from 27 to 19. Topics have been brought together to create more logical groupings and more seamless transitions.

In addition to the reorganization, content has been updated throughout with the latest research findings; over four hundred new references are cited in this edition. There is also new practical content, including new or expanded information on such topics as job placement, gender and sexual orientation, leadership and sporting news, parental involvement in sports, burnout, drug abuse, and pain management. Some of the important changes and additions to the text are as follows:

Part 1: Understanding Sport Psychology

Part 1 includes three chapters. Chapter 1, "Foundations of Sport Psychology," focuses on introductory material, such as history, professional issues, and multicultural issues; new material has been added on job placement and on issues of gender and sexual orientation. Chapter 2, "Psychology of the Athlete," includes material previously contained in chapters 10 and 11. This change allows for a smooth transition from athlete disposition to athlete response to environmental changes. New coverage includes information on the effects of personality and mood on performance, emotional intelligence, and mental toughness. Chapter 3, "Leadership and Communication in Sport," contains material covered in chapter 23 in the previous edition, with additional information on communication. Some material on leadership in the context of youth sports (chapter 7 in the previous edition) has also been merged into this chapter. Material on coaching efficacy has been added, and leadership issues related to current events in sports have been updated.

Part 2: Motivation in Sport and Exercise

Chapter 4, "Causal Attribution in Sport," contains new material on the Causal Dimensions Scale–II (CDSII). Chapter 5, "Self-Confidence and Intrinsic Motivation," includes material from chapters 2, 5, and 7 in the previous edition. The revision allows for a clearer presentation of how athletes develop intrinsic motivation and how it is affected by external motivation. New material on Vealey's Multidimensional Model of Sport-Confidence has been added, and new coverage of parental concerns and involvement has been included in the section on youth sports. Chapter 6, "Goal Perspective Theory" (previously chapter 3), contains three new figures and a new section on goal orientation and moral functioning (sportspersonship). The importance of the mastery motivational climates has been highlighted.

Part 3: Effects of Arousal and Anxiety on Performance

Part 3 includes two chapters that combine material from four chapters in the previous edition. Chapter 7, "Neurophysiology of Arousal and Attention" (previously chapters 8 and 9), treats these two mental and physiological phenomena in a unified way, showing how they are related in a manner that supports concept building. Chapter 8, "Anxiety, Arousal, and Stress Relationships" (previously chapters 12 and 13), focuses on the effects of stress and anxiety on performance. Alternatives to inverted-U theory are brought together in chapter 8, and information on Flow has been moved to this chapter. New figures bring clarity to topics associated with attentional style, the zone of optimal functioning, and directional concerns in the measurement of anxiety.

Part 4: Cognitive and Behavioral Interventions

Part 4 includes four chapters. Chapter 9, "Coping and Intervention Strategies in Sport," brings together material from the chapters on coping, relaxation, and arousal energizing strategies (chapters

14, 15, and 16 in the previous edition). Self-talk is now included in this chapter, and a new figure on the Interactional Model of the Stress Process has been added. Chapter 10, "Goal Setting in Sport" (formerly chapter 6), has been updated with new research and new figures. Chapter 11, "Imagery and Hypnosis in Sport," combines chapters 17 and 18 and includes updated material. Chapter 12, "Psychological Skills Training" (formerly chapter 19), has been updated with new material on the characteristics of the successful elite athlete, the sport psychology consultant, and generalization of psychological skills training to other nonsport applications.

Part 5: Social Psychology of Sport

Three chapters are included in part 5. Chapter 13, "Aggression and Violence in Sport" (chapter 20 in the previous edition); chapter 14, "Audience and Self-Presentation Effects in Sport" (chapter 21 in the previous edition); and chapter 15, "Team Cohesion in Sport" (chapter 22 in the previous edition), all have been updated with new material. A new section on self-presentation and self-attention has been added to chapter 14 as an alternative explanation for the effects of audience on athletic performance.

Part 6: Psychobiology of Sport and Exercise

The order of the four chapters in part 6 remains unchanged. Chapter 16, "Exercise Psychology" (formerly chapter 24), includes a section on exercise self-schemata theory as an additional theory of exercise behavior. The Physical Self-Description Questionnaire is introduced in this chapter, and self-presentation is reintroduced as a way of conceptualizing social physique anxiety. Chapter 17, "Burnout in Athletes" (formerly chapter 25), contains a new figure showing how coping resources and social support interact with overtraining stress to cause athlete burnout, as well as new text sections on coach burnout and athletic career termination. Chapter 18, "The Psychology of Athletic

Injuries" (formerly chapter 26), includes new coverage of pain catastrophizing as a way of understanding pain management by injured athletes. Chapter 19, "Drug Abuse in Sport and Exercise" (formerly chapter 27), includes new material and a figure on the Drugs in Sport Deterrence Model.

Using the New Edition of *Sport Psychology* in Your Class

The smaller number of chapters in this edition is a function of planned reorganization rather than any reduced coverage of content. Because a variety of concepts are included in different topic areas, the 19 chapters vary in length. Instructors may want to adjust assignments accordingly in adapting the text to a 15-week semester or a 10-week quarter. Through creative management, the text can readily be used in a variety of class configurations.

Pedagogical Aids

Several pedagogical aids are included in the text for the benefit of students, instructors, and coaches. Most significantly, many sports-related examples are included to illustrate chapter topics. In addition, "Concept and Application" boxes appear throughout the chapters, following the introduction of major themes and topics. As noted earlier, the concepts are derived from pertinent scientific literature, and the applications are designed to assist practitioners in making practical use of research findings in their day-to-day teaching and coaching activities.

Also included in each chapter are a list of key terms, a chapter summary, critical thought questions, and a glossary of terms. The key terms are listed at the beginning of the chapter to focus students' attention on the important ideas they will encounter in the chapter; terms appear in boldface type when they are introduced and are defined in the chapter-end glossary.

Supplements

Available with *Sport Psychology* are on Online Learning Center and an Instructor's Resource CD. The student side of the Online Learning Center includes a recommended reading list for each chapter. The instructor side of the Online Learning Center includes such instructor resources as sample course syllabi and PowerPoint slide presentations for each chapter. The Instructor's Resource CD includes all these materials, as well as a Test Bank containing multiple-choice and short-answer questions.

Organizations Associated with Sport Psychology

For additional information on topics in sport and exercise psychology, instructors may wish to consult any of the following Web sites.

Sport Psychology Organizations

- Association for the Advancement of Applied Sport Psychology (AAASP) www.aaasponline. org/asp/health_and_exercise/index.php
- Division 47 of the American Psychological Association (APA) www.psyc.unt.edu/ apadiv47/
- North American Society for the Psychology of Sport and Physical Activity (NASPSPA) www.naspspa.org/
- Canadian Society for Psychomotor Learning and Sport Psychology (SCAPPS) www. scapps.org/info.html

National Organizations with a Sport Psychology Sub-focus

- American Alliance for Health, Physical Education, Recreation and Dance (AAHPERD) www.aahperd.org/
- American College of Sports Medicine (ACSM) www.acsm.org/index.asp

Coach Training Web Sites

- American Sport Education Program
  www.asep.com/

- Coaching Association of Canada
  www.coach.ca/

- Program for Athletic Coaches' Education
  (PACE) http://ed-web3.educ.msu.edu/
  ysi/SpotlightWin97/pace.html

- Coach Effectiveness Training (CET)
  www.wardepub.com/smithsmoll.html

I am indebted to a host of people who have contributed to the completion of this work. First of all, I am grateful to my wife, Linda, and my four children, Candice, Clayton, Ryan, and David, for their patience and forbearance.

Second, I am indebted to the reviewers of both this and the previous edition, who went the extra mile to ensure that the work would be a success:

Terry Brown
Faulkner University

Peggy A. De Cooke
Purchase College, SUNY

M.L. De Furia
Syracuse University

Tami Eggleston
McKendree College

David Furst
San Jose State University

Andy Gillentine
University of Miami

Eric D. Hall
Elon University

Brad Hatfield
University of Maryland

Marion Johnson
Colorado State University

Paul Rhoads
Williams Baptist College

Jay Shaw
Eastern Montana College

Third, I want to thank my colleagues, who were always willing to share ideas and resources.

Finally, I am grateful to the reserve librarians at the University of Missouri–Columbia, who were more than happy to help me locate foreign and other references not in the library.

Richard H. Cox

Understanding Sport Psychology

Part 1 of this text is composed of three distinct chapters. The first chapter, "Foundations of Sport Psychology," provides a framework for understanding, among other things, what sport psychology is; where it came from (a brief history); what professional organizations and journals are involved; how one becomes a sport psychologist; the role of multicultural education; and gender issues that impact the lives of athletes, coaches, and everyone interested in the sport and exercise culture. The second chapter, "Psychology of the Athlete," focuses on the individual characteristics of the athlete. Here, we will be concerned about not only the personality of the athlete, but also ways in which the athlete responds to environmental stimuli, and how these psychological responses affect athletic performance. Chapter 3, Leadership and Communication in Sport," focuses upon the coach and other team leaders in terms of how the leader interacts with athletes and/or teammates. In this regard, effective communication is embedded within effective leadership, as an integral part of that leadership. The following historical event provides an example of why sport is so exciting, and why sport psychologists are interested in understanding everything they can about the personality and psychology of athletes at all levels, from youth sport to professional sport.

In the 1999 National League Professional Baseball Championship Series, the Atlanta Braves were pitted against the New York Mets. Atlanta won the first two games in Atlanta and won the third game in New York. The Mets won game four in New York. The Braves led the series 3–1 before game number five at New York's Shea Stadium. Game number five was to become one of the most exciting baseball games ever played in Major League Baseball history. As described by Bamberger (1999), "On Sunday night at half past nine on the East Coast, time stopped." The New York Mets were at bat and the Atlanta Braves were in the field. The lead-off hitter was Shawon Dunston, with his team trailing 2 to 3 in the bottom of the fifteenth inning.

Dunston fouled off pitch after pitch and finally stroked a single to center field. Dunston stole second and later walked home to tie the score at 3 to 3. Now it was Robin Ventura's turn to bat. Bases were loaded and Ventura was facing rookie right-hander Kevin McGlinchy. Ventura was 1 for 18 thus far in the series. With two strikes against him, he made the swing that a ballplayer dreams about. He hit a two-strike pitch into the rain and through the night over the right center field wall. It was a grand slam! After reaching first base Robin was mobbed by players and fans, so he never made it to home plate—or second base, for that matter. The official score was 4–3, and Ventura was credited with a single to end the longest postseason game ever, five hours and forty-five minutes. During the game 126 batters came to the plate, but only seven scored (officially). ∞

CHAPTER 1

Foundations of Sport Psychology

KEY TERMS

Accreditation
Acculturation
Clinical/counseling sport
  psychologist
Cultural compatibility model
Cultural competence
Diversity
Educational sport psychologist
Enculturation
Feminism
Gay
Griffith, Coleman
Heterosexist behavior
Heterosexual
Homophobia
Homophobic behavior
Homosexual
Inclusiveness
Lesbian
Martens, Rainer
Multicultural training
Ogilvie, Bruce
Race thinking
Racist thinking
Research sport psychologist
Sexism
Sexual orientation
Sport Psychology Registry
Triplett, Norman
Universalistic model
USOC
White privilege

Hardly a subject associated with sport is more intriguing than the subject of sport psychology. Perhaps this is so because it is a subject coaches, athletes, and fans feel comfortable discussing. The average spectator does not usually venture to offer a biomechanical explanation for an athlete's achievement of a near-superhuman feat, yet the same spectator is often willing to give a psychological explanation (e.g., mental toughness, motivation, strength of character). Every four years, sport fans from all over North America become transfixed by the spectacle of the Summer or Winter Olympic Games. Throughout the television broadcasts of these games, viewers are exposed to frequent references to athletes who train with the aid of professional sport psychologists. Many times the sport psychologist will be identified as the camera zooms in on the individual athlete. It is also becoming somewhat common for television crews to identify professional golfers who employ the services of sport psychologists. Somewhat recently, a sport psychologist was given credit for the Indianapolis Colts' decision to select Peyton Manning over Ryan Leaf in the 1998 professional football draft (Carey, 1999). Manning went on to stardom in Indianapolis, while Leaf continued to struggle for several years with the San Diego Chargers. Over the years, selected professional baseball teams have acquired the services of applied sport psychologists. At the present time there are many young people seeking to earn a living providing sport psychology services to professional, Olympic, or even collegiate sports teams. Hopefully, these young people will acquire the knowledge, experience, and certification/licensure that will allow them to realize their dreams.

One wonders, however, who will provide sport psychology services to the coaches and players of millions of youth and high school sports teams that do not have the financial resources to employ a full- or even part-time sport psychologist. The goal of providing sport psychology services to every coach and athlete is unrealistic. A better goal might be to train coaches and athletes to serve as their own sport psychology consultants and to train one another. As advocated by Martin, Thomson, and McKnight (1998), the ultimate goal of a sport psychology consultant should be to teach clients to teach or counsel themselves.

Think of the marvelous example of coaching that was provided by UCLA's legendary John Wooden, and contrast that with the intimidation style of former Indiana and current Texas Tech coach Bob Knight. Either John Wooden was a great applied sport psychologist, or he had someone on his staff who was. Knight, on the other hand, has been an example of a coach in desperate need of a sport psychologist to help him relate in a positive way with his athletes and fellow coaches. Bill Walton said it best:

> With Coach Wooden, an Indiana native, life was always fun, always upbeat, always positive, always about the team, always about the greatness of the game. Sadly you don't get any sense of that from Knight. There's no joy. Even worse, there's no happiness on the faces of his players (Walton, 2000, p. 96).

As a student of sport psychology, you may not go on to become a consultant to a professional team, but hopefully you will be able to apply what you have learned from this book and to share it with others.

This text offers the prospective coach and scholar the opportunity to learn correct concepts and applications of sport psychology, even though sport psychology is not a perfect science. We have a great deal to learn about mental preparation for sport competition. We will always have a need for the scientist who is interested in discovering new knowledge. As you read this text, keep an open mind and become interested in sport psychology as a science.

In the paragraphs that follow, a number of peripheral issues will be discussed that provide background information for the study of sport and exercise psychology. Specifically, this chapter provides a definition of sport psychology; sketches a brief history of sport psychology in North America, including development of professional organizations; discusses the issue of certification; reviews various roles of the sport psychologist; discusses ethics associated with applied sport psychology; broaches the issue of accreditation; and concludes with a discussion of multicultural issues that relate to race and gender.

Sport and Exercise Psychology Defined

Sport psychology is a science in which the principles of psychology are applied in a sport or exercise setting. These principles are often applied to enhance performance. However, the true sport psychologist is interested in much more than performance enhancement and sees sport as a vehicle for human enrichment. A win-at-all-costs attitude is inconsistent with the goals and aspirations of the best sport psychologist. The sport psychologist is interested in helping every sport participant reach his or her potential as an athlete. If helping a young athlete develop self-control and confidence results in superior athletic performance, this is good. However, it is also possible that a quality sport experience can enhance an athlete's intrinsic motivation without the athlete's necessarily winning. Taken as a whole, sport psychology is an exciting subject dedicated to the enhancement of both athletic performance and the social-psychological aspects of human enrichment.

Stated more simply, sport and exercise psychology is the study of the effect of psychological and emotional factors on sport and exercise performance, and the effect of sport and exercise involvement on psychological and emotional factors. This is an easy-to-understand definition that shows clearly the interactive relationship between sport and exercise involvement and psychological and emotional factors. It is upon this basic construct that this book is based. Athletic performance is influenced by psychological and emotional factors that can be fine-tuned and learned. Conversely, involvement in sport and exercise activities can have a positive effect upon an individual's psychological and emotional makeup.

History of Sport Psychology in North America

Sport psychology as a distinct field of study is extremely young and is evolving. Perhaps the first clear historical example of research being conducted in the area of sport psychology was reported by **Norman Triplett** in 1897. Drawing upon field observations and secondary data, Triplett analyzed the performance of cyclists under conditions of social facilitation. He concluded from this "milestone" research that the presence of other competitors was capable of facilitating better cycling performance (Davis, Huss, & Becker, 1995).

While Triplett provided an example of one of the earliest recorded sport psychology research investigations, he was not the first person to systematically carry out sport psychology research over an extended period of time. This distinction is attributed to **Coleman Griffith,** often referred to as the "father of sport psychology in North America" (Gould & Pick, 1995). Griffith is credited with establishing the first sport psychology laboratory at the University of Illinois in 1925. Griffith, a psychologist, was selected by George Huff, head of the Department of Physical Education at the University of Illinois, to develop this new laboratory based on Huff's vision. Dr. Griffith's laboratory was devoted to solving psychological and physiological problems associated with sport and athletic performance. Over an extended period of time, Griffith studied the nature of psychomotor skills, motor learning, and the relationship between personality variables and physical performance. Thus, the historical trend for the next sixty years was established in this early event. Physical Education, a cross-disciplinary entity, would provide the academic home for the application of psychology to sport and athletics.

Along with developing the first sport psychology laboratory at the University of Illinois, Griffith was also the first psychologist hired by a professional sports team in the United States. In 1938, P. K. Wrigley, owner of the Chicago Cubs, hired him to be the team sport psychologist and to improve performance. Resisted by the team manager, Charlie Grimm, Griffith did not enjoy great success with the Chicago Cubs, but his scientific approach to the psychology of coaching has emerged as the current model for sport psychologists working with professional teams (Green, 2003).

While Coleman Griffith was credited with the development of the first sport psychology research laboratory, others would follow his lead. Following World War II, such notables as Franklin M. Henry at the University of California, John Lawther at Pennsylvania State University, and Arthur Slater-Hammel at Indiana University pioneered graduate-level courses and developed research laboratories of their own.

Many women were also instrumental in the early development of sport psychology in North America. Such notables as Dorothy Harris, Eleanor Metheny, Camille Brown, Celeste Ulrich, and Aileen Lockhart could all be considered the "mothers of sport psychology," with Dorothy Harris also being the "mother of applied sport psychology" (Gill, 1995; Granito, 2002; Oglesby, 2001). Women such as Diane Gill, Tara Scanlan, Jean Williams, Bonnie Berger, and Carole Oglesby not only made significant contributions to the development of modern sport psychology, but remain to this day leaders in the field (Gill, 1995).

Dan Landers (1995) referred to the period of time from 1950 to 1980 as the "formative years" for sport psychology. During this time, sport psychology began to emerge as a discipline somewhat distinct from exercise physiology and motor learning. This is especially true of "applied" sport psychology. Prior to the emergence of applied sport psychology, most research related to sport psychology was conducted within a laboratory setting and was referred to as motor learning research.

During the formative years, a number of important research initiatives and textbooks were published. These early sporadic initiatives paved the way for the emergence of sport psychology as an academic subdiscipline within physical education and psychology. Some of the early textbooks included *Psychology of Coaching,* by John D. Lawther (1951); *Problem Athletes and How to Handle Them,* by Bruce Ogilvie and Tom Tutko (1966); *Motor Learning and Human Performance,* by Robert Singer (1968); *Psychology of Motor Learning,* by Joseph B. Oxendine (1968); *Psychology and the Superior Athlete,* by Miroslaw Vanek and Bryant Cratty (1970); *Social Psychology and Physical Activity,* by Rainer Martens (1975); and *Social Psychology of Sport,* by Albert Carron (1980).

As mentioned earlier, the book titled *Problem Athletes and How to Handle Them* was authored in 1966 by Thomas Tutko and Bruce Ogilvie. This book and the authors' personality inventory for athletes—the Athletic Motivation Inventory (AMI)—caught on with coaches and athletes. Notwithstanding the popularity of the book and the inventory with the athletic community, Tutko and Ogilvie's work was not well received by the sport psychology community of scholars at the time. For reasons to be discussed in detail in the chapter on personality, the AMI and the book on how to handle problem athletes were deemed by the scientific community to be overly simplistic and not based on good science. Interestingly, Bruce Ogilvie's work as an applied sport psychologist is much better received by the scientific community today than it was in the 1960s. Because of his pioneering work with personality and applied sport psychology, **Bruce Ogilvie** is referred to as the father of applied sport psychology in North America.

If Coleman Griffith is the father of sport psychology in North America and Bruce Ogilvie the father of applied sport psychology, then the title "father of modern sport psychology" should go to **Rainer Martens,** former professor of sport psychology at the University of Illinois and founder of Human Kinetics Publishers. In modern times,

Baseball is an excellent game in which to observe sport psychology in action. Courtesy Ball State University Sports Information.

Rainer Martens has done more for the development of sport psychology in North America than any other single individual. This assessment is based upon his research initiatives while a professor at Illinois, and on the fact that the students that he mentored are now leaders in the field throughout the world.

Development of Professional Organizations

A number of professional sport psychology organizations have evolved since the 1960s. In 1965 the *International Society of Sport Psychology* (ISSP) was formed. Organized in Rome, the purpose of ISSP is to promote and disseminate information about the practice of sport psychology throughout the world. In North America a small group of sport psychologists from Canada and the

United States met in Dallas, Texas, to discuss the feasibility of forming a professional organization distinct from the American Alliance for Health, Physical Education, Recreation, and Dance (AAHPERD). The efforts of this small group came to fruition in 1966 when it was recognized by ISSP. The name of this new organization was the *North American Society for the Psychology of Sport and Physical Activity* (NASPSPA). The first annual meeting of NASPSPA was held prior to the 1967 AAHPER National Convention in Las Vegas. Since that time, NASPSPA has evolved into an influential academic society focusing on sport psychology in the broadest sense. NASPSPA provides a forum for researchers in the areas of sport psychology, sport sociology, motor learning, motor control, and motor development to meet and exchange ideas and research. Shortly after the emergence of NASPSPA in the United States, another significant professional organization came into existence in Canada in 1969. This organization was named the *Canadian Society for Psychomotor Learning and Sport Psychology* (CSPLSP). CSPLSP was originally organized under the auspices of the Canadian Association for Health, Physical Education, and Recreation (CAHPER), but became an independent society in 1977. Somewhat concurrent with the emergence of the Canadian society, the *Sports Psychology Academy* (SPA) emerged in the United States as one of six academies within the National Association for Sport and Physical Education (NASPE). NASPE is an association within AAHPERD. In order to better address the interests and needs of sport psychologists interested in applying the principles of psychology to sport and exercise, the *Association for the Advancement of Applied Sport Psychology* (AAASP) was formed in the fall of

1985 (Silva, 1989). AAASP emerged in the 1990s as the dominant association for the advancement of applied sport psychology as well as research in North America, and perhaps in the world.

In addition to the specialized organizations mentioned above, two significant North American–based associations created interest areas dedicated to sport psychology within their organizations. These include the American Psychological Association (APA) with its Division 47 (formed in 1986), and the American College of Sports Medicine (ACSM). Paralleling the emergence of professional sport psychology organizations are journals that provide an outlet and forum for research generated by members of these organizations.

As a summary, table 1.1 lists professional organizations partially or completely dedicated to sport and exercise psychology. This table also indicates the year each organization was formed. Table 1.2 provides an incomplete list of research

TABLE 1.1 | Summary of Major Professional Societies That Are Dedicated or Partially Dedicated to the Discipline/Profession of Sport Psychology

Genesis	Name of Association or Society
1954	American College of Sports Medicine (ACSM)
1965	International Society of Sport Psychology (ISSP)
1967	North American Society for the Psychology of Sport and Physical Activity (NASPSPA)
1977	Canadian Society for Psychomotor Learning and Sport Psychology (CSPLSP)
1977	Sport Psychology Academy (SPA) (Division within AAHPERD)
1985	Association for the Advancement of Applied Sport Psychology (AAASP)
1986	Division 47 of the American Psychological Association (APA)

TABLE 1.2 | Incomplete List of Journals Completely or Partially Dedicated to the Advancement/Application of Knowledge in Sport and Exercise Psychology

Journal Name	Affiliation
International Journal of Sport Psychology (IJSP)	ISSP
Journal of Applied Sport Psychology (JASP)	AAASP
Journal of Sport Behavior (JSB)	None
Journal of Sport & Exercise Psychology (JS&EP)	NASPSPA
Medicine and Science in Sports and Exercise (MSSE)	ACSM
Research Quarterly for Exercise and Sport (RQES)	AAHPERD
The Sport Psychologist (TSP)	None

journals that are partially or completely dedicated to sport and exercise psychology.

Issue of Certification

Historically, sport psychology emerged as a discipline from physical education. In recent years, however, a significant interest in the discipline has developed among individuals prepared in psychology and counseling. This has raised the issue among practicing sport psychologists as to which people are qualified to call themselves "sport psychologists" and to provide services to athletes.

Some have gone so far as to argue that only licensed psychologists should be allowed to call themselves sport psychologists, and suggest that the appropriate title for a nonlicensed "sport psychologist" would be "mental training consultant." Most agree, however, that even licensed psychologists should have significant academic training in the exercise and sport sciences before practicing applied sport psychology (Taylor, 1994).

A partial solution to the issue of professionalization of sport psychology was presented by the **United States Olympic Committee (USOC)** (1983) and clarified by May (1986). The USOC developed the **Sport Psychology Registry** to identify three categories in which a person can demonstrate competence. These categories correspond to three types of sport psychologists: the clinical/counseling sport psychologist, the educational sport psychologist, and the research sport psychologist. The purpose of the Sport Psychology Registry was to identify individuals in the area of sport psychology who could work with specific national teams within the Olympic movement. The registry was not meant to be a licensing or authorizing committee.

The AAASP took the issue of who is qualified to deliver sport psychology services one step further. It adopted a certification document outlining the process an individual must take to be given the title "Certified Consultant, Association for the Advancement of Applied Sport Psychology." As one of the certification criteria, the applicant is required to hold a doctorate in an area related to sport psychology (e.g., psychology, sport science, or physical education). In addition, numerous specific courses and experiences are identified. While this certification process adopted by the AAASP may not be the final one, it is a good beginning, since it recognizes that an individual needs specialized training in psychology and physical education (sport and exercise science) to be certified as a practicing sport psychologist.

It should be mentioned, however, that not all sport psychologists are in agreement about the merits of the AAASP certification process. Anshel (1993), for example, argued that the AAASP certification process is discriminatory and counterproductive. He argues that there is scant evidence that certified consultants make better consultants than noncertified consultants. Nevertheless, it appears that the AAASP certification initiative is a move in the right direction. It requires both licensed and unlicensed psychologists to meet minimum standards in order to be certified by AAASP.

The issue of what sport psychology is and who is qualified to practice applied sport psychology was addressed by the European Federation of Sport Psychology (FEPSAC, 1996). This body took the position that the term *sport psychology* was properly used in a broad sense, and included all qualified persons, independent of their specific academic fields. It did, however, acknowledge that different countries and different states within the U.S. may have restrictions on the use of the term *psychologist*.

What Does the Sport Psychologist Do?

In an effort to promote the virtues of sport psychology to coaches, athletes, and prospective students, many thoughtful professionals have suggested contributions that sport psychologists can make to sport. In the paragraphs that follow, different roles and functions of the sport psychologist are outlined. Generally, these roles and functions describe the sport psychologist in the categories of clinician, educator, and researcher.

The Clinical/Counseling Sport Psychologist

The clinical/counseling sport psychologist is a person trained in clinical or counseling psychology and may be a licensed psychologist. Generally, the clinical/counseling sport psychologist also has a deep interest in and understanding of the athletic experience. Training may also include coursework and experience in sport psychology from programs in physical education. Clinical/counseling sport psychologists are individuals who are prepared to deal with emotional and personality disorder problems that affect some athletes. The athletic experience can be very stressful to some athletes, and can negatively affect their performance or their ability to function as healthy human beings. In these cases, sport psychologists trained in counseling psychology or clinical psychology are needed.

The Educational Sport Psychologist

Most sport psychologists who received their academic training through departments of physical education (i.e., sport and exercise science) consider themselves to be educational sport psychologists. These individuals have mastered the knowledge base of sport psychology and serve as practitioners. They use the medium of education to teach correct principles of sport and exercise psychology to athletes and coaches. In general, their mission and role is to help athletes develop psychological skills for performance enhancement. They also help athletes, young and old, to enjoy sport and use it as a vehicle for improving their quality of life.

The Research Sport Psychologist

For sport and exercise psychology to be a recognized and respected science, the knowledge base must continue to grow. It is the scientist and scholar who serves this important role. For the practicing sport psychologist to enjoy professional credibility, there must exist a credible scientific body of knowledge.

Given the different roles that sport psychologists can play, it is of interest to note the kinds of jobs that recent graduates are placed in and their job satisfaction. For the years 1994 to 1999, a recent study reported that 73 percent of individuals who graduated with a doctoral degree in a sport psychology–related field found employment in academia. Almost half of the students with a master degree found jobs in sport psychology–related fields. A large portion of the remainder found jobs related to their academic training. Students who graduated during the indicated timeframe also reported improved job satisfaction and success in achieving career goals, as compared to those who graduated between the years 1989 and 1994 (Anderson, Williams, Aldridge & Taylor, 1997; Williams & Scherzer, 2003).

Ethics in Sport Psychology

While the ethical application of sport psychology principles is discussed throughout this text, and specifically in the chapter on psychological skills training, it is important to emphasize the topic. In recent years it has become clear that theories and techniques derived from the study of sport psychology can provide the winning edge for athletes and athletic teams. In this text, you will learn many of the psychological theories and techniques that can make you a more effective teacher and/or coach. This does not mean, however, that you will be qualified to provide psychological services to coaches and athletes. It takes much more than one course in sport psychology to become a consulting sport psychologist. This is true despite the fact that at the present time there are limited licensing procedures in sport psychology; almost anyone can claim to be a sport psychologist. However, without certain minimal qualifications this would be unethical. When one considers the dangers involved in the inappropriate application of psychological theory, personality assessment, and intervention strategies, it is no wonder that many professionals are concerned.

The practice of sport psychology, whether by a coach or by a licensed psychologist, involves two diverse components. The first has to do with teaching, while the second is clinical in nature.

For example, the sport psychologist uses teaching principles to help an athlete learn how to use imagery and/or relaxation techniques effectively. A well-trained and informed coach or teacher should be able to give such service. However, when the sport psychologist is called upon to provide clinical services such as crisis counseling, psychotherapy, or psychological testing, it is important that that person be specifically trained and licensed. To do otherwise would be unethical and irresponsible.

Accreditation Issues in Sport Psychology

The issue of who is qualified to deliver sport psychology services has been addressed to some degree by AAASP with its certification program and by the USOC with its classification of three different kinds of sports psychologists. The issue still remains, however, as to who is qualified to prepare or train sport and exercise psychologists. Silva, Conroy, and Zizzi (1999) have argued that AAASP should provide leadership for a movement to accredit university sport psychology programs. They argue that **accreditation** is the only way to ensure quality and consistency of academic training. Students graduating from accredited programs would be prepared to become certified AAASP consultants. Arguments in favor of accreditation are bolstered by research that shows that of 79 programs listed in the fifth edition of the *Directory of Graduate Programs in Applied Sport Psychology* (see the AAASP Web site), only 27 percent offer coursework in all of the 12 different content areas mandated by AAASP for certification (Van Raalte et al., 2000).

In response to arguments in favor of accreditation, Hale and Dannish (1999) respond that the issue of accreditation is premature and naive relative to the complex issues involved. They point out that unless an academic program is viewed as "critical" to the mission of a university, the university will be reluctant to pay the cost of accreditation.

Second, they point out that accreditation would certainly raise the issue of who is qualified to call himself or herself a "psychologist." The APA and departments of psychology would resist accreditation of programs that produce sport psychologists who are not licensable as psychologists. Third, the debate over accreditation standards within, AAASP would be costly, from both a monetary and an emotional perspective. Finally, they argue that the impact of accreditation upon university programs would be to reduce academic freedom and program flexibility. While it is true that most programs in sport psychology continue to be in departments of physical education (e.g., kinesiology, exercise and sport science, etc.), the trend is moving slowly toward having departments of psychology, and particularly counseling psychology, provide training in sport psychology. It would be difficult for faculty from such diverse program areas to agree upon accreditation standards that they could take back and sell to their university deans and department chairs.

Multicultural Issues That Relate to Race

In this section we talk first about why race is an issue in sport psychology, and then about different multicultural training models that can be developed. In a subsequent section we will address multicultural issues related to gender, but in this section the focus is upon racial issues. In the broad sense, multicultural issues go well beyond race to include the concepts of **diversity** and **inclusiveness** (Sue & Sue, 1999). Diversity implies that people from diverse cultural background are represented in any group; inclusiveness implies that individuals are not excluded from a group because of their race, ethnic background, gender, sexual orientation, or religion. Sport psychology clients include individuals of different races, different cultures, different sexual orientations, and they have different ways of thinking about sport and the world we live in.

The Issue of Race in Applied Sport Psychology

An important goal of applied sport psychology should be to attract into the field more individuals from different races. This is important because the vast majority of sport psychologists are Caucasians from a European background, while many college and professional athletes are African American blacks (Kontos & Breland-Noble, 2002). This not to say, however, that a white sport psychologist cannot provide excellent services to black or non-white athletes. Until more African Americans and members of other ethnic groups enter the discipline of sport psychology, those who are Caucasian must focus upon understanding and accepting cultural differences. Butryn (2002) addresses this difficult issue by reporting on a life history interview with a white male sport psychologist consultant and a male African American athlete, in which they discussed racial awareness and the notion of **white privilege** in North America, and particularly in the United States. Butryn argues that it is not enough to be "color blind." The white sport psychologist must also come to recognize the fact that he is privileged simply by having been born white. Butryn insists, "White people carry with them a host of unearned, largely unconscious privileges, which are conferred upon them simply because they were born with a white skin" (2002, p. 318). He goes on: ". . . white people may not recognize that the way whiteness is represented in the consciousness of many black people are [is] profoundly negative and intimately connected with the systematic and destructive oppression of African-Americans by white people throughout history" (p. 318).

What is the white sport psychologist to do? One cannot stop being white, but one can come to recognize why resentment and distrust may exist between white consultant and black athlete. Furthermore, it is important to recognize the difference between **race thinking,** which is not racist, and **racist thinking,** which is. For a white sport psychologist to work with a black athlete, she must engage in race thinking. A failure to engage in race thinking is illustrated in a study reported by Ram, Stareck, and Johnson (2004). In this study, the researchers reviewed 982 articles published in *The Sport Psychologist, Journal of Applied Sport Psychology,* and the *Journal of Sport & Exercise Psychology* from 1987 to 2000 inclusive, relative to reference to race/ethnicity or sexual orientation. Results of the study showed that only 20 percent made reference in any way to race/ethnicity, while only 2 percent made substantive reference to sexual orientation. The results were even worse relative to sexual orientation, where only 12 articles out of 982 made any reference at all to sexual orientation issues.

In a thoughtful article, Kontos and Breland-Noble (2002) discuss the meaning of **cultural competence** and the ways a person becomes culturally competent. Cultural competence means that the coach or sport psychologist understands his client's racial identity, his own racial identity, and the role that race and cultural ethnicity play in the athlete/consultant relationship. The distinction between acculturation and enculturation is made. An individual is encultured, or experiences **enculturation,** simply by being born and raised in a particular group or culture. Conversely, **acculturation** implies learning to look at the world through a multicultural lens. It involves assimilation, truly understanding the culture of other ethnic groups, developing a world view of multiculturalism, and focusing upon the individual and not the group.

Multicultural Training in Sport Psychology

An accreditation issue that must be addressed, either formally or informally, is the issue of **multicultural training.** Graduates of sport psychology programs should be adequately trained in issues that relate to culture and race. According to Martens, Mobley, and Zizzi (2000), multicultural counseling is defined as counseling that takes place among individuals from different cultural/racial backgrounds.

Sports competition brings out the best in athletes, regardless of racial background. Courtesy University of Missouri–Columbia Sports Information.

Multicultural training of sport psychology students should be provided in four domains. First, students should experience a heightened awareness of and sensitivity to cultural groups different from their own. Second, they should gain knowledge about people who belong to cultures different from their own. Third, students should learn helping and intervention skills through the process of role playing and simulated interaction. Finally, each prospective graduate should experience a supervised practicum to gain hands-on experience working with members of a different culture or race.

According to census reports, approximately 29 percent of all people in the United States belong to racial and/or ethnic minorities. Yet, in some National Collegiate Athletic Association sports, the proportion of racial minorities is much greater than 29 percent. For example, in men's basketball, it is estimated to be as high as 68 percent; in football, 57 percent; and in women's basketball, 43 percent. Contrast this to the fact that most sport psychologists are white, and you see a clear need for multicultural training. Martens et al. identified two basic strategies for addressing the cultural disparity between athletes and applied sport psychologists. The **universalistic model** endorses the concept of teaching prospective sport psychologists cultural sensitivity and how to be culturally competent. In the absence of more minority sport psychologists, this is the model that must be aggressively promoted. The **cultural compatibility model** proposes to address multicultural issues by matching the background of the counseling sport psychologist with that of the athlete. Given an increase in the number of minority sport psychologists, a combination of the two models would seem to be most appropriate. If sport psychologists are truly sensitive and educated relative to racial/cultural issues, it should not matter what race or culture the athlete and psychologist belong to.

A number of different multicultural training designs may be implemented. Four different designs are listed in table 1.3. They range from the least preferred design (workshop) to the most preferred (integrated model). Where there is no formal course or concentration for teaching multicultural issues, then workshops may be organized and provided. While a workshop is better than no training at all, this method of delivery does not assure that participants gain a desired level of

CONCEPT It is the responsibility of the coach and team leaders to foster multiculturalism in sport teams with respect to accepting diversity and being inclusive when it comes to individuals from different racial and ethnic backgrounds.

APPLICATION Acculturation must take place among the athletes and between athletes and coaches. This means that team members learn to look at the world through a multicultural lens. They do this by understanding themselves first, and then taking the time to learn and understand the cultures that other teammates belong to.

TABLE 1.3 | Multicultural Training Designs in Sport Psychology

Design	Design Characteristics
1. Workshop Model	One- or two-day workshops are provided as needed.
2. Separate Course Model	Free-standing semester-long course on multicultural issues is provided.
3. Area of Concentration	Several free-standing courses and experiences are provided as part of a program concentration.
4. Integrated Model	Multicultural training is provided through all of the above, as well as integrated within each course in the curriculum.

knowledge and sensitivity to issues. A separate semester-long course dedicated to multicultural issues would be much more likely to successfully enhance cultural sensitivity. An even better approach would be to provide students with an area of concentration that focuses upon different aspects of multicultural issues. Finally, the integrated model endorses the concept that multicultural issues be addressed in all courses within the sport psychology curriculum. In addition, the integrated model would use workshops, dedicated courses, and the area of concentration concept to make sure that all sport psychology students were thoroughly immersed in multicultural issues.

Multicultural Issues That Relate to Gender

In the previous section of this chapter, we talked about multicultural issues in sport psychology that relate to race. In this section we turn our attention to multicultural issues in sport that relate to gender and to sexual orientation within gender.

Gender and Feminist Issues in Sport Psychology

As pointed out by Oglesby (2001), women have been largely overlooked and unrecognized in any historical discussion of the development of sport psychology in North America. As defined by Bell (2000), **feminism** is "a movement to end sexism, sexist exploitation, and oppression" (p. viii). Leaving the contribution of women out of a historical description of the development of sport psychology in North America would be an example of unintentional **sexism.** Volume 15 (issue 4) of the 2001 edition of *The Sport Psychologist* is edited by Diane Gill and is dedicated to feminism in sport psychology. Gill (2001) identifies four themes drawn from feminist theory and sport psychologist scholarship:

1. Gender is relational rather than categorical.
2. Gender is inextricably linked with race/ethnicity, class and other social identities.
3. Gender and cultural relations involve power and privilege.
4. Feminism demands action.

Consistent with Diane Gill's item number two, Hall (2001) makes the inextricable connection between gender and race in this way:

> When we discuss women or feminism, the focus is on white women. Conversely, when we discuss athletes of color, the focus is on males, especially African-American males. As a result, women of color frequently feel isolated and are treated as if their race and/or gender are non-issues, or at the very least have little relevance to these respective groups. Consequently, women of color frequently feel alienated in the sport arena and in the sport psychology literature. (p. 391)

Past research and practice in sport psychology focused almost exclusively on a masculine perspective and utilized male participants to a large degree. This has changed a great deal in recent years, as university human subject committees require justification for excluding either male or female participants. The feminist movement has served as an effective reminder to researchers and practitioners to avoid sexist practices or sexist language in all aspects of sport psychology. When conducting research, sport psychologists can (a) include males and females, people of color, and people with diverse sexual orientations as participants; (b) include gender and race as categorical variables; (c) include references that address race and gender; and (d) include substantive discussions related to race and gender (Ram et al., 2004). We will return to this important topic throughout the text, as gender issues are woven into the fabric of every chapter in the book.

Sexual Orientation in Sport Psychology

The multicultural concepts of diversity and inclusiveness extend to the inclusion of individuals who have a **sexual orientation** that may be different from the traditional heterosexual one. By definition, males who embrace a homosexual sexual orientation describe themselves as **gay,** while women who embrace a homosexual sexual orientation describe themselves as **lesbian.** For an individual to describe him or herself as gay or lesbian is to indicate sexual attraction to members of his or her own sex. Thus, to be **heterosexual** is to be sexually attracted to members of the opposite sex, while to be **homosexual** is to be sexually attracted to members of the same sex. To be inclusive is to accept both heterosexual and homosexual individuals into a group.

Homophobic behavior is defined as harmful behavior directed at individuals who are believed to be gay or lesbian, or such behavior directed at organizations or groups that support gay and lesbian people (Morrow & Gill, 2003). Examples of homophobic behavior include, but are not limited to, name calling, physical assaults, and destruction of property. As it relates to gay and lesbian people, inclusive behavior is behavior that is accepting and non-prejudiced. **Homophobia** is defined as irrational fear and intolerance of homosexual individuals or organization (Roper, 2002). While not as directly harmful as homophobic behavior, **heterosexist behavior** is more insidious. Heterosexist behavior is behavior that implies that everyone in a group is heterosexual, or that everyone lives in a traditional family or is attracted to someone of the opposite sex (Morrow & Gill, 2003). In many ways, this is more damaging than homophobic behavior, because it marginalizes people and forces them into thinking of themselves as "other" (Krane, 2001).

In a study involving a sample of high school physical education teachers and college students asked to reflect on the high school experience, Morrow and Gill (2003) reported that (a) homophobic behavior is as common in physical education

CONCEPT It is the responsibility of the coach and team leaders to foster multiculturalism in sports teams with respect to being accepting of homosexual individuals and being inclusive when it comes to sexual orientation.

APPLICATION Coaches and team leaders can cultivate multiculturalism with respect to different sexual orientations by educating athletes about homophobic behavior and about what it means to practice heterosexist behavior. Once this is accomplished, the focus should be upon treating every athlete with respect and dignity and upon valuing the athletic abilities of each athlete, regardless of sexual orientation.

---

classes as in the wider school population; (b) homophobic and heterosexist behavior is a regular part of the secondary school experience; and (c) despite the high level of homophobic and heterosexist behavior that exists, few teachers or students regularly confront the behaviors. The researchers reported that the most dramatic finding of the study was the great disparity between teachers' perception and students' perception of the creation of a psychologically "safe environment" for the students by the teachers.

Research also shows that the media treat men and women differently when it comes to athletic accomplishments and athletic prowess (Knight & Giuliano, 2003). Male athletes are perceived and assumed by the media to be heterosexual. Consequently, the media don't focus upon sexual orientation, but move on immediately to the athletic achievements of the male athletes. However, with female athletes, the media has a tendency to "heterosexualize" women by emphasizing their relationships with men. An emphasis on a woman's athletic prowess is secondary to an emphasis on her sexual orientation. This occurs because the media is anxious to overcome the image of homosexuality among women athletes. This research further showed that male and female athletes described as clearly heterosexual were perceived more favorably than athletes with an ambiguous sexual orientation.

Another concern related to sexual orientation is the rising number of male coaches who date, fall in love with, and sometimes marry the female athletes they train. This is a practice that has the potential of disrupting careers, interfering with performance, and leaving teammates angry and disillusioned (Wahl, Wertheim & Dohrmann, 2001). Relative to this practice, Mary Jo Jane, Director of the Tucker Center for Research on Girls and Women in Sport at the University of Minnesota, made the following observation: "But because of homophobia in and around women's sports, if it is a lesbian relationship, the negative perception is exacerbated—it quietly moves from the arena of bad judgment to the arena of deviance and immorality" (quoted in Wahl et al., 2001, p. 63).

Finally, we conclude this section with information derived from a qualitative investigation reported by Krane and Barber (2005). The daily identity tension of 13 lesbian college coaches was investigated. Results revealed that lesbian coaches are constantly negotiating with themselves about their social identities associated with being coaches of young women and being lesbians. They are confronted on the one hand, with the need to fight against homophobia; on the other hand with the need to protect their professional careers (i.e., remain silent). Results also show that these lesbian coaches did not passively accept their fate, but rather they fought against the prevailing heterosexist atmosphere and worked to create positive social change.

Summary

Sport and exercise psychology is the study of the effect of psychological and emotional factors on sport and exercise performance, and the effect of sport and exercise involvement on psychological and emotional factors.

Norman Triplett (1897) is cited as the first individual to conduct sport psychology research. Triplett analyzed the performance of cyclists under conditions of social facilitation. Coleman Griffith established the first sport psychology laboratory at the University of Illinois in 1925. In recent years, numerous scholarly societies have emerged to represent the discipline and application of sport psychology. In the United States, the most prominent are the North American Society for the Psychology of Sport and Physical Activity (NASPSPA) and the Association for the Advancement of Applied Sport Psychology (AAASP).

The issue of who is qualified to provide sport psychology services has been addressed by numerous professional organizations. The United States Olympic Committee developed the Sport Psychology Registry to identify individuals qualified to work with Olympic athletes. The AAASP developed procedures whereby qualified individuals could earn the title "Certified Consultant, AAASP." The roles and functions of the sport psychologist fall into the categories of clinical/counseling services, education, and research.

Concern is emerging over ethics associated with providing applied sport psychology services. In this regard the APA and AAASP have published ethical guidelines for providing services to clients. The AAASP guidelines will be discussed in a later chapter on psychological skills training.

As sport psychologists deal with the issue of certification and ethics, some have called for AAASP to spearhead a movement to accredit university sport psychology programs. Pros and cons of this proposed initiative were discussed.

Multiculturalism as it relates to both race and gender was discussed. Multiculturalism includes the concepts of diversity and inclusiveness relative to being accepting of people of different race, gender, and sexual orientation. The distinction between race thinking and racist thinking was made. Individuals are encultured merely by being born and raised in a particular group or culture. Acculturation, however, implies learning to look at the world through a multicultural lens.

An accreditation issue that must be addressed, either formally or informally, is multicultural training. Students preparing for careers as applied sport psychologists should receive training in multicultural counseling. Two models for addressing multicultural issues in practice include the universalistic model and the cultural compatibility model.

In the context of multiculturalism, both feminism and sexual orientation were discussed. Feminism is a movement to end sexism, sexist exploitation, and oppression. Heterosexual individuals are attracted to members of the opposite sex, while homosexual individuals are attracted to members of the same sex. Homophobic behavior was described as harmful behavior directed at individuals or groups who are believed to be gay or lesbian. Heterosexist behavior is behavior that implies that everyone in a group or team is heterosexual.

Critical Thought Questions

1. Considering the roles that physical education (kinesiology) and psychology have played in the development of sport psychology, what roles do you feel these two groups should play in defining sport psychology for the future?

2. Do you think that an individual trained in the exercise and sport sciences (physical education) should be able to use the word "psychologist" to describe what he does in sport? How do you think this issue is addressed within AAASP?

3. Do you think AAASP should champion a move to accredit university sport psychology programs? If so, how do you think it should proceed?

4. Do you think multicultural training can help members of diverse teams be more accepting of one another? In your opinion, what must be done to accomplish this goal?

5. What is your opinion of the two approaches for providing multicultural training to minority athletes (universal versus cultural compatibility)?

6. What is the root cause of homophobia on sport teams? What steps must be taken to overcome homophobia and heterosexism?

Glossary

accreditation A process in which a professional organization establishes guidelines and then determines whether programs seeking accreditation meet the guidelines.

acculturation Learning to look at the world through a multicultural lens.

clinical/counseling sport psychologist The type of sport psychologist that is required to be licensed and have specialized training in clinical and/or counseling psychology.

cultural compatibility model A consulting model in which the racial/ethnic identity of the athlete is matched with the racial/ethnic identity of the sport psychology consultant.

cultural competence An individual is understanding of her own racial identity, other people's racial identities, and the role that race and cultural ethnicity play in a relationship.

diversity The representation in a group of people from diverse cultural backgrounds.

educational sport psychologist The type of sport psychologist that uses education as a medium for teaching athletes and coaches correct principles associated with sport psychology.

enculturation Values and attitudes one receives by being born into a specific culture.

feminism A movement to end sexism, sexist exploitation, and oppression.

gay A male who embraces a homosexual sexual orientation.

Griffith, Coleman The father of sport psychology in North America. In 1925, while at the University of Illinois, he established the first sport psychology laboratory in North America.

heterosexist behavior Behavior that implies that everyone in a group is heterosexual, or that everyone lives in a traditional family or is attracted to individuals of the opposite sex.

heterosexual Sexually attracted to members of the opposite sex.

homophobia Irrational fear and intolerance of homosexual individuals or groups.

homophobic behavior Harmful behavior directed at individuals who are believed to be gay or lesbian, or at groups that support such individuals.

homosexual Sexually attracted to members of the same sex.

inclusiveness Individuals are not excluded from a group because of their race, ethnic background, gender, sexual orientation, or religion.

lesbian A female who embraces a homosexual sexual orientation.

Martens, Rainer A former professor of sport psychology at the University of Illinois, identified in this book as the "father of modern sport psychology."

multicultural training Training that prepares sport psychologists to counsel athletes from different cultural/racial backgrounds.

Ogilvie, Bruce The father of applied sport psychology in North America.

race thinking Thinking about race issues in a nonracist way.

racist thinking Thinking in ways that discriminate against people of other races or cultures.

research sport psychologist The type of sport psychologist who is mainly interested in research and in expanding the knowledge base in sport psychology.

sexism Intentionally or unintentionally overlooking or minimizing the contributions of the opposite sex, and/or saying or implying derogatory things about the opposite sex.

sexual orientation The ways individuals come to feel about their own sexuality, whether heterosexual, homosexual, or transsexual in nature.

Sport Psychology Registry A list of individuals in the area of psychology of sport who are qualified to work with Olympic athletes. The registry was initiated by the USOC.

Triplett, Norman The person who conducted and published what appears to be the first clear example of sport psychology research in North America.

universalistic model A consulting model in which athlete and sport psychologist are not matched according to cultural background; rather, the sport psychologist is trained in multicultural sensitivity issues.

USOC United States Olympic Committee.

white privilege The condition of being privileged simply by being white, compared to those who are not white.

Psychology of the Athlete

KEY TERMS

Able-bodied athlete
Athletic Motivation Inventory
Athletic pyramid
Big five personality traits
Cattell 16 PF
Competitive situation
Conceptual model
Disabled athlete
Disposition
Effect size
Global personality traits
Gravitational hypothesis
Iceberg profile
Interactional model
Mental health model
Meta-analysis
MMPI
Moderating variable
Mood profile
Mood state
Multivariate approach
Personality
Personality profile

Personality trait
Physically challenged athlete
Precompetitive mood
Primary personality factors
Profile of Mood States
Projective procedures

Psychological profile
Rorschach test
Situation
Thematic Apperception Test
Troutwine Athletic Profile
Winning Profile Athletic Instrument

In this chapter we discuss two categories of psychological factors that may affect performance in various sport- and exercise-related activities. The first category deals with enduring personality characteristics called traits or dispositions, while the other category deals with less stable psychological states that are influenced by the environment. In this chapter we will refer to these psychological states as mood states. Mood states are psychological responses that are less stable than personality traits but more stable than emotions (Mellalieu, 2003). We will introduce and discuss the concept of emotions in a later chapter on the topic of anxiety, arousal, and stress relationships (chapter 8). At this point it is important to understand that personality characteristics are psychological factors that are stable and enduring, while psychological mood change may be influenced by the environment. In the section on personality, we go to some length to introduce theories of personality that come from the study of psychology generally. These theories also represent many of the basic theories of psychology that will be discussed throughout the text. While sport psychology research has utilized all of these theories to some degree in the study of personality, the focus has been upon what has come to be referred to as trait theory. Trait theory has tended to dominate personality research because of the emphasis that has been placed in psychology on the development of inventories that measure identified personality traits.

Personality and the Athlete

Sport psychologists have long been intrigued with the question of whether or not successful athletic performance can be accurately predicted on the basis of personality or psychological assessment. Personality assessment was apparently a factor in the Indianapolis Colts professional football team's decision to select Peyton Manning over Ryan Leaf to be its first-round draft pick in 1998 (Carey, 1999; Rand, 2000). History records that Manning went on to stardom with the Colts, while Ryan Leaf continued to struggle with the San Diego Chargers and later was traded. Ryan Leaf retired in the year 2002 after a lack-luster career (King, 2002). This single event is built up in the press as evidence of the effectiveness of psychological testing in predicting athletic success. Apparently, a large percentage of professional teams use psychological testing to assist them in making personnel decisions. Not everyone, however, agrees with this practice. The following observation was made by Ralph Wilson, owner of the Buffalo Bills professional football team:

> We lost a lot of good players giving those psychological tests. I can remember one. I won't mention

his name, but we dropped him from our list. Now he is All-Pro. (Psychological Profiles, 1997, p. 26).

In the 1960s and 1970s, research involving the athlete and personality assessment was very popular. Ruffer (1975, 1976a, 1976b), for example, cited 572 sources of original research in a compilation of references on the relationship between personality and athletic performance. In recent years, however, interest in this kind of research has waned because of a lack of consistent correlation between personality factors and athletic prowess. However, in view of the current practice of many teams in the National Football League to include personality assessment in decision making, it behooves the sport psychology student to be knowledgeable about personality and personality assessment in sport.

Concepts to be introduced and studied in this section include (a) a definition of personality, (b) theories of personality, (c) measurement of personality, and (d) personality and sport performance. As we shall learn, personality assessment involves measuring relatively stable personality traits, and not unstable mood states. Discussion of the relationship between mood states and athletic performance will be reserved for section two of this chapter. In this way we will distinguish between the practice of relating athletic performance to personality traits and that of relating performance to mood states. It will be the goal of this chapter to clearly distinguish between these two practices. As a general observation, we can note that most preselection inventories used by professional teams are basically personality inventories. That is, they measure *general* attitudes, beliefs, and behavioral characteristics, as opposed to situation-specific feelings or moods.

Personality Defined

As defined by Kalat (1999, p. 477), **personality** is "all the consistent ways in which the behavior of one person differs from that of others, especially in social situations." The key words in this definition are the words "consistent" and "differs."

Athletes also exhibit interesting personality styles. Courtesy Kansas State University Sports Information.

An individual's personality defines the person in unique ways that remain stable and consistent over time. If an athlete consistently exhibits the characteristics of being assertive on and off the athletic field, we might say that he is an assertive person.

One of the difficulties scientists have in determining the personality characteristics of an individual is that the individual may purposefully or inadvertently "mask" her true personality. Hollander (1976) wrote about this problem when he said that *typical responses* and *role-related behaviors* don't always reflect a person's true personality, or *psychological core*. A typical response is indicative of how an individual usually behaves in a social setting, while a role-related behavior is indicative of how the person behaves in various specific situations. Consider the example of the athlete who is being recruited to play football at a major university. The university representative asks the high school football coach about the athlete's personality. The coach responds that he is very quiet, but hard-working. When this same question is asked of

the athlete's girlfriend, she replies that he is actually very sociable and outgoing.

Theories of Personality

In this section we will consider four major theoretical approaches to the study of personality: psychodynamic theory, social learning theory, humanistic theory, and trait theory. Each will be briefly discussed.

Psychodynamic Theory   Sigmund Freud's psychodynamic theory (1933) and his method of treating personality disturbances were based primarily upon self-analysis and extensive clinical observation of neurotics. Two distinguishing characteristics of the psychodynamic approach to personality have been its emphasis upon in-depth examination of the *whole* person, and its emphasis upon unconscious motives.

In Freud's view, the id, ego, and superego form the tripartite structure of personality. The id represents the unconscious instinctual core of personality; in a sense, the id is the pleasure-seeking mechanism. In contrast, the ego represents the conscious, logical, reality-oriented aspect of the personality. The superego represents the conscience of the individual; it is the internalized moral standards of society impressed upon the person by parental control and the process of socialization. Freud proposed that the ego aids in the resolution of conflicts between the id and the superego. Essentially, Freud advocated a conflict theory of personality. In this respect, the three parts of the psychic structure are always in conflict. The individual's personality is the sum total of the dynamic conflicts between the impulse to seek release and the inhibition against these impulses.

The individual's unconscious sexual and aggressive instincts are major determinants of behavior, according to Freud. Athletic aggression represents a potential example of this approach. Instinct theory provides one explanation for the phenomenon of violence in sport, as we will later learn.

Social Learning Theory   From the viewpoint of social learning theory, behavior is not simply a function of unconscious motives (as in psychoanalytic theory) or underlying predispositions. Rather, human behavior is a function of social learning and the strength of the situation. An individual behaves according to how she has learned to behave, as this is consistent with environmental constraints. If the environmental situation is prominent, the effect of personality traits or unconscious motives upon behavior should be minimal.

The story is told of the boy who brought his report card to his father and wanted to know if his poor performance was inherited or due to his social environment. This was certainly a no-win situation for the father. However, from a social learning theory perspective, the answer would clearly be his social environment. According to social learning theory, a child's performance and behavior are a function of the child's experiences and environment.

The origin of social learning theory can be traced to Clark Hull's 1943 theory of learning and to B. F. Skinner's (1953) behaviorism. Hull's stimulus-response theory of learning was based on laboratory experimentation with animals. According to stimulus-response theory, an individual's behavior in any given situation is a function of his learned experiences. Other researchers, such as Miller and Dollard (Miller, 1941), Mischel (1986), and Bandura (1977, 1986), extended the Hullian notions of complex human behavior.

Two of the primary mechanisms through which individuals learn are modeling and social reinforcement. *Modeling,* or imitative behavior, refers to the phenomenon of learning through observation. Albert Bandura's social learning theory is based primarily upon this important concept. According to Bandura, behavior is best explained as a function of observational learning. *Social reinforcement* is based upon the notion that rewarded behaviors are likely to be repeated.

A youth league football player observes on television that professional athletes are often able to intimidate quarterbacks and wide receivers through aggressive hard-hitting tackles. Using the professional athlete as his model, he tries the same tactics on his youth league team and is reinforced by the coach with a pat on the back. This example illustrates how, through modeling and social reinforcement, young athletes develop questionable behaviors that may eventually define their personalities.

Humanistic Theory   The major proponents of the humanistic theory of personality are Carl Rogers and Abraham Maslow. Unlike the pessimistic Freud, Rogers and Maslow argued that human nature is inherently healthy and constructive. At the center of the humanistic theory of personality is the concept of *self-actualization.* The human organism possesses an innate drive or tendency to enhance itself, to realize capacities, and to act to become a better and more self-fulfilled person. In the developing personality, openness to experiences that then shape the individual is of critical importance. It is not necessarily the experience that shapes the individual, but the individual's perception of that experience. Self-actualization is an

CONCEPT   Four basic approaches for explaining the phenomenon of personality are the psychodynamic, social learning, humanistic, and trait theories.

APPLICATION   In attempting to explain behavior on the basis of personality, it is important to recognize the ramifications of adopting one theoretical approach over another. The teacher's or coach's belief system will influence athlete-coach interactions.

ongoing process of seeking congruence between one's experiences and one's self-concept. Rogers's influence on the development of the humanistic theory of personality is largely due to his method of psychotherapy, which is nondirective and client-centered. The therapist does not attempt to impose her values on the client, but rather helps the client to find her own solutions to problems. Further, the therapist is accepting, empathetic, and honest, and expresses unconditional positive regard for the client. Maslow's contribution to the humanistic theory is in the development of his hierarchical motive system based on the notion of hierarchical needs. For Maslow, the end goal of all human experience is self-actualization, but to get there the person must first have lesser needs fulfilled.

Trait Theory   The basic position of trait or factor theory is that personality can be described in terms of traits possessed by individuals. These **personality traits** are considered synonymous with **dispositions** to act in a certain way. Traits are considered to be stable, enduring, and consistent across a variety of differing situations. Those who exhibit the trait or need to achieve success, for example, can be expected to have a disposition toward competitiveness and assertiveness in many situations. A disposition toward a certain trait means not that the individual will *always* respond in this manner, but that a certain likelihood exists.

Among the most ardent advocates of trait psychology are psychologists such as Gordon Allport, Raymond Cattell, and Hans Eysenck. Cattell (1965, 1973) identified 35 different traits that he believed describe a personality. Using a

similar approach, British psychologists (Eysenck & Eysenck, 1968) concentrated on the dimensional traits of neuroticism-stability and introversion-extraversion.

Since the notion of an enduring, somewhat genetically founded, trait approach to personality offends the social learning theorist, it is important to point out that Cattell never ignored the importance of the environment. Cattell (1965) believed that typical responses are a function of both the situation (environment) and the personality disposition. This is evident from his formula, $R = S \times P$, in which R = response, S = situation, and P = personality. This revelation may be somewhat startling to social learning advocates who oppose trait theory on the grounds that it does not consider the environment.

The 35 specific personality traits originally identified by Cattell in 1965 form the basis of the fifth edition of the 16 PF to be discussed in the measurement section. In recent years, trait psychologists claim to have identified the **big five personality traits** (John & Srivastava, 1999; Kalat, 1999). The big five traits, which are believed to represent a consolidation of Cattell's original 35 personality traits, are the following: neuroticism, extraversion, agreeableness, conscientiousness, and openness to new ideas.

The great strength of the trait theory of personality is that it allows for the easy and objective measurement of personality through the use of inventories. If it can be demonstrated that a collection of traits can accurately describe a person's psychological profile, then this certainly is superior to a psychoanalytic approach, in which personality is inferred through less objective techniques. Conversely, the weakness of the trait approach is that it may fail to consider the whole person, since according to this approach, personality is represented by a collection of specific traits. As we shall see, the trait approach to studying personality has dominated the sport psychology literature.

The Measurement of Personality

This section will identify and briefly discuss various techniques used for assessing personality. It should be pointed out that the various methods of assessing personality correspond closely to the basic personality theories we have just discussed. For example, projective tests such as the Rorschach test are closely linked to the psychoanalytic theory of personality. Conversely, the various paper-and-pencil inventories are linked to trait theory. In this brief overview of personality measurement techniques, the reader should be aware that many issues regarding personality assessment remain unresolved. The methods outlined here are not perfect; nor do psychologists agree on the meaning of the results of any particular test.

Three basic classes of measurement techniques may be identified. These are (1) rating scales, (2) unstructured projective tests, and (3) questionnaires. Each of these three categories will now be discussed, with particular emphasis upon the questionnaire method. The questionnaire method is highlighted because it is the measurement technique most commonly used by sport psychologists today.

Rating Scales Characteristically, *rating scales* involve the use of a judge or judges who are asked to observe an individual in some situation. The judges employ the use of a checklist or scale that has been predesigned for maximum objectivity. Usually, if the checklist is used properly and the judges are well trained, the results can be fairly reliable and objective.

Typically, two types of situations are involved in personality assessment using rating scales. These are the *interview* and the *observation of performance.* In the interview, the judge asks the subject numerous open-ended and specific questions designed to ascertain personality traits and general impressions. Generally, several interviews are necessary to gain impressions about underlying motives (the core of personality). If the interview is conducted properly, carefully, and systematically, the results can be reliable and valid. However, much depends upon the skill and sensitivity of the person conducting the interview.

Observation of a subject during some type of performance situation is the second kind of rating system used for ascertaining personality. As with the interview, observations can be effective if the checklist being used is well designed and planned, and if the observer is highly trained. Typically, for personality assessment, the checklist would contain specific traits and behaviors that the observer would look for. These traits, as they were observed, would then be rated in terms of strength and clarity.

Unstructured Projective Procedures The foregoing rating methods are generally used for ascertaining data on traits of personality, although in many instances inferences may be made concerning underlying motives. **Projective procedures** may also be used to identify traits, but they are commonly used to determine information about underlying motives. Projective techniques allow subjects to reveal their inner feelings and motives through unstructured tasks. These unstructured techniques are used primarily in clinical psychology and are somewhat synonymous with the psychoanalytic and humanistic approaches to explaining personality. The underlying assumption in the unstructured test situation is that if subjects perceive that there are no right or wrong responses, they will likely be open and honest in their responses.

Several kinds of unstructured tests have been developed. Among them are the Rorschach Test

(Sarason, 1954), the Thematic Apperception Test (Tompkins, 1947), the Sentence Completion Test (Holsopple & Miale, 1954), and the House-Tree-Person Test (Buck, 1948). For our purposes, only the Rorschach (also known as the "inkblot") and Thematic Apperception Tests (TAT) will be discussed. The inkblot and the TAT are by far the most commonly used projective tests.

The Rorschach Test   Herman Rorschach, a Swiss psychiatrist, was the first to apply the inkblot to the study of personality (Kalat, 1999). The **Rorschach test** was introduced in 1921, and remains the most famous of all the projective testing devices. The test material consists of ten cards. Each card has an inkblot on it, which is symmetrical and intricate. Some of the cards are entirely in black and white, while others have a splash of color or are nearly all in color. The cards are presented to the subject one at a time and in a prescribed order. As the cards are presented, the subject is encouraged to tell what he sees. The tester keeps a verbatim record of the subject's responses to each, and notes any spontaneous remarks, emotional reactions, or other incidental behaviors. After all the cards have been viewed, the examiner questions the subject in a systematic manner regarding associations made with each card.

The Rorschach test has not been used extensively by sport psychologists to evaluate personality in athletes. There is no doubt that the responses that clients give to the Rorschach test contain a wealth of personal information. The question is whether the psychologist can accurately interpret the responses. Research (Weiner, 1994) suggests that when the Rorschach is used as an objectively scored test, as recommended by Exner (1986), it is a reliable and psychometrically sound test. Still, questions remain as to the validity of the conclusions derived from the Rorschach test (Kalat, 1999).

The Thematic Apperception Test   The **Thematic Apperception Test,** developed by Henry Murray and his associates in 1943 at the Harvard University Psychological Clinic, has been used almost as extensively as the Rorschach test. The TAT is composed of nineteen cards containing pictures depicting vague situations, and one blank card. The subject is encouraged to make up a story about each picture. In contrast to the vague blots in the Rorschach test, pictures in the TAT are rather clear and vivid. For example, the sexes of the characters in the pictures and their facial expressions are generally identifiable. It is believed that subjects reveal or project important aspects of their personalities as they weave the characters and objects in the pictures into either an oral or a written story.

Like the Rorschach test, the TAT has not been used extensively by sport psychologists to measure personality in athletes. This is not to say that it should not be used; however, its validity and reliability are highly dependent upon the skill and training of the individual administering and interpreting the results.

Structured Questionnaires   The structured questionnaire is a paper-and-pencil test in which the subject answers specific true-false or Likert scale–type statements. A typical Likert scale–type statement is illustrated in the following example:

In athletic situations, I find myself getting very uptight and anxious as the contest progresses.

DEFINITELY FALSE				*DEFINITELY TRUE*
1	2	3	4	5

There are many different kinds of questionnaire-type personality inventories. Certain specific personality characteristics or traits are believed to be identified through the administration of these questionnaires. For our purposes we will focus our discussion on the three most commonly used personality inventories. One of these inventories was developed to be used with individuals suffering from personality disorders, while the other two were developed for normal populations. All of these inventories are of interest, because both have been used in sport-related research involving athletes.

Minnesota Multiphasic Personality Inventory
The Minnesota Multiphasic Personality Inventory
(**MMPI**) is the most widely used of all personality
inventories. The MMPI consists of a series of
true-false questions designed to measure certain
personality traits and clinical conditions such as
depression. The original version of the MMPI,
composed of 550 items, was developed in the
1940s and is still in use (Hathaway & McKinley,
1940). A revised version of the inventory, composed of 567 items, was developed in 1990 and
named the MMPI-2 (Butcher, Graham, Williams,
& Ben-Porath, 1990). These authors also developed a new form of the inventory to be used with
adolescents (MMPI-A). Traits measured by the
MMPI-2 include the following: hypochondria, depression, hysteria, psychopathic deviation, mas-
culinity-feminity, paranoia, obsessive-compulsive
behavior, schizophrenia, hypomania, and social
introversion. The inventory also includes items to
detect lying and faking good/bad scores. While
the MMPI-2 was designed specifically for use
with clinical populations, it may be used with

normal individuals (Hathaway & McKinley,
1967).

Cattell's Sixteen Factor Personality Inventory
Developed by Robert Cattell (1965), the Sixteen
Factor Personality Inventory (**Cattell 16 PF**) is
based upon 35 personality traits originally identified by Cattell. Through a statistical process known
as factor analysis, Cattell reduced the 35 specific
traits to 16 broader traits or factors. The 16 factors
measured by the 16 PF are believed to be personality traits exhibited by normal individuals. The current edition of the 16 PF is titled the 16 PF Fifth
Edition (Russell & Karol, 1994), and is composed
of 185 items. The 16 PF takes from 35 to 50 minutes to complete and is designed for adults, or
those aged 16 years and over. An adolescent version of the 16 PF is available for individuals ranging from ages 12 to 18. The 16 PF measures 16 **primary personality factors;** it also includes a social
desirability index to assess faking good or bad. The
primary personality factors measured by the 16 PF
are displayed in the left column of table 2.1.

TABLE 2.1 | Primary and Global Personality Traits Associated with the 16 PF,
as Well as Personality Traits Associated with the "Big Five"

16 PF Primary Traits	16 PF Global Traits	Big Five Traits
1. Warmth	1. Extraversion	1. Extraversion
2. Reasoning	2. Anxiety	2. Neuroticism
3. Emotional Stability	3. Tough-Mindedness	3. Conscientiousness
4. Dominance	4. Independence	4. Openness
5. Liveliness	5. Self-Control	5. Agreeableness
6. Rule-Consciousness		
7. Social Boldness		
8. Sensitivity		
9. Vigilance		
10. Abstractedness		
11. Privateness		
12. Apprehension		
13. Openness to Change		
14. Self-Reliance		
15. Perfectionism		
16. Tension		

Cattell believed that the 16 traits measured by the 16 PF could be further condensed down to five secondary or **global personality traits.** It is interesting to compare Cattell's five global traits with the big five traits presented earlier. Cattell's global traits and the big five traits are presented in table 2.1 along with Cattell's 16 primary traits. In comparing the descriptions of the Cattell global traits with those of the big five traits, it is clear that they are not exactly the same. However, extraversion appears on both lists, and neuroticism and anxiety are essentially the same.

From Cattell's perspective, it is interesting to look at table 2.1 to see what factors constitute what we call personality. Of even greater interest is the plotting of the an individual's standardized scores for each of the 16 personality traits on a line graph. Plotted standardized scores produce what sport psychologists call a **personality profile.** A standardized score is a score that has been converted from a raw score so that it indicates whether an individual is high or low in a characteristic relative to other individuals of the same gender, age, and academic background. A hypothetical personality profile is illustrated in figure 2.1.

NEO–Five Factor Personality Inventory   The NEO–Five Factor Personality Inventory (NEO-FFI)

is a 60-item personality inventory designed to measure the Big-Five Personality Traits of extraversion, neuroticism, conscientiousness, openness, and agreeableness. The 60-item NEO-FFI is extracted from the more comprehensive NEO Personality Inventory-R (Costa & McCrae, 1992). Personality factors believed to relate to *Extraversion* include warmth, gregariousness, assertiveness, activity, excitement seeking, and positive emotions. Personality factors believed to relate to *Neuroticism* include anxiety, angry hostility, depression, self-consciousness, impulsiveness, and vulnerability. Factors believed to relate to *Conscientiousness* include competence, order, dutifulness, achievement striving, self-discipline, and deliberation. Personality factors believed to underlie *Openness* include fantasy, aesthetics, feelings, actions, ideas, and values. Finally, personality factors believed to relate to *Agreeableness* include trust, straightforwardness, altruism, compliance, modesty, and tendermindedness.

Hughes, Case, Stuempfle and Evans (2003) utilized the NEO-FFI in a study that involved 28 men and 7 women who participated in the Iditasport Ultra-Marathon. The Iditasport Ultra-Marathon is a grueling 100-mile race that begins in Big Lake, Alaska and takes place over trails that wind through the Alaskan wilderness in all

FIGURE 2.1 | Personality profile showing how an athlete's scores compare to the population mean (zero).

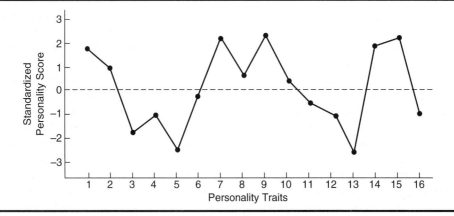

kinds of weather. Using cross-country skis, snowshoes, a bicycle, or their feet, the participants must complete the race within 48 hours while carrying their own supplies. Results of the study showed that these athletes score higher than a norm group in extraversion and openness. No significant differences were noted for any personality factor as a function of gender, age, or race division.

Structured Questionnaires Designed for Athletes   In addition to the MMPI and the 16 PF, sport psychologists use other inventories that may be considered personality inventories. For example, in chapter 5 we will learn that we can measure sport self-confidence using Vealey, Knight, and Pappas' (2002) Sport-Confidence Inventory. In chapter 6 we will learn that we can measure task and ego goal orientation using either the Task and Ego Orientation in Sport Questionnaire (TEOSQ; Duda 1989), or the Perceptions of Success Questionnaire (POSQ; Roberts, 1993). In chapter 7 we will learn that we can measure attentional focus using Nideffer's (1976) Test of Attentional and Interpersonal Style (TAIS). Each of these previously mentioned inventories was designed to measure specific personality dispositions or traits. Throughout the book you will be introduced to numerous inventories designed to measure specific personality traits. For example, when we cover anxiety you will learn about inventories designed to measure the personality trait of anxiety. When we cover aggression you will learn about inventories designed to measure the personality trait of aggressiveness.

In addition to the specific trait inventories identified in the previous paragraph, sport psychologists have developed personality inventories designed to measure personality traits in athletes. These inventories have generally been developed for the purpose of studying the relationship between personality and athletic performance. A few of these inventories will be introduced here. The reader is referred to Ostrow (1996) and LeUnes (2002) for a more complete description of available personality inventories.

Before we begin this discussion, you should know that *no scientific study to date has shown a strong statistical relationship between personality variables and athletic ability*. We will look at the evidence on this matter later in the chapter, but for now it is important for you to understand this fact about personality testing. This statement casts doubt on the practices of professional teams that use psychological testing for the purposes of team selection, especially if they give significant weight to results of the testing. Personality and psychological testing can play an important role in player development, but no evidence exists to justify its use in making personnel decisions. If a test developer believes that he has developed an inventory that can accurately predict athletic success, he has the responsibility to put it to the test and make the data available to scientists. Three personality/psychological inventories will be mentioned in this section, along with a brief discussion of two inventories designed to measure a single personality trait.

Athletic Motivation Inventory The **Athletic Motivation Inventory** (AMI) was developed by Thomas Tutko, Bruce Ogilvie, and Leland Lyon at the Institute for the Study of Athletic Motivation at San Jose State College (Tutko & Richards, 1971, 1972). According to its authors, the AMI measures a number of personality traits related to high athletic achievement: drive, aggression, determination, responsibility, leadership, self-confidence, emotional control, mental toughness, coachability, conscience development, and trust.

The reliability and validity of the instrument have been questioned by Rushall (1973), Corbin (1977), and Martens (1975). However, Tutko and Richards (1972) say that thousands of athletes have been tested and that the AMI was originally based upon the 16 PF and the Jackson Personality Research Form (Ogilvie, Johnsgard & Tutko, 1971).

Perhaps the real concern of sport psychologists is not that the test is more or less reliable than other personality inventories, but that the developers implied that it could predict athletic success. No other organization, researcher, or promoter has made similar claims about other more distinguished personality inventories. The unsubstantiated claims of the developers of the AMI hurt the field of sport psychology in terms of legitimacy.

A study by Davis (1991) supports this position. Davis studied the relationship between AMI subscales and psychological strength in 649 ice hockey players who were eligible for the National Hockey League (NHL) entry draft. The criterion measure of psychological strength was based on an evaluation of on-ice play by NHL scouts. The results showed that less than 4 percent of the variance in scout ratings was accounted for by AMI scores ($r = .20$). This outcome suggests that the AMI is a poor predictor of psychological strength of ice hockey players.

Winning Profile Athletic Instrument The **Winning Profile Athletic Instrument** (WPAI) was developed by Jesse Llobet of PsyMetrics. The WPAI is a fifty-item inventory that measures conscientiousness and mental toughness. Llobet (1999) reported

internal reliability coefficients of .83 and .87 for these two factors respectively. When completing the instrument, athletes are asked to use their own sport as a frame of reference for answering questions. In one investigation, Llobet (1999) reported correlations of between .30 and .43 between WPAI scores and coaches' ratings for conscientiousness and mental toughness. In a second study, Paa, Sime, and Llobet (1999) administered the WPAI to high school, collegiate, semiprofessional, and professional athletes. Results showed significant differences between the mean total WPAI scores for high school athletes and all other groups, and between collegiate athletes and professional athletes.

Troutwine Athletic Profile The **Troutwine Athletic Profile** (TAP) was developed by Bob Troutwine, a professor of psychology at William Jewell College (Carey, 1999; Rand, 2000). According to news reports, the TAP was used by the Indianapolis Colts to help them make their decision to select Peyton Manning over Ryan Leaf in the 1998 professional football draft. Psychometric properties of the TAP have not been published in any of the mainline sport psychology journals; nor has anything scientific been published about the validity of the test in terms of predicting athletic success.

Emotional Intelligence Scale The 32-item Emotional Intelligence Scale (EIS; Schutte et al., 1998) was designed to measure the personality trait of emotional intelligence. Emotional intelligence, or what has come to be called EQ, is defined as "an individual's capacity to recognize and utilize emotional states to change intentions and behavior" (Zizzi, Deaner, & Hirschhorn, 2003, p. 262). In a study involving 40 collegiate baseball hitters and 21 pitchers, it was observed that EQ was correlated with pitching but not hitting. Included in EQ is the ability to contend with emotions in the following areas: (1) perceiving emotion, (2) integrating emotions in thought, (3) understanding emotion, and (4) managing emotion. Because these four factors take time to be integrated, it is thought that pitching would have the advantage in terms of EQ. This

TABLE 2.2 | Attributes of Mental Toughness Listed in Order of Descending Importance

1. Having an unshakable self-belief in your ability to achieve your competitive goals
2. Bouncing back from performance setbacks as a result of increased determination to succeed
3. Having an unshakable self-belief that you possess unique qualities and abilities that make you better than your opponents
4. Having an insatiable desire and internalized motives to succeed
5. Remaining fully focused on the task at hand in the face of competition-specific distractions
6. Regaining psychological control following unexpected, uncontrollable events
7. Pushing back the boundaries of physical and emotional pain, while still maintaining technique and effort under distress in training and competition
8. Accepting that competition anxiety is inevitable and knowing that you can cope with it
9. Not being adversely affected by others' good and bad performances
10. Thriving on the pressure of competition
11. Remaining fully-focused in the face of personal life distractions
12. Switching a sport focus on and off as required

is because the pitcher determines how much time he needs to prepare for the next pitch, whereas the hitter must be ready when the pitcher is ready.

Measuring Mental Toughness A personality inventory does not exist to measure the trait of mental toughness independent of other personality traits, yet it is deemed by many coaches and sport psychologists to be an important athlete characteristic. Jones, Hanton, and Connaughton (2002) conducted a qualitative investigation designed to identify what makes up the construct of mental toughness. As a result of interviewing 10 elite international athletes, the following definition emerged for mental toughness:

> Mental toughness is having the natural or developed psychological edge that enables you to (a) generally, cope better than your opponents with the many demands (competition, training, lifestyle) that sport places on a performer, and (b) specifically, be more consistent and better than your opponents in remaining determined, focused, confident, and in control under pressure. (p. 209)

Based on the results of the investigation, 12 characteristics of athletes who exhibit the personality trait of mental toughness emerged. These 12 characteristics are illustrated in table 2.2 in order of importance. It is conceivable that these 12 characteristics may form the basis of an inventory designed to measure the trait of mental toughness.

Personality and Sport Performance

Since 1960, several comprehensive literature reviews have been completed in an attempt to clarify the relationship between personality and sport performance (Cofer & Johnson, 1960; Cooper, 1969; Hardman, 1973; Ogilvie, 1968, 1976; Morgan, 1980b). Of these, the review by Morgan (1980b) provided the most comprehensive treatment of the subject. While not fully endorsing the position that personality profiles can accurately predict sport performance, Morgan argued that the literature shows a consistent relationship between personality and sport performance when (a) response distortion is removed, and (b) data are analyzed

John McEnroe dominated men's professional tennis in the 1980s though superior skill and a volatile personality. Courtesy Kansas State University Sports Information.

using a multivariate approach. A **multivariate approach** is used when multiple measures of personality are analyzed simultaneously, as opposed to separately. Since personality is multifaceted and complex, it is appropriate that statistics used to analyze personality measures also be complex. While it is good to remember that the relationship between sport performance and personality is far from crystal clear, it seems equally true that certain general conclusions can be drawn. In the paragraphs that follow, sport personality research will be synthesized and general conclusions drawn on several topics of interest.

Athletes Versus Nonathletes   Athletes differ from nonathletes on many personality traits (Gat & McWhirter, 1998). It is often a matter of conjecture whether these differences favor the athletes or the nonathletes. Schurr, Ashley, and Joy (1977) clearly showed that athletes who

participate in team and individual sports are more independent, more objective, and less anxious than nonathletes. From Hardman's (1973) review it is also clear that the athlete is often more intelligent than average. Additionally, Cooper (1969) describes the athlete as being more self-confident, competitive, and socially outgoing than the nonathlete. This is supportive of Morgan's (1980b) conclusions that the athlete is basically an extravert and low in anxiety.

In several recent investigations, a number of comparisons have been made between an athlete's score on various personality and psychological inventories and scores associated with norm groups. For example, compared to published normative data, the scores of professional cowboys indicate that they tend to be alert, enthusiastic, forthright, self-sufficient, reality based, and practical (McGill, Hall, Ratliff & Moss, 1986). Compared to norm groups, elite rock climbers exhibit low anxiety, emotional detachment, low superegos, and high levels of sensation seeking (Robinson, 1985).

While the evidence favors the conclusion that the athlete differs from the nonathlete in many personality traits, the problem arises in the definition of what constitutes an athlete. In the Schurr et al. (1977) research, an athlete was defined as a person who participated in the university intercollegiate athletic program. This would seem to be a viable criterion. However, this classification system has not been universally adopted by researchers. Some studies, for example, have classified intramural and club sports participants as athletes. Other studies have required that participants earn awards, such as letters, in order to be considered athletes. Until some unifying system is adopted, it will always be difficult to compare results from one study with those from another.

Developmental Effects of Athletic Participation upon Personality   Given that athletes and nonathletes differ on the personality dimensions of extraversion and stability, is this due to the athletic experience (learning), or to a natural selection

CONCEPT Generally speaking, athletes differ from nonathletes in many personality traits. For example, it can be demonstrated that athletes are generally more independent, objective, and extraverted than nonathletes, but less anxious.

APPLICATION As a coach, expect your athletes to be generally higher in such traits as independence, extraversion, and self-confidence, and lower in anxiety, than nonathletes. One cannot, however, rank athletes on the basis of these traits or make team roster decisions based on them. A statistical relationship (often low) does not suggest a cause-and-effect relationship.

CONCEPT Athletes tend to be more extraverted, independent, and self-confident than nonathletes because of a process of "natural selection," and not necessarily due to learning. Individuals who exhibit certain personality traits may tend to gravitate toward athletics. An important exception to this principle occurs in the formative years before the young athlete reaches maturity. During the early maturing years, the youth sport experience is critical in forming positive personality traits such as self-confidence and independence.

APPLICATION Coaches and teachers who work with young boys and girls must be very careful that the athletic experience is a positive one in the lives of young people. Athletic programs designed for youth should place a premium on the development of feelings of self-worth, confidence, and independence, and relegate winning to a position of secondary importance. Winning must not be more important than the needs of the boys and girls.

process in which individuals possessing certain personality traits gravitate toward athletics? Perhaps an unequivocal answer to this question will never be known; however, the evidence typically supports the genetic or **gravitational hypothesis** (Morgan, 1974). Individuals who possess stable, extraverted personalities tend to gravitate toward the athletic experience. As the competitive process weeds out all but the keenest of competitors, those who remain are those having the greatest levels of extraversion and stability. This could be described as sort of an athletic Darwinism (survival of the fittest). Some of the studies that support the gravitational model are those by Yanada and Hirata (1970), Kane (1970), and Rushall (1970).

The viability of the gravitational model, however, does not preclude the possibility that sport participation can enhance personality development. In this respect, Tattersfield (1971) has provided longitudinal evidence that athletic participation before maturity has a developmental effect upon personality. Specifically, Tattersfield monitored the personality profiles of boys participating in an age-group swimming program across a five-year training period. Significant changes toward greater extraversion, stability, and dependence

CONCEPT Generally speaking, it can be demonstrated that differences exist in the personalities of athletes who engage in different types of sports. Perhaps the clearest distinction occurs between athletes involved in team sports and those involved in individual sports. For example, team sport athletes are more extraverted, dependent, and anxious than individual sport athletes. Certainly, one might expect some differences to emerge between football players and tennis players in terms of personality traits.

APPLICATION Personality profiles may be used by trained sport psychologists to help athletes decide which sports to devote their energies to, but they should never be used to coerce the athletes into making such decisions. If a young athlete with a tennis player's personality wants to be a golfer, so be it. Occasionally, an athlete reaches a juncture in her athletic career when she must decide between two sports in order to devote adequate time to academic work. Perhaps consideration of the athlete's personality profile would be useful at this point.

were observed in the boys during this period. From an educational perspective, all but the factor of dependence would be considered positive in nature.

Personality Sport Type Can personality profiles of athletes in one sport be reliably differentiated from those of athletes in another sport? Perhaps the first real attempts to answer this question were made with bodybuilders. Research by Henry (1941), Thune (1949), and Harlow (1951), for example, suggested that bodybuilders suffer from feelings of masculine inadequacy, and are overly concerned with health, body build, and manliness. A study by Thirer and Greer (1981), however, would tend to cast doubt on these earlier stereotypes. In a well-conceived and controlled study, the authors concluded that intermediate and competitive bodybuilders were high in achievement motivation and resistance to change, but relatively normal in all other traits measured. They found no support for the previous generalities and negative stereotyping sometimes applied to bodybuilders.

Kroll and Crenshaw (1970) reported a study in which highly skilled football, wrestling, gymnastic, and karate athletes were compared on the basis of Cattell's 16 PF. The results showed that when the football players and wrestlers were contrasted with the gymnasts and karate participants,

significantly different personality profiles emerged. The wrestlers and football players had similar profiles, while the gymnasts and karate athletes differed from each other, as well as from the wrestlers and football players.

Similarly, Singer (1969) observed that collegiate baseball players (a team sport) differed significantly from tennis players (an individual sport) in several personality variables. Specifically, tennis players scored higher than baseball players on the desire to do one's best, desire to lead, and ability to analyze others, but were less willing to accept blame.

Schurr, Ashley, and Joy (1977), in their signal research, clearly demonstrated that personality profile differences exist between players of team and individual sports, and between players of direct and parallel sports. Team sport athletes were observed to be more anxious, dependent, extraverted, and alert-objective, but less sensitive-imaginative, than individual sport athletes. Direct sport athletes (basketball, football, soccer, etc.) were observed to be more independent and to have less ego strength than parallel sport athletes (volleyball, baseball, etc.).

Clingman and Hilliard (1987) examined the personality characteristics of super-adherers and found them to differ significantly from the population norm in the personality traits of achievement,

CONCEPT   In many cases, athletes playing different positions on the same team can be differentiated as a function of personality characteristics. This is especially pronounced in sports in which athletes are required to do very different kinds of things. Point guards in basketball, setters in volleyball, quarterbacks in American football, and goalies in soccer and/or ice hockey can be expected to exhibit personality characteristics decidedly different from those of some other position players.

APPLICATION   Personality characteristics of athletes can and should be considered in the selection of players for certain specialized positions. Results of personality tests and the like may be helpful in identifying a self-confident, energetic, and outgoing extravert to run your multiple offense in volleyball or your motion offense in basketball. You may also ascertain that an individual has these same important characteristics by simply observing athletes in competitive situations. It may not take a pencil-and-paper test to tell you that Mary excels at taking charge of the team when she is on the court. One should not forget, however, that physical characteristics such as speed, power, and quickness are also critically important.

aggression, autonomy, dominance, endurance, harm avoidance, and play. Super-adherers are runners, swimmers, cyclists, and triathletes who are dedicated to endurance activities. While data were not provided, the expectation is that the super-adherer would also differ from athletes in other sports in certain personality traits.

The literature shows that athletes in one sport often differ in personality type and profile from athletes in other sports (Franken, Hill & Kierstead, 1994). It seems reasonable, for example, to expect a football player to be more aggressive, anxious, and tolerant of pain than a golfer or a tennis player. However, the point still needs to be made that the state of the art (or science) is still not so refined that one could feel justified in arbitrarily categorizing young athletes based on their personality profiles.

Player Position and Personality Profile   In the previous section, the notion of personality types among athletes of differing sports was discussed. It was concluded that in many circumstances, differences exist between the personality profiles of athletes from different sports. The same concept can be applied to whether athletes of a certain sport exhibit different personality profiles based on player position.

In recent years we have experienced an age of superspecialization in team sports. In baseball, outfielders are inserted based on whether they hit left- or right-handed. In football, the offense and defense of the same team rarely come in contact with each other. In volleyball, hitters and setters have specialized roles that dictate the sorts of defensive and offensive assignments they fulfill. Similar kinds of specializations can be observed with most other team sports.

While this area of research would seem to be of interest to coaches and athletes, very little has been reported on it. Cox (1987) asked the following question relative to the sport of volleyball. Do center blockers, strong-side hitters, and setters display different psychological profiles due to their different assignments? The subjects were 157 female volleyball players who participated in an invitational volleyball tournament. The results indicated that the three groups of athletes were very similar in terms of their psychological profiles, with the exception of certain attentional focus variables. Compared to middle blockers and strong-side hitters, setters were observed to have a broad internal focus and be able to think about several things at one time. The setter on a volleyball team is like the point guard on a basketball team or the quarterback on a football team. She must be cognizant at all times of what plays to call and of the strengths and weaknesses of front-line attackers, as well as the strengths and weaknesses of the opposing team's blockers and defensive alignment.

In a similar study reported by Schurr, Ruble, Nisbet, and Wallace (1984), a comparison was made between player position in football and personality traits. Using the Myers-Briggs Type Inventory (MBTI), the authors concluded that linesmen differ significantly from backfield players in terms of judging and perceiving traits. Linesmen tend to be more organized and practical, while defensive and offensive backs are more flexible and adaptable. Interestingly, no reliable differences were noted between offensive and defensive linesmen, while offensive backs tended to be more extraverted and defensive backs more introverted.

Personality Profiles of Athletes Differing in Skill Level The ability to distinguish between successful and unsuccessful athletes in any particular sport using personality traits has never been particularly successful (Davis & Mogk, 1994; Morgan, 1980b). For example, Kroll (1967), using collegiate wrestlers, and Kroll and Carlson (1967), using karate participants, could not successfully distinguish between the successful and unsuccessful performers. Rushall (1972), using football players, and Singer (1969), using tennis and baseball players, likewise could not distinguish between the successful and unsuccessful players. In addition, Craighead, Privette, and Byrkit (1986) were unable to distinguish between starters and nonstarters in high school boys' basketball.

Added to this lack of relationship between personality traits and skill level are the results of the Schurr et al. (1977) research. Successful and unsuccessful sport participation in this study was determined based on whether or not the athlete earned a letter or award. The results of this comparison using the global factors of the 16 PF failed to show a significant relationship between performance and personality. It does not seem reasonable to expect that a group of first-string athletes

could be separated from a group of second-string athletes based solely on personality traits. Both of these groups consist of highly skilled athletes in the first place, or they would not be on the team. Additionally, the task of differentiating between two groups of relatively successful performers on the basis of skill itself is a very tenuous and arbitrary task. Why, then, should a coach expect to be able to do the same thing based on personality traits? A study by Williams and Parkin (1980) provides credence to this line of reasoning. Specifically, they compared the personality profiles (Cattell's 16 PF) of 18 international-level male hockey players with those of 34 national-level and 33 club players. Their results showed that the international players had significantly different profiles from the club players, but that the national-level players could not be distinguished from players in either of the other two groups.

Research by Garland and Barry (1990) and Davis (1991) does little to alter this view. Garland and Barry (1990) categorized 272 American collegiate football athletes on the basis of skill (e.g., regulars, substitutes, or survivors). Results showed that the personality traits of tough-mindedness, extraversion, group dependence, and emotional stability accounted for 29 percent of the variance in skill ($R = .54$). While this is not a high correlation, it is higher than those reported in earlier investigations. Davis (1991), however, reported that skill level in prospective professional ice hockey players could not be predicted as a function of personality traits.

One exception to the general rule that skill level cannot be differentiated as a function of personality may occur when *elite athletes* are compared with athletes of lesser ability. Notice that in the Williams and Parkin (1980) study cited above, international-level hockey players exhibited personality profiles that differed from those of club-level players, but not national-level players. Silva (1984) provided a plausible explanation for this phenomenon. As illustrated in figure 2.2, as aspiring elite athletes move up the **athletic pyramid,** they become more alike in their

and the game on the line. As the TV cameras zeroed in on the batter, you could see clearly the total concentration and attention that he was giving to the pitcher. Dane let the first pitch, a fastball, go by. Then he stroked the next pitch into right field for a game-winning single. He was a hero! As history has recorded, the Kansas City Royals went on to win the seventh game and the World Series.

Dane may or may not have been an anxious person, as determined by a personality inventory, but it would be impossible for him not to be tense and anxious in this specific situation. The power and influence of this historic baseball situation were far more forceful than any general disposition to respond in a certain way.

Just as the effects of personality on athletic behavior can be determined and measured, so also can the effects of the **situation** (environment) on athletic behavior be determined. To accomplish this, we must first find a way to represent the effects of the situation. One way that sport psychologists do this is through the measurement of mood. Mood states fluctuate as the situation changes. In the baseball example, tension increased as a result of the extreme pressure of the **competitive situation.**

In the pages that follow we will discuss (a) ways in which sport psychologists measure mood state, (b) Morgan's mental health model, (c) research and the Profile of Mood States, (d) the interactional model, and (e) the mood profile of the elite disabled athlete.

Ways in Which Sport Psychologists Measure Mood State

Our focus in this chapter will be upon research that has utilized the Profile of Mood States (POMS) for measuring mood states. Nevertheless, the student should be aware that there are numerous other inventories that measure mood states. An incomplete list of such instruments is provided in table 2.3.

The **Profile of Mood States** (POMS) is by far the most commonly used instrument for measuring mood states in sport psychology. LeUnes and Burger (1998) noted that the POMS was first used in sport in 1975, and has been associated with 257 published articles between 1975 and 1998. Originally developed by McNair, Lorr & Droppleman (1971, 1981, 1992), the POMS is composed of 65 items that measure six mood states: tension, depression, anger, vigor, fatigue, and confusion. Five of these mood states are negative in nature, while one is positive (vigor). Since the original development of the POMS in 1971, two additional authorized versions of the POMS have been developed. One of them was a bipolar version with 72 items (Lorr & McNair, 1988), and the other was a short-form version with 30 items (McNair et al., 1992). The same basic six mood states are measured in each version. In addition to the three authorized versions of the POMS, independent researchers have developed four other shortened versions (LeUnes & Burger, 2000; Terry, 1995). These four versions, along with the three authorized

TABLE 2.3 | An Incomplete List of Psychological Instruments That Measure Mood State

Type	Inventory
General	1. Activation-Deactivation Adjective Check List (Thayer, 1986)
	2. Beck Depression Inventory (Beck, Ward, Mendelsohn, Mock, & Erbaugh, 1961)
	3. Multiple Adjective Checklist (Nowlis, 1965)
	4. Positive Affect Negative Affect Scale (Watson, Clark, & Tellegen, 1988)
	5. Profile of Mood States (McNair, Lorr, & Droppleman, 1971, 1981, 1992)
Exercise Specific	1. Exercise-Induced Feeling Scale (Gauvin & Rejeski, 1993)
	2. Subjective Exercise Experience Scale (McAuley & Courneya, 1994)

TABLE 2.4 | Authorized and Independently Developed Versions of the Profile of Mood States (POMS)

Category	Items	POMS Version
Authorized	65	Profile of Mood States (McNair et al., 1971, 1981, 1992)
	72	Profile of Mood States—Bipolar (Lorr & McNair, 1988)
	30	Profile of Mood States—Short version (McNair et al., 1992)
Independent	37	Shortened Version of POMS (Shacham, 1983)
	40	Abbreviated POMS (Grove & Prapavessis, 1992)
	27	Short POMS for Young Athletes (Terry, Keohane & Lane, 1996)
	06	Brief Assessment of Mood (Whelan & Meyers, 1998)

FIGURE 2.3 | Illustration of the iceberg profile of the elite athlete.

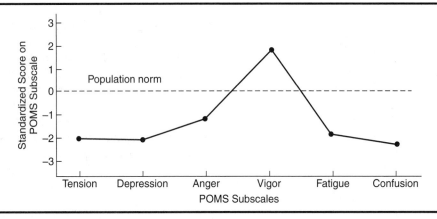

versions, are listed in table 2.4. Research has shown that all of the shortened versions, including the bipolar version, are highly correlated with the original 65-item POMS.

The Profile of Mood States and Morgan's Mental Health Model

It appears that Bill Morgan (1979) was one of the first to utilize the Profile of Mood States (POMS) in sport- and exercise-related research. Morgan plotted standardized POMS scores for elite athletes and noted that (a) elite athletes exhibited a **mood profile** that was lower in negative moods and higher in vigor than a normative sample, and (b) elite athletes also exhibited a more mentally healthy mood profile than less successful athletes. Morgan referred to the notion that the successful athlete exhibits a more healthy mood profile than less successful athletes or a normative population as the **mental health model.** According to this model, the successful athlete is viewed as a mentally healthy individual relative to psychological mood. When the standardized POMS scores of the elite athlete are plotted as in figure 2.3, they take the form of an iceberg, with all of the negative moods falling below the population norm and the vigor score falling well above the norm. This

CONCEPT Researchers cannot consistently and effectively discriminate between athletes of differing skill level on the basis of mood state scores alone.

APPLICATION You will note that we observed a similar outcome when we tried to discriminate between athletes of different skill level based on personality. While the mental health model does discriminate between athletes and nonathletes, it is not a reliable predictor of whether an athlete belongs to a high achievement group or a low achievement group. As with personality, coaches should not use POMS scores to make personnel decisions.

---

mood profile has come to be referred to as the **iceberg profile.**

Research has been very supportive of the notion that the successful athlete exhibits an iceberg profile relative to the population norm (average of the population), but not so supportive in terms of discriminating between successful and less successful athletes. We will discuss the issue of discriminating among athletes in the next section.

Terry and Lane (2000), however, found strong support for the notion that the athlete exhibits a mood profile that is superior to that of the population norm. They administered the POMS to 2,086 athletes and found differences between the athletic sample and the existing population norm for all mood subscales. Consistent with the mental health model, athletes exhibit lower negative mood states and a higher vigor score compared to a POMS normative sample of a similar age group.

Research and the Profile of Mood States

As with personality research, investigators have been interested in studying the relationship between **precompetitive mood** and athletic performance. One approach has been to determine if athletes belonging to different achievement levels can be differentiated based on mood state measures. A second approach has been to determine if performance outcome can be predicted based on precompetitive mood. In this section, we will consider both of these approaches. In addition, a conceptual

model for studying the relationship between mood and performance will be considered.

Mood States and Achievement Levels In this line of research, investigators attempted to show that scores on the POMS could discriminate among groups of athletes of different skill levels. That is, can mood differentiate between starters and nonstarters on an athletic team? This is a situation in which athletes of clearly different skill levels are given the POMS to see if the scores of the differently skilled groups differ.

Beedie, Terry, and Lane (2000) reported the results of a **meta-analysis** (statistical summary of studies) that included 13 studies, 90 effect sizes (mean comparisons), and 2,285 participants. The overall **effect size** for this investigation was .10, which is considered to be very low (Cohen, 1992). Except for a small difference in vigor scores, athletes at different levels of achievement report essentially the same moods. These results are consistent with earlier reviews by Landers (1991); Rowley, Landers, Kyllo, and Etnier (1995), and Prapavessis (2000). Apparently, it is not possible to consistently differentiate between athletes of differing skill level, as earlier suggested by Morgan and the mental health model.

Mood States and Performance Outcome In the previous section, we considered whether athletes of differing achievement or skill levels could be differentiated on the basis of POMS scores.

CONCEPT   A weak to moderate relationship exists between precompetitive mood and performance outcome. This relationship is enhanced when performance is measured subjectively as opposed to objectively.

APPLICATION   An athlete's mood prior to an athletic contest is related to athletic performance. The less negative mood and the more positive mood the athlete experiences, the better he is likely to perform. This relationship is not so strong, however, that the coach should use it to predict objective performance outcome.

CONCEPT   Depression moderates the relationship between the other mood states and athletic performance. In the presence of depression, the increased levels of negative mood will have a debilitating effect on performance. Increased depression is also associated with reduced vigor, which results in a reduced facilitative effect.

APPLICATION   Coaches and athletes must be concerned about the debilitating levels of depression. Depression can negatively influence the other moods, as well as performance. If high levels of depression are suspected, the athlete may need to seek professional help from a counseling or clinical sport psychologist.

In this section we consider whether the performance outcome of athletes of a similar skill level can be predicted based on POMS scores. If I know an athlete's precompetitive mood profile, can I use it to predict how she will do in the competition?

Beedie, Terry, and Lane (2000) reported the results of a second meta-analysis that included 16 studies, 102 effect sizes, and 1,126 participants. The overall effect size for this investigation was .35, which is considered to be small to medium. In addition, some moderating variables were identified. A **moderating variable** is a variable that determines the relationship between two other variables. Moderating variables included type of sport and how performance was measured.

Type of Sport   Performance was predicted a little better in open skills as opposed to closed skills. Closed skills are believed to be closed to the environment (e.g., bowling, clean-and-jerk), while open skills are believed to be open to the environment (e.g., tennis, soccer). Effects were slightly larger for individual sports compared to team sports, and effects were larger for short-duration sports (rowing, wrestling) compared to long-duration sports (e.g., basketball, volleyball).

Measurement of Performance   Effects were larger when performance outcome was conceptualized as subjective and self-referenced, as opposed to objective. An objective outcome would be whether you won or lost a contest, or whether you recorded a better time than another athlete in a contest. Examples of subjective self-referenced outcomes include (a) a post-event self-rating of performance, (b) percentage of a personal best, and (c) comparison to expectations. In post-event self-rating, an athlete has an opportunity to subjectively indicate how she feels she performed independent of objective outcome (win/loss). In the percentage of personal best method, performance is measured as a percentage of how the athlete did compared to her personal best. If she lost a race, but performed at 95 percent of her personal best, this may be a better performance outcome than the 90 percent of personal best displayed by the winner. Finally, in the comparison to expectations method, the athlete compares her performance with how she expected to perform. For example, an athlete's expected performance in golf is her golf handicap. If she normally shoots seven over par and she shoots four over par today, she has had a good performance, regardless of objective outcome.

A stronger relationship exists between mood and performance when performance is measured subjectively than when it is measured objectively. If you are simply trying to predict whether an athlete wins or loses a contest or finishes higher than another runner in a race, mood is a relatively weak predictor of performance (effect size = .28). If you are trying to predict if an athlete will perform up to personal expectations and past performance, then the relationship between mood and performance is a little stronger (effect size = .37). Cohen (1992) has indicated that effect sizes of .20, .50, and .80 are considered to be small, medium, and large, respectively.

A Conceptual Model for Predicting Performance

Based on the literature, Lane and Terry (2000) proposed a **conceptual model** for explaining the relationship between precompetitive mood and performance. At the present time the model should be considered to be theoretical in nature. A theory allows investigators to test various aspects of a model to either modify it, verify it, or reject it. For this reason, a testable theory is very important to the advancement of science.

Lane and Terry propose that depression is a moderator between other manifestations of mood and athletic performance. As can be observed in figure 2.4, *high levels of depression* are associated with increased anger, tension, confusion, and fatigue, but with reduced vigor. The increased levels of negative mood have a debilitative effect upon performance, while reduced vigor has a reduced facilitative effect upon performance.

In the *absence of depression,* vigor will have a facilitative effect on performance, fatigue and confusion will have a debilitative effect upon performance, and anger and tension will have a curvilinear effect upon performance. Note that fatigue and confusion are predicted to have a debilitative effect upon performance regardless of whether the athlete is depressed or not. Anger and tension, in the absence of depression, can actually facilitate performance up to a point, but when they get too high they will cause a decrement in performance.

Some of the tenets of the conceptual model were tested by Lane, Terry, Beedie, Curry, and Clark (2002) utilizing a large sample (N = 451) of school-age children. Mood was assessed, using an adolescent version of the POMS, 10 minutes prior to a running competition in which participants completed a self-referenced race for distance or time. Consistent with the conceptual model, participants categorized as depressed scored higher on anger, confusion, fatigue and tension, but lower in vigor compared to the nondepressed group. Also consistent with the conceptual model, larger correlations were observed among the moods of anger, tension, confusion, fatigue, and vigor for the depressed mood group compared to the non-depressed group. As predicted, vigor significantly predicted increased performance regardless of level of depression; however, confusion and fatigue did not lead to a reduction in performance as expected. Finally, in the depressed group, anger predicted reduced performance as expected, but anger in the no-depression group and tension in both groups failed to influence performance as expected. Overall, this study provided support for some aspects of the Lane and Terry (2000) conceptual model, partial support for others, and no support for the notion that a curvilinear relationship would exist between anger and tension with

FIGURE 2.4 | Lane and Terry's (2000) conceptual model to predict performance from precompetitive mood.

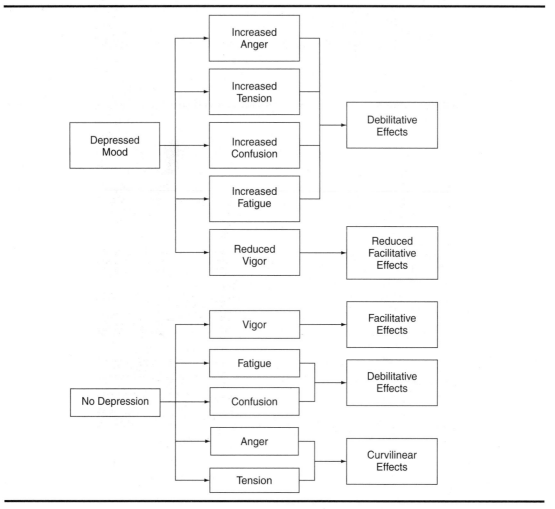

Reproduced with permission.

performance in the no-depression group. Finally, it is important to note that while many predicted relationships were significant, due to a large sample size, many of the significant effects were very weak. Clearly, the model needs further testing before we can conclude that depression acts as a moderator of the relationship between mood state and athletic performance.

The Interactional Model

In the previous section on personality, we learned that personality alone is a weak predictor of athletic behavior (performance). In this chapter we have learned that the situation, as measured by mood, is also a relatively weak predictor of athlete behavior. It is believed, however, that the sum of

Does this highly successful collegiate athlete exhibit the mood state "iceberg profile" of the elite athlete? Courtesy University of Missouri–Columbia Sports Information.

the two plus their interaction would be a stronger predictor of athletic behavior. The notion that the personality interacts with situation to predict performance is known as the **interactional model.** Information about personality plus information about the environment (situation) plus the interaction between the two is a better predictor of athlete behavior than personality or the situation alone. This relationship is represented in the following formula:

$$Behavior = Personality + Situation + P \times S + Error$$

The error in the formula represents all of the *unmeasured* factors that may contribute to athletic behavior. One way to measure the effects of the environment (situation) is by measuring mood, as we have learned to do in this chapter.

FIGURE 2.5 | Illustration showing the contribution of personality and situation to total athlete behavior.

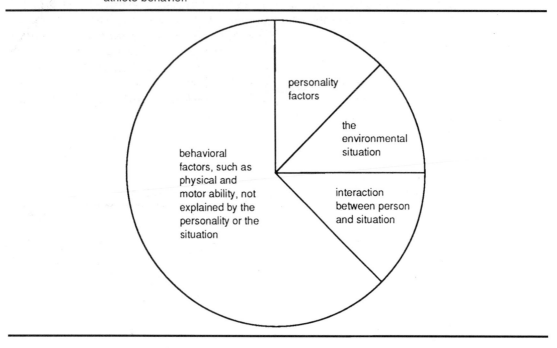

personality
factors

the
environmental
situation

behavioral
factors, such as
physical and
motor ability, not
explained by the
personality or the
situation

interaction
between person
and situation

The relationship between the personality of the individual and the situation is illustrated in figure 2.5. In this figure, the total pie represents all the factors that can contribute to athletic behavior or performance. Only a small part of the total pie is due to factors associated with the athlete's personality. Another small portion is due to factors directly related to the situation and independent of or unrelated to the person. Next, a certain part of the pie is represented by the interaction between the personality and the situation. When factors associated with the athlete's personality, the environmental situation, and the interaction between these three are summed, approximately 30 percent of the athlete's behavior is accounted for. If we were to consider only the athlete's personality, then we could explain only about 10 to 15 percent of the athlete's performance or behavior.

The interactive relationship between personality traits and mood states is evident in the literature (Prapavessis & Grove, 1994a, 1994b). When athletes are categorized as high or low on some personality variable, it is observed that these diverse groups may also differ on selected mood states. For example, rifle shooters categorized as high on the personality characteristic of commitment also score high on the precompetitive measure of tension.

Utilizing the interactional model, sport psychologists have been able to identify a **psychological profile** for the elite athlete. Four of the ten psychological factors illustrated in figure 2.6 are personality traits, while the remaining six are mood states. Together, selected personality traits and mood states are effective predictors of athletic ability. Silva, Shultz, Haslam, and Murray (1981) reported being able to accurately classify

CONCEPT   The combined and interactive effects of personality and the environment constitute a stronger predictor of athletic performance than personality alone.

APPLICATION   The fact that Linda is an anxious person may not be predictive of athletic performance, but the fact that Linda is an anxious person *and* that she gets very anxious in competitive situations might be. These two factors together, and the interaction between them, may create a situation that will not be conducive to consistent ground stroking in competitive tennis. The coach needs to know more about Linda than that she is generally an anxious person. The coach also needs to know how she responds in a specific competitive situation.

FIGURE 2.6 | Interactive psychological profile of a mentally healthy elite athlete.

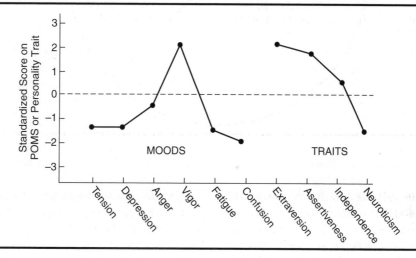

80 percent of a group of elite wrestlers using the interaction model. Similarly, Silva, Shultz, Haslam, Martin, and Murray (1985) demonstrated that 78 percent of a group of qualifiers for the United States Olympic Wrestling Team could be accurately classified using an interactional model. For both studies, the percentage of correct classification increased when physiological variables were also included.

In summary, the successful world-class athlete is low in the trait measures of anxiety and neuroticism, and high in extraversion. In terms of psychological mood states, the world-class athlete is low in anxiety, tension, depression, anger, fatigue, and confusion, but high in vigor. In total, the psychological profile of the successful world-class athlete is consistent with positive mental health.

Psychological Profile of the Elite Disabled Athlete

The interaction approach in sport psychology has focused primarily on the elite **able-bodied athlete.** In recent years, however, more attention has been

CONCEPT   The psychological profile of the elite physically challenged athlete is similar to that of the elite able-bodied athlete. Both groups of athletes exhibit the iceberg profile relative to mood states.

APPLICATION   When working with elite disabled athletes, it is important to recognize that they do not suffer from psychological disabilities as well. They are mentally healthy individuals who have overcome tremendous adversity to become elite athletes.

devoted to describing the psychological characteristics of the elite **disabled** or **physically challenged athlete.** This surge of interest in the disabled athlete is due partly to the encouragement of notable sport psychologists who have argued that this group of athletes has been ignored (Ogilvie, 1985).

Interestingly, the elite disabled athlete exhibits a psychological profile that is very similar to the profile of the elite able-bodied athlete (Asken, 1991; Shephard, 1990). Elite wheelchair athletes, for example, exhibit personality characteristics that are similar to those of able-bodied athletes, but dissimilar to those of disabled wheelchair nonathletes. Wheelchair athletes are higher in self-esteem and physical orientation than disabled nonathletes (Roeder & Aufsesser, 1986).

In addition, the iceberg profile of the elite able-bodied athlete (see fig. 2.3) is readily observed in elite disabled wheelchair athletes (Greenwood, Dzewaltowski & French, 1990; Henschen, Horvat, & French, 1984). As with the elite able-bodied athlete, the physically challenged elite athlete is generally a mentally healthy individual who displays low levels of tension, depression, anger, fatigue, and confusion. These findings are very striking, considering the extreme physical and psychological trauma that many of these remarkable athletes have had to overcome (Asken, 1991).

The iceberg profile of the elite athlete has also been observed in elite visually impaired male athletes (Mastro, Sherrill, Gench, & French, 1987).

Visually impaired female athletes, however, possess psychological characteristics typical of average nonathletic females. In a follow-up investigation, Mastro, Canabal, and French (1988) studied mood states of sighted and unsighted "beep baseball" players. Beep baseball is an interesting game in which the catcher, the pitcher, and two outfield spotters are sighted; the remaining defensive players are unsighted. Mastro et al. observed that the sighted and unsighted players exhibited similar mood state profiles. Although both groups reported mood state scores that were below the population norm (able-bodied), the unsighted players reported being more tense and depressed when compared to the sighted players.

While unrelated to mood state, an interesting investigation by Cox and Davis (1992) compared the psychological skills of elite wheelchair athletes to those of able-bodied collegiate-level athletes. Psychological skills measured included anxiety control, concentration, confidence, mental preparation, motivation, and team emphasis. The wheelchair athletes displayed psychological skills that were superior to those of a group of collegiate track and field athletes, as well as a group of collegiate athletes from four sports combined. It was hypothesized that the differences in psychological skill were due to relative skill level. The wheelchair athletes were competing for berths on the United States Seoul Paralympics team, while the collegiate athletes represented a skill level clearly below elite for the able-bodied athlete.

Summary

Personality is defined as all the consistent ways in which the behavior of one person differs from that of others especially in social situations. An individual's personality defines the person in unique ways that remain stable and consistent over time. A person's typical responses and role-related behaviors don't always reflect that person's true personality.

Four theories or approaches to studying personality were reviewed. These were (1) the psychodynamic approach, (2) social learning theory, (3) humanistic theory, and (4) trait theory approach. A number of different approaches to measuring personality were also discussed. These included rating scales, projective procedures, and pencil-and-paper inventories. A number of different personality inventories were described, including the Minnesota Multiphasic Personality Inventory, Cattell's 16 PF, the NEO–Five Factor Personality Inventory, the Athletic Motivation Inventory, the Winning Profile Athletic Instrument, and the Troutwine Athletic Profile.

Several factors were considered concerning whether a relationship exists between athletic performance and an athlete's personality. The following conclusions were drawn: (1) athletes differ from nonathletes on many personality traits; (2) athletes who exhibit certain personality traits gravitate toward athletic involvement; (3) athletes in one sport often differ in personality, type, and profile from athletes in other sports; (4) an association exists between personality and player position in some sports; (5) it is difficult to discriminate between players of differing skill level based purely upon personality variables; (6) elite athletes can be discriminated from athletes of low ability based on personality variables; and (7) female athletes are very similar to male athletes in the general conclusions that have been drawn.

Whereas a personality trait is believed to be a relatively permanent disposition, a mood state is believed to be a situation-specific, somewhat transient psychological response to an environmental stimulus.

While there are many different kinds of inventories available to measure mood, the one most commonly used in sport and exercise is the Profile of Mood States (POMS).

The plotting of the six POMS mood subscales yields a mood profile. Morgan proposed that the mood profile of the elite athlete represented a mentally healthy profile, and referred to this as the mental health model. The mood profile of the elite athlete is referred to as an iceberg profile, because all negative moods are below the mean of the population norm and vigor is above the population norm. The notion that the successful athlete exhibits a mood profile that is different from the population norm of nonathletes is supported by research.

Results of meta-analyses of completed studies show that athletes of different achievement or skill levels cannot be reliably differentiated on the basis of mood states. A weak to moderate relationship, however, exists between precompetitive mood and performance of athletes who are of a similar skill level. The way in which performance is measured moderates the relationship between mood and performance outcome. The relationship between mood and performance outcome is stronger when performance is subjectively determined.

Lane and Terry (2000) proposed a conceptual model showing how mood affects athletic behavior. In the model, depression is a moderating variable that determines how the other moods affect performance. Depression is believed to increase the negative effects of mood upon athlete behavior.

An interactional model proposes that the combined and interactive effects of personality and mood (situation) have a greater impact upon athlete behavior than either has alone. The psychological profile of the elite athlete includes both mood states and personality traits. The psychological and mood profile of the elite disabled athlete is very similar to that of the elite able-bodied athlete.

Critical Thought Questions

1. Why do you think the big five personality traits do not agree exactly with Cattell's five global traits?

2. Now that you have studied the various ways that sport psychologists measure personality, which inventory would you recommend for use? Why?

3. Given that research does not support the use of personality or psychological profiles for making athlete personnel decisions, why do you think the practice persists?

4. Provide a summary statement about the existence and strength of the relationship between personality and athletic performance.

5. Mood fluctuation is one way that the effect of the environment situation can be measured. Can you think of other ways in which situational variables could be represented and measured?

6. Why do you think the POMS features five negative moods and only one positive mood? Some sport psychologists believe this is a weakness of the POMS. What do you think?

7. Can the POMS predict athletic success any better than a personality inventory? Explain.

8. Why do you think depression would moderate or determine the relationship between mood and behavior?

9. Why would the interactional model improve the prediction of athletic performance? Do you think it improves it enough to make the model useful for personnel decisions about athletes?

Glossary

able-bodied athlete An athlete who does not possess physically challenging disabilities.

Athletic Motivation Inventory A personality inventory designed to predict athletic success (Institute for the Study of Athletic Motivation).

athletic pyramid A pyramid showing less-skilled players at the base and more highly skilled players at the top. Athletes at the bottom are more heterogeneous in terms of personality characteristics, while those at the top are more homogeneous.

big five personality traits Trait psychologists identified the five major personality traits to be neuroticism, extraversion, agreeableness, conscientiousness, and openness.

Cattell 16 PF Cattell's Personality Factor Questionnaire, measuring the 16 source traits of personality.

competitive situation An environmental situation that is competitive in nature.

conceptual model In the case of mood and athletic behavior, a model that explains conceptually and theoretically how different variables operate on each other to affect performance.

disabled athlete See physically challenged athlete.

disposition A tendency to behave in a certain manner. Also called a personality trait.

effect size The number of times that a pooled standard deviation can be divided into the difference between two means (Cohen, 1992).

global personality traits Cattell's version of the big five personality traits: extraversion, anxiety, tough-mindedness, independence, and self-control.

gravitational hypothesis The notion that athletes possessing stable, extraverted personalities gravitate toward athletics.

iceberg profile A profile of the elite athlete on the six mood states measured by the POMS. Vigor is the only state for which elite athletes score well above the population mean, causing the profile to resemble an iceberg when charted on a graph.

interactional model An approach to sport personality based on the notion that both personality traits and situational states should be used in any prediction equation.

mental health model Developed by Morgan, a model proposing that the elite athlete is a mentally healthy individual.

meta-analysis A statistical summary and comparison of independent samples associated with a literature review.

MMPI Minnesota Multiphasic Personality Inventory; a 12-scale test designed for clinical populations.

moderating variable A variable that determines or moderates the relationship between one variable or set of variables and another variable or set of variables.

mood profile Plotting of standardized mood state scores on a graph.

mood state A situation-specific, somewhat transient, psychological response to an environmental stimulus.

multivariate approach The practice of measuring and analyzing correlated dependent variables simultaneously, as opposed to separately, as in the univariate approach.

personality All the consistent ways in which the behavior of one person differs from that of others, especially in social situations.

personality profile The plotting of an athlete's standardized personality scores on a line or bar graph.

personality trait A disposition to exhibit certain personality characteristics.

physically challenged athlete An athlete possessing physically challenging disabilities.

precompetitive mood An athlete's mood immediately before a competitive event.

primary personality factors The 16 personality factors or traits that Cattell arrived at when he reduced the original 35 traits he had identified.

Profile of Mood States A 65-item inventory designed to measure a person's mood states on six subscales.

projective procedures Psychological tests commonly used to determine information about underlying motives. Responses are unstructured and open-ended.

psychological profile Plotting of standardized mood state and personality trait scores on a graph.

Rorschach test A projective test in which the subjects describe an inkblot.

situation The effects of the environment at a specific point in time.

situation The effects of the environment at a specific point in time.

Thematic Apperception Test A personality test in which the personality is projected through storytelling.

Troutwine Athletic Profile A personality inventory designed to predict athletic success (Troutwine).

Winning Profile Athletic Instrument A personality inventory designed to predict athletic success (PsyMetrics).

Leadership and Communication in Sport

KEY TERMS

Centrality
Chelladurai's multidimensional model
Coach-athlete compatibility
Coach Effectiveness Training (CET)
Coaching Behavior Assessment System (CBAS)
Coaching efficacy
Conceptual model of coaching efficacy
Consideration
Fiedler's contingency theory
Functional model of leadership
"Great man" theory of leadership
Initiating structure
Leadership behavior model
Life cycle theory
Path-goal theory
Positive sandwich approach
Propinquity
Relationship motivation
Situational behaviors

Situational traits
Situation-specific behavior theories
Stacking
Task dependence

Task motivation
Team building
Universal behavior theory
Universal behaviors
Universal traits

I t is much easier to point to examples of great leadership than it is to explain what great leadership is. For example, in sport, it would be hard to find greater examples of successful leader-ship than Vince Lombardi, Pat Head Summitt, and John Wooden. The critical questions, however, are these: Why were they great leaders, and can we learn from them?

Vince Lombardi will forever be linked with the unprecedented success of Green Bay Packers professional football. Lombardi had an unquenchable desire to succeed, to excel, and to win. He was famous for slogans placed in locker rooms and upon walls where the players could see them. One of his favorite slogans was, "Winning is not everything. It is the only thing." (Kramer, 1970; Wiebush, 1971). Not to be outdone by Vince Lombardi, George Steinbrenner, principal owner of the New York Yankees baseball team, was quoted as saying, "For us, winning isn't the only thing, it's second to breathing" (Kepner, 2003).

Pat Head Summitt, women's basketball coach at the University of Tennessee, has enjoyed unprecedented success as a leader and coach. Coach Summitt is one of the most successful coaches in America and ranks with any male coach in terms of success (Wrisberg, 1990).

John Wooden, the most successful basketball coach in college history, won ten NCAA national championships at UCLA. Seven of those wins were in a row, beginning in 1967 and ending in 1973. On Wooden's coaching style, Bill Walton (2000) said this of his former college coach:

> Wooden was a teacher. He taught on a constant basis, from showing us how to put our shoes and socks on, to building a foundation based on the human values and personal characteristics embodied in what he called his Pyramid of Success. All of this was done in the subtlest of ways. While our practices were the most demanding endeavors, both physically and emotionally, that I've ever been a part of, there was always the sense of people having fun playing a simple game.

Sometimes, though, leaders lead simply by example. Pat Tillman's story is both tragic and inspirational (Smith, 2004). While on patrol in the mountains of Afghanistan with other United States Army Rangers, he was killed by friendly fire. This was tragic, but the rest of the story was truly inspirational. Prior to interrupting his National Football League (NFL) career with the Arizona Cardinals, he had signed a three-year, 3.6-million-dollar contract.

He gave this up to volunteer for the Army Rangers to fight the Taliban and Al-Qaeda in Afghanistan.

In some ways, the complexity of the concept of leadership is overwhelming. It is like a puzzle that makes little sense until each piece is put in its place. In an attempt to master this puzzle, this chapter has been organized into three sections. The first addresses the major theories of leadership that have evolved. The second section deals with the nature of coach-athlete compatibility and communication. The third discusses player position, leadership opportunity, and stacking.

While the concept of coach-athlete communication is not formally introduced in this chapter until section 2, it is important to understand that effective communication is a requirement of effective leadership. Effective leaders communicate effectively to their followers, and this is especially true in the coach-athlete relationship. As we shall learn, however, there are many modes of positive and negative communication. Body language and facial expression are two of the most important forms of communication. The concept of communication will also be addressed in chapter 15, when we introduce the concept of team cohesion, which involves communication among members of a team.

Theories of Leadership

Early interest in leadership centered on the traits or abilities of great leaders. It was believed that great leaders were born and not made. Since these early beginnings, leadership research has evolved from an interest in the behavior of leaders to the notion of situation-specific leadership. The notion of an evolution in leadership thought is useful, but it suggests that the early researchers were somehow naive and behind the times. But a careful analysis of the early writings of some of the great researchers reveals that they were as aware of our "modern" concerns for situation-specific leadership as we are today. For example, Metcalf and Urwick (1963, p. 277) quoted management theorist Mary Parker Follett as saying, "Different situations require different kinds of knowledge, and the man

FIGURE 3.1 | A classification scheme for four types of leadership theories.

Characteristics of leaders

		Traits	**Behaviors**
Generality of situation	**More universal**	Trait or "great man" theory • Great leaders are born with personality traits that lead to success in all situations.	Michigan and Ohio State studies • Great leaders possess general behavioral characteristics that can be learned.
	More specific	Fiedler's contingency theory • Personality traits that lead to leader effectiveness in one situation may lead to failure in another.	Situation-specific theories • Effective leadership is a function of learned behaviors that are situation specific.

From O. Behling and C. Schriesheim, *Organizational behavior: Theory, research, and application.* Copyright © 1976 Allyn and Bacon, Inc. Used with permission.

possessing the knowledge demanded by a certain situation tends in the best managed business . . . to become the leader of the moment." Stogdill (1948) expressed similar sentiment when he suggested that a successful leader in one situation may not necessarily be successful in other situations.

Perhaps the most significant contribution to understanding the various approaches to categorizing leadership theory has come from Behling and Schriesheim (1976). They developed a typology of leadership theory that is illustrated in figure 3.1. Their typology categorizes the four major approaches to studying leadership, according to whether the theory deals with leadership traits or leadership behaviors, and whether the traits or behaviors are universal or situation specific in nature.

Leadership traits are relatively stable personality dispositions such as intelligence, aggressiveness, and independence. *Leadership behaviors* have to do with the observed behavior of leaders and have little to do with their personalities. Traits found in *all* successful leaders are referred to as **universal traits,** as opposed to **situational traits.** Situational traits and **situational behaviors** are

those traits and behaviors that may help make a leader successful in one situation, but are of little value in another. Research reported by Cratty and Sage (1964) underscores the time-honored importance of this concept. They conducted a study in which a fraternity pledge class (led by the pledge class president) competed against a loosely organized group of students who did not know one another. The task consisted of going through a maze while blindfolded. The a priori hypothesis was that the pledge class would do better because of their well-established lines of communication and leadership. In fact, the group having no previous association with each other outperformed the pledge class. The reason for this finding was the quality of the leadership. The pledge group tended to rely on the pledge president, who had no specific experience with such things as navigating a maze blindfolded. However, from the independent group, a leader quickly emerged who had obvious skills at navigating the maze. The members of this group turned to him for instructions and tips that allowed them to outperform their competitors. They were not hampered by a leader who had no useful skills for this task.

CONCEPT   There are four possible explanations for effective leadership. These explanations are that (a) the leader possesses universal personality traits that will make her successful in any situation, (b) the leader possesses universal behaviors that will make her successful in any situation, (c) the leader possesses specific personality traits that will make her successful in some situations but not others, and (d) the leader possesses specific behaviors that will make her successful in some situations but not others.

APPLICATION   There are many different theories of leadership. The important principle to understand is that they all can be categorized using the Behling and Schriesheim classification system. Once this has been accomplished, then it is possible to study and test a theory consistent with predictions. In considering a successful leader, it is instructive to see how they fit into the typology illustrated in figure 3.1.

Universal Trait Theories of Leadership

> I think there are people God put on this earth to be natural-born leaders, and Gary is one of them (Matt Simon's assessment of Gary Pinkel, football coach, University of Missouri–Columbia; Matter, 2000, p. B1).

Trait theory has its origin in the **"great man" theory of leadership,** which suggests that certain great leaders have personality traits and personality characteristics that make them ideally suited for leadership. The heyday of trait leadership theory began with the development of objective personality tests in the 1920s and lasted until the end of World War II. Proponents of trait theory believe that successful leaders have certain personality characteristics or leadership traits that make it possible for them to be successful leaders in *any* situation. Since these personality traits are relatively stable, it should be possible to identify potential leaders simply by administering a personality inventory. This approach had a great deal of support from social scientists prior to and during World War II, but after the war, support waned rapidly.

The beginning of the decline in trait leadership theory occurred shortly after Stogdill (1948) published his review of 124 trait-related studies. His review and general conclusions led social scientists to discredit the universal trait theory of leadership. It was simply not possible to demonstrate that successful leaders possessed a universal set of leadership traits. A comparable review of sport-related literature led Sage (1975) to make the same conclusion relative to leadership in sport.

Since the early 1970s there has been a sharp decline in the number of sport studies investigating trait leadership theory. In some ways this is appropriate, since there does not seem to be a *universal* set of personality traits that would set the successful leader or coach apart from less successful colleagues. However, in some respects, this is also unfortunate. While there may not be a universal set of traits associated with successful leadership, this is not to say that certain combinations of universal traits might not be beneficial in more than one situation. Vince Lombardi had unprecedented success as the coach of the Green Bay Packers, but his subsequent leadership attempts in corporate America and with another professional football team were only moderately successful. Conversely, Joe Gibbs is an example of a successful professional football coach who did find success in another setting. Gibbs won three National Football League Super Bowls in ten years as coach of the Washington Redskins. He walked away from the Redskins in 1993 and became a successful NASCAR auto racing owner. The pressure of being a successful NASCAR owner requires meticulous skill at organization, which was Gibbs's strength (McCafferty, 2000).

After being away from professional football for 11 years, Joe Gibbs returned to be the head

CONCEPT There is no such thing as a universal set of personality traits common to all successful leaders.

APPLICATION Prospective coaches should not be discouraged if they do not share common personality traits with the famous leaders and coaches in sport.

CONCEPT Leadership behaviors can be learned, while personality traits cannot.

APPLICATION The distinct advantage of the behavioral approach to effective leadership as opposed to the personality trait approach is that leader behaviors can be learned. Coaches who lack the necessary skills to be effective leaders can learn these skills by studying the universal behaviors possessed by successful leaders.

coach of the Washington Redskins for the 2004–05 football season. His first season back proved to be the worst of his professional football career, making it a building year.

Universal Behavior Theories of Leadership

Shortly after World War II, the focus in leadership research turned from universal traits to **universal behaviors** of successful leaders. It was believed that successful leaders had certain universal behaviors. Once these universal behaviors were identified, they could be taught to potential leaders everywhere. This approach to leadership was very optimistic, since anyone could learn to be a successful leader simply by learning certain predetermined behavioral characteristics. If these universal behaviors could be mastered, then anyone could be a successful leader. Unlike trait theory, the belief was that *leaders are made, not born*. The driving force behind this approach to leadership came from two different sources at approximately the same time: Ohio State University and the University of Michigan.

Two important products or concepts emerged from the universal behavior research conducted at Ohio State University and the University of Michigan during the 1950s and early 1960s. First was the development and refinement of the Leader Behavior Description Questionnaire (LBDQ), from which most of the universal behavior research was derived (Halpin, 1966). Second was the identification of consideration and initiating structure as the two most important factors characterizing the behaviors of leaders. **Consideration** refers to leader behavior that is indicative of friendship, mutual trust, respect, and warmth between the leader and subordinates. Conversely, **initiating structure** refers to the leader's behavior in clearly defining the relationship between the leader and subordinates, and in endeavoring to establish well-defined patterns of organization, channels of communication, and methods of procedure.

These two kinds of behavior are considered to be relatively independent but not necessarily incompatible. That is, a leader could be high in both consideration and initiating structure. It is not necessary, according to the construct, to be high in

CONCEPT   Consideration and initiating structure are the two most important factors characterizing the behavior of leaders.

APPLICATION   Coaches and leaders of sport teams should strive to establish well-defined patterns of organization and communication, while at the same time displaying the behaviors of friendship, trust, respect, and warmth.

TABLE 3.1 | Leadership Styles Equivalent to Consideration and Initiating Structure

Consideration	Initiating Structure
Relationship motivated	Task motivated
Democratic	Autocratic
Egalitarian	Authoritarian
Employee oriented	Production oriented

FIGURE 3.2 | Predicting leadership effectiveness as a function of the universal behaviors of consideration and initiating structure.

one and low in the other. Interestingly, the Michigan studies resulted in two nearly identical universal behaviors associated with leadership (Kahn & Katz, 1960).

The two general dimensions of leadership behavior identified in the Ohio State and Michigan studies have provided a basic framework for many leadership theories. Often the terms *initiating structure* and *consideration* have not been used, but compatible terms have been. Yet the general nature of these two categories has resulted in confusion about the terms used to describe them. Table 3.1 presents some of these terms in relation to the labels that have been used. Such leadership styles as authoritarianism, production orientation, and autocratic leadership are roughly equivalent to the notion of initiating structure. Leadership styles with such labels as democratic, egalitarian, and employee oriented reflect the notion of consideration. Leadership styles that are basically autocratic in nature tend toward behavior that can best be explained in terms of initiating structure or production emphasis. Leadership styles that are basically democratic in nature tend toward behavior

that can best be explained in terms of consideration and employee orientation.

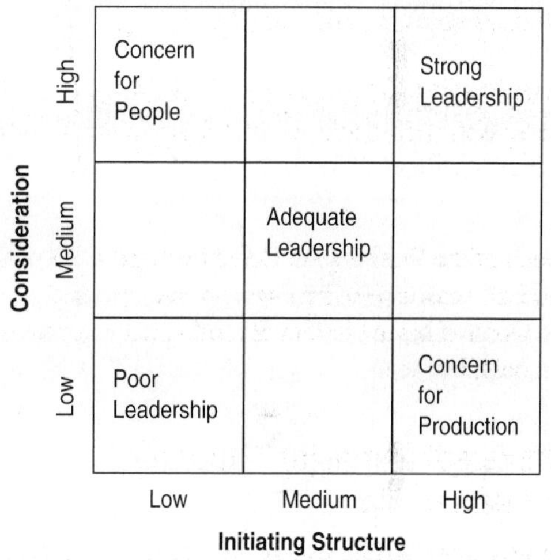

If you believe in the **universal behavior theory** of leadership, then you believe that individuals can be taught to be effective leaders by learning how to exhibit the behaviors of consideration and initiating structure in the proper proportions. Organizations that believe in the universal behavior theory conduct management and leadership seminars to teach their managers how to be effective leaders. Theoretically, the most effective leader would exhibit high levels of both consideration and initiating structure. As reflected in figure 3.2, this would be the leader who is able to maintain a strong interest in the welfare of employees while at the same time maintaining a strong concern for productivity. Blake and Mouton (1985, 1994) have developed a theory of management that appears to be based on research that came out of the Ohio State leadership studies.

Reflecting the belief of its management in universal leadership behaviors, the Philadelphia Eagles National Football League (NFL) professional football team hired the untested Andy Reid to be the head coach in 1999. Those who selected Reid looked at the characteristics of other successful NFL coaches and tried to identify someone with those same behavioral characteristics. What were those characteristics? In the words of the Eagles Team President, successful NFL coaches ". . . have exceptional leadership skills, are not afraid to be

wrong or make a mistake, are self-confident, have a strong conviction, are detail oriented, straightforward and honest" ("Chosen One," 2002, 4b). In a qualitative investigation involving behavioral characteristics possessed by leader-athletes, in-depth interviews were conducted with six leader-athletes from selected Canadian volleyball, basketball, or ice hockey college teams (Wright & Cote, 2003). The results identified four behavioral characteristics possessed by these six student-athlete leaders. The four characteristics were these:

1. Possesses exceptional sport skill
2. Possesses a strong work ethic
3. Possesses an enriched cognitive understanding of their sport
4. Possesses exceptional rapport with teammates, coaches and people in general

Coaches exhibit coaching behaviors. Courtesy University of Missouri–Columbia Sports Information.

It was concluded that an athlete who possesses these four behavioral characteristics would emerge as a team leader.

Behling and Schriesheim (1976) have argued that it is difficult to find a single leader who can exhibit strong concern for both people and productivity at the same time. For this reason they proposed a **functional model of leadership** in which two or more individuals are appointed who have different strengths. As a management team, one leader may be strong in the behavior of consideration while another may be strong in initiating structure. Working as a cohesive team, the several managers are able to address both consideration and initiating structure at the same time. Applied to sport, if the head basketball coach is strong in initiating structure, he would be wise to hire at least one assistant coach who is strong in the universal behavior of consideration.

Fiedler's Contingency Theory

Fiedler's contingency theory provides an excellent example of a leadership theory that is situation specific, but retains the notion of personality traits (see fig. 3.1). Fiedler's theory is one of many that use the contingency approach. The contingency approach to leadership suggests that leader effectiveness is somehow situation specific, and that leaders that are effective in one situation may not be in another. In a sense, effective leadership depends on specific environmental situations. However, Fiedler's theory differs from most situational theories, since the emphasis is on relatively stable personality traits, as opposed to behaviors. Thus, a particular personality disposition that seems to be effective in one leadership situation may not be effective in another.

According to Fiedler (1967), the contingency model of effective leadership posits that the effectiveness of a group is *contingent* on the relationship between leadership style (personality traits) and the degree to which the situation enables the leader to exert influence. The theory holds that the effectiveness of a group depends on two factors: the personality of the leader, and the degree to which the situation gives the leader power, control, and influence over the situation.

In terms of the personality, Fiedler believes that leaders are either relationship motivated or task motivated. **Relationship motivation** refers to concern with the interpersonal relationships between leader and followers. Successful performance of the task is of secondary importance to this type of leader. **Task motivation,** on the other hand, refers to the leader's concern with accomplishing the task at hand. The satisfactory completion of the task is important to this type of leader, while establishing and maintaining positive interpersonal relationships are secondary.

To measure these two personality types, Fiedler developed the Least Preferred Co-Worker (LPC) scale, which measures the leader's empathy for her least preferred team member. A high score on the LPC would indicate that the leader is able to have positive feelings toward a weak or nonproductive member of the group, and thus is relationship motivated. A low score on the LPC would indicate that the leader is unable to rate the least preferred co-worker very high, and thus is task motivated.

The second major factor in Fiedler's contingency model is *situational favorableness.* This construct indicates the degree to which the situation gives the leader control and influence over the environment. According to Fiedler, situational favorableness depends upon three subfactors: leader-member relations, task structure, and leader position power.

The interaction between the leader's personality style and the favorableness of the situation is graphically illustrated in figure 3.3. The horizontal axis indicates the situational favorableness dimension, with the left side of the graph representing the most favorable situation and the right side the least favorable situation. The vertical axis represents performance effectiveness for the relationship-oriented person (high-LPC leader) and the task-oriented person (low-LPC leader). The two curves in figure 3.3 represent Fiedler's basic predictions.

CONCEPT Leaders tend to be endowed with a disposition toward task motivation or relationship motivation.

APPLICATION Coaches should learn to recognize their own personality dispositions and work to compensate for their weaknesses through personal adjustments or through the help of assistant coaches. If the head coach is a task-motivated person, a relationship-motivated assistant coach might be hired to provide the personal touch. Coaches should also work to improve the favorableness of the situation.

FIGURE 3.3 | Fiedler's contingency model for leadership.

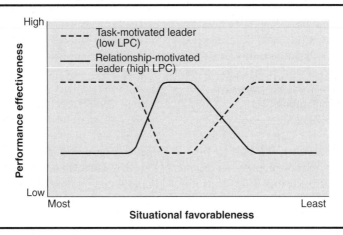

From F. E. Fiedler, The contingency model—new directions for leadership utilization. *Journal of Contemporary Business, 4,* 65–79, 1974. Adapted with permission.

Specifically, relationship-oriented leaders perform best in situations of moderate favorableness, while task-oriented leaders perform best in either favorable or unfavorable situations.

Fiedler's contingency theory has intuitive appeal and some research support (Fiedler, Chemers & Mahar, 1977). Perhaps the most controversial aspect of the theory is the basic proposition that *leadership training programs are of little value.* Leadership training programs only help the leader learn how to enhance power and influence. However, increased power and influence would not benefit the relationship-oriented person, who does best in a moderately favorable situation. Therefore, Fiedler proposes that there are only two

ways to improve leadership effectiveness. The first involves changing a leader's personality. This is unlikely to happen, since core personality dispositions cannot be easily changed. The second approach involves modifying the degree to which the situation is favorable to a certain type of leader. Fiedler suggests that this could be done by adjusting some aspect of organizational structure, or looking for leaders who possess personality characteristics consistent with existing structure and situational favorableness.

Intuitively, one can think of many examples in which Fiedler's theory could apply in sport. Doug Collins, a former coach of the Chicago Bulls professional basketball team, provides a good

CONCEPT The basic proposition of path-goal theory is that the function of the leader is to assist the follower in achieving his goals.

APPLICATION To be an effective leader, the coach must assist the athlete in selecting worthwhile goals and by pointing out the "path" to follow to successfully reach goals.

example. Because of the nature of his emotional volatility, Collins was able to take a young team to near stardom during his early years with the Bulls. His volatile personality was useful in motivating a young and unpredictable team. However, this same personality characteristic became a liability as the Bulls matured as a team and began to tune him out (McCallum, 1991). History records that Collins was fired after the 1988–89 season and replaced by Phil Jackson. It was Jackson who eventually led the Bulls to six World Championships.

A second example would be Johnny Keane. Following the failure of the New York Yankees to win the World Series in 1964, the Yankees fired Yogi Berra, a manager with a light touch, and hired the rules-conscious Johnny Keane.

> It would be the wrong team for him. He was a manager who was better with younger players than older ones, and this was a team of aging stars whose best years were behind them (Halberstam, 1994, p. 352).

The Yankees finished the 1965 season with a losing record of 77–85, and Johnny Keane was fired the following year.

Situation-Specific Behavior Theories of Leadership

Many contingency theories of leadership, or theories that hypothesize an interaction between the leader and the situation, have been studied. The basic difference between Fiedler's contingency theory and those that are to be discussed in this section is that Fiedler insists on looking at relatively stable personality traits, as opposed to behaviors. The theories in this section view leadership as a function of the interaction between *leader behavior* in a specific situation and the situation itself.

Some of the **situation-specific behavior theories** are these: path-goal theory (House & Mitchell, 1974); life cycle theory (Hersey & Blanchard, 1977); adaptive-reactive theory (Osborn & Hunt, 1975); leader-member exchange theory (Case, 1998); and the normative model of decision making (Vroom & Yetton, 1973). Unfortunately, space does not allow a thorough review of each of these theories; the first two will be considered because of their potential application to athletics. In addition, Chelladurai's (1978) multidimensional model of leadership, and Smoll and Smith's (1989) Model of Leadership Behaviors in Sport will be introduced as examples of leadership theory that has evolved from the sport sciences.

Path-Goal Theory In Fiedler's theory, the emphasis is on the personality of the leader and the favorableness of the situation. In **path-goal theory,** the emphasis is on the needs and goals of the subordinate or the athlete. In other words, the leader is viewed as a *facilitator.* The coach or leader helps athletes realize their goals. The leader's success is viewed in terms of whether or not the subordinates achieve their goals. Thus, the basic proposition of path-goal theory is that the function of the leader is to provide a "well-lighted path" to assist the follower in achieving goals. This is done by rewarding subordinates for goal attainment, pointing out roadblocks and pitfalls on the path to success, and increasing the opportunities for personal satisfaction. For example, if an athlete's goal is to break a school record in the mile run, it is the coach's job to provide a training program that is rewarding and enables the athlete to accomplish this goal.

CONCEPT The type of leadership behavior appropriate for any given situation may be mediated by the maturity level of the athlete.

APPLICATION While it is difficult to predict which leadership behavior is best for specific maturity levels, coaches and leaders must be sensitive to the maturity level of the athlete.

Path-goal theory has not been investigated much either in or out of sport environments, perhaps due to its lack of clarity. However, Chelladurai and Saleh (1978) looked at the theory from a sport context and reported partial support for path-goal theory. Individuals who demonstrated a preference for team sports also indicated a preference for leader behavior that was calculated to improve performance through training procedures. Thus, leader behavior correlated with the athlete's preference for an interdependent type of sport. As predicted by the theory, a particular athlete personality consistently preferred a particular leader behavior.

Life Cycle Theory Like path-goal theory, **life cycle theory** places the emphasis in leadership behavior on the subordinates and not on the leader. The appropriate leadership style for any specific situation depends on the maturity of the subordinate. Two types of leadership behavior, conceptualized in terms of relationship behavior (consideration) and task behavior (initiating structure), are possible. The appropriate combination of task and relationship behavior depends on the maturity of the follower. Maturity is defined in terms of the capacity to set and obtain goals, willingness and ability to assume responsibility, and education and/or experience. According to this model, the need for task structure behavior decreases with increased maturity. However, the need for relationship behavior forms an inverted U relative to maturity. At low and high levels of maturity, relationship behavior should be low, but at the moderate levels of maturity it should be high.

Case (1987) reported an investigation in which the basic tenets of Hersey and Blanchard's life cycle theory were tested in an applied setting. Leadership behaviors of successful head basketball coaches were ascertained. A total of 399 basketball players completed a leader behavior inventory regarding their respective coaches. Athletes were categorized according to the maturity dimensions of junior high, high school, college, and AAU participation. Initiating structure (task behavior) and consideration (relationship behavior) leadership scores were calculated for 40 coaches and then categorized according to maturity (competitive) level. The results revealed a quadratic relationship between maturity and relationship behavior and between maturity and task behavior. Task behavior of successful coaches was low at the junior high and AAU levels of maturity and high for the high school and collegiate levels. Conversely, relationship behavior of successful coaches was high at the junior high and AAU levels of maturity and low for the high school and collegiate levels. These results led Case to propose the life cycle model, illustrated in figure 3.4.

The Case model requires additional testing before it can be used for prediction purposes. Intuitively, the model is appealing because it is somewhat consistent with expectations. Young athletes who lack maturity and highly skilled and mature athletes would not be expected to respond well to a great deal of task structure. Yet, these same athletes might be expected to respond well to an environment in which concern for the athlete was openly expressed. Moderately mature athletes (high school and collegiate level) would require a fair amount of task structure in order to perform well. In this case, relationship behavior might appear to be less pronounced and less important.

FIGURE 3.4 | Successful combinations of task and relationship behavior for different levels of maturity (Case, 1987). For example, the task behavior of successful coaches is highest for high school and college, but low for junior high and AAU.

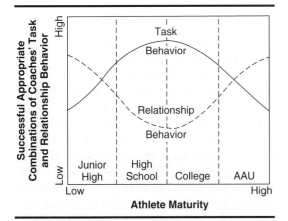

Chelladurai's Multidimensional Model of Leadership

Chelladurai's (1978, 1993) **multidimensional model** of leadership, illustrated in figure 3.5, provides an interactional approach to conceptualizing the leadership process. In this model, athlete satisfaction and performance are viewed as the products of the interaction of three components of leadership: prescribed leader behavior, preferred leader behavior, and actual leader behavior. *Prescribed leader behaviors* are those that conform to the established norms of the organization. In the military, for example, officers are expected to behave in a certain manner in the presence of their subordinates. *Preferred leader behaviors* are those behaviors that are preferred by the athletes. For example, members of a rugby team might prefer that the coach socialize with the team after a game. Finally, *actual leader behaviors* are those behaviors that the leader exhibits, irrespective of the norms or preferences of the team.

FIGURE 3.5 | Chelladurai's multidimensional model of leadership.

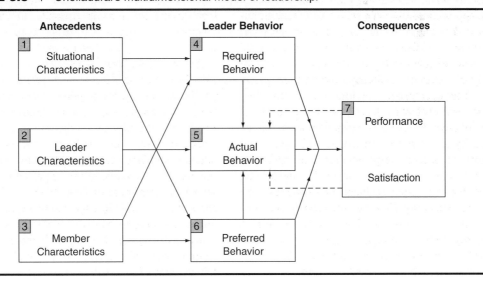

FIGURE 3.6 | Leader behavior congruence and outcomes.

Leader Behavior			Outcome
Prescribed	Actual	Preferred	
+	+	+	Ideal
−	−	−	Laissez-faire
+	−	+	Removal of leader
+	+	−	Performance
−	+	+	Satisfaction

+ Congruence with other types of behavior

− Lack of congruence with other types of behavior

From P. Chelladurai and A.V. Carron, *Leadership.* Copyright © 1978 by the Canadian Association for Health, Physical Education and Recreation. Used with permission of the publisher.

Based on the model illustrated in figure 3.5, Chelladurai hypothesized certain consequences of the *congruence* among the three types of leader behavior. As can be observed in figure 3.6, congruence between all three types of leader behavior should promote ideal performance and satisfaction. A laissez-faire outcome is predicted when all three leader behaviors are incongruent with one another. If actual behavior is incongruent with both prescribed and preferred leader behavior, it is expected that the leader will be removed. If the prescribed and actual behaviors are congruent, but both are incongruent with preferred behavior, performance may be high, but athletes may be dissatisfied. Finally, if actual and preferred behavior are congruent, but prescribed behavior is incongruent, athletes may be satisfied, but performance may suffer.

The Leadership Scale for Sport (LSS) was developed by Chelladurai and Saleh (1980) for measuring coaching behavior in sport. Composed of 40 items, the LSS measures the following five coaching behaviors: training behavior, autocratic behavior, democratic behavior, social support, and rewarding behavior. Preferred and actual coaching behaviors are determined by administering the LSS to athletes and asking them to complete the inventory according to the coaching behaviors they prefer or according to the coaching behaviors they actually observe in their coach. Prescribed

coaching behaviors are determined by administering the LSS to coaches and asking them to complete the inventory relative to how they believe they coach. Recently, the LSS was revised (RLSS) by Zhang, Jensen, and Mann (1997). The RLSS is composed of 60 items measuring six behaviors. The six behaviors measured by the RLSS include the original five, plus situational consideration behavior.

General support for Chelladurai's multidimensional model has been forthcoming on several fronts. The notion that congruence among the three types of leader behavior leads to improved athlete performance and satisfaction is well established (Riemer & Chelladurai, 1995; Riemer & Toon, 2001; Vealey, Armstrong, Comar, & Greenleaf, 1998). Athletes do better and are more satisfied when actual and prescribed coaching behavior of coaches agree with the athletes' own preferred coaching behaviors. Another well-established notion derived from the Chelladurai model is that coaching behaviors lead to either satisfaction or dissatisfaction (Allen & Howe, 1998; Vealey et al., 1998). Compared to parents' preferences for their children, boys and girls prefer higher levels of decision making, a democratic style of coaching, and a warm and positive group atmosphere from the coach (Martin, Jackson, Richardson, & Weiller, 1999). Prescribed behaviors of coaches tend to be similar for males and females, but coaching behaviors differ as a function of coaching level (Jambor & Zhang, 1997). High school coaches exhibit a greater degree of democratic behavior than college coaches, and junior high coaches exhibit lower levels of training/instruction behavior and social support than do high school and college coaches. This finding leads to the possible conclusion that junior high school coaches are so busy dealing with large numbers of athletes that they do not find the time for proper instruction and social support.

Most recently, preferred leader behaviors of NCAA Division I and II coaches were ascertained

Communication between coach and athlete is important.
Courtesy University of Missouri–Columbia Sports Information.

by administering the RLSS to 408 male and female athletes (Beam, Serwatka, & Wilson, 2004). Male student athletes were observed to prefer autocratic and social support behavior from their coaches, while female athletes preferred situational consideration and training instruction behavior. Compared to interdependent sport (team sport) athletes, independent sport (individual sport) athletes had a greater preference for democratic behavior, positive feedback, situational considerations, and social support from their coaches. Furthermore, male closed sport athletes (those in sports closed to the environment, e.g., golf) indicated a greater preference for autocratic behavior than did female closed sport athletes. Male open sport athletes (those in sports open to the environment, e.g., tennis and basketball) showed a greater preference for democratic behavior than female open sport athletes.

Finally, as it relates to performance of elite Olympic athletes, 46 U.S.A. coaches from the 1996 Atlanta Summer Olympics and 19 from the 1998 Nagano, Japan Winter Olympics were interviewed about coach behaviors that affect performance Gould, Greenleaf, Guinan & Chung (2002). Based upon these interviews, it was concluded that the following coach behaviors have a strong influence on coach effectiveness and athlete performance:

1. Establishing a high level of trust and credibility with athlete
2. Staying cool under pressure
3. Making fair but decisive decisions
4. Creating and functioning in a positive team environment
5. Keeping things simple
6. Realistic expectations for athletes
7. Following a performance plan
8. Providing sport psychology support for athletes

Leadership Behavior Model   As proposed by Smoll and Smith (1989), the **leadership behavior model** is based upon situation-specific behaviors

CONCEPT Discrepancies between an athlete's preferred coaching behavior and actual or prescribed coaching behavior have a measurable effect on the athlete's performance and/or satisfaction.

APPLICATION Athletes enter into the athletic environment with certain predetermined expectations about coaching behavior. Coaches should take this into account as they attempt to motivate athletes to superior performance.

FIGURE 3.7 | Leadership behavior model.

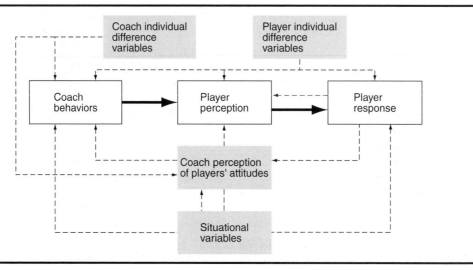

of the leader. As illustrated in figure 3.7, the model's central process is defined with solid lines leading from *coach behaviors* to *player perception* of coach behaviors to *player responses*. The dotted lines in the model represent the effect of various other variables upon the central process. In the model, coach individual difference variables include such factors as goals, intentions, perceptions of self/athletes, and gender. Player individual difference variables include such things as age, gender, perceptions about coach, motivation, anxiety, and self-confidence. Situational factors include things like nature of the sport, competitive

level, success/failure, and team cohesion. The dotted line leading from player individual difference variables to coach behaviors was added to the model to reflect research by Kenow and Williams (1992). Coach behavior is influenced by the coach's perception of the individual athlete. A coach may treat an athlete who exhibits high anxiety or low self-confidence differently from other athletes. The model provides a framework for leadership behavior research in sport.

Coaching Behavior Assessment System Coaching behaviors have been studied extensively by

CONCEPT A low correlation exists between a coach's actual behavior and his perception of coaching behaviors.

APPLICATION In order to be effective, a coach needs to be more aware of actual coaching behaviors and less influenced by inaccurate self-perceptions of his behavior. Coaches of youth sports teams could take turns observing each other's reactive and spontaneous behaviors and recording them. The CBAS is very easy to learn. All verbal and body-language responses are categorized into one of 12 categories.

Smith and Smoll (1997a). Their research, based upon the **Coaching Behavior Assessment System (CBAS)** as illustrated in figure 3.8, focuses upon reactive and spontaneous behavior of coaches. In the CBAS, a trained observer keeps track of eight different types of reactive behaviors and four different types of spontaneous behaviors.

Reactive behaviors are coach reactions to player or team behaviors. For example, a player makes a mistake and the coach responds by verbally chastising the player. **Spontaneous behaviors** are initiated by the coach and do not occur in response to player behavior.

Research with the CBAS has revealed a number of interesting relationships. When they are working with youth sports athletes, the dominant behaviors of coaches are positive reinforcement, general technical instructions, and general encouragement. The behaviors of keeping control (maintaining order) and administering punishment (punitive behavior) are perceived by players to occur much more often than they actually do. Another interesting finding is that coaches of youth sports teams spend a greater amount of their time providing technical instruction and feedback to low-expectation youth than to high-expectation youth. In other words, the coach does not favor the athletes she expects to be the better performers (Horn, 1984; Smoll, Smith, Curtis, & Hunt, 1978).

The CBAS has also been utilized as a measurement tool to determine if behavioral training programs are effective in teaching youth sports coaches to be better and more effective

FIGURE 3.8 | Coaching behavior assessment system.

Class I. Reactive behaviors
A. Player performs well
   1. Positive reinforcement (R)
   2. Nonreinforcement (NR)
B. Player makes mistake
   3. Mistake-contingent encouragement (EM)
   4. Mistake-contingent technical instruction (TIM)
   5. Punishment (P)
   6. Punitive TIM (TIM + P)
   7. Ignoring mistakes (IM)
C. Player misbehaves
   8. Keeping control (KC)
Class II. Spontaneous behaviors
A. Game-related
   9. General technical instruction (TIG)
   10. General encouragement (EG)
   11. Organization (O)
B. Game-irrelevant
   12. General communication (GC)

From Ronald E. Smith, Frank L. Smoll, and Earl Hunt, 1977. A system for the behavioral assessment of athletic coaches. *Research Quarterly, 48,* 401–407. Reprinted by permission of the publisher, the American Alliance for Health, Physical Education, Recreation and Dance.

leaders of youth. Research has demonstrated that well-conceived, well-planned efforts to train coaches are effective. Desirable coaching behaviors can be identified and conveyed to new coaches. Furthermore, improved coaching behaviors result

CONCEPT Well-planned leadership training programs are effective in teaching coaches how to be good leaders.

APPLICATION Effective coaching behaviors can be learned. Therefore, coaches should be encouraged to attend training sessions designed to teach effective leadership skills.

in benefit to the young athletes in the form of greater satisfaction and reduced anxiety (Barnett, Smoll, & Smith, 1992; Smith, Smoll, & Barnett, 1995; Smith, Smoll, & Curtis, 1979).

More recently, research with the CBAS shows that coaches who engage in high frequencies of supportive behaviors, such as positive reinforcement and mistake-contingent encouragement, facilitate the development of teams whose members like the coach and like playing with each other. Conversely, negative interpersonal coaching behaviors, such as punishment and negative criticism, promote the development of teams whose members don't like the coach and don't like playing with each other (Smith & Smoll, 1997a). Perhaps the most consistent finding involving the use of the CBAS with youth coaches is that there is very little relationship between behaviors actually exhibited by coaches and the coaches' perceptions of their own behaviors. Conversely, children's perception of coaches' behaviors are more highly correlated with actual coaching behaviors. This finding underscores the critical need for objectively recording behaviors of coaches, as their own perception of their behavior is not always accurate. Coaches are simply unaware of how often they really use different kinds of reactive and spontaneous behaviors (Smoll & Smith, 1999).

While the CBAS has been the most widely studied system for observing and documenting coaching behaviors in youth sports, it is not the only one. A case in point is the Arizona State University Observation Instrument (ASUOI) developed by Lacy and Darst (1984). The ASUOI is composed of 17 behavioral categories, seven of which are directly related to instruction. It has

been utilized in studying coaching behaviors in American football, tennis, gymnastics, basketball, and soccer. Research with the ASUOI has tended to focus upon behaviors of coaches of adult athletes as opposed to those of youth sport athletes

In addition to the CBAS and the ASUOI, the Coaching Behavior Quest (CBQ) was developed by Kenow and Williams (1992) to measure athlete perceptions of coaches' behavior. Composed of 28 items, the CBQ measures the perceived coaching behaviors of negative activation and emotional composure. The proposed two-factor structure of the CBQ was confirmed by Williams, Jerome, Kenow, Rogers, Sartain and Darland (2003). As a result of their investigation, Williams et al. (2003) proposed minor modifications in the Smoll and Smith (1989) leadership behavior model (fig. 3.7).

As an extension of the CBAS, Coach Effectiveness Training (CET) was developed to assist coaches in learning leadership skills appropriate for youth sports. A summary of their research findings and the foundation of CET is captured in the following quotation from Smith and Smoll (1997a, p. 17):

> Not surprisingly, we found that the most positive outcomes occurred when children played for coaches who engaged in high levels of positive reinforcement for both desirable performance and effort, who responded to mistakes with encouragement and technical instruction, and who emphasized the importance of fun and personal improvement over winning. Not only did the children who had such coaches like their coaches more and have more fun, but they also liked their teammates more.

CONCEPT Coach effectiveness training is based upon five basic principles derived from research using the Coaching Behavioral Assessment System (CBAS). Two of the principles deal with the importance of deemphasizing winning, and the importance of focusing upon only positive coaching behaviors (positive reinforcement, encouragement, sound technical instruction).

APPLICATION The use of the "positive sandwich approach" provides a means whereby the coach can give reinforcement, encouragement, and technical instructions to an athlete in a completely positive and complimentary way. Young athletes frequently interpret technical instructions to be a form of criticism, so it is important for the youth coach to master and refine her ability to deliver a technical instruction sandwiched between two complimentary statements.

Coach Effectiveness Training The Coach Effectiveness Training (CET) program is based upon over twenty years of research with the CBAS. The stated purpose of the CET is to teach youth coaches how to engage in team building. Effective **team building** results in teams that have a positive climate, whose members enjoy a sense of satisfaction, and feel attraction to the team as well as to other team members. The purpose of team building is not necessarily a better win/loss record, but the promotion of a more enjoyable and valuable developmental experience for coaches and athletes (Smith & Smoll, 1997a; Smoll & Smith, 1998; Smoll & Smith, 1999).

A CET workshop lasts approximately two and a half hours. Behavioral guidelines for effective coaching are presented and discussed. The behavioral guidelines are based on a set of five coaching principles, as outlined below (Smith & Smoll, 1997a):

1. *"Winning" is defined not in terms of win-loss records, but in terms of giving maximum effort and making improvements.* The emphasis in the first principle is in creating a mastery climate as opposed to a competitive climate. Coaches learn to make having fun, deriving satisfaction, learning new skills, and developing greater self-confidence and self-esteem the primary goals of the youth sports experience.

2. *Coach-athlete interactions are based on a positive approach that emphasizes positive reinforcement, encouragement, and sound technical instruction.* The three supportive behaviors of positive reinforcement, encouragement, and sound technical instruction represent the three primary ways that coaches should interact with athletes. When they provide corrective instruction, it is recommended that they use the **positive sandwich approach.** In this approach, the coach starts with a compliment, gives a future-oriented instruction, and ends with another compliment. In this way, the instruction is "sandwiched" between two positives. For example, in a tennis-related setting the coach might say this:

   (a) "Way to hustle! You really look strong when you approach the net."

   (b) "Now, if you will stop and square yourself to the net you will look just like a pro when you make your volley shot."

   (c) "Keep up the hard work; you are really improving fast."

3. *Norms are established that emphasize athletes' mutual obligations to help and support one another.* Developing social support, attraction among teammates, and commitment to the team is as much an athlete's responsibility

FIGURE 3.9 | The conceptual model of coaching efficacy.

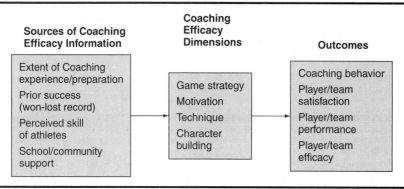

Reproduced with permission of the publisher from Feltz, D. L., Chase, M. A., Moritz, S., & Sullivan, P. (1999). Development of the multidimensional coaching efficacy scale. *Journal of Educational Psychology, 91,* 765–76. Published by the American Psychological Association (APA).

as a coach's responsibility. The coach learns this principle and establishes expected norms for athletes in sharing the responsibility for team building.

4. *Compliance with team roles and responsibilities is promoted by involving athletes in decisions regarding team rules and compliance.* If the athletes are involved in decisions about team rules and expected compliance, they will be able to share in this responsibility. The coach does not want to be placed in a position of using punitive measures to punish noncompliance to team rules.

5. *Coaches obtain behavioral feedback and engage in self-monitoring to increase awareness of their own behaviors.* Coaches are taught how to use the CBAS system, or some simple variation of it, to monitor their positive and negative coaching behaviors. Coaching feedback is critical to the success of the CET program.

Coaching Efficacy as a Predictor of Coaching Behavior   Coaching behavior has been discussed in the last two sections as being important for facilitating athlete performance and athlete satisfaction. In this section, we back up a step and

ask the question of what leads to the formation of specific coaching behaviors. Research by Feltz, Chase, Moritz, and Sullivan (1999) and Sullivan and Kent (2003) suggests that coaching efficacy is a strong predictor of athlete behavior as well as athlete/team satisfaction, performance, and efficacy. As initially proposed by Feltz et al. (1999), the **conceptual model of coaching efficacy** is illustrated in figure 3.9. In this model, coaching efficacy predicts coaching behavior, but it is in turn predicted by efficacy sources such as coaching experience, prior success, perceived skill of athletes, and school/community support. As defined by Feltz et al. (1999, p. 765), **coaching efficacy** is "the extent to which coaches believe they have the capacity to affect the learning and performance of their athletes."

In order to measure coaching efficacy, Feltz et al. (1999) developed the 24-item Coaching Efficacy Scale (CES). The CES measures the coaching efficacy factors of (a) game strategy, (b) motivation, (c) technique, and (d) character building. Sullivan and Kent (2003) utilized the CES to test the model illustrated in figure 3.9 in terms of predicting coaching behaviors. In this study, coaching behaviors were measured by administering the Leadership Scale for Sports (LSS) to 224 college coaches. Study results provided evidence for the conceptual model of coaching efficacy, in that coaching efficacy for motivation and technique were observed to be significant predictors of the coaching behaviors of training instruction and positive feedback.

Coach-Athlete Compatibility and Communication

An important factor linked with leader effectiveness is **coach-athlete compatibility,** or the quality of the relationship between the coach and the athlete. Compatibility between coach and athlete has been shown to be an important determinant of team success and satisfaction. In studying coach-athlete compatibility, researchers compare behaviors of effective *coach-athlete dyads* with those of less effective dyads. Dyads (pairs) may be formed and compared utilizing an instrument called the Fundamental Interpersonal Relations Orientation-Behavior Questionnaire (FIRO-BQ). The FIRO-BQ was developed by Schutz (1966) to measure the levels of affection, control, and inclusion that exist between members of a dyad. *Affection* refers to close personal emotional feelings between two people, while *control* refers to the perception of power, authority, and dominance. *Inclusion* refers to positive association among people and is related to communication, openness, and two-way interaction.

As illustrated in figure 3.10, compatible coach-athlete dyads are characterized by good communication and the presence of rewarding behavior flowing from coach to athlete. Conversely, incompatible coach-athlete dyads are characterized by a lack of communication and rewarding behavior. In compatible dyads, coach and athlete freely interact with each other. There is a feeling of mutual respect, an appreciation of each other's roles, and a desire to communicate honest feelings. These feelings are not present in the incompatible dyads. Rather, there is a feeling of detachment and isolation from each other. Effective and open communication cannot take place in an environment of exclusion. Compatible dyads are also

FIGURE 3.10 | Some characteristics of compatible and incompatible dyads.

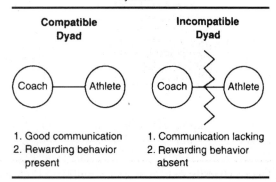

Compatible Dyad	Incompatible Dyad
1. Good communication	1. Communication lacking
2. Rewarding behavior present	2. Rewarding behavior absent

characterized by coaches who consistently reward athletes for effort and performance. Rewards come in the form of praise, acknowledgment of effort, and recognition for outstanding performance. An enthusiastic "pat on the back" is characteristic of compatible coach-athlete dyads (Horne & Carron, 1985; Kenow & Williams, 1999).

As is clear from figure 3.10, one critical aspect of coach-athlete dyad compatibility is good communication. An in-depth investigation of a coach-athlete dyad in crisis supported this notion, as the relationship suffered from poor communication as well as emotional isolation and frequent disagreements (Jowett, 2003). Communication among members of a team or between coach and athlete is more than a transfer of knowledge from one person to another. It includes all of the ways that individuals interact to create a new body of knowledge and ways of understanding each other (Arripe-Longueville, Saury, Fournier, & Durand (2001). Good communication leads to a feeling of positive rapport between coach and athlete. An investigation reported by Baker, Coté, and Hawes (2000) showed that an absence of rapport, or negative rapport, between coach and athlete is associated with an increase in state anxiety by both parties.

Sport psychologists and coaches have come to admire the accomplishments of John Wooden, a

CONCEPT The quality of coach-athlete interaction is a critical factor in team success and satisfaction.

APPLICATION Perhaps the most important factor in improving coach-athlete interaction is communication. Coaches must encourage two-way communication between themselves and their athletes. If the athletes feel that the coach values their input, they will feel comfortable in a two-way interaction.

former coach of the University of California at Los Angeles (UCLA) men's basketball team, and they have wondered about his coaching behaviors. An early study by Tharp and Gallimore (1976) indicated that 75 percent of all verbal utterances by the coach to his players were instructional in nature, with very little use of praise or reproofs (14 percent). In a later, in-depth interview, Coach Wooden said that he did not praise his starters much because they did not need it. He said that they got plenty of that from the media and fans. He went on to say that he reserved most of his praise for his bench players, because they needed it the most (Gallimore & Tharp, 2004). Clearly, Coach Wooden understood the importance of quality communication with his athletes.

Investigations have shown that significant disparity exists between coach and athlete perceptions of coaching behaviors and the environment. Coaches tend to view the environment as ideal, while athletes often see a great disparity between what is happening and what they think should be happening (Smith & Smoll, 1997b).

Quality interaction, communication, and respect between coach and athlete lead to athlete satisfaction and improved performance. The importance of coach-athlete compatibility was highlighted in a study involving married couples as coach-athlete dyads. Effective married couple coach-athlete dyads are characterized by emotional closeness, good communication, trust, and cooperation (Jowett & Meek, 2000). Consistent with Chelladurai's multidimensional model of leadership, Kenow and Williams (1999) noted that athlete satisfaction is a strong predictor of coach-athlete compatibility. Regarding feedback to athletes from coaches, research clearly suggests that a good performance should be followed by praise and helpful information about the performance. In response to a poor performance, the coach should provide encouragement and information that will help the athlete succeed (Allen & Howe, 1998; Amorose & Weiss, 1998).

In correcting a mistake, a coach needs to be assertive, yet avoid damaging the athlete's self-esteem. Miller (1982) suggests assertiveness training for coaches to help them relate better to athletes. According to Miller, assertiveness training involves appropriate expressions of thoughts and feelings on the part of the coach so that the athlete is instructed in a non-threatening way. Overly assertive coaches may damage interpersonal relationships, while underassertive coaches may fail to make an important correction. In Miller's *assertiveness training* module, the athlete is instructed in three specific steps. Using a volleyball example, actual execution of the model might involve the following three steps:

1. Describe the situation to the athlete. "Your assignment was to cover the power angle of that spike."

2. Tell how it affects the team. "When you follow through with your assignment, it provides the coverage necessary for an effective defense."

3. Tell what you think should be done. "Focus your attention on your specific assignment and trust your teammates to take care of their assignments."

CONCEPT Each and every coach-athlete interaction is important in developing trust, respect, and cooperation. Of particular concern is the way in which coaches choose to correct athletes' mistakes.

APPLICATION Miller's three-step assertiveness training approach should be used when interacting with athletes. Coaches should learn how to assertively correct athletes' errors and mistakes without coming across as demeaning or threatening.

As explained by Yukelson (2006, p. 174), "Communication is what teamwork and group chemistry are all about. From a group perspective, it is tied to oneness of thought and everyone being on the same page." In a 2005 National Football League playoff game between the Minnesota Vikings and the Philadelphia Eagles, the Vikings tried a fake field goal attempt with the holder passing the ball to a wide receiver. However, when the holder turned to pass the ball to the wide receiver, there was no one there. Due to a series of miscommunications, there was an extra player on the field, so the wide receiver had walked off the field just before the ball was centered to the holder.

Communication can be defined in many different ways, but it essentially describes the process of conveying information, thoughts, and feelings in verbal and nonverbal ways. Nonverbal communication can take place through body language, facial expression, and other symbolic gestures. Body language and facial expression are particularly powerful forms of communication, although often expressed in unintended ways. As explained by Yukelson (2001), coaches have the responsibility to create an environment that encourages athletes to initiate communication freely. Communication between the coach and athlete must be a two-way street. The athlete must truly believe that he can voice his feelings and concerns openly without reprisal. From the perspective of the coach, table 3.2 contains a number of suggestions for interventions that can facilitate coach-athlete communication (Orlick, 1990; Yukelson, 2006).

Player Position, Leadership Opportunity, and Stacking

Beginning with Grusky (1963), a body of literature has evolved that relates an athlete's playing position to future leadership opportunity and to racial bias

TABLE 3.2 | Selected Practical Suggestions for Facilitating Coach-Athlete Communication (coaches' perspective)

1. Recognize individual differences among athletes.
2. Use a style of communication that is comfortable.
3. Be honest, sincere, and genuine, but never sarcastic.
4. Be generous with praise and encouragement.
5. Make sure nonverbal communication is consistent with verbal communication (avoid mixed signals).
6. Exercise personal self-control at all times.
7. Be supportive and empathetic to athlete needs.
8. Openly discuss communication needs and shortcomings with individual athletes, as well as with team as a whole.

CONCEPT The coach can develop leadership skills in young athletes by placing them in team positions requiring observability, visibility, and task dependence.

APPLICATION It is usually the athlete who already possesses leadership ability that becomes the quarterback in football or the catcher in baseball. Coaches should use this knowledge to help their players develop leadership skills. Young athletes who lack leadership ability could benefit from playing point guard on the basketball team or quarterback on the football team.

(stacking). We will first consider the leadership opportunity aspect of this research area, and then consider stacking.

Playing Position and Leadership Opportunity

Most of the research dealing with playing position and leadership opportunity has focused on the sport of professional baseball (Chelladurai & Carron, 1977; Grusky, 1963; Loy & Sage, 1970), but more recently studies have been reported dealing with football (Bivens & Leonard, 1994) and soccer (Norris & Jones, 1998). Basically, what these investigations show is that athletes who play in certain central positions on the playing field benefit from greater leadership opportunity. In the case of professional baseball, it has been clearly demonstrated that former catchers and infielders are selected to be major league managers more often than athletes who played other positions.

Of the six major league managers hired following the strike-shortened 1994 season, four had been catchers in their playing days. Bob Boone, a manager of the Kansas City Royals, said of his playing days as a catcher, "I managed every game I played in. I just didn't have the control." Dan Duquette, Boston Red Sox general manager, was quoted as saying, "The catcher is involved with every pitch, every pitcher, and he's the only player on the field who has the whole field in front of him" (Chass, 1994, pp. 1, 4).

As illustrated in figure 3.11, and explained by Chelladurai and Carron (1977), the critical factors associated with these findings are task dependence and propinquity. **Task dependence** refers to interaction between players of the same team. Higher task dependence is associated with greater interaction and greater dependence between players. The

FIGURE 3.11 | Categorization of baseball positions on the basis of propinquity and task dependence.

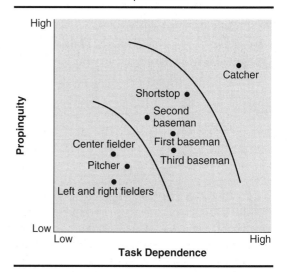

From P. Chelladurai and A. V. Carron, A reanalysis of formal structure in sport. *Canadian Journal of Applied Sport Sciences, 2,* 9–14, 1977. Reproduced by permission of the publisher.

CONCEPT   Position on an athletic team should be determined on the basis of skill, physical attributes, and athlete preference, and never upon the basis of race, ethnicity, or color of skin.

APPLICATION   There are a lot of myths associated with playing positions on athletic teams. Neither coaches nor athletes should give credence to these myths. An athlete should be given an opportunity to compete for any position on an athletic team. It is generally the coach that makes the final determination as to where an athlete plays. For this reason, it is also the coach that is ultimately responsible for making sure that stacking does not occur.

catcher in baseball interacts with players on her team to a greater extent than any other player. Thus, catching is a position with high task dependence, whereas playing in the outfield is a position with low task dependence. **Propinquity** refers to observability and visibility on the playing field. In baseball and softball, the catcher is the most visible and observable player on the team from the perspective of her teammates. The same could be said for the quarterback in football, the point guard in basketball, the setter in volleyball, and the center halfback in soccer. Athletes enjoying the greatest amounts of task dependence and propinquity have greater leadership responsibility as well as greater leadership opportunity.

Playing Position and Stacking

Related to the concept of playing position and leadership opportunity is the notion of playing position and stacking. **Stacking** refers to the disproportionate placement of blacks or minorities into positions of low **centrality** relative to task dependence and propinquity. If stacking does occur in sport, African Americans should be underrepresented in positions of high centrality. A position of high centrality would be a position exhibiting high propinquity and high task dependence, such as catcher in baseball. Studies of centrality and racial segregation have shown that minority players are underrepre-

sented in central positions, where opportunities for leadership are greatest (Hallinan, 1998; Norris & Jones, 1998). Tangential to this issue is the finding by Hallinan (1998) that women are underrepresented in positions deemed central to the smooth operation of recreation programs.

Perhaps of even greater concern than stacking in Major League Baseball (MLB) is the fact that fewer and fewer African American athletes are choosing to play baseball. At the midpoint of the 2003 MLB season, there were only 90 blacks playing in the major leagues, or 10 percent of players on 25-man rosters. This is down from 19 percent in 1995 and down from 27 percent in 1975 (Verducci, 2003a). Possible reasons suggested by Verducci for this disturbing trend include the following: (a) for financial reasons, many blacks are being denied access to expert instruction and groomed playing fields associated with the "pay-for-play" mentality of modern suburbia; (b) there are so few blacks in MLB that there are few role models for young black athletes to emulate; (c) baseball can't match the "buzz"-producing marketing and excitement of football and basketball; and (d) baseball does not provide the opportunity for instant fame and fortune that the National Basketball Association afforded Labron James of the Cleveland Cavaliers. It would seem, however, that the latter two reasons might discourage white as well as black athletes from focusing on baseball.

Summary

Consistent with Behling and Schriesheim's leadership theory classification system, four different categories of leadership were discussed. These included universal trait theories, universal behavior theories, Fiedler's contingency theory, and situation-specific behavior theories.

Universal trait theory is based upon the notion that great leaders are great men or women who possess universal personality traits that would make them great leaders in any situation. Universal behavior theories are based upon the notion that certain universal behaviors exist that define effective leaders. Research has shown that the universal behaviors are consideration and initiating structure. Individuals can learn to be effective leaders by learning to exhibit these two behaviors, regardless of the situation. Fiedler's contingency theory is based on the notion that leaders possess personality dispositions that will help them be effective leaders in one situation, but not in another. Thus, leadership is contingent upon possessing a certain personality trait suitable for a specific situation.

Situation-specific behavioral theories are based on the notion that specific behaviors will help an individual be an effective leader in one situation but not another. Leadership theories discussed under this category included path-goal theory, life cycle theory, Chelladurai's multidimensional theory, and Smoll and Smith's leadership behavior model. Each of these theories proposes a situation-specific relationship between a leader's behaviors and effective leadership. Multidimensional theory posits that effective leadership is a function of congruence between prescribed leader behavior, actual leader behavior, and preferred leader behavior. Coaching efficacy was introduced as a predictor of coaching behaviors.

Coach-athlete compatibility and communication are based upon good communication between coach and athlete and effective rewarding behavior. Quality interaction, communication, and respect between coach and athlete lead to athlete satisfaction and improved performance. Coach assertiveness training was suggested as a way for a coach to learn to interact effectively with athletes. Suggestions were given for facilitating coach-athlete communication.

Finally, player position, leadership opportunity, and stacking were discussed. Athletes who play in central positions relative to propinquity and task dependence are given greater opportunities for growth as leaders. Minorities are underrepresented in central positions on athletic teams.

Critical Thought Questions

1. Which of the four basic categories of leadership theories do you relate to best? What role would leadership training play in your leadership theory of choice?

2. Think about coaching staffs that you are familiar with. To what degree is the functional model of leadership being applied in these coaching staffs? Based on this theory, how could the leadership effectiveness of this coaching staff be improved?

3. Discuss what you like most and least about Fiedler's contingency theory of leadership. Explain your answers.

4. Based on Case's version of life cycle theory, how would you coach children differently than you would coach high school athletes or professional athletes, and why?

5. What do you think the strengths and weaknesses of Chelladurai's model are? Explain why.

6. There is little congruence between an athlete's perception of a coach's behaviors and the coach's own perception of his behaviors. Why do you think this is the case?

7. Discuss the value of utilizing the Coaching Behavior Assessment System (CBAS) as a research tool as well as a practical application tool in sport.

8. Discuss the utility of adopting the Coach Effectiveness Training program for preparing coaches. Think of other approaches that could be used, and put in writing your ideas for a program to train coaches.

9. How could the conceptual model of coaching efficacy be used to develop positive coaching behaviors in a coaching staff?

10. Coach-athlete compatibility and communication are essential for athlete satisfaction and athlete success. Discuss ways that a positive coach-athlete dyad can be developed and maintained.

11. Do you think stacking is a problem in youth sports? How about professional sports? Why do you feel this way?

Glossary

centrality The condition of playing in a position that is highly visible, interactive, and associated with high task interdependence.

Chelladurai's multidimensional model A leadership model in which athlete performance and satisfaction are viewed as products of the congruence of prescribed leadership behavior, actual leadership behavior, and preferred leadership behavior.

coach-athlete compatibility The quality of the relationship between the coach and the athlete.

Coach Effectiveness Training (CET) A coach training system that is based upon 20 years of research with the CBAS.

Coaching Behavior Assessment System (CBAS) A recording system designed to categorize the behavior of coaches during practices and games.

coaching efficacy The extent to which coaches believe they have the capacity to affect the learning and performance of their athletes.

conceptual model of coaching efficacy A conceptual model that predicts that coaching efficacy leads to effective coaching behaviors.

consideration Leader behavior that is indicative of friendship, mutual trust, respect, and warmth between the leader and subordinates.

Fiedler's contingency theory A leadership theory that is situation specific, but retains the notion of personality traits.

functional model of leadership A team approach to leadership in which one individual is strong in consideration while another is strong in initiating structure.

"great man" theory of leadership A theory of leadership based on the notion that great leaders are born, not made.

initiating structure A leader's behavior in clearly defining the relationship between the leader and subordinates, and in endeavoring to establish well-defined patterns of organization, channels of communication, and methods of procedure.

leadership behavior model The Smoll and Smith model of leadership based upon situation-specific behaviors of the leader.

life cycle theory A theory of leadership proposing that the appropriate leadership style for any specific situation depends on the maturity of the athlete.

path-goal theory A theory of leadership in which the emphasis is upon the needs and goals of the athlete. The leader is a facilitator.

positive sandwich approach Form of instruction in which the coach starts with a compliment, gives a future-oriented instruction, and ends with another compliment.

propinquity Observability and visibility on the playing field.

reactive behaviors Coach reactions to player or team behavior.

relationship motivation Concern with interpersonal relationships between leader and followers (see consideration).

situation-specific behavior theories Theories that view leadership as a function of specific behaviors effective in one situation but not another.

situational behaviors Behaviors that may help leaders be effective in some situations but not others.

situational traits Personality traits or dispositions that may help leaders be effective in some situations but not others.

spontaneous behaviors Behaviors initiated by the coach that do not occur in response to a players behavior.

stacking The disproportionate placement of blacks or other minorities into positions of low centrality relative to propinquity and task dependence.

task dependence The degree of interaction between members of the same team while executing a task.

task motivation A leader's concern with accomplishing the task at hand (see initiating structure).

team building A process that results in teams that have a positive climate, whose members enjoy a sense of satisfaction and feel attraction to the team as well as to other team members.

universal behavior theory Theory of leadership that proposes the existence of a set of universal leadership behaviors.

universal behaviors Leadership behaviors found in all successful leaders.

universal traits Personality traits found in all successful leaders.

PART 2

Motivation in Sport and Exercise

It is difficult to imagine anything being more important to success in sport than motivation. Sometimes we assume that great sport performances are based upon innate natural ability. Some might think, for example, that Tiger Woods' recent domination of the professional golf tour is somehow due to physical abilities that he was born with. Or we might believe that Michael Jordan's stature as perhaps the greatest basketball player in the history of the game was somehow based on innate physical abilities. However, close scrutiny of the training and preparation habits of all great performers can be traced to a combination of physical ability and *a drive to be the very best*. When Michael Jordan finished his college career at North Carolina, he possessed only an average outside jump shot. Through thousands of hours of practice and working on technique, he became a complete player. Defensive players feared his fall-away jump shot as much as they feared his explosive drive to the basket.

The athletic literature and folk history are full of examples of athletes who have excelled because of an internal desire, as opposed to physical attributes such as size, strength, power, and quickness. Former Boston Celtic great Larry Bird may be a case in point. Bird was never accused of possessing great quickness, speed, or vertical jumping ability, yet he remains one of the greatest basketball players of all time. Much of his greatness can be attributed to an intense internal desire to work hard and to achieve success. Examples of motivation are not restricted to sport. An admirer once remarked to a highly accomplished concert pianist, "I would give half my life to play as you do." The pianist responded, "That's exactly what I did." What is it that motivates an individual to give much of her life to accomplish a goal? For some reason (or reasons), the individual comes to believe that the goal is worth spending a lifetime and large amounts of money to achieve.

Motivation comes in many forms. Sometimes it is internal in nature and comes from a personal desire to find success independent of external rewards and enticements. Sometimes it is external in nature and comes from a desire to gain notoriety, fame, or financial rewards. Evidence exists to suggest that external rewards are often only fleeting motivators, and can in the end actually undermine intrinsic, or internal, motivation. In the chapters that follow, we will examine the literature and unravel many of the mysteries surrounding the sometimes elusive concept of motivation.

Insight into the deeper meaning of motivation comes from the early work of psychologists such as Hull (1943, 1951) and Spence (1956), who demonstrated that animals will go to extraordinary lengths to reduce an internal drive such as hunger or thirst. Drive theory, as proposed by these psychologists, is a theory of motivation based upon the notion of drive reduction. Drive theory states that motivation is related to a desire to reduce or satisfy an internal drive. In the case of sport, the drive may be to become an All-American track star or to make a high school basketball or football team. Motivation to achieve success in sport, however, is not simply an innate drive, such as the drive to satisfy hunger or thirst, but one that is

developed and learned. The root of the word *motivation* is the word *motive*. The Latin form of this word is *movere*, meaning "to move." The desire to move, as opposed to remaining stationary, is the essence of motivation.

Another insight into the basic concept of motivation comes from the classic work of Abraham Maslow (1970, 1987). Maslow's concept of motivation is based upon a needs hierarchy. A person must first satisfy lower-level needs before he can turn his attention to satisfying higher-level needs. Lower-level needs include the basic need to feel safe and the needs to satisfy the cravings of hunger and thirst. Once these fundamental needs have been satisfied, the individual can turn his attention to satisfying higher-level human needs, such as the needs to be loved, to feel worthy, to feel competent, and to realize self-fulfillment. Maslow's higher-level needs are the ones that can be achieved through involvement in sport and exercise. Maslow's hierarchy of needs is helpful, however, as it demonstrates that it is difficult to focus upon a higher need such as competence and self-fulfillment if you are hungry, thirsty, or fearing for your personal safety.

Building upon the theories of Hull (1943, 1951) and Spence (1956), Atkinson (1964) and

McClelland (McClelland, Atkinson, Clark, & Lowell, 1953) developed what was to be called the McClelland-Atkinson model of motivation. This model was based upon two basic psychological constructs that remain important in understanding motivation to this day. The first is the construct of intrinsic motivation, or what McClelland and Atkinson called the motive to achieve success; and the second was anxiety, or what they called fear of failure. The theory was an approach-avoidance model in the sense that an individual makes a decision to either engage in (approach) or withdraw from (avoid) an achievement situation based upon the magnitude or strength of the two psychological constructs. If the individual's intrinsic motivation to take part in an achievement situation were greater than her fear of failing at it, she would take part. Conversely, if the individual's fear of failure were stronger than her intrinsic motivation to take part, she would withdraw from the situation. In its simplest form, the model is represented by the following equation:

Participation = intrinsic motivation − fear of failure

As the McClelland-Atkinson model evolved, it took on added features, referred to as elaborations. While thoroughly studied between 1950 and 1970, the theory has been largely abandoned by most psychologists and sport psychologists in favor of more situation-specific theories. One reason the theory was abandoned was its complexity and the difficulty of measuring its psychological constructs. The one redeeming characteristic of the theory, however, was that the specific psychological constructs were systematically identified and studied in an attempt to explain the phenomenon of human motivation.

In this part of the book, motivation in sport will be thoroughly investigated and explained through three important chapters. The three chapters will cover the important topics of causal attribution, self-confidence and intrinsic motivation, and goal perspective in sport. Each of these chapters will explain motivation from the perspective of sport and exercise involvement. We seek to understand what motivation is and how it can be developed in sport and exercise. ➷

4

Causal Attribution in Sport

KEY TERMS

Accurate optimist
Attribution theory
Attributional training
Causal Dimension Scale
Competitive situation
Controllability
Covariation principle
Dysfunctional attribution
  strategy
Ego-enhancing strategy
Ego-protecting strategy
Functional attribution strategy
Hopefulness
Hopelessness
Illogical model
Learned helplessness
Locus of causality
Locus of control
Logical attribution
Logical model
Maladaptive attributional
  pattern
Self-serving hypothesis
Stability

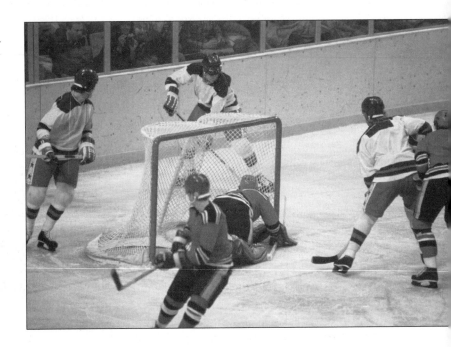

The key element in *attribution theory* is perception. When athletes are asked, "To what do you attribute your great success?" they are being asked for their perceptions. The fact that their perceptions of why they are successful may be debatable is beside the point. The manner in which athletes answer questions like these reveals their perceptual beliefs.

Consider the following scenario. Two experienced volleyball players were matched against a pair of less experienced players in intramural doubles competition. The outcome was predictable: the

CONCEPT   Attributions that athletes select to explain their outcomes reveal much about their motivational constructs.

APPLICATION   Coaches should not disregard the kinds of attributions athletes use to explain their outcomes. Instead, coaches should analyze them to understand the athletes' basic attribution structures. Athletes who give inappropriate attributions may need help in explaining their outcomes.

experienced team won the match easily. After the match, the losers explained to the victors that they had lost because one of them had injured his shoulder and they had had a bad day. In point of fact, they had lost because they had played a team with far greater ability. However, this was not apparent to the losers, who attributed their loss to bad luck and an injured shoulder. In so doing, they were subconsciously protecting their egos. While this may not have made them better volleyball players, it served to protect their self-esteem.

Consider a second example, a variation that occurs regularly in youth sports competition. A group of youngsters was returning home after suffering a humiliating 17–0 soccer defeat at the hands of a superior team. As the children began to give causes for the defeat, it became apparent to the father of two of the youngsters that each child had a little different perception of the cause of the loss. One child explained that they lost because of poor officiating. A second and a third exclaimed that they thought they lost the match because of the poor condition of the playing field. A fourth child reported, with tears in her eyes, that they lost because they weren't any good. Each response revealed important information about the way children attempt to make sense out of outcomes.

Attribution theory is a cognitive approach to motivation. It assumes that people strive to explain, understand, and predict events based upon their cognitive perception. According to attribution theory, the intent of every human being is to explain his own actions in terms of their perceived causes. Fritz Heider (1944, 1958), the originator of attribution theory, described his theory as one of common sense, or "naive psychology."

However, as viewed by Weiner (1985) and Roberts (1982), attribution theory is far more than a layperson's understanding of perceived motivation. It is a complex theory in which perceived attributions are viewed as greatly influencing a person's actions, feelings, confidence, and motivation. How

Athlete's affect associated with outcome is indicative of perceived cause. Courtesy Kansas State University Sports Information.

an athlete feels about herself is directly related to the athlete's perception of cause and effect.

Most of the research that uses attribution theory deals with understanding when and why people select certain categories of attribution. For example, if an athlete systematically attributes failure to bad luck, we might suspect an unwillingness to accept responsibility. The attributions that athletes select reveal their motivational constructs. Furthermore, helping athletes to change their perceptions can have a significant effect on their motivation to achieve. For this reason, motivation and attribution theory are very closely related. For example, some young people feel they fail because they lack innate ability. Since innate ability is relatively permanent, it is hard for those children to see that things will ever change for the better. However, if young athletes can be encouraged to consider bad luck or lack of effort as a cause for their failure, they need not feel that things cannot change. After all, luck can improve, and one can always try harder.

This chapter further explains the essence of attribution theory under four broad subheadings: historical development of the attribution model in sport, causal attributions in competitive situations, attributional training, and egocentrism in attribution.

> A common wisdom among basketball coaches is that shooting a basketball is luck, and that the more one practices the luckier one becomes (Miserandino, 1998, p. 287).

The Attributional Model

The basic attribution model was proposed by Heider (1944, 1958). However, several significant contributions by Weiner (1972, 1979, 1985) have made it much more applicable to the sports realm. Most recently, contributions by Russell (1982) and by McAuley, Duncan, and Russell (1992) have improved our ability to measure attribution in sport and exercise.

Fritz Heider's Contribution

The basis for Heider's model was the notion that people strive for prediction and understanding of daily events in order to give their lives stability and predictability. A simplified version of Heider's basic model is illustrated in figure 4.1.

Outcomes are attributed internally to the person (personal force) or externally to the environment (environmental force). Effective personal force is composed of the attributional factors *ability* and *effort,* while effective environmental force is composed of the attributional factors *task difficulty* and *luck.*

According to Heider, an interaction occurs between the personal force of ability and the environmental force of task difficulty that yields a separate dimension referred to as *can* (or *cannot*). If a task is difficult and yet is accomplished, it must be due to great ability. However, depending on the difficulty of the task and the ability of the subject, several other attributions can give rise to the *can* or (*cannot*) dimension.

The highly unstable factor of luck also enters into many attribution situations. Luck is an environmental factor that can favorably or unfavorably change an outcome in an unpredictable way. However, keep in mind that what one person calls luck another person may call ability. For example, a tennis player who consistently places the first serve into the deep backhand corner of the opponent's serving area should be considered skilled. However, the opponent may continue to attribute the event to luck. All these factors (effort, ability, task difficulty, and luck) combine to result in a behavioral outcome, to which an individual attributes a cause. Heider reasoned that the personal and the environmental components of causation are summative. Thus, the following formula represents his reasoning:

Behavioral outcome = Personal force
+ Environmental force

FIGURE 4.1 | Simplified schematic of Heider's (1958) model of causal attributions.

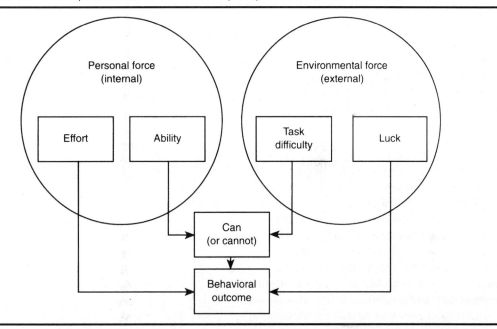

Bernard Weiner's Contributions

Using Heider's basic formulation, Weiner (1972) made several significant contributions to the attribution model that made it easier to understand and apply in achievement situations. Weiner took Heider's four main factors and restructured them into two main causal dimensions. These two dimensions he labeled **stability** and **locus of control.** As can be observed in figure 4.2, stability is composed of stable and unstable attributes, while locus of control includes internal and external loci of control. Locus of control is a psychological construct that refers to people's belief about whether they are personally responsible for what happens to them. Athletes who exhibit internal control tend to believe their behaviors influence outcomes. Those who exhibit external control tend to attribute their outcomes to outside forces such as fate, chance, and other people.

Weiner then incorporated Heider's four main factors (effort, ability, task difficulty, and luck)

FIGURE 4.2 | Weiner's classification scheme for causal attributions.

| | **Locus of control dimension** | |
	Internal	External
Stability dimension Stable	Ability (internal/stable)	Task difficulty (external/stable)
Stability dimension Unstable	Effort (internal/unstable)	Luck (external/unstable)

into his two-dimensional classification scheme for causal attribution. Ability was classified as being internal and stable, effort as internal and unstable, task difficulty as external and stable, and luck as external and unstable.

Within this four-choice framework, Weiner envisioned that people would generally attribute their successes and failures to one of the four factors depicted in figure 4.2. If a sprinter loses a race to a faster opponent and then reasons that the loss is due to bad luck, what she is really saying is that the cause is external and unstable, and given another chance she would win. But if she loses and attributes the loss to a lack of ability, she is saying the cause is internal and is not going to change; if she ran the race a second time, she would still lose.

For many years, research in attribution focused upon Weiner's two-dimensional classification scheme. However, limitations of the two-dimensional scheme became apparent. Frieze (1976) originally found support for the model when she reported that 85 percent of the attributions reported in her research could be categorized into one of the four cells in figure 4.2. Conversely, Roberts and Pascuzzi (1979) reported that only 45 percent of attributions made by children in youth sport settings could easily be categorized as being due to ability, effort, task difficulty, or luck.

In his later writings, Weiner (1979, 1985) clarified that a third dimension named **controllability** must be included in the attribution model. He argued successfully in favor of a three-dimensional model, as illustrated in figure 4.3. The inclusion of this third dimension created a few conceptual problems that had to be addressed. The first

FIGURE 4.3 | Weiner's (1985) three-dimensional model of causal attribution.

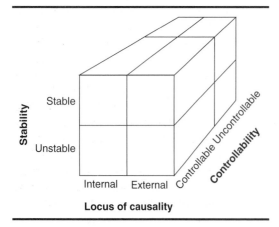

problem was how to differentiate between the dimension of locus of control and the new dimension of controllability. He solved this problem by renaming the locus of control dimension **locus of causality** and clarifying the distinction between the two dimensions. He explained that locus of causality has to do with whether an outcome was perceived by the individual to be internally or externally caused, whereas controllability has to do with whether an outcome was perceived by the individual to be controllable or uncontrollable. An attribution such as effort might be considered to be under volitional control (controllable), whereas mood or fatigue might not (uncontrollable). Math aptitude might be a good example of an internal (locus of causality) but uncontrollable attribution. The student recognizes that his lack of math aptitude is an internal attribution, but does not feel that he has any personal control over aptitude. Similarly, an athlete might lose a 100-meter race to a faster opponent, attribute the loss internally to low ability (speed), yet feel that she doesn't have control over how fast she can run.

Another issue that Weiner became uncomfortable with, relative to the two-dimensional model, was the implication that the four attributions shown in figure 4.2 always fit the two-dimensional model. For example, ability (an aptitude), classified in the model as being stable, could be considered by an individual to be unstable if learning is possible. Effort, categorized as unstable, could be viewed as stable by individuals who always try hard. Tasks considered to be difficult in one instance could become, with practice, less difficult. Finally, luck, normally considered to be external and unstable, could actually be considered by an individual who believes himself to be a "lucky person" to be stable.

Dan Russell's and Ed McAuley's Contributions as They Relate to Measurement

Traditionally, there have been three ways of measuring causal attribution. The first was the structural rating scale method, in which the athlete was

CONCEPT   Formal attempts to measure an athlete's attribution structure should employ an open-ended system in conjunction with the Causal Dimension Scale.

APPLICATION   Open-ended attributions allow freedom of choice. In conjunction with the Causal Dimension Scale, these freely selected attributions can be correctly categorized. Although it is usually reserved for researchers, the practice of gathering data on perceived causality can be a valuable source of information for the coach.

asked to rate several attributions in terms of how they apply to an event. The list of attributions usually included ability, effort, difficulty, and luck. The second method was the structural percentage rating scale method. With this the attributions were again supplied, but the subject rated them in terms of percentage of contribution. The third method was referred to as an open-ended system. The athletes made their own attributions or selected them from a long list of potential attributions. The researcher then assigned the open-ended statements to specific categories of the attribution model shown in figures 4.2 or 4.3.

The weakness of the two structural methods of assessing attributions is that they are too constraining. Participants are forced to select attributions from a list that may not contain a statement that matches their perception of what caused an event. The weakness of the open-ended system is that it leaves the sport psychologist with the task of assigning attributions to the appropriate dimensions. The sport psychologist and the athlete may not agree on the meaning of a causal attribution, and too often the open-ended attributions are ambiguous.

To deal with attribution distortion and misclassification, Russell (1982) developed the **Causal Dimension Scale** (CDS). In using the CDS, athletes are asked to indicate their perceived cause for an outcome, and then to rate the cause relative to nine questions. The scale is composed of three questions for each of the dimensions of locus of causality, stability, and controllability. The score range for each dimension is between 3 and 27. The higher the score, the more internal, stable, and controllable the athlete perceives the attribution to be. Thus, if an athlete attributed her outcome to "I had a good day" and then received a locus score of 25, a stability score of 21, and a controllability score of 10, you could label her attribution as internal, stable, and uncontrollable.

After its development in 1982, the Causal Dimension Scale was used extensively by researchers. As a result, it became apparent that the controllability dimension of the scale was defective. Psychometric investigations revealed that the controllability dimension of the scale exhibited low internal consistency and a propensity to correlate highly with the locus of control dimension (Russell, McAuley, & Tarico, 1987).

An article by McAuley, Duncan, and Russell (1992) documents the development of the Causal Dimension Scale II (CDSII), a revision of the original version of the scale. The revised version differs from the original in that it comprises four rather than three causal dimension scales. The four dimensions of the CDSII are locus of causality, stability, personal control, and external control. The original CDS scale failed to distinguish adequately between causes that were controlled by the individual and those controlled by other people. Attributions were simply controllable or uncontrollable, with no clear indication of who was controlling the cause. As indicated in figure 4.4, the CDSII measures four specific dimensions of causality.

The actual inventory is composed of twelve items, with three items representing each of the dimensions of locus of control, stability, external control, and personal control. Values for each dimension can range from 3 to 27, with higher values representing attributions that are more internal, stable, controllable by others, and personally controllable. A sample item from the personal control dimension is as follows:

Is the cause something:

YOU CAN							YOU CANNOT	
REGULATE								REGULATE
9	8	7	6	5	4	3	2	1

As with the original Causal Dimension Scale (CDS), the Causal Dimension Scale II (CDSII) also has some psychometric problems that need to be resolved. Crocker, Eklund, and Graham (2002) reported an investigation in which the four-factor structure of the CDSII (see fig. 4.4) was tested using a statistical procedure called confirmatory factor analysis. The results of this investigation varied as a function of the samples that were analyzed. When the sample was composed of team sport athletes (e.g., hockey/soccer), the results provided strong support for the four-factor structure of the 12-item CDSII. However, when the sample was composed of individual sport athletes (e.g., swimming/track & field), a less-than-ideal fit to the data was observed. The degree to which the data fit in the four-factor model was significantly improved, however, when a particular stability item was removed. This particular stability item correlated highly with locus of causality, personal control, and stability, even though it theoretically measured the stability dimension. This problem was further highlighted by the observation that the locus of causality dimension and the personal control dimension were highly correlated with each other. Theoretically, the four causal dimensions illustrated in figure 4.4 should be somewhat independent of one another.

Other Considerations

The process of identifying and categorizing causal attributions has come a long way since Heider first defined it. However, a number of conceptual problems persist. For instance, researchers and practitioners may fail to recognize that the kinds of attributions people make are based on a socialization

FIGURE 4.4 | Attributional Dimensions of the CDSII. These four dimensions are used to measure causality in the revised Causal Dimension Scale (CDSII).

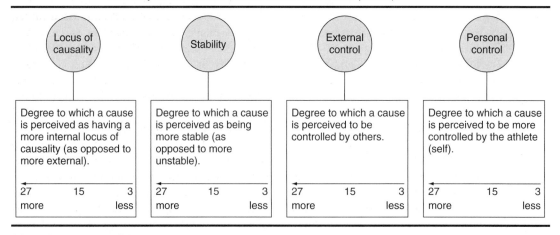

Source: McAuley, Duncan, & Russell (1991).

process that may vary across cultures. Socialization plays an important part in the emphasis that we place on attributions. Attributions depend on what we learn to value. For example, ability is very important for Iranian children, and evolves as an important attribution regardless of whether a child fails or succeeds (Salili, Maehr, & Gillmore, 1976). American children, on the other hand, tend to value effort and intent regardless of innate ability. These socialization differences will undoubtedly affect the kinds of attributions made.

In addition to social-cultural differences, we also have evidence of differences due to race and ethnicity. Morgan, Griffin, and Heyward (1996), for example, observed that young track and field athletes' attributions do not differ as a function of gender, but do differ as a function of race/ethnicity. Young Anglo athletes perceive success as internal and stable to a greater degree than African or Native American athletes do. This certainly is an advantage for the young Anglo athletes. They perceive success as something that they can control and that will likely occur again.

A second problem that has often plagued attribution research is that the experimenter can bias a subject's perception of outcome. In many sports-related attribution studies, subjects do not perceive themselves to be succeeding or failing until the researcher biases their perceptions by asking, "To what do you attribute your success (or failure)?" Sometimes success and failure are perceived differently by researcher and athlete. For example, let's say I play tennis with one of the world's best players. I don't expect to win, but if I can win one or two games, I will consider myself a success.

Causal Attributions in Competitive Situations

A **competitive situation** is defined as one in which participants expect that their performance will be evaluated by others in some way. It is an opportunity to compete with others for some internal or external reward. The competitive situation provides rich opportunities in which to study attribution theory. There are usually a perceived winner and loser, and an opportunity for participants to explain reasons or causes for outcomes. In this section we look specifically at internal/external locus of causality, emotional response, and stability considerations in competitive situations.

Internal/External Attributions

Regarding the internal and external dimensions of attribution, several lines of research have evolved. Two are of particular interest to us in this section. One has dealt with the notion of locus of causality to the exclusion of the stability dimension. The second has concentrated on the notion of covariation.

Locus of Causality   Previously called locus of control, locus of causality is the extent to which people believe they are responsible for their behavioral outcomes. A vast body of psychological literature exists dedicated to this concept in and of itself. To avoid confusion between the terms *locus of control* and *controllability,* we have taken Weiner's advice and renamed the locus of control dimension "locus of causality." Throughout this section, we will refer to the construct as locus of causality, even though in the literature it is generally named locus of control. As discussed earlier, people with an internal locus of causality tend to believe their behaviors influence outcomes, while those with an external locus of causality tend to attribute outcomes to outside forces such as fate, chance, and other people. This dichotomy closely resembles DeCharms and Carpenter's (1968) origin-pawn relationship. People who are *origins* like to be in control and originate their own behavioral outcomes. Those who are *pawns* feel powerless and acted on by external sources.

Perhaps the person most responsible for developing the conceptual framework for the locus of causality dimension in attribution was Julian B. Rotter (1966, 1971). Rotter (1966) developed the

CONCEPT   An internal locus of control is typically a more mature orientation.

APPLICATION   Externals can be identified by using Rotter's Internal-External Locus of Control Scale or by observing that the athletes attribute most outcomes to external causes. These athletes can be encouraged to adopt a more internal orientation through the development of self-confidence and of the habit of attributing outcomes internally when appropriate.

29-item Internal-External Locus of Control Scale to measure the extent to which people believe they possess some control over their lives. The Rotter scale has been used by many researchers to classify subjects on the basis of the locus of causality dimension. After using the scale for many years, Rotter (1971) stated the following generalities about locus of causality: (1) children coming from a lower socioeconomic environment tend to be external, (2) children tend to become more internal with age, and (3) highly external people feel they are at the mercy of their environment and are continually being manipulated by outside forces.

As an alternative to the Rotter scale for measuring locus of control, Levenson (1981) developed the Levenson IPC scale. It measures the internal (I) dimension in much the same way the Rotter Scale does, but breaks the external dimension down into two important subdivisions. These two subdivisions are powerful others (P) and chance (C). Levenson reasoned that individuals with an external locus of causality view their lack of control as being orderly and predictable (controlled by powerful others), or unordered, unpredictable, and out of control (chance).

While it is not appropriate for human beings to always give internal attributions to outcomes, research makes it abundantly clear that in the sports environment it is better to have an internal as opposed to an external locus of causality. It is better that young athletes and people in general view themselves as in control of their own destiny, as opposed to seeing themselves as at the mercy of external events. Accepting credit for a success is psychologically preferred to attributing the success to some external force, such as luck or the actions of others. While painful, it is also desirable that we accept responsibility for our actions when we fail. If we do not accept responsibility for our errors and failures, how can we possibly improve and become stronger? The key is to accept responsibility for our failures when appropriate, but to do so in such a way that the attribution does not suggest that failure is inevitable for the future. This approach can be instilled in children by teaching them to use internal but unstable (changeable) attributions for failure. We will discuss the stability dimension in greater detail in a subsequent section of this chapter.

Research suggests that an internal orientation is more mature than an external orientation (Rotter, 1971). Consequently, we should expect that children's attributions should shift toward a more internal orientation as they mature (Jambor & Rudisill, 1992; Ntoumanis & Jones, 1998). Furthermore, we have evidence that sports and exercise can have the effect of shifting a child's locus of causality from the external to the internal. Duke, Johnson, and Nowicki (1977) monitored the locus of control of 109 children ages six to fourteen during an eight-week sport fitness camp, and observed a significant shift toward internal causality as a result of the experience.

In keeping with the theme that an internal locus of causality is more mature than an external locus of causality, two studies are of interest. Scheer and Ansorge (1979) noted that gymnastic coaches typically rank-order their gymnasts from poorest to best for gymnastic meets, on the theory that judges expect scores to improve as the meet

CONCEPT According to the covariation principle, outcomes that agree with the performance of others usually result in external attributions, while outcomes that disagree usually result in internal attributions.

APPLICATION This principle can help the coach tell when the athlete is making inappropriate attributions for success and failure. For example, if an athlete hits a home run off a pitcher who strikes most batters out, this outcome should be attributed internally.

progresses. Interestingly, the results showed that judges who themselves had an internal locus of control were uninfluenced by order. Conversely, judges who had an external locus of control were influenced by order. This suggests that the judges who had an internal orientation were able to overcome the order bias and judge solely on the basis of performance. Another study showed that captains (leaders) of female adult volleyball teams exhibit a greater tendency toward internal locus of control than their teammates (Aguglia & Sapienza, 1984). More recently, Ntoumanis and Jones (1998) reported that youth sport participants score higher on internal locus of causality than do nonparticipants.

Even though an internal locus of causality appears to be preferable to an external locus of causality, this should not be construed to mean that all external attributions are immature. Sometimes external attributions are appropriate and expected. For example, it would be completely normal for athletes to complain that they lost because of poor officiating if their team had been called for twice as many fouls as the other team.

Covariation Principle A person's attributions for success or failure can be predicted on the basis of the performance of others on the same task. This phenomenon has been named the **covariation principle.** According to this principle, when the performance of others agrees (covaries) with the performance of the participant, attributions will be external. If the performance of others disagrees (lacks covariation)

with the performance of the participant, attributions will be internal. For example, if I beat someone in tennis whom everyone else has lost to, I will certainly attribute my victory to an internal cause such as superior ability. Conversely, if I defeat someone in tennis whom everyone else has also defeated, I will likely attribute my success to an external cause, such as my opponent's low ability. Because there is logic in these predicted attributions, they are referred to as **logical attributions.** The covariation principle is illustrated in figure 4.5. When your performance agrees with the performance of others, your attributions are likely to be external in nature (e.g., task difficulty or luck). Conversely, when your performance disagrees with the performance of others, your attributions are likely to be internal in nature (e.g., ability or effort).

Perceived Causality and Emotional Response

Emotional response to athletic outcomes occurs on two different levels (Weiner, 1985). At the initial or primitive level, emotional responses are said to be *attribution free.* The initial response of an athlete to success is generally happiness or joy. The initial response of an athlete to failure is generally disappointment or sadness. This initial emotional response is given before the athlete has had a chance to consider the cause of the outcome. At the second level, emotional responses arise in direct response to causal attributions as to why the outcome occurred. These emotions are *attribution*

FIGURE 4.5 | Illustration of the covariation principle applied to sport.

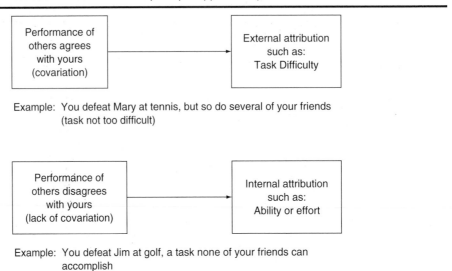

Example: You defeat Mary at tennis, but so do several of your friends
(task not too difficult)

Example: You defeat Jim at golf, a task none of your friends can
accomplish

dependent, and are said to be distinct and separate from the initial attribution-free emotional response. These attribution-dependent emotions reveal a great deal about how the athlete feels about why the outcome occurred.

The affect-attribution relationship provides the coach or sport psychologist with an excellent tool for understanding the cognitions and thoughts of the athlete. If an athlete hides his emotions well, you might be able to determine how he is feeling by asking him to tell you why he feels he either won or lost a match. Conversely, if an athlete does not like to explain why he feels he won or lost a match, you can deduce a great deal about the hidden attributions by his emotional responses to either success or failure.

The kinds of affective responses you can expect from athletes, as a function of attribution, are illustrated in figure 4.6 (Weiner, 1985). Internal locus of causality attributions are linked to the emotions of pride and self-esteem. If an athlete succeeds and attributes the cause to be internal, she will usually respond with increased feelings of pride and self-esteem. Conversely, if the athlete fails and attributes the cause to be internal, she will

usually respond with decreased feelings of pride and self-esteem. If an athlete either succeeds or fails and attributes the cause externally, there is no reason why she should take it personally, so no particular affective response is predicted in terms of pride and self-confidence.

Controllability attributions are primarily linked to the emotions of anger, gratitude, guilt, pity, and shame. Failure that is linked to personal controllability should result in the emotions of shame, guilt, and perhaps depression. This is the case because the athlete believes that he had personal control over the outcome and failed. Conversely, if an athlete succeeds and attributes the cause to personal control, we should expect her to exhibit affect associated with increased self-confidence and competence. Failure that is linked to a perceived uncontrollable cause (e.g., other people) should give rise to the emotional response of anger, or perhaps to surprise and astonishment. Anger is a typical response when an athlete feels that failure can be blamed on an incorrect call by an official. Conversely, if the athlete succeeds and attributes the success to an uncontrollable cause, the emotions of gratitude or pity are predicted.

FIGURE 4.6 | Illustration showing affect associated with various combinations of outcome and attribution.

Outcome

	Success	Failure
Internal	pride self-esteem satisfaction	reduced pride reduced self-esteem reduced satisfaction
External	no feelings about self	no feelings about self

Locus of Causality

If athlete internalizes the cause of success or failure, significant affect in form of pride and self-esteem will follow.

Outcome

	Success	Failure
Controllable	confidence competence	shame guilt depression
Uncontrollable	gratitude pity for opponent	anger surprise astonishment

Controllability

Emotional response to success or failure depends a great deal on athlete's perception of who (self or others) was in control (or not) of outcome.

Outcome

	Success	Failure
Stable	hopefulness	hopelessness
Unstable	uncertainty	hopefulness

Stability

Athletes tend to feel either hopeful or hopeless toward prospect of future success depending on stability attribution.

CONCEPT The kinds of attribution that athletes make for success and failure are closely associated with their emotions.

APPLICATION Coaches should learn to recognize athletes' unspoken attributions from the athletes'

emotional responses. If an athlete hides emotions, the coach should be able to predict how that person is feeling based upon the attributions the athlete makes.

Gratitude may be the expected affective response if a success occurred because of a particularly good play by your teammate, or by an error made by an opponent (or perhaps you may feel pity for the opponent).

Stability dimensions are linked to feelings of hopefulness or hopelessness. If you lose and attribute the cause to something that is not going to change (stable cause), then **hopelessness,** or the feeling that failure will continue, is the expected affective response. Conversely, if you win and attribute the cause to a stable attribution, the expected emotional response is **hopefulness,** or the expectation that you will continue to win. If an athlete loses but attributes the cause to something that is unstable and can change (not enough effort), then he can be hopeful that things will be different next time with a little more effort. Finally, if success is the outcome and an attribution is made to an unstable cause (good luck), then the expected affect is uncertainty.

The kinds of attributions that young athletes make in response to success and failure are closely linked to their feelings of self-esteem and self-confidence. Individuals suffering from low self-esteem are more likely than individuals high in self-esteem to internalize a failure and respond with negative affect. Losers are much more likely to search for reasons they failed than winners are to search for reasons they succeeded. This is especially true if a negative outcome was unexpected. If you lose a contest that you expected to win, you want to know why (Biddle & Hill, 1992).

Stability Considerations

In the previous two sections we considered practical applications associated with locus of causality research and psychological affect. In this section we will turn to a discussion of the stability dimension of causal attribution.

Expectancy and Attribution The attributional position is that the stability of a cause, rather than its locus or causality, determines *expectancy* shifts. We actually introduced this concept in the lower part of figure 4.6, where it was shown that stability attributions give rise to feelings of hopefulness and hopelessness. A hopeful individual has expectations that future contests will result in success, whereas a hopeless individual has expectations that future contests will result in another defeat or failure.

An athlete's expectation for future success or failure is largely based on the stability attribution that she gave for previous outcomes. If the athlete gives a stable attribution for an outcome, she is saying that the conditions or causes that brought this outcome about are not going to change; therefore, the expectation is that the next outcome will be the same. If the previous outcome was a success, then the expectation for the future is success. Conversely, if the previous outcome was failure, then the expectancy for the future is failure.

If an athlete gives an unstable attribution for an outcome, he is saying that the conditions or causes that brought this outcome about are going to change; therefore, the expectation is that the

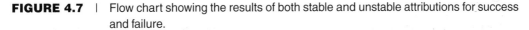

FIGURE 4.7 | Flow chart showing the results of both stable and unstable attributions for success and failure.

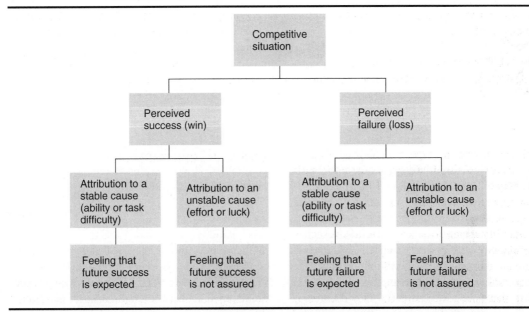

next outcome will be different. If the previous outcome was success, then the expectation for the future is uncertainty. Conversely, if the previous outcome was failure, then the expectancy for the future may be success.

Given that attributions are linked to emotions and that emotions are linked to cognitions, we can see the critical importance of the kinds of stability attributions that athletes give for athletic outcomes. As a coach, I would want every one of my athletes approaching every game from the perspective of hopefulness and optimism. The research support for the link between stability attributions and expectancy is so strong that Weiner (1985) characterized the relationship as a fundamental psychological law or principle. The basic application of this principle is illustrated in figure 4.7.

Learned Helplessness Seligman's (1995) notion of **learned helplessness** is somewhat related to Weiner's use of the term "hopelessness" to describe the affective response to failure when linked to a stable cause. The term "learned helplessness," however, is developed to a greater extent and contains a more specific and foreboding meaning.

Seligman defines learned helplessness in terms of the phrase "giving up without even trying." It is caused by the perception that one has no control over events. Seligman's research began with dogs in a laboratory. Some dogs when shocked would do nothing about it and passively accept the pain. Seligman's later research with humans linked pessimism and depression with learned helplessness and even with physical illness and a reduced or compromised immune system. Seligman's research and writing is about teaching children to become **accurate optimists.** Children must be taught how to interact with their environment in an optimistic but realistic way. False optimism will eventually be exposed, but accurate optimism is about knowing yourself and taking an active stance to shape your own life. Rather than being a passive recipient of what

CONCEPT "Changes in expectancy of success following an outcome are influenced by the perceived stability of the cause of the event" (Weiner, 1985, p. 559).

APPLICATION The coach or sport psychologist should monitor the attributions that athletes give for competitive outcomes. If attributions to failure are stable in nature, proactive steps should be taken relative to attribution training. Athletes must be taught to make unstable attributions to negative outcomes. Failure to do so will result in a feeling of hopelessness on the part of the affected athletes. Attribution training is the topic of the next section of this chapter.

happens in life, the child must learn to be an optimist.

"Learned helpless" children who show a deterioration of performance under the threat of failure tend to attribute their failure to stable factors such as lack of ability. Conversely, "learned helpless" children who show enhanced performance under the threat of failure tend to choose unstable factors such as luck or lack of effort (Dweck, 1980). Attributing success to stable factors suggests to the child that success is a realistic expectation for the future; attributing failure to stable factors suggests to the child that failure is a realistic expectation for the future.

A coach or teacher should promote feelings of self-efficacy and self-confidence by encouraging children to make appropriate attributions for success and failure. Children who succeed should be encouraged to view the success as both stable and internal—internal, because the child needs to feel pride in their accomplishment; stable, because the child needs to feel that success is likely to occur again. Attributing success to ability should be beneficial, since it is both internal and stable. Children who experience repeated failure should be encouraged to select an unstable and perhaps internal attribution (Grove & Pargman, 1986). Such an attribution will assure the child that failure is not inevitable, because the cause is not stable. But an internal attribution will help the child accept responsibility for the results. It would not be wise to continually encourage an external/unstable attribution, because the child may come to feel that bad luck or poor officiating are the cause of all disappointments. However, a good mix of internal and external unstable attributions may prove beneficial.

Dweck (1975) proposed and tested such a therapeutic strategy. A sample of "learned helpless" children were categorized into a failure deprivation condition and an attribution retraining condition. In the deprivation condition, the children's confidence was bolstered through programmed success. The children in the attribution retraining condition were told after experiencing a failure to attribute the failure to an unstable cause such as effort. The results showed that by the end of the training period, the attribution retraining children fared far better than the success-only children in the face of a contrived failure. Therefore, helping children to change their attributions may be more beneficial than merely manipulating success. This does not mean that experiencing success is not important. It is. But performance and self-efficacy can also be enhanced by helping children make confidence-building or confidence-protecting attributions.

Attributional Training

Research with **attributional training** has clearly shown that planned interventions can alter ways that an athlete perceives outcome, and also alter actual performance (Miserandino, 1998; Orbach, Singer, & Murphey, 1997; Orbach, Singer, & Price, 1999). In each of these studies functional and dysfunctional attributional strategies were contrasted. A **functional attribution strategy** is one in

CONCEPT Attributing failure to an internal/stable cause is potentially damaging to a young athlete's self-esteem.

APPLICATION Young athletes should be encouraged to attribute failure to unstable causes that can be expected to change. For example, insufficient effort would be an ideal attribution for failure.

CONCEPT Attributing success to an internal/stable cause such as ability is good for a young athlete's self-confidence.

APPLICATION The development of self-confidence is the most important goal of any youth sport program. Coaches should encourage athletes to take credit for their successes.

which athletes are taught to explain the causes of a failure outcome as being controllable and unstable in orientation. A **dysfunctional attribution strategy** is one in which athletes are taught to explain the cause of a failure outcome as being uncontrollable and stable. In each of the investigations cited above, it was demonstrated that the two strategies result in athletes giving attributions that mirror their training, and that participants in functional attribution strategy groups exhibited superior performance scores. Furthermore, functional attributional training groups exhibited higher expectations for success and were more hopeful and more optimistic.

Research with children suggests that attributional training can positively influence a child's future expectations and performance (Rudisill, 1988). Attributional training can also be effective with adults, although not so effective as it is with children. Adults respond well to attributional training as long as their perceived competence is not too low. Athletes who suffer from maladaptive attributional patterns exhibit attributional styles that differ from those of nonmaladaptive athletes. Athletes with **maladaptive attributional patterns** give failure attributions that are more internal, stable,

uncontrollable, and global than those of the nonmaladaptive athletes (Prapavessis & Carron, 1988). This means that the athlete who suffers from maladaptive attributional patterns attributes failure to causes that are personal (internal), are unchanging (stable), are out of his control (uncontrollable), and apply generally to his life (global). For an example, an athlete with low self-esteem with a history of failure might explain a recent failure thus: "I am just no good at this." This explanation, correctly interpreted, may tell the coach that this young person believes that he is responsible for the failure, there is no likelihood for change in the future, he has no control over the situation, and he is likely to experience failure in most athletic mastery attempts.

If the athlete suffering from maladaptive attributional patterns wins a contest, he is likely to attribute the success to causes that are impersonal (external), changing (unstable), out of his control (uncontrollable), and specific to the event. In this case, the individual suffering from learned helplessness might explain a recent unexpected success this way: "Everyone gets lucky sometime." Correctly interpreted, this explanation may tell the coach that this young person believes that he was not

Women athletes learn to attribute success to internal causes. Courtesy University of Missouri–Columbia Sports Information.

responsible for the success, it is not likely to happen again, he has no control over it, and the success is not likely to have a positive effect on his life generally.

In attribution training, it is a good idea to objectively determine the nature of attributions given by individuals for outcomes. Earlier we introduced the Causal Dimension Scale (CDS) and the CDSII as means for determining the true nature of attributions given. One of these instruments, or an appropriate adaptation, can be used to assist in correctly interpreting the true meaning of attributions given by young athletes for outcomes (Grove & Prapavessis, 1995).

Once it has been determined that attributions given by a maladaptive athlete are indeed counterproductive and potentially damaging to the individual, steps should be taken to restructure how the person perceives attributions. Consider the following hypothetical script:

> COACH: "Sally, it appears that you feel that your failure to return serve in your last match was due to lack of skill."
>
> SALLY: "Not just skill. I really don't have what it takes to be a good tennis player. I'm just not coordinated and never will be."
>
> COACH: "Actually, I've known lots of good tennis players who felt that way when they first started. I'm sure you are no different."
>
> SALLY: "Do you really think so?"
>
> COACH: "Yes, I do. You have a whole week before your next match. I'll work with you on your footwork. I'm sure you will do better next time. Practice really helps, but it does take time."

In the prior script, the coach has subtly suggested to the athlete that the cause of her failure may be something that can change (skill), and that she can do something about it (practice). The coach did not encourage Sally to reject responsibility for her outcomes (bad luck), but suggested that the outcome can change (unstable attribution) and that Sally is in control. The coach must be very patient and positive when engaging in attribution training. One should not expect an athlete to immediately alter a long-standing maladaptive attribution pattern. It takes patience and time. To help students and athletes choose suitable attributions, the following steps are recommended:

1. Record and classify attributions that students and athletes make to successful and unsuccessful outcomes.

2. For each outcome, discuss with the athlete causes or attributions that might lead to a greater expectancy for success and increased effort.

3. Provide an attributional training program for athletes who consistently give attributions that lead to negative implications for future outcomes.

CONCEPT Attributional training is effective in helping young athletes overcome feelings of learned helplessness. Attributional training involves teaching individuals to adopt more appropriate and positive explanations for their successes and failures.

APPLICATION The first step in attributional training is to pay attention to the reasons young athletes give for outcomes. Attributions provide valuable information about the way young people see themselves. If properly used, attributional information can be used to understand an athlete and to help her appropriately restructure the way she views reasons for success and failure.

Egocentrism in Attribution

People are assumed to follow logic when they make attributions to behavioral outcomes. For example, in regard to the covariation principle, it was observed that people tend to make attributions consistent with a certain logic. That is, if a person "aces" a test, but then realizes that everyone else has aced it too, that person will ascribe the cause externally (e.g., an easy test). This is considered to be a **logical model** for making attributions to outcomes.

However, evidence suggests that people are not always entirely logical in making causal attributions for their behavior. Instead of making logical attributions, they often make self-serving ones. In this regard, a person might attribute successes to internal causes and failures to external causes. Attributing all successes to internal causes is called **ego-enhancing strategy,** while attributing all failures to external causes is called **ego-protecting strategy.** Both strategies are self-serving and are considered **illogical models** of attribution. Mann (1974) observed this strategy among football fans. Mann found that fans of winning football teams tended to attribute game outcomes to internal causes, such as ability, while fans of losing teams tended to attribute game outcomes to external causes, such as luck and biased officiating.

Perhaps the first serious review of the available literature on the **self-serving hypothesis** was conducted by Miller and Ross (1975). In their review, they pointed out that for the illogical model to be true, it must be shown that people indulge in both ego-protective attributions under conditions of failure and ego-enhancing attributions under conditions of success. Their basic conclusion was that the self-serving bias proposition was largely unsupported, since the literature provided strong evidence that people use ego-enhancing strategies under conditions of success, but only minimal evidence that they use ego-protective strategies under conditions of failure.

A review of the sport psychology literature since Miller and Ross's (1975) seminal work reveals a continued interest in the self-serving hypothesis, but does little to clarify the issue. Of the articles reviewed, only one demonstrated unambiguous support for the illogical hypothesis for both the ego-enhancing and the ego-protecting notions (Zientek & Breakwell, 1991). As with the Miller and Ross conclusions, studies generally showed that people experiencing success typically attributed their success to internal factors such as effort and ability. But when it came to the ego-protecting bias, the results tended to be qualified in terms of some situational factor.

In a study by Gill (1980), the question of self-serving bias was investigated in regard to team outcomes rather than individual outcomes. Participants were members of women's basketball teams. After winning or losing, players were asked to assign primary responsibility for success or failure either to their own team or to their opponents. Results showed that players attributed success to

CONCEPT Athletes are not always completely logical in their attributions. They will often engage in illogical or ego-enhancing strategies to explain events.

APPLICATION Athletes who make self-serving attributions for every event are in danger of losing contact with reality. After all, losing is not always something or someone else's fault. However, to a certain extent, self-enhancing and self-protecting strategies are good for the athlete's self-esteem.

their own team and failure to the other team. Thus, in terms of group attributions, the self-serving hypothesis seemed to be supported. In another part of the study, players were asked to assign primary responsibility for success or failure to themselves (an internal attribution) or to their teammates (an external attribution). The results failed to support the self-serving hypothesis. Members of winning teams assigned primary responsibility to their teammates and members of losing teams assigned primary responsibility to themselves. Thus in this case, a reverse egocentric pattern emerged.

A recent investigation by DeMichele, Gansneder, and Solomon (1998) was interesting in that the attributions of stability and controllability were also included. Using the CDSII (fig. 4.4), causal attributions of wrestlers were requested and measured following each athlete's first match of the year. The authors hypothesized that consistent with the self-serving hypothesis, winners should exhibit higher attribution scores on locus of control (more internal), stability (more stable), and personal control (more controllable), but a lower attributional score on external control (less controllable). The results of the investigation supported the authors' hypotheses relative to the self-serving hypothesis in all cases but one. As hypothesized, winners exhibited higher internal locus of control, higher stability, and higher personal controllability. However, in terms of external controllability, winners exhibited more controllability, not less, as hypothesized. Apparently,

winners were acknowledging the weaknesses of their opponents and giving them credit (external control) for their victories.

In summary, the attributional process is probably neither purely logical nor purely illogical (self-serving). Rather, the disposition to use a self-serving strategy is within each individual to some degree. Some people will rarely use it, preferring to accept responsibility for their own actions in most cases. However, others may find it comforting to reject personal responsibility for outcomes in order to protect delicate egos.

It is good to remember at this point in our discussion that Dweck (1980) suggested that "learned helpless" children can be helped by being taught to attribute their failures to unstable internal factors such as low effort. It is also important to keep in mind that an ego-enhancing/ego-protecting approach to attribution may be useful from the standpoint of improving self-efficacy. Athletes should learn to accept responsibility for their own performances, but not at the expense of their self-confidence. It is better to hear young athletes state that they struck out in baseball because of a bad call or because of a great curve ball than that they struck out because of a lack of ability (even if they do lack ability). It is good for athletes to ascribe failure to ability *if* they perceive ability to be something they can improve on. In this case, ability would be an unstable attribution, since it could be changed. Unfortunately, young athletes often fail to see skill as dynamic and changing.

Summary

Attribution theory is based on the kinds of perceptions people have of why they succeed or fail. Attributions are causal explanations for outcomes. Fritz Heider is the acknowledged founder of attribution theory, but Bernard Weiner is credited with making significant contributions to it in terms of interpretation and application. People are believed to make attributions along three dimensions: locus of causality, stability, and controllability. Dan Russell and Ed McAuley are credited with making significant contributions relative to the accurate assessment and measurement of attributions.

Attribution theory is very useful in understanding behavior exhibited in competitive situations. Locus of causality is a basic dimension used by athletes in explaining causality. A person who believes she is responsible for her own destiny exhibits an internal locus of causality, while one who feels at the mercy of outside forces exhibits an external locus of causality. A person's attributions for success or failure can be predicted on the basis of the performance of others on the same task. This is known as the covariation principle.

The kinds of attributions that people give for outcomes are linked to specific emotional responses. Locus of causality attributions give rise to the emotions of pride and self-esteem; controllability gives rise to the emotions of shame, guilt, and confidence; stability is associated with hopefulness and hopelessness.

The stability dimension predicts expectancy. An athlete's expectation for future success or failure is largely based on the stability dimension of attribution. A stable attribution gives rise to the expectancy that outcome in the future will not change. An unstable attribution gives rise to the expectancy that conditions as well as outcome can change. The stability dimension in attribution theory is important in helping children overcome feelings of hopelessness and learned helplessness.

Attributional training is effective in teaching athletes how to develop functional attribution strategies. Controllable and unstable attributions are important in helping young athletes feel optimistic about future achievement situations.

Egocentrism in attribution suggests that athletes give self-serving internal attributions for success and self-serving external attributions for failure. While it is true that some athletes do adopt an egocentric approach to attribution, most take a more logical approach to attribution.

Critical Thought Questions

1. Students often have a difficult time distinguishing between the causal dimensions of locus of causality and controllability. Think of some attributional examples that could help clarify this distinction for another student.

2. Distinguish between the way researchers measure attributions today as compared to 20 years ago. What are the critical differences? Why are these differences important?

3. As a disposition or way of looking at things, research supports the position that an internal locus of causality is preferred to a external locus of causality. Can a person learn to be more internal in terms of locus of causality? Explain and justify your answer.

4. Why would a person who experiences success attribute the cause of that success to an unstable dimension? What sort of affect would you expect to be associated with this attributional situation?

5. Do you know a child who suffers from learned helplessness? Do you think

attributional training would be effective in helping this child become more hopeful? If so, how would you approach this specific problem?

6. Do you know anyone who is truly egocentric in all attributions? Why do you think the person is this way? Do you think attributional training would be of benefit? Why or why not?

Glossary

accurate optimist According to Seligman, a person who knows her strengths and weaknesses and takes an active stance in shaping her life for the good.

attribution theory A cognitive approach to motivation in which perceived causation plays an important role in explaining behavior.

attributional training A process by which attributions given for failure are manipulated in order to overcome feelings of learned helplessness.

Causal Dimension Scale A scale developed by Russell for assigning attributions to one of three dimensions: locus of control, stability, and controllability.

competitive situation A situation in which participants expect their performance to be evaluated in some way.

controllability An attributional dimension in which causes for events are perceived to be either within or beyond a person's control.

covariation principle The principle that when the performance of others agrees (covaries) with the performance of the athlete, attributions about that performance will be external.

dysfunctional attribution strategy An attribution strategy in which athletes are taught to explain the cause of a failure outcome as uncontrollable and stable.

ego-enhancing strategy A strategy by which one attributes all success to internal causes.

ego-protecting strategy A strategy by which one attributes all failures to external causes.

functional attribution strategy An attribution strategy in which athletes are taught to explain the

cause of a failure outcome as controllable and unstable.

hopefulness Hope for the future, or the belief that you will succeed in the future.

hopelessness Lack of hope for the future, or the belief that you will not succeed in the future.

illogical model An ego-enhancing or ego-protecting strategy for selecting attributions.

learned helplessness A condition in which people feel that they have no control over their failures, and that failure is inevitable.

locus of causality A psychological construct referring to whether an outcome is perceived to be internally or externally caused (see locus of control).

locus of control A psychological construct that refers to people's beliefs about whether they are personally responsible for what happens to them.

logical attribution An attribution one would expect an individual to give if not biased by a desire to enhance or protect the ego.

logical model The notion that people make logical attributions about outcomes.

maladaptive attributional pattern The pattern in which an athlete gives attributions for both success and failure that lead to feelings of low self-esteem and future failure.

self-serving hypothesis The observation that people will sometimes make illogical attributions to enhance or protect their egos.

stability An attributional dimension that suggests that an outcome will either change or remain stable.

CHAPTER 5

Self-Confidence and Intrinsic Motivation

KEY TERMS

Achievement situation
Additive principle
Amotivation
Autonomy
Cognitive evaluation theory
Collective self-efficacy
Competence motivation
Controlling aspect of extrinsic
  motivation
Discounting principle
Efficacious pawn
External regulation
Extrinsic motivation
General-sport dropout
Global self-confidence
"Hot hand" myth
Identified regulation
Informational aspect of
  extrinsic motivation
Integrated regulation
Internalization
Intrinsic motivation
Introjected regulation
Motives for participation
Multiplicative principle
Overjustification principle
Parents' code of conduct
Participatory modeling
Precipitating event
Professional sports model
Psychological momentum
Reflected appraisal process

Relatedness
Reversed-dependency trap
Self-determination
Self-determination continuum
Self-efficacy
Situation-specific self-confidence
Social comparison

Specific-sport dropout
Sport-confidence
Surface reasons for withdrawal from sport
Underlying psychological reasons for
  withdrawal from sport
Youth sports
Youth sports model

Self-confidence and motivation are not synonymous concepts, but they are very closely related. Athletes who are highly motivated tend to be very self-confident about their abilities. Yet, a distinction must be made between **global self-confidence** and **situation-specific self-confidence.** Global self-confidence is more of a personality trait or disposition. One can exhibit a great deal of global self-confidence and not be successful at a specific sport or physical activity. Global self-confidence is an important personality characteristic that facilitates daily living. It can be instrumental in encouraging a young person to try new things, but it is not the same as believing that you can succeed at a specific task. The basketball player who enjoys situation-specific self-confidence truly believes that she can make her free throws when the game is on the line. In the closing moments of a close competition between two teams, the coach wants the ball in the hands of the individual who believes completely in his ability to succeed. This is situation-specific self-confidence.

In this chapter we will (a) provide an in-depth discussion of self-confidence and the role it plays in the development of intrinsic motivation, (b) discuss sport psychology topics related to sport psychology, (c) introduce the integrated theory of motivation in sport, and (d) conclude with a discussion of the relationship between motivation and youth sport. It is often thought that self-confidence is something that the skilled athlete exhibits, but in reality self-confidence is a fundamental building block in the development of motivation. Athletes are motivated to practice and to perform because they possess confidence that they can eventually succeed and excel at their sport. It is critical that athletes develop both situation-specific self-confidence and global self-confidence. A historical example of an athlete who possessed overwhelming skill as well as extreme self-confidence is Jack Morris. Morris was the winning pitcher in game 7 of the 1991 World Series between the Minnesota Twins and the Atlanta Braves. "In perhaps the best World Series game ever played, the Twins' Jack Morris gave us one final glimpse of a dying breed: a pitcher who was

determined to finish whatever he started" (Verducci, 2003, p. 71). Following the game which the Twins won 1–0 in the tenth inning, Jack Morris made the following statement in a post-game interview: "I never had as much will to win a game as I did on that day. I was in trouble many times during the game but didn't realize it because I never once had a negative thought" (Jack Morris, Minnesota Twins pitcher, in Verducci, 2003, p. 71).

Models of Self-Confidence

In this section a number of cognitive models will be introduced that use terms essentially equivalent to the concept of situation-specific self-confidence. These include Bandura's *self-efficacy,* Harter's *competence motivation,* and Vealey's *sport-confidence.* Each reflects the notion of situation-specific self-confidence, as opposed to a global personality trait. In addition, the confidence-related topics of psychological momentum and women in sport will be discussed.

Bandura's Theory of Self-Efficacy

Bandura (1997) defines **self-efficacy** as "beliefs in one's capabilities to organize and execute the courses of action required to produce given attainments" (p. 3). As such, self-efficacy is a form of situation-specific self-confidence. Self-efficacy is the critical component of what Bandura refers to as social cognitive theory. Other important components of social cognitive theory are agency and personal control. In order for self-efficacy to develop, the individual must believe that she is in control and that acts she performed were performed intentionally. The power and will to originate a course of action are the key feature of personal agency. If a person believes she is in control and that she has the power to produce specific results, she will be motivated to try to make things happen. Thus the importance of self-efficacy. If an athlete perceives or believes that she can influence for good the outcome of a contest, she will eagerly enter into the competition. Thus, an efficacious athlete is a

Many concerned individuals contribute to the development of motivation and self-confidence. Courtesy Kansas State University Sports Information.

motivated athlete. The athlete is motivated to work hard to ensure success because she believes that she can succeed.

Bandura (1977, 1982, 1986, 1997) proposes four fundamental elements effective in developing self-efficacy (see fig. 5.1). Each of these elements is critical in understanding how an athlete can develop self-efficacy and self-confidence:

1. *Successful Performance*   The athlete must experience success in order for self-efficacy to develop. With a difficult task, this is an unrealistic expectation, so the coach or teacher must ensure success by initially reducing the difficulty of the task. An example of how this can be accomplished is found in tennis and volleyball instruction. A beginner may not be able to successfully serve a volleyball across the net on a regulation court, but when the coach encourages the athlete to step into the court several meters, it can be accomplished. The teacher must find a way for beginners to find success, or they will come to believe that they cannot succeed, and quit trying. The difficulty

of the task can be increased as the simpler tasks are mastered.

2. *Vicarious Experience*   Beginning athletes can experience success through the use of models. In learning a new skill, the learner needs a template or model to copy. This can be provided by the instructor, a skilled teammate, or a film or video of a skilled performer. In this respect, an important component of Bandura's theory is the concept of participatory modeling. In **participatory modeling,** the learner first observes a model perform a task. Then the model or instructor assists the subject in successfully performing the task. The vicarious experience of success will provide a good foundation for the experience of success in a real situation. For example, in teaching a young athlete how to hit a ball with a bat, the teacher will actually help the child hold the bat as it moves towards the ball. In this way, the child learns how it feels to hit the ball. Without this sort of assistance, the child might not experience success.

FIGURE 5.1 | Relationship between factors leading to self-efficacy beliefs and athletic performance.

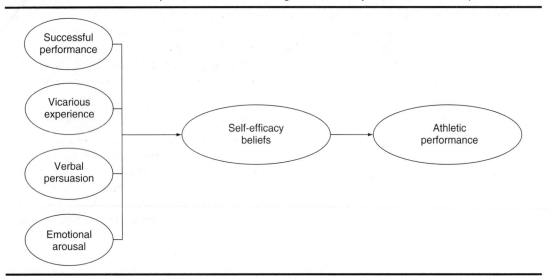

3. *Verbal Persuasion*   Verbal persuasion usually comes in the form of encouragement from the coach, parents, or peers. Helpful verbal statements that suggest that the athlete is competent and can succeed are most desirable. Negative comments should always be avoided. Coaching tips can be given in such a way that they do not convey negativism. For example, the coach could say, "Good swing, Mary; now remember to keep your eyes on the ball." Verbal persuasion can also take the form of self-persuasion. This is referred to as self-talk, and will be discussed in greater detail in chapter 9.

4. *Emotional Arousal*   Emotional and physiological arousal are factors that can influence readiness for learning. Details as to exactly how this can happen will be discussed in a subsequent chapter. For now, it is important to understand that we must be emotionally ready and optimally aroused in order to be attentive. Proper attention is important in helping the athlete to master a particular skill and develop a feeling of efficacy.

The efficacy of Bandura's model in the sport setting is well documented. Perceived self-efficacy is a strong and consistent predictor of individual athletic performance (Escarti & Guzman, 1999; Krane, Marks, Zaccaro, & Blair, 1996; Moritz, Feltz, Fahrbach, & Mack, 2000; Schunk, 1995; Treasure, Monson, & Lox, 1996). As a general rule, compared with persons who doubt their capabilities, those exhibiting high self-efficacy work harder, persist in the task longer, and achieve at a higher level. Furthermore, logic and some evidence suggest that situation-specific self-confidence can generalize to other situations and to global self-confidence (Zinsser, Bunker & Williams, 1998). Every child should become competent in at least one sport or activity. This will provide the foundation for the development of self-efficacy in other areas, as well as increasing global self-confidence.

Sport-related research continues to inform our understanding of the relationship between self-efficacy and athletic performance. Research shows that self-efficacy beliefs are influenced by perceived outcome. Experimentally manipulated success results in increased self-efficacy beliefs, but

CONCEPT Development of perceived self-efficacy and self-confidence is closely associated with the level of success experienced by the athlete.

APPLICATION Find ways to help the athlete experience success. You can accomplish this by reducing the initial difficulty of the task, or through participatory modeling, in which the instructor or model assists the athlete in learning the skill.

manipulated failure results in decreased self-efficacy. This may seem obvious, but of interest is research reported by Gernigon and Delloye (2003) showing that the causal attribution of stability moderates or determines the nature of that relationship in male but not female national-level sprinters. As the attribution for success becomes more stable (less changing), the resultant self-efficacy for the next attempt becomes stronger. Conversely, when the attribution for perceived failure becomes more stable, the resultant self-efficacy goes down. For female sprinters, causal attribution does not serve as a moderator between perceived outcome and self-efficacy, but the attribution of personal control has a direct effect on self-efficacy.

Research utilizing long-distance wheelchair athletes revealed that self-efficacy beliefs about meeting performance goals, overcoming performance obstacles, and training under difficult conditions were all related to outcome confidence and positive affect (Martin, 2002). Given that self-efficacy is important for athletic success, what are some of the strategies that coaches say they find most effective for enhancing self-efficacy? Male and female Division I and II collegiate coaches from the sports of baseball, basketball, softball, and soccer believe that the most effective strategies for enhancing self-efficacy are (a) instruction drilling, (b) acting confident themselves, and (c) encouraging positive self-talk (Vargas-Tonsing, Myers, & Feltz, 2004). Self-talk, as a way to develop self-efficacy and situation-specific self-confidence, will be discussed at length in a later chapter on coping and intervention strategies in sport.

The benefits of perceived self-efficacy are not limited to the individual. Groups that collectively exhibit high self-efficacy also tend to perform at a higher level than groups exhibiting low collective self-efficacy (George & Feltz, 1995). This confidence in the team is referred to as **collective self-efficacy.** Just as it is important to develop self-efficacy in individual athletes, it is also important to develop a sense of collective self-efficacy in a team. In later chapters we will introduce and develop the related concepts of team building and team cohesion.

Harter's Competence Motivation Theory

Patterned after White's (1959) theory of effectance motivation, Harter (1978) proposed a theory of achievement motivation that is based on an athlete's feeling of personal competence. According to Harter, individuals are innately motivated to be competent in all areas of human achievement. To satisfy the urge to be competent in an achievement area such as sport, the person attempts mastery. An individual's self-perception of success at these mastery attempts develops feelings of positive or negative affect. As illustrated in figure 5.2, successful attempts at mastery promote self-efficacy and feelings of personal competence, which in turn foster high competence motivation. As **competence motivation** increases, the athlete is encouraged to make further mastery attempts.

Conversely, if a young athlete's attempts at mastery result in perceived rejection and failure, then low competence motivation and negative affect will be the end product. It is hypothesized that

FIGURE 5.2 | Harter's competence motivation theory.

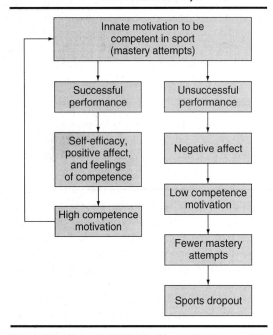

Source: From Harter, S. (1978). Effectance motivation reconsidered. *Human Development, 21,* 34–64. Adapted by permission of S. Karger AG, Basel.

low competence motivation will result in a youth sport dropout.

The importance of developing competence motivation in sport has been verified by Weiss and Horn (1990). This investigation underscored the importance of accurately assessing personal competence. Boys and girls who underestimate their own competence tend to be candidates for dropping out of sports. Girls who underestimate their own competence tend to drop out of sport involvement, suffer from high trait anxiety, prefer unchallenging activities, and be controlled by external forces. The effect of underestimation on boys seems to be less damaging. Generally, children who accurately assess their own ability feel more in control and seek involvement in challenging activities.

An investigation by Black and Weiss (1992) reaffirmed the importance of significant others in developing competence motivation in young athletes. Young athletes who perceive their coaches as individuals who give positive feedback and encouragement are the same athletes who perceive themselves as highly motivated. The importance of a supportive coach or teacher cannot be overestimated. Coaches, teachers, and leaders must recognize that helping young people develop confidence in themselves is time well spent.

In Harter's model, high competence motivation leads to successful task performance, much as high self-efficacy leads to successful performance. Three relatively recent investigations suggest ways in which an individual's competence motivation can be enhanced. Weigand and Broadhurst (1998) demonstrated that competence motivation is influenced by intrinsic motivation, years of soccer playing experience, and perceived control. Allen and Howe (1998) demonstrated that after controlling for ability of the female adolescent field hockey player, perceived coaching behaviors were predictive of competence motivation. Specifically, they reported that in response to a good performance, praise and technical information had the effect of increasing competence motivation. Conversely, in response to a poor performance, praise and technical information had the effect of decreasing competence motivation. This result would suggest that supportive silence might be the best strategy for enhancing perceived competence following a poor performance. Smith (1999) conducted an investigation, grounded in Harter's theoretical perspectives, that suggests that friendship and peer group acceptance are important variables in enhancing competence motivation among youth sport participants. The acceptance and support of friends are very important to teenagers. Enhancing peer group acceptance of a young person's sport participation is a good way to positively influence attitude and self-confidence.

Athletes with more positive perceptions of competence demonstrate greater motivation to train and participate in their sport. Amorose (2003) provides evidence to support the position that significant others play an important role in informing the athlete about his competence. The process by which an individual comes to see himself as competent has been referred to as the reflected appraisal process. The **reflected appraisal process** is a function of the actual appraisal of others, one's own appraisal of self, and one's perception of how others appraise him. Using 325 Division I college athletes as participants, Amorose demonstrated that the reflected appraisal of parents and sport-related significant others predicts an athlete's self-perception of competence.

Vealey's Multidimensional Model of Sport-Confidence

The multidimensional model of **sport-confidence** is a revision of Vealey's (1986, 1988b) model of sport-confidence. The original model conceptualized trait sport-confidence, state sport-confidence, and competitive orientation as predictors of satisfaction and performance success. Limitations of the original model included inability of state sport-confidence (as measured by the State Sport-Confidence Inventory) to predict performance, and failure of the model to conceptualize measures of sport-confidence as being multidimensional in nature. To address these shortcomings in the original model, Vealey, Knight, and Pappas (2002) developed the Multidimensional Model of Sport-Confidence. The *Multidimensional Model of Sport-Confidence (MMSC)* is a model in which multidimensional sport-confidence is conceptualized as being more dispositional (trait) or state-like across a continuum of time.

As illustrated in figure 5.3, the rectangle in the middle shows three source domains of sport-confidence (Vealey, Hayashi, Garner-Holman, & Giacobbi, 1998), as well as three types of sport-confidence. Together, the sport-confidence source domains and sport-confidence types are referred to as the *sport-confidence rectangle*. Constructs within the sport-confidence rectangle influence and are influenced by *characteristics of the athlete* (personality traits, attitudes, values), *demographic characteristics* (age, sex, ethnicity, culture), and *organizational culture* (competitive level, motivational climate, program goals). The three source domains of sport-confidence are identified in the figure as *achievement* (mastery and demonstration of ability), *self-regulation* (physical/mental preparation, physical self-presentation), and *social climate* (social support, coaches' leadership, vicarious experience, environmental comfort, situational favorableness). In the model, the sources of sport-confidence both influence and are influenced by the three types of sport-confidence. The three types of sport-confidence (SC) are *SC–cognitive efficiency* (decision making, thought management, maintaining focus), *SC–physical skills/training* (skill execution and training), and *SC-resilience* (overcoming obstacles, overcoming setbacks, overcoming doubts, refocusing after errors).

As also illustrated in figure 5.3, the self-confidence rectangle and, specifically, multidimensional sport-confidence determine how athlete and demographic characteristics and organizational culture influence the affect, behavior, and cognitions of the athlete (triangle). Affect, behavior, and cognition in turn influence athlete performance, which is also influenced by uncontrollable external

FIGURE 5.3 | Vealey's multidimensional model of sport-confidence.

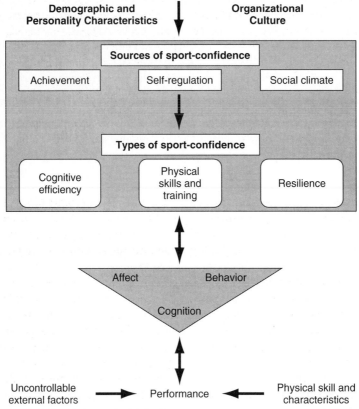

Source: Reproduced with permission from Vealey, R. S., Knight, B.J., & Pappas, G. (2002, November). Self-confidence in sport: Conceptual and psychological advancement. Paper presented at the annual convention of the Association for the Advancement of Applied Sport Psychology, Tucson, AZ.

factors and the physical skill and characteristics of the athlete. While focusing upon sport-confidence, the model depicted in figure 5.3 has ramifications associated with psychological constructs that have not yet been fully explored.

In order to measure multidimensional sport-confidence and to test various aspects of the sport-confidence model, it was necessary to develop a sport-confidence inventory. The development of the Sport-Confidence Inventory (SCI) is chronicled in Vealey et al. (2002). The resultant SCI is composed of 14 items anchored to a 7-point Likert scale that ranges from "Totally Certain" to "Can't Do It At All." The stem for all 14 item is "How certain are you that. . .", and a sample item might be ". . . can you successfully perform the physical skills required in your sport?" While the inventory appears to be both reliable and valid, further testing is recommended. Initial research suggests that the subscales in the SCI are predictive of athletic performance across time. The utility and elegance of the model are that it shows how different types of sport-confidence are developed and how sport-confidence influences athletic performance.

In support of the model, a number of recent investigations have shown a consistent relationship between an athlete's self-confidence and athletic performance (Beattie, Hardy, & Woodman, 2004; Craft, Magyar, Becker, & Feltz, 2003; Woodman & Hardy, 2003). Using slalom canoeists as participants, Beattie et al. (2004) showed that it is not just self-confidence that is related to performance, but also the discrepancy between an athlete's perception of ideal self-confidence and actual measured self-confidence. A small discrepancy is correlated with athletic performance. In other words, best performance occurs when ideal self-confidence is the same as actual self-confidence.

Sport Psychology Topics related to Confidence

So far in this chapter, we have discussed three main models that explain how athletes develop self-confidence and self-efficacy. In this subsection we turn our attention to two topics that are closely related to confidence in sport. The first deals with the important concept of psychological momentum, and the second with the development of confidence as it relates to sex and gender.

Psychological Momentum in Sport

Among other things, athletes report a feeling of increased confidence during periods of perceived psychological momentum. For this reason, we are going to consider psychological momentum as a subsection in the section on self-confidence. It is hard to escape experiencing the phenomenon of momentum as either a performing athlete or a spectator. Television announcers frequently use the term to describe an apparent shift in good fortune for an athlete or an athletic team. Athletic teams often seem to behave like giant boulders rolling down a mountain, gaining speed and momentum as they move downward. As the boulder picks up speed and is assisted by gravity, it seems unstoppable. Often, however, the boulder crashes into other large boulders or trees that slow its momentum and, in many cases, stop its downward plunge altogether.

Psychological momentum is a phenomenon that has been documented in the literature relative to tennis (Burke, Edwards, Weigand, & Weinber, 1997; Silva, Hardy & Grace, 1998), basketball shooting (Burke, Burke, & Joyner, 1999; Shaw, Dzewaltowski, & McElroy, 1992), volleyball (Burke & Houseworth, 1995), ice hockey (Gayton, Very, & Hearns, 1993), pocket billiards (Adams, 1995), and riflery (Kerick, Iso-Ahola, & Hatfield, 2000).

As defined by Taylor and Demick (1994), **psychological momentum** is "a positive or negative change in cognition, affect, physiology, and behavior caused by an event or series of events that will result in a commensurate shift in performance and competitive outcome" (p. 54). The key element in this definition is the *precipitating event* that leads to the "momentum chain." An important mediating variable is the experience of the athletes involved (both teams, or both opponents). Experienced athletes are better able to recognize and act upon precipitating events, more likely to possess the skills necessary to take advantage of precipitating events, and better able to mobilize defenses against negative momentum. *Negative momentum* may be characterized as conditions necessary to precipitate positive momentum on the part of the opposition. Examples of precipitating events in tennis might include a dramatic shot, breaking an opponent's serve, winning game after long deuce, a critical unforced error, and not converting 15–40, 0–40 break serve opportunities. Examples of precipitating events in basketball might include a slam-dunk, a critical 3-point play or shot, a steal and conversion, and making the first free throw in a one-and-one situation.

Models of Psychological Momentum
Researchers have proposed three different models to explain the psychological momentum phenomenon. The three models are the *antecedents-consequences model* (Vallerand, Colavecchio, & Pelletier, 1988), the *multidimensional model* (Taylor & Demick, 1994), and the *projected performance model* (Cornelius, Silva, Conroy, & Peterson, 1997).

Antecedents-Consequences Model In this model, a situational antecedent event such as a dunk in basketball or an ace serve in tennis precipitates the perception of psychological momentum. Psychological momentum results in feelings of goal progression, self-confidence, motivation, and energy. Whether or not psychological momentum will translate into actual performance enhancement depends upon the actions of the opposing players as well as personal and situational context variables. Response of the crowd, importance of the game, and skill level of the performers are all variables that will either facilitate or dampen the performance enhancement consequences of psychological momentum.

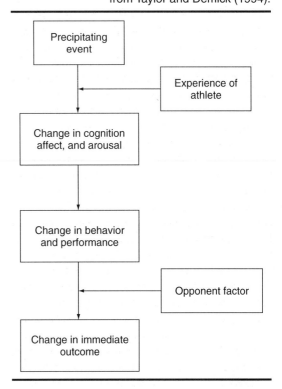

FIGURE 5.4 | Illustration showing the multidimensional model of psychological momentum as adapted from Taylor and Demick (1994).

Multidimensional Model In the multidimensional model, psychological momentum is defined as being either positive or negative. The key element in the model is the **precipitating event,** which leads to a momentum chain. As illustrated in figure 5.4, the momentum chain includes a simultaneous change in cognition, affect, and physiological arousal, followed by a change in behavior, a change in performance, and finally, a change in immediate outcome (success/failure). Two variables are hypothesized to moderate the effects of the momentum chain. The moderator variables are experience of the performers on the momentum team and opponent factors. For the sake of an illustration, let's say a positive precipitating event occurs during a basketball game (e.g., runaway slam dunk that also results in a made free throw). Depending on the experience of the momentum team, team members should collectively experience an increase in self-confidence, positive affect, increased attention, and increased physiological arousal. This jump in confidence, positive mood, and arousal should result in a noticeable change in behavior and performance. Depending on how the opponents respond, increased performance should result in a positive change in immediate outcome (e.g., more points being scored by the team enjoying the surge in momentum). Research reported by Mack and Stephens (2000) provides partial support for the model, in that a precipitating event leads to a change in cognition.

Projected Performance Model   Failing to show a clear cause-and-effect relationship between psychological momentum and improved performance, Cornelius, Silva, Conroy, and Peterson (1997) proposed a model that hypothesizes that the popular notion of psychological momentum has little effect on performance. According to the projected performance model, positive and negative psychological momentum are only labels used to describe performance, and are the result of extremely good or bad performance. Large positive fluctuations in performance above the mean performance zone are labeled positive psychological momentum, while large negative fluctuations below the mean are labeled negative psychological momentum. In the course of an athletic contest, teams and players cycle through phases of good and bad performance. These cycles are often labeled positive and negative momentum, but there is no cause-and-effect relationship between the labels and actual performance.

Psychological Momentum: Fact or Fiction?

Sufficient research exists to conclude that the concept of psychological momentum is real and that it is associated with changes in athletic performance. In an important study, Perreault, Vallerand, Montgomery, and Provencher (1998) contrasted the predictions of the above three models using bogus 12-minute bicycle races. Arguing that the

link between psychological momentum and increased performance had not yet been clearly established, the researchers designed a study to address this issue. The purpose of the study was to examine the psychological momentum–performance relationship in a laboratory setting to determine if the precipitating event of coming from behind to tie an opponent in a bicycle race elicited changes in perceived momentum, and if changes in momentum resulted in measured changes in cycling performance. The results showed that the presentation of the precipitating event did result in an increase in psychological momentum, which in turn was associated with an increase in performance. The authors concluded that their research supported the antecedent consequences model and the multidimensional model of psychological momentum, but not the projected performance model.

Of related interest is the finding by Eisler and Spink (1998) that team cohesion and psychological momentum are related. Teams that enjoy high levels of task-related team cohesion are more likely to experience psychological momentum during competition than are less cohesive teams. This finding suggests a minor modification in the multidimensional model of psychological momentum as illustrated in figure 5.4. The important concept of team cohesion will be discussed in a later chapter of the book.

While research seems to support the concept of psychological momentum in sport, the same does not seem to be true for the concept of the "hot hand" in basketball and other related sports. The notion of a **hot hand** describes the belief that performance of an athlete temporarily improves following a string of success. Koehler and Conley (2003) studied the phenomenon of the hot hand in conjunction with the annual National Basketball Association (NBA) long-distance shootout contest held during the all-star game. Result of the investigation failed to provide evidence for the myth of the "hot hand." The authors of the research suggested that the declaration of "hotness" in basketball be best viewed as historical commentary, as opposed to prediction about future performance.

CONCEPT Elicited by a precipitating event, psychological momentum leads to a change in behavior which may result in an immediate positive outcome.

APPLICATION Teams and individuals must be taught how to prepare for the onset of psychological momentum from the perspective of the momentum team as well as the opposing team. A precipitating event may set up the conditions necessary for psychological momentum to occur, but it will not occur unless the athletes are sufficiently skilled and mentally prepared to take advantage of it. Conversely, if you are on the receiving end of the opponent's surge in confidence and momentum, your team must be taught how to break the momentum of the other team. Slowing the game down, calling a time out, and playing with greater discipline are all strategies used to break the other team's psychological momentum and confidence.

Gender and Self-Confidence

> I have decided that it is not my own gender or anyone's gender, that makes the important difference. Instead, it is gender in society that opens opportunities, imposes limits, and makes a difference in the real world of sport and exercise (Diane Gill, 1999, pg. 134).

Nineteen seventy-two was a landmark year for girls and women in sport in the United States of America. This was the year that the government passed Title IX, the federal act that mandated nondiscrimination in federally funded education programs. This single historic event did more to expand opportunities for sport involvement for women than any other combination of events or social changes in America before or since. Many aspects of sport and exercise in the United States are measured in terms of being before or after the passage of Title IX.

As we contemplate the effects of Title IX on women sports, it is interesting to think of the impact that individual athletes have upon sport. For example, in the United States one cannot think about great male athletes without thinking about Michael Jordan in basketball and Babe Ruth in baseball. Similarly, as one contemplates great female athletes, the name of Mia Hamm comes to mind. It has been said of Hamm that she "represented the possibilities—college scholarships, achievement, recognition, respect, commercial endorsements—available to women after the passage of the gender-equity legislation known as Title IX" (Longman, 2004b, C11). The world's largest sporting event for women (the 1999 World Soccer Cup) was built on Mia Hamm's reputation, as was the U.S. Women's United Soccer Association and the professional league that followed. Mia Hamm is the best-known soccer player in the United States, regardless of sex.

Much of what we know and understand about women and self-confidence in achievement situations comes from the classic writings of Ellen Lenney (1977). Lenney's writings and conclusions are based upon research conducted prior to 1977, and many of them emerged prior to the passage of Title IX. Consequently, many have wondered if anything has changed relative to Lenney's observations since that time. Somewhat of a revisionist, Lenney concluded that while men and boys generally score higher than women and girls on measures of self-confidence, this observation is not true in all achievement situations. An **achievement situation** was defined by Lenney as one in which **social comparisons** are being made. Competitive sports would qualify as an achievement situation by this definition. Lenney argued that women and girls suffer from reduced levels of self-confidence when one or more of three situational variables are present. If these situational variables are not present, then girls and women should enjoy self-confidence equal to that of men and boys. These three situational variables relate to (a) the nature of the task, (b) ambiguity of available information, and (c) social comparison cues.

Nature of the Task   While it is not clear exactly what types of tasks are associated with reduced levels of self-confidence, it does seem clear that women respond to some tasks with a great deal of confidence, but to others with little confidence. For example, a woman might be expected to respond with a low level of confidence to a task that she considered inappropriate to her gender role. The kinds of tasks that a girl or woman considered to be gender-role inappropriate would probably vary from individual to individual. Body building (not training) was once considered to be gender inappropriate for women, although even this perception is changing rapidly. In a relatively recent investigation, Riemer and Visio (2003) gave children in grades K–12 the opportunity to answer questions about gender-appropriate sporting activities. The results show that K–12 students continue to gender-type boxing, football, and wrestling as sports that are appropriate for boys, and aerobics and gymnastics as appropriate for girls.

Ambiguity of Available Information   Self-confidence in girls and women depends on the availability of clear and unambiguous information. Females provided with clear feedback regarding their performance will exhibit as much self-confidence as men. However, if the feedback is unclear and ambiguous, women tend to have lower opinions of their abilities and to respond with lower levels of self-confidence than men. For example, women might be more likely to show a lack of confidence if they were asked to execute a sideward roll in volleyball without being told

what was good or bad, or for what purpose they were doing it.

Social Comparison Cues   When girls and women work alone or in a situation not involving social comparisons, they are likely to respond with self-confidence levels equal to those of men and boys. This would suggest a situation in which cooperation instead of competition is emphasized. When placed in a situation where performance is compared with that of others in a social context, girls and women are expected to respond with lower levels of self-confidence than those of men in a similar situation.

Lenney's hypotheses regarding women and self-confidence were derived primarily from research in which cognitive (non-motor) tasks were studied. Lirgg (1991) conducted a meta-analysis to determine if research involving physical activity would also support Lenney's assertions. Being tested were Lenney's assertions that females would be less confident than males when the task was male-appropriate or when the situation was competitive in nature. The results of the meta-analysis supported Lenney's hypothesis that females will show lower self-confidence than males when performing male-appropriate tasks. As long as the task was not female-inappropriate, however, the analysis did not support Lenney's contention that females will be less confident than males in competitive (social comparison) situations. While research shows that females do not lack self-confidence in all situations, strategies to increase self-confidence in women may be beneficial. Suggested strategies include these:

1. Ensure success through participatory modeling.

2. Avoid gender-inappropriate activities.

3. Avoid ambiguity through effective communication.

4. Use effective modeling of correct performance.

5. Decrease competitive situations during learning.

CONCEPT   Girls and women participating in sport and exercise activities may not always exhibit the same level of self-confidence as boys or men in the same situation. Factors that tend to lower self-confidence in girls and women include nature of the task, feedback ambiguity, and social comparison cues.

APPLICATION   Being aware of factors that can inhibit self-confidence in girls and women should make it possible to implement strategies to control for these factors. Women should be allowed to select the sports and activities in which they participate and compete. As with all learners, pertinent feedback should be provided. During learning, reduce the amount of competition that participants are exposed to. Learning experiences that emphasize cooperation among participants as opposed to competition should be emphasized.

An investigation reported by Lirgg, George, Chase, and Ferguson (1996) provides additional insight into the issue of gender-inappropriate tasks and self-confidence (self-efficacy). Self-efficacy of men and of women was assessed relative to performing a decidedly feminine task (baton twirling) or a decidedly masculine task (kung fu) under conditions of differing beliefs about ability. Results showed that men were unswayed by either the gender-inappropriate nature of the task or their conception about ability. Conversely, women were affected by both the nature of the task and their conception about ability. The combination of a perceived masculine task and a belief that ability is unchangeable (innate) leads to lower self-efficacy in women. Women, however, respond with significantly higher levels of self-efficacy if they believe ability or skill on the masculine task can be learned.

An Integrated Theory of Motivation in Sport and Exercise

At the fundamental core, intrinsic motivation is little more than taking part in an interesting activity simply because of love for the activity or for the game. The story of Jim Morris, "the oldest rookie," warms your heart and makes you believe that all things are possible. Jim was a guy who wanted to play major league baseball, but his dream ended in 1987 when he couldn't get his fastball to move faster than 88 mph. So Jim gave up his dream to be a major league pitcher after a short stint in the minor leagues. But he didn't give up his love for baseball. Several years later he became the boys' baseball coach at a high school in Big Lake, Texas. The team had only had three wins in three years, but that was changing fast as the boys found that hitting other teams' pitching was easy compared to trying to hit Jim Morris's batting practice pitches. They knew that his pitches were major league scary. One day when Jim was giving his team a pep talk to follow their dreams, the boys challenged him to follow his own dreams and try out for a major league team. Morris answered a radio ad for a tryout with the Tampa Bay Devil Rays. With his mitt and three young children in tow, he went to the tryout and shocked the scouts by throwing 12 pitches at 98 mph. In 1999 Jim Morris became the oldest rookie in three decades; in relief, he struck out Royce Clayton of the Texas Rangers with a 96 mph fastball (Stein, 1999). *The Rookie* is now a major motion picture.

The integrated theory of motivation includes the notions of intrinsic and extrinsic motivation, but the focus is upon motivation that is long term and persistent. Until recently, motivation has been a very difficult concept to operationally explain. Most people have an idea as to what it means to be motivated, but very few have more than a cloudy idea as to how motivation can be developed and maintained over a lifetime. We have learned a lot about motivation from our previous discussions on the topics of self-confidence and attribution theory. We need, however, a unifying theory of motivation that puts all previous concepts into perspective relative to an overall theory. That theory is the *integrated theory of motivation in sport,* based upon the centerpiece of self-determination. **Self-determination** is the unifying psychological construct that brings meaning to the overall concept of motivation.

Self-determination theory is based upon the writings of Deci and Ryan (1985, 1991) and Deci, Vallerand, Pelletier, and Ryan (1991). Vallerand (1997) was the author of the hierarchical model of intrinsic and extrinsic motivation that includes Deci and Ryan's concepts of self-determination as well as the notion that there are three hierarchical levels to the theory (global, contextual, specific). Vallerand and Losier (1999) are the authors of the integrated theory of motivation in sport that is the focus of this section. The central core of Vallerand and Losier's integrated theory is Deci and Ryan's concept of self-determination applied to the sport environment (situation-specific level). The theory, in model form, is shown in figure 5.5. Social factors and psychological mediators are seen as determinants of motivation that lead to certain consequences. Psychological mediators are viewed as mediating the relationship between social factors and motivation. In the model, self-determination appears specifically as autonomy or agency and also brings meaning to what we will later call the self-determination continuum relative to motivation.

Social Factors

Social factors facilitate or cause feelings of competence, autonomy, and relatedness. The specific social factors identified in the model include experiences of success and failure, experiences with competition and cooperation, and coaches' behaviors. This is an incomplete list of possible social factors, but they represent the most common examples.

Success and Failure As athletes participate in sport, they will have many opportunities to experience failure or negative feedback, as well as success or positive feedback. As we know from Harter's competence motivation theory, Bandura's theory of self-efficacy, and Vealey's multidimensional model of sport-confidence, successful experiences lead to the belief that one is competent and efficacious relative to skills being learned and performed. Conversely, failure feedback leads to a reduction in the belief that one is competent and efficacious. In addition to directly affecting competency, success and failure experiences have an effect upon the perceptions of autonomy and relatedness. Athletes want to have a choice in their actions and want to feel connected with others.

FIGURE 5.5 | Vallerand and Losier's (1999) integrated theory of intrinsic and extrinsic motivation in sport.

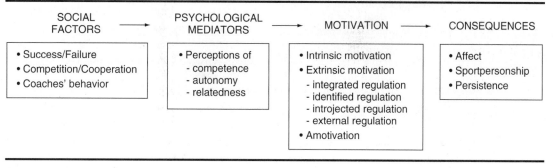

Source: Adapted with permission of publisher.

Competition and Cooperation   Achievement situations tend to focus upon either competition or cooperation. In competitive situations, the goal is often to win or to defeat the other person or team in order to appear superior in a social comparison sense. Because of this focus upon an external reward (social comparison), many researchers believe that an athlete may suffer a loss in intrinsic joy of playing a sport. Conversely, when cooperation is the focus of sport involvement, many researchers believe that the focus is upon demonstrating improvement and making a contribution to the team. This is the reason competition and cooperation are important predictors of psychological mediators that help develop intrinsic motivation.

Coaches' Behavior   Coaches' behavior is another social factor that can influence an athlete's perception of competence, autonomy, and relatedness. A controlling or dictatorial style of coaching can undermine an athlete's intrinsic motivation by taking away her perception of autonomy or of being in control. At the risk of overgeneralizing, there appear to be two broad categories of coaches. One category of coach insists on being in complete control and determining, even down to the last detail, exactly what transpires on the playing field or practice field. The other category of coach is more democratic in nature, and is willing to share the perception of control with his players and assistant coaches. The controlling coach risks destroying the intrinsic motivation of the athlete for the sake of personal control or even perhaps more wins. Again, it is worth quoting Bill Walton in his now-classic contrast between the coaching styles of John Wooden of UCLA basketball fame and Bobby Knight of Indiana basketball fame:

> Wooden fostered hope, Knight represents the death of hope, the stifling control freak. Look at his coaching style: "Get the ball, and look over here at me, and I'll tell you what to do. I'll put you in a position where you can win by one or two points, because it's my strategy in the end."

Wooden gave you the freedom to perform. He was the conductor of a free-form symphony. He always said, "Don't look over here at the sideline. I've already done my job. When the game starts, it's about you guys having fun playing a game and doing your best." (Walton, 2000, p. 96).

History records that Bobby Knight was eventually fired as head men's basketball coach at the University of Indiana, but his stalled coaching career was largely resurrected at Texas Tech University. Despite Knight's successes in the win column, the famous temper that got him into trouble at Indiana is like a time bomb. In December of 2003, Knight went into a profanity-filled tirade after an ESPN reporter asked about his relationship with former Indiana player Steve Alford; then, in February of 2004, he got into a "verbal spat" with the university chancellor at a grocery store in Lubbock (Knight is under review, 2004).

Psychological Mediators

As illustrated in figure 5.5, social factors (success/failure, competition/cooperation, coaches' behavior) determine the beliefs that athletes have about themselves. It is these resultant beliefs or psychological mediators that determine motivation. Self-determination theory focuses on three innate human needs: the needs for competence, autonomy, and relatedness. To the extent that social factors do not allow for the satisfaction of these three basic psychological needs, they will result in diminished motivation, impaired psychological development, alienation, and perhaps poor performance (Deci et al., 1991; Vansteenkiste, Simons, Soemens, & Lens, 2004).

Competence   The concepts of perceived competence and self-efficacy were discussed at length in previous chapters and are central to many current theories of motivation, including Bandura's theory of self-efficacy and Harter's theory of competence motivation.

This is what Rick McGuire, head track and field coach in the University of Missouri–Columbia, says about competence: "Competence builds confidence. Having competence means you've worked hard and mastered a skill. If you don't get up early and run the miles, you have no right to be confident on the starting line" (quoted in Smith, 2005, p.34). Self-determination theory values competence as a prerequisite for motivation, but by itself it is not a sufficient condition for its development. It is clear that competence (self-confidence) is critical to the development of intrinsic motivation, but without autonomy you do not have self-determination, and without self-determination you do not have intrinsic motivation in the truest sense. To paraphrase Deci et al. (1991, p. 339), competence without autonomy gives rise to the **efficacious pawn.** In the efficacious pawn, you have an individual who is confident that he can successfully perform a task, but who is doing it for an external reason. When the external reason is removed, he will no longer be motivated to perform the task, although he may continue to do it without enthusiasm or real motivation.

Autonomy   The concept of autonomy is central to self-determination theory. You cannot exhibit self-determination without **autonomy,** or without what has been referred to as "agency." If you are an agent unto yourself, then you are in control of your destiny and your actions. According to self-determination theory, every individual has the basic innate need to be an "origin" and not a "pawn" (DeCharms & Carpenter, 1968). You will recall that the concept of origin and pawn was introduced in the previous chapter on attribution theory, when we discussed locus of causality. In order for an athlete to develop a mature feeling of internal motivation, she must believe that she has a voice, or input in determining her own behavior. In the sport of volleyball, every player has a specific assignment on defense. This assignment often requires each athlete to be at certain spots on the floor at specific points in time. Coaches will often place physical marks on the practice court to remind the athletes exactly where they are to be. Sometimes these marks will become so important

to the coach that athletes will be pu are not on their marks when they a be. If the athletes come to believe "pawns" in this exercise, they will behave as robots on the floor and play without enthusiasm. This same illustration of tactics can be observed in many other sports and situations.

Relatedness   The third innate psychological need is the need for relatedness. Along with competence and autonomy, relatedness is necessary for a person to be self-actualized, or to realize his full potential as an athlete and as a human being. **Relatedness** has to do with the basic need to relate to other people, to care for others and have others care for you. Humans are social animals and have a basic need to interact in positive ways with other humans. In sport it is interesting to see how athletes support each other on the playing field. To a large extent, an athlete's enjoyment in sport is associated with how she relates to other athletes on her team, as well as to the coaches and support personnel. In the case of youth sports, relationships with parents and peers are also critical to children's satisfaction with the sport experience.

Motivation

Looking at figure 5.5, we understand that social factors and psychological mediators are determinants of motivation. We should understand that competence, autonomy, and relatedness are psychological perceptions that mediate the relationship between social factors and the manifestation of motivation.

We should further understand that the degree to which an athlete feels competent, autonomous, and related depends on the quality of the social experiences that she has had. These social experiences come in the form of perceptions of success and failure, competition and cooperation, and coaching behaviors. This explains why the motivational climate created by the coaches is so critical to the development of motivation in athletes.

Looking again at figure 5.5, we can see that social factors and psychological mediators lead to

FIGURE 5.6 | The self-determination continuum and the different types of motivation.

AMOTIVATION	EXTRINSIC MOTIVATION				INTRINSIC MOTIVATION
Amotivation	External	Introjected	Identified	Integrated	- knowledge - accomplishment - stimulation

THE SELF-DETERMINATION CONTINUUM

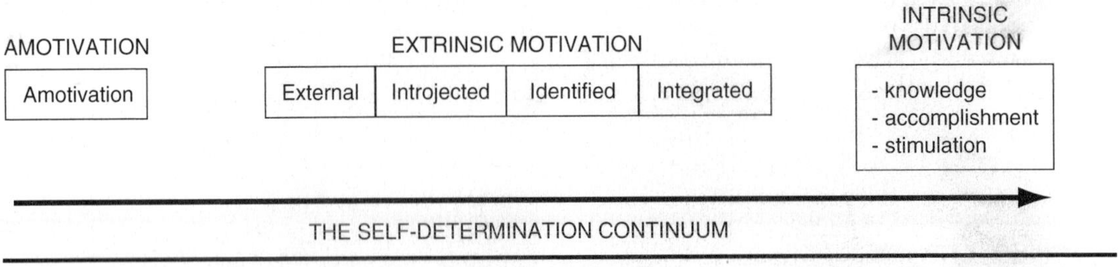

Source: Adapted from Vallerand and Losier (1999) with permission of publisher.

motivation, but we can see also that there are different kinds of motivation. We have already alluded to many of these different types of motivation. It is now time to discuss and define each type of motivation and explain how they relate to self-determination and to each other.

Motivation as it relates to self-determination is best conceptualized as a continuum. This is illustrated in figure 5.6 as the **self-determination continuum.** What this figure illustrates is that the less self-determining forms of motivation are found to the far left of the continuum (amotivation), while the most self-determining forms of motivation are found to the far right of the continuum (intrinsic motivation). At various stages along the middle of the continuum you have different kinds of extrinsic motivation. Some kinds of extrinsic motivation are associated with more self-determination, while others are associated with less self-determination.

Amotivation   The least self-determining kind of motivation is no motivation at all. This is referred to as amotivation. **Amotivation** refers to behaviors that are neither internally nor externally based. It is the relative absence of motivation. Relative to playing tennis, an amotivated athlete might say that he doesn't know why he plays tennis and that he doesn't see any particular benefit associated with it. In practice this seems to be a relatively rare form of motivation. Amotivated individuals usually will not even bother to become involved in sport. From a starting sample of 390 14- and

15-year-old children, Ntoumanis, Pensgaard, Martin, and Pipe (2004) identified 21 children who were categorized as being nearly devoid of motivation (amotivation). Through semistructured interviews, it was confirmed that all 21 children were low in need for autonomy, feeling of competence, and relatedness.

Intrinsic Motivation   The kind of motivation that exhibits the highest level of self-determination or agency is referred to as being intrinsic or internal in nature. **Intrinsic motivation** is motivation that comes from within. Intrinsically motivated individuals engage in activities that interest them, and they engage in them freely, with a full sense of volition and personal control. There is no sense of engaging in the activity for a material reward or for any other kind of external reward or motivation. Intrinsic motivation is believed to be multidimensional in nature, or composed of more than one dimension. The three aspects or manifestations of intrinsic motivation are motivation toward knowledge, toward accomplishment, and toward experiencing stimulation.

Intrinsic motivation *toward knowledge* reflects an athlete's desire to learn new skills and ways of accomplishing a task. For example, it is intrinsically motivating for a basketball player to learn a new way to deny an offensive player an open lane to the basket. Intrinsic motivation *toward accomplishment* reflects an athlete's desire to gain mastery over a particular skill and the pleasure that comes from reaching a personal goal for mastery.

CONCEPT   Motivation that comes from within is intrinsic in nature. Tasks that are intrinsically motivating are tasks that are interesting and that are performed by the athlete because they are interesting. Personal volition and control are critical components of intrinsic motivation. An athlete spontaneously engages in an activity that is intrinsically motivating. There is no need for rewards or any sort of external control to motivate an athlete to engage in an intrinsically motivating behavior.

APPLICATION   People readily participate in activities that they perceive to be interesting and unthreatening. Most young athletes start this way. A child wants to play baseball because it looks like a lot of fun and it is very interesting. The single most important goal of youth sport programs should be to retain a young person's intrinsic motivation and love for sport. Coaches and youth leaders should study the sport experience and focus on those activities and experiences that would cause a child to retain his intrinsic motivation.

For example, it is intrinsically motivating for a tennis player to spend countless hours trying to refine her slice serve, and to finally feel that she has accomplished this goal. Intrinsic motivation *toward experiencing stimulation* reflects the feeling that an athlete gets from physically experiencing a sensation innate to a specific task. For example, there is a certain exhilaration associated with the raw feeling of "driving" a pitcher's best fastball for a line drive into the gap in right/center field.

Extrinsic Motivation   While amotivation and intrinsic motivation lie at the two extremes of the self-determination continuum, extrinsic motivation falls in the large middle area. By definition, **extrinsic motivation** refers to motivation that comes from an external as opposed to an internal source. Extrinsic motivation comes in many forms, but common examples include awards, trophies, money, praise, social approval, and fear of punishment. As you will notice in figure 5.6, intrinsic and extrinsic motivation are not dichotomous concepts, as they were once believed to be. There are many degrees of extrinsic motivation. As one moves closer to the far right on the self-determination continuum, extrinsic motivation and intrinsic motivation become more alike in terms of self-

determinism. Deci and Ryan (1991) identified four different types of extrinsic motivation. These four different types of extrinsic motivation are titled external regulation, introjected regulation, identified regulation, and integrated regulation. The term *regulation* refers to the perception that a behavior is either internally or externally regulated. External regulation is believed to be the furthest removed from intrinsic motivation, while integrated regulation is believed to be the most closely associated with intrinsic motivation in terms of self-determinism. With this concept clearly in mind, the notion that intrinsic and extrinsic motivation are dichotomous in nature loses meaning.

External Regulation   **External regulation** describes the least self-determined form of extrinsic motivation. A behavior that is performed only to obtain an external reward or to avoid punishment is said to be externally regulated. For example, an externally regulated runner takes part in a weekend 10-kilometer race because of the promise of a trophy and a cash reward. An externally regulated basketball player carefully avoids the appearance of "slacking off" to avoid the punishment of running extra exhausting sprints after practice. Neither of these behaviors leads to

CONCEPT A skilled athlete who performs a behavior purely for external reasons is an efficacious pawn. Externally regulated behavior is behavior that is controlled by external sources.

APPLICATION Locus of causality shifts from an internal to an external cause when an athlete performs a behavior for purely external reasons. This shift may result in the athlete's losing a sense of personal control over her environment. Before engaging in a system of external rewards or punishment, the coach should always ask the following question: "If I quit rewarding the athlete or quit threatening punishment, will this athlete perform the desired behavior?" If the answer to that question is "no" or "probably not," then the coach is engaging in coaching behaviors that are undermining the athlete's intrinsic motivation for the activity. Once an athlete's intrinsic motivation has been severely diminished, it is only a matter of time before the athlete either gives up the activity or performs it without passion. It is difficult to say which outcome is worse.

Basketball players motivating each other. Courtesy University of Missouri–Columbia Sports Information.

self-determination and the perception of being in personal control. The athletes in these two examples are pawns in terms of exercising personal control of their behavior.

Together, the last three types of extrinsic motivation (introjected, identified, integrated) represent various levels of internalization. **Internalization** is a natural outcome of integration that comes as people obtain meaningful relationships with others. Rewards and other forms of extrinsic motivation become less external and more internal through the process of internalization. The process of internalization involves assimilation. External motives become assimilated as they are accepted as one's own and become part of the person.

Introjected Regulation Extrinsic motivation that has undergone **introjected regulation** is only partially internalized. It evokes a greater degree of self-determination than an externally regulated motive, but it is still not completely assimilated. In this state of assimilation, the athlete still struggles with the notion of causality. He has partially internalized a motive, but he still perceives the motivation as controlling. An example might be the degree to which an athlete feels that he practices daily to please his coach, as opposed to practicing to become a better player because he wants to become a better player. The motive has become partially internalized or regulated.

Identified Regulation   When an athlete comes to "identify" with an extrinsic motivation to the degree that it is perceived as being her own, it is referred to as being an **identified regulation.** Identified regulation is present when an athlete engages in an activity that she does not perceive as being particularly interesting, but does so because she sees the activity as being instrumental for her to obtain another goal that is interesting to her. An example might be a soccer player who lifts weight in the off-season to improve her kicking power. She participates in soccer because it is an interesting activity. She wants to excel in soccer, so she engages in what she perceives to be an uninteresting activity to obtain her goal.

Integrated Regulation   The most internalized form of regulation is referred to as **integrated regulation.** When regulatory mechanisms are well integrated, they become personally valued and freely done. At this level of integration, a behavior previously considered to be externally controlled becomes fully assimilated and internally controlled. From the perspective of self-determination, the fully integrated extrinsic motivation can hardly be distinguished from intrinsic motivation. At this stage the athlete perceives a coach's controlling behaviors as being completely consistent with his

own aspirations and goals and no longer perceives them as being externally controlling.

Consequences of Motivation

Referring back to figure 5.5, we see that there are hypothesized consequences associated with motivation. High levels of intrinsic motivation and internalized extrinsic motivation should lead to positive affect, positive behavioral outcomes, and improved cognition. Research shows (Vallerand & Losier, 1999) that athletes who engage in sport for self-determined reasons experience more positive and less negative affect, have greater persistence, and exhibit higher levels of sportspersonship (why you play determines how you play).

Research Support for the Integrated Model

Pelletier et al. (1995) reported on the development of the Sport Motivation Scale (SMS), designed to measure the different aspects of motivation that are illustrated in figure 5.6. The factor structure and internal consistency were confirmed on the English version of the SMS. In addition, self-determination as measured by the SMS was shown to be associated with selected motivational consequences. The SMS measures amotivation, intrinsic motivation, and three of the four types of external motivation. The authors explained that integrated regulation was not included in the inventory because of the difficulty of measuring this construct.

While the Sport Motivation Scale has been largely embraced by researchers seeking to measure motivation within the self-determination model, a study reported by Martens and Webber (2002) casts some doubt on the factor (subscale) structure of the scale. Specifically, they reported that the amotivation and external regulation scale items were problematic in terms of fitting the data, derived from 270 U.S. college athletes, to the theoretical model.

Markland (1999) reported on an investigation that demonstrated that self-determination moderates the relationship between perceived competence and intrinsic motivation. They observed that when self-determination is high, intrinsic motivation is high, regardless of the level of perceived competence. Furthermore, they observed that when self-determination was low, the level of perceived competence was important in predicting intrinsic motivation. Specifically, high levels of competence predict high levels of intrinsic motivation, while low levels of competence predict low levels of intrinsic motivation. Consistent with the integrated theory of motivation, this study illustrated the critical importance of both perceived competence and self-determination in the development and prediction of intrinsic motivation. In a related investigation, Gagne, Ryan, and Bargmann (2003) observed that by giving children choices and by creating an autonomous and self-determined environment, the self-determination of the child is enhanced.

Kowal and Fortier (2000) reported on an investigation that provided strong support for both the integrated model of Vallerand and Losier (1999) and Vallerand's hierarchical model of intrinsic and extrinsic motivation. Kowal and Fortier provided convincing evidence that social factors predict the psychological mediators of autonomy, competence, and relatedness, and that these mediators in turn predict intrinsic and extrinsic motivation. In support of Vallerand's hierarchical model, they were able to demonstrate that the important mediating characteristics of autonomy, competence, and relatedness occur on a general level of involvement in swimming, as well as a situation-specific level in swimming.

Ferrer-Caja and Weiss (2000) utilized 407 male and female high-school-age physical education students in an investigation designed to test selected aspects of Vallerand and Losier's (1999) integrated model of intrinsic and extrinsic motivation in sport. The results of the investigation supported the model generally, but found only partial support for the self-determination construct. Self-determination was measured as a function of the degree to which students perceived they had a choice in taking the physical education class, and the degree to which they felt they had a choice in selection of activities once in the course. In retrospect, this probably was not a valid measure of self-determination, because physical education was a mandatory course of study for the students. In explaining why the investigation failed to observe the expected hypothetical relationship between self-determination and intrinsic motivation, the authors wrote, "Perhaps because the course was mandatory, students may not have perceived choices to participate in decision making. In this vein, the required nature of the class could have obscured the potential effect of self-determination on intrinsic motivation." Even with an invalid measure of self-determination, the researchers observed a weak but significant association between self-determination and intrinsic motivation for females, but not for males.

Cognitive Evaluation Theory

Cognitive evaluation theory is a subtheory to the integrated theory of intrinsic and extrinsic motivation. Notions of cognitive evaluation theory were developed in the 1980s by Deci and Ryan (1985), but were later assimilated into the broader theory of self-determination (Deci & Ryan, 1991) that is the centerpiece for the integrated theory of motivation presented in this chapter. To give the reader a sense of the importance and influence of cognitive evaluation theory, consider that Vallerand reported in 1997 that over eight hundred studies had been published on this psychological topic alone. Research support for cognitive evaluation theory is strong, as evidenced by a recent meta-analysis and other investigations (Deci, Koestner, & Ryan, 1999; Ryan, 2000).

When someone engages in an interesting activity for its own sake and not for any other reason, we may conclude that she engages in the activity with an intrinsic motivation. On the other hand, if someone has an external reason for engaging in the activity, we would agree that she is externally motivated. If the external motivation is a reward, then it can be assumed that the reward may be part of the reason the person is participating.

It is appealing to assume that extrinsic rewards can enhance motivation. But what happens to an athlete's motivation if the rewards are withdrawn? Can external rewards actually damage rather than enhance motivation? Research on attribution theory indicates that external rewards can damage a young athlete's intrinsic desire to compete. The kinds of attributions that people give for receiving external rewards may have a negative impact on their intrinsic motivation.

According to the **additive principle,** a young athlete who is low in intrinsic motivation will participate in an achievement situation if there is sufficient reward or extrinsic motivation for doing so. Yet a great deal of research evidence seems to cast doubt on the additive principle. Specifically, it has been argued that the relationship between intrinsic and extrinsic motivation is multiplicative, not additive. That is, extrinsic rewards can either add to or detract from intrinsic motivation. This principle is illustrated in the story of a retired psychologist who wanted to chase away some noisy children who liked to play near his home (Siedentop & Ramey, 1977). The man tried several strategies to get the boys to play elsewhere, but to no avail. Finally, he came up with a new and interesting strategy. He decided to pay the boys to play near his house! He offered them 25 cents apiece to return the next day. Naturally, the boys returned the next day to receive their pay, at which time the man offered them 20 cents to come the following

day. When they returned again he offered them only 15 cents to come the next day, and he added that for the next few days he would give them only a nickel for their efforts. The boys became very agitated, since they felt their efforts were worth more than a nickel, and they told the man that they would not return!

The boys in this story came to believe that the reason they were playing near the man's house was for pay and not for fun. Therefore, their perceived locus of causality shifted from an internal to an external source. When this happens, an activity can lose its intrinsic value. Is it possible that this is happening today in professional sports? There are no doubt many highly paid athletes who have shifted their locus of control from an internal source—love of the game—to an external source. If the high salaries were withdrawn, how many would continue playing the game?

A similar thing could be happening to our young athletes as they receive trophies, money, pins, and awards for athletic participation. Is the relationship between intrinsic and extrinsic rewards additive, or is it multiplicative? The **multiplicative principle** suggests that the interaction between intrinsic and extrinsic rewards could either add to or detract from intrinsic motivation.

Embedded in attribution theory are the **principles** of **discounting** and **overjustification** (Lepper & Greene, 1975, 1976). These concepts suggest that adding external rewards as an incentive to participate in an otherwise interesting activity may represent an overjustification for participating, leading to a discounting, or reduction, in intrinsic motivation. For example, if a child begins playing baseball for fun but then is induced to do so for a trophy, this trophy may represent an overjustification for playing baseball. The child may come to perceive that she is playing for the purpose of receiving a trophy rather than for intrinsic reasons. Whenever an individual comes to believe that she is participating in an otherwise interesting activity for external rewards, intrinsic motivation is minimized.

The overjustification principle plays a role in the weakening of intrinsic motivation within adults

Can trophies such as this one contribute to a decrease in intrinsic motivation?
Courtesy Kansas State University Sports Information.

as well as children. Consider the destructive effect that big salaries associated with free agency have had upon major league baseball players. In a moment of unusual candor, Candy Davis, wife of big-league relief pitcher Mark Davis, said of his new $13 million contract with the Kansas City Royals: "You'd think he discovered the cure for cancer or something." As history records, Mark Davis did not live up to his multimillion-dollar contract (Neff, 1990). This observation is further supported by research reported by Sturman and Thibodeau (2001). Archival data obtained on 33 major league baseball free agents for two seasons prior to and two seasons after the signing of a substantial free agent contract revealed a substantial decrease in immediate post-contract performance. In some cases the performance improved back to pre-contract levels during the second year following the signing of the contract.

Perhaps the single most important contribution to our understanding of the relationship between intrinsic motivation and extrinsic rewards comes from **cognitive evaluation theory.** Cognitive evaluation theory (Deci & Ryan, 1985) is deeply seated in attribution theory, and in the locus of causality origin-pawn relationship introduced in the previous chapter on attribution theory.

Deci theorized that extrinsic rewards can affect intrinsic motivation in two ways. The first is to produce a decrement in intrinsic motivation; this occurs as people perceive a change in locus of causality from an internal to an external one. That is, when people come to perceive that their behavior is controlled by external forces, they respond with decreased levels of intrinsic motivation. This is referred to as the **controlling aspect of extrinsic motivation,** and serves to place an athlete in the position of a pawn who is acted upon. The second effect of extrinsic rewards is informational in nature, and results in an increase in intrinsic motivation. If an external award provides feedback to the person and enhances that person's sense of

CONCEPT An extrinsic reward that encourages athletes to attribute their participation to external causes can reduce intrinsic motivation.

APPLICATION Coaches should discourage any form of extrinsic reward that athletes may perceive to be more important than athletic participation itself.

competence and self-determination, increased intrinsic motivation will be the end result. This is referred to as the **informational aspect of extrinsic motivation,** and it places an athlete in the position of an originator who does the acting.

Consider the following situation: A 10-year-old boy agrees to run in a five-mile road race with his father. As further incentive to train and finish the race, the father promises the boy 10 dollars. Later on, the boy passes up a second opportunity to run in a race with his father because, as he puts it, "Why, what's in it for me?" This may seem like an extreme example, yet situations like this occur every day. Why did this boy lose interest in this intrinsically interesting activity? Because he came to perceive that the primary reason for his running in the race was money. The money, not the intrinsic fun of running, became the source of his motivation. Once the shift in locus of causality was made from the internal cause to the external cause, the boy came to feel controlled by the external reward. He was running for the money and not for the intrinsic value of the experience; consequently, when the salient external motivation was withdrawn, intrinsic motivation was insufficient.

Let us consider a second example. A 12-year-old girl competed in a singles tennis tournament and won an award for accomplishment. The inscription on the award said, "In recognition of your placing in the top ten of the City Tournament." This positive feedback about her performance gave the girl a feeling of competence and self-determination. She was proud of the award and went on to participate in several more tennis tournaments that year. Because she perceived that the award provided her positive information about her ability as a tennis player, it became intrinsically motivating.

Research has also linked intrinsic motivation to goal orientation, a topic we will discuss in chapter 6. Individuals displaying a mastery orientation enjoy enhanced intrinsic motivation because of the self-referenced and self-determined nature of their involvement. Conversely, individuals displaying a competitive orientation suffer a loss of intrinsic motivation because of the controlling nature of their involvement. A competitive orientation can be controlling because the goal to demonstrate competence in an event becomes more important than the event itself (Frederick & Ryan, 1995; Walling, Duda, & Chi, 1993). Competition may lead to a reduction in intrinsic motivation because of its controlling nature. When athletes compete only for the purpose of winning and demonstrating superiority over others, the main reason for their participation is an external reward (winning), and not the joy of participation. Fortier, Vallerand, Briere, and Provencher (1995) reported that French Canadian recreational athletes enjoy higher levels of intrinsic motivation for their sport involvement than do competitive collegiate athletes. Ryan (1980) reported that scholarship football players exhibit lower intrinsic motivation than nonscholarship wrestlers and female athletes.

These two studies by Fortier et al. (1995) and Ryan (1980), and an earlier study by Ryan (1977), seem to suggest that collegiate scholarship athletes suffer a loss of intrinsic motivation due to the controlling nature of being paid to play sports. Receiving financial support to play collegiate sports, however, should also provide information to the athlete that would be suggestive of competence and self-determination. Consequently, it does not follow that scholarship athletes should necessarily exhibit lower levels of intrinsic motivation than nonscholarship athletes.

CONCEPT Extrinsic rewards (such as praise, awards, ribbons, and trophies) that athletes view as rewards for competent performance and encouragement for further participation will enhance intrinsic motivation.

APPLICATION Coaches and teachers should carefully consider the perceptions that young athletes have about extrinsic rewards. If the rewards are perceived to represent excellence, they can be valuable. However, if they become more important than the sport itself, they can be damaging.

| 5.11 | **CONCEPT & APPLICATION** |

CONCEPT The development of an athlete's intrinsic motivation and self-confidence is the ultimate goal of youth sport programs.

APPLICATION Coaches and administrators should define program goals in terms of the intrinsic values the participants will gain.

An important study reported by Amorose and Horn (2000) seems to provide important insight into the relationship between intrinsic motivation and rewards in the form of an athletic scholarship. Participants for this research were 386 Division I collegiate athletes participating in the sports of football, field hockey, gymnastics, swimming, and wrestling. Athletes completed the Intrinsic Motivation Inventory (McAuley, Duncan, & Tammen, 1989), designed to measure five aspects of intrinsic motivation, and were classified as having a full, a partial, or no scholarship. Results of the investigation revealed that male athletes exhibit higher levels of intrinsic motivation than female athletes, and that scholarship athletes exhibit higher levels of intrinsic motivation than nonscholarship athletes. The authors concluded that scholarships may actually serve to enhance intrinsic motivation by conveying positive information suggesting a higher level of competence. While it is true that a scholarship may in some instances convey to the athlete a sense of being controlled by an external force, it is by no means a necessary outcome. As this study clearly shows, it is more likely that a

scholarship will convey to the athlete a feeling of competence and personal control that translates into higher levels of intrinsic motivation.

In a follow-up investigation involving collegiate male and female collegiate gymnasts, Amorose and Horn (2001) reported that there was no difference between scholarship and nonscholarship athletes on any of the five aspects of intrinsic motivation measured by the Intrinsic Motivation Inventory. In this same investigation, Amorose and Horn also studied the relationship between intrinsic motivation and perceived coaching behaviors. The results of this analysis showed that athletes who perceived that their coaches provided high levels of training/instruction and low levels of autocratic behavior and social support showed an increase in intrinsic motivation from the beginning to the end of the competitive season.

Youth Sports

"If you want to teach kids to hit, you tell them, 'Wait for a good pitch to hit.' If you want to win, you tell them, 'I want you to take [don't swing] until you get two strikes,' but in the end, what have you got? You haven't taught them how to hit, only how to draw a walk and run the bases" (Cal Ripken, Jr., in Menez, 2003, p. 65).

Most people, when they think of applied sport psychology, think of elite athletes and how to improve athletic performance. This is certainly the focus of sport psychology during the winter and summer Olympic Games that so captivate the nation and the world. However, when you consider that approximately thirty-five million children between the ages of 6 and 18 participate in agency-sponsored youth sport programs each year, and another ten million 14- to 18-year-old youth participate in school-sponsored programs (Smoll & Smith, 1998), you see the tremendous potential for human enrichment and development. If every child who participated in sport emerged with increased self-confidence, greater perceived ability, increased intrinsic motivation, and greater self-esteem, the world and society would certainly be better for it. Unfortunately, this is not always the case, as the following two true stories reveal.

This is the story of a child named Johnny who had not yet succeeded in hitting a baseball off a tee (T-ball). One day, after several attempts, the boy, for the first time in his young life, succeeded in hitting the ball. Overcome with happiness and joy, the boy jumped up and down with glee as his parents and other fans cheered his success. In his excitement, however, he forgot that he was supposed to run to first base. In anger, his volunteer coach grabbed him and said "Johnny, you dummy, you can't even run to first. You will never get another chance to bat on my team." Needless to say, Johnny became a sports dropout. Johnny's experience could have been one of the greatest in his life, but an untrained, insensitive volunteer coach turned it into one of his worst (K. Dimick, Personal Communication, September 1990).

Candice [name changed] was a 10-year-old soccer player. Her first soccer coach was more interested in winning than in teaching skills and building self-confidence. The coach yelled at the girls

constantly throughout each game. In one championship game, Candice scored a goal about four minutes into the game. She was beaming with pride at her accomplishment. The coach, however saw it differently. He took her out of the game, stating for all to hear, "Candice, that was a goal the goalie should have stopped. The next time I want to see you score a goal the goalie can't stop!"

Candice now has a new coach. On the first day of practice, the coach talked to the players and told them not to yell at the kids from the sidelines during the game, and if they did say anything, to make it positive. He also explained to them that confidence building and enjoyment, and not winning, were most important at this age. After the first practice Candice exclaimed to her mother, "Mom, the coach thinks we're all good players! It was fun! Wow!!" (D. Wright, Personal Communication, September 17, 2004).

Historically, youth sport originated in the United States free from adult surveillance, in settings as diverse as New York City, southern slave communities, and western frontier towns (Wiggins, 1996). Children enjoyed unsupervised marbles, crack-the-whip, capture-the-flag, soccer, and all sorts of variations of baseball and other sports. "The essential wonderment of the games we played is that we played them blessedly free from adults. There were no soccer moms or Little League dads. For better and for worse, we defined and lived in our own world." (Maraniss, 2001, p. 86).

Over time, adults saw the need to provide organized and supervised sport programs for youth. Adults were motivated then, as now, along various lines of thinking. Sometimes they promoted sports for educational and moral development reasons, but at other times competition itself was their goal. Interestingly, highly competitive youth sport programs emerged in the United States as early as the 1920s and 1930s, prompting educators to warn against the dangers of highly competitive sport. The Youth Sport Institute at Michigan State University set the stage for programs designed to study ways in which youth sport could be developed for the maximum personal benefit of the youth participants. This program emerged in 1978 under the leadership of Vern Seefeldt (Wiggins, 1996).

While the primary focus of this section will be upon the potential psychological benefits of youth sport participation, potential health benefits should also be mentioned. Pate, Trost, Levin, and Dowda (2000) hypothesized that sport participation was related to positive health benefits. Data for this investigation came from a nationally representative sample of 14,221 U.S. high school students in grades nine through twelve. Results showed that approximately 70 percent of male students and 53 percent of female students reported participating in one or more sport teams in school and/or non-school settings. Male sport participants were more likely than male nonparticipants to report daily fruit and vegetable consumption, and less likely to report cigarette smoking, cocaine and other illegal drug use, and trying to lose weight. Female sport participants were more likely to report daily consumption of vegetables, and less likely to report having had sexual intercourse during the previous three months. Additional health benefits were noted for white male and female sport participants. A few associations with negative health behaviors were observed in African American and Hispanic subgroups, but overall, sport participation is associated with positive health behaviors. The authors recommended that physicians encourage young people to take advantage of opportunities to join sport teams. Unfortunately, many youth who would like to participate in organized school sport programs are unable to because of limited school resources and the sizes of their schools. In large city schools, coaches are forced to discriminate among interested youth on the basis of skill and of body size or type.

Clearly, there are two types of youth sport programs. One is sponsored by the schools, and the other is sponsored by agencies and city recreation departments. *School-sponsored programs* generally have the luxury of dedicated facilities and qualified coaches, although this is not always the case. State high school athletic associations mandate a certain level in the qualifications of coaches. Requirements for coaches of school-sponsored teams vary from state to state. The standard for a head coach of a major sport is usually a teaching certificate, with some coaching experience and training desired. In some states the requirements are even higher, but hardship exceptions are routinely given, as school administrators are hard pressed to find coaches for all the sports. Theoretically, the higher coaching standards in the school-sponsored programs result in better, more educationally sound programs, but this is not always true. Because school administrators can hire and fire coaches, they have a level of control that is not often available in nonschool youth sports programs. However, stipends for coaching are often so low that they offer little encouragement to coaches to meet desired coaching standards.

Nonschool youth sports programs operate in quite a different way. These programs use volunteers as coaches, and it is often difficult for teams to find places to practice. The primary focus of this chapter on youth sports is upon nonschool youth sports programs, so we will simply refer to them as **youth sports** throughout the rest of the chapter. The very nature of youth sports is very dynamic, as it brings together all aspects of society. The only paid participants in the youth sports experience are the organizers (e.g., city recreation department staff) and the referees and officials. The participants, coaches, parents, and other interested adults are all volunteers with various levels of expertise. What typically happens in a youth sports program, such as a basketball program, is that a call goes out from the organizers for youth participants and coaches. Coaches are selected and the youth are assigned or drafted into teams (this process varies greatly from program to program). The organizers have an important voice in determining who will be selected for coaches, but if they have a shortage of volunteers their options are limited. Typically, an adult volunteer is assigned to coach a team that includes the coach's own son or daughter. This, of course, is the primary motivation of the adult to volunteer to spend hundreds of hours of his free time coaching children. Coaching is an opportunity to be with his child, as well as an opportunity to have a major voice in how much playing time his child gets. It is a very interesting cultural experience. While the youth participants are playing, some of the parents are coaching, and other parents are in the stands either supporting or not supporting the decisions of the volunteer coach on the field.

With the scenario just described, there is tremendous opportunity for human development and enrichment to take place as children, parents, coaches, and officials interact to provide a learning experience for the children. Overall, the experience is a positive one and a marvel to behold, but there are many opportunities for and examples of abuse. In this section we will learn more about the youth sports experience by discussing (a) benefits of youth sports and reasons children participate, (b) potential negative factors associated with the youth sports experience, (c) why youth drop out of sports, (d) training volunteer coaches, (e) coach-parent relationships, and (f) parental concerns and involvement.

Benefits of Youth Sports and Reasons Children Participate

Numerous investigations have been reported in which youth sport participants were asked to give or identify reasons why they participate in sport (Ewing & Seefeldt, 1996; Gill, Gross, & Huddleston, 1983; Lee, Whitehead, & Balchin, 2000; Wankel & Kreisel, 1985; White, Duda, & Keller, 1998). While the studies do not yield identical reasons for participation, there are common themes. The number one reason children give for participating in youth sports is "to have fun." When it isn't fun anymore, the young athletes will find something else to do. Based on numerous investigations, the following **motives for participation** have been identified repeatedly by youth sports participants:

1. To have fun and to enjoy participating in sport

2. To learn new skills and to improve on existing sports skills

Children who participate in sports have fun and learn new skills. Source: © Royalty-Free Corbis.

3. To become physically fit and to enjoy good health

4. To enjoy the challenge and excitement of sports participation and competition

5. To enjoy a team atmosphere and to be with friends

In addition to representing motives for participation, the above list represents some of the perceived benefits of youth sports participation. The benefits of youth sports participation include having fun, learning new sports skills, getting physically fit, experiencing the excitement of competition, and making new friends. This is, however, an incomplete list of the potential benefits of youth sport participation. The intangibles that children do not list include things like learning to cooperate

CONCEPT   The motives that young athletes have for participating in youth sports programs are the same motives that lead to the development of intrinsic motivation and self-confidence.

APPLICATION   Youth sport promises an exciting and challenging environment in which participants can realize enhanced self-esteem and motivation.

Some youth sports programs may be based on participation motives of organizers and parents that are not consistent with the motives of the participants themselves. In order to assist participants in the development of intrinsic love for sport and increased self-confidence relative to sport participation, the participant's motives for participation must be of primary concern.

with teammates and coaches, learning what it means to be a good sport, and developing a sense of perceived competence and self-efficacy. A positive youth sports experience will enhance intrinsic motivation, which will in turn lead to continued participation in sports throughout a lifetime. Interestingly, "winning" or "to win" is seldom at the top of any child's list of reasons for participating (Lee et al., 2000).

Potential Negative Factors Associated with the Youth Sports Experience

If youth sports programs are properly organized and supervised by responsible adults, there is no reason why there should be any negative outcomes associated with the experience. To avoid negative experiences in the youth sports experience, organizers should host two mandatory educational sessions. One training session would be held for youth sports coaches and the other for all parents of youth participants. The focus of these two sessions should be, first, how to make the youth sports experience a positive one for the participants, and second, how to avoid negative consequences associated with youth sports.

What are the potential negative consequences of youth sports participation? We will focus upon three negative consequences here. They are (a) too much competition and focus upon winning, (b) too much distress and anxiety in the minds and bodies

of the participants, and (c) violence involving adults.

Competition and Focus upon Winning   If kept within the appropriate bounds, competition satisfies one of the motives of youth sports participation, which is to enjoy challenging and exciting competition. Competition gives the youth sports participants an opportunity to put all of their practice and hard work to the test. A loss should mean not that a player has low ability, but that through hard work she can improve. This is where attribution training comes into play. The problem arises when winning becomes so important that it becomes the sole purpose of competition. When winning becomes that important, it forces an external locus of causality, and the athlete's sense of self-determination and autonomy is diminished, as is intrinsic motivation.

Who decides that winning is the only reason that a team plays a basketball game against an opponent? How do the youth sports participants come to believe that winning is the primary reason that they are involved in youth sports? These are good questions that have fairly complex answers. We should look first of all to the organizers of the youth sports league to see how important winning is to such things as the format for postseason play, selection to all-star teams, and efforts made to equalize teams on the basis of skill and maturity. Organizers can deemphasize the importance of winning by allowing all teams to go into a playoff round and to equalize skill level among teams so that no one team has an unfair advantage to begin with.

Next, we can look to the coaches of the youth sports teams to see what their motivations are. Why should a coach believe that winning is so important that only the most skilled players get to play most of the time? What effect does sitting on the bench and watching his peers play most of the game have on the perceived confidence of a young athlete? There is a clear message here, and it is not lost on the young athlete—or his parents. The athlete suffers a loss of perceived ability, and he comes to fear competition for fear of failing. Some organizers of youth sports programs will require that every athlete get a chance to play in every game, but they need to take that policy a little further and require that every youth has an equal opportunity to play. Still, even with all the safeguards against unequal opportunity, an overemphasis on the importance of winning ruins the experience for many of the participants.

Just as athletes can be competition or "win" oriented as opposed to mastery oriented, so can coaches be win oriented. To the competition-oriented coach, coaching ability is associated with defeating another team or another coach. It has nothing to do with improving the skill level of an entire group of young people, including those with very little skill. The mastery-oriented coach is going to look at competition and winning from a totally different perspective from that of the competition-oriented coach. She will take satisfaction in seeing a group of youngsters learn to work together and improve their individual and team skills, independent of the final game score. Winning the contest is a secondary goal to the mastery-oriented coach.

> Children want and need positive experiences in sport. They want to play, not watch others play; they want to achieve their own goals, not adult goals; they want less emphasis on winning and more freedom to have fun. Unfortunately, what children want from sport is often overshadowed by what some adults have done to children's sport (Orlick & Zitzelsberger, 1996, p. 330).

Distress and Anxiety   Too much emphasis upon competition and winning leads to increased levels of distress and anxiety. A detailed explanation of the meaning of distress and anxiety will be given in a later chapter, but for now it is sufficient to understand that these terms are related to a child's fear of failure and worry about disappointing others. The primary reason that youth sports participants give for involvement in sport is to have fun; distress and anxiety are certainly not fun. You simply cannot enjoy playing a baseball or softball game if you are fearful every time it is your turn to bat, or are worrying that the ball might be hit to you when you are in the field.

Over time, with the proper coaching and experience, young athletes can learn to appreciate and enjoy the excitement of competition as an end in itself. Everyone enjoys the euphoria and thrill of victory, but in reality it cannot be fully appreciated unless one has experienced defeat. More important than the actual winning or losing of an athletic contest is the pure joy of being part of the experience.

Violence Involving Adults

> The rising tide of violence and verbal abuse by adults at youth sports events reached its terrible peak this month when one hockey father killed another (Nack & Munson, 2000, p. 87).

The whole topic of sport aggression among players and fans will be discussed in detail in a later chapter of the text, but for now our focus is upon violence in youth sports. Violence among adults in youth sports is truly reprehensible and must be stopped. Unfortunately, according to the national news media, it is something that is increasing rather than decreasing (Nack & Munson, 2000).

- April 1999, Albany, Georgia: Ray Knight, former Cincinnati Reds third baseman and manager, and father of a 12-year-old girl, punched the father of a girl belonging to an opposing softball team following a heated exchange.

CONCEPT An inordinate focus upon winning leads to a negative experience for youth sports participants.

APPLICATION The number one reason children give for participating in sports is to have fun. This number one reason for participating in youth sports is sacrificed when coaches and adults overemphasize the importance of winning. The adults set the tone, from the organizers down to the coaches and the parents. Adult training sessions for parents and coaches are ways to teach adults how to make the sports experience a joyful one for their children.

CONCEPT Distress and anxiety, when associated with the youth sports experience, are almost always caused by an overemphasis upon competition and winning.

APPLICATION Rather than trying to reduce distress through some sort of psychological intervention, why not go right to the heart of the problem and reduce the emphasis placed upon winning? Ask yourself why it is so important to win this game, match, or contest. This question should not be asked repeatedly before each competition, because then it is too late. This question needs to be asked early on, when team and individual goals are being set and when organizers are planning postseason tournaments and determining what the purposes of youth sports should be. If organizers decide that the youth sports experience is for the purpose of identifying the best players and winning postseason tournaments, then the participants should be informed early on of this fact.

- October 1999, Swiftwater, Pennsylvania: Police were called in to stop a brawl between parents and players following a football game between 11- to 13-year-olds.
- January 1999, Staten Island, New York: Following a hockey game for 11- and 12-year-old boys, a father struck his son's coach in the face with two hockey sticks.
- April 1999, Sacramento, California: Following a Little League game, a father who was coaching his son's team beat up the manager of the opposing team.
- September 1999, Eastlake, Ohio: A soccer dad punched a 14-year-old boy who had scuffled for the ball with the man's 14-year-old son.
- October 1999, La Vista, Nebraska: A former corrections officer assaulted a 16-year-old referee at a flag football game for 6- and 7-year-old boys.

These are just some of the examples of adult violence associated with youth sport. Perhaps the most outrageous and flagrant example of adult violence took place in July 5, 2000 at the Burbank Ice Arena in Reading, Massachusetts. The altercation,

CONCEPT   Incidents of sport violence in youth sports usually involve fathers of the youth participants.

APPLICATION   There are really only two potential solutions to this dilemma. One is to ban parents from youth sports involvement altogether, and the second is to require in-service training of parents, similar to that in the Jupiter, Florida experiment. Most parents are wonderful, well-behaved supporters of the youth sports experience, but it is the volatile exception that causes all of the problems. Parents must be firmly taught that if they cannot control their emotions, tempers, and egos, they are not welcome on the field, on the floor, or at any other place their son or daughter is performing.

involving two fathers, occurred in front of his three sons. The altercation began on the ice, when the assailant accused the victim of not controlling rough play among the boys during an ice hockey team practice. Hard feelings and words continued outside of the arena at the pop machine following the practice. The assailant knocked the smaller man down, pinned him to the floor with his knee, and beat him to death with his fists while the boys watched in horror. History records that Thomas Junta was convicted of involuntary manslaughter for his role in this event (Youth Sport Parent Convicted, 2002).

As may be noted, all of these examples but one involved parents of youth sports participants. Somewhat tongue-in-cheek, Rick Reilly (2000) wrote an editorial titled "Bringing Parents Up to Code," in which he wrote a code of conduct for parents of youth sports participants. His fourth code of conduct goes like this: "I'll realize that the guy behind the umpire's mask, whom I've been calling 'Jose Feliciano' and 'Coco, the talking ape,' is probably just a 15-year old kid with a tube of Oxy 10 in his pocket, making $12 the hard way. I'll shut up." (Reilly, 2000, p. 88.) In this same editorial, Reilly mentions the fact that the athletic association of the town of Jupiter, Florida requires parents of all youth sports participants to view a film on sportspersonship and to sign a code of conduct.

Taking it one step further, the New Brunswick, New Jersey Recreation Department has designed and built unique raised baseball fields. The fields at their new parks are raised 10 feet above the ground. Anyone standing behind the backstop can't see the action. The design places the bleachers well down the foul line into the outfield, separating parents from the dugouts (Bach, 2002).

Why Do Youth Withdraw from Sport?

The answer to this question is partly the reverse of all the motives that children give for wanting to be involved in youth sport. Children's **surface reasons for withdrawal from sport** are as follows:

1. Participating in sport not being fun anymore
2. Failure to learn new skills or to improve on existing skills
3. Lack of physical activity
4. Lack of thrills, challenges, and excitement
5. Poor team atmosphere, not making friends

In addition to surface reasons for why young people withdraw from sports are the **underlying psychological reasons for withdrawal from sport.** First, you have the distress and worry associated with too much emphasis upon winning and competition. These factors undermine a child's intrinsic motivation or love for an activity. There is no longer an intrinsic reason to continue sports participation, and the external rewards are insufficient motivators.

Another surface reason youth sports participants give for dropping out is described by

CONCEPT   Youth withdraw from the sport experience for surface as well as underlying psychological reasons.

APPLICATION   Research shows that the dropout rate for organized youth sport programs is 35 percent for any given year (Gould & Petlichkoff, 1988). Youth sports leaders should consider a complete dropout from sport for any reason other than "change of interest" or "other things to do" to be of major concern. Dropping out for surface reasons such as "not having fun" or "not learning new skills" suggests weaknesses in the program, while dropping out for underlying psychological reasons suggests insensitivity to the psychological needs of children. When young people drop out of sports, a systematic follow-up should be made to determine why they have dropped out. A simple, confidential questionnaire could be developed for this purpose.

age-group swimmers as simply "change of interest" or "other things to do" (Butcher, Linder & Jones, 2002; Gould, Feltz, Horn, & Weiss, 1982). An athlete's decision to drop out of swimming, however, does not mean that he is a dropout from all youth sport activities. Swimming is a very demanding activity involving little social interaction. Consequently, it is important to determine if a youth sport dropout is a **specific-sport dropout** or a **general-sport dropout.** Withdrawing from one sport to participate in another is less of a concern to sport psychologists than dropping out of sports altogether.

It is believed that one of the strongest benefits of youth sports participation is an increase in perceived competence and self-confidence associated with a positive sports experience. In this regard, it is most discouraging when a child drops out of sports, because this implies that the child will not enjoy this benefit. In fact, Weiss and Chaumeton (1992) showed that children who do not participate in sports or who drop out suffer from lower levels of perceived competence than those youth who persist. The implication is that some youth may withdraw from sports because of some experience or combination of experiences that has caused them to lose self-confidence. Such things as too much emphasis upon winning, too much pressure and anxiety, or an aversion to a competitive climate could lead to a perception of lowered competence.

Children who succeed in sports gain the admiration of their friends and peers. This opens up tremendous social opportunities for them, and has considerable influence on their psychological development. Conversely, if a child is perceived by herself and her peers as having low skill, she may suffer a loss of friends, a loss of self-confidence, and an increase in anxiety about competition. Adults associated with youth sport programs must make every effort to make them meaningful, positive experiences for each participant. Withdrawal from sport for underlying psychological reasons is more serious than withdrawal out of simply losing interest or finding other things to do (Brustad, 1996b; Passer, 1996).

Training Volunteer Coaches

The best way to assure a quality youth sport program is to provide quality training and supervision of volunteer coaches (Smith & Smoll, 1997b). A number of formal coach training programs have been developed in the United States to assist youth coaches in creating a positive and enjoyable athletic experience. Examples include these:

1. American Sport Education Program (ASEP; Martens, 1987).
2. Program for Athletic Coaches' Education (PACE; Seefeldt & Brown, 1992).
3. Coach Effectiveness Training (CET; Smith & Smoll, 1997b).

Each of these coach training programs provides excellent guidelines for the effective training of youth sport coaches. Because of its close association with the Coaches Behavior Assessment System (CBAS), the Coach Effectiveness Training (CET) program was discussed in some detail in the earlier chapter on leadership (chap. 3). Research reported by Malete and Feltz (2000) demonstrated the effectiveness of the Program for Athletic Coaches' Education (PACE) to increase coach efficacy in terms of teaching strategies and technique.

Coach-Parent Relationships

In youth sports, coaches are also often parents, so the relationship between coach and parent is a very sensitive one. To a large extent, problems in youth sport come from two basic sources. The first is a failure on the part of coaches and parents to distinguish clearly between the youth sports model and the professional model of sport, and the second is what Smith and Smoll (1996) have named the "reversed-dependency trap."

The **youth sports model** provides an educational setting for the development of desirable physical and psychosocial characteristics in young athletes. Conversely, the **professional sports model** is a commercial enterprise in which the stated goals are to entertain and to make money. Sometimes parents and coaches fail to see the distinction between the two and act as if they are one and the same.

The **reversed-dependency trap** describes a situation in youth sport in which the child becomes an extension of the parent. A parent comes to define his own sense of self-worth in terms of the success and failure of his son or daughter. When this happens, the parent becomes a "winner" or a "loser" through his young athlete. A parent may seek to experience through his child the success he never knew as an athlete. This is often referred to as the "frustrated jock syndrome" (Smoll, 1998).

Hanlon (1994) and Smoll (2001) list ten standards of conduct that a parent should follow. Adherence to these ten standards will greatly enhance the quality of the coach-parent relationship. Ideally, these ten standards should be presented to the parents in a preseason parents' and coaches' training session lasting about one hour. As adapted from Smoll (1998), the **parents' code of conduct** is displayed in table 5.1. The basic premise of the code of conduct is that nothing in a parent's behavior should detract from or interfere with any child's enjoyment of sport.

The guiding principle for a coach-parent relationship is that communication should take place, and that it is a *two-way street*. Coaches must take the initiative to encourage communication, but at the same time they must identify the parameters for when the communication should take place. Discussions between coach and parent should never take place in front of a child, should never take

TABLE 5.1 | Parents' Code of Conduct

1. I will remain in the spectator area during games.
2. I will not advise the coach on how to coach.
3. I will not direct derogatory comments toward coaches, officials, or players of either team.
4. I will not try to coach my child during the course of a contest.
5. I will not drink alcohol at contests or come to a contest having drunk too much.
6. I will cheer for my child's team and give them my support.
7. I will show interest, enthusiasm, and support for my child.
8. I will be in control of my emotions at all times.
9. I will help when asked by coaches or officials.
10. I will thank coaches, officials, and other volunteers who conducted the event.

Source: Smoll (1998, p. 67).

CONCEPT   The key to a good coach-parent relationship is effective and open communication. The lines of communication must be kept open and encouraged by the coach. Parents must be informed about when it is inappropriate to enter into a dialogue with the coach.

APPLICATION   The coach should call a coach-parent meeting before the season begins. At this

meeting the parents' code of conduct, as outlined in table 5.1, should be reviewed. In addition, the coach should use this time to encourage two-way communication with the parents and to clarify the purpose of the youth sports program. Parents should be employed as valuable resources to assist the coach in achieving the objectives of the youth sports program.

place during a game, and should rarely take place during practice. The one topic about which coaches and parents will often disagree is a given athlete's ability. Coaches must learn to listen patiently, thank the parents for their thoughts, and assure them that their input will be given every consideration. Parents will often present some very challenging problems for coaches. Some common types of "problem parents" and suggestions on how to handle them are identified in table 5.2.

Parental Concerns and Involvement

Notwithstanding the challenges that overinvolved parents give to youth sport teams, organized youth sport programs could not survive in the absence of parental support. This support comes in the form of such things as transportation, fundraising, and

volunteer coaches. Parent involvement and support also permeate every aspect of the social fabric of the youth sport experience. Parent and family socialization of the youth sport experience can be organized around the three components of (a) parents as role models, (b) parents as interpreters of experience, and (c) parents as providers of experience (Fredricks & Eccles, 2004). Current knowledge of the effects of parental socialization in the youth sport experience is summarized in table 5.3.

Of particular interest to parents and children alike is athletic success. Children's primary motivation for sport and exercise participation is fun and enjoyment, but they have more fun if they can experience some success. For example, it is fun to shoot baskets in a game of basketball, but it is even more fun if some of those shots actually go into the basket. Holt and Morley (2004) conducted an

TABLE 5.2 | Common Types of "Problem Parents" and How to Handle Them

Problem Type	How to Handle Them
1. Disinterested	1. Try to find out what the problem is and encourage their involvement.
2. Overcritical	2. Explain damaging effect of criticism on their child.
3. Scream from behind bench	3. During break in action tactfully explain that loud behavior is distracting.
4. Sideline coaches	4. Privately explain to parent how confusing it is to child to have two coaches.
5. Overprotective	5. Reassure parent that the event is fairly safe as long as child is attentive.
6. Abusive	6. With the assistance of a program supervisor, privately assure parent that their behavior will not be tolerated. If not curtailed, they will be given a police escort off the premises.

Source: Smoll (2006, pp. 197–198).

TABLE 5.3 | Synthesis of Knowledge Associated with How Parent Socialization Affects the Youth Sport Experience

PARENTS AS ROLE MODELS

1. Active parents have active children.
2. Parent participation in athletics is particularly important for girls.
3. Female athletes are more likely to have parents who participate in athletics than are female non-athletes.

PARENTS AS INTERPRETERS OF EXPERIENCE

1. Higher parental pressure is related to negative child outcomes.
2. Low to moderate levels of parental pressure is related to children's higher enjoyment of athletics.
3. Parental beliefs are positively related to children's own competency beliefs, interests, and participation.
4. Parents hold gender-stereotyped beliefs, believing that athletics is more important for boys than for girls and that boys have more athletic talent than girls.
5. Children's perceptions of parents' beliefs are more strongly related to children's self-perceptions than are parent-reported beliefs.

PARENTS AS PROVIDERS OF EXPERIENCE

1. Parents support and encourage children's athletic involvement in a variety of ways, from time involvement to monetary support.
2. Parental encouragement is positively related to children's sports involvement.
3. Parents are gender-typed in their behaviors. They encourage their sons to be physically active more than they encourage their daughters.
4. Over-involvement by parents can contribute to children's negative emotional reactions to sports and ultimately to athlete burnout.

Source: Fredericks, J. A. and Eccles, J. (2004). Parental influences on youth involvement in sports. In M. R. Weiss (Ed.), *Developmental sport and exercise psychology: A lifespan perspective* (pp. 145–164). Morgantown, WV: Fitness Information Technology. Reproduced with permission of the publisher.

in-depth qualitative investigation in which they identified nine major psychosocial theme categories related to athletic success. Associated with these nine theme categories were 28 specific factors. The theme categories included ambitions, choice of sport, motives, success attributions, sacrifices, obstacles, emotional support, informational support, and tangible support. Specific factors identified by more than 45 percent of the sample were (a) elite athlete ambitions, (b) enjoyment, (c) practice, (d) physical attributes, (e) parents and family, (f) practice partner, and (g) coaches.

Parents are becoming concerned about two troubling trends in youth sport participation. These include the trend toward early participation in competitive sport and the trend toward year-long involvement in a single sport (Pennington, 2003). Many parents worry that if they don't start their children young, the children will not be able to play their sports when they get into high school. Consequently, children start playing at a young age, often at the expense of school and other social activities. The trend toward year-long involvement in a single sport is particularly stressful on parents and children. In many cases different sports compete for a child's time, with parents frantically running to and fro to get the kids to practice and games. Too much sport involvement can lead to burnout in sport, a topic we will address in detail in chapter 17.

Summary

Three models of self-confidence were discussed. They included Bandura's theory of self-efficacy, Harter's competence motivation theory, and Vealey's multidimensional model of sport-confidence. Self-efficacy is the belief an individual holds that he can accomplish a specific task, and as such, is a form of situation-specific self-confidence. Factors required to develop self-efficacy include successful performance, vicarious experience, verbal persuasion, and emotional arousal. Harter's competence motivation theory is based upon mastery attempts and an individual's innate desire to be competent. Vealey's sport-confidence model shows how sources of sport-confidence lead to sport-confidence, which leads to enhanced performance.

Psychological momentum was defined as "a positive or negative change in cognition, affect, physiology, and behavior caused by an event or series of events that will result in a commensurate shift in performance and competitive outcome." Three different models for explaining psychological momentum were discussed. The three models were the antecedents-consequences model, the multidimensional model, and the projected performance model. Research supports the antecedents-consequences and multidimensional models over the projected performance model.

Notwithstanding the passage of Title IX, girls and women still lag behind men in the development of self-confidence relative to sport and exercise participation. Factors that contribute to this phenomenon include nature of the task, ambiguity of feedback information, and social comparison cues.

Vallerand and Losier's (1999) integrated model of intrinsic and extrinsic motivation is presented in this chapter as a unifying theory of motivation that includes the concepts of self-confidence, goal perspective, and attribution, with self-determination at its core. In the integrated theory, social factors and psychological mediators are conceptualized as determinants of motivation.

Self-determination and choice are best conceptualized as being on a continuum relative to motivation. The most self-determining kind of motivation is intrinsic motivation. Extrinsic motivation may be conceptualized as being completely external in nature and therefore low in self-determination, or it may be conceptualized as being internalized and having increasingly greater levels of self-determination.

Cognitive evaluation theory is a subtheory to Vallerand and Losier's integrated theory of motivation. Cognitive evaluation theory posits that extrinsic motivation has the potential of diminishing an individual's intrinsic motivation. There are two components to the theory. The controlling aspect of the theory predicts that intrinsic motivation will be reduced if extrinsic motivation is perceived as being controlling. The informational aspect of the theory predicts that extrinsic motivation will actually enhance intrinsic motivation if an external reward is perceived as being suggestive of personal competence.

Historically, youth sports originated in the United States free from adult supervision. Children enjoyed unsupervised marbles, crack-the-whip, capture-the-flag, soccer, and all sorts of variations of baseball and other sports. Highly competitive youth sports programs emerged in the United States as early as the 1920s and 1930s.

The benefits of sports and the reasons youth participate in sports include having fun, learning new sport skills, getting physically fit, experiencing the excitement of competition, and making new friends. Other benefits include learning to cooperate, learning to be a good sport, and gaining self-confidence and self-esteem.

There are also potential negative consequences associated with youth sports participation. These include an inordinate focus upon competition and winning, increased anxiety and stress associated with a competitive sports climate, and violence among adults.

Research shows that the dropout rate for organized youth sport programs is 35 percent for any given year. Surface as well underlying psychological causes were discussed as reasons children drop out of a specific sport or out of sport altogether. Perhaps the major reasons children drop out of sport are "a change of interest" or simply "other things to do."

A number of programs have been developed for training youth sport volunteer coaches. These include the American Sport Education Program (ASEP), the Program for Athletic Coaches' Education (PACE), and Coach Effectiveness Training (CET).

The chapter concluded with a discussion of ways in which coach-parent relationships can be enhanced. The guiding principle for effective coach-parent relationships is good communication. Coaches must take the initiative to encourage communication, but at the same time they must identify the parameters for when the communication should take place. A parents' "code of conduct" was discussed. Different types of problem parents were described and ways to handle them were suggested.

Finally, a section was devoted to parental concerns and involvement in youth sport.

Critical Thought Questions

1. How do you think situation-specific self-confidence can be best developed in athletes? Provide a model and a theory.

2. Do you think that situation-specific self-confidence developed in one sport situation can be transferred to another situation or even to global self-confidence? Explain and defend your response.

3. Is psychological momentum fact or fiction? How do you feel about the projected performance model of psychological momentum?

4. Do you think the effects of Title IX on sport have completely eliminated the disparity in self-confidence sometimes exhibited by men and women? Explain and defend your answer.

5. Using the integrated theory of motivation as your knowledge base, describe the steps you would follow in making sure that your own child is motivated to succeed in some particular sport or activity.

6. What can coaches do to make sure that their athletes develop the characteristic and perception of being autonomous in the way they interact with their environment?

7. From a practical perspective, discuss steps you as a coach or parent can take to make sure that extrinsic motivation does not have the undesirable effect of reducing an athlete's intrinsic motivation.

8. Some people believe that the only way to have a good non-school-sponsored youth sports program is to deny parents access to it. How do you feel about this argument? Does it make sense? Can there be a volunteer youth sports program without parents?

9. Discuss ways in which youth sports programs can feature healthy, stimulating competition without focusing upon winning. Is this possible?

10. Other than banning parents, how do you solve the problem of adult violence in youth sports?

11. What would you include in a training session for volunteer coaches if you were in charge?

Glossary

achievement situation A condition of expectation that one's performance will be subject to evaluation.

additive principle The notion that an athlete low in intrinsic motivation will participate in a competitive situation if there is an extrinsic reward or motivation.

autotelic experience An experience that is entered into as an end in itself. The doing is its own reward.

amotivation The complete lack of any kind of motivation.

autonomy The belief a person has that she is in control of her destiny and her own actions and choices.

cognitive evaluation theory A theory that proposes that external rewards may have either a controlling or an informational effect upon the person receiving the reward.

collective self-efficacy The collective exhibition by a team of the perception of self-confidence, or self-efficacy.

competence motivation An individual's belief that he is competent, which leads to the motivation to try to learn new tasks.

controlling aspect of extrinsic motivation A term describing the tendency of people who come to perceive that their behavior is controlled by external forces to respond with decreased levels of intrinsic motivation.

discounting principle The notion that intrinsic motivation is reduced, or discounted, when rewards are not justified.

efficacious pawn A competent individual who performs a task for an external reason or cause.

external regulation The least self-determined form of extrinsic motivation.

extrinsic motivation Motivation that comes from an external as opposed to an internal source.

general-sport dropout A child who withdraws from sport participation altogether.

global self-confidence A personality trait or disposition to be a self-confident person.

"hot hand" myth The belief that performance of an athlete temporarily improves following a string of success.

identified regulation The process by which an athlete engages in an activity that he doesn't perceive as being particularly interesting, but does so because he sees the activity as being instrumental to obtaining another goal that is interesting to him.

informational aspect of extrinsic motivation A term describing the tendency of people who come to perceive that extrinsic motivation provides them with information that suggests personal competence to respond with increased levels of intrinsic motivation.

integrated regulation The process by which an extrinsic motivation has been fully integrated or internalized by the individual. In terms of self-determination, it is very similar to intrinsic motivation.

internalization The process by which rewards and other forms of extrinsic motivation become less external and more internal.

intrinsic motivation Motivation that comes from within the individual.

introjected regulation Extrinsic motivation that has undergone only partial internalization.

motives for participation Reasons children give for why they participate in sports. They may also be considered benefits of sports participation.

multiplicative principle The notion that extrinsic motivation interacts with intrinsic motivation to either add to or detract from it.

overjustification principle The excessive or inappropriate giving of external rewards as an incentive to participate in an otherwise interesting activity. To the extent that this represents an over-justification for participating, it may result in a reduction in intrinsic motivation.

parents' code of conduct Ten standards of conduct that a parent of a youth in sports agrees to respect.

participatory modeling The learner first observes a model perform a task, then the model or instructor assists the athlete in successfully performing the task.

precipitating event An important event in an athletic contest that precipitates psychological momentum.

professional sports model Model of a commercial sports enterprise in which the stated goals are to entertain and to make money.

psychological momentum A positive or negative change in cognition, affect, physiology, and behavior that will result in a shift in performance and outcome.

reflected appraisal process An appraisal process that is a function of the actual appraisal of others, one's own appraisal of self, and one's perception of how others appraise him.

relatedness The basic need to relate to other people, to care for others and have others care for you.

reversed-dependency trap A situation in which a parent comes to define his own sense of self-worth in terms of the success and failure of his son or daughter.

self-determination A unifying concept that brings meaning to the overall concept of motiva-

tion. It refers to a person's having autonomy and agency to act for herself and to make her own decisions.

self-determination continuum The notion that extrinsic motivation lies on a continuum relative to self-determination and to the degree that extrinsic motivation has been internalized.

self-efficacy A person's belief that she is competent and can succeed in a particular task.

situation-specific self-confidence The sense of sureness a person has that he can be successful at a specific task or sport.

social comparison Comparing one's own performance with another person's performance.

specific-sport dropout A child who withdraws from participation in one specific sport, but not from participation in all sports.

sport-confidence The perception of confidence in a sport-related achievement situation.

surface reasons for withdrawal from sport The reasons that children give for withdrawling from sport, which seldom reflect deeper psychological reasons.

underlying psychological reasons for withdrawal from sport "Deeper" reasons children drop out of sports: stress, fear of failure, loss of self-esteem, and loss of self-confidence.

youth sports Nonschool youth sports programs, designed to develop desirable physical and psychosocial characteristics in young athletes.

youth sports model Sports model dedicated to the development of desirable physical and psychosocial characteristics in young athletes.

Goal Perspective Theory

KEY TERMS

Achievement motivation
Adaptive motivational pattern
Cognitive restructuring
Competitive climate
Competitive orientation
Differentiated goal perspective
Ego involvement
Ego goal orientation
Goal involvement
Goal orientation
Maladaptive motivational
  pattern
Mastery climate
Mastery orientation
Matching hypothesis
Motivational climate
Perceived ability
Social approval goal orientation
Sportspersonship
Task involvement
Task goal orientation
Undifferentiated goal
  perspective

In this chapter we will introduce a theory of motivation that focuses upon the different ways children and adults think about their own competence and about the different ways they conceptualize ability. The phrase *goal perspective theory* was introduced by researchers to describe this approach to theorizing about motivation. The word "goal" in the phrase is a little confusing because goal perspective theory is not about setting goals; it is about the different ways that athletes approach and think about achievement situations. By way of example, consider the goal perspective orientations of two hypothetical athletes. Joe is 16 years old and has been playing tennis competitively for four years. His friends describe him as being a highly competitive person because he becomes very distraught if he loses a match. Winning seems to mean everything to him. For example, he once commented to a friend that he didn't care how he played the game, just as long as he was victorious. Contrast this orientation with that of Mary, a 16-year-old gymnast who has been competing for eight years but approaches every tournament from the perspective of having fun and doing her very best. Because of her work ethic and desire to excel, she puts in many hours of practice, but never seems to get overly upset when she does not win a competition. Her friends describe her as a person who strives for perfection but does not seem to be caught up in defeating her opponent. Her focus always seems to be on self-improvement and working hard. With this lay introduction to goal perspective theory, let us now turn our attention to a more theoretical discussion of goal perspective theory.

Nicholls' (1984, 1989) theory of motivation provides a framework for considering individuals' motivational perspectives across the lifespan. Nicholls' developmentally based theory of **achievement motivation** is a logical extension of both Bandura's theory of self-efficacy and Harter's theory of competence motivation. According to Nicholls (1984) and Duda (1989), the defining feature of achievement motivation is the way children come to view their own **perceived ability.** In goal perspective theory, the nature of perceived ability changes initially as a function of developmental level of the child, and later as a function of learning and **cognitive restructuring.** The sections of this chapter are logically developed to assure a systematic and clear understanding of the important concepts that make up Nicholls' goal perspective theory. Important concepts to be discussed in this chapter include (a) achievement goal orientations, (b) the developmental nature of goal orientation, (c) measuring goal orientation, (d) goal involvement, (e) goal orientation and moral reasoning, and (f) characteristics of task and ego goal orientation.

Athletes exhibiting a mature goal orientation understand the difference between ability, effort, and luck. Courtesy University of Missouri–Columbia Sports Information.

Achievement Goal Orientation

There are two **goal orientations** mentioned by Nicholls. They are task orientation and ego orientation. These two orientations are referred to as goal orientations because they differ as a function of the individual's achievement goal. In the case of **task goal orientation,** the goal is mastery of a particular skill. Perceived ability for the task-oriented individual is a function of perceived improvement from one point in time to the next. The task-oriented athlete perceives herself to be of high ability if she can perform a task better today than she could one week ago. The task-oriented individual continues to work for mastery of the skill she is working on, and enjoys feelings of self-efficacy and confidence in so doing.

At this point, you are probably thinking that everyone must be task oriented, because everyone enjoys mastering a task. Not necessarily. At some point in our lives we become aware of the consequences of social comparison. When we start to make social comparisons, we adopt a different sort of goal orientation. It is no longer enough simply to gain mastery over a skill and make personal improvements. We must also demonstrate that we can outperform another individual or other individuals. For the person with an **ego goal orientation,** perceived ability is measured as a function of outperforming others, as opposed to self-improvement. In some ways, this is a sorry state of affairs, as the ego-oriented individual's perceived ability and self-confidence is tied to how he compares with others as opposed to objective improvement in skill.

> Life used to be so simple. When I was a child I thought I was doing pretty good if I could skip a rock across a small stream. Now things are different. Not only do I have to skip the rock across the stream, but I have to do it better than the guy next to me (Anonymous).

Traditionalists such as Treasure, Duda, Hall, Roberts, Ames, and Maehr (2001) argue persuasively that there are only two basic goal orientations (task and ego goal orientation), while researchers such as Harwood, Hardy, and Swain (2000) have argued that a third or even fourth goal orientation might exist. For example, Gernigon, d'Arripe-Longueville, Delignieres, and Ninot (2004) conducted a qualitative study on judo competitors who they claimed revealed a third perspective for conceptualizing goal orientation. They described this third goal orientation to be ego involved in nature, but with a focus on avoiding embarrassment or defeat, as opposed to wanting to outperform the opponent. Two other groups of researchers identified **social approval goal orientation** to be a third goal perspective (Schilling & Hayashi, 2001; Stuntz & Weiss, 2003). Social goal orientation emphasizes the desire for social

acceptance through conformity to norms while displaying maximum effort.

Developmental Nature of Goal Orientation

According to Nicholls (1984, 1989), a child two to six years old views perceived ability in terms of how well she performed the task the last time. If the child notices an improvement in performance from time one to time two, she naturally assumes that ability has increased and that she is competent at performing the task. High amounts of effort in mastering the task are perceived by the child as evidence of high ability and competence. Competence is perceived by the child as a function of hard work and absolute capacity. At this early age, the child is said to be task oriented, as opposed to ego oriented.

At the age of six or seven, the child begins to view perceived ability in terms of how other children perform. The child becomes ego oriented, as opposed to task oriented. No longer is it enough to perform the task better than she performed it the last time; the child must now perform the task better than other children do. Perceived ability is now a function of one's own capacity as it is relative to that of others, as opposed to being a function of absolute ability. High ability and competence are only perceived as such if they are better than the performance of others.

After age 11 or 12, the child may exhibit either a task- or an ego-involved disposition, depending upon the situation at hand. Environmental factors causing a person to focus upon social comparisons will result in an ego-oriented disposition, while situations causing a person to focus upon personal mastery and improved performance will foster a task-oriented disposition.

From a developmental perspective, children mature with respect to how well they are able to differentiate between the concepts of effort, ability, and outcome. According to Nicholls, children pass developmentally through four levels as they

CONCEPT   Children pass through four developmental levels in terms of their understanding of the concepts of effort, ability, and outcome. In Level 1 they cannot differentiate among concepts of effort, ability, and outcome; by Level 4, they can.

APPLICATION   Knowing where a child is in the developmental hierarchy will help the adult leader to plan activities for children. Keeping score with children in Level 1 makes no theoretical sense. If all the children try equally hard, they should exhibit the same ability and have the same score. That is how children in the first level see things, and forcing them to think in terms of winning and losing is only confusing.

come to fully understand these three concepts, as well as the concepts of luck and task difficulty.

Level 1   At this early level, the child views effort, ability, and outcome as the same thing. At this level of development, the child is said to have an **undifferentiated goal perspective.** To the child at this age level, effort, or trying hard, is the same as ability or having a successful outcome. Furthermore, the child has no concept of how luck differs from ability or how one task can be more difficult than another.

Level 2   At Level 2, the child is beginning to recognize that there is a difference between effort and ability, but the child believes that effort is the major determinant of achieving success. If you try hard and expend lots of effort, you will find success.

Level 3   The third level is transitional, in the sense that the child is beginning to differentiate between ability and effort. Sometimes the child will recognize that effort is not the same as ability, but at other times he will revert back to an undifferentiated conceptualization of the two.

Level 4   Children and adults in Level 4 have a **differentiated goal perspective.** At around age 12, the child can clearly distinguish among the concepts of ability, effort, luck, and outcome. She also clearly understands the ramifications of task difficulty and recognizes that some tasks (opponents) will be more difficult than others. For example, the child understands that effort enhances performance of tasks requiring high ability (skill), but not that of tasks requiring luck. Furthermore, the child understands that low effort coupled with strong performance is probably indicative of high ability.

Research by Fry (2000) and Fry and Duda (1997) shows support for Nicholls' developmental theory of achievement motivation in the physical or sport and exercise domain. Children do in fact pass through these four developmental levels. Children in Level 1 exhibit a task goal orientation, but this is not by choice. The child simply cannot differentiate between effort and ability, so he thinks only in terms of mastery and trying hard. Children and adults in Level 4 have a mature concept of the meaning of effort and ability, and can therefore learn to exhibit either a task or an ego orientation toward achievement or competitive situations.

As a child matures, he will go from being task goal oriented to being more ego goal oriented. After the age of around 12, however, goal orientations fluctuate as a function of life's experiences as well as personality characteristics. Of interest is the effect that significant others may have on goal orientation in children. Carr and Weigand (2002) studied the relationship between the goal orientation of students ages 11 to 15 with their perception of their teachers, coaches, peers and sport heroes' goal orientations. Results showed that task-oriented children perceive significant others and sport heroes to favor a task-oriented learning environment.

Young children cannot differentiate between ability and effort, perceiving that trying hard is the same as ability. Conversely, older children can differentiate between effort and ability, recognizing that great effort may not mean success if ability is lacking. In a study reported by Chase (2001), measures of effort and persistence, future self-efficacy, and attributions for failure were obtained on 289 children of different sexes and ages (grades 3, 5, and 8) following a failure scenario. Dividing participants as a function of current self-efficacy, it was observed that (a) younger children score higher on effort than older children, and (b) low self-efficacy children attributed perceived failure to lack of ability more than high self-efficacy children did.

Measuring Goal Orientation

In order to determine whether individuals exhibit task and/or ego goal orientations, a number of inventories have been developed. These are the Task and Ego Orientation in Sport Questionnaire (TEOSQ), the Perceptions of Success Questionnaire (POSQ), and the Sports Orientation Questionnaire (SOQ). The TEOSQ (Duda, 1989; White & Duda, 1994) is composed of 15 items that measure task and ego orientation. The POSQ (Roberts, 1993; Roberts & Treasure, 1995) is composed of 12 items that measure competitiveness (ego orientation) and mastery (task orientation). The SOQ (Gill, 1993; Gill & Deeter, 1988) is composed of 25 items and purports to measure competitiveness, win orientation, and goal orientation. It is unclear, however, exactly how each of these factors compares with basic task and ego orientations (Marsh, 1994). Similar to the TEOSQ, a new 10-item inventory called the Goal Orientation in Exercise Scale (GOES; Kilpatrick, Bartholomew, & Reimer, 2003) was developed to measure task and goal orientation in the exercise as opposed to the sport environment.

The TEOSQ and the POSQ result in separate scores representing an athlete's level of task orientation and ego orientation. Somewhat confusing is the fact that in the POSQ, task orientation is named **mastery orientation** and ego orientation is named **competitive orientation.** It would appear, however, that the mastery and competitive orientation labels are more descriptive of the concepts being measured. While somewhat controversial (Harwood, Hardy, & Swain, 2000; Pierce & Burton, 1998), the two goal orientations are conceptualized as being independent of each other. An individual can be high on both orientations, low on both, or some combination of high and low on both.

The notion that task and ego goal orientations are independent, or orthogonal to each other, is supported in the sport psychology literature (Gernigon et al., 2004; Harwood & Hardy, 2001; Harwood & Swain, 2001). This means that an athlete can be task and ego goal oriented at the same time. In other words, being high on task orientation does not necessarily mean that that you have to be low on ego goal orientation. The two goal orientations are not at opposite ends of the same continuum. This concept is illustrated clearly in figure 6.1.

FIGURE 6.1 | Task and goal orientation are independent or orthogonal to each other.

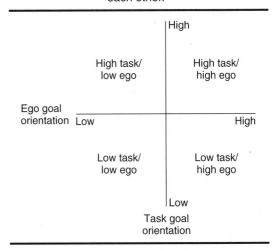

Goal Involvement

Related to the measurement issue is the observation by Nicholls (1989) and L. Williams (1998) that there are really two types of goal perspective. One is referred to as goal orientation as described above, and the other is called goal involvement. Instruments such as the TEOSQ and POSQ measure goal orientation (i.e., task and ego orientation) and represent dispositional or personality traits relative to the two orientations. Conversely, **goal involvement** is a situation-specific state measure of how an individual relates to an achievement situation at a specific point in time.

According to Nicholls (1989), situations that heighten awareness of social evaluation induce a state of **ego involvement,** accompanied by feelings of increased anxiety. Conversely, situations that do not heighten an awareness of social evaluation evoke a state of **task involvement,** accompanied by feelings of low anxiety. To be ego involved is to display characteristics of an ego-oriented person in a specific situation. To be task involved is to display characteristics of a task-oriented person in a specific situation. As might be surmised, goal involvement is greatly influenced by the motivational climate or environment, a topic we will discuss in the next section.

L. Williams (1998) reported an investigation in which the concept of goal involvement was measured and studied in a sport-related environment. In this investigation, goal involvement was measured using the Goal Involvement in Sport Questionnaire (GISQ), which is nothing more than the TEOSQ with situation-specific instructions. Instead of asking an athlete how she generally felt relative to an item on the TEOSQ, Williams asked the athlete to indicate how she felt "right now" on the same item relative to a current situation. In the Williams study, the "current situation" was either a team practice or a team competition. The results of the investigation confirmed that athletes exhibit higher levels of task involvement and lower levels of anxiety prior to a practice than prior to an actual game.

Motivational Climate

We don't really look at 8–0, we look at each match. We try to prepare for each match that we are going to play, and our focus is what we're doing out on the court. Regardless of the opponent we've got to prepare to play and we've got to take care of business. And if we work hard hopefully good things will happen (Susan Kreklow, Volleyball Coach, University of Missouri–Columbia, Hopp, 2000).

Perhaps of greater import than whether an individual is task or ego oriented is the **motivational climate** that the individual is placed in. Just as individuals can be task or ego oriented, learning environments can also be task or ego oriented. An ego-oriented environment, with its emphasis upon social comparison, can be particularly harmful to low-ability youth. Conversely, high-ability children seem to thrive in either environment. The effects of a mastery-, or task-oriented, learning environment can reverse the negative effects of an ego orientation (Amos, 1992).

The Perceived Motivational Climate on Sport Questionnaire (PMCSQ; Seifriz, Duda, & Chi, 1992) and the PMCSQ–2 (Newton, 1994; Newton, Duda, & Yin, 2000) were developed to assess an athlete's perception of whether a motivational climate emphasized mastery-based (task orientation) or competitive-based (ego orientation) goals. A **mastery climate** is one in which athletes receive positive reinforcement from the coach when they (a) work hard, (b) demonstrate improvement, (c) help others learn through cooperation, and (d) believe that each player's contribution is important. A **competitive climate** is one in which athletes perceive that (a) poor performance and mistakes will be punished, (b) high-ability athletes will receive the most attention and recognition, and (c) competition between team members is encouraged by the coach. For purposes of clarification, it should be noted that in the literature "competitive climate" is often referred to as "performance climate."

As one reflects upon the differences between the two climates, it is instructive to reflect back once again on Bill Walton's contrast of the coaching styles of his own college coach, John Wooden, and Bobby Knight. In light of what is written above about the two contrasting motivational climates, consider Bill Walton's poignant statement:

> We all need motivation. It's a particularly important aspect of sports because the tiniest of margins often separates the winners from the losers. Yet with Knight, we're not talking about a constructive approach to making people perform by challenging them on their positions or on their failures in life. Knight does it to denigrate. Doesn't Indiana know that universities are supposed to be about how you teach? Teaching is about building confidence, about making people feel better about what they do and who they are (Walton, 2000, p. 96).

In explaining goal perspective theory, we have introduced and explained two different kinds of goal orientation, two different kinds of goal involvement, and two different kinds of motivational climate. These several concepts are summarized in table 6.1.

Epstein (1989) and Treasure and Roberts (1995) have proposed that a mastery-oriented climate can be created by the coach or teacher that will be instrumental in developing and fostering self-confidence and intrinsic motivation in youth sport participants. As originally coined by Epstein,

the acronym TARGET has come to represent the manipulation of environmental conditions that will lead to a mastery climate conducive to the development of intrinsic motivation. It is proposed that coaches address each of these conditions in order to create a mastery environment. The conditions are as follows:

1. *Tasks*—Tasks involving variety and diversity facilitate an interest in learning and task involvement.

2. *Authority*—Students should be given opportunities to participate actively in the learning process by being involved in decision making and monitoring their own personal progress.

3. *Reward*—Rewards for participation should focus upon individual gains and improvement, and away from social comparisons.

4. *Grouping*—Students should be placed in groups so that they can work on individual skills in a cooperative learning climate.

5. *Evaluation*—Evaluation should involve numerous self-tests that focus upon effort and personal improvement.

6. *Timing*—Timing is critical to the interaction of all of these conditions.

Motivational climate is important because it can influence both goal orientation (disposition) and goal involvement (state). Over time, an emphasis on a mastery or task goal climate can cause an athlete to have more of a mastery goal

TABLE 6.1 | Characteristics of Different Types of Goal Orientation, Goal Involvement, and Motivational Climate

Goal Orientation (Personality Trait)	Goal Involvement (Psychological State)	Motivational Climate (Environment)

1. Task or Mastery Orientation
   a. Effort important
   b. Mastery important
	1. Task or Mastery Involvement
	   a. Athlete works hard
	   b. Athlete strives for mastery
		1. Mastery Climate
		   a. Effort rewarded
		   b. Cooperation emphasized

2. Ego or Competitive Orientation
   a. Social comparisons important
   b. Winning important
	2. Ego or Competitive Involvement
	   a. Athlete defines ability as winning
	   b. Athlete strives to win
		2. Competitive Climate
		   a. Mistakes punished
		   b. Competition encouraged

CONCEPT The climate and environment created by the coach or teacher can be a powerful determinant as to whether a young athlete will increase in intrinsic motivation and self-confidence.

APPLICATION TARGET structures provide specific suggestions as to how the coach can create an atmosphere conducive to the development of self-confidence and the motive to achieve success.

Factors such as making practices interesting, involving athletes in decision making, basing rewards on individual gains, and creating an atmosphere of cooperation are all important TARGET structures. Other strategies used by coaches to enhance self-confidence include (a) instruction/drilling, (b) encouraging positive self-talk, (c) acting self-confident, (d) liberal use of praise, and (e) physical conditioning sessions.

CONCEPT Perceived ability moderates the effect that a high competition motivational climate will have on self-esteem. Those most vulnerable to a loss of self-esteem associated with an ego-involved competitive environment are the low-ability athletes.

APPLICATION Coaches must be mindful that a planned competitive environment affects each member of a team differently. High-ability athletes will probably not be negatively affected by

an ego-involved climate, but they can benefit from a mastery climate. Because a mastery climate promises beneficial outcomes for all athletes, the focus of practice situations should be upon teamwork, skill mastery, and cooperative behavior that will be beneficial to the whole team. Competitive game-like situations can be beneficial to all athletes if they are organized in a way that does not always result in the low-ability athletes' losing or coming up second best.

orientation (Gano-Overway & Ewing, 2004; Harwood & Swain, 2002; Weigand & Burton, 2002). With this in mind, it is useful to examine the positive benefits of creating a mastery-focused motivational climate for athletes. Some of the benefits associated with a mastery motivational climate include enhanced perception of competence, increased satisfaction, reduced boredom, perceived ability, reduced rough play, heightened effort, greater enjoyment, and increased self-esteem (Boixados, Cruz, Torregrosa, & Valiente, 2004; Halliburton & Weiss, 2002; Weigand & Burton, 2002). An investigation reported by

Reinboth and Duda (2004) is of particular interest, as it shows how motivational climate can interact with perceived ability to affect self-esteem. A motivational climate that is highly ego involved (competitive environment) can have a deleterious effect upon self-esteem, but only when associated with perceived low ability. This means that in the presence of an ego-involved environment, self-esteem is protected if the athlete enjoys the perception of high personal ability. As illustrated in figure 6.2, this also means that the low-ability athlete is particularly vulnerable to a decline in self-esteem in the presence of a competitive environment.

FIGURE 6.2 | The deleterious effects of an ego-involved competitive climate on a perceived low-ability athlete's self-esteem.

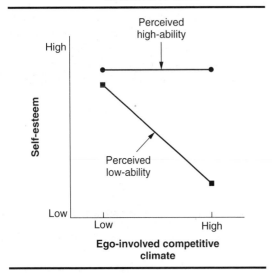

Source: Reinboth & Duda, 2004.

Goal Orientation and Moral Functioning

In this section we relate the concept of moral functioning with the concept of good or bad **sportspersonship.** Athletes who perform with a high level of moral functioning are said to exhibit good sportspersonship, while those exhibiting a low level of moral functioning are said to exhibit unsportspersonlike behavior. Low moral functioning is linked to goal orientation; because "the ego-oriented athlete's perceptions of competence are dependent on outdoing others, he or she may be more likely to break the rules and behave in an unsportspersonlike fashion when winning is at stake" (Kavussanu & Ntoumanis, 2003, p. 503). Conversely, task goal orientation is linked to sportspersonlike behavior because the athlete's focus is upon the task at hand and whether or not she performs up to her potential. With these basic

concepts in place, let's look at some of the recent literature on the subject.

Research by Kavussanu and Ntoumanis (2003) showed that participation in contact sports is predictive of an ego goal orientation, which in turn is predictive of lower levels of moral functioning in terms of judgments, intentions, and actual behaviors (more willingness to break rules, risk injury, and deliberately hurt opponents). This research showed a strong relationship between an ego goal orientation and reported low levels of moral functioning, while task orientation had the opposite effect. After reviewing the related literature, Kavussanu, Roberts, and Ntoumanis (2002) observed that unbridled competition reduces prosocial behavior, whereas cooperation enhances prosocial behavior. Observing the frequency of unsportspersonlike behaviors in competitive sport, they conclude with the following statement:

> The roots of unsportspersonlike conduct encountered in the sport context may reside within one's own athletic team. Many of the inappropriate actions we observe in the sport realm might be the result of certain social norms that become predominant in each team over time thereby reinforcing unsportspersonlike behaviors (Kavussanu et al., 2002, p. 362).

Lemyre, Roberts and Ommundsen (2002) measured dispositional goal orientation, perceived ability, and moral functioning in 511 male youth soccer players. Moral functioning was measured as a function of respect for social conventions, respect for rules and officials, respect for one's full commitment toward sport, and true respect and concern for the opponent. Results showed that (a) ego goal orientation has a negative effect on all four measures of sportspersonship, (b) perceived ability has a positive significant effect on all four measures of moral reasoning, and (c) perceived ability moderates (determines) the relationship between ego goal orientation and respect for rules and officials. The highest respect for rules and officials occurs with low ego goal orientation and

CONCEPT   An ego goal orientation and focus upon a competitive environment are related to low moral functioning and low sportspersonship. This relationship is due to the focus upon outperforming or defeating the opposition that is present in ego goal oriented/involved achievement situations.

APPLICATION   If as a coach or teacher you are concerned about the unsportspersonlike behavior of your athletes you must turn your attention to the kind of social environment that is fostered during practices and games. If the social norm is to win at all costs, then the seeds of unsportspersonship are embedded within the fabric of the team. This can only be reversed by changing the motivational climate of the team from being focused on competition and winning at all costs to one of cooperation and a focus upon effort, teamwork, and skill improvement.

---

high perceived ability, whereas the lowest respect occurs with high ego goal orientation and low perceived ability.

Similarly, Stuntz and Weiss (2003) studied the relationship between goal orientation (including social approval goal orientation) and moral functioning as measured by an instrument designed to measure legitimacy of and intention to use unsportspersonlike play during competition. Results showed that goal orientation predicts unsportspersonlike behavior, with an ego orientation being positively related to bad intentions, and task orientation being negatively related to bad intentions. For boys, but not girls, social approval goal orientation was predictive of bad intentions. If coach, friends, or peers approve, boys indicate a willingness to engage in unsportspersonlike behavior. Kavussanu and Roberts (2001) noted a sex difference relative to how male and female collegiate basketball players think about moral functioning. The female basketball players in this sample were more task goal oriented than the males and had higher levels of moral functioning. Utilizing a sample of young urban tennis players (50 percent African American), Fry and Newton (2003) reported that perceiving the tennis environment to be task involving is associated with liking the instructor and having a sense of sportspersonship. Conversely, perceiving the environment as ego involving was associated with not liking the instructor and poor sportspersonship.

Characteristics of Task and Ego Goal Orientations

A task or mastery goal orientation is associated with the belief that success is a function of effort and mastery. Mastery-oriented individuals feel most successful when they experience personal improvement that they believe is due to their hard work and effort. They gain a sense of accomplishment through learning and mastering a difficult task. Task-oriented individuals, regardless of their perception of personal ability, tend to exhibit **adaptive motivational patterns.** This means that they choose to participate in challenging tasks that allow them to demonstrate persistence and sustained effort. As a general rule, a mastery goal orientation is associated with positive perceptions and behaviors. Mastery-oriented persons focus on developing skill, exerting effort, and self-improvement (Carpenter & Yates, 1997; Fry & Duda, 1997; Williams, 1998).

An ego or competitive goal orientation is associated with the belief that success is a function of how well a person performs relative to other people. Ability is independent of effort. If a person performs well against other competitors, yet does not expend much effort, this is evidence of great ability. Thus, for the ego-oriented athlete, success is outperforming an opponent using superior ability as opposed to high effort or personal improvement.

CONCEPT & APPLICATION

An ego-oriented individual who has high perception of ability should exhibit adaptive motivational patterns (engage willingly in challenging tasks). However, an ego-oriented individual who has low perception of ability should exhibit a **maladaptive motivational pattern.** Because his motivation is to win and he does not believe he can win, he will not likely take part in a challenging activity. The obvious disadvantage of an ego orientation is that it discourages participation simply for the fun of it unless one is certain of experiencing success. In summary, ego-oriented individuals focus on beating others with minimal effort in order to enhance their social status (Carpenter & Yates, 1997; Fry & Duda, 1997; Williams, 1998).

Research on goal orientation has revealed that individuals who are high in task orientation can also be high in ego orientation; other combinations of the two orientations are also possible. In other words, the two orientations are independent of each other. The best combination is for a young athlete to be high in both orientations (Dunn, Dunn, Syrotuik, 2002). Individuals with high task and ego orientations exhibit the highest levels of motivation and perceived competence. The worst combination in terms of motivation and perceived competence is to be low in both task and ego orientations. Individuals in this category tend to be primarily young women. Children dominated by a task orientation tend to be more motivated than children dominated by an ego orientation (Fox, Goudas, Biddle, Duda, & Armstrong, 1994).

Several studies point to the superiority of a task orientation over an ego orientation in athletes. King and Williams (1997), utilizing martial arts students as participants, demonstrated that task but not ego orientation was related to martial arts performance. Furthermore, they observed that task orientation but not ego orientation was related to students' perceptions of satisfaction and enjoyment. Similarly, Vlachopoulos and Biddle (1999) reported a large-scale study in which goal orientation was measured in over one thousand British physical education students. The results of the investigation led investigators to conclude that a task orientation should be promoted for physical education students and athletes. Their data indicated that task and not ego orientation has the potential to promote success and positive affect in young athletes, independent of perceived ability.

While it sometimes appears from the literature that an ego goal orientation is usually undesirable, this conclusion is oversimplified and could be misleading. An ego goal orientation in the presence of a very low task goal orientation is undesirable, but in combination with a high level of task orientation, this is not necessarily the case. Using a statistical procedure called cluster analysis, Hodge and Petlichkoff (2000) grouped 257 rugby players into distinct goal orientation group combinations.

CONCEPT   It is not desirable for an athlete to be highly ego oriented if he harbors feelings of low ability. However, if an athlete perceives that he is highly skilled, then to be ego oriented is not entirely undesirable, especially if the athlete is also highly mastery oriented.

APPLICATION   It is always important to remember that the two types of goal orientation are independent of each other. Research has shown that in terms of performance, satisfaction, and enjoyment, it is best to be high in both task and ego orientation. The athlete's perception of his own ability is of critical importance. An athlete who is ego oriented and has low perception of ability is at risk of avoiding competitive challenges for fear of failing. For this reason, it is important for the coach or sport psychologist to be aware of an athlete's goal orientation and perception of ability.

(*Cluster analysis* magnifies differences between athletes in different groups while at the same time minimizing differences between athletes that are within the same cluster.)

The results showed that high levels of perceived rugby ability are associated with a high degree of ego orientation when coupled with high or moderately high levels of task orientation. Thus, in terms of perceived ability and competence, high levels of ego orientation are not necessarily bad. Cluster analysis further showed that level of ego orientation, and not level of task orientation, may be the critical factor in predicting perceived ability in rugby players. A moderate level of task orientation and high level of ego orientation yielded the highest level of perceived ability in the cluster analysis.

The observation that an ego goal orientation is not always bad was further clarified in a study reported by Wang and Biddle (2001). The focus of this investigation was upon goal orientation in combination with conceptions of ability and self-determination theory. In this study, 2,969 British students (ages 11–15) completed inventories measuring goal orientation, conceptions of ability, self-determination, and perceived competence. Using cluster analysis procedures, the researchers were able to differentiate five distinct cluster profiles ranging from highly motivated to amotivated. The two highest motivational clusters were characterized as being high in task goal orientation, able to view ability as changeable, high in self-determination, and high in perceived competence. The next-to-highest motivational cluster, however, was also high in ego goal orientation, making it clear that an ego goal orientation in combination with a high task orientation is associated with high levels of motivation.

Interaction between Goal Orientation and Motivational Climate

Based upon theory, it may be hypothesized that the best combination of goal orientation and motivational climate is to be task and ego oriented in conjunction with a mastery climate. This combination should yield the highest levels of actual performance, personal satisfaction, and enjoyment. Following this, in terms of desirability, would be the combination of high task orientation, low ego orientation, and a mastery climate. The least desirable combination would be to be low in both task and ego orientation and be placed in a competitive climate. The interaction between goal orientation and motivational climate is illustrated in figure 6.3 along with predictions of best performance, satisfaction, and enjoyment. As can be observed in this figure, best performance,

FIGURE 6.3 | In terms of a goal orientation by motivational climate interaction, best outcomes in terms of performance, satisfaction, and enjoyment are expected at cell 3 and 4, while the worst are expected at cell 5.

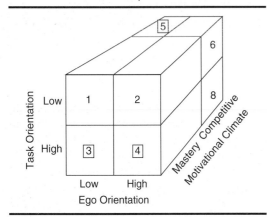

satisfaction, and enjoyment are predicted to occur in cells 3 and 4, with worst in cell 5. Research to confirm or modify these theoretical predictions in the physical domain has just recently begun to emerge.

Treasure (1997) measured elementary-age children's perceptions of motivational climate and related these perceptions to the children's perceptions of ability, satisfaction, attitudes, and boredom. A perceived climate that was high in competition but low in mastery yielded feelings of low effort, high ability, and high boredom. A perceived climate that was moderately high in competition and high in mastery yielded feelings associated with high satisfaction, belief that both ability and effort were important for success, and belief that the participant was high in ability. Treasure concluded that a mastery climate should be promoted and that a competitive climate should be deemphasized in order to increase motivation and self-confidence in children.

Treasure and Roberts (1998) measured perceived motivational climate and goal orientations of adolescent females. It was observed that a strong mastery climate was associated with feelings that effort was important for success, and a strong competitive environment was associated with feelings that ability and deception were important. Additionally, they were able to identify two interactions that support the hypothesis that an interactive relationship exists between goal orientation and motivational climate. In terms of predicting the belief that ability was important for success, it was observed that motivational climate interacts with goal orientation. Specifically, ego orientation moderates the relationship between a competitive climate and the belief that ability is important. If ego orientation was low, a competitive climate did not predict the importance of ability; if ego orientation was high, a competitive climate did predict the importance of ability. Furthermore, in terms of predicting the belief that mastery experiences were important for success, it was again observed that motivational climate interacts with goal orientation. Specifically, task orientation moderates the relationship between a mastery climate and the belief that mastery experiences were important. The perception that mastery experiences were important increased as the perception of mastery climate increased for both high and low task-oriented females, but at a faster rate for high task-oriented individuals.

Bar-Eli et al. (1997b) categorized male high school participants as being low task and low ego oriented, low task and high ego oriented, high task and low ego oriented, and high task and high ego oriented. They then had the participants from each goal orientation category participate in four separate 1600-meter races in which competitive and mastery climate conditions were manipulated. Best running times were recorded for the competitive conditions compared to the mastery conditions, with no evidence of an interaction with goal orientation. These results were counter to the expected results shown in figure 6.3.

CONCEPT   It is hypothesized that an interactive relationship exists between goal orientation and motivational climate in predicting such things as satisfaction, beliefs about success, performance, and enjoyment. The exact nature of this relationship, however, is not known at this time.

APPLICATION   It is important for the coach or sport psychologist to be aware of the goal orientation of the athletes, but also to be aware of the motivational climate that is being created for the athletes. The coach must recognize and be sensitive to issues raised by the athletes relative to a disparity between goal orientation and the motivational climate. Knowing why an ego-oriented athlete might object to a mastery-oriented climate should be of great use to the coach.

In an investigation reported by Newton and Duda (1999), the interaction between motivational climate and goal orientation was studied using junior female volleyball players. They investigated the hypothesis that best results in terms of predicting intrinsic motivation and expectations of success would occur in situations in which the motivational climate was matched with the goal orientation. In this model, best results should occur under conditions of high task orientation in a mastery climate and conditions of high ego orientation in a competitive environment. Looking at figure 6.3, best outcome would be expected in cells 3 and 4 when high task orientation and high mastery climate are matched; and in cells 6 and 8 when high ego orientation and high competitive climate are matched. The **matching hypothesis** was not supported in this research, but the investigators did observe that greater intrinsic motivation was observed in conditions of task orientation and mastery climate than in conditions of ego orientation and competitive climate. A significant interaction was observed between task orientation and task climate in predicting the belief that effort leads to success. Specifically, task orientation moderates the relationship between mastery climate and the belief that effort is important in determining success. As a perception of mastery climate increases, so does the perception that effort is important. But the strength of this relationship increases as task orientation increases from low to high. A high level of mastery environment in combination with a high level of task orientation yields the highest level of effort belief.

Related to the matching hypothesis, introduced above, is an important study underscoring the importance of goal orientation, perceived ability, and task difficulty to exerted effort and wall-climbing performance. In this investigation, the dispositional goal orientations and perceived ability of 500 French school boys ages 12 to 16 were measured (Sarrazin, Roberts, Cury, Biddle, & Famose, 2002). Based on these results, 78 boys with extreme scores in goal orientation and perceived rock climbing ability were assigned to one of four groups: (a) High Task (low ego) and High Perceived Ability (HPA); (b) High Task (low ego) and Low Perceived Ability (LPA); (c) High Ego (low task) and High Perceived Ability (HPA); and (d) High Ego (low task) and Low Perceived Ability (LPA). Following this, all 78 participants completed five 8-meter-high rock wall climbing courses (random), with their exerted effort (percentage of heart rate reserve) and performance recorded. During these five climbs, a motivational climate was created to match the group that they were assigned to (e.g., a mastery climate was created for boys high in task goal orientation). Results of the experiment were similar for both performance and exerted effort, with the results for effort illustrated in figure 6.4. Differences in exerted

FIGURE 6.4 | Effects of task difficulty, goal orientation, and perceived ability on exerted effort.

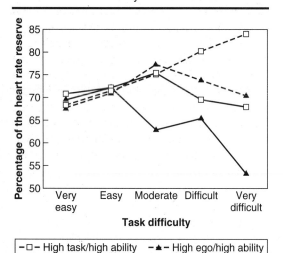

Task difficulty

-□- High task/high ability   -▲- High ego/high ability
-□- High task/low ability   -▲- High ego/low ability

Source: Adapted with permission from Sarrazin, P., Roberts, G., Cury, F., Biddle, S., & Famose, J.P. (2002). Exerted effort and performance in climbing among boys: The influence of achievement goals, perceived ability, and task difficulty. *Research Quarterly for Exercise and Sport, 73* (4), 425–36.

effort (HR reserve) do not become evident until the moderately difficult rock climbing courses are attempted. As the course becomes more difficult, the superiority of the group high in task goal orientation in combination with high perceived ability becomes more evident. Similarly, the inferiority of the group high in ego orientation and low in perceived ability becomes more evident as the task becomes more difficult. Perceived ability moderates (determines) the relationship between task difficulty and goal orientation on exerted effort and performance. Children who suffer from perceived low ability simply do not do well or try hard when confronted with a difficult climbing task. This is further exacerbated by having a disposition toward an ego goal orientation. In terms of goal orientation, it is important to note that this study does not address the situation that would occur if children were categorized as being high in both task and ego goal orientation at the same time (or vice versa). As indicated earlier, we would expect children high in perceived ability, task orientation, and ego orientation to perform well and to exert effort in challenging situations.

Summary

Goal perspective theory is a developmentally based theory of achievement motivation. Children pass through four developmental levels as they move from not being able to differentiate between ability and effort to being able to differentiate between the two at about 12 years of age. Three psychological constructs are important in understanding goal perspective theory. These three constructs are goal orientation, goal involvement, and motivational climate.

There are two dispositional goal orientations mentioned by Nicholls. These two are task orientation and ego orientation. The goal orientation that an athlete has determines how she will evaluate her own ability. Task-oriented children perceive ability as being a function of effort and mastery. Ego-oriented children perceive ability as being a function of social comparison. The terms *task* and *ego orientation* are used interchangeably with the terms *mastery* and *competitive orientation*. Additional goal orientations are suggested by some researchers.

Goal orientation is a personality disposition, whereas goal involvement is a situation-specific state, or way of responding to an achievement situation at a specific point in time. There are two kinds of goal orientations. They are task or mastery goal orientation and ego or competitive goal orientation.

Just as individuals can be task or ego oriented, motivational climates can be task or ego oriented. A task-oriented environment is referred to as a mastery climate, while an ego-oriented environment is referred to as a competitive climate. A mastery climate is one in which effort, mastery, and cooperation are emphasized. A competitive or performance climate is one in which social comparison and competition are emphasized. Research supports the efficacy of providing a mastery climate for enhancing learning, self-confidence, and perceived ability.

New research relating the concept of moral functioning to sportspersonship was discussed.

Research suggests a link between sportspersonship and task and ego goal orientation. Contact sports are linked to an ego goal orientation, which is predictive of lower levels of moral functioning in terms of judgments, intentions, and actual behaviors.

An important area of needed research is to study the interaction between goal orientation and motivational climate. Theory suggests that certain goal orientation dispositions should do best in certain motivational climates relative to success, satisfaction, and enjoyment. Sustained research in this area will be important in identifying the best strategies to help young athletes to become confident and motivated.

Critical Thought Questions

1. Goal orientations are described as being relatively stable personality dispositions. Yet, research suggests that a person's disposition to be ego involved can be changed over time to be more mastery oriented through long-term exposure to a mastery climate. Critically discuss this paradoxical issue.

2. It seems as though a child moves developmentally from having a task orientation relative to perceived ability to having an ego orientation at about age 12. Yet, a task orientation is often described as being more desirable than an ego orientation in terms of developing self-confidence and experiencing satisfaction and enjoyment in sport. Are we saying that moving backwards developmentally is desirable? Explain.

3. What do you think is the most desirable motivational climate for developing self-confidence and motivation in children and young athletes? Explain why you think this is so. Provide a detailed description of your ideal motivational climate.

4. Why would an ego goal orientation or competitive orientation be more associated with poor sportspersonship than a mastery goal orientation? What is there about the ego orientation that causes an athlete to be more willing to break rules and perhaps inflict harm on another athlete?

5. Bill Walton's discussion of the differences between the legendary John Wooden and Indiana's Bobby Knight seems to parallel the distinction between the two motivational climates described in this chapter. How do you feel about this comparison? How do you feel about Bill Walton's assessment of the two coaches? Incidentally, approximately three months after Walton wrote his article in *Time* magazine, Bobby Knight was fired as the men's basketball coach at Indiana. As we mentioned in an earlier chapter, he was later hired as head men's coach at Texas Tech University.

6. Develop and discuss your own theory as to how goal orientation and motivational climate should interact relative to success, satisfaction, and enjoyment.

Glossary

achievement motivation An athlete's predisposition to approach or avoid a competitive situation.

adaptive motivational pattern Motivation to participate in challenging activities.

cognitive restructuring The use of cognitive or mental skills to restructure or change the way one views certain situations.

competitive climate An environment in which athletes perceive that mistakes will be punished and competition between teammates will be encouraged.

competitive orientation Goal disposition that perceives ability as a function of outperforming others as opposed to self-improvement (see ego orientation).

differentiated goal perspective Ability of a child to clearly distinguish or differentiate among the concepts of ability, effort, luck, and outcome.

ego involvement A situation-specific manifestation of being ego- or competition-oriented. Similar to ego orientation.

ego goal orientation Goal disposition that perceives ability as being a function of outperforming others as opposed to self-improvement (see competitive orientation).

goal involvement A situation-specific state measure of how an individual relates to an achievement situation at a specific point in time.

goal orientation A person's disposition to be task goal oriented and/or ego goal oriented.

maladaptive motivational pattern Lack of motivation to participate in challenging activities.

mastery climate Environment in which athletes receive positive reinforcement from the coach

when they work hard, cooperate, and demonstrate improvement.

mastery orientation Goal disposition to view perceived ability as a function of effort and improvement (see task orientation).

matching hypothesis As used in this chapter, the term relates to matching a person's goal orientation with a person's motivational climate to bring about maximum achievement benefits.

motivational climate The motivational environment a person is placed in relative to factors that relate to mastery or competition.

perceived ability A conceptualization of ability that is based upon how a person views the relationships between ability, effort, mastery, and social comparison.

social approval goal orientation The desire for social acceptance through conformity to norms while displaying maximum effort.

sportspersonship Performance of athletic tasks with a high level of moral functioning. Those exhibiting a low level of moral functioning are said to exhibit unsportspersonlike behavior.

task involvement A situation-specific manifestation of being task- or mastery-oriented; similar to task orientation.

task goal orientation Goal disposition to view perceived ability as a function of effort and improvement (see mastery orientation).

undifferentiated goal perspective Point of view in which a child cannot distinguish or differentiate among the concepts of ability, effort, luck, and outcome.

PART 3

Effects of Arousal and Anxiety on Performance

Part III of the text is composed of two related chapters. Chapter 7 is devoted to a discussion of the neurophysiology of arousal and attention. The concepts of arousal and attention are covered in the same chapter because of their interrelatedness. The very act of focusing one's attention on an object is associated with a neurophysiological response. This response is commonly referred to as arousal or activation. Imagine that you are sitting at your computer writing a term paper when suddenly you hear a loud explosion outside your window. At the same time that your attention is diverted from your computer to the loud explosion, you experience a sudden increase in a number of physiological indicators of physiological arousal (e.g., heart rate and blood pressure). To make it possible for the student to more fully comprehend the concept of attention, we begin with a brief discussion of the neurophysiology of arousal. Building on our understanding of the physiology of arousal and attention, chapter 8 is dedicated to a discussion of anxiety, arousal, and stress relationships, and in particular, how they affect athletic performance. ∞

Neurophysiology of Arousal and Attention

KEY TERMS

Acetylcholine
Adrenal medullae
Arousal
Arousal response
Ascending reticular activating
   system
Associators
Attention control training
Attentional flexibility
Attentional focus
Attentional narrowing
Attentional style
Automatic processing
Autonomic nervous system
Bit
Capacity model
Centering
Central nervous system
Cerebral cortex
Chunking
Cognitive interference
Controlled processing
Cue utilization
Direction of attention
Dissociators
Distractibility
Electroencephalograph
Electromyograph
Epinephrine

Fight or flight response
Galvanic skin response
Gate out
Hypothalamus
Individual differences
Information conveyed
Information processing
   model
Long-term memory
Memory storage
Norepinephrine

Palmar sweating
Parasympathetic nervous
   system
Peripheral scanning
Playing in the zone
Processing capacity
Reaction time probe
Retrieval
Selective attention
Sensory register
Short-term memory

Skin conductivity
Skin resistance
Stress response
Sympathetic alarm
   response
Sympathetic nervous
   system
Thought stopping
Width of attention

Standing on the San Diego Chargers' 21-yard line with one minute remaining, down by 8 points and deadlocked with Dan Marino for the most touchdown passes in a season, [Peyton] Manning disregarded the play that was being shouted in his headset. He blocked out the 57,330 fans at the RCA Dome who stood in anticipation. He ignored his parents, Archie and Olivia, who had arrived with eight minutes left. Manning, famous for his onfield intensity and his intricate audibles, casually walked over to wide receiver Brandon Stokley and whispered an instruction heard more often in backyard touch football games than N.F.L. stadiums: Run a post. (Jenkins, 2004)

The brief story about Peyton Manning epitomizes the real-life manifestation of physiological arousal and attentional control. On December 26, 2004, in Indianapolis, Peyton Manning threw his 49th touchdown of the season, surpassing Dan Marino's record by one. This was not just a touchdown to set a record, however; it was also a score that put his team in position to win the game against San Diego. To win, the Colts needed (and achieved) a two-point conversion and a field goal in overtime to defeat San Diego 24 to 31. This interesting story sets the stage for the rest of this chapter.

Neurophysiology of Arousal

The story is told of an African hunter who, after losing his weapon, was pursued by a lion. He was running as fast as he could with the lion in hot pursuit, when he spotted a tree limb about 12 feet off the ground. Without breaking stride, he leaped with all his might, hoping to jump higher than he had ever imagined possible. As luck would have it, he missed the limb going up, but he caught it coming down! This tale illustrates an interesting fact about the phenomenon of arousal. When extremely aroused, we are capable of astonishing feats. However, note that the hunter in the story *missed* the tree limb going up. Luckily for him he caught it on the way down—but what does this say about his accuracy?

This section of the chapter is devoted to equipping the student with a basic understanding of the neurophysiology of arousal. This discussion does not include an in-depth discussion of the anatomical and physiological components of the human nervous system. For example, we will not be talking about the individual neurons, synapses, or neural transmission. The student is referred to a textbook on gross anatomy and physiology for such a discussion. Rather, we will focus upon basic structures in the central nervous system. In the second section of the chapter, we will engage in a fairly detailed discussion of attention and concentration as they relate to human performance psychology.

The neurophysiology of arousal is a little like the internal workings of an automobile engine. The engine may run at extremely high speeds, but without the transmission engaged, the car will not go anywhere. Similarly, an individual may be highly aroused as evidenced by heart rate, brain waves, and blood pressure, but without a purpose or goal, this energy is wasted. This analogy can be extended a little further by asking what happens to an engine if the transmission is engaged while the brakes are applied. This would put a great deal of stress on the engine, to the point that it could burn up. In the case of the individual, the brakes could be thought of as negative thoughts and feelings that interact with arousal to burn up the athlete (Landers & Arent, 2006).

If this book were about the automobile, this chapter would focus only upon the gas combustion engine. This chapter is about the neurophysiology of arousal and about a specific factor that interacts in arousal: attention. We will discuss other interacting factors in chapter 8. **Arousal** is a neutral physiological phenomenon that is associated with increases in heart rate, blood pressure, respiration, metabolism, and other indicators of activation. In chapter 8, arousal will be associated with negative and positive affective states, without being synonymous with either. The intent in this section is to give the reader a basic understanding of arousal from a neurophysiological perspective. Without this basic understanding, the student would not be able to fully appreciate the role that arousal and activation play in sport and exercise psychology. The reader is referred to Guyton (1991) for a more comprehensive treatment of the topic.

Major Divisions of the Nervous System

There are three major divisions of the nervous system. These three are (a) the central nervous system (CNS), (b) the peripheral nervous system, and (c) the autonomic nervous system. The CNS is composed of the brain, the brain stem, and the spinal cord. The peripheral nervous system provides innervation from the brain and spinal cord to all of the skeletal muscles of the body. It is the peripheral nervous system, through efferent pathways, that instructs skeletal muscles to contract and relax. It is the peripheral nervous system, through afferent pathways, that returns information from the skeletal muscles and joints back to the CNS. The autonomic nervous system innervates the glands and visceral organs of the body.

In this chapter we will focus upon specific parts of the CNS that are closely associated with the neurophysiology of arousal, and upon the autonomic nervous system. While the peripheral nervous system is certainly affected by arousal, it plays no role in the onset of the arousal response in humans. For this reason we will focus the balance of this section upon the CNS, the autonomic nervous system, the arousal response, and electrophysiological indicators of arousal.

Central Nervous System Structures Controlling Arousal

Fundamental to the concept of arousal is the notion that levels of activation come under the control of progressively higher levels of the nervous system. Structures of the **central nervous system** (CNS) that are closely related to the onset of the arousal response in humans include the cerebral cortex and hypothalamus in the brain, and the ascending reticular activating system in the brain stem (the area between the brain and the spinal cord). While these three CNS structures are most closely associated

with the neurophysiology of arousal, it would be simplistic to rule out the involvement of other parts of the CNS in affecting arousal.

Cerebral Cortex   The **cerebral cortex** is the area of the brain responsible for higher brain functions and conscious thought processes. The functional part of the cerebral cortex comprises a thin layer of neurons about 6 mm thick. The cerebral cortex contains 50 to 80 billion neurons and is divided up into frontal lobes, parietal lobes, occipital lobes, and temporal lobes. The frontal lobes contain areas that control thoughts, emotions, and skilled movements. The electrical activity of the cortex is measured with the electroencephalograph (EEG), from which an electroencephalogram is derived. The EEG can monitor frequency and amplitude of electrical potential changes in the brain. High states of arousal are associated with EEG waves that are asynchronous, fast, and of low amplitude. Low states of arousal are associated with a synchronous pattern of EEG waves (Guyton, 1991). The cerebral cortex is illustrated in figure 7.1.

FIGURE 7.1 | Three important brain structures associated with arousal.

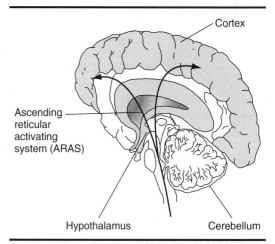

Source: From Philip W. Groves and Kurt Schlesinger, *Introduction to biological psychology,* 2nd ed. © 1979, Wm. C. Brown Publishers, Dubuque, Iowa. All rights reserved. Reprinted by permission.

Hypothalamus   The **hypothalamus,** located in the midbrain, represents less than one percent of total brain mass, yet plays a major role in controlling many bodily functions, including emotions and arousal. For example, stimulation of the lateral hypothalamus has been shown to result in increased activity and arousal, sometimes leading to rage and fighting behavior. Stimulation of other areas of the hypothalamus has been shown to result in reduced arousal, tranquility, eating behaviors, fear, and sexual drive. The location of the hypothalamus relative to the cerebral cortex is illustrated in figure 7.1.

Ascending Reticular Activating System

The reticular formation is a complex set of neurons and nuclei that extends throughout the brain stem and on up to the posterior hypothalamus. This network of neurons sends diffuse fibers throughout the nervous system and cerebral cortex. It appears that the reticular formation organizes sensorimotor behavior through its interconnections with the cerebral cortex, hypothalamus, and CNS. Along with the cortex and the hypothalamus, the activity of the reticular formation, and more specifically the **ascending reticular activating system** (ARAS), is closely associated with the onset of arousal. The ascending axons of the ARAS facilitate the activation of higher brain center neurons. Stimulation of the ARAS of sleeping animals results in EEG waves resembling those they would have if awake (Milner, 1970). When an individual perceives a situation to be threatening, the ARAS is activated, which in turn governs the sequence of neurological events leading to the arousal response. The ARAS is illustrated in figure 7.1 relative to the cortex and hypothalamus.

Autonomic Nervous System

The part of the nervous system that controls visceral and glandular functions of the body is called the **autonomic nervous system** (ANS). This system helps control arterial blood pressure, heart rate, urinary bladder emptying, body temperature, sweating, and many other body functions that are generally considered to be involuntary in nature. They are involuntary in the sense that you don't consciously increase arterial blood pressure in the same way that you flex a skeletal muscle. This is not to say, however, that many functions of the autonomic nervous system cannot be consciously controlled. Later in the text we will talk about managing stress, a concept based on the notion that many functions of the autonomic nervous system can be controlled.

One of the interesting characteristics of the ANS is how quickly and intensely it can change visceral and glandular functions. Within only a few seconds, the heart rate can be doubled, the bladder can empty, or palmar sweating can begin. Arterial blood pressure can double within ten seconds, or decrease in only five seconds to a level that can cause fainting. It is these rapid changes brought about by the ANS that are measured by the lie detector (polygraph) test. Changes in how people feel in response to certain questions can elicit significant changes in their physiological responses. With practice, however, some people can mask their true feelings and also how they respond physiologically to questions.

There are two major divisions to the ANS. The first is named the **sympathetic nervous system** and the second is the **parasympathetic nervous system.** The terminal nerve endings of all parasympathetic neurons secrete **acetylcholine,** while most sympathetic nerve endings secrete norepinephrine. These hormones act on different organs and glands to bring about their respective sympathetic and parasympathetic effects.

Sympathetic stimulation has an excitatory effect on some organs but an inhibitory effect on others. This is true also of parasympathetic stimulation. In some cases the sympathetic and parasympathetic systems operate reciprocally to each other. For example, the sympathetic nervous system causes the pupil of the eye to dilate, while the parasympathetic system causes it to constrict. In most cases, however, organs are dominantly controlled by one system or the other. Sweat glands are stimulated by the sympathetic nervous system, but not necessarily by the same hormone. Most sweat glands are activated by acetylcholine, but sweat glands in the palms are activated by norepinephrine. Sweating of the hands and palms is associated with increased anxiety and worry.

In contrast to the peripheral nervous system, the ANS requires only small amounts of neural stimulation to maintain normal bodily functions. The parasympathetic nervous system acts in very specific ways on organs and glands. Conversely, the sympathetic system often discharges as a complete unit in a massive and powerful way. This generally occurs when the hypothalamus is activated in response to fear or severe pain. The result is a widespread bodily reaction called the **sympathetic alarm response,** or the sympathetic **fight or flight response.** The sympathetic alarm reaction literally prepares the body to make a powerful physical response to protect against a perceived threat. Changes that take place in response to the fight or flight response include some or all of the following:

1. Increased blood flow to skeletal muscles
2. Increased rates of cellular metabolism
3. Increased arterial pressure and blood flow
4. Increased heart rate and force of contraction
5. Increased concentration of glucose in the blood
6. Increased eye pupil dilation
7. Increased cellular metabolism
8. Increased stimulation of the adrenal medullae
9. Decreased blood flow to organs and glands not essential to fighting against a perceived threat

The Adrenal Medullae and the Stress Response

All of the factors listed above come in response to simultaneous and massive stimulation of the organs innervated by the sympathetic nervous system. One pair of organs that is innervated by the sympathetic nervous system is the adrenal medullae. Each of the two **adrenal medullae** sits on top of a kidney. When stimulated by the sympathetic nervous system, the adrenal medullae release large amounts of **epinephrine** and **norepinephrine** into the bloodstream. The bloodstream carries these two hormones to all tissues in the body, where they affect the organs in the same way as does direct sympathetic nerve stimulation. The effects, however, of epinephrine and norepinephrine in the bloodstream last five to ten times as long, due to the time required to remove them from the blood (Guyton, 1991). The effects of epinephrine and norepinephrine on organs are nearly identical, except that epinephrine has a greater effect on stimulating the heart, while norepinephrine has a greater effect in terms of constricting arterial blood vessels in the muscles.

The total effect of massive stimulation of organs by the sympathetic nervous system and the adrenal medullae is to bring about the **stress response,** which has also been referred to as the alarm reaction, or fight or flight response. The neurophysiological events that lead up to the stress response are illustrated in figure 7.2. In considering the concepts illustrated in this figure, it is important to understand that the stress response is not the end product *every time* the sympathetic nervous system is activated. Most of the time, the parasympathetic and sympathetic nervous systems work together to bring about a state of homeostasis, or regularity, of bodily functions. What we might call the **arousal response** is the result of ANS activity, which ranges on a continuum from deep sleep to extreme excitement.

This chapter began with a story about a hunter who, running for his life, "missed his target going up but caught it on the way down." This phrase should have greater meaning now, because you understand how the activation of the sympathetic nervous system gave the fictional hunter the superhuman strength to avoid certain death. The phrase also has meaning in terms of the hunter's failure to accurately grasp the tree limb on the way up,

CONCEPT   When the brain senses danger, the sympathetic nervous system is activated in a massive way, producing the stress response or alarm reaction that prepares the individual for "fight or flight."

APPLICATION   The stress response is nature's way to prepare an individual to defend herself against harm and danger. Understanding the neurophysiology of arousal makes it possible for the sport psychologist to help an athlete cope with the extreme pressures of competition.

FIGURE 7.2 | Anatomical and physiological basis of the stress response.

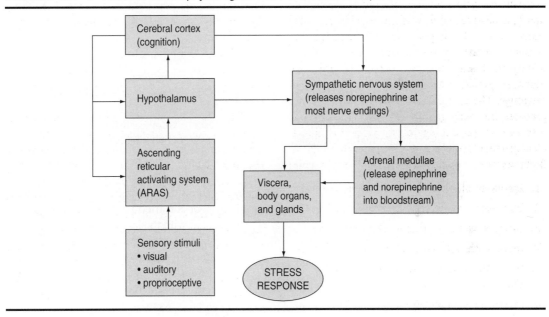

as he had intended. Researchers have consistently demonstrated that organisms seek to obtain a level of arousal that is ideal for the task at hand. This is generally considered to be a moderate level of arousal—not too much and not too little. The notion that both too little arousal (deep sleep) and too much arousal (terror) inhibit performance, while some moderate level of arousal facilitates performance, is the basis of the classic Yerkes-Dodson Law, to be discussed in chapter 8.

Electrophysiological Indicators of Arousal

Many electrophysiological methods exist for measuring arousal level. Some of the more common methods will be outlined here. We should remember, however, that no single measure of arousal can be considered completely accurate, as correlations among the various measures of arousal are very low (Tenenbaum, 1984). This means, for example, that an athlete exhibiting an increased heart rate might not necessarily exhibit increased arterial blood pressure or decreased palmar sweating. Understanding how physiological arousal is measured provides the student with additional insight into the arousal process and associated mechanisms.

1. *Electrocortical Activity in the Brain*   As discussed earlier, the electrical activity of the cerebral cortex can be measured by an **electroencephalograph** (EEG), which measures the amount and type of electrical activity put out between scalp electrodes. Alpha, beta, delta, and theta waves are observed in normal persons. Brain waves that differ in amplitude, frequency, and rhythmicity are given different names to distinguish them from each other. Generally, delta waves are of low amplitude and are associated with deep sleep. Beta and theta waves are generally associated with some level of stress or tension. When in a resting but awake state, normal individuals typically display rhythmic alpha waves. When they become suddenly alert, the synchronous and rhythmic alpha waves are replaced with asynchronous, higher-frequency beta waves. A skilled technician is required to interpret the meaning of the various brain waves (Guyton, 1991).

2. *Biochemical Indicators*   The arousal, or activation, response in the brain triggers the release of epinephrine and norepinephrine in the bloodstream by the adrenal medullae. Thus, one way to determine arousal levels is to directly measure the amount of epinephrine and norepinephrine in the blood. The accurate assessment of these hormones in the blood requires immediate blood samples, as they readily diffuse into body tissue.

3. *Heart Rate*   The heart rate of an aroused person is easily obtained with an electrocardiograph (ECG), a device for measuring the electrical activity of the heart. The heart rate can also be indirectly measured with a pulse monitor or by finger palpation. The heart

rate is not considered to be a good single indicator of arousal. Its correlation with other more viable indicators is quite low.

4. *Muscle Tension*   The electrical potential of muscles can be measured with an **electromyograph** (EMG), a device that measures electrical activity in a muscle. Woodworth and Schlosberg (1954) have shown that muscle tension levels are roughly equivalent to levels of arousal. Kavussanu, Crews, and Gill (1998) successfully used electromyography in research involving free-throw shooting ability in basketball.

5. *Respiration Rate*   Rate of respiration is not entirely under the control of the autonomic nervous system, but it is still a fairly reliable indicator of heightened arousal. With a spirometer, a person's respiratory rate, tidal volume, inspiratory reserve volume, expiratory reserve volume, inspiratory capacity, and vital capacity can be measured.

6. *Blood Pressure*   Arterial blood pressure can be measured with a sphygmomanometer. Blood pressure is an indication of the relative dilation or constriction of the blood vessels associated with the autonomic nervous system. Since blood pressure is generally monitored through repeated application of the pressure cuff and stethoscope, only intermittent recordings can be obtained. For this reason, blood pressure is not considered to be a very good measure of arousal.

7. *Palmar Sweating*   In a threatening situation, increased levels of activation are associated with an increase of sweat from sweat glands on the hands. According to Harrison and MacKinnon (1966), sweat glands of the human palm do not function in response to environmental changes, but are activated by alerting stimuli. Techniques for counting palmar sweat glands are detailed by Sutarman and Thompson (1952), Johnson and Dabbs (1967), and Dabbs, Johnson, and Leventhal (1968).

8. *Galvanic Skin Response*   Associated with increased **palmar sweating** during periods of heightened anxiety is a corresponding change in the resistance of the skin to the passage of an electrical current (ohms of resistance). Increased palmar sweating causes a decrease in skin resistance, or galvanic skin response (GSR). A decrease in **skin resistance** to the passage of electricity from one electrode to another is equal to an increase in **skin conductivity.** The **galvanic skin response** is mediated through the sympathetic nerve supply to the skin and is attributed to changes in the number of active sweat glands. Therefore, increased skin conductivity is directly related to an increase in the number of active palmar sweat glands.

Attention and Concentration in Sport

The concept of concentration, or what may be referred to as applied attention, epitomizes the accomplishments of Tiger Woods during the year 2000 professional golf tour. Tiger started his incredible year by winning the U.S. Open at Pebble Beach by 15 strokes over his nearest competitor. Thirty-five days later he won the British Open by eight strokes. In so doing, he accomplished a career grand slam at age 24, two years younger than Jack Nicklaus was when he accomplished it. In golf, the Grand Slam includes the Masters, the U.S. Open, the British Open, and the PGA Championship. Within one month Tiger won the PGA Championship for the second time in two years, making him the only other golfer besides Ben Hogan to win three majors in a single year. Besides being incredibly talented, Tiger accomplished this task by being completely focused and single-minded on each hole, and even each stroke (Hoffer, 2001). Prior to the U.S. Open, Tiger skipped a special ceremony honoring the late Payne Stewart, the 1999 U.S. Open winner. Responding to criticism, Tiger later said in his defense, "I felt going would be more of a deterrent for me during the tournament, because I don't want

To succeed, the quarterback in American football must concentrate and effectively narrow his attentional focus.
Courtesy Kansas State University Sports Information.

to be thinking about it" (Garrity, 2000, p. 61). Commenting on Tiger's demeanor at the U.S. Open, Scotty Bowman, the USGA scorer, said, "His eye contact is right with his caddie and nowhere else when he's preparing to hit a shot. He's oblivious to everyone else" (Garrity, p. 61). While Tiger Woods dominated the PGA from 1999 to 2001, his dominance has waned since that time. This is not necessarily a bad thing. When Woods won 7 of 11 majors, there was little opportunity for anyone else (Brown, 2004). Since he won the United States Open in 2002, nine different players have won a major PGA championship. Nevertheless, Tiger Woods is still one of the best golfers on the professional tour, recently winning the 2005 British Open.

According to William James (1890), attention is "the taking possession by the mind, in clear and vivid form, of one out of what seem several simultaneously possible objects or trains of thought. . . . It implies withdrawal from some things in order to deal effectively with others" (pp. 403–4). In sport, nothing can be more important than paying attention to the object at hand. On the surface, the idea of paying attention seems simple enough, but psychologists have long recognized that the attention process can be very complex. In discussing the complex nature of attention, this section is divided into several related subsections. Each section builds upon the previous section and helps explain why attention is important in sport. Important concepts to be introduced include the following: information processing, memory systems, measuring information, selective attention, information processing capacity, attentional narrowing, being in the zone, measuring attentional focus, attention control training, and associative versus dissociative attentional styles.

Information Processing

Perhaps the most critical difference between the modern game of volleyball and the same game many years ago is in the complexity of the offense. Many years ago, volleyball was a relatively predictable game in which the spiker attacked from one of two positions on the court. These two positions were the left and right sides of the court near the sidelines. The ball was always set high and there was never any deviation from this pattern. This changed in the late 1960s and early 1970s, when the Japanese revolutionized the game with their version of the multiple offense. In this remarkable offense, attackers spiked the ball from numerous positions at the net. In so doing, the spikers often switched attack positions and called for sets of varying heights and speeds. The result was predictable. Defensive net players were jumping at the wrong time, responding to the wrong attackers, crashing into their own players, and generally falling all over themselves. From an information processing point of view, they were simply overwhelmed. Up to this point, the blockers had

only been required to attend to one or two spikers at a time. But now they had to deal with three or four times as much information. Later on, when opposing teams were able to study the multiple offense, defensive players were taught to ignore irrelevant movement and fakes and to concentrate on the important elements of the attack.

In a very general way, there are two basic approaches to explaining behavior. The first and probably better understood is the behavioral, or stimulus-response, approach. In this way of looking at things, the world is explained through a series of stimulus-response (S-R) connections. In fact, psychologists such as B. F. Skinner (1938) would have us believe that all behavior can be reduced to a mathematical model in which specific stimuli go in and predicted responses come out. With animals, this approach has been extremely successful. However, for human beings this approach seems too simplistic. There seems to be more to human behavior than the simple act of strengthening the bond between a stimulus and a response. Certainly, a great deal goes on in the brain between the time that a stimulus is given and the time that a response is initiated. This notion is well accepted by cognitive psychologists, and is illustrated below. It is referred to as the **information processing model** of behavior. The information processing model contains a stimulus and a response, but a large number of mental operations occur between the two.

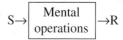

For a person to experience a stimulus and respond to it at a later time, there must be a **memory storage** capability. That is, the person must have a memory, or place to save important information. Once the information has been saved, the person must be able to reactivate or retrieve it. **Retrieval** enables us to use the information to make decisions about forthcoming responses. A football quarterback stores thousands of pieces of information about offenses and defenses. As he approaches the line of scrimmage after calling one play in the huddle, he may observe the defensive alignment and change the play prior to the snap (this is termed "calling an audible"). What has happened here? The answer is simple. Previously stored information about the opposing team was retrieved from memory and used to initiate a different but appropriate response. This is information processing in action, and it takes place constantly on the athletic field or court. The concept is based on the notion of a storage or memory system, which we will discuss next.

Memory Systems

One basic question we may ask about memory is whether there is one memory system, or are there several? While many researchers have tried to show that the different types of memory are clearly distinct from one another, the current thinking is that the distinction among memory systems is for convenience and should not be interpreted to mean that they reside in different parts of the brain. With this in mind, the three basic memory systems will be described.

Sensory Information Store   The first stage in the human memory system is the sensory information store, sometimes called the **sensory register.** This storage system is capable of holding large amounts of sensory information for a very brief amount of time before most of it is lost (Kalat, 1999). Information is thought to remain in the sensory register for up to one-half second before it is either lost or transferred to a more permanent storage system. The limitations of the sensory register are illustrated in a volleyball officiating situation. Events often occur so rapidly in a play at the net that it is hard for the referee to make an immediate decision. However, if the decision is not immediate, the referee will discover that the image is no longer available. The same situation occurs in basketball officiating when the ball is knocked out of bounds by one of two opposing players. The information in the sensory register decays very rapidly, and may be effectively scanned for only about one-half second. That portion of the information that we can effectively attend to is passed on to a short-term memory system for further processing.

Short-Term Memory (STM)   The **short-term memory** (STM) is the center, or crossroads, of activity in the information processing system. Information comes into STM for rehearsal from both the sensory store and permanent memory. Information that comes into STM from the sensory store is often new or original information. If we do not rehearse and memorize it quickly, we will likely forget it. For example, when a telephone operator gives us a new telephone number for a friend, we repeat it several times while dialing. If we did not repeat it, we would forget the number before we could dial. This is an example of rehearsing new information in STM. Conversely, a quarterback uses STM to rehearse information already permanently stored in memory. For example, just before a game, the quarterback will retrieve from memory the plays that he has learned and will rehearse them to make sure he knows them well. This process tends not only to refresh his memory of the plays, but also to strengthen their representation in memory. Generally, if a person can rehearse new information for 20 to 30 seconds in STM, it will be sufficiently learned to be passed on to long-term memory for permanent storage. Quality of rehearsal will determine whether or not information in STM will be passed on to long-term memory. Short-term memory is often referred to as "working memory," to emphasize the dynamic nature of this memory system.

The absolute capacity of short-term memory is relatively limited. It would be very difficult, for example, for the average person to retain more than seven separate words or numbers in STM at one time. However, through the process of chunking, it is possible for an individual to retain far more than this. **Chunking** is the process of combining several separate pieces of information into larger ones. The larger chunks are combined in such a way that they can be rehearsed as a unit. Key words or phrases are then used to represent and recall the larger

CONCEPT   The working capacity of short-term memory can be effectively enhanced through the process of "chunking."

APPLICATION   Grouping separate words, thoughts, ideas, and motor movements into meaningful wholes is a skill that can be learned. The wholes, or "chunks," can be memorized, rehearsed, and practiced much more efficiently in this way. Athletes should be taught how to utilize this skill when trying to learn and manage large amounts of verbal or motor information.

chunks. In the sport of football, for example, a single number or phrase is often used to represent a complex series of actions on the part of several players. In this way it is possible for the quarterback to rehearse in memory several complex plays without getting them confused. He rehearses the plays as chunks, or units. The details of each chunk (play) do not immediately need to be scrutinized. In this manner, the capacity of short-term memory can be greatly increased.

Long-Term Memory (LTM)   Whereas information in short-term memory is present for only a brief period of time, information in **long-term memory** (LTM) is relatively permanent. The purpose of the memory system is to store information in LTM. Once information is stored in LTM, it is theoretically permanent. This may seem difficult to understand, since we all have occasionally had trouble remembering things we thought were permanently learned. In conjunction with STM, information in long-term memory can be continually updated, reorganized, and strengthened. New information can also be added to LTM. The relationship between the three basic memory systems is illustrated in figure 7.3.

FIGURE 7.3 | The three stages of memory, showing rehearsal in STM and retrieval in LTM.

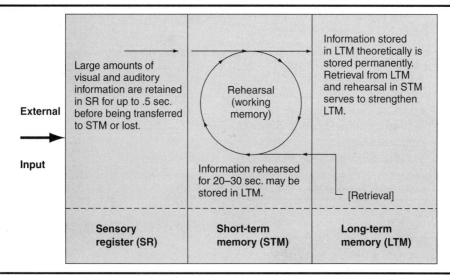

FIGURE 7.4 | Pitcher A has four pitches at his command. The probability of his throwing any one of the pitches is 25 percent. What is the average amount of information conveyed?

Pitcher *A*

Changeup 25%	Slider 25%
Curve 25%	Fastball 25%

Measuring Information

Psychologists can measure the amount of information that is conveyed by a particular problem or task. The amount of **information conveyed** or transmitted by a particular problem is measured in **bits** of information, (short for "binary digit"). Intuitively, bits of information conveyed is equal to the number of questions that would have to be systematically asked to solve the problem.

Illustrated in figure 7.4 is a rectangle divided into four quadrants. Each quadrant shows the probability that a particular major league pitcher throws each of four pitches. From this diagram we know that the pitcher has command of four pitches that he uses with equal probability. If the balls and strikes count is 3 and 2 and you guess that he is going to throw you a fastball, you have a 75 percent chance of being wrong.

This is a difficult problem that conveys or transmits two bits of information. How do we know that this problem conveys two bits of information? Because it would take two "planned" questions to correctly solve the problem. Now, understand, this is not how you determine which pitch he is going to throw, but how you determine *the number of bits of information conveyed by the problem.* Okay, so what are the two questions? Question one might be, "Are you going to throw either a slider or a fastball?" If his answer to that question is no, then *one column* is eliminated and we can focus on the other column. The second question might be, "Are you going to throw a changeup?" If he answers yes, we know he is going to throw a changeup. If he answers no, we know he is going to throw a curve ball, and no further questions are required. How much information would be conveyed by a pitcher who only had one pitch, say, a fastball? No questions would have to be asked, so if you said zero, you would have been correct. A major league pitcher who had only one pitch would certainly be in trouble after just a few innings.

This same logic could be used to determine bits of information conveyed by a 2-, 8-, 16-, 32-, or even 64-pitch or decision problem, as long as each pitch had an equal probability of occurring. See if you can logically and systematically determine bits of information conveyed by each of these situations. As you will note, as long as the probabilities are equal, and as long as the number of pitches can be expressed as the log to the base of 2 (e.g., $2 = 2^1$; $4 = 2^2$; $8 = 2^3$; $16 = 2^4$; $32 = 2^5$; $64 = 2^6$), you will be able to logically determine bits of information conveyed.

The more bits of information conveyed, the more difficult the problem being presented. We have illustrated this concept using a pitcher in baseball, but you could apply the same principle to other sports. The defensive player in basketball looks at the point guard and wonders if she is

CONCEPT An athletic response can be made more difficult to interpret in terms of information conveyed.

APPLICATION Let's use the baseball pitching example. Your pitcher's difficulty in terms of information conveyed can be increased in three ways.

First, the pitcher must master as many different pitches as possible. Second, the pitcher must throw each pitch with equal probability.

Finally, the delivery should provide no cues to the batter as to which pitch is coming. A combination of these three factors maximizes the amount of information conveyed.

going to drive right, drive left, or pull up and shoot a jump shot. The defensive back in football looks at the wide receiver and wonders if he is going to execute any number of inside/outside moves, or if he will go long, or if he will execute a button hook. The more quality moves an offensive player has, the more information is conveyed, and the more difficult it will be to defend.

Now look at figure 7.5. In this illustration the pitcher also has four pitches at his command, but he throws them with *unequal* probability. This makes the pitcher easier to outguess and hit against, but it makes it more difficult to calculate information conveyed. The actual information conveyed in this problem is 1.25 bits of information, which is less than that conveyed by pitcher A in the equal probability case. The reason that

pitcher B conveys less information is that he throws his fastball 70 percent of the time, so if in doubt, you can guess fastball, and you will be right 70 percent of the time. In the unequal probability case, bits of information cannot be calculated using the number of questions method. Rather, it is necessary to apply a formula as detailed in Fitts and Posner (1967) and Cox (1985).

This discussion was not presented so that you could calculate information conveyed, but so that you can clearly understand the relationship between an athlete's skill and information conveyed. As skill increases, information conveyed increases. The more information conveyed by an offensive player, the more difficult it is going to be for the defensive player to respond.

FIGURE 7.5 | Pitcher B has four pitches at his command. However, the probabilities are not equal. What is the average amount of information conveyed?

Pitcher *B*

Changeup 5%	Slider 15%
Curve 10%	Fastball 70%

Selective Attention

Humans' ability to **gate out,** or ignore, irrelevant sensory information, and to pay **selective attention** to relevant information, is of incalculable value. Perhaps the best way to dramatize this point is to consider the schizophrenic patient who may suffer an impaired capacity to sustain attention. At one extreme, the patient may attend to some internal thought to such an extent that she becomes catatonic. At the other extreme, the patient may be incapable of selectively attending to anything. Although young schizophrenic patients describe their difficulties in different ways, the following extract is considered typical (McGhie & Chapman, 1961):

> I can't concentrate. It's diversion of attention that troubles me . . . the sounds are coming through to me but I feel my mind cannot cope with everything. It is difficult to concentrate on any one sound . . . it's like trying to do two or three different things at one time. . . . Everything seems to grip my attention although I am not particularly interested in anything. I'm speaking to you just now but I can hear noises going on next door and in the corridor (p. 104).

Each of us has experienced the feeling of over-stimulation that can result in an inability to concentrate, but can you imagine experiencing this problem every waking hour? If it were not for our ability to concentrate on one or two relevant items at a time, we simply could not function. While you are reading this page, you are selectively attending to one thing at the expense of several others.

The ability to selectively attend to the appropriate stimuli is critical in most athletic situations. In basketball, the athlete must concentrate on the basket while shooting a free throw rather than being distracted by the noise from the crowd. In volleyball, the athlete must selectively attend to the server instead of being distracted by thoughts of a previous play. In baseball, the base runner must attend to the pitcher, and not to the jabbering of the second baseman. In football, the quarterback must selectively attend to his receivers, while gating out the sights and sounds of the huge defensive linesmen who are lunging at him. Of course, some athletes are better than others at selectively attending to important cues. This is one difference between the good athlete and the outstanding athlete.

As we watch sport on television and in person, many times we can observe athletes engaging in various psychological ploys to gain an advantage. Usually these ploys are manifested in some sort of verbal dialogue, such as commenting on things unrelated to the contest. In baseball, base runners have been picked off first or second base while engaging in innocent chatting with infielders. When and if these ploys (intentional or otherwise) are successful, this is usually related to inappropriate selective attention. The athlete simply is not attending to the appropriate stimuli. This, as well as information overload, will cause a delay in responding.

A number of complex models have been proposed to explain the phenomenon of selective attention. These models include the Broadbent Model (1957, 1958), Norman's Pertinence Model (1968), and Treisman's Attenuation Model (1965). Each of these models propose mechanisms that allow us to selectively attend to one item at the expense of several others, while at the same time allowing for a shift in attention from one important item to an even more important item. A concrete sports-related example of this would be the defensive basketball player intent upon cutting off the passing lane to the person she is guarding, only to be beaten by the back-door play. In this example, the shift from selectively attending to cutting off the passing lane to anticipating the back-door play was too slow.

For highly trained and skilled athletes, the process of selective attention is very efficient. When skilled basketball players step up to the free throw line, they refuse to allow anyone or anything besides the task at hand to capture their attention. Coaches refer to this process as "concentration." However, some athletes never do learn how to

CONCEPT   Selective attention is perhaps the single most important cognitive characteristic of the successful athlete.

APPLICATION   All sporting events contain critical "keys," or cues, that must be selectively attended to. In volleyball, blocking may be the most decisive offensive weapon in scoring points, because a team is generally blocking when it is serving. To take advantage of this situation, the blockers must selectively attend to the assigned attacker and must not be distracted by actions of the setter, by fakes by other spikers, or even by the ball.

cope with distraction. Every little event distracts them, or they concentrate on the wrong things (e.g., dribbling), and miss relevant cues.

One concluding comment about selective attention is in order. Our ability to selectively attend to stimuli is based on the correct distribution of neurochemicals in the brain. A disruption in the balanced distribution of dopamine and norepinephrine is associated with an inability to selectively attend to stimuli, and with mental disorders such as schizophrenia, depression, and attentional deficit disorder. Various prescription drugs have been developed to control symptoms associated with attentional disruption, but sometimes even these drugs have unfortunate movement disorder side effects (Posner & Raichle, 1997). We mention this so that the sport psychologist is aware of the critical importance of selective attention, and is aware that the inability to selectively attend to instructions is not always due to a lack of effort on the part of the athlete.

Limited Information Processing Capacity

An alternative approach to studying attention is to view it in terms of information **processing capacity,** or *space.* In the previous section we discussed attention in terms of our ability to selectively gate out irrelevant information. In this section, we are concerned with the capacity to attend to more than one thing at a time. In view of our discussion of selective attention, this may seem paradoxical. However, we can readily see that human beings

Digging a hard-driven spike is a complex information problem that requires the athlete's undivided attention. Courtesy Kansas State University Sports Information.

CONCEPT   Selective attention is a skill that can be learned.

APPLICATION   There is no doubt that some athletes are better at selective attention than others. However, there is no reason to believe that this skill cannot be learned. The secret is for the coach to identify the important cues and then to provide drills that require the athlete to selectively attend to them. A good example might be shooting free throws in basketball. The key, of course, is to concentrate on the basket. However, few athletes learn to do this during practice, since there are rarely any distractions to cause their attention to wander. A game-like situation with fans and opponents would help the athlete to learn selective attention.

seem to be able to attend to more than one thing at a time. For example, a skilled basketball player can dribble a basketball, hold up one hand to signal a play, and respond to a teammate who is cutting to the basket. A person driving a car can carry on a conversation with a passenger, steer the car, and shift gears all at the same time. How can this be? Didn't we just conclude that the human mind can attend to only one piece of information at a time? Not necessarily; we concluded only that the human mind is *capable* of selectively attending to one thing at a time. Several possibilities exist. An athlete might (a) be compelled to selectively attend to only one action at one time because it consumes all of his attention, (b) choose to selectively attend to one action or thought to avoid distraction, or (c) simultaneously attend to more than one thought or action because he is able to.

Keele (1973) was one of the first psychologists to introduce the notion that individuals may be limited by the amount of processing space available to them. In this way of looking at attention, we think in terms of different mental and motor tasks requiring a finite amount of information processing space. If a specific task requires all of the information processing space, then that specific task is selectively attended to at the expense of all others. If a specific task does not require all of the available information processing space, then more than one task can be attended to at one time, depending upon the attentional demands of the second task. This is referred to as the **capacity model** of selective attention. The great Boston Celtics basketball star Bill Russell used different words to describe it, but he had a similar concept in mind when he said this:

> Remember, each of us has a finite amount of energy, and things you do well don't require as much. Things you don't do well take more concentration. And if you're fatigued by that, then the things you do best are going to be affected. (Deford, 1999, p. 110)

In the capacity model of attention, more than one piece of input can be attended to at one time and more than one response can be made at one time, if the demands on available space are not too severe. If any particular task requires all available space, then only that task will be attended to, and all others will suffer a performance decrement.

The concepts of selective attention and limited information processing capacity are germane to the sport psychologist, coach, or teacher who is interested in improving athletic performance. Wrisberg and Shea (1978) demonstrated through the use of the **reaction time probe** that the attentional demands of a motor act decrease as learning increases. In other words, as a motor act becomes automatic or learned, the demands on the limited information processing capacity of the athlete decrease, and the athlete can attend to other cues. In the reaction time probe procedure, the subject must perform a simple reaction time task while at the same time performing a primary motor task. If reaction time is slower than normal, then the primary task is judged to require

CONCEPT Each athlete's information processing capacity, or space, is limited.

APPLICATION If, as a coach, you require athletes to attend to more information than they have processing space to handle, you are inviting failure. Processing space is not the same as intelligence.

attention, and hence, information processing space. The significant difference between a beginning basketball player and a skilled one appears in the demands placed on information processing space. In a game, dribbling requires nearly all of the available processing space of the beginner. She cannot hear the coach, see the basket, see other players, or do anything except attend to the task of dribbling. On the other hand, the skilled player has reduced the attentional demands of dribbling to such a degree that she can see and hear all kinds of relevant cues while dribbling. The important concept of processing space is illustrated in figure 7.6.

The capacity model of attention takes into consideration the notion that the information processing requirements of tasks are modified by learning. That is, information processing demands of a specific task (e.g., dribbling in basketball)

may be reduced over time. Another factor that should be considered when conceptualizing the capacity model of attention is the notion of **individual differences** (Keele & Hawkins, 1982). No two individuals are alike in terms of the amount of attention required to deal with more than one task at a time. Therefore, you should not assume that two athletes possessing an equal amount of playing experience will perform the same when confronted with a multiple-task problem. One person may experience task interference in attempting tasks A and B together, but experience no difficulty with tasks A and C together. Conversely, a second athlete may experience an entirely different set of problems relative to the same tasks. Coaches must be particularly sensitive and aware of individual differences when teaching athletes how to manage multiple-task athletic situations. Basketball and soccer are sports that are very similar in this

FIGURE 7.6 | Relative amounts of available information processing space for a beginning basketball player and a skilled player.

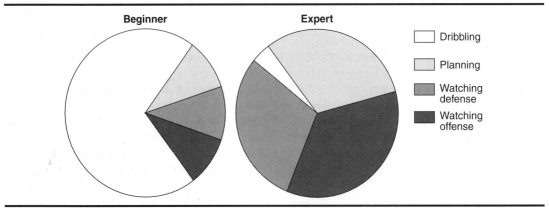

room for nothing else. The athlete will not be able to pass to the open player, see plays develop, or even avoid an opponent. However, once the player has mastered the skill of dribbling, he will be able to do all of this and more. It is not that information processing space has increased, but that the information content of dribbling has been reduced to nearly zero.

respect: an athlete must be able to control a ball while at the same time planning and taking into consideration offensive and defensive players around her.

Two recent investigations illustrate how the use of the reaction time probe has enhanced our understanding of the information processing demands of selected tasks. In the first study, horseshoe pitching performance served as the primary task and reacting to an auditory signal served as the secondary reaction time (RT) probe task. In this study by Prezuhy and Etnier (2001), an auditory signal was presented to the pitcher at three distinct times during the throwing motion. The participant's task was to depress a RT button in his non-throwing hand when he heard the signal. Longer RT would indicate that the primary task required more information processing space or attention at a particular point in the throwing motion. Results showed that more attention to the primary task is required at the initiation of the backward motion and just before the release, compared to the backward extension of the motion. This study also showed that a difficult horseshoe-tossing task (short peg) requires more attention than an easy task (high peg).

In a study reported by Sibley and Etnier (2004), the primary task was setting a volleyball and the secondary task was again the auditory reaction time probe. To begin with, the study demonstrated that a simple predetermined front or back set required less information processing space than a complex set in which a front or back choice was required. The results showed that the

complex setting task required more attention than the simple set, but it also showed that attention demands changed as a function of ball flight prior to the set. Probe position 1 (PP1) was placed at the initiation of the ball toss to the setter, while PP2 was prior to the peak, PP3 was just after the peak, and PP4 was just prior to ball contact by the setter. For both simple and complex setting tasks, attention demand (longer RT) was greatest at initiation of the ball toss. This result led the researchers to conclude that "performers do not need to track the entire ball flight but rather that skilled sport participants track the initial flight of the ball, and then their eyes 'shoot ahead' to the final portion of flight" (p. 102).

Attentional Narrowing

An athlete's ability to attend to appropriate stimuli during competition has been termed **attentional focus.** The concept of attentional focus includes the ability of an athlete to both narrow and broaden her attention when necessary. For example, in basketball, the guard who initiates a fast break must be able to broaden her attentional focus in order to see teammates on either side as they break toward the basket. This same player must be able to narrow attentional focus while shooting free throws in order to gate out distractions from the crowd.

The notion of **attentional narrowing** is best understood in terms of **cue utilization.** As explained by Easterbrook (1959), attentional narrowing is a function of available cues. Environmental

FIGURE 7.7 | Cue utilization and the arousal-performance relationship.

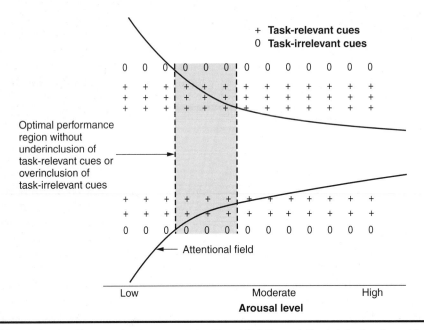

Source: From Daniel M. Landers, The arousal-performance relationship revisited. *Research Quarterly for Exercise and Sport,* 1980, *51,* 77–90. Reproduced by permission of the publisher, the American Alliance for Health, Physical Education. Recreation and Dance, 1900 Association Dr., Reston, VA 22091.

cues provide the athlete with needed information for a skilled performance. In any sport task, many cues are available to the athlete. Some are relevant and necessary for quality performance; others are irrelevant and can damage performance. Under conditions of low arousal, the athlete picks up both relevant and irrelevant cues. The presence of irrelevant cues should result in a decrement in performance. As arousal increases, the athlete's attention begins to narrow. At some optimal point, attentional narrowing gates out all of the irrelevant cues and allows the relevant cues to remain. At this point performance should be at its best. If arousal increases still further, attention continues to narrow and relevant cues will be gated out, causing a deterioration in performance.

High levels of arousal may also lead to the phenomenon of **distractibility.** In addition to

gating out potentially relevant cues, high arousal may also decrease an athlete's ability to selectively attend to one stimulus at a time. Rather, the athlete's attention shifts randomly from stimulus to stimulus. Distractibility has the effect of decreasing the athlete's ability to discriminate between relevant and irrelevant cues, and to focus upon relevant cues. The athlete who is suffering from distractibility tends to experience sudden and significant decrements in performance. The phenomenon of attentional narrowing is illustrated in figure 7.7.

When a quarterback drops back for a pass, he needs a relatively wide band of attentional focus in order to pick up his receivers. However, if the band is too wide, he will pick up such irrelevant cues as the noisy crowd and the cheerleaders. This will cause a decrement in performance (arousal level is

CONCEPT Attentional narrowing has the effect of reducing cue utilization.

APPLICATION Broad attentional focus allows the athlete to attend to important cues, but the distraction of irrelevant cues can hurt performance. Narrow attentional focus allows the athlete to attend to only the most critical cues, but can also hurt performance, because many relevant cues can be eliminated. Successful athletes are often required to adjust their attentional focus so that it is appropriately narrow in one situation, yet broad in another. A point guard in basketball must have broad attentional focus to be able to pass to the open player on offense, but must have a narrow band of attention on the foul line.

too low). As arousal level increases, attention narrows and irrelevant cues are eliminated. However, in a very intense game situation, arousal may be very high. Consequently, further narrowing of attention may cause the quarterback to gate out such relevant cues as the secondary receivers, the position of defensive backs, and the possible outlet pass.

Performing in an athletic event requires an athlete to narrowly focus upon the task at hand in order to realize success. Quality attentional focus can gate out the debilitating effects of distractors and irrelevant cues. As the time to execute a skill gets closer, the requirement to narrowly focus attention increases. The ability to focus narrowly on relevant cues is a skill that can be learned, but also a skill that is influenced by arousal. Too much arousal undermines the athlete's ability to narrowly focus attention in a quality manner, while too little arousal may introduce unwanted competition between irrelevant and relevant cues.

Easterbrook's notion that increased arousal is associated with narrowing of attentional focus, as illustrated in figure 7.7, has been consistently supported in the literature. Most recently, Janelle, Singer, and Williams (1999) reported the results of an experiment in which increased arousal decreased performance on both a central car driving task and a peripheral reaction time task. Similarly, Williams and Elliot (1999) demonstrated that under conditions of increased arousal and decreased attentional narrowing, karate performers

altered the way in which they scan peripheral information. Under conditions of low arousal, athletes focused their eyes on the chests of the opponents and picked up the movements of the hands and feet of opponents using peripheral vision (broad focus). Under conditions of elevated arousal, however, athletes again focused their eyes on the chests of the opponents, but used **peripheral scanning** to see the hands and feet of the opponents (narrow focus). Because their attention was narrowed due to increased arousal, they could not see the movements of the opponents' hands and feet unless their eyes actually fixated on them for brief periods of time.

In recent years, interest has been shown in the concept of attentional flexibility, an individual difference characteristic believed to be possessed in different amounts by individuals. **Attentional flexibility** refers to the ability of athletes to quickly and effectively shift their attention from one location to another. Another proposed characteristic of attentional flexibility is the ability of individuals to shift from a very narrow attentional focus to a very broad focus. It is believed that athletes who are high in this characteristic should have an advantage in certain athletic contests and tasks. Keele and Hawkins (1982) report that the characteristic does exist in athletes, but that it is difficult to find meaningful correlations between the characteristic and specific physical abilities. Conversely, Turatto, Benso, and Umilta (1999) reported a relationship between attentional flexibility and level of skiing ability. They compared a group of nonelite female amateur skiers to a group of elite Italian female skiers, and found that the elite skiers scored higher in attentional focusing skills.

Finally, Hatzigeorgiadis and Biddle (1999) reported an interesting connection between cognitive interference and goal orientation. **Cognitive interference** was defined as "thoughts of escape" and "task-irrelevant thoughts." Any random thought or event that would tend to break an athlete's concentration could be considered cognitive interference. A case in point is an incident related by Schmid and Peper (1998) in which a 16-year-old U.S. rhythmic gymnast lost her poise and concentration when a loud teenage voice yelled a lewd comment as she walked toward the mat in an international meet. In the Hatzigeorgiadis and Biddle investigation, snooker and tennis players who were high in task orientation exhibited low levels of cognitive interference. That is, they were less likely to be negatively influenced by random cognitive thoughts. Conversely, individuals who were high in ego orientation and low in perceived ability (a deadly combination) exhibited high levels of cognitive interference. You will recall from our earlier chapter on goal perspective in sport that an individual high in ego orientation tends to focus upon social comparisons and upon winning.

When Athletes Are in the Zone

> When the body is brought to peak condition and the mind is completely focused, even unaware of what it's doing, an individual can achieve the extraordinary. (Tolson, 2000, p. 38)

The above statement was made by the author of a popular news magazine article following Tiger Woods' extraordinary performance at the U.S. Open Golf Tournament at Pebble Beach. Tiger won this tournament by 15 strokes over his nearest competitor. In that same tournament, John Daly, another golfing great, dropped out of the tournament on the first day, after posting 14 strokes on the 18th hole. The title of Tolson's article was "Into the Zone." A question you might ask relative to Tolson's quote is, "Is an athlete ever unaware of what his body is doing?" An athlete's mind may not be consciously thinking about what his left arm is doing during a golf swing, but it is highly likely that the brain is always aware, on some level, of what the body is doing. The brain is continually receiving sensory information from muscles, joints, and ligaments about body movement.

Tolson is not the first person to use the phrase **playing in the zone** to refer to extraordinary performance of an athlete. The concept of a zone of optimal functioning may have been first introduced by Russian psychologist Yuri Hanin (1980) when he presented his theory of optimal functioning relative to state anxiety. This is a topic that we will discuss in greater detail in chapter 8.

In an article written in *The New York Times,* Gould (2000) takes particular issue with the notion that skilled athletic performance is somehow wholly associated with "bodily intelligence." He argues that skilled athletic performance reflects close coordination between mind and body, and that it is demeaning to the intelligence of athletes to suggest that it is just a physical thing. Supporting Gould's contentions, Gladwell (1999) wrote a highly insightful article titled "The Physical Genius." In his article, Gladwell provides a very intelligent research-based discussion of exactly what great athletes, great surgeons, and great musicians have in common. He suggests that there are three things that go into making the physical genius. First are the raw physical and mental abilities that the athlete or surgeon is born with. Second is the time spent in practicing to become the best in the world. Tiger Woods got to be a "physical genius" by physically and mentally practicing golf for thousands and thousands of hours, and after that he practiced another thousand hours. It is no accident that an elite athlete plays in the "zone," because he is potentially in the zone every time she performs. Third is what Gladwell calls "imagination." The great athlete has imagined every possible situation that could occur in a game.

There are no surprises to the elite athlete. In describing the mindset of the great athlete, Gladwell quotes Wayne Gretzky, one of the greatest ice hockey players ever to have set foot or the ice:

> People talk about skating, puck-handling, and shooting, but the whole sport is angles and caroms, forgetting the straight direction the puck is going, calculating where it will be diverted, factoring in all the interruptions. (p. 59)

Regarding this last area of imagination, Gladwell makes an insightful comparison between the great basketball player, Karl Malone, and the greatest basketball player of all time, Michael Jordan. Malone had raw ability and work ethic equal to those of Michael Jordan, but he never had an imagination to equal Jordan's. Gladwell points to the sixth game of the 1998 World Championships in Salt Lake City. The game came down to a few seconds in which the Utah Jazz and Karl Malone had both the ball and the lead. Malone, unaware of where Jordan (Chicago Bulls) was on the court, jockeyed for position in the low post with Dennis Rodman. Using the imagination that he had, Michael came up on Malone's blind side and stripped the ball from him. Malone never saw it coming—but he should have. This is what is meant by imagination. Jordan went on to make the final shot of the game and sealed the victory and championship for Chicago. Being a "physical genius" is not just being in the "zone"; it is perfecting your game mentally and physically, so that you are in the "zone" when you need to be. For the accomplished surgeon, it means being in the "zone" all of the time.

What about the notion of "automaticity," the idea that while in the "zone" the athlete is somehow disconnected from interference of conscious thought? After an amazing play by Michael Jordan, the announcer comments that he is playing "unconscious." After an errant throw by an otherwise steady second baseman, the announcer implies that the conscious brain interfered. These statements are best understood within the framework of the information processing model and allocated attention. While not an expert in human movement, Bandura (1997), a social psychologist, made the following insightful observation:

> Partial disengagement of thought from proficient action has considerable functional value. Having to think about the details of every skilled activity before carrying it out in recurrent situations would consume most of one's precious attentional and cognitive resources and create a monotonously dull inner life. After people develop adequate ways of managing situations that recur regularly, they act on their perceived efficacy without requiring continuing directive or reflective thought. (p. 34)

As explained by Smith (1996), cognitive psychologists distinguish between controlled and automatic processing of information. In learning a new sports skill, an athlete must focus upon **controlled processing** of information. This means that the athlete must attend to the details of executing the skill to be learned. This is what is happening to the beginning basketball player in figure 7.6. Almost all of the athlete's attention is focused on learning how to dribble a basketball, to the exclusion of other important cues. Controlled processing is relatively slow and effortful, consuming most of the available information processing capacity of the individual.

Once a sport skill is mastered, it comes under **automatic processing.** The execution of the skill is still being monitored by the brain, but because it is well learned it requires little conscious attention. Again, as illustrated in figure 7.6, the skilled basketball player may now focus most of the available information processing space upon other relevant basketball-related cues. One of the vulnerabilities of automatic processing is that if the smooth operation of the task is interfered with, it is susceptible to error. It is a little like reciting a poem. If you make an error and forget where you are in the poem, you often have to start over to get back on track. So it is with completing a double play in baseball or softball. You don't want to hesitate or entertain a negative thought about the throw to first base, because if you do you may upset the automatic processing of the skill.

None of this discussion about automatic processing of a skilled movement implies that the brain of an individual is not involved; it only clarifies the nature and level of conscious involvement. The perfect execution of a sports skill is best thought of as an elegant interaction between mind and body. Describing a peak performance as simply being in the "zone," as if there is a separation of the mind from the body, diminishes the immense preparation that goes into training to become an elite athlete, at any level of competition.

Having established that the brain is not disengaged during skilled athletic performance, it is also important to note that the brain is essentially in a "do not interfere" mode. This is why superior performers typically indicate an absence of conscious regulation during an outstanding performance. This concept was experimentally observed in a laboratory investigation by Deeny, Hillman, Janelle and Hatfield (2003). In this study, EEG recordings were monitored in expert and less skilled rifle marksmen during competitive shooting. Results showed less intercortical communication in the expert shooters compared to the less skilled, which implies decreased cognition during highly skilled motor processes.

Gladwell (2000) also makes some interesting observations regarding the difference between *choking* and *panicking*. Gladwell links the common occurrence of choking with the shifting of attention from the automatic mode (implicit learning) to the controlled process mode (explicit learning) when the athlete starts to think too much. This can occur with the pitcher who, in an effort to throw a perfect strike, goes into a control mode and tries to guide the pitch to its target with disastrous results. Thus, choking is associated with thinking too much, while panicking is associated with thinking too little. In a panic attack, the athlete reverts to instinct and quits thinking logically. In sport the difference between choking and panicking might not matter much; you lose the point or miss the shot in either case. However, in flying

an airplane or in SCUBA diving, the difference between choking and panicking is a life-and-death matter. If her equipment fails in SCUBA diving, the diver can go back to a controlled processing mode and fall back on a checklist to save his life. However, if the SCUBA diver or pilot panics and reverts to instinct, the outcome could be death. For example, the airplane pilot must not revert to instinct when he experiences vertigo in a storm.

Measuring Attentional Focus

Landers (1988) identified three primary ways in which attention may be measured by sport psychologists. In method one, a *behavioral* assessment of attention is made using the reaction time probe technique. In this procedure, attention demands of a primary task are estimated based on a subject's performance on a secondary reaction time task.

The second method used by sport psychologists for assessing attention is the use of *physiological indicators*. As illustrated in figure 7.7, physiological arousal and attentional focus are closely related. As the level of arousal increases, an individual's attentional focus tends to narrow (Landers, 1980).

The third method identified by Landers for assessing attention is the use of the *self-report*. While behavioral and physiological indicators of attention tend to measure attentional abilities at a specific point in time, the self-report method has tended to be more of an indicator of attentional focus as a personality trait or disposition. The primary originator of the self-report method for assessing attentional focus is Robert Nideffer (1976). Nideffer called his self-report inventory the Test of Attentional and Interpersonal Style (TAIS). Basing his research on reviews by Silverman (1964) and Wachtel (1967), Nideffer reasoned that an athlete's attentional processes could be represented as a function of two independent dimensions. The first he called *width* and the second he called *direction*. The width dimension of the athlete's attentional focus ranges from narrow to broad, while the direction dimension varies from internal to external.

FIGURE 7.8 | Attentional focus varies as a function of width and direction.

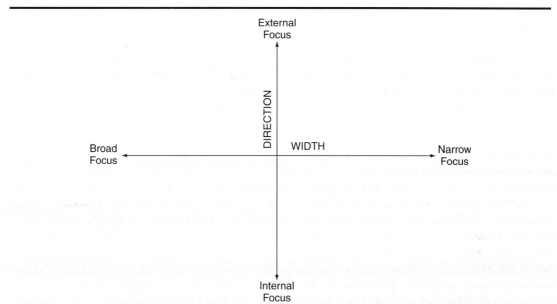

The width and direction dimensions of attentional focus are illustrated in figure 7.8. We were previously introduced to the notion of **width of attention** in figure 7.7. This dimension implies that an athlete's attentional focus can range from broad to narrow, and that it is closely associated with arousal. The **direction of attention** dimension, however, is new, and implies that an athlete can be internally or externally focused. In internal focus, the athlete's thoughts and feelings are directed inward; in external focus, the athlete's attention is directed to external cues such as the ball and the opponents.

Related to direction of attention is a study reported by Perkins-Ceccato, Passmore, and Lee (2003). In their investigation they asked 10 highly skilled and 10 less skilled golfers to practice pitching golf balls from varied distances towards a target using one of two different directional focus methods. In the internal focus method, the golfers were asked to focus internally, on their form and the force to be applied; in the external focus method, they were asked to focus externally, on hitting the ball as close to the target as possible. Results of the study suggested that skilled golfers do best while using an external focus, while less skilled golfers performed best under the internal focus condition.

Nideffer's TAIS was developed, in part, to measure an athlete's disposition to be narrowly or broadly focused and to be internally or externally focused. The TAIS is composed of 144 items which purport to measure seventeen subscales, six of which are attentional subscales. The six attentional subscales are identified in table 7.1, along with identifying characteristics. Three of the attentional subscales measure positive aspects of attentional focus (BET, BIT, NAR), while three measure negative aspects (OET, OIT, RED). In addition, table 7.1 provides a brief description of each scale, including dimension measured. Except for the BET and BIT, the six dimensions do not allow for a clear categorization into the four quadrants of attentional focus illustrated in figure 7.8.

Unfortunately, studies have failed to support the factor validity of the six attentional subscales

TABLE 7.1 | Description and Classification of Attentional Subscales as Measured by the Test of Attentional and Interpersonal Style

Scale	Name	Type	Dimension Measured	Scale Description
BET	Broad-External	Positive	Dir/Width	Environmental awareness
BIT	Broad-Internal	Positive	Dir/Width	Analytical planning skill
NAR	Narrow-Focused	Positive	Width	Avoid distractions and ability to stay focused
OET	External-Overload	Negative	Direction	Inappropriate attention to external stimuli
OIT	Internal-Overload	Negative	Direction	Inappropriate attention to internal stimuli
RED	Reduced Attention	Negative	Direction	Inability to shift direction (internal/external)

Source: Nideffer, R. N., & Sagal, M. (2006). Concentration and attentional control training. In J. M. Williams (Ed.), *Applied sport psychology: Personal growth to peak performance* (pp. 382–403). McGraw-Hill.

of the TAIS (Bergandi, Shryock, & Titus, 1990; Dewey, Brawley, & Allard, 1989; Landers, 1982; Van Schoyck & Grasha, 1981). Instead of measuring six subscales or factors reflective of width and direction, the TAIS actually measures a subscale that might be named "scanning," and another that might be named "focusing." Landers (1982) concluded that the TAIS is able to accurately measure the width dimension of attentional focus, but not the direction dimension.

Perhaps more important than an athlete's disposition toward a particular attentional profile is that athlete's ability to adopt an effective attentional focus for specific situations. In dynamic team sports such as basketball and football, an athlete's ideal attentional focus may change from moment to moment, as well as situation to situation. From an attentional perspective, the challenge faced by the quarterback in American football is particularly intriguing. In a pass play, the quarterback must simultaneously disregard the sights and sounds of charging defensive linesmen, and expand his field of vision so that he can see all of his receivers either directly or peripherally. We will discuss this problem further in the next section, on attention control training.

Attention Control Training

Sport psychologists have written extensively about attention control training (Nideffer, 1992;

Nideffer & Sagal, 2006; Schmid & Peper, 1998; Zinsser, Bunker, & Williams, 2001). The primary component of **attention control training** (ACT) is the process of narrowing or widening attention through arousal management strategies. As illustrated in figure 7.7, attention narrows as arousal increases. Also illustrated in this figure is the very clear concept that best performance occurs at an optimal level of arousal. The different interventions used to achieve optimal arousal are discussed in detail in part 4 of this book.

Focusing Attention   Let us return briefly to figure 7.8 and consider the challenges that confront the quarterback in American football. When the quarterback drops back for a pass play, he must gate out the sights and sounds of the attacking defensive line, while at the same time maintaining a broad external focus so that he will be able to see all of his potential receivers. If the quarterback fails to gate out the sights and sounds of the charging linemen, an incomplete pass, an interception, or a sack is a high probability. If the quarterback maintains an external focus that is too narrow due to high arousal, he will likely stare at a single receiver and be intercepted. The primary intent of attention control training for the quarterback should be to (a) teach him to have confidence in his offensive line so that he can gate out the sights and sounds of charging defensive linemen, and (b) teach him to control his emotions and arousal so that he can

CONCEPT Thought-stopping and centering skills help an athlete avoid errors caused by negative thoughts and diverted attention.

APPLICATION Thought-stopping and centering skills practiced and developed prior to competition can be used when they are needed. Specific positive thoughts, relevant cues, and task-oriented suggestions should be practiced and readied for competition.

create an optimal width of attention focus. Due to individual differences, the optimal band of attention will vary from athlete to athlete and from situation to situation.

The concepts introduced in figure 7.8 about attention can be applied to any sport or performance situation. Every sport situation requires an optimal level of arousal to create an optimal width of attention focus (narrow/broad). As an athlete prepares for competition, she will focus her attention internally, as she considers thoughts and feelings associated with analyzing and rehearsing; and externally, as she assesses the situation, teammates, and opponents. Attention control required for actual competition is generally externally focused and ranges from narrow to broad, depending on the situation.

Thought Stopping and Centering

In addition to arousal management, attention training must teach the athlete how to eliminate negative thoughts. It is critically important that the athlete learn to use attention to stop negative thoughts and to focus on positive thoughts. This is a problem that confronts athletes regularly. To overcome feelings of self-doubt, it is necessary to apply the principles of selective attention as discussed in this chapter. In other words, the athlete must develop a high degree of attentional control. As defined by Nideffer & Sagal (2006), attention control is a technique designed to keep the athlete from slipping into a cycle of anxiety and self-doubt.

It is important that the athlete approach every sport situation with a positive attitude and belief that she will succeed. When negative thoughts come into consciousness, they must be removed or displaced with positive thoughts. The process of stopping a negative thought and replacing it with a positive one is referred to as **thought stopping** (Zinsser et al., 2001). It is a basic principle of psychology that an athlete cannot give quality attention to more than one attention-demanding task at a time. In this case, it is the mental task of thinking a positive as opposed to a negative thought. Once the negative thought has been displaced, the athlete centers her attention internally. The process of **centering** involves directing thoughts internally. It is during the internal process of centering that the athlete makes conscious adjustments in attention and arousal. According to Nideffer and Sagal (2006), the process of centering involves being consciously aware of the body's center of gravity, while at the same time internalizing thought processes. Immediately following the centering process, the athlete narrowly focuses her attention on a task-relevant external cue. It is at this point that she takes skilled action. Any delay between directing attention externally and skill execution will only invite distractions in the form of negative thoughts or unwanted environmental stimuli.

Let's take a specific example. Say you are standing at the foul line and are about to shoot a game-winning (or game-losing) foul shot. The thought goes through your mind, "I'm going to miss, I can feel it. The basket is too small, it's a mile away, and I'm scared!" You are losing control. To successfully use the thought-stopping and centering procedure, you must first use the principle of selective attention to drive out the negative thought with a positive thought. You might say to yourself, "No, I'm an excellent shooter; I'm the best person on the team to be shooting in this situation." At this point you center your attention internally as you make minor adjustments in your level of arousal. Many athletes accomplish this by taking a deep breath and exhaling slowly. Then you turn your attention to the basketball hoop and focus upon a task-oriented suggestion, such as "follow through, and put a little backspin on the ball." By using the thought-stopping and centering procedure correctly and practicing it in many different situations, you will have an instant weapon to use against the occasional loss of attentional control.

The following basic steps are used in the thought-stopping and centering procedure:

1. Displace any negative thought that comes into your mind with a positive thought.
2. Center your attention internally while making minor adjustments in arousal.
3. Narrowly focus your attention externally on a task-relevant cue associated with proper form.
4. Execute the sport skill as soon as you have achieved a feeling of attentional control.

Learning the thought-stopping and centering procedure takes practice. The critical point to understand is that negative thoughts can be displaced, and that through the process of centering, the thoughts that capture attention can be controlled. The conscious process of thought stopping and centering will divert the athlete's attention from threatening thoughts and anxiety-producing stimuli. Selective attention will effectively gate out the unwanted thoughts if the correct thoughts are pertinent and meaningful to the athlete (Singer, 2002).

Associative versus Dissociative Attentional Style

Morgan (1978) hypothesized that marathon runners adopt one of two **attentional styles** to assist

them in training and competition. He defined **associators** as those runners who *internalize* the direction dimension of attention and focus on the body's sensory feedback signals. Conversely, he defined **dissociators** as those runners who *externalize* the direction dimension of attention and gate out or block out sensory information from the body. It was Morgan's basic hypothesis that elite marathon runners tend to be associators, while less elite runners tend to be dissociators. He further hypothesized that associators would be less prone to injury due to their monitoring of sensory feedback. Morgan's basic theory has generated a great deal of interest on the part of sport psychologists and runners. In 1998, Masters and Ogles (1998a) cited 26 separate investigations on this topic alone. There have been many more articles published on the topic since then.

Terminology and Classification   Since 1978, the basic concept of associators versus dissociators has persisted, but there has been concern expressed about terminology. Masters and Ogles (1998a) point out that the term "dissociative" is confusing, because it is so similar to the term "dissociative disorder" in clinical psychology. In response, Stevinson and Biddle (1999) suggested that the term "dissociation" be replaced with the term "distraction," and that both association and distraction be divided into internal and external components. In this regard, Couture, Jerome, and Tihanyi (1999) noted that working on a math problem or reciting poetry would be examples of internal distraction, while attending to scenery, trees, and the environment would be examples of external distraction.

Consistent with suggestions made by Masters and Ogles (1998b) and Stevinson and Biddle (1999), figure 7.9 illustrates the two-dimensional model of attentional strategy. In this model, the term "distraction" replaces the controversial term "dissociative"; and both "associative" and "distraction" are conceptualized as having internal and external direction components. Prior to the introduction of the two-dimensional model, everything

FIGURE 7.9 | Stevinson and Biddle's (1999) two-dimensional classification system for conceptualizing attentional strategy.

	Direction of attention	
	Internal	External
Associative	Associative–Internal	Associative–External
	Focus on form, how muscles feel, and breathing	Focus on time splits, distance completed, and strategy
Distraction	Distraction–Internal	Distraction–External
	Daydreaming, fantasizing, and problem solving in the mind	Focus on external or environmental stimuli, such as scenery and wildlife

*(Row label group: **Task Relevance**, with rows **Associative** and **Distraction**)*

Source: Stevinson, C.D., & Biddle, S.J.H. (1999). Cognitive strategies in running: A response to Masters and Ogles. *The Sport Psychologist, 26:* page 236, figure 1. Adapted with permission from Human Kinetics (Champaign, IL)

that was previously labeled associative would fit into the single cell labeled associative-internal, while everything else would be considered dissociative (the other three cells). Later we will report on an investigation that used the two-dimensional attentional strategy model (Connolly & Janelle, 2003).

Measurement of Attentional Style

Masters and Ogles (1998a) noted that researchers have utilized six different methods of measuring attentional style. Methods of measurement include pencil-and-paper inventories, structured interviews, tape recordings during running, objective data, subjective data, and experimenter rating. Pencil-and-paper inventories include the Running Style Questionnaire (RSQ; Silva & Appelbaum, 1989), the Attentional Focus Questionnaire (AFQ; Brewer, Van Raalte, & Linder, 1996), and the Thoughts During Running Scale (TDRS; Goode & Roth, 1993).

Research Findings In the following paragraphs, research findings related to attentional style will be discussed as a function of attentional preferences, performance relationships, and link to injuries.

Attentional Preferences Marathon runners and other long-distance runners use both associative and dissociative styles of attention. During competition, the vast majority of running time is linked to the associative attentional style. Conversely, during training runs, the vast majority of running time is linked to the dissociative style. Increased exertion and running intensity are linked to the associative attention style (Bachman, Brewer, & Petitpas, 1997; Schomer, 1990; Tammen, 1996). Runners prefer the associative style for competition and the dissociative style for practice runs (Masters & Ogles, 1998a). It is believed that the greater intensity needed for competition can be best obtained by internally associating with sensory feedback from the body (Nietfeld, 2003). The dissociative style is believed to be more relaxing and preferred during training and recreation runs. The dissociative style allows the body to either disregard sensory feedback or simply drift off to more pleasant and distracting thoughts.

Performance Relationships Masters and Ogles (1998a) note that for laboratory-controlled muscular endurance (leg extension) tasks, the dissociative style yields the best performance. However, because marathoners prefer the associative style during competition, it can be inferred that this style yields superior running times. This inference is supported by research involving swimming (Couture et al., 1999) and rowing (Scott, Scott, Bedic, & Dowd, 1999).

Earlier in our discussion on attentional style, we introduced Stevinson and Biddle's (1999) two-dimensional classification system for conceptualizing attentional strategies (see figure 7.9). Utilizing the two-dimensional classification system, Connolly and Janelle (2003) conducted an investigation using male and female collegiate

CONCEPT   The proportion of associative (internal) attentional focus is directly related to perceived exertion in skilled marathoners and long-distance runners. Consequently, the proportion of internal focus increases during competition, but decreases during training runs.

APPLICATION   In order to be an effective long-distance runner, it is important that the athlete be able to internally focus a large proportion of the time. Through careful coaching, the athlete can learn to use an associative attentional strategy. It would be a mistake, however, to insist that an athlete associate all of the time. Dissociating is more relaxing, and provides a needed psychological break for the marathoner.

rowers. Using a rowing ergometer machine, the participants completed a baseline piece and four experimental pieces that were each 2000 meters in distance. For each rowing piece, the participants were asked to try to keep their heart rates at between 160 and 180 beats per minute. Time to complete the rowing piece (performance), heart rate, and rating of perceived exertion were monitored for the baseline and experimental rowing pieces. The four experimental rowing sessions were presented in a counterbalanced order over a four-week period. Each experimental rowing piece represented one of the cells in the two-dimensional classification system shown in figure 7.9. Thus, the participants completed their four experimental rowing sessions using the following attentional strategies in counterbalanced order: Associative-Internal, Associative-External, Distraction-Internal, Distraction-External. Compared to the two distraction conditions, the two associative conditions were superior in terms of performance, heart rate (faster), and effort. Thus, the results of this investigation are similar to earlier studies, in that the associative attentional strategy yields greater performance and effort compared to the dissociative (distraction) condition. However, this investigation provides additional insight into the nature of attentional strategy as it relates to rowing. An associative style that focuses upon strategies necessary to do well at the task (associative-external) is as effective as a style that focuses upon the body's sensory feedback (associative-internal).

Finally, a recent study by Baden, Warwick-Evans, and Lakomy (2004) provided new and interesting information that related attentional strategy and effort expenditure with expected exercise duration. The investigation provided evidence that exercisers run with greater effort and with a greater percentage of associative style when they believe the trial run is of short as opposed to long duration. Conversely, if they believe the trial run is of long duration, they tend to pace themselves (less effort expenditure) and to dissociate more during the run.

Link to Injuries   Morgan (1978) hypothesized that the greater incidence of injuries would be linked to the dissociative style of running, because the athlete is not attending to his body signals. Research, however, has failed to support this hypothesis. Research and literature reviews by Masters and Ogles (1998a, 1998b) provide strong evidence that the associative strategy has a stronger link to physical injuries than the dissociative strategy. It is believed that athletes engaging in a dissociative style of attentional focusing are running with less intensity in a more relaxed mode, and therefore are less susceptible to injury. Conversely, the associator is running with great intensity, and is therefore more susceptible to athletic injury, even though she is attending to body signals.

Summary

The intent of the first part of this chapter is to give the reader a basic understanding of arousal from a neurophysiological perspective. Without this basic understanding, the student would not be able to fully appreciate the role that arousal and activation play in sport and exercise psychology.

There are three major divisions of the nervous system. These three are (a) the central nervous system (CNS), (b) the peripheral nervous system, and (c) the autonomic nervous system. The CNS is composed of the brain, the brain stem, and the spinal cord. The peripheral nervous system provides innervation from the brain and spinal cord to all of the skeletal muscles of the body. The autonomic nervous system innervates the glands and visceral organs of the body. Structures of the central nervous system (CNS) that are closely related to the onset of the arousal response in humans include the cerebral cortex and hypothalamus in the brain, and the ascending reticular activating system in the brain stem.

There are two major divisions to the autonomic nervous system. The first is named the sympathetic nervous system, and the second is the parasympathetic nervous system. The terminal nerve endings of all parasympathetic neurons secrete acetylcholine, while most sympathetic nerve endings secrete norepinephrine. These hormones act on different organs and glands to bring about their respective sympathetic and parasympathetic effects.

When stimulated by the sympathetic nervous system, the adrenal medullae release epinephrine and norepinephrine into the blood stream. The total effect of massive stimulation of organs by the sympathetic nervous system and the adrenal medullae is to bring about the stress response, often referred to as the alarm reaction, or fight or flight response. The section is concluded with a discussion of electrophysiological indicators of arousal.

The focus of the second part of this chapter was upon attention and concentration in sport. The information processing model of attention recognizes the presence of many variables and processes between a stimulus and a response. Memory plays an important role in information processing. The three types, or stages, of memory are the sensory register, short-term memory, and long-term memory. Information is measured in bits. The amount of information conveyed by a particular problem can be quantified in terms of questions asked, or in terms of a mathematical formula.

The ability to gate out irrelevant information and attend to important information is called selective attention. A number of structural models of selective attention have been proposed. Three models mentioned in this chapter were the Broadbent model, Norman's pertinence model, and the Triesman model.

The notion of limited information processing capacity helps explain the difference between skilled and unskilled athletes. If a particular task requires all of a person's information processing space, then none will be left over for attending to other tasks that also require attention.

Easterbrook's cue utilization theory deals with the phenomenon of attentional narrowing. As an athlete's arousal increases, the athlete's attentional focus narrows. The narrowing process tends to gate out irrelevant cues, and sometimes relevant ones as well.

The perfect execution of a sports skill is best thought of as an elegant interaction between mind and body. Describing a peak performance as simply being in the "zone," as if there is a separation of the mind from the body, diminishes the immense preparation that goes into training to become an elite athlete, at any level of competition.

Attentional focus is measured through behavioral assessment (e.g., reaction time probe), physiological indicators, and pencil-and-paper self-report. The most common self-report method is Nideffer's Test of Attentional and Interpersonal Style (TAIS). While the factor structure of the attentional components of the TAIS is not well established, the TAIS continues to be a popular inventory for assessing width and direction of attention.

The primary component of attention control training (ACT) is the process of narrowing or widening attention through arousal management strategies. Every sport situation requires an optimal level of arousal to create an optimal width of attention focus. In addition to arousal management, attention training teaches the athlete how to eliminate negative thoughts. This is accomplished through thought stopping and centering.

Marathon runners tend to both internalize (associate) and externalize (dissociate) in terms of attentional focus. Marathoners prefer the associative style for competition and the dissociative style for practice runs and training. Because marathoners prefer the associative style during competition, it can be inferred that this style yields superior running times. This inference is supported by research in swimming and rowing. Athletes engaging in a dissociative style of attentional focusing are running with less intensity, in a more relaxed mode, and therefore are less susceptible to injury.

The chapter was concluded with a discussion of the two-dimensional classification system for conceptualizing attentional strategy.

Critical Thought Questions

1. From a neurophysiological perspective, you should now understand the events leading up to the stress response. From a neurophysiological perspective, how would you propose that the physiological indicators of the stress response be reversed?

2. Research has shown that the various neurophysiological indicators of arousal are not highly correlated. Why do you think this is the case, and how do you think this would affect the way in which sport psychologists measure arousal?

3. What does knowing how to calculate bits of information conveyed in a sports situation have to do with athletic performance? Provide examples to support your arguments.

4. Can an athlete gate out distracting information while at the same time maintain a broad external focus of attention? If so, give examples in sport where this occurs.

5. What does it mean to you when a sports announcer says that an athlete is in the "zone"? Do you think this term represents an oversimplification of a complex interaction between mind and body? What is an athlete's mind doing when the athlete is in the "zone"?

6. Distinguish between effects, causes, and mechanisms associated with "choking" and "panicking" in human performance. Give examples.

7. What are your feelings about using the TAIS to evaluate an athlete's attentional abilities?

8. Develop thought-stopping and centering scenarios for five different sporting situations. Assume you are the coach and you are doing this for your athletes.

9. Why is the research on attentional style important to the coach and the athlete?

10. Discuss the two dimensional classification system for conceptualizing attentional strategy as it relates to performance, effort, and environmental application.

Glossary

acetylcholine The cholinergic hormone released at the nerve endings of the parasympathetic nerves.

adrenal medullae Two organs that sit one on top of each kidney, which are innervated by the sympathetic nervous system. They release epinephrine and norepinephrine into the bloodstream.

arousal   A neutral physiological phenomenon that is associated with increases in heart rate, blood pressure, respiration, metabolism, and other indicators of activation.

arousal response   End product of autonomic nervous system activity, which ranges from deep sleep to extreme excitement.

ascending reticular activating system   That part of the reticular formation that stimulates the hypothalamus and cerebral cortex when arousing stimuli are present. Located in the brain stem.

associators   Long-distance runners who internalize, or adopt an internal attentional focus.

attention control training   The process of teaching athletes how to narrow and widen their attention focus and to control their thoughts.

attentional flexibility   The ability of athletes to quickly and effectively shift their attention from one location to another.

attentional focus   In sports, an athlete's ability to focus on relevant information during competition.

attentional narrowing   The narrowing of an athlete's attentional focus due to an increase in arousal.

attentional style   An athlete's particular style of attending to stimuli.

automatic processing   The execution of a skill that, although it is being monitored by the brain, requires little conscious attention because it is well learned.

autonomic nervous system   That part of the nervous system that controls visceral and glandular functions of the body.

bit   A term that stands for binary digit, a unit of information measurement. The number of bits corresponds to the number of questions needed to accurately predict the occurrence of an event.

capacity model   A model of attention based on limited information processing space.

centering   The process whereby an athlete's attention is brought to focus on an important task-oriented suggestion.

central nervous system   That part of the nervous system that is composed of the brain, brain stem, and spinal cord.

cerebral cortex   The area of the brain responsible for higher brain functions and conscious thought processes.

chunking   The cognitive process of combining several separate pieces of information into larger ones.

cognitive interference   Random thought or distraction that breaks an athlete's concentration.

controlled processing   An athlete's necessary attentional focus on the details of executing a skill that is being learned.

cue utilization   According to Easterbrook, the process of narrowing attention to gate out environmental cues.

direction of attention   An athlete's attentional focus, categorized as being internal or external.

dissociators   Long-distance runners who externalize, or adopt an external attentional focus.

distractibility   An athlete's inability to selectively attend to relevant stimuli due to very high levels of arousal.

electroencephalograph   The machine, using scalp electrodes, that measures the amount and type of electrical activity generated by the brain.

electromyograph   Machine, using electrodes, that measures the electrical activity generated by a muscle.

epinephrine   The adrenergic hormone released into the bloodstream by the adrenal medullae.

fight or flight response   The widespread bodily reaction to a stimulus that is synonymous with the sympathetic alarm reaction or stress response.

galvanic skin response   A decrease in skin resistance associated with an increase in palmar sweating. Measured with skin electrodes.

gate out Exclude or ignore irrelevant sensory information.

hypothalamus An area of the brain that plays a major role in controlling many bodily functions, including emotions and arousal. Located in the midbrain.

individual differences The differences between individual athletes in the amount of processing capacity they have available, as well as in how they utilize the capacity they have.

information conveyed The amount of information, in bits, contained in a particular problem. For example, a reaction-time problem containing four lights conveys two bits of information if all four lights are equally likely to flash.

information processing model A model based on the theory that humans process information rather than merely responding to stimuli. Many cognitive processes are involved. For example, information must be stored, retrieved, and rehearsed.

long-term memory Long-term or permanent memory.

memory storage Capacity to store all information reaching memory for future recall.

norepinephrine The adrenergic hormone released at the nerve endings of the sympathetic nerves, as well as into the bloodstream by the adrenal medullae.

palmar sweating The activation of sweat glands in the hands by the sympathetic nervous system in response to a threat.

parasympathetic nervous system The division of the autonomic nervous system that secretes acetylcholine at its nerve endings and operates in some cases in a fashion reciprocal to the sympathetic nervous system.

peripheral scanning Instead of seeing objects peripherally while focusing on a central task, the athlete repeatedly scans peripheral objects and then quickly returns to the central task.

playing in the zone A nondescriptive term that refers to extraordinary performance of an athlete.

processing capacity The limited amount of space people have available for the processing of information.

reaction time probe A procedure used in attention research to determine if a certain primary task requires information processing space.

retrieval The mental process of retrieving information to make decisions about forthcoming responses.

selective attention The capability of humans to attend to one stimulus to the exclusion of others.

sensory register A short-term sensory store that effectively retains information for about one-half second before it is lost or transferred to a more permanent storage system.

short-term memory The working memory, or the center of activity in the information processing system.

skin conductivity The ease with which a small charge of electricity can pass between two skin electrodes. Skin conductivity is increased when palmar sweating is increased.

skin resistance Resistance to a small charge of electricity that passes between two skin electrodes. Skin resistance is decreased when palmar sweating is increased.

stress response The widespread bodily reaction to a stimulus that is synonymous with the sympathetic alarm reaction or fight or flight response.

sympathetic alarm response The widespread bodily reaction to a stimulus that is synonymous with the stress or fight or flight response.

sympathetic nervous system The division of the autonomic nervous system that secretes norepinephrine at most nerve endings and is often associated with the fight or flight response.

thought stopping In sport, the process of replacing a negative thought with a success-oriented, positive thought.

width of attention An athlete's attentional focus, ranging from broad to narrow.

CHAPTER 8

Anxiety, Arousal, and Stress Relationships

KEY TERMS

Affect
Antecedent
Anxiety
Autotelic experience
Catastrophe theory
Cognitive anxiety
Competitive situation
Competitive state anxiety
Direction component
  of anxiety
Distress
Drive
Drive Theory
Emotion
Eustress
Flow
Hysteresis
Individual zone of optimal
  functioning
Intensity component
  of anxiety
Intraindividualized scores
Inverted-U theory
Ipsative z-score
Metamotivational
Multidimensional
Multidimensional anxiety
  theory

Neurotic perfectionism
Organizational stress
Paratelic-dominant
  individual
Perfectionism
Precompetitive state anxiety
Prestart state anxiety
Primary appraisal
Psychological reversal
Recall method
Reversal theory

Secondary appraisal
Signal detection theory
Somatic anxiety
Standard deviation
State anxiety
Stress
Stress process
Telic-dominant individual
Trait anxiety
Yerkes-Dodson law
z-score

The following story about a young athlete illustrates the potentially debilitating effects of anxiety on athletic performance. Ryan is a physically gifted 16-year-old athlete. He participates in several sports for his high school during the academic year and plays summer baseball as well. Some of the team sports he excels in are football, basketball, and baseball. However, his favorite sport is track and field, which is primarily an individual sport.

Ryan is a highly anxious young man with a tendency toward perfectionism. In Ryan's particular case, these traits had very little negative effect on his performance in the team sports he played. He would often get uptight about a big game, but he could always rely upon his teammates to help him out. The fact that team games involved other players seemed to help control the negative impact his anxiety could have had on his performance. Ryan occasionally "clutched" during baseball games, but the outcome of the game was rarely affected. Usually, only Ryan and Ryan's parents were aware of the anxiety and tension that were boiling within.

However, track and field was a different matter. Ryan was a sprinter and hurdler. His physical power and mesomorphic build made him especially well equipped for running and jumping events that required speed and leg power. Unfortunately, his basic anxiety and worry about failing had a serious effect on his performance during competition. During practice, Ryan always did well. In fact, during three years of high school Ryan had never lost a race to a teammate during practice. In actual competition, things were different. Ryan began preparing mentally for his races days in advance of the actual competition. During the days and hours preceding competition, his anxiety would rise to fearful levels. By the time actual competition came, Ryan could hardly walk, let alone run or jump. Several times he had to vomit before important races. His coach talked to him a great deal about learning to relax and not worry about the race, but didn't give him specific suggestions on how to accomplish this. Finally, the coach decided to remove Ryan from his favorite events because he was actually a detriment to the team. This was more than Ryan could take. He approached the coach one day and announced that he was going to give up athletics altogether and concentrate on his studies. This story has a successful conclusion, but it will be shared later, at the beginning of the cognitive and behavioral intervention section of the book (part 4).

In explaining the relationships between anxiety, arousal, and stress, and their relationship to athletic performance, it is important that we understand a number of conceptual relationships. Therefore, this chapter is divided into the following seven sections: (a) differentiating among the terms *anxiety, arousal,* and *stress;* (b) the multidimensional nature of anxiety; (c) antecedents of anxiety; (d) measurement of anxiety; (e) time-to-event nature of precompetitive anxiety; (f) the relationship between anxiety and performance; and (g) alternatives to inverted-U theory.

Differentiating among Anxiety, Arousal, and Stress

The focus of this chapter is upon the emotion of anxiety and how it affects athletic performance. The problem, however, is that the term "anxiety" is closely associated with the terms "arousal" and "stress." In this section we are going to clarify the ways in which these terms are similar and the ways in which they differ. To accomplish this it will be useful to focus our discussion upon emotions and mood, Selye's concept of stress, and Lazarus's concept of the stress process.

Emotions and Mood

Lazarus (2000a) defines an **emotion** as "an organized psychophysiological reaction to ongoing relationships with the environment, most often, but not always, interpersonal or social" (p. 230). Lazarus identifies 15 different emotions and core themes associated with each emotion. One of these emotions is **anxiety,** which he defines as "facing

CONCEPT Anxiety is one of many emotions that may arise in response to a competitive situation.

APPLICATION In this chapter our focus will be upon the emotion of anxiety and its effects upon athletic behavior. However, it is important to remember that there are many other emotions, and that each may have a little different effect upon behavior. Emotion is a complex experience that arises in response to appraisal of the environmental situation as well as to an evaluation of coping resources.

uncertain, existential threat" (p. 234). An emotion, such as anxiety, occurs following appraisal and an evaluation of coping resources. A similar chain of events occurs for the emotion of anger, which he defines as occurring in response to "a demeaning offense against me or mine." The point is that each emotion occurs as a discrete response to an environmental event following appraisal of the situation (Mellalieu, 2003).

Lazarus identifies anxiety as one of the emotions that may have substantial impact upon how an athlete performs. Other emotions, such as anger, guilt and shame, relief, happiness, and pride, may also have a powerful influence upon performance. Lazarus (2000a, 2000b) argues, however, that emotions should not be lumped into positive and negative groups when one is assessing their effect upon athletic performance. Rather, the different emotions should be considered as discrete emotions having discrete effects upon performance. Anger, for example, is often considered a negative emotion, yet it may have either an inhibitory or a facilitatory effect upon performance (Cerin, 2003; Cerin, Szabo, Hunt, & Williams, 2000).

Anxiety, then, is an emotion that arises in response to how we interpret and appraise an environmental situation such as competition. **Affect** is a generic term used to describe emotions, feelings, and moods. In a previous chapter we discussed the effect that moods have on athletic performance. What is the difference, you might ask, between the terms "emotion" and "mood"? These two are differentiated as a function of time (Vallerand & Blanchard, 2000). Emotions are sudden reactions to a situation that last only for seconds, minutes, or perhaps hours. Moods, however, are more diffuse, and may last for weeks or even months. Depending upon how the inventory is worded, the Profile of Mood States (POMS), for example, may actually measure emotions more than it measures moods.

An emotion, such as anxiety, occurs as a momentary response to something, whereas a mood is longer in duration and may persist. Jones (2003) further clarifies that an emotion is composed of three main elements. First, an emotion is associated with a physiological change. For example, anxiety would be associated with an increase in arousal, whereas sadness might be associated with a decrease in arousal. Second, an emotion is associated with a subjective experience. For example, an athlete might experience anger due to missing a tackle in football. Third, an emotion is associated with an action tendency. Experiencing the emotion of exhilaration might energize an athlete to a successful spike in volleyball. While our focus in this chapter is on the emotion of anxiety, it is important to be able to generalize to other emotions. This will become even more evident later on in this chapter, when we talk about the zone of optimal functioning.

Selye's Concept of Stress

Hans Selye (pronounced "sale-ye") (1983, p. 2) defined **stress** as the "nonspecific response of the body to any demand made upon it." In a sense, what Selye is saying is that when aroused, the body is under stress regardless of whether the

FIGURE 8.1 | The stress process and not the competitive situation determines the extent of the stress response.

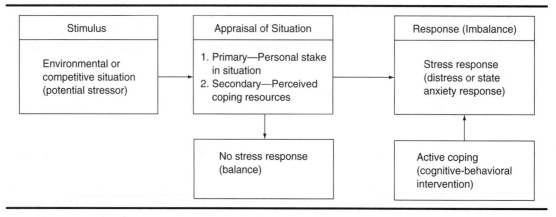

cause is something negative like anger or positive like joy. The point is that the "engine" is running at a high rate of speed in either case. It can be argued, however, that anger and anxiety are much harder on the body than are joy and happiness. To take these factors into consideration, Selye allowed that there must be two different kinds of stress. The "good stress" he labeled **eustress,** and the "bad stress" he labeled **distress.** In this chapter distress will be considered to be synonymous with what we will later define as state anxiety.

While distress and arousal (defined in chapter 7) are not identical concepts, it is generally understood that the two are correlated. That is, a high level of distress or state anxiety is associated with an increase in physiological arousal. This is consistent with our understanding of the stress response as illustrated previously in figure 7.2. The most prevalent coping strategy for reducing the debilitating effects of the stress response is to reduce arousal through relaxation. We will talk about reducing the debilitating effects of anxiety through relaxation in part 4 of the text.

The Stress Process

The best way to understand stress is to conceptualize it as a process, as opposed to an outcome. The

stress process, as illustrated in figure 8.1, is really the information processing model in action. The stress process begins with the stimulus (competitive situation) on the left and results in the response (stress response) on the right. In between the stimulus and the response is cognition, or thought processes. Cognition determines how the athlete will respond (Lazarus, 2000a, 2000b; Lazarus & Folkman, 1984).

The stress process begins with the environmental or competitive situation on the left. This is the stimulus. The **competitive situation** is not by itself stressful. It is how the athlete interprets the situation that determines whether or not the situation is stressful. Consider the situation in which an athlete finds himself on the foul line in a basketball game with the outcome of the game resting upon his performance. To most people this would be an extremely stressful situation. However, to many basketball players this is exactly the kind of situation that they seek. The situation is not intimidating because they have supreme confidence in their skill and the thought of failure does not enter their minds.

In October of 2004, the Boston Red Sox made history by defeating the New York Yankees in seven games to get into baseball's World Series. There were many heroes in that series, but none

CONCEPT Whether or not an athlete responds to a threatening situation with high levels of state anxiety will depend entirely on the athlete's perception of the situation.

APPLICATION Each athlete is unique and should be treated as an individual. Do not attempt to predict an athlete's anxiety response to a competitive situation based on your own perception of the same situation. The athlete's own perception of the situation will determine the level of anxiety response, if any.

greater than David Ortiz. What Ortiz accomplished in the face of potential extreme anxiety and tension speaks to his ability to manage the stress process. In game four of the American League Championship Series (ALCS), and down three games to none, David Ortiz hit a walk-off home run in the 12th inning to win the game and stave off what seemed to be a sure four-game sweep by the Yankees. Then, in game five, Ortiz hit a single in the bottom of the 14th inning to win the game and keep the seven-game series alive (Kepner, 2004).

Consider a nonathletic situation. Suppose you walk into an old abandoned home and notice that right on the ceiling above you is a very large spider. Does this evoke the stress response in your body? For most people it would, but not for all. Some individuals are not afraid of spiders because of their experiences with them. They know that most spiders are harmless and that this one is big and harmless. The difference is in perception. To understand this we look at the middle panel of figure 8.1.

Upon being confronted with a *potentially* stressful situation, the individual conducts an instantaneous appraisal or evaluation of the situation. Appraisal of the situation occurs on two levels. The first is referred to as primary appraisal, and the second as secondary appraisal. In **primary appraisal,** the athlete determines if she has a personal stake in the outcome. If the athlete determines that the outcome is very important to her, then secondary appraisal becomes important. In **secondary appraisal,** the athlete evaluates her personal coping resources to deal with the competitive situation. The outcomes of the primary and secondary appraisals determine whether the stress response will or will not occur.

If an athlete determines either that it makes no difference to him personally if he makes a play, or that he is perfectly capable of coping with the situation, then the stress response does not occur. In this case, we say that there is a *balance* between the stressful nature of the competitive situation and the athlete's perceived ability to cope with the situation. If, however, the athlete determines that he does not have the resources (skill, confidence, experience) to cope with the situation, the stress response will occur. In this case we say that there is an *imbalance* between the stressful nature of the competitive situation and the athlete's perceived ability to cope. The stress response is equated with Selye's concept of distress, or what we will later define as state anxiety.

Also shown in figure 8.1 is a box labeled "active coping." If the state anxiety response proves to be detrimental to performance, it may become necessary to intervene in some way to reduce debilitating anxiety. We will discuss active coping, or cognitive-behavioral interventions, in part 4 of the text.

An anecdote related by Fisher (1976) serves to clarify the relationships illustrated in figure 8.1. Two researchers were studying the effects of fear of drowning on the physiological responses of a subject. The subject was strapped to the side of a swimming tank with the water steadily rising. For some reason the researchers left the test area and forgot about their subject. When they remembered, they were aghast and numb with fear. Dropping everything, they raced to the test area to find the water level dangerously high. Quickly, they unstrapped the subject and pulled him from the water. Safe on the pool deck, they asked the subject if he was frightened. The subject responded that he wasn't at all worried, because it was just an experiment and he knew that the researchers wouldn't let any harm come to him! The subject perceived the test situation to be nonthreatening, and therefore the state anxiety reaction was not evoked.

To this point, all of our discussion on the stress process has focused on the individual athlete relative to figure 8.1, but there is another kind of stress that we have not talked about, and that is the stress placed on the athlete by the organizing body. **Organizational stress** is the stress placed on the athlete by the competitive sport environment, not just the coaches or a specific competitive event (Fletcher & Hanton, 2003; Noblett & Gifford, 2002; Woodman & Hardy, 2001). Fletcher and Hanton (2003) identified four sources of potential organizational stress: (a) environmental issues

(selection, travel, accommodations, competitive environment, etc.), (b) personal issues (nutrition, injury, goals, expectations, etc.), (c) leadership issues (coaches and coaching style, etc.), and (d) team issues (team atmosphere, support network, roles, communication, etc.). Taken together, issues associated with organizational stress can take their toll on the athlete.

The Multidimensional Nature of Anxiety

Anxiety is **multidimensional** in two different ways. Like all other emotions, anxiety has both a trait component and a state component. The trait component is like a personality disposition, whereas the state component is a situation-specific response. **State anxiety** is an immediate emotional state that is characterized by apprehension, fear, tension, and an increase in physiological arousal. Conversely, **trait anxiety** is a *predisposition* to perceive certain environmental situations as threatening and to respond to these situations with increased state anxiety

FIGURE 8.2 | Both trait and state anxiety exhibit cognitive and somatic anxiety components.

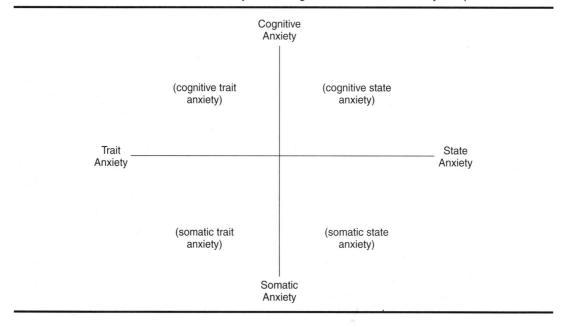

(Spielberger, 1971). If an athlete has a high level of competitive trait anxiety, she is likely to respond to an actual competitive situation with a high level of competitive state anxiety.

Anxiety is also multidimensional in the sense that it is believed that there are both cognitive and somatic components to anxiety (Endler, Parker, Bagby, & Cox, 1991). **Cognitive anxiety** is the mental component of anxiety caused by such things as fear of negative social evaluation, fear of failure, and loss of self-esteem. **Somatic anxiety** is the physical component of anxiety and reflects the *perception* of such physiological responses as increased heart rate, respiration, and muscular tension. Both state and trait anxiety are believed to have cognitive and somatic components. In the sport psychology literature, the notion that anxiety has both cognitive and somatic components is referred to as *multidimensional anxiety theory* (Martens, Vealey, & Burton, 1990). The bipolar, multidimensional nature of anxiety is illustrated in figure 8.2.

Antecedents of Precompetitive State Anxiety

Competitive state anxiety that occurs prior to a competitive situation is referred to as **precompetitive state anxiety.** According to Endler (1978, 1983), there are five specific **antecedents,** or factors that lead to an increase in anxiety in anticipation of

an achievement situation. These five factors are as follows:

1. *Fear of performance failure*   Fear of getting defeated by a weaker opponent could pose a threat to an athlete's ego.
2. *Fear of negative social evaluation*   Fear of being evaluated negatively by thousands of spectators could pose a threat to self-esteem.
3. *Fear of physical harm*   Fear of being hit in the head by a 90 mph fastball could pose a serious threat.
4. *Situation ambiguity*   Not knowing if she is going to start a match is sometimes stressful to an athlete.
5. *Disruption of well-learned routine*   Being asked to change the way he does things without practice and warning could be threatening to an athlete.

Research has identified fear of failure and fear of negative social evaluation as the most likely causes of state anxiety in ice hockey athletes (Dunn, 1999). Even though ice hockey is a very physically demanding sport, the athletes were not particularly worried about being harmed physically. Another antecedent or cause of state anxiety is the perceived importance of a competition (Marchant, Morris, & Anderson, 1998). Athletes who exhibit high levels of competitive trait anxiety and perceive an event to be important are more likely to perceive it as stressful. In addition, Thuot, Kavouras, and Kenefick (1998) observed that high school basketball players exhibit elevated levels of state anxiety in response to perceived skill level of their opponents. Consistent with the stress process illustrated in figure 8.1, Hammermeister and Burton (2001) noted that in addition to perceived threat, perceived lack of control and coping resources may be considered antecedents to a state anxiety response. Research has also demonstrated that situation ambiguity in sport is a viable antecedent and predictor of state anxiety (Beauchamp, Bray, Eys, & Carron, 2003; Eubank, Collins, & Smith, 2002).

In addition to situation factors as identified above, a number of personality variables have been identified as being antecedents, or predictors, of competititive state anxiety. These include competitive trait anxiety, goal orientation, and perfectionism. In women's softball, athletes categorized as optimists exhibited lower levels of precompetitive state anxiety than pessimists (Wilson & Steinke, 2002). In golf, individuals who were high in competitive trait anxiety were observed to exhibit higher levels of state anxiety prior to an achievement situation (Marchant et al., 1998). In a study involving cross-country runners, Hall, Kerr, and Matthews (1998) observed that individuals who were high in ego goal orientation were higher in precompetitive state anxiety than individuals low in ego orientation. An ego-oriented athlete is likely to approach a cross-country competition with a focus upon outcome as opposed to mastery. In this same study, involving high-school-age runners, perfectionism was also observed to be a predictor of cognitive state anxiety.

Perfectionism involves the setting of exceptionally high performance standards for oneself. Researchers have identified two specific types of perfectionism: normal and neurotic. Normal or adaptive perfectionism is typically possessed by highly motivated and achieving athletes. Conversely, **neurotic perfectionism** is a destructive personal characteristic that is associated with inflexibility and a variety of other maladaptive cognitions and affective responses, such as low self-esteem, guilt, and shame. In the Hall et al.

(1998) investigation, neurotic perfectionism was predictive of cognitive state anxiety.

Just as perfectionism is linked to trait and state anxiety, perfectionism is also linked to goal orientation. In a study involving Canadian football players, it was observed that there is an association between an adaptive perfectionist orientation with a task goal orientation, and an association between a maladaptive perfectionist orientation with ego goal orientation (Dunn, Dunn, & Syrotuik, 2002). In addition, athletes who exhibit a maladaptive perfectionist orientation also tend to be low in self-esteem. Instruments used to measure perfectionism include the Frost–Multidimensional Perfectionism Scale (Frost, Martens, Lahart & Rosenblate, 1990) and the Hewitt–Multidimensional Perfectionism Scale (Hewitt & Flett, 1991).

Measurement of Anxiety

In recent years, the preferred method of measuring trait and state anxiety has been through the use of pencil-and-paper inventories. For your perusal a number of the most common anxiety inventories as used or developed by sport psychologists are listed in table 8.1. For a more comprehensive description and listing of anxiety inventories, see Ostrow (1996).

While pencil-and-paper inventories are the most common measures of anxiety, behavioral and physiological assessment can be very effective. One category of behavioral measurement is direct observation, where the experimenter looks for objective signs of arousal in the subject and records them. Such things as nervous fidgeting, licking the lips, rubbing palms on pants or shirt, and change in respiration could all be interpreted as behavioral signs of activation. Such a system was developed and used by Lowe (1973) for ascertaining arousal through "on-deck activity" of batters in Little League baseball.

Along these lines, table 8.2 displays a list of overt behavioral responses that can be used by the athlete to identify indicators of distress, or state anxiety. The list is arranged in alphabetical order and may be used by the athlete as a checklist to monitor state anxiety response during practice, immediately before competition, and during competition.

TABLE 8.1 | Common Anxiety Inventories Utilized or Developed by Sport Psychologists

Trait/State	Dimension	Inventory	Reference
TRAIT	*Unidimensional*	Spielberger's Trait Anxiety Inventory (TAI) Sport Competition Anxiety Test (SCAT)	Spielberger (1983) Martens et al. (1990)
	Multidimensional	Cognitive Somatic Anxiety Questionnaire (CSAQ) Sport Anxiety Scale (SAS)	Schwartz, Davidson, and Goleman (1978) Smith, Smoll, and Schutz (1990)
STATE	*Unidimensional*	Spielberger's State Anxiety Inventory (SAI) Competitive State Anxiety Inventory (CSAI)	Spielberger (1983) Martens (1977, 1982)
	Multidimensional	Activation-Deactivation Checklist (AD-ACL) Competitive State Anxiety Inventory-2 (CSAI-2) Revised Competitive State Anxiety-2 (CSAI-2R)	Thayer (1986) Martens et al. (1990) Cox, Martens, and Russell (2003)

TABLE 8.2 | Incomplete Checklist for Monitoring Distress-Related Behavioral Responses of the Athlete

_____	Clammy Hands	_____	Nausea
_____	Diarrhea	_____	Need to Urinate
_____	Dry Mouth	_____	Physical Fatigue
_____	Fidgeting	_____	Rapid Heart Rate
_____	Increased Respiration	_____	Scattered Attention
_____	Irritability	_____	Tense Muscles
_____	Jitters	_____	Tense Stomach
_____	Licking of Lips	_____	Trembling Legs
_____	Mental Confusion	_____	Unsettled Stomach
_____	Mental Fatigue	_____	Voice Distortion

From the perspective of applied (nonlaboratory) field research, pencil-and-paper inventories and behavioral assessment techniques seem most feasible. This will remain true as long as electrophysiological indicators require expensive instruments. Advances in the field of applied psychophysiology, however, may change this perspective. Improvements in the use of telemetry will make it possible to monitor an athlete's heart rate, blood pressure, and muscular tension while she is competing in such dynamic activities as swimming, batting in baseball, and sprinting in track. It has long been argued that both physiological and psychological assessments of anxiety should be taken to measure anxiety and arousal. In this regard, however, it is important to point out

that the correlation between physiological and psychological measures of state anxiety is quite low (Karteroliotis & Gill, 1987). Consequently, if both physiological and psychological measures of state anxiety are recorded simultaneously, it is possible that conflicting results may be obtained (Tenenbaum, 1984).

Multidimensional anxiety theory has precipitated the development of anxiety inventories that measure both trait and state anxiety, as well as cognitive and somatic anxiety. Referring again to table 8.1, we can note that several of the inventories are identified as being multidimensional in nature, as opposed to unidimensional. A multidimensional measure of trait or state anxiety partitions the construct into at least two components: cognitive and

CONCEPT In addition to situational variables as described by Endler, various personality characteristics are predictive of competitive state anxiety. These include competitive trait anxiety, ego goal orientation, and neurotic perfectionism.

APPLICATION Knowing what personality characteristics predispose an athlete to respond to competitive situations with increased levels of state anxiety should help the athlete as well as the coach to cope with the stress of competition. Inventories are available for measuring all three of these personality constructs. If it is suspected that an athlete's state anxiety response may be partially due to a personality characteristic, steps should be taken to ascertain its extent through measurement.

CONCEPT The state anxiety response to stressful situations can be observed and recorded through the use of a behavioral checklist.

APPLICATION The athlete should systematically chronicle anxiety-related behavioral responses. Once these are recorded, the coach will be able to help an athlete identify and control competitive stress.

somatic. A *unidimensional* measure of trait or state anxiety makes no attempt to partition the construct into multiple parts. Among the trait inventories, those that measure anxiety as a multidimensional construct include the Cognitive Somatic Anxiety Questionnaire (CSAQ) and the Sport Anxiety Scale (SAS). Among the state inventories, those that measure anxiety as a multidimensional construct include the Activation-Deactivation Checklist (AD-ACL), the Competitive State Anxiety Inventory-2 (CSAI-2), and the Revised Competitive State Anxiety-2 (CSAI-2R).

Since 1990, the CSAI-2 has been the instrument of choice for measuring multidimensional competitive state anxiety. The CSAI-2 is composed of 27 items that measure cognitive state anxiety, somatic state anxiety, and self-confidence. Recent research with the CSAI-2, however, failed to confirm the hypothesized three-factor structure of the inventory (Cox, 2000; Lane, Sewell, Terry, Bertram, & Nesti, 1999). Consequently, the Revised Competitive State Anxiety Inventory–2 (CSAI-2R) was developed by Cox, Martens, and Russell (2003). The CSAI-2R is composed of 17 items that measure the constructs of cognitive anxiety (5 items), somatic anxiety (7 items), and self-confidence (5 items). Items that were removed were items that tended to be highly correlated with more than one construct or subscale. Both the CSAI-2 and the CSAI-2R take several minutes to administer, so they can be a distraction to athletes who are preparing for competition. To address this shortcoming, several very short versions of the CSAI-2 have been developed. They include the Mental Readiness Form (Murphy, Greenspan, Jowdy, & Tammen, 1989); the Anxiety Rating Scale (Cox, Robb, & Russell, 2000, 2001); the Immediate Anxiety Measurement Scale (Thomas, Hanton, & Jones, 2002); and the Sport Grid (Raedeke & Stein, 1994; Ward & Cox, 2004). A 15-item version of the CSAI-2 (CSAI-2C) has also been developed for children (Stadulis,

Eidson, & MacCracken, 1994). Finally, the CSAI-2 can be modified to provide a multidimensional measure of competitive trait anxiety. This is accomplished through a simple modification of premeasurement instructions (Albrecht & Feltz, 1987). Instead of being asked to respond as to how she feels "at this moment" relative to a competition, the athlete is asked to respond to how she "usually feels" about competition in general.

Time-to-Event Nature of Precompetitive Anxiety

Our ability to obtain independent measures of cognitive and somatic state anxiety has greatly enhanced our knowledge about the athletic situation. One of the factors that is believed to significantly influence the quality of the athletic experience is the level of state anxiety during the time leading up to competition. We have already referred to this as precompetitive anxiety. We now know quite a bit about the temporal changes in anxiety during the period of time leading up to and immediately following the beginning of the event. Precompetitive cognitive anxiety starts relatively high and remains high and stable as the time of the event approaches. Conversely, somatic anxiety remains relatively low until approximately 24 hours before the event, and then increases rapidly as the event approaches. Once performance begins, somatic anxiety dissipates rapidly, whereas cognitive state anxiety fluctuates throughout the contest as the probability of success/failure changes (Fenz, 1975; Hardy & Parfitt, 1991; Jones & Cale, 1989; Jones, Swain & Cale, 1991; Martens et al., 1990; Schedlowski & Tewes, 1992; Parfitt, Hardy, & Pates, 1995; Swain & Jones, 1992; Wiggins, 1998). The relationship between competitive state anxiety and time-to-event is graphically illustrated in figure 8.3.

FIGURE 8.3 | Changes in competitive state anxiety prior to competition (decline in cognitive anxiety fluctuates with probability of success/failure).

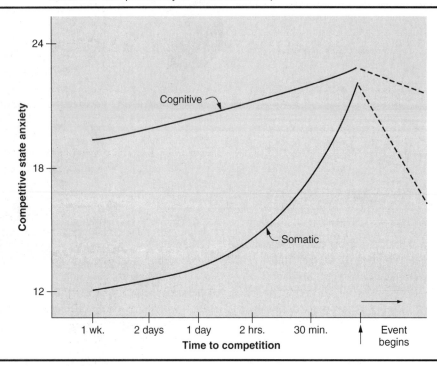

The Relationship Between Arousal and Athletic Performance

Throughout this chapter, an effort has been made to avoid confusing the terms *anxiety* and *arousal*. In this section, however, it will be necessary to use the term *arousal* as somewhat synonymous with *state anxiety*. This is the case because researchers have routinely employed a test of state anxiety as the primary means for determining a subject's arousal level. Consequently, most of the reported research will relate negative anxiety (state anxiety) to sport and motor performance. This practice, however, is consistent with our understanding that anxiety (emotion) is associated with a physiological change (Jones, 2003).

The primary focus of this section will be upon two main theories that purport to explain the relationship between arousal and athletic performance: inverted-U theory and drive theory. **Inverted-U theory** includes many subtheories that explain why the relationship between arousal and performance is curvilinear as opposed to linear in nature. Conversely, **drive theory** proposes a linear relationship between arousal and performance. In the most elementary case, the distinguishing characteristics of inverted-U and drive theory are illustrated in figure 8.4.

Inverted-U Theory

The inverted-U theory has been around for as long as the arousal/performance relationship has been studied. It simply states that the relationship between performance and arousal is curvilinear as opposed to linear, and takes the form of an inverted U (fig. 8.4). While it is described as a theory or hypothesis, researchers such as Duffy

FIGURE 8.4 | Relationship between drive and inverted-U theories.

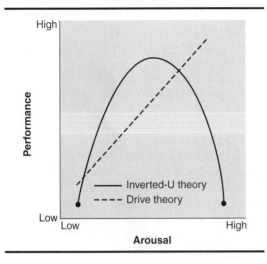

(1957) and Malmo (1959) consider it to be an observed fact.

One of the difficulties encountered in testing the inverted-U theory with humans is our inability to precisely measure arousal. For example, if in a particular study researchers fail to demonstrate that heightened arousal causes a decrement in performance, it is not particularly damaging to the theory. The reason for this is that it can always be argued that for that particular task, arousal was not high enough. If it had been higher, we may argue, performance would have declined. The problem is that from the perspective of protecting the human participant, the amount of arousal researchers can induce is limited. For example, if arousal is induced through electrical shock, how much can the researcher elevate the voltage

Athlete exhibiting emotional response. Courtesy University of Missouri–Columbia Sports Information.

CONCEPT The relationship between athletic performance and arousal takes the form of the inverted U.

APPLICATION Preparing athletes for competition involves more than psyching them up. It involves finding the optimal level of arousal for each athlete.

FIGURE 8.5 | Results of the Yerkes-Dodson (1908) research showing the effect of arousal and task difficulty on performance.

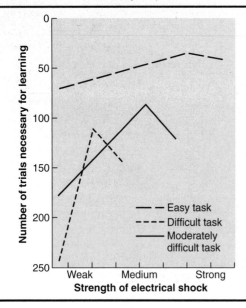

Source: From R. M. Yerkes and J. D. Dodson, The relationship of strength of stimulus to rapidity of habit formation, *Journal of Comparative Neurology and Psychology*, 1908, *18*, 459–482. Adapted with permission of Alan R. Liss, Inc., publisher and copyright holder.

without violating the participant's rights? Not very much.

The foundation for inverted-U theory is the classic work of Yerkes and Dodson (1908). Using dancing mice as subjects, Yerkes and Dodson set out to discover the relationship between arousal and task difficulty in their effect on performance. Performance was measured as the number of trials needed for the mice to select the brighter of two compartments. Arousal consisted of high, medium, and low intensities of electrical shock. Task difficulty was manipulated in terms of the differences in brightness between two compartments (high, medium, and low difficulty). Results showed that the amount of practice needed to learn the discrimination task increased as the difference in brightness between the two compartments diminished. These findings led to the **Yerkes-Dodson law,** which is this:

> an easily acquired habit, that is, one which does not demand difficult sense discrimination or complex associations, may readily be formed under strong stimulation, whereas a difficult habit may be acquired readily only under relatively weak stimulation (pp. 481–2).

The results of the Yerkes-Dodson research are illustrated in figure 8.5. As can be observed in this figure, the optimal level of electrical shock (arousal) for a difficult task was much lower than that needed for an easy task. Additionally, an optimal level of arousal (electrical shock) is indicated for each task. Before and after the optimal point, performance drops off. This is the inverted U.

In terms of practical sport application, the Yerkes-Dodson law is illustrated in figure 8.6. This figure shows that as the complexity of a skill increases, the amount of arousal needed for optimal performance decreases.

As can be observed in figure 8.6, a high level of arousal is necessary for the best performance in gross motor activities such as weight lifting. Conversely, a lower level of arousal is best for a fine motor task such as putting in golf. Each sport skill has its theoretical optimal level of arousal for best performance. Regardless of which type of skill is

FIGURE 8.6 | Application of the Yerkes-Dodson law in athletic events.

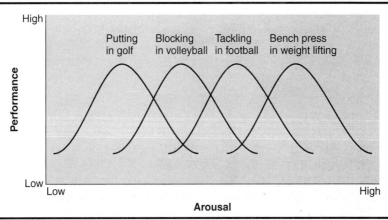

FIGURE 8.7 | Application of the Yerkes-Dodson law to tennis players at various skill levels.

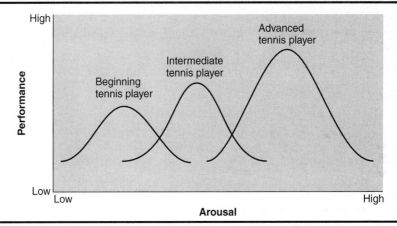

being performed, they all conform to the inverted-U principle. Specifically, performance is lowest when arousal is very high or very low, and highest when arousal is moderate, or optimum.

Another important consideration relating to the Yerkes-Dodson law is skill level. Just as putting in golf is a complex activity compared to weight lifting, learning to dribble a basketball is more difficult for a beginner than for someone performing the same task as an expert. The optimal level of arousal for a beginner should be considerably lower than the optimal level for an expert performing the same task. As

illustrated in figure 8.7, this concept explains why highly skilled athletes often perform better in competitive situations than do novices (Oxendine, 1970).

Evidence of an inverted-U relationship between athletic performance and arousal is documented in the literature. Klavora (1978) and Sonstroem and Bernardo (1982) were able to demonstrate that basketball performance is related to level of arousal, with best performance occurring at moderate levels of arousal and poorest performance at high or low levels. Similarly, Gould, Petlichkoff, Simons, and Vevera (1987) and Burton (1988) reported that best

CONCEPT   The optimal level of arousal varies as a function of the complexity of the task and the skill level of the athlete.

APPLICATION   Highly skilled athletes and athletes performing simple tasks need a moderately high level of arousal for maximum performance. Less skilled athletes and athletes performing complex tasks require a relatively low level of arousal for maximum performance.

performance in pistol shooting and swimming, respectively, were related to somatic anxiety in a way consistent with inverted-U predictions. In a related study, Beuter and Duda (1985) observed that heightened arousal has a detrimental effect on the motor performance of children. Under conditions of optimal arousal, children perform smooth and automatic movement patterns. However, under conditions of high arousal, movement patterns come under volitional control and are observed to be less smooth and efficient. The inverted-U relationship between performance and arousal has also been documented with nonathletic tasks such as reaction time (Lansing, Schwartz, & Lindsley, 1956; Arent & Landers, 2003); auditory tracking (Stennet, 1957); and hand steadiness (Martens & Landers, 1970).

While it seems relatively clear that the nature of the relationship between athletic performance and arousal takes the form of the inverted U, it is not clear why this occurs. In the following subsections, three theories that predict the inverted-U relationship will be briefly reviewed.

Easterbrook's Cue Utilization Theory
Easterbrook's (1959) notion of cue utilization theory was introduced in chapter 7 and illustrated in figure 7.7. The basic premise of cue utilization or attentional narrowing theory is that *as arousal increases, attention narrows*. The narrowing of attention results in some cues being gated out, first irrelevant cues and later relevant cues. From figure 7.7 it should be clear that attentional narrowing predicts an inverted-U relationship between arousal and performance. When arousal is low, the attentional band is wide, and both irrelevant and relevant cues are available. The presence of the irrelevant cues is distracting and causes a decrement in performance. At a moderate, or optimal, level of arousal, only the irrelevant cues are eliminated, and therefore performance is high. Finally, when arousal is high, attentional focus is narrow, and both relevant and irrelevant cues are gated out. This results in a decrement in performance, as predicted by the inverted-U theory.

Cue utilization theory also addresses the problem of task complexity and learning. With a complex or unlearned motor skill, there are a greater number of task-relevant cues to manage. Consequently, with increased arousal, the probability of errors increases at a faster rate than it would for a simple motor skill. Because there are so many task-relevant cues to manage, the relevant as well as irrelevant cues get gated out as arousal increases and attention narrows.

Signal Detection Theory
Another theory that predicts a curvilinear relationship between arousal and performance is signal detection theory (SDT). **Signal detection theory** is a theory of perception that predicts that increased decision errors will occur when an individual is either insensitive to a physical stimulus (stringent response criterion) or supersensitive to a physical stimulus (lenient response criterion). The lowest number of decision errors should occur with an optimal, or balanced, sensitivity to stimuli.

According to signal detection theory, the response criterion, or sensitivity to a physical stimulus, changes as a function of physiological

CONCEPT Increased arousal has the effect of narrowing an athlete's attention.

APPLICATION Athletes who participate in a sport that requires broad attentional awareness need lower levels of arousal for best performance. The setter in volleyball must be particularly aware of all aspects of the game. Narrow vision would seem to be particularly damaging to the setter's play selection.

CONCEPT Decreased arousal has the effect of broadening an athlete's attentional focus.

APPLICATION Athletes who participate in a sport that requires narrow attentional focus need appropriately increased levels of arousal for optimal performance. An athlete attempting a single feat of power and force will need a narrowed focus of attention.

arousal. At a very low level of arousal, the individual exhibits a stringent response criterion and is insensitive to signals from the environment (errors of omission). At a very high level of arousal, the individual exhibits a lenient response criterion and is very sensitive to signals from the environment (errors of commission). At a moderate level of arousal, the individual exhibits an optimal, or balanced, response criterion (fewer errors). Thus, low and high levels of arousal are associated with a large number of signal detection errors, while an optimal or moderate level of arousal is associated with fewer signal detection errors. This pattern of errors is consistent with inverted-U theory.

Consider an example in American football. The defensive lineman is interested in exploding out of his ready position and across the line of scrimmage when he detects the ball has been snapped. There is considerable advantage to be gained from exploding across the line of scrimmage before the offensive line can block movement. If the linesman is underaroused, he will not get across the line as quickly as he should; this represents an error of omission. If the linesman is overaroused, he will explode across the line of scrimmage too quickly and be called for being offside. This would be an error of commission. If the linesman is optimally aroused with a moderate level of arousal, he will move with the snap of the ball and make fewer errors of either commission or omission. For a detailed review of signal detection theory applied to sport, see Cox (1998).

Information Processing Theory The basic predictions of information processing theory for the arousal/performance relationship are identical to those of signal detection theory. Both theories predict the inverted-U relationship between performance and arousal, and both support the Yerkes-Dodson law. Welford (1962, 1965) gives a

211

CONCEPT   Athletes in sports that require instant decisions require a moderate level of arousal to avoid errors of commission or omission.

APPLICATION   An overly aroused batter in baseball will tend to swing at bad pitches (error of commission), while an underaroused hitter will allow called strikes (error of omission). A moderate level of arousal will tend to balance out the two kinds of decision errors.

---

basic outline of the theory's predictions. However, the theory is presented without the support of research evidence in the motor domain.

According to Welford (1962, 1973), brain cells become active with increased levels of arousal, and they begin to fire. As this happens, the information processing system becomes noisy, and its channel capacity is reduced. At low levels of arousal, the system is relatively inert and performance is low. At high levels of arousal, a performance decrement occurs because of the reduced information processing capacity of the channels. At some optimal level of arousal, the information processing capacity of the system is at its maximum, and performance is at its best.

Drive Theory

Perhaps the great contribution of drive theory is that it helps to explain the relationships between learning and arousal, and between performance and arousal. Many young athletes are just beginning the process of becoming skilled performers. The effect of arousal upon a beginner may be different from its effect upon a skilled performer. The basic relationship between arousal and an athlete's performance at any skill level is given in the following formula:

$$Performance = Arousal \times Skill\ Level$$

As developed by Hull (1943, 1951) and Spence (1956), drive theory is a complex stimulus-response theory of motivation and learning. It is a theory of competing responses, in which increased **drive** (arousal) facilitates the elicitation of the dominant response. The basic tenets of drive theory are as follows:

1. Increased arousal (drive) will elicit the dominant response.

2. The response associated with the strongest potential to respond is the dominant response.

3. Early in learning or for complex tasks, the dominant response is the incorrect response.

4. Late in learning or for simple tasks, the dominant response is the correct response.

We can make several practical applications of these drive theory tenets. First, heightened levels of arousal should benefit the skilled performer, but hamper the beginner. The coach with a relatively young team should strive to create an atmosphere relatively low in anxiety and arousal. Low levels of arousal should increase the beginner's chances of a successful performance. In turn, the experience of success should strengthen self-confidence. Skilled athletes, on the other hand, will benefit from an increase in arousal. Similar applications can be made to the performance of simple and complex tasks. For example, a complex task, such as throwing a knuckleball in baseball, will always require a low level of arousal. Conversely, a very simple task, such as doing a high number of push-ups, would seem to benefit from arousal. A case in point is a reported study by Davis and Harvey (1992). Utilizing drive theory predictions, the researchers

CONCEPT The effect of increased arousal on an athlete performing a complex task or learning a novel task will be to elicit an incorrect response, which is the dominant response.

APPLICATION With beginners it is important that the environment be one of low arousal and stress. Young athletes tend to make more mistakes if they become excited and overly activated.

CONCEPT The effect of increased arousal on an athlete performing a simple or well-learned task will be to elicit a correct response, which is the dominant response.

APPLICATION Highly skilled athletes will often benefit from increased arousal. Psyching up a basketball star like Michael Jordan could have grave consequences for the opposing team.

hypothesized that increased arousal caused by major league baseball pressure situations would cause a decrement in batting (a complex task). Four late-game pressure situations were compared with nonpressure situations relative to batting performance. Results showed a decrement in batting performance associated with increased arousal, as predicted by drive theory.

Drive theory received tremendous amounts of attention from researchers between 1943 and 1970. However, since then, interest in the theory has diminished significantly. The theory was extremely difficult to test, and the tests that were conducted often yielded conflicting results. For an in-depth review of research associated with drive theory, the reader is referred to Cox (1990).

Alternatives to Inverted-U Theory

In the previous section we learned that the primary theory sport psychologists have used to explain the relationship between anxiety and performance is inverted-U theory. For a number of reasons, however, sport psychologists have turned to other more

complex theories to explain this relationship. It is believed by many that the inverted-U theory is a simple theory that does not capture or explain the complexities of the anxiety-performance relationship.

As you look back to figure 8.4, relative to inverted-U theory, you will note that the hypothesized relationship between anxiety and performance is smooth, suggesting that smooth and measured changes in performance occur in conjunction with gradual and measured increases in anxiety/arousal. We can think of many examples that would suggest that changes in performance associated with changes in anxiety are anything but smooth. A case in point is the real-life experience (or rather, nightmare) of professional golfer Greg Norman (Reilly, 1996). After the third round of the 1996 Masters golf tournament, Greg Norman held a six-shot lead over his nearest competitor, with just one round (18 holes) to go. On Sunday, during the final and fourth round, came the most "catastrophic" four holes in Greg's professional career. On the ninth through the twelfth holes, he surrendered his six-stroke lead to Nick Faldo. He then went on to lose the Masters by five strokes.

Whether the theories that we will discuss in this chapter are really alternatives to inverted-U theory or just modifications is a matter of discussion by sport psychologists. Clearly, you will see some aspects of inverted-U theory in all of the theories that we will discuss. These are the six anxiety-performance theories that we will discuss in this section Martens' multidimensional anxiety theory, Fazey and Hardy's catastrophe theory, Hanin's individual zone of optimal functioning theory, Csikszentmipalyi's concept of Flow, Jones's directionality theory, and Apter's reversal theory.

Martens' Multidimensional Anxiety Theory

Multidimensional anxiety theory (Martens et al., 1990) is based upon the notion that anxiety is multidimensional in nature, composed of a cognitive anxiety component and a somatic anxiety component. As you will recall, multidimensional anxiety

theory and the multidimensional nature of anxiety were introduced early in this chapter. At that time, however, we did not discuss the specific anxiety-performance relationship that is hypothesized by multidimensional anxiety theory. Relative to anxiety, multidimensional theory specifically hypothesizes these things:

1. A negative linear relationship exists between cognitive state anxiety and athletic performance.

2. An inverted-U relationship exists between somatic anxiety and performance.

The two basic principles of multidimensional anxiety theory are illustrated in figure 8.8. The relationships displayed in this figure are consistent with research conducted by Burton (1988) using swimmers and by Gould, Petlichkoff, Simons, and Vevera (1987) using pistol shooting. While this relationship is very appealing and seems to make practical sense, many investigators have failed to confirm multidimensional anxiety theory as

FIGURE 8.8 | Multidimensional theory relationship between athletic performance and state anxiety.

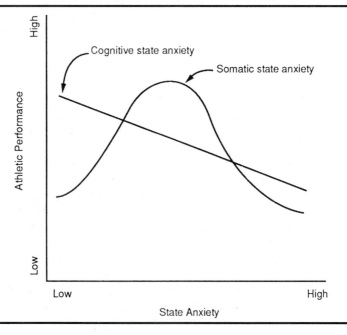

CONCEPT   According to multidimensional anxiety theory, an inverted-U relationship should exist between athletic performance and somatic state anxiety. Conversely, a negative linear relationship should exist between cognitive state anxiety and athletic performance.

APPLICATION   Consistent with predictions of multidimensional anxiety theory, an athlete should seek to obtain a moderate level of somatic anxiety or perceived arousal (heart rate, tension, jitters, etc.), and a low level of cognitive state anxiety (fear of failure, fear of performing poorly, etc.). Ideally, a low level of cognitive state anxiety should also be associated with a high level of self-efficacy and confidence.

---

illustrated in figure 8.8. See Jerome and Williams (2000) for a review.

The study reported by Jerome and Williams (2000) is worth discussing in some detail, as it raises a number of important issues relative to studying the anxiety-performance relationship. Jerome and Williams studied semiprofessional and recreational bowlers and found that an inverted-U relationship exists between precompetitive cognitive state anxiety and bowling performance, and that a negative linear relationship exists between somatic state anxiety and bowling performance. This is pretty much the exact opposite result to that illustrated in figure 8.8. You might ask, why would the differences be so extreme? A couple of things come to mind. First, relationships between anxiety and performance may vary for different sports. Second, bowling performance was conceptualized as a difference score between the score for the game and average score accumulated across a season. Thus, the way in which performance was measured may have contributed to different results. Third, the exact time before competition that the anxiety inventory (CSAI-2) was administered may have varied. Fourth, a single performance and anxiety observation was recorded for each bowler. It is possible that a very different result might have been obtained if a different game observation had been used. In recent years, most anxiety-performance studies have measured an athlete's performance and associated anxiety repeatedly, and then converted them into intraindividualized

ipsative z-scores. This variation in procedure may also have contributed to the different results.

Because **intraindividualized scores** or ipsative z-scores are routinely mentioned in the sport psychology literature, it is useful for the beginning sport psychology student to be familiar with how these scores are computed. As you are probably aware, a **z-score** is a standardized score formed by subtracting the mean (m) of a group of scores from a single subject's score (x) and dividing by the group **standard deviation** ($z = x - m \div sd$). By way of illustration, assume you have 100 anxiety scores from 100 different athletes. From these 100 scores you could easily calculate a mean, a standard deviation, and a z-score. If the mean were 20, the standard deviation were 4, and a specific individual's score were 24, then that individual's z-score would be 1.00 ($24 - 20 \div 4 = 1.00$). If you did this for all 100 athletes, you would have 100 z-scores, the mean of which would be zero and the standard deviation of which would be one.

In the case of the **ipsative z-score,** you do the same thing as with a regular z-score, but you use the mean and standard deviation associated with a specific individual's multiple observations. By way of illustration, assume that an athlete completed an anxiety inventory 25 times over a three-week period. This would yield 25 separate anxiety scores for this one athlete. Assume that the mean and standard deviation for the 25 observations were 30 and 5, respectively, and that the athlete's anxiety score for the 10th observation was 25.

The ipsative z-score for this specific observation would be -1.00 $(25 - 30 \div 5 = -1.00)$. You could then calculate the ipsative z-scores for all 25 observations. In any subsequent data analysis, it would be the ipsatized or intraindividualized scores that would enter into the analysis.

Fazey and Hardy's Catastrophe Theory

A fundamental weakness of Martens' multidimensional theory is the notion that cognitive anxiety and somatic anxiety have independent effects upon athletic performance. Looking at figure 8.8, consider the case in which an athlete exhibits a high level of cognitive anxiety and a moderate level of somatic anxiety. What would be the predicted level of performance in this case? If you looked at the prediction line for cognitive anxiety, you would predict poor performance. Conversely, if you looked at the prediction line for somatic anxiety, you would predict high performance. Can you have it both ways? Not likely. Cognitive and somatic anxiety must work together in some interactive way to affect performance. What is needed is a theory that can consider the independent effects of anxiety and physiological arousal in the same model. Fazey and Hardy's catastrophe theory is just such a model.

As illustrated in figure 8.4, inverted-U theory predicts a smooth bell-shaped (inverted U) curve relationship between physiological arousal and athletic performance. The basic assumptions of the theory are that (a) small incremental increases in arousal result in small incremental increases or decreases in performance, and that (b) moderate arousal results in optimal performance. **Catastrophe theory** questions both of these basic assumptions, but more specifically, the notion that small incremental increases in arousal result in small changes in performance. At critical points in the performance curve, quite the opposite may be observed. When faced with debilitating stress and arousal, athletes do not experience small incremental decreases in performance; they suffer large and dramatic decrements that may be described as

catastrophic in nature. In addition, once the athlete suffers a catastrophic decrement in performance, small incremental reductions in arousal rarely bring performance back to the pre-catastrophic level (Fazey & Hardy, 1988). Inverted-U theory cannot account for these sudden and extreme reductions in performance. A case in point is the Greg Norman golf example that we discussed at the beginning of this chapter. Greg Norman's golf performance did not decline in small measured amounts; instead, he suffered a catastrophic drop-off in performance.

Another golf example of a catastrophic drop in performance was Jean Van de Velde's collapse on the final hole of the 1999 British Open. All Van de Velde needed on the final hole to win the British Open was a double bogey. Instead, he shot a triple bogey to tie, and then lost a four-hole playoff to Paul Laurie. Perhaps the most famous catastrophic team collapse in history involved the New York Yankees and the Boston Red Sox in the 2004 American League Championship Series. As you will recall, the Yankees lost the series in seven games after leading three games to none (Behrendt, 2004).

Unfortunately, the complexity of the catastrophe model is so high that students are typically "discouraged" before they come to appreciate the elegant predictions of the theory. Before we begin a more detailed discussion of the model, it is well that we look at it in a more simplified fashion. In figure 8.9 (a, b, c), the model is represented as a function of level of cognitive anxiety. The basic variables of the model include cognitive anxiety, physiological arousal (not somatic anxiety), and performance.

At the top, figure 8.9 (a) shows that under conditions of *low cognitive anxiety,* the relationship between physiological arousal and athletic performance takes the form of a well-proportioned bell-shaped curve. When cognitive anxiety is very low, the model predicts a smooth inverted-U relationship between performance and arousal. This is the performance situation in which the athlete is not worried about performance outcome or negative

FIGURE 8.9 | Simplified illustration of the catastrophe model at different levels of cognitive anxiety.

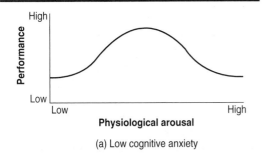

(a) Low cognitive anxiety

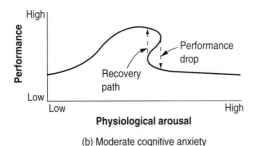

(b) Moderate cognitive anxiety

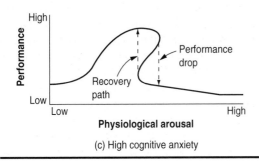

(c) High cognitive anxiety

social evaluation, yet arousal is free to fluctuate from low to high.

In the middle of figure 8.9, illustration (b) shows that under conditions of *moderate cognitive anxiety,* the relationship between physiological arousal and athletic performance takes the form of a somewhat distorted bell-shaped curve. At a moderate level of cognitive anxiety, the model predicts an increase in performance with increased arousal, but then a fairly significant drop-off in performance

as arousal gets too high. As the figure shows, arousal will have to return to a level below that where the drop-off occurred in order for the athlete to get back to a high level of performance (recovery path).

At the bottom of figure 8.9, section (c) indicates that under conditions of *high cognitive anxiety,* the relationship between physiological arousal and athletic performance takes the form of a very distorted inverted U. At a high level of cognitive anxiety, the model predicts an increase in performance with increased arousal, but then a *catastrophic* drop in performance as arousal gets too high. Again, as the figure shows, arousal will have to return to a level well below that where the drop-off occurred for the athlete to get back to a high level of performance (recovery path).

Fazey and Hardy's catastrophe model is illustrated in figure 8.10. In this model, physiological arousal is represented on the back horizontal edge of the floor of the three-dimensional model (X). Cognitive anxiety is represented as being at a right angle to arousal and on the left edge of the floor of the model (Y). Performance is represented as being the height of the performance surface (Z). For every (X, Y) coordinate on the floor of the model, a point exists on the performance surface directly above it.

If cognitive anxiety is very low, the relationship between arousal and performance is predicted to take the form of the traditional inverted U, as represented by the back edge of the performance surface. Cognitive anxiety is represented in the model as the decisive factor for determining whether performance changes will be smooth and small, abrupt and large, or somewhere in between. With increasing physiological arousal, a catastrophe is predicted to occur at point (X_2), when cognitive anxiety is high. At this point, performance drops over the edge of the upper fold's performance surface down to a very low point on the same surface. Thus, with a very small increase in physiological arousal, a very large and abrupt decrease in performance occurs. Notice that the severity of the catastrophic decrease in performance depends on

FIGURE 8.10 | Fazey and Hardy's (1988) catastrophe model of the relationship between anxiety and performance.

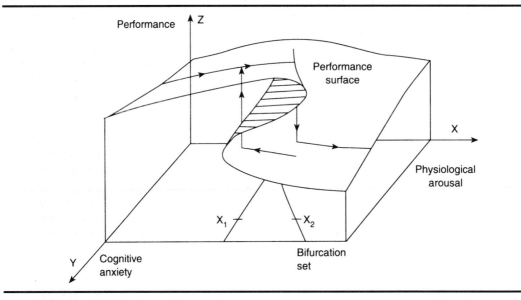

Source: From J. Fazey and L. Hardy, 1988. The inverted-U hypothesis: A catastrophe for sport psychology? *Bass Monograph No. 1.* Leeds, U.K.: British Association of Sports Sciences and National Coaching Foundation. Reprinted with permission.

the level of cognitive anxiety. A small decrease in physiological arousal will not result in performance returning to its former lofty height, even though a small incremental increase in physiological arousal resulted in the performance catastrophe in the first place.

If cognitive anxiety remains high (unchanged), a significant decrease in physiological arousal will be necessary to return performance back to a position on top of the upper fold of the performance surface. The point where this occurs is represented as (X_1) on the floor of the three-dimensional model. Notice that the distance between point one (X_1) and point two (X_2) on the floor of the model is a function of cognitive state anxiety. The distance between this "bifurcation set" increases as cognitive anxiety increases. When physiological arousal recedes to point one (X_1), with no change in cognitive anxiety, performance jumps abruptly back to its pre-catastrophic level. The requirement that discontinuity (represented by sudden large jumps)

occurs at different points along the normal factor (physiological arousal) is known as **hysteresis.**

Another subtle prediction of the model is that when physiological arousal is very low, an increase in cognitive anxiety will result in an increase in performance (the height of Z is greater at the front of the model than at the back). Conversely, when physiological arousal is very high, a decrease in cognitive anxiety will result in increased performance (the height of Z is greater at the back than at the front). This aspect of the model was supported by research involving netball players (Edwards & Hardy, 1996).

The basic tenets of Fazey and Hardy's catastrophe model were tested by Hardy and Parfitt (1991) and Hardy, Parfitt, and Pates (1994). In both of these studies, cognitive anxiety and physiological arousal were manipulated. Setting cognitive anxiety at a high level and systematically increasing physiological arousal resulted in catastrophic decrements in basketball and bowling performance.

CONCEPT   If cognitive state anxiety is high, an increase in physiological arousal can result in a sudden and large decrement in athletic performance.

APPLICATION   Large and sudden decrements in performance will not occur if cognitive state anxiety can be minimized or eliminated. Failing this, it will be necessary to closely monitor physiological arousal to avoid triggering a catastrophe in performance. If a catastrophe in performance does occur, it is best to give the athlete a rest to allow physiological arousal to return to a low level.

Minimal changes in performance were observed when cognitive anxiety was low and physiological arousal was systematically increased. Both of these studies provided strong support for the basic tenets of catastrophe theory. A more recent investigation by Cohen, Pargman, and Tenenbaum (2003), however, failed to obtain experimental support for the model. In the Cohen et al. investigation, arousal was manipulated via treadmill walking while cognitive anxiety was manipulated using threat of random electrical shock. It was difficult to be convinced, however, that cognitive anxiety was effectively manipulated.

Several investigators have replaced physiological arousal with somatic anxiety and tested the revised catastrophe model in competitive situations. In these investigations, cognitive and somatic state anxiety were measured immediately before batting in softball (Krane, Joyce, & Rafeld, 1994), or before diving off a 3-meter board (Durr, 1996). In the Krane et al. (1994) investigation, very minimal support was found for the revised model, in that somatic anxiety was related to batting performance in certain critical game situations (situations in which cognitive anxiety would be expected to be high). As somatic anxiety increased, performance increased to a point, but then began to decline (a curvilinear relationship).

Technically, the three-dimensional model illustrated in figure 8.10 describes what has been called the "cusp" catastrophe model. Higher-order models in which variables such as personal control and self-confidence are included are called "butterfly" catastrophe models (Edwards, Kingston, Hardy, & Gould, 2002; Hardy, Woodman, & Carrington, 2004). Utilizing driving off a tee in golf, Hardy et al. (2004) demonstrated that self-confidence moderates the relationship between arousal, cognitive anxiety, and performance. Specifically, with a high level of self-confidence, a catastrophe in performance would not be observed unless both somatic and cognitive anxiety were very high.

Hanin's Individual Zone of Optimal Functioning (IZOF) Theory

I couldn't have played any better. In the beginning, in the middle of the second set, I was on fire. In all aspects of my game, from my serving to my groundstrokes, I was playing in a zone. It was as well as I could play, plain and simple.

(Pete Sampras on winning Wimbledon against Andre Agassi in Alexander, 1999.)

Developed by Yuri Hanin (1989), **individual zone of optimal functioning** (IZOF) theory also questions the two basic assumptions of inverted-U theory, but more specifically the notion that a moderate level of state anxiety results in best performance. IZOF theory postulates that the level of optimal state anxiety best for one athlete may be very different from that optimal for the next athlete. Hanin (1986), for example, reported that a group of 46 elite female rowers had a mean optimal **prestart state anxiety** (precompetitive) of 43.80, with individual levels ranging from 26 to 67. Thus, for some athletes, the optimal level of state anxiety was very low, while for others it was very high.

Playing "in the zone" requires outstanding skill as well as optimal positive and negative affect. Courtesy Ball State University Sports Information.

State anxiety was measured using a Russian version of Spielberger's State Anxiety Inventory (SAI). Hanin's concept of a zone of optimal functioning has been discussed in detail by Raglin and Hanin (2000).

According to Hanin, if an athlete's optimal prestart state anxiety level can be determined, it should be possible to help an athlete achieve that ideal level through arousal control techniques. An athlete's optimal prestart anxiety level can be determined either directly or *retrospectively.* Direct measurement of optimal prestart anxiety level is accomplished by actually measuring state anxiety immediately before a number of competitions and determining the level of anxiety that corresponds to the best performance. Since this method of determining optimal prestart anxiety is often time-consuming and impractical, the retrospective or **recall method** offers an attractive alternative. In the recall method, athletes are merely asked to reflect upon past performances and to complete the SAI according to how they remember feeling immediately before their best-ever performance. Hanin (1986) reported data showing that actual and restrospective measures of state anxiety are identical in some situations. In other situations, retrospective measures of state anxiety tend to be inflated relative to actual measures.

The notion that an individual's recalled optimal precompetitive anxiety level is essentially the same as that obtained through actual observation has been the topic of several investigations (Annesi, 1997; Harger & Raglin, 1994; Imlay, Carda, Stanbrough, Dreiling, & O'Connor, 1995; Russell & Cox, 2000; Tenenbaum & Ebran, 2003; Tenenbaum, Lloyd, Pretty, & Hanin, 2002). Correlations between actual and recalled optimal precompetitive anxiety are relatively high (r = .95) when the recalled information is obtained within two days of the target competition. Correlations drop off significantly, however, with an increase in the time interval between actual event and recalled optimal precompetitive anxiety. Annesi (1997) provided evidence that shows, however, that the recall method is most effective when a unidimensional measure of anxiety is used (e.g., SAI) as compared to a multidimensional measure of anxiety (e.g., CSAI-2). Annesi recommended that the recall method not be used if anxiety is measured using the CSAI-2. In a laboratory investigation, Russell and Cox (2000) reported that recalled optimal positive affect scores tend to be larger than actual scores, and that the correlation between recalled and actual optimal positive and negative affect is about .75. In summary, the use of recalled optimal affect scores is a viable option if the actual scores cannot be obtained, but their accuracy may be limited in some cases.

CONCEPT In the absence of an actual ideal precompetitive state anxiety score, an estimate may be obtained by asking the athlete to complete a state anxiety inventory relative to how she retrospectively recalls feeling before her best performance.

APPLICATION Once the ideal precompetitive anxiety score is identified, a zone of optimal functioning can be easily formed by adding and subtracting .5 standard deviations. In the case of Spielberger's SAI, the zone would range from four points below to four points above the ideal score.

Once optimal prestart state anxiety is determined, a zone of confidence (confidence interval) is placed around it. The upper and lower boundaries of the IZOF are established by adding and subtracting four points to or from the optimal prestart state anxiety score. This procedure allows for error in selecting the optimal level of anxiety. Hanin reported that four anxiety points correspond to a .5 standard deviation of observed precontest optimal state anxiety scores. Therefore, an IZOF is defined as an individual's optimal prestart level of state anxiety, plus or minus a population estimate of a .5 standard deviation. It is not known whether the standard deviation would change as a function of nationality, gender, sport, or skill level. If an athlete exhibited an optimal prestart state anxiety level of 60, her ZOF would be 56 to 64. Based on Hanin's theory, it would be expected that best performance would be achieved when state anxiety was within this zone, as opposed to some "moderate" level of state anxiety. By monitoring an athlete's prestart state anxiety, it should be possible to utilize some form of intervention to increase or decrease state anxiety to move it into the IZOF. The concept of the IZOF, relative to precompetitive state anxiety, is illustrated in figure 8.11 for two different athletes.

Hanin also presented data to suggest that prestart state anxiety can be accurately predicted by the athlete as much as one week in advance.

FIGURE 8.11 | Two athletes (A and B) exhibit different bell-shaped curves relative to state anxiety and performance. Best performance occurs within IZOF for each athlete.

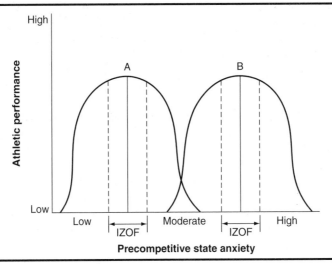

In this case, the athlete is asked to complete the state anxiety inventory (SAI) according to how he thinks he will feel before the start of an important upcoming competition. Again, if the predicted level of prestart anxiety is outside of the IZOF, then the coach can utilize some form of intervention to assist the athlete in adjusting anxiety as the competition approaches. If the athlete reports that he expects prestart anxiety to be low, the coach can work on ways to increase state anxiety before the competition begins.

Strong support for the concept of an individual zone of optimal functioning (IZOF) has been reported by Prapavessis and Grove (1991), Raglin and Turner (1993), and Turner and Raglin (1996). In all three of these investigations, predictions based upon IZOF theory were compared to predictions based upon Morgan's mental health model approach (discussed in chapter 2) or upon inverted-U theory. In each case, the results favored IZOF theory. In the case of the two Raglin and Turner articles, track and field performance scores associated with state anxiety that fell within a predetermined IZOF were significantly larger than those for which anxiety levels fell outside of the zone. Conversely, performance scores associated with state anxiety that fell within a normatively based moderate zone of functioning were not significantly larger than those falling outside of that zone.

Of particular interest to IZOF theory is an applied investigation reported by Annesi (1998). In this study, Annesi patiently identified the actual IZOFs of three elite adolescent tennis players. After establishing the IZOF for each athlete, the athlete was instructed in anxiety adjustment techniques. In the second phase of the investigation, athletes self-measured anxiety level prior to competitive matches and used their anxiety adjustment skills to move precompetitive anxiety into their predetermined IZOF. Results of the study showed that the self-monitored intervention was successful in bringing their tennis performance to a level above where it had been before the intervention started. This was an important study, because it demonstrated that Hanin's concepts could be applied by athletes prior to competition.

The individual zone of optimal functioning theory is a viable theory for explaining the anxiety-performance relationship. It is important to recognize, however, that some investigations have failed to find support for the theory (Randle & Weinberg, 1997), while others have reported only partial or weak support for Hanin's predictions (Russell & Cox, 2000; Woodman, Albinson, & Hardy, 1997). An interesting study reported by Raglin and Morris (1994) provides some perspective. They showed that collegiate volleyball players tended to perform within their predetermined IZOF when they were playing difficult matches against highly skilled opponents. When they were playing easy matches against less skilled opponents, however, their precompetitive anxiety levels tended not to be in their predetermined IZOF. It is not generally necessary that athletes be in their zones of optimal functioning against lesser competition. They will likely prevail anyway. This explains, however, why it is possible for a weaker team to defeat a stronger team on occasion. If a strong team overlooked a supposedly weak team or failed to take it seriously, it is possible that its players could suffer an unexpected loss before they could appropriately adjust their arousal levels. We will discuss more on this important topic in part 4 of the text.

In Hanin's original research, his focus was upon state anxiety and upon forming an IZOF around an optimal level of competitive state anxiety to predict performance. In recent years, however, Hanin and others have moved from a focus upon state anxiety to a focus upon emotions in general, of which anxiety is just one example. It makes sense that both positive and negative emotions, as opposed to just the negative emotion of anxiety, should be in an optimal zone prior to competition; and that the particular pattern of emotions would be different for each athlete (D'Urso, Petrosso, & Robazza, 2002; Hanin & Stambulova, 2002; Hanin & Syrja, 1995;

CONCEPT   An athlete will perform best if her state anxiety is within a certain zone of optimal functioning.

APPLICATION   Once an athlete's zone of optimal functioning has been determined (directly or

through retrospection), arousal control techniques can be utilized to assist the athlete in achieving the optimal-level prestart state anxiety. Some athletes monitor prestart pulse rate as a means of determining if they are within their IZOF.

CONCEPT   Just as an IZOF can be formed around an optimal level of competitive anxiety, an IZOF also can be formed around the more general notions of positive and negative affect. The athlete who is playing at peak performance is probably in the zone of optimal performance relative to a whole array of distinct emotions, and not just anxiety.

APPLICATION   Precompetitive measures of positive and negative affect can be obtained using the Positive and Negative Affect Scale (PANAS; Watson, Clark, & Tellegen, 1988). Through practice, an athlete can learn to recognize when she is in her personal zone of optimal functioning. Once the zone is determined, interventions such as those discussed in part 4 of the text can be applied to increase or decrease various emotions.

Kamata, Tenenbaum, & Hanin, 2002; Raglin & Hanin, 2000; Robazza & Bartoli, 2003; Robazza, Bartoli, & Hanin, 2004; Ruiz & Hanin, 2004; Russell & Cox, 2000). Theoretically, it would be possible to create an IZOF around multiple individual emotions, but this would be impractical. In addition, several researchers have expanded the list of potential predictors and suggested that physical measures such as reaction time, power, skill, endurance and heart rate be included in individual zones of optimal functioning (D'Urso et al., 2002; Robazza & Bartoli, 2003; Robazza et al., 2004).

While the problem is complex, Kamata, Tenenbaum, and Hanin (2002) have proposed a probabilistic approach to looking at the formation of an individual zone of optimal functioning (IZOF) while simultaneously looking at an individual

zone of dysfunction (IZDF). The probability of falling into the IZOF or the IZDF is a function of combined idiosyncratic emotional intensity, which varies for each athlete. Initially, the process of establishing an athlete's IZOF was as simple as determining the level of state anxiety associated with optimum athletic performance and then forming a zone around that optimal level of anxiety. To take into account multiple emotions, Hanin (2000) introduced the notion of idiographic (individualized) scaling procedures, in which the athlete is asked to identify affect descriptors (words) that exert an influence on performance, and then later rate these descriptors relative to a particular performance. Using these scaling procedures with 374 male and female athletes, Robazza and Bartoli (2003) were able to conclude that compared with nonelite performers, elite performers exhibit (a) higher positive emotions and bodily somatic symptoms, (b) lower levels of anxiety and higher self-confidence, and (c) higher hedonic tone (more pleasure).

Flow: The Psychology of Optimal Experience

Mihaly Csikszentmihalyi (pronounced cheeks-sent-me-high) is credited with being the origina-tor of the Flow concept. Flow is not an acronym, but a way of expressing a sense of seemingly effortless and intrinsically joyful movement. As originally conceptualized by Csikszentmihalyi (1990), an individual experiences **Flow** when engaged in an interesting activity for its own sake and for no other external purpose. In recent years, however, Flow has been associated with Hanin's notion of an individual zone of optimal functioning (IZOF). Thus, the term "peak perfor-mance" is often used to describe the concept of Flow. In reality, however, it is not necessary to have a peak or optimal performance in order to experience Flow.

The individual most responsible for applying the principles of Flow to sport and exercise is Susan Jackson (1992, 1995, 1996). As defined by Jackson (1995), "Flow is a state of optimal experiencing involving total absorption in a task, and creating a state of consciousness where optimal levels of functioning often occur" (p. 138). In his original conceptualization of the Flow construct, Csikszent-mihalyi (1990) described Flow as an end in itself, something that is to be enjoyed and appreciated. The key term in the Flow construct is that of the **autotelic experience.** An autotelic experience is "a self-contained activity, one that is done not with the expectation of some future benefit, but simply because the doing itself is the reward" (p. 67). The nine defining characteristics of the Flow experience are these (Csikszentmihalyi, 1990):

1. Requirement of a challenge/skill balance.
2. Merging of action and awareness (sense of automaticity and spontaneity).
3. Goals that are clearly defined.
4. Clear, unambiguous feedback.
5. Total concentration on the skill being performed.
6. Sense of being in control without trying to be in control (paradox of control).
7. Loss of self-awareness (becoming one with the activity).
8. Loss of time awareness.
9. Autotelic experience (end result of all of the above).

The nine defining characteristics of the Flow experience form the basis of an instrument devel-oped by Jackson and Marsh (1996) for measuring Flow. The Flow State Scale (FSS) is composed of 36 items that measure the nine dimensions identi-fied by Csikszentmihalyi. Each item is set to a 5-point Likert scale (1 = strongly disagree to 5 = strongly agree). A sample item on the FSS might be as follows:

My concentration was focused entirely on the task at hand

STRONGLY DISAGREE				*STRONGLY AGREE*
1	2	3	4	5

Most recently, the Flow State Scale (FSS) was revised and is now named the Flow State Scale–2 (FSS-2). In revising the FSS, five of the original items were replaced with five new items, keeping the FSS-2 inventory to 36 items in length. As men-tioned earlier, it has been tempting for some au-thors to use the terms "peak experience" or "peak performance" as identical to the Flow experience. Flow is a combination of emotional ecstasy and personal best performance (Kimiecik & Stein, 1992; McInman & Grove, 1991). An athlete may perform a personal best in a track and field event, yet not really consider the total experience as a peak moment. Conversely, one may experience an au-totelic experience in sport and not realize a personal best score in terms of performance. In studying the

CONCEPT When the conditions are just right, the athlete may enjoy a psychological experience that yields both high performance and personal ecstasy. Flow is an end in itself, something that is to be enjoyed and appreciated. It is sometimes, but not necessarily, associated with peak performance.

APPLICATION Conditions necessary for Flow to occur are listed in table 8.3. They include a positive mental attitude, positive affect, attentional focus, perception of being well prepared physically, and a oneness with teammates and/or coach. These are all attributes that an athlete should strive for at all times. If at some time they yield the ecstasy of the Flow experience, this is all the better.

TABLE 8.3 | Factors Believed to Facilitate or to Prevent the Occurrence of the FLOW State

Effect on FLOW State	Factor
Facilitate	1. Development of a positive mental attitude. 2. Positive precompetitive affect. 3. Positive competitive affect (during contest). 4. Maintaining appropriate attentional focus. 5. Physical readiness (perception of being prepared). 6. Unity with teammates(s) and/or coach.
Prevent	1. Experiencing physical problems and mistakes. 2. Inability to maintain appropriate attentional focus. 3. Negative mental attitude. 4. Lack of audience response.

Flow experience, Jackson identified factors believed to facilitate Flow, as well as other factors believed to prevent the occurrence of the Flow state. These factors are listed in table 8.3.

One interesting way to view the Flow experience is as a positive interaction between skill and challenge (Kimiecik & Stein, 1992; Stein, Kimiecik, Daniels, & Jackson, 1995). This concept is illustrated in figure 8.12. The Flow experience is most likely to occur when the athlete is highly skilled, yet feels personally challenged by the competition that she faces. If the athlete feels personally challenged by the competition, yet feels that her skills are not up to the challenge, anxiety is likely to occur. Apathy is the likely outcome when an individual with a low skill level is confronted with a nonchallenging situation. Finally, boredom

will likely ensue when a highly skilled athlete is confronted with a nonchallenging competitive situation (Fave, Bassi, & Massimini, 2003).

Flow was originally measured as a situation-specific state measure (e.g., Flow state). By changing instructions, the 36-item FSS became the 36-item Trait Flow Scale (TFS; Jackson, Ford, Kimiecik, & Marsh, 1998), later renamed the Dispositional Flow Scale (DFS). The DFS was revised recently by revising five of the original items, and renaming it the DFS-2 (Jackson & Eklund, 2002). So now we have the FSS-2 and the DFS-2, both being 36 items in length.

In an investigation reported by Jackson et al. (1998), dispositional Flow was measured in 398 athletes participating in Masters Games in a setting separate from competition. Measures of trait

FIGURE 8.12 | Flow in sport is associated with a high level of skill and a high level of personal challenge.

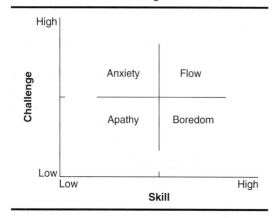

anxiety, goal orientation, intrinsic motivation, and perceived ability were taken on the athletes at the same time dispositional Flow was measured. In addition, Flow state was measured for all participants immediately after a competitive event associated with the games. Three important findings emerged from this research:

1. Both trait and state measures of Flow are correlated with perceived ability. This finding supports the concept illustrated in figure 8.12 that Flow is associated with high levels of skill and challenge.

2. Both trait and state measures of Flow are negatively correlated with competitive trait anxiety. This confirms the notion, listed in table 8.3, that positive and not negative affect facilitates the Flow experience. It also suggests that anxiety (worry) is the antithesis of Flow.

3. Both trait and state measures of Flow are positively correlated with intrinsic motivation. By definition, the Flow experience should be related to intrinsic motivation, because it occurs while one is performing a task that is interesting and enjoyable.

As listed in table 8.3, certain precompetitive factors are believed to be associated with the precipitation of the Flow experience. In this regard, an interesting confirmatory study was reported by Catley and Duda (1997). In this investigation, 163 recreational golfers completed instruments designed to measure precompetitive physical and mental readiness factors. Specific factors measured included calmness, confident readiness, the absence of pessimism, and positive focus. Following a round of golf, participants completed two instruments designed to provide state measures of the Flow experience. Results of the study confirmed that the Flow experience is associated with all four precompetitive readiness factors, but most closely with confident readiness and positive focus.

While Flow has been discussed in this chapter in association with the individual zone of optimal functioning, it is well to remember that Flow is closely linked with intrinsic motivation (Martin & Cutler, 2002). That is, Flow is best experienced in a situation in which a person engages in an interesting activity for its own sake and for no other external purpose. Additional insight into the Flow experience is provided by Jackson, Thomas, Marsh, and Smethurst (2001). Flow state and dispositional flow are highly correlated with each other. Flow factors account for almost 50 percent of the variability of subjective performance and 13 percent of the variability of objective performance. Finally, Flow correlates with self-concept and with the ability to cope with adversity (Jackson et al., 2001).

Jones's Directionality Theory

> People are a little nervous right now, but that can be a good thing. You can turn that anxiety into competitiveness on the court and that helps you out.
>
> (Logan Tom, member of year 2000 USA Women's Olympic Volleyball team; cited in Moore, 2000.)

When an athlete completes a precompetitive anxiety inventory such as the CSAI-2, two anxiety scores emerge. These two scores represent the absolute perceived intensity of the athlete's cognitive and somatic state anxiety. Jones (1991) reasoned that the absolute **intensity component of anxiety** was not nearly so important as the athlete's perception of whether his anxiety intensity was facilitative or debilitative relative to a subsequent competitive event. Jones labeled this facilitative or debilitative perception the **direction component of anxiety.** Thus, the important question is not whether an athlete has a high or low level of anxiety, but whether he perceives that this specific level will help him perform better.

To test this theory, Jones and Swain (1995) modified the Competitive State Anxiety Inventory-2 (CSAI-2) to include the directionality construct. Recall that the CSAI-2 is a 27-item inventory that measures cognitive anxiety, somatic anxiety, and self-confidence. Each item on the CSAI-2 is anchored by a four-point Likert scale (1 = not at all, 2 = somewhat, 3 = moderately so, 4 = very much so). In the modified CSAI-2, the athlete is asked to indicate whether she perceives her intensity response to be debilitative or facilitative to her upcoming performance. The directionality scale requires the athlete to indicate on a seven-point scale (−3, −2, −1, 0, +1, +2, +3) whether she considers her response on the intensity of anxiety item to be debilitative (negative rating) or facilitative (positive rating).

The Jones group reported several studies that showed that successful athletes could be differentiated from less successful athletes based upon anxiety direction scores, but not intensity scores (Jones & Hanton, 1996; Jones, Hanton, & Swain, 1994; Jones & Swain, 1995). Also in support of the directionality concept, Perry and Williams (1998) demonstrated that novice and skilled tennis players could be differentiated on the basis of directionality scores. However, they also were able to discriminate between the two groups using intensity scores. Furthermore, they provided evidence that would suggest that intensity and directionality scores were correlated. Finally, it should be mentioned that a study reported by Jerome and

Williams (2000) using bowlers found only limited support for directionality theory.

Going on the assumption that directionality was a predictor of athletic performance, Page, Sime, and Nordell (1999) designed a study to see if negative perceptions about precompetitive anxiety could be changed through imagery (imagery will be discussed in part 4 of the text). Following five weeks of imagery training, the authors found that negative perceptions of anxiety in collegiate swimmers could be made to be more positive. That is, following the imagery intervention, the swimmers came to view precompetitive anxiety as being conducive to good performance.

From an applied perspective, clear differences emerge between Hanin's theory of individual zones of optimal functioning and Jones's theory of directionality. In the case of IZOF, obtained precompetitive state anxiety is compared with an established zone of optimal functioning relative to state anxiety. If this obtained anxiety score is either below or above the predetermined IZOF, behavioral and/or cognitive interventions are applied to raise or lower precompetitive anxiety. A markedly different strategy emerges if you subscribe to the directionality theory of precompetitive anxiety. Instead of concluding that high anxiety is a negative thing, the athlete is taught to view anxiety as a natural by-product of competition. The athlete is taught to view high levels of anxiety as being facilitative to best performance. Athletes are taught to restructure their conscious thought relative to experiencing either somatic or cognitive state anxiety prior to competition (Eubank, Collins, & Smith, 2000).

The application of directionality theory in sport is illustrated in two studies reported by Hanton and Jones (1999a, 1999b). In the first investigation, ten elite male international swimmers who exhibited facilitative direction scores on the CSAI-2D were studied. Through qualitative research procedures, it was determined that this group of elite athletes (a) experienced early unwanted negative feelings about precompetitive anxiety; (b) learned, early in their careers, that

CONCEPT Intensity of competitive state anxiety is an indicator of the absolute level of state anxiety associated with a competitive situation, whereas direction of competitive state anxiety is the athlete's perception of whether the indicated intensity is debilitative or facilitative relative to performance.

APPLICATION From the perspective of individual differences, it is more important for the coach or teacher to know whether an athlete perceives a certain level of anxiety to be positive or negative than for her to know the absolute level. Two athletes may exhibit high levels of somatic and cognitive anxiety immediately prior to competition, but one of them may view these high levels as having a positive, or facilitative, influence on the competition. This knowledge should provide the coach with valuable information as to how to best prepare the athlete for competition.

---

feelings of apprehension, worry, and physiological arousal were normal and that they should view them as being positive and necessary precursors to good performance; (c) possessed well-developed precompetitive mental routines that helped them use positive and negative affect to their advantage; and (d) learned to use precompetitive jitters and nerves to their advantage, and did not try to reduce the symptoms. In the second investigation, four regional/national level male swimmers who consistently interpreted precompetitive state anxiety as debilitating to performance were retained as subjects. A multimodal single-subject design with staggered start times was used to test directionality theory. One participant served as the control, while the other three received intervention strategies designed to teach them the use of mental skills as well as awareness of the positive benefits of precompetitive anxiety symptoms. All participants competed in ten swim meets in which their times were recorded. Each of the three experimental participants started the intervention at a different time along the ten-meet schedule. Results of the investigation clearly showed that precompetitive directionality scores changed from being negative (debilitative) to positive (facilitative) after participants received the intervention. No change was observed for the control subject. While not tested statistically, data also indicated that swimming performance improved following intervention for all experimental participants.

While IZOF and directionality theory tend to force us to think differently in terms of the effect of anxiety/emotions on performance, a number of researchers have looked for commonalities between the two theories. Using high school competitive swimmers as participants, Davis and Cox (2002) demonstrated that best objective performance generally occurs when an athlete is within her predetermined cognitive anxiety IZOF. However, they also reasoned that direction scores that fell within the IZOF would also be higher than those that fell out of the zone (e.g., more facilitative). This expectation was not confirmed. Robazza and Bartoli (2003) utilized Hanin's IZOF notion of idiographic scaling in conjunction with directionality theory to study the relationship between hedonic tone and functionality. Athletes were presented with lists of emotion-laden words and body/somatic symptom words and asked to categorize them as being pleasant or unpleasant (hedonic tone) and as being facilitative or debilitative (functionality) to a good performance in their sport. The results of this investigation, relative to most often selected emotion-laden words/phrases, are illustrated in figure 8.13. In addition to demonstrating that selected emotions are not universally categorized by all athletes in the same way, the results illustrated differences between elite and nonelite athletes in terms of hedonic tone and functionality. The intensity scores of emotions/somatic symptoms categorized as being both facilitative

FIGURE 8.13 | Emotion/affect–laden words most often categorized as being facilitative/inhibiting and pleasant/unpleasant.

Functionality (Direction)

	Facilitative	Inhibiting
Pleasant	• Motivated • Focused • Energetic • Secure • Determined	• Calm • Relaxed • Serene • Cheerful • Pleased
Unpleasant	• Tense • Nervous • Enraged • Aggressive • Worried	• Unfocused • Unconfident • Insecure • Tired • Uncertain

Hedonic tone

Source: Based on Robazza & Bartoli, 2003.

and pleasant were higher for elite athletes. Elite athletes enjoyed lower anxiety intensity scores and higher self-confidence intensity scores, as well as more facilitative and more pleasant scores. Similar results to these were also reported by Mellalieu, Hanton, and Jones (2003).

Two separate studies by Butt, Weinberg, and Horn (2003) and Thomas, Maynard, and Hanton (2004) provide new and interesting insight as to how directional scores change across time. Using the traditional modified CSAI-2 inventory, Thomas et al. (2004) measured intensity, direction, and frequency of state anxiety 7 days, 48 hours, 24 hours, and 1 hour before an important competition for 60 national- and regional-level athletes. Frequency was measured as a function of how often an athlete experienced a particular anxiety-related emotion on a scale of 1 to 7. Results show that the directional scale is flat for self-confidence, cognitive anxiety, and somatic anxiety up to 24 hours before competition, but then one hour before competition, the directional scales for all three decline, or get

less facilitative. Frequency for cognitive and somatic anxiety increases linearly across time, while it remains flat and high for self-confidence. Using the Mental Readiness Form (MRF) and an attached directional scale, Butt, Weinberg, and Horn (2003) measured anxiety/confidence intensity and direction retrospectively across a field hockey game for 62 female collegiate athletes. Results showed that somatic and cognitive anxiety declined across time (pregame, 1st half, 2nd half, postgame), while self-confidence increased across time. Conversely, little change was observed across time for direction (functionality) of anxiety or self-confidence.

Finally, Hanton and Connaughton (2002) reported an interesting study involving swimmers in which perceived personal control serves as a moderator variable between intensity and direction. A moderator variable determines how another variable (intensity) affects a third variable (direction). As illustrated in figure 8.14, somatic and cognitive anxiety have a facilitative effect on performance and self-confidence if the athlete perceives that he has the ability to control the debilitating effects of state anxiety. Conversely, if the athlete does not feel that he has personal control over the debilitating effects of anxiety, then a decline in performance and self-confidence will follow.

Apter's Reversal Theory

Reversal theory, as proposed by Apter (1982), is as much a theory of personality as it is a theory of arousal. Individuals are described as being either telic or paratelic dominant. **Telic-dominant individuals** have a goal-directed orientation toward life, while **paratelic-dominant individuals** are fun-loving and have a "here-and-now" orientation. At the same time, however, Apter notes that the telic and paratelic orientations are not enduring traits or personality dispositions. While an individual tends to be dominant in either the telic or the paratelic orientation, each person has the capability to switch back and forth between the two. **Reversal theory** receives its name from this proclivity toward switching back and forth between the two

FIGURE 8.14 | Whether anxiety is perceived as facilitating or debilitating depends on perception of personal control.

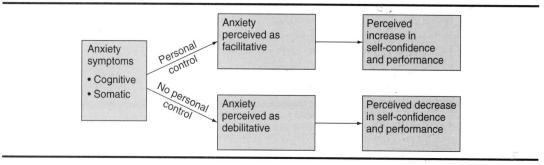

Source: Based on Hanton & Connaughton, 2002.

A paratelic orientation may be conductive to a Flow experience. Courtesy University of Missouri–Columbia Sports Information.

orientations. Apter's concept of reversal theory is described in detail by Apter (1984) and by Kerr (1997).

Reversal theory is described as having characteristics associated with both drive theory and inverted-U theory. In drive theory, the organism seeks to reduce drive (anxiety) by satisfying the craving for such needs as food, water, or sex. Drive reduction has the effect of moving an organism from a state of being aroused to a state of relaxation. In inverted-U theory, the organism seeks to overcome boredom by increasing arousal. In this case, a moderate increase in arousal brings on the desirable psychological state of excitement. Combining these two conditions into a single theory (reversal theory) produces a hedonic goal (pleasure seeking) to bring about a situation of relaxation or excitement, as opposed to anxiety or boredom. Reversal theory as explained in these terms is illustrated in figure 8.15. As can be observed in this figure, the objective is to increase hedonic tone, not to increase or decrease arousal.

The two curves in figure 8.15 are representative of the two frame-of-mind orientations in reversal theory. The orientation leading from anxiety (an unpleasant condition) to relaxation is labeled the telic mode, while the orientation leading from boredom (also an unpleasant condition) to

FIGURE 8.15 | The hypothesized relationship between arousal and hedonic tone (pleasure seeking) for the anxiety-avoidance (telic) and the excitement-seeking (paratelic) systems.

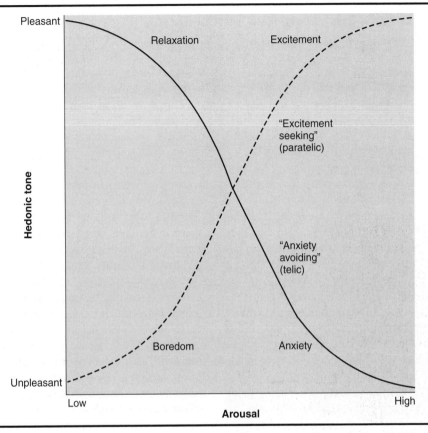

Source: Adapted from Apter, M. J. (1982), *The experience of motivation: The theory of psychological reversals*, New York: Academic Press.

excitement is labeled the paratelic mode. The telic mode is goal oriented and serious. While in this frame of mind, the individual views increased arousal to be unpleasant and stressful. Conversely, the paratelic mode is activity oriented and excited with the here-and-now. Increased arousal could be viewed as threatening and stressful in the telic mode and as exciting and exhilarating in the paratelic mode.

Because reversal theory hypothesizes the involuntary switching back and forth between the telic and paratelic orientations, it is referred to as being **metamotivational** as opposed to motivational in nature. Three factors interact with one another to bring about a **psychological reversal** (Apter, 1984). These three factors are (a) contingent events, (b) frustration, and (c) satiation.

An example of a *contingent event* might be as follows. An athlete enters a game situation where the atmosphere is extremely tense and competitive. This is a situation conducive to a telic orientation. Midway through the game, however, her team starts to gain momentum as they score one important point after another. The athlete's mood, along with the moods of her teammates, begins to shift noticeably toward the paratelic mode and away from the telic mode. High levels of arousal and excitement are still present, but her mood has changed, and the emotional environment has shifted from one of high anxiety and tension to one of fun and excitement.

The following describes an infamous Olympic incident that could be an example in which *frustration* caused a reversal. In the 1972 Munich Olympic Games, members of the U.S.A. men's basketball team leaped and hugged one another with joy (paratelic mode) when they believed they had won the gold medal against the then Soviet Union. This psychological frame of mind quickly changed to the telic mode when they were informed that the game was not over and that three seconds were being put back on the clock. It was during these last three seconds, and the third questionable opportunity to inbound the ball, that the Soviets won the game by one point. The U.S. players boycotted the medals ceremony, refusing to accept the silver medal for second place (Smith, 1992).

The third factor that can bring about a change in metamotivational mode is *satiation,* or an innate dynamic force for change. As the period of time an individual spends in one metamotivational mode increases, the probability of a reversal also increases. This situation might occur with a tennis player who has just spent two hours working on refining his backhand drive down the line (telic mode). Taking a water break, he meets some friends who invite him to join in a friendly game of mixed doubles. Partly from satiation and partly from a desire for a change, the tennis player experiences a metamotivational reversal from the telic to the paratelic mode. Suddenly, the tension and singlemindedness of his practice session shifts to a carefree feeling of enjoyment, enthusiasm, and excitement about the game of tennis.

The attractiveness of reversal theory is closely associated with its flexibility and dynamic nature. The theory underscores the importance of taking a situation-specific and individualistic approach to studying the relationship between arousal and performance. If an athlete is in the telic mode, increased arousal could result in a state anxiety level that could cause a decrement in performance. Conversely, if an athlete is in the paratelic mode, decreasing arousal through some sort of intervention could actually bring about boredom. Neither of these scenarios is likely to have a facilitative effect upon athletic performance. A great deal of care must be used to determine the appropriate approach to use with an athlete who is suffering from a decrement in athletic performance. From a reversal theory perspective, figure 8.16 illustrates the various options that are available to the athlete who is experiencing either debilitating state anxiety or boredom.

An athlete suffering from debilitating anxiety while in the telic mode has two possible options open to her. The first option is to decrease the level of arousal through a stress management strategy (progressive relaxation). The second option is to induce a reversal to the paratelic mode. If this can be accomplished, the athlete will view the anxiety-provoking situation as exciting and challenging (pleasurable), as opposed to threatening and unpleasant. The psychological reversal can be triggered through a reinterpretation of the unpleasant high arousal. For example, the athlete might engage in some sort of pleasant fantasy that is associated with high arousal (e.g., dunking the basketball).

Similarly, an athlete who is suffering from boredom while in the paratelic state has two options available to her. The first option is to increase the level of arousal to induce a sense of excitement (psyching-up strategy). The second option is to induce a reversal to the telic state. If this can be accomplished, the athlete will view the unpleasant situation as relaxing and tranquil as opposed to boring. For example, the athlete might reflect upon the peacefulness of the moment and imagine she is relaxing in a hot tub.

As shown in figures 8.15 and 8.16, reversal theory posits that athletes seek an increase in hedonic tone as they strive for excellence. The bored athlete strives for more excitement and enthusiasm, and the distressed athlete strives for calm and

PART 4

Cognitive and Behavioral Interventions

In an earlier chapter on anxiety, arousal, and stress relationships (chapter 8), the case study of a young high school athlete named Ryan was introduced. Recall that Ryan was an extremely gifted multiple-sport athlete who experienced difficulty in dealing with anxiety while competing in track events. Specifically, he would become so anxious prior to sprinting and hurdling events that he literally could not run efficiently. During practices, however, Ryan experienced little or no tension and anxiety. During three years of high school track, he had never lost a race during practice with teammates.

It was clear that Ryan was going to be a track "dropout" if some sort of intervention were not provided. Ryan's father talked to a professor of sport psychology at the local college to find out if something could be done to help Ryan. After three weeks of studying Ryan's anxiety response to competition, the sport psychologist concluded that an individualized intervention program could be developed to help him. The program that was recommended was one very similar to autogenic training, described in chapter 9. In this program, Ryan learned what caused his anxiety and how to cope with it when it occurred. Ryan's success at reversing the damaging effects of anxiety did not happen overnight. However, during his senior year he made up for many of his earlier failures by setting a state record in the 200-meter sprint.

In part 3 of the text, we discussed the concepts of arousal and anxiety in great depth. You are now familiar with both of these terms and aware of several theories that purport to explain the relationship between arousal/anxiety and performance. Too much or too little arousal may result in poor athletic performance. Consequently, the goal for the athlete and the coach is to identify the optimal level of arousal for any particular event.

The purpose of this part of the book is to introduce and explain various coping and intervention strategies designed to control or modify anxiety, arousal, and stress as defined in part 3 of the text. Topics to be addressed in chapters 9 through 12 include (a) coping and intervention strategies in sport, (b) goal setting in sport, (c) imagery and hypnosis in sport, and (d) psychological skills training. ∞

CHAPTER 9

Coping and Intervention Strategies in Sport

KEY TERMS

Abdominal breathing
Affirmation statements
Anxiety/stress spiral
Approach style of coping
Autogenic training
Avoidance style of coping
Biofeedback
Bulletin board
Chest breathing
Coping
Coping conceptual framework
Coping strategies
Coping style
Deep breathing
Dispositional hypothesis
Dynamic hypothesis
Emotion-focused coping strategy
Fan support
Generalizability of coping skills
Immediate mobilization
Individual self-energizing strategies
Mantra
Matching hypothesis
Meditation
Mental device
Pep talk
Precompetition workout
Problem-focused coping strategy
Progressive relaxation
Relaxation response
Self-activation
Self-energizing strategies
Self-talk
Self-thought
Stress management
Team energizing strategies
Transcendental meditation

In this very important chapter on coping and intervention strategies in sport, we are going to introduce and discuss four major topics that relate to coping and intervention. These include (a) coping strategies in sport, (b) self-talk as an intervention, (c) relaxation strategies used in sport, and (d) arousal energizing strategies. Subsequent chapters in this part of the text will build on the behavioral and cognitive interventions introduced in this chapter.

While it may seem obvious to most students of sport psychology, it is important to briefly distinguish between the concepts of behavioral and cognitive interventions. A behavior is something that can be observed, so when we talk about a behavioral intervention we are talking about an intervention that changes the way an athlete behaves. This usually involves changing the environment in some way, or changing the way an athlete prepares for competition. For example, teaching an athlete how to breathe in preparation for a free throw in basketball would be a behavioral intervention. Conversely, a cognitive intervention has to do with the way athletes think and analyze situations. We can observe the effects of a cognitive intervention, but we can't see an athlete think. That is, we can't get inside of the athlete's head and observe how she thinks. Nevertheless, restructuring how an athlete thinks about competition or how she thinks about confidence can have a powerful effect on behavior or performance. For example, the use of imagery as a way to improve technique in a sport skill would be a cognitive intervention. Sometimes cognitive and behavioral interventions are combined and intertwined into a single intervention.

Another important concept to understand before we begin this chapter is the distinction between the terms *psychological intervention* and *coping strategy*. While these two terms are very similar and are often used interchangeably, there are some important differences. Think of a psychological intervention (behavioral or cognitive) as something that the coach or sport psychologist uses to intervene on the athlete's behalf. For example, if the sport psychologist uses a stress management technique to

teach an athlete how to reduce pregame anxiety, this would be an example of an intervention designed by someone else to help the athlete. However, if the athlete is able to personalize and claim ownership of the newly discovered stress management skills and to integrate them into her own repertoire of psychological skills, then they become personal coping skills. So, what was once an intervention provided by the coach or sport psychologist can later become a personal coping strategy or skill.

Coping Strategies in Sport

> My third maxim was to endeavor always to conquer myself rather than the order of the world, and in general accustom myself to the persuasion that except our own thoughts, there is nothing absolutely in our power. (René Descartes, *Discourse on Method,* Part III)

Coping has been defined by Lazarus and Folkman (1984) as "constantly changing cognitive and behavioral efforts to manage specific external and/or internal demands that are appraised as taking or exceeding resources of the person" (p. 141). Referring back to figure 8.1, we are reminded that the stress response is the end result of a perceived imbalance between the demands of the situation and an appraisal of coping resources. To address the debilitating effects of the stress response, the athlete intervenes with active coping responses.

Consistent with the stress process shown in figure 8.1 is the interaction model shown in figure 9.1. As an extension of Cerin et al. (2000), the interaction model was proposed by Mellalieu (2003) to show how the stress process is influenced by mood state, personal factors, situational factors, and attentional processing; all of these are factors we have discussed in previous chapters. The stress process, including coping, is shown as the central feature in the interactional model. Thus, figure 9.1 shows a much more complex and complete picture as to how coping plays a central role in the stress process, and how emotions influence performance. Research confirms that cognitive appraisals of

FIGURE 9.1 | The Interactional Model of the Stress Process, showing how coping with emotions is influenced by mood, attention, personality, and situational factors.

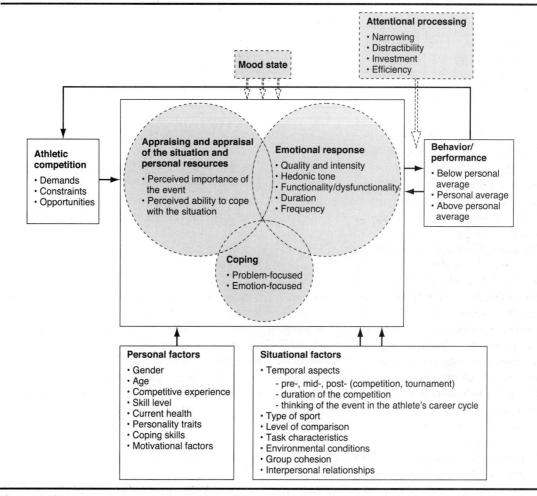

Source: Mellalieu, S.D. (2003). Mood matters: But how much? A comment on Lane and Terry (2000). *Journal of Applied Sport Psychology, 15,* 99–114. Reproduced with permission of Taylor & Francis, Inc. http://www.taylorandfrancis.com

stressful situations influence the use of coping strategies (Anshel, Jamieson, & Raviv, 2001), and that unexpected stressors present additional challenges to the coping process (Dugdale, Eklund, & Gordon, 2002).

Coping involves a personal response on the part of the athlete to address the stress response. The athlete feels anxious in a competitive situation and tries to use personal coping resources to reduce the anxiety. The use of various relaxation or arousal management procedures to reduce anxiety is commonly referred to as **stress management.** When an athlete uses a stress management technique or any other cognitive or behavioral intervention, this is a form of coping. Thus, any sort of intervention, if it is self-applied, can appropriately be called a coping skill. Sometimes, however, an athlete's coach may determine that the athlete's own coping attempts are not working and decide to intervene with a planned cognitive or behavioral intervention.

In the balance of this section we will focus our discussion on (a) a conceptual framework for coping strategies and styles, (b) measurement of coping skill, (c) the dynamic nature of coping skill, (d) factors that enhance the generalizability of coping, (e) factors that influence coping effectiveness, (f) the relationship between emotion and coping, and (g) examples of coping by elite athletes. In subsequent chapters of part 4 of the text, we will address other ways of preparing athletes for optimal performance.

Conceptual Framework for Coping Strategies and Styles

Lazarus and Folkman (1984) indicated that **coping strategies** are of two types: problem-focused and emotion-focused. **Problem-focused coping strategies** center on alleviating the environmental stimulus that is causing the stress response. If a right-handed baseball player is very anxious when batting against left-handed pitchers, an appropriate problem-focused coping strategy might be to get more experience hitting against left-handed pitchers during practice. Other common names for problem-focused coping include the terms "task-focused coping" and sometimes "action-focused coping." These are all considered to be synonymous terms.

Emotion-focused coping strategies seek to regulate emotions in order to reduce or manage cognitive distress. In the baseball example, the batter would focus his coping on controlling his emotions through anxiety reduction techniques. Instead of attacking the source of the problem, the athlete seeks to reduce or eliminate the symptoms associated with the stress.

Several authors have proposed a third coping strategy and called it "avoidance coping" (Endler & Parker, 1990; Grove & Heard, 1997). Anshel,

Williams, and Hodge (1997), however, have pointed out that rather than being a coping strategy, avoidance coping is really a **coping style.** Two different coping styles are identified: approach coping and avoidance coping. Some athletes prefer an **approach style of coping,** in which their coping preference is to address the stressful situation directly. Conversely, some athletes prefer an **avoidance style of coping,** in which their preferred coping style is to solve the problem by avoiding the problem. Avoidance coping is also referred to as repression, disengagement, or rejection.

Anshel et al.'s (1997) two-dimensional **coping conceptual framework** for studying coping styles and strategies is illustrated in figure 9.2. As can be observed in this figure, four different categories of coping styles and strategies can be identified. The four different coping strategies include (a) approach/problem-focused coping, (b) approach/emotion-focused coping, (c) avoidance/problem-focused coping, and (d) avoidance/emotion-focused coping. Examples of each of these four different coping

FIGURE 9.2 | Conceptual framework for studying coping styles and strategies and examples.

| | Coping styles | |
	Approach	Avoidance
Problem Focused	Analyze reasons why errors were made and correct them	Apply a mental distraction
Emotion Focused	Use progressive relaxation to reduce stress	Vent unpleasant emotions, cry

Coping strategies

CONCEPT Athletes cope with stress by either approaching or avoiding the situation. Within this framework, they will adopt either an active problem-solving strategy or an emotion-focused strategy.

APPLICATION An avoidance style of coping may be effective in some situations, but it does not provide a long-term solution to the problem. Rather than solving the problem, avoidance only represses the problem or puts the solution off. Coaches should assist athletes in developing coping strategies that can either reduce or eliminate the stress response.

---

strategies are provided within the cells of the conceptual framework.

Measurement of Coping Skill

Several different pencil-and-paper inventories have been developed to measure coping resources. Among them are the Ways of Coping Checklist (WOCC; Crocker, 1992; Folkman & Lazarus, 1985); the COPE and MCOPE instruments (Carver, Scheier, & Weintraub, 1989; Crocker & Graham, 1995); Coping Inventory for Stressful Situations (CISS; Endler & Parker, 1990); the Coping Style in Sport Survey (CSSS; Anshel, Williams, & Hodge, 1997); the Coping Function Questionnaire (CFQ; Kowalski & Crocker, 2001); and the Coping Inventory for Competitive Sport (CICS; Gaudreau & Blondin, 2002).

The Coping Style in Sport Survey (CSSS) was developed by Anshel et al. (1997) to reflect the coping styles and strategies conceptual framework illustrated in figure 9.2. The CSSS is composed of 134 items associated with seven common sports-related stressors. The athlete's task is to indicate how she would usually respond relative to the following acute stressors:

1. After making a physical or mental error
2. After being criticized by the coach
3. After observing my opponent cheat
4. After experiencing intense pain or injury
5. After receiving a "bad" call by the official
6. After successful performance by an opponent

7. After poor environmental conditions such as bad weather, poor ground/court conditions, or negative crowd reactions

The Dynamic Nature of Coping Styles and Strategies

Sport psychologists have been interested in knowing if athletes' coping strategies are dispositional in nature or if they are consistent with a dynamic process. The **dispositional hypothesis** posits that athletes have a certain learned or innate way of coping with all stress-related situations. Conversely, the **dynamic hypothesis** posits that athletes' coping responses are dynamic and fluid, changing from situation to situation.

Applied research has generally supported the hypothesis that coping strategies and styles are dynamic and fluid. Research involving U.S. Olympic wrestlers, U.S. National Champion figure skaters, and elite Korean athletes all confirms this hypothesis. Elite athletes do not simply apply the same coping strategy to every situation, but rather select different strategies to fit different situations (Gould, Eklund, & Jackson, 1993; Gould, Finch, & Jackson, 1993; Park, 2000). The dynamic hypothesis was also supported by research reported by Crocker and Isaak (1997) and by Grove and Heard (1997). A study that seemed to provide evidence favoring the dispositional hypothesis was reported by Giacobbi and Weinberg (2000). They based their conclusion on the presence of moderate-sized correlations between coping strategies reported at three different points in time. These

CONCEPT Athletes utilize a dynamic as opposed to dispositional approach to coping with stress. Different situations require different coping applications.

APPLICATION The dynamic nature of coping and the principle of specificity highlight the importance of learning many different kinds of coping styles and strategies. If an athlete has numerous ways in which to cope with adversity, she will be more likely to find one that will be effective in a specific situation.

CONCEPT Factors such as stimulus generality, broad application, personal significance, being in control, and learned resourcefulness are all important in enhancing the generalizability of coping skills.

APPLICATION As coaches teach and athletes learn coping skills, it is important to understand the broad potential application of these skills. In a sense, all coping skills should be taught with the thought in mind that they should transfer to other situations as well. Coping skills learned in sport situations should generalize to the nonsport environment, and vice versa. To accomplish this, the athlete and coach must think in terms of broad application and ways of enhancing generalizability.

conclusions were made despite the presence of significant differences between coping strategy scores reported at the three different times. Consequently, the case can be made that even this study provides support for the dynamic hypothesis.

Factors that Enhance the Generalizability of Coping

The skills athletes acquire to deal with anxiety, low self-confidence, and other stressful sport-related situations may generalize to other more global life situations. This means that if an athlete can learn to cope with failure (or success) in an athletic situation, the coping skill may be transferred to another sport situation or even a stressful nonsport situation (e.g., illness, financial setback, loss of job, loss of friend).

In this regard, Smith (1999) identifies five different factors that can facilitate the **generalizability of coping skills** to other situations. These factors are as follows:

1. *Recognition of stimulus generality* Many stressful life situations are very similar to athletic situations. Recognizing the similarity and recalling the specific coping strategy that was effective in the athletic situation will facilitate transfer of coping skill to another situation.

2. *Broad application of coping skill* Some coping skills are very specific to a specific athletic situation, but others are very broad. Progressive relaxation, for example, is a broad coping skill that should generalize to numerous sport and nonsport situations.

3. *Personal significance of coping application*
A coping skill that was effective in reducing stress related to an issue of great personal significance will be remembered. Coping skills that have proven to be personally important will generalize to other situations.

4. *Internal locus of control of coping skill*
When an athlete claims "ownership" of a coping skill, it is more easily transferred to other situations.

5. *Learned resourcefulness*   Learning a specific coping skill to address a specific life stress is effective, but it is narrow-minded. The resourceful individual looks for broader application of all coping skills and learning experiences.

Factors That Influence Coping Effectiveness

As reported by Hammereister and Burton (2004), coping effectiveness is related to the sex of the athlete. For example, their research suggests that female athletes utilize emotion-focused coping strategies more effectively than male athletes.

Women also reportedly benefit more from social support than do the male athletes. Another factor that can influence coping effectiveness is related to the matching hypothesis. The **matching hypothesis** suggests that coping responses that match the stressor are most effective (Campen, Carrie, & Roberts, 2001). For example, a cognitive or problem-focused coping strategy should be more effective in addressing the debilitating effects of cognitive anxiety than an emotion-focused coping strategy. Some coping strategies have been shown to be effective in the short term but not the long term. Kim and Duda (2003) showed that both approach and avoidance styles of coping are effective in reducing stress in the short term, but only the approach (problem- and emotion-focused) style of coping is effective long term. Avoidance and withdrawal styles of coping have little effect upon long-term satisfaction, enjoyment, and desire to continue with an activity.

Related to motivation is the observation that the effectiveness of coping in sport is related to an athlete's perception of self-determination (Amiot, Gaudreau, & Blanchard, 2004). As illustrated in figure 9.3, scoring high in self-determination is positively associated with an active approach style

FIGURE 9.3 | Model illustrates the association between self-determination in sport, coping style, and goal attainment.

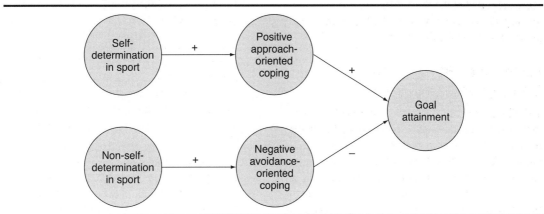

Source: Adapted with permission from Amiot, C.E., Gaudreau, P., & Blanchard, C.M. (2004). Self-determination, coping and goal attainment in sport. *Journal of Sport & Exercise Psychology, 26,* 396–411. Adapted with permission from Human Kinetics Publishers.

CONCEPT   Factors such as sex of athlete, match between stressor and coping strategy, coping strategy (approach/avoidance), and self-determination (intrinsic motivation) all have an influence on the effectiveness of an athlete's attempts to cope with adversity.

APPLICATION   From an applied perspective, nothing can be done about the sex of the athlete, but a great deal can be done about matching the coping strategy with the stressor, developing self-determination, and ultimately influencing the long-term effectiveness of coping. An approach coping style should be encouraged by coaches, as this will lead to greater likelihood of goal attainment. Furthermore, as we learned in chapter 5, coaches must continually focus on the development of intrinsic motivation, as opposed to a reliance on external rewards.

of coping, which is positively associated with goal attainment. Conversely, scoring low in self-determination is positively associated with an avoidance/disengagement style of coping, which in turn is negatively associated with goal attainment. The student is referred back to chapter 5 for a review of self-determination theory.

The Relationship Between Emotion and Coping

"And that hit me when I realized I was out of control with my emotions. I knew I was scared to death and I couldn't make myself not scared. And I walked up there and I was like, 'God I don't want to be here, I'm scared.' I felt completely, 100 percent out of control. I had very rarely ever in my life felt that way. I don't know how to stop it from happening." (Quote from unidentified athlete from Poezwardowski & Conroy, 2002.)

The dynamic relationship between emotion and coping is illustrated in figure 9.1. Several investigations have been reported that refine our understanding about that relationship. These studies have tended to utilize ideographic scaling techniques introduced in chapter 8 under the heading "Individual Zones of Optimal Functioning." Recall that we previously learned about the process of emotion profiling wherein emotions experienced by athletes were categorized in terms of functionality and hedonic tone. Ntoumanis and Biddle (2000) studied the relationship between competitive state anxiety and coping strategies. Athletes were categorized, for both somatic and cognitive anxiety, into high- and low-intensity groups, and as viewing anxiety as being facilitating or debilitating (direction). Results showed that high levels of cognitive anxiety were associated with avoidance and venting coping strategies, whereas cognitive anxiety perceived as being facilitative (functional) was associated with high levels of problem solving and approach coping. Relative to somatic anxiety, results showed an association between intensity and functionality with an approach style of coping. Similarly, Pensgaard and Duda (2003) utilized ideographic scaling to categorize emotions in terms of direction (functional/dysfunctional) and hedonic tone (pleasant/unpleasant). Results showed a positive association between emotions that were both functional and pleasant and the most effective coping strategies (e.g., approach strategies). As illustrated in figure 9.1, coping resources moderate (determine) the relationship between the situation and emotional response, but as Skinner and Brewer (2004) point out, inadequate coping will lead to an increase in negative emotion.

Athletes learn how to cope with rough play. Courtesy University of Missouri–Columbia Sports Information.

Coping Strategies Used by Elite Athletes

Athletes who possess well-developed and practiced coping skills will be more effective in managing the stress and demands of training and competition. Gould and colleagues (Gould, Eklund, & Jackson, 1993; Gould, Finch, & Jackson, 1993) studied coping strategies reported by Olympic wrestlers and National Champion figure skaters. Thirty-nine different coping themes were reported by the wrestlers. The 39 themes reduced down to four broad dimensions: (a) thought control strategies (e.g., self-talk, positive thinking, thought control), (b) attentional focus strategies (e.g., concentration control, tunnel vision), (c) emotional control strategies (e.g., arousal control, relaxation, visualization), and (d) behavioral strategies (e.g., set routines, rest, control of the environment). With the exception of the seeking of social support, coping strategies reported by figure skaters tended to be similar to those reported by wrestlers. Seeking of social support was not one of the themes reported by wrestlers, but was a consistent theme reported by figure skaters. The observation that females utilize social support as a coping strategy to a greater degree than males was reported by Crocker and Graham (1995).

Park (2000) studied the coping strategies of 180 elite Korean athletes representing 41 different sports. Some athletes identified as few as two coping strategies, while others identified as many as 15. Park identified 156 raw data themes or unique coping strategies that reduced to 25 first-order themes, 11 second-order themes, and finally, 7 general coping dimensions. The seven coping dimensions and percentages of each included psychological training (49.7 percent), physical training and strategizing (15.6 percent), somatic relaxation (14.4 percent), hobby activities (7.8 percent), social support (6.1 percent), prayer (5.2 percent), and substance use (1.2 percent). By far the most used coping strategy was the application of some form of psychological training (e.g., imagery, meditation, self-talk, positive thinking, attention, self-confidence, repression, goal setting, and willpower). Physical training and strategizing followed psychological training in importance (e.g., practicing hard, preparing for the next contest, watching films of opponents). Next in importance to training/strategies was somatic relaxation (e.g., progressive relaxation, massage, sleeping). These three categories of coping strategies accounted for 79.9 percent of all coping strategies cited. These results were similar to those reported by Gould and his colleagues.

CONCEPT Elite athletes tend to use an approach style of coping, with the majority of the strategies being problem or action focused. The vast majority of coping strategies may be categorized under the heading of psychological training, physical training and strategizing, and somatic relaxation.

APPLICATION While coping strategies tend to be of the approach variety, they vary greatly from situation to situation and athlete to athlete. The coach should help the athlete identify coping strategies that she is comfortable with and that she has personal control over. Remember, coping is primarily a dynamic process that requires a great deal of flexibility in style and application.

Finally, Dale (2000) reported the results of studying the coping practices of seven elite decathlon athletes. The decathlon track and field event is composed of ten different events across two days of competition (day 1: 100-meter run, long jump, shot put, high jump, 400-meter run; day 2: 110-meter hurdles, discus throw, pole vault, javelin throw, 1500-meter run). The athletes were asked to describe their experiences and thoughts associated with their most memorable performance. The open-ended response format yielded 32 raw data themes that could be considered distractions or things to overcome. From these 32 distractions, eight higher-order distraction themes emerged (lack of confidence, fatigue, a bad event, pain, fear, weather, other competitors, the 1500-meter run). The open-ended response format also yielded 24 raw data coping strategies. From these 24 coping strategies, six higher-order coping strategies or ways of addressing distractors emerged (visualization, focus on relevant cues, competing against self, confidence in training, consistency of effort, camaraderie).

In addition to the above examples of coping strategies used by elite athletes, examples from the sports of soccer and golf may be added. Holt and Hogg (2002) reported on stress experienced and coping strategies used by seven members of a women's international soccer team in preparation for the 1999 World Cup. Stress themes identified included (a) coach/player communication, (b) pace and demand of international soccer, (c) competitive stressors (anxiety, mistakes, evaluations, not starting, etc.),

and (d) fatigue and opponent distractions. Four main coping strategies included (a) application of learned mental skills, (b) social support resources, (c) practice and performance preparation, and (d) blocking out relevant and irrelevant stimuli.

Pensgaard and Duda (2002) focused upon the coping strategies used by a single female member of the Norwegian 2000 Olympics soccer team (eventual gold medal winner). Results showed that this athlete experienced stress associated with self-doubts, dissatisfaction with her own performance, and occasional discontent with team philosophy. Results also showed that she used a wide array of different approaches (problem and emotion focused) and avoidance strategies to overcome stress. Although this athlete experienced minor fluctuations in mood throughout the 25-day preparation period, she maintained positive response outcome expectancy (PROE) throughout.

Finally, Giacobbi, Foore, and Weinberg (2004) reported on the coping strategies employed by both skilled and moderately skilled golfers. The four general stress themes that emerged from this qualitative study were (a) being evaluated by others, (b) specific performance challenges, (c) psycho-emotional concerns, and (d) competitive stress. The six coping strategies identified by these golfers for addressing stress included (a) cognitive adjustment techniques (problem focused), (b) relaxation techniques (emotion focused), (c) off-course efforts to improve golf ability (problem focused), (d) situation golf course strategies (problem focused), and (e) general emotion-focused strategies.

As with all of the cognitive-behavioral interventions discussed in this section, for best results, coping strategies must be developed, practiced, and refined. Danish, Petitpas, and Hale (1992) suggest the use of life development intervention (LDI) specialists to assist individuals in developing strategies for coping with distress. The LDI specialist must possess (a) counseling skills, (b) the ability to assist in setting and attaining goals, and (c) proficiency in helping individuals identify existing coping skills and transfer them from one domain to another. A sport psychologist with LDI training should be available to youth and adult athletes.

Self-Talk as an Intervention

> When you step into the water you have to tell yourself a thousand times "I can swim the channel. I can swim the channel." I can't tell you how many times over the past year, two years I have said that to myself. (An athlete's self-talk thoughts on preparing to swim the English Channel, a distance of approximately 27 miles; Hollander & Acedvedo, 2000, p. 6)

It is an observed fact that athletes engage in self-talk during practice and competition (Van Raalte, Brewer, Rivera, & Petitpas, 1994; Van Raalte, Cornelius, Brewer, & Hatten, 2000). Sometimes the self-talk is positive in nature and sometimes it is negative in nature. Among junior tennis players, negative self-talk occurs twice as frequently as positive self-talk (Van Raalte et al., 1994). Nevertheless, the focus of this section is going to be on positive self-talk designed to enhance athletic performance, and not upon negative self-talk. Once mastered, positive self-talk may become an effective coping strategy to overcome anxiety, increase self-confidence, and improve technique. Consistent with Hardy, Gammage and Hall (2001), we will define **self-talk** as overt or covert personal dialogue in which the athlete interprets feelings, perceptions, and convictions and gives himself instructions and reinforcement. Perhaps one of the best explanations of the nature and function of self-talk was provided by Hardy et al.

(2001). In this excellent paper, the authors discuss research that focuses upon the where, when, what, and why of self-talk. Consistent with Munroe, Giacobbi, Hall and Weinberg (2000), they referred to these factors as the 4 Ws of self-talk.

The Where and When of Self-Talk

Athletes use self-talk in both sports-related and non-sports-related venues. Sports-related venues include such places as the practice environment, the competitive environment, the dressing room, and the bench. Non-sports-related venues include the home or any quiet place (Hardy et al., 2001). Next to sports-related venues, the home is the second most common place for self-talk to take place (Hardy et al., 2001). Within the sports-related environment, the most common time for self-talk to take place is during competition, with "during practice" being a distant second. Self-talk takes place equally either before or during competition (Hardy et al., 2001). Relative to the competitive season, self-talk increases linearly as the season progresses from preseason through early season to late season. Individual sport athletes report using self-talk to a greater degree than team sport athletes, and more highly skilled athletes use it more frequently than less skilled athletes (Hardy, Hall, & Hardy, 2004).

The What of Self-Talk

The what of self-talk represents the content of self-talk. By far, the most documented "what's" are structure and task instruction. Structure of self-talk describes the use of cue words, phrases, and sentences, of which phrases are the most common. Task instruction is usually specific as opposed to general in nature (Hardy et al., 2001).

Self-talk can be in the form of words actually spoken, or in the form of thoughts that come into one's mind. These thoughts can be either positive or negative. As a psychological method for improving self-confidence, self-talk must be positive in nature and lead to positive feelings about an athlete's ability. Evidence exists to support the use of self-talk for the purpose of enhancing self-confidence.

Self-talk is a strategy used by both junior and professional tennis players (DeFrancesco & Burke, 1997; Gould, Russell, Damarjian, & Lauer, 1999). In addition to demonstrating the effectiveness of self-talk in a study involving female collegiate tennis players, Landin and Herbert (1999) discuss the different types of self-talk as well as guidelines for its implementation. Three primary categories of self-talk include task-specific statements, encouragement and effort, and mood words. These three categories are further clarified below:

1. *Task-specific statements relating to technique* This category of self-talk refers to words or statements that reinforce technique. For example, in the tennis volley, the word "turn" might be used in association with preparation for stepping into the volley.

2. *Encouragement and effort* This category of self-talk refers to words or statements that provide self-encouragement to persevere or to try harder. For example, the phrase "You can do it" might be used in preparation for an anticipated play at home plate in softball.

3. *Mood words* This category of self-talk refers to words that precipitate an increase in mood or arousal. For example, the mood words "hard" or "blast" might be used in conjunction with a play in football or soccer.

For self-talk to be effective, it is suggested that self-talk statements be (a) brief and phonetically simple, (b) logically associated with the skill involved, and (c) compatible with the sequential timing of the task being performed. In the Landin and Herbert (1999) investigation, the skill being practiced was the tennis volley. Two important components of executing the volley are the split stop, referring to the position of the feet prior to executing the volley, and the shoulder turn in preparation for the actual stroke. Key words used for self-talk were "split" and "turn," spoken in rhythm with the timing of the actual execution of the skill.

The Why of Self-Talk

The why of self-talk describes its role and function. The two main functions of self-talk are cognition and motivation. The cognitive component of self-talk is used to assist in skill development, skill execution, improvement in performance, and execution and planning of strategy. The motivational component of self-talk is instrumental in developing self-confidence, focusing attention, controlling arousal, and maintaining drive (Hardy et al., 2001).

Zinsser, Bunker, and Williams (2006) identify specific uses or functions of self-talk. From their perspective, one of the most important uses of self-talk is the building and enhancing of self-efficacy and self-confidence. This position is further reinforced by Conroy and Metzler (2004), who studied the association between self-talk and state anxiety. An association between self-talk and reduced anxiety would also provide evidence of an association between self-talk and self-confidence, because of the strong negative association between state anxiety and self-confidence (Cox et al., 2003). A partial summary of the Zinsser et al. (2006) list is as follows:

1. *Building and developing self-efficacy* Self-talk is effective in stimulating thoughts and feelings that lead to the belief that a person is competent and able to perform a task efficiently and effectively.

2. *Skill acquisition* Learning a new skill requires persistence, effort, and dedication. Self-talk can be effective in helping the athlete to continue to work hard in order to achieve a worthwhile goal. In becoming proficient in a new skill, the athlete changes bad habits and learns new good habits.

3. *Creating and changing mood* Effective use of mood words can either create a desired mood or change an undesirable one. Words are powerful motivators because of the meaning that they convey. In an effort to increase power needed to get out of a sprinter's block quickly, the athlete might say the words "go" or "explode" as she powers forward.

TABLE 9.1 | Examples of Self-Affirmation Statements to Be Used by the Athlete

Sport Situation	Affirmation Statement
Goalie in Soccer	"Nothing gets by me"
Server in Tennis	"I can hit a strong and accurate first serve"
Shooter in Basketball	"Nothing but net for me"
Receiver in Volleyball	"I am a consistent and accurate passer"
Quarterback in Football	"I have a cannon for a throwing arm"
Wrestler	"I am strong as a bull"
Golf	"I have the perfect swing"

4. *Controlling effort*   Athletes need to be able to sustain effort throughout long practices or competitions. Self-talk can suggest to the athlete the need to increase effort when it is needed or to sustain effort when it is deemed beneficial for performance learning or enhancement. During long practices, boredom can be a challenge that must be overcome. Self-talk words and phrases such as "pick it up," "stay with it," or "pace" can be effective in controlling effort.

5. *Focusing attention or concentration*   As with maintaining effort, it is often necessary to remind yourself to stay focused or to concentrate on the task at hand. Athletes often get tired, and when this happens, their concentration can easily wander. If the mind wanders when the coach is teaching an important concept relating to the athlete's role on the team, it is imperative that he heighten and maintain concentration. Such words and phrases as "focus," "stay with it," or "now" can help the athlete stay focused.

Feelings of confidence, efficacy, and personal control will be enhanced if coaches and sport psychologists assist the athlete in preselecting and constructing **affirmation statements** that can be used during competition or during preparation for competition. These are statements that affirm to the athlete that she possesses the skills, abilities, positive attitudes, and beliefs necessary for successful performance. These self-affirmation statements must be both believable and vivid. Do not leave it to the athlete to come up with these important thoughts or statements at the exact moment that they are needed, but prepare them in advance. Some examples are illustrated in table 9.1.

Research Support for Self-Talk

Theodorakis, Weinberg, Natsis, Douma, and Kazakas (2000) provide an excellent review of research that shows general support for the use of self-talk strategies to improve performance in exercise and sport tasks. In addition, they report the results of four experiments designed to contrast the efficacy of "motivational" and "instructional" self-talk strategies compared to a control condition. Self-talk strategies were contrasted in four separate studies involving soccer accuracy, badminton serving skill, sit-ups for endurance, and knee extension for strength and endurance. Results showed that the instructional self-talk strategy (technique) was superior to the control condition in both sport skill tasks and the knee extension task. Both the motivational (increase effort) and the instructional self-talk strategies were superior to the control condition relative to the knee extension task. The authors concluded that the instructional or technique-related self-talk strategy was superior to the motivational strategy and a control condition when the task involved fine motor control and skill, as did the soccer and badminton skills. However, when the task required strength and endurance, both the motivational and the instructional strategy self-talk strategies were equally effective in improving performance.

CONCEPT Self-talk is an effective technique to control thoughts and to influence feelings. Thoughts and feelings can influence self-confidence as well as performance.

APPLICATION Thoughts that come into an athlete's mind during competition can be either positive or negative. These thoughts are a form of self-talk. The athlete must learn to control his thoughts and to structure them to his advantage. This is effectively accomplished through self-talk. The athlete must carefully preselect the actual words and phrases used during self-talk and consider them for maximum effectiveness. The coach or sport psychologist can assist the athlete in this regard.

In this investigation, the motivational self-talk strategy utilized an efficacious statement such as "I can . . ." to bolster a participant's self-confidence and effort. The instructional self-talk statement utilized a technique-related phrase such as "I see the net, I see the target" to focus attention on the task, as well as bolster self-confidence. This study provides strong evidence that self-talk is effective in enhancing performance, but it also enlightens us on the interactive relationship between self-talk strategies and nature of the task. With tasks involving fine motor control and skill, self-talk for purposes of instruction and technique is most effective.

Research by Hatzigerorgiadis, Theordorakis, and Zourbanos (2004) provides strong experimental support for the efficacy of self-talk as an intervention or coping strategy for improving athletic performance. Utilizing water polo athletes and two different water polo tosses, they investigated the relative effectiveness of two different types of self-talk (instructional/motivational) on tossing performance. Results showed that instructional self-talk was most effective in improving performance on a precision accuracy tossing task, whereas motivational self-talk was most effective in a toss for distance. Both types of self-talk were more effective than a control group for improving either tossing task. The study also showed a significant decline in attentional distraction during experimental testing compared to the control group, leading the researchers to conclude that reduced attentional distraction was one important explanation for the effectiveness of self-talk. Similarly, experimental support for the efficacy of self-talk in improving basketball performance has been reported (Perkos, Theodorakis, & Chroni, 2002; Theodorakis, Chroni, Laparidis, Bebetos, & Duoma, 2001).

Additional support for the efficacy of using self-talk to improve athletic performance has been reported using a single-subject multiple-baseline design. As reported elsewhere in this book, this design involves having athletes start a self-talk intervention following experimentally manipulated different time lengths of performing in a control condition. If athletes improve performance following the intervention compared to their control performance, this is evidence of the effectiveness of self-talk. In a study involving five junior ice hockey goaltenders, goal save performance was monitored across a six-month season. Results showed that self-talk was effective in improving goal-tending performance across the season (Rogerson & Hrycaiko, 2002). Similarly, in a study involving four elite female youth soccer players, soccer goal shooting performance was improved compared to a control subject as well as to their own preintervention (self-talk) performance (Johnson, Hrycaiko, Johnson, & Halas, 2004).

Relaxation Strategies Used in Sport

I think a lot of it has to do with me pressing. It's in my head. I'm trying harder, and the harder I try, the worse it goes. I've just got to try and relax.

CONCEPT   An important part of any relaxation procedure is to focus attention on a mental device.

APPLICATION   Two mental devices are highly recommended for the athlete. The first is to take a deep breath and exhale slowly, and the second is the use of a *mantra,* or key word or phrase. Athletes can focus on the key phrase and slow air release as they relax.

Athletes engage in self-talk to help them prepare to execute a skill. Courtesy University of Missouri–Columbia Sports Information.

But the more I miss, the harder it is to relax, so it's just a vicious circle.

(Jeff Jaeger, place kicker,
Cleveland Browns, 1987.)

While some athletes may suffer from low levels of arousal, the more difficult problems occur with athletes who experience excessively high levels of anxiety and tension. For these athletes, any strategy calculated to heighten arousal can only cause greater anxiety and tension. Typically, what happens is that an initial increase in anxiety leads to a decrease in performance. This decrease in performance itself results in even greater anxiety, resulting in the **anxiety/stress spiral.** There is only one way out of this spiral, and that is to reverse the process by reducing the anxiety and tension. *Relaxation procedures* can effectively reduce tension and anxiety associated with sport. In this section, we will discuss some of them.

Four prevalent relaxation procedures can be adequately categorized under the broad heading of relaxation. These are (1) progressive relaxation, (2) autogenic training, (3) meditation, and (4) biofeedback. Each procedure is unique, but they all yield essentially the same physiological result. That is, they all result in the **relaxation response.** The relaxation response consists of physiological changes that are opposite to the "fight or flight" response of the sympathetic nervous system. Specifically, procedures such as progressive relaxation, autogenic training, and meditation result in decreases in oxygen consumption, heart rate, respiration, and skeletal muscle activity, while they increase skin resistance and alpha brain waves (see chapter 7).

Four different factors are necessary for eliciting the relaxation response. Each of these factors is present to some degree in the specific relaxation techniques that we will discuss. These four elements or factors are (1) a **mental device,** (2) a passive attitude, (3) decreased muscle tone, and (4) a quiet environment. The mental device is generally some sort of word, phrase, object, or process used to shift attention inward.

Before discussing specific relaxation procedures, it is essential that the issue of *need* be addressed. Except in a general way, athletes who are *not* overly aroused may not benefit from relaxation intervention. In fact, the danger exists that an athlete who is "misdiagnosed" by his coach as tense and anxious may become drowsy and broadly focused as a result of arousal reduction. This problem is identified because coaches are inaccurate estimators of athletes' competitive state and trait anxiety (Hanson & Gould, 1988). Using two well-known sport-specific anxiety inventories, coaches were asked to complete the inventories as they thought an athlete would. The results showed that a large discrepancy exists between a coach's perception and an athlete's perception of the athlete's anxiety level. A coach should make sure that an athlete is actually suffering from anxiety and tension before applying an arousal adjustment intervention.

In this section we will discuss specific relaxation techniques that are designed to bring about the relaxation response. These techniques include progressive relaxation, autogenic training, meditation, and biofeedback. Mastering the technique of **deep breathing** for the purpose of relaxation and relieving tension is an important component of each of the relaxation techniques we will discuss. As explained by Davis, Eshelman, and McKay (1995), two patterns of breathing are typically used: chest or thoracic breathing, and abdominal or diaphragmatic breathing. **Chest breathing** is usually associated with emotional distress and is often shallow, irregular, and rapid. Conversely, **abdominal breathing** is associated with relaxation and is often deep, regular, and slow. In practicing the relaxation procedures introduced in this chapter, the athlete must practice relaxing through deep breathing. The process of deeply inhaling and exhaling in a slow rhythmic fashion is very relaxing to the body and mind. Deep breathing can be practiced at any time or in any place (e.g., a basketball free-throw line), but it is most effective while sitting or lying down on one's back in a comfortable position. Each time the athlete breathes out, she should imagine that she is expelling tension from her body. When practicing deep breathing, place one hand lightly on your chest and the other on your diaphragm. You should feel small amounts of movement under the hand resting on the chest, and large rhythmic movement under the hand on the diaphragm.

When learning relaxation strategies for the purpose of performance enhancement, it is critical that the athlete have in mind some optimal level of arousal or relaxation that he is seeking. Becoming too relaxed just before an event requiring great physical exertion may be worse than being overly aroused or anxious. In this regard, advice given by Dan O'Brian, the U.S. 1996 Olympic decathlon champion, is instructive (O'Brian & Sloan, 1999). Dan mentioned two principles that he believes are of great importance when preparing for optimal performance in the decathlon:

1. "The athlete has to be able to turn it on and then turn it off in a short period of time."

2. "Give me a 90 percent effort, not 100 or 110, for best performance."

Dan's first principle underscores the importance of mastering relaxation and arousal energizing strategies for the purpose of immediate application. During one phase of preparation for competition, an athlete is trying to relax and conserve energy. Yet in another phase, perhaps separated by minutes, he has to be able to activate the arousal response in anticipation of maximal effort. Dan's second principle underscores the important concept that best performance, regardless of activity, is probably not at a super-aroused level. Baseball pitchers routinely comment that they have their best "stuff" when they are a bit fatigued and not trying to throw 100 mph fastballs. With these preliminary principles and reminders firmly in mind, we now turn to a discussion of specific relaxation strategies used by athletes to reduce anxiety and to control physiological arousal.

Progressive Relaxation

Modern progressive relaxation techniques are all variations of those outlined by Edmond Jacobson (1929, 1938). Jacobson began his work with progressive relaxation in the early part of the twentieth century. It was Jacobson's basic thesis that it is impossible to be nervous or tense in any

CONCEPT   It is difficult for a coach to accurately estimate an athlete's level of competitive state anxiety.

APPLICATION   If a coach believes that an athlete is suffering a decrement in performance due to elevated competitive state anxiety, she should consider recommending an arousal control intervention. However, before actually referring the athlete for treatment, the coach should make sure that she has not misdiagnosed the athlete. This can be accomplished through the administration of a state anxiety inventory, discussed in chapter 8.

CONCEPT   Deep breathing is associated with relaxation and involves expanding the abdominal area more than the chest.

APPLICATION   The athlete should practice deep breathing in order to feel the difference between breathing with the diaphragm and breathing with the chest. Deep breathing involves rhythmic breathing as opposed to shallow, irregular, fast breathing. In deep breathing, each phase of expiration should be mentally linked with the feeling of expelling pent-up tension and anxiety.

part of the body where the muscles are completely relaxed. In addition, Jacobson believed that nervousness and tenseness of involuntary muscles and organs could be reduced if the associated skeletal muscles were relaxed. According to Jacobson, an anxious mind cannot exist in a relaxed body.

Jacobson's **progressive relaxation** procedure requires that subjects lie on their backs with their arms to the side. Occasionally a sitting posture in a comfortable chair is recommended. In either case, the room should be fairly quiet and arms and legs should not be crossed, to avoid unnecessary stimulation. While the goal of any progressive relaxation program is to relax the entire body in a matter of minutes, it is essential that in the beginning the subject practice the technique for at least one hour every day. Once the relaxation procedure is well learned, the relaxation response can be achieved in a few minutes.

Jacobson's method calls for the subject to tense a muscle before relaxing it. The tensing helps the subject recognize the difference between tension and relaxation. Once the subject can do this, he should be able to relax a limb completely without tensing it first. Jacobson warns that only the first few minutes of any relaxation session should be devoted to muscle tensing. The remaining time should be devoted to gaining complete relaxation. For a muscle to be considered relaxed, it must be completely absent of any contractions and must be limp and motionless.

Jacobson's full progressive relaxation procedure involves systematically tensing and relaxing specific muscle groups in a predetermined order. Relaxation begins with the muscles of the left arm and proceeds to those of the right arm, left and right legs, abdomen, back, and chest and shoulders, concluding with the neck and face muscles. The full training procedure lasts many months. In the beginning stages, an entire session should be devoted to the total relaxation of a single muscle group. While it is unrealistic to expect an athlete to devote this much time to learning to relax, Jacobson's point is well taken. A well-developed

CONCEPT   Learning how to relax the muscles of the body is a foundation skill for all stress management and intervention strategies.

APPLICATION   As a first step in learning how to control anxiety and stress, the athlete must become proficient at relaxing the mind and the body.

relaxation training program requires a great deal of practice in the beginning. It is unrealistic to expect an athlete to elicit the relaxation response at will after only one or two 15-minute practice sessions. However, after several months of practice and training, it should be possible to evoke the relaxation response in a matter of seconds.

Abbreviated versions of Jacobson's full 40-session procedure have been proposed (Davis et al., 1995; Greenberg, 1996). A review by Carlson and Hoyle (1993) provided evidence that abbreviated progressive relaxation training procedures are effective in reducing anxiety, tension, and stress. Numerous variations of Jacobson's original progressive relaxation procedure have proved to be effective. For example, it is not necessary that the procedure always start with the left arm. And in some cases a muscle contraction could be best accomplished by applying resistance to an immovable object.

The ultimate goal of any relaxation training program is to evoke the relaxation response to counter stress in a specific situation. For example, a professional golfer does not have 30 minutes to relax prior to a $15,000 putt. The golfer must be able to accomplish this while waiting to putt, a skill that takes many hours of practice to master.

Research has clearly shown that progressive relaxation procedures are effective in eliciting the relaxation response. Additionally, numerous investigations have shown that when used in conjunction with other cognitive or arousal control interventions, it is associated with increased sports performance. Greenspan and Feltz (1989) critically reviewed nine investigations in which forms of relaxation intervention were involved. The majority of the studies showed that increased performance was associated with arousal control in combination with some other cognitive technique. Few studies,

however, have shown that progressive relaxation procedures alone effectively enhance performance. For example, Wrisberg and Anshel (1989) showed that relaxation used in conjunction with imagery was effective in enhancing the basketball shooting performance of young boys. Neither imagery nor relaxation training alone was effective in enhancing shooting performance. In conjunction with adequate preparation, muscle relaxation training is effective in enhancing an athlete's tolerance to pain (Broucek, Bartholomew, Landers, & Linder, 1993).

Autogenic Training

Autogenic training and progressive relaxation both elicit the relaxation response. Whereas progressive relaxation relies upon dynamic contracting and relaxing of muscles, **autogenic training** relies upon feelings associated with the limbs and muscles of the body. Autogenic training is very similar to autohypnosis, and is based upon early research with hypnosis. The procedure was first developed by the German psychiatrist Johannes Schultz (Schultz & Luthe, 1959). In working with hypnotized patients, Schultz noted that they invariably reported two bodily sensations associated with the relaxation response. These two sensations were heaviness in the limbs and a feeling of general warmth in the body, arms, and legs. In its simplest form, autogenic training consists of a series of mental exercises designed to bring about these two bodily states. Limbs feel heavy because of a total lack of muscle tension, and the body feels warm due to dilation of blood vessels (a parasympathetic nervous system response).

Various authors have suggested different exercises and self-statements to bring about the relaxation response using autogenic training (Davis,

Eshelman, & McKay, 1995; Greenberg, 1996). Essentially, autogenic training is composed of three component parts that are often intermingled. The first and most important part is the six initial steps designed to suggest to the mind a feeling of warmth in the body and heaviness in the limbs. These six self-statement steps are as follows:

1. Heaviness in the arms and legs (beginning with the dominant arm or leg)

2. Warmth in the arms and the legs (again, beginning with the dominant arm or leg)

3. Warmth in the chest and a perception of reduced heart rate

4. Calm and relaxed breathing

5. Warmth in the solar plexus area

6. Sensation of coolness on the forehead

The second component part of autogenic training involves the use of imagery. In this step, the subject is encouraged to visualize images of relaxing scenes while at the same time focusing upon feelings of warmth and heaviness in the arms and legs. The third component of autogenic training involves the use of *specific themes* (Davis et al., 1995) to assist in bringing about the relaxation response. One particularly effective specific theme is the use of self-statements to suggest to the mind that the body is indeed relaxed.

As with progressive relaxation, research has clearly shown that when used properly, autogenic training is effective in bringing about the relaxation response (Benson et al., 1974). Autogenic training requires several months and a great deal of practice to master. Once mastered, it can be utilized to bring about the relaxation response in a matter of minutes. Whereas the relaxation benefits of this technique are well documented, very little evidence exists to suggest that autogenic training by itself enhances athletic performance. Spigolon and Annalisa (1985) provide anecdotal evidence to suggest that autogenic training is related to improved athletic performance.

More recently, Groslambert, Candau, Grappe, Duque, and Rouillon (2003) provided evidence that demonstrated the effectiveness of autogenic training in the French Biathlon. The biathlon is a winter sport that combines cross-country skiing with rifle marksmanship. Compared to a classical training condition, a condition that included six weeks of classical training plus autogenic training demonstrated greater improvement in terms of standing stability control while shooting. No difference, however, was noted for marksmanship.

Various authors have outlined autogenic training and relaxation programs that can be adopted by the athlete (Nideffer, 1985; Orlick, 1986). Table 9.2 includes a series of instructions and statements that can be used for teaching athletes to relax using autogenic training. Using this list and others, the athlete could develop and record her own autogenic training tape.

Meditation

Meditation, as a form of relaxation, is tied directly to the concepts of selective attention discussed in chapter 7. In practicing **meditation,** the individual attempts to uncritically focus his attention on a

TABLE 9.2 | Suggested Instructions and Statements That May Be Included in an Autogenic Training Presentation

1. Locate a quiet room or environment where you will not be disturbed.
2. Find a comfortable area where you can sit or lie down on your back.
3. Close your eyes and put away thoughts of the outside world.
4. Begin by practicing some deep breathing to help you to relax.
5. Slowly inhale, exhale, inhale, exhale, inhale, exhale.
6. Each time you exhale, *feel* the tension being expelled from your body.
7. Now that you are feeling relaxed and your breathing has stabilized, begin suggesting to yourself that your limbs are beginning to feel heavy.
8. "My right arm feels heavy," "my left arm feels heavy," "both of my arms feel heavy," "my right leg feels heavy," "my left leg feels heavy," "both of my legs feel heavy," "my arms and legs feel heavy."
9. "My right arm feels warm," "my left arm feels warm," "both of my arms feel warm," "my right leg feels warm," "my left leg feels warm," "both of my legs feel warm," "my arms and legs feel warm."
10. "My chest area feels warm and my heartbeat feels slow and regular."
11. Focus for a few minutes upon your heart rate, while at the same time repeating to yourself that your heartbeat feels slow and regular.
12. Focus for a few minutes upon your breathing, while at the same time repeating to yourself that your respiration feels calm and relaxed.
13. Repeat several times: "My stomach area feels warm."
14. Repeat several times: "My forehead feels cool."
15. While experiencing feelings of warmth and heaviness in your limbs, warmth in your solar plexus and coolness in your forehead, imagine to yourself that you are on a warm sandy beach enjoying a cool lemonade while watching the waves flow in and out.
16. While enjoying this relaxing visual image (or some other one), repeat relaxing statements to yourself.
17. "I feel quiet."
18. "I feel warm and relaxed."
19. "My mind is at ease."

single thought, sound, or object. Meditation will result in the relaxation response if practiced in a quiet environment that is associated with a passive attitude and decreased muscle tone.

The practice of meditation as a form of relaxation and thought control had its origin in Eastern cultures more than four thousand years ago. The individual most responsible for exporting meditation to the Western cultures was Maharishi Mahesh Yogi of India. Referred to as **transcendental meditation,** Maharishi Mahesh Yogi's brand of meditation has been widely accepted in the United States and throughout the world. Other forms of Eastern culture meditation practices include Chakra yoga, Rinzai Zen, Mudra yoga, Sufism, Zen meditation,

and Soto Zen (Greenberg, 1996). The most common *mental device* used in transcendental meditation is the repetition of a **mantra.** The mantra is a simple sound selected by the instructor as a mental concentration device. One such sound, "om" or "ahhom," has been popular (Nideffer, 1976). Other mental devices that have been used in meditation include the *mandala* (a geometric figure), *nadam* (imagined sounds), and *pranayama* (breathing).

In practice, the subject sits in a comfortable position with eyes closed. The subject concentrates on deep breathing while at the same time repeating the mantra. Reportedly, the sound of the mantra soon disappears as the mind experiences more subtle thought levels and finally arrives at the source of the thought. While most Oriental approaches teach a sitting meditation position, both Zen and transcendental meditation emphasize that standing or sitting are acceptable. Davis et al. (1995) and Greenberg (1996) offer excellent ideas for enhancing and facilitating the meditation experience. Similar to transcendental meditation, Tai Chi is a moving form of meditation which originated in China. The stress reduction effects of Tai Chi are comparable to those received from moderate physical exercise.

While it is clear that the various forms of meditation can reduce anxiety and tension by evoking the relaxation response, it is not clear whether its practice has a facilitative effect on athletic performance. Like the effects of other forms of relaxation, the effects of meditation upon athletic performance are likely to be indirect. Meditation has a direct effect on reducing anxiety, tension, and stress, which in turn should have a facilitative effect on the performance of the anxiety-prone athlete. Attempts to link meditation training directly with improved athletic performance have met with mixed success. Meditation seems to be beneficial for performing gross motor skills such as the 50-meter dash, agility tasks, standing broad jump, and coordination tasks (Reddy, Bai, & Rao, 1976). But it seems to be of little facilitative value for performing fine motor tasks such as the rotary pursuit, mirror tracing, or pistol shooting (Hall & Hardy, 1991).

Biofeedback Training

It has been demonstrated that humans can voluntarily control functions of the autonomic nervous system. Biofeedback is a relatively modern technique that is based upon this principle (Davis et al., 1995; Greenberg, 1996; Tenenbaum, Corbett, & Kitsantas, 2002).

Biofeedback training uses instruments to help people control responses of the autonomic nervous system. For example, a subject monitors an auditory signal of her own heart rate and experiments with different thoughts, feelings, and sensations to slow the heart rate. Once the subject learns to recognize the feelings associated with the reduction

of heart rate, the instrument is removed and the subject tries to control the heart rate without it. This is the goal of the biofeedback therapist. People suffering from chronic anxiety or illnesses caused by anxiety can often benefit from biofeedback training, because when they learn to reduce functions of the sympathetic nervous system, they are indirectly learning to reduce anxiety and tension. Biofeedback is essentially the same as progressive relaxation, autogenic training, and meditation. Using the latter three techniques, the subject relaxes; this lowers arousal and decreases the activity of the sympathetic nervous system. With biofeedback, the subject begins by lowering certain physiological measures with the help of an instrument. This decreases arousal and increases relaxation.

Instrumentation Theoretically, biofeedback can be very useful to athletes who suffer from excessive anxiety and arousal. If athletes could be trained to control their physiological responses in the laboratory, they should be able to transfer this ability onto the athletic field. The main drawback to biofeedback in athletics is expense. The cost of purchasing a machine for measuring heart rate, EEG, EMG, or GSR changes is out of reach for the average school's athletic budget. However, not all biofeedback measurement techniques are expensive, and many are still in the experimental stages. Some of the basic measurement techniques used in biofeedback training are as follows.

Skin Temperature The most commonly used and least expensive form of biofeedback is skin temperature. When an athlete becomes highly aroused, additional blood is pumped to the vital organs. Part of this additional blood supply comes from the peripheral blood vessels, leaving the hands feeling cold and clammy. Thus, the effect of stress is to decrease the skin temperature of the extremities. Subjects can monitor skin temperature to discover what kinds of responses, thoughts, and autogenic phrases are most effective in increasing it. Typically, subjects are trained to use progressive relaxation techniques and autogenic phrases to assist them in the biofeedback process. Although

CONCEPT   Biofeedback is an effective and powerful tool for reducing the debilitating effects of anxiety and stress.

APPLICATION   If an athlete cannot control anxiety and stress using progressive relaxation, autogenic training, or meditation, then biofeedback training should be attempted. To begin biofeedback training, it may be necessary to identify a professional therapist. Equipment necessary for biofeedback training may not be readily available to the athlete or coach.

FIGURE 9.4 | Skin temperature can be monitored with a cardboard-backed thermometer.

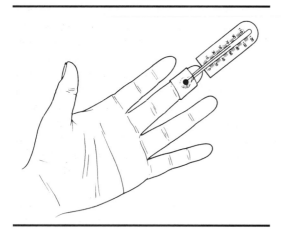

Source: From *Biofeedback: An introduction and guide* by David Danskin and Mark Crow. Reprinted by permission of Mayfield Publishing Company. Copyright © 1981 by Mayfield Publishing Company.

sophisticated instruments are available, a simple and inexpensive cardboard-backed thermometer can be used to monitor skin temperature. The cardboard is cut off just above the bulb and the thermometer is taped to the finger, as illustrated in figure 9.4. Similarly, small skin sensors can be attached to the fingers to register temperature changes.

Electromyography   Another very popular biofeedback technique employs the use of an electromyographic feedback instrument (EMG). Electrodes are attached to a particular group of muscles in the arm or forehead, and the subject tries to reduce muscular tension by using auditory or visual cues of muscle electrical activity. Auditory cues typically come through earphones in the form of clicks. Visual cues come through an oscilloscope that the subject watches.

Electroencephalogram   A third major instrument used for biofeedback is the electroencephalogram (EEG). Use of the EEG is commonly called brainwave training. Tiny electrical impulses from billions of brain cells can be detected by electrodes placed on the scalp and connected to an EEG. Four basic types of brain waves are associated with EEG recordings. Beta waves predominate during periods of excitement and high arousal. Alpha waves predominate when the subject relaxes and puts his mind "in neutral." It is the alpha waves that the subject tries to produce.

Other Methods   While skin temperature, EMG, and EEG are the most common methods used in biofeedback training, several others are used to a lesser degree. These are the galvanic skin response (GSR), heart rate, and blood pressure. Other methods of biofeedback training techniques are of potential use. One is the use of a stethoscope to monitor heart rate. Still others involve monitoring of respiration rate, vapor pressure from the skin, stomach acidity, sphincter constriction, and blood chemistry.

Biofeedback and Performance   In a laboratory setting, the athlete learns to control the autonomic nervous system. The feelings and experiences associated with learning how to reduce sympathetic nervous system responses in the

CONCEPT   Biofeedback training is effective in facilitating athletic performance.

APPLICATION   The use of biofeedback equipment for learning how to monitor and manipulate physiological arousal as a means of controlling and elimi-nating debilitating negative affect has proven to be very effective. If an athlete's performance is negatively influenced by inappropriate high (or low) levels of arousal, then biofeedback training can help. The availability of biofeedback equipment and trained clinicians should be investigated.

laboratory are then transferred to the athletic environment. In some cases, biofeedback may be practiced in the athletic environment. For example, Costa, Bonaccorsi, and Scrimali (1984) reported the use of biofeedback training with team handball athletes to reduce precompetitive anxiety.

The difference between success and failure of two equally matched athletes often depends on an individual's ability to cope with the perceived stress of competition. Biofeedback provides a way for athletes to determine their levels of physiological arousal and to learn how to make conscious changes calculated to reduce anxiety and improve performance. A number of scientific investigations have been conducted to determine the effect of biofeedback on athletic performance. Zaichkowsky and Fuchs (1988) reviewed 42 studies that examined the effect of biofeedback training on sports and athletic performance. Of these 42 studies, 83 percent found biofeedback training to be successful in facilitating sport and athletic performance, as well as beneficial to the athlete's well-being. More recently, Petruzzello, Landers, Kubitz, and Salazar (1991), Boutcher and Zinsser (1990), and Blumenstein, Bar-Eli, and Tenenbaum (1995) have reported that biofeedback training is highly effective in eliciting the relaxation response and moderately effective in facilitating improved performance in athletes.

Arousal Energizing Strategies

In the previous section we discussed strategies that athletes use to relax and to reduce anxiety and arousal associated with the stress response. In this section we will discuss arousal energizing strategies needed to obtain peak performance. Often athletes need to be "psyched up" or energized to prepare them for competition. As Dan O'Brian said in the previous section, the athlete needs to be able to "turn it on and then turn it off." The skill, however, comes in knowing when to turn it on and when to turn it off or down. In this chapter we will be talking about "turning it on," but at the same time we need to be aware of the dangers of getting the athlete overly energized and psyched up. Let us discuss this issue a little more before moving on to a discussion of specific psyching-up strategies.

It was reported several years ago (McCallum, 1994) that the Milwaukee Brewers professional baseball team brought in a California motivational group called Radical Reality to "motivate" its players. During one of the presentations, one of the Radicals ripped a phone book in two with his bare hands. The next day, one of the team's pitchers tried to duplicate the phone book stunt and dislocated his left shoulder. The rookie right-hander was scratched from his next scheduled pitching rotation and reassigned to a minor league team. This example of misdirected "psyching up" underscores the danger of undifferentiated attempts to raise or lower the arousal level of athletes.

Coaches have been looking to the sport psychologist to learn how to maintain optimal levels of arousal in athletes. This is a most promising development, since many coaches have improperly prepared their athletes for competition. The typical approach has been to "psych up" the athlete through various kinds of pep talks and activation techniques. There is, of course, a proper time to get

FIGURE 9.5 | The effects of a pep talk on the activation levels of four different athletes.

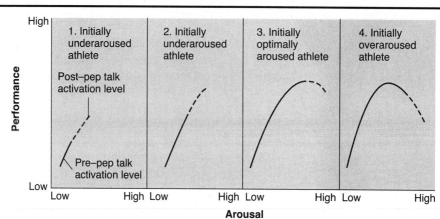

athletes excited and aroused, but often these techniques are applied at the wrong time. It is commonplace, for example, to see high school volleyball coaches leading their players in cheering and psyching-up sessions immediately before a match. Generally, these athletes have only an intermediate level of skill, and the extra arousal serves only to induce unforced errors. This problem is illustrated in figure 9.5. Each athlete in this figure begins with a different initial level of arousal. Increasing arousal affects each athlete differently. In most cases, intervention procedures are best applied on an individual basis; each athlete should be treated differently. Some will need a pep talk, but others may need an entirely different form of intervention.

As can be observed in figure 9.5, using a pep talk to increase the arousal level of four different athletes has interesting ramifications. Only in situations 1 and 2 did the pep talk have the desired effect. In situation 3, the athlete was already at an optimal level of activation, and it was destroyed by the coach's pep talk. In situation 4, the athlete was overactivated to begin with; the intervention was totally inappropriate. How many coaches overactivate their athletes by their pregame locker room pep talks? It is also important to recall the important lesson learned from our earlier discussion on catastrophe theory (chapter 8). When an athlete has a high level of cognitive state anxiety, it is

possible that even a small increase in physiological arousal could result in a large catastrophic decrement in performance.

The indiscriminate use of relaxation or arousal energizing strategies has prompted sport psychologists to promote a closer match between precompetitive affect and psychological adjustment. This practice has come to be referred to as the matching hypothesis. In the *matching hypothesis,* care is taken to make sure that the intervention selected to relax or energize the athlete is matched to the specific symptoms. This concept has more often been applied to situations associated with anxiety reduction, but it also applies to situations requiring increased levels of arousal. Relative to anxiety reduction, it is recommended that relaxation be used to counter high levels of somatic state anxiety, while cognitive restructuring be used to counter high levels of cognitive state anxiety (Maynard, Hemmings, & Warwick-Evans, 1995; Maynard, Smith, & Warwick-Evans, 1995).

This chapter will be divided into two major sections: (a) team energizing strategies, and (b) individual energizing strategies. **Team energizing strategies** are those strategies that deal with the team as a whole and are generally orchestrated by the coach. They include such things as team goal setting; pep talks; bulletin boards; publicity and news coverage; fan support; coach, athlete, and

CONCEPT   Group activation strategies such as pep talks may help some athletes reach an optimal level of arousal, but may cause others to become overaroused.

APPLICATION   Indiscriminate use of activation procedures to psych up athletic teams should be avoided. Instead, help each athlete to find her own optimal arousal level.

parent interactions; and precompetition workouts. **Individual self-energizing strategies** are those strategies that the individual uses to induce immediate activation and alertness. From the perspective of the individual, these latter techniques are also referred to as individual psyching-up strategies.

Team Energizing Strategies

As a coach prepares for the season, she recognizes the need to set into motion a number of initiatives designed to keep the team focused and energized for the entire season. At the beginning of the season, the athletes are generally energized and excited about the new season and the new challenges. This initial enthusiasm and excitement, however, can diminish across a long season if efforts are not set into motion to maintain it. This is especially true if the team or individual athletes get mired in a losing streak or a period of energy-draining situations.

Team Goal Setting   As proposed by Locke and Latham (1990), goal setting is motivational in nature and is used by athletic teams as a way to energize individual athletes. Chapter 10 of the text is dedicated to the details of the goal-setting process. The coach should provide the leadership in this process, but the athletes must be equal partners in deciding what they want to accomplish as a team and as individuals during the current competitive season. The coach then lays out for the team a plan whereby the goals set by the team can be accomplished. While outcome goals must be addressed, the main focus should be upon process and performance goals that give the team a chance to succeed. Goals are then monitored on a regular basis so that progress can be determined.

In preparing a highly seeded basketball team with 28 wins and 2 losses to play an unranked team in the NCAA playoffs, the coach must do something to keep the team from overlooking a potential "giant killer." One useful strategy is to help each member of the team to set personal performance goals for the game. The star rebounder might be challenged to accept the personal goal of getting thirteen "bounds" in the game. Similarly, the guards might be challenged to keep their turnovers below three between them. With each member of the team working to achieve realistic but moderately difficult goals, it is likely that the team as a whole will perform well.

Pep Talks   A **pep talk** by the coach or a respected member of the team is the most common method now used to increase the activation level of athletes. But like any verbal communication, it can be either effective or ineffective. Perhaps the most important element of the pep talk is an emphasis on the ingredient that is lacking in the team. If the team is obviously taking an opponent lightly, it must be impressed upon them that on a given night, any team can pull off an upset. Some of the elements of an effective pep talk may include personal challenges, stories, poems, silence, reasoning, and voice inflections.

Bulletin Boards   In many ways the messages on a **bulletin board** are identical to those in a pep talk, but they are visually rather than verbally conveyed. Poster-board displays should be placed where team members cannot miss them. Such places as locker room dressing areas and confined training areas are ideal. The bulletin board should always convey positive, motivating thoughts and ideas. Catchy phrases such as "when the going gets tough, the tough get going" can be effective. Athletes remember these simple phrases and will

FIGURE 9.6 | Poster showing performance goals for a volleyball team.

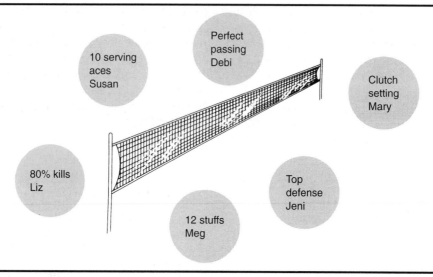

Source: From C. Voelz, 1982, *Motivation in coaching a team sport.* Reprinted by permission of American Alliance for Health, Physical Education, Recreation and Dance, 1900 Association Drive, Reston, Virginia 22091.

repeat them later, when they need reinforcement. Other messages on the display board might include personal challenges to members of the team. One such display for a volleyball team might look like the one in figure 9.6. This poster could either reflect great performances for the season or challenge performances for the next match.

Challenging or inflammatory statements by opposing teammates or coaches should also appear on the bulletin board. If an opponent is quoted as saying that she will dominate a certain player, this should be posted for all to see. It will give the team something to get excited about. A case in point was game six of the first round of the 2003 National Basketball Championship (NBA) series between the Portland Trail Blazers and the Dallas Mavericks. In response to a blowout victory against Dallas in game six of the series, Portland guard Ruben Patterson was quoted in the news coverage as saying that he could see fear in the eyes of the Dallas players. Dallas coach Don Nelson prominently displayed the quote in the Dallas locker room in preparation for game seven in Dallas. The Dallas Mavericks eliminated Portland with a 107–95 game seven victory (Thamel, 2003).

Publicity and News Coverage The school newspaper and other advertisements can be very helpful in generating a team spirit. If the members of the team sense that the student body is behind them, they will work harder to get prepared. Ads can be placed in the newspaper by the coach to call attention to an important game or contest. These same ads can be used to recruit new players for the team. For many teams, publicity comes easy, but for others it does not. It may be necessary to cultivate a close relationship with the media and school sports reporters. Invite them to games and send them positive information about players and upcoming contests.

Fan Support Those who enjoy sport for its recreational value do not need people watching in order to enjoy the game. However, if you practice 10 to 15 hours a week and have a 20-game schedule, it doesn't hurt to have **fan support.** Fans

CONCEPT Goal setting, pep talks, bulletin boards, publicity and news coverage, fan support, coach and parent interaction, and precompetitive workouts are all effective ways to energize and motivate athletic teams during a long season.

APPLICATION Goal setting, pep talks, and precompetitive workouts are all energizing strategies that a coach can manage without much help. All of the other energizing strategies, however, take time and organization and will require the assistance of student support groups, parent support groups, assistant coaches, and the school administration. A team booster club could be organized by an assistant coach or a group of supportive parents. The booster club could organize and facilitate energizing strategies.

---

tell the athletes that what they are doing is important to people other than themselves. A full season of daily basketball, football, or tennis can burn out many players. Those responsible for promoting the team must do all they can to get people to support the team by coming to watch them.

Coach, Athlete, and Parent Interaction

The interactions between an athlete's parents, the athlete, and the coach are an often-overlooked source of motivation for an athlete. Coaches are often wary about the overinvolved and demanding parent. However, often just the opposite situation occurs, and parents are excluded from active involvement in motivating a young athlete. Parents provide tremendous support for an athlete's involvement that sometimes goes completely unnoticed. Parents provide transportation for games and practices, and sacrifice vacations and leisure time to watch their son or daughter perform. When called on, they are observed serving as scorekeepers, "water boys," bus drivers, and sometimes assistant coaches. What a tremendous source of support and motivation a parent can be when properly nurtured and appreciated!

Precompetition Workout

In the mid-sixties when the Japanese were dominating the international volleyball scene, an interesting phenomenon was observed. Prior to an international men's match between the United States and Japan, the Japanese team came out two hours early and went through a full workout. This was no warm-up as typically observed prior to competition, but a full-blown practice session to exhaustion. The Japanese team went on to defeat the U.S.A. in three relatively easy games.

Husak and Hemenway (1986) were apparently thinking along similar lines when they tested the effects of competition-day practice on the activation and performance of collegiate swimmers. In this investigation, members of a collegiate swimming team engaged in brisk workouts four to six hours prior to competition. The results did not yield a significant performance effect, but they did show a reduction in feelings of tension and anxiety on the part of the precompetition workout group. Because tension and anxiety can easily hamper performance in swimming competition, precompetition workouts could be an effective tool for preparing an athlete for competition. **Precompetition workouts** that enhance and increase activation are apparently effective in reducing precompetitive anxiety.

Immediate Self-Energizing Strategies

In the paragraphs above we talked about team strategies for energizing athletes for the duration of a season. Individual athletes, however, also need to be able to energize themselves for **immediate mobilization.** A basketball player who sits on the bench for three-quarters of the game and is then inserted into the lineup is not ready to play mentally or physically. A tennis player who finds his

CONCEPT Personal goal setting, self-talk, attentional focus, imagery, and self-activation are effective in energizing the athlete to greater levels of activation.

APPLICATION Dan O'Brian's wise statement that you have to be able to "turn it on and then turn it off" when you need to is extremely appropriate here. Athletes are not always optimally aroused for competition. Sometimes they are overaroused and sometimes they are underaroused. When the athlete is underaroused and needs to be immediately energized, a pep talk from a coach or another athlete might help, but usually it is a personal thing. The athlete has to be able to "turn it on" when she needs to. The methods reviewed above are all effective in energizing athletes. Coaches should help athletes learn how to use these energizing techniques to their advantage.

two-game lead in the final set slipping away has to energize himself to stop the backward slide. An earlier quote by Dan O'Brian is of particular significance here. Recall that he said you have to be able to "turn it on and then turn it off." We learned how to turn it off earlier in this chapter, and now we learn how to turn it on. Most of the strategies we will mention in the following paragraphs have already been introduced in earlier sections and chapters of the book. **Self-energizing strategies** to be discussed include individual goal setting, self-talk, attentional focus, imagery, and self-activation.

Individual Goal Setting Individual athletes set long-term goals to help motivate them for the long haul across a season. However, successful athletes also use goal setting to motivate and energize them for an approaching competition. To be effective, these immediate goals must be phrased silently or verbally just before the event occurs. Goal setting that is contiguous with an event is a form of positive self-talk containing specific goal parameters. For example, when the "hit and run" play is on in baseball, the batter's stated goal might be, "Make contact." In tennis, the serve receiver's goal on the first serve might be, "Block it back." In the waning moments of a basketball game, the power forward's goal might be, "Take it hard to the rim and score." Goal setting, even in acute situations, is highly motivating and energizing, and should be used often.

Self-Talk Self-talk was introduced earlier in this chapter as an intervention strategy. Here we introduce the concept as a means of energizing the athlete to greater activity and effort. Self-talk, or even **self-thought,** should always be used with a positive frame of reference. Actually phrasing and verbally stating cues that remind the athlete of the need to generate greater energy can be effective. As the fullback leads the way into the defensive line in football, he picks his target and thinks or says, "Explode." As the basketball player sets a blind screen in anticipation of hard contact, she says or thinks, "Hold." As the tennis player aims for a backhand passing shot down the line, he says or thinks the word, "Blast." Other key words that are symbolic of greater energy and activation include "now," "go," "deep," "hit," and "power."

Attentional Focus Attentional focus was introduced in chapter 7 of the text. Increased attention is associated with increased physiological arousal. Consequently, strategies designed to increase or narrow attention will also result in activation and greater energy. Narrowed attention occurs when we gate out irrelevant cues that may serve as distractors. It is instructive to think of the linebacker in American football as he focuses his attention on the running back and says to himself, "You are mine." The goalie in soccer focuses her attention on the ball and says to herself, "Be fearless and smother the ball." There are certain situations in sport in which maximum effort and maximum arousal are necessary for success. When these situations occur, the athlete has to be fully attentive and fully activated.

Imagery   As we will learn in chapter 11 of this book, imagery has both a cognitive and a motivational function. It is the motivational function that makes imagery a viable energizer. As the tennis player prepares for an important serve, he visualizes the ball "leaping" off his racket and "exploding" into the backhand corner of the opponent's receiving court. As the spiker in volleyball approaches the net, she visualizes herself "smashing" the ball over the block and into the unprotected deep down-the-line corner of the opponent's court. In golf, the golfer sees himself "drive" the ball in a low trajectory deep into the middle of the fairway. Visualizing successful outcomes in situations requiring activation and strong effort is motivating and energizing.

Self-Activation   In addition to all of the energizing techniques mentioned above, successful athletes develop their own methods for energizing themselves on a moment's notice. This is called **self-activation.** Jimmy Conners, a former tennis great, would slap himself on the thigh in conjunction with various self-talk statements to get himself activated late in the match. Dennis Rodman, of Chicago Bulls basketball fame, had the curious habit of going back into the tunnel leading to the locker room and riding a stationary bicycle at high speeds to elevate his heart rate. John Rocker, fiery reliever for the Atlanta Braves baseball team, liked to sprint onto the field for his relief appearances. Every successful athlete learns ways to self-activate and energize himself when he needs to.

Summary

Coping has been defined by Lazarus and Folkman (1984) as "constantly changing cognitive and behavioral efforts to manage specific external and/or internal demands that are appraised as taking or exceeding the resources of the person."

Coping strategies are of two types: problem focused and emotion focused. Problem-focused coping centers on alleviating the environmental stimulus that is causing the stress response, whereas emotion-focused coping seeks to regulate emotions in order to reduce cognitive stress.

Two types of coping style are identified: the approach style and the avoidance style. The approach style of coping involves addressing the stressful situation directly, whereas the avoidance style of coping involves avoiding or repressing the stressful situation. Coping style and coping strategies together represent the two dimensions of the conceptual framework for coping.

Coping by athletes is believed to be dynamic as opposed to dispositional in nature. Coping strategies used by athletes are very dynamic and flexible. For this reason, it is advantageous for athletes to develop and refine a multitude of coping resources. Coping skills can also generalize to other sport and nonsport life situations. Five different factors are identified that facilitate the transfer of coping skills to nonsport situations.

Elite athletes tend to use an approach style of coping, with the majority of the strategies being problem or action focused. The vast majority of coping strategies may be categorized under the heading of psychological training, physical training and strategizing, and somatic relaxation.

The where, when, what, and why of self-talk were discussed. The what of self-talk deals with structure and content of self-talk. Self-talk can be in the form of words actually spoken, or in the form of thoughts that come into the athlete's mind. Categories of self-talk include statements related to technique, statements used for encouragement, and words that change mood. The why of self-talk includes the following uses or functions: (a) building and developing self-efficacy, (b) skill acquisition,

(c) creating and changing mood, (d) controlling effort, and (e) focusing attention or concentration.

Relaxation procedures discussed in this chapter include progressive relaxation, autogenic training, meditation, and biofeedback. Common to all of these procedures is the relaxation response. Factors necessary to precipitate the relaxation response include a mental device, a passive attitude, decreased muscle tone, and a quiet environment. Mastering the technique of deep breathing for the purpose of relaxation and relieving tension is an important component of each of the relaxation techniques discussed.

Jacobson's full progressive relaxation procedure involves systematically tensing and relaxing specific muscle groups in a predetermined order. Relaxation begins with the muscles of the left arm and proceeds to those of the right arm, left and right legs, abdomen, back, and chest and shoulders, concluding with the neck and face muscles. Abbreviated versions and variations of Jacobson's procedures are also effective in reducing anxiety, tension, and stress.

Autogenic training and progressive relaxation both elicit the relaxation response. Whereas progressive relaxation relies upon dynamic contracting and relaxing of muscles, autogenic training relies upon feelings associated with the limbs and muscles of the body. Autogenic training is very similar to autohypnosis, and is based upon early research with hypnosis. In autogenic training, the athlete focuses upon achieving a sensation of heaviness in the limbs and a feeling of general warmth in the body, arms, and legs.

Meditation is tied directly to the concept of selective attention. In practicing meditation, the individual attempts to uncritically focus his attention on a single thought, sound, or object. Meditation will result in the relaxation response if practiced in a quiet environment that is associated with a passive attitude and decreased muscle tone.

Biofeedback training uses instruments to help people control responses of the autonomic nervous system. For example, an athlete monitors an auditory signal of her own heart rate and experiments with different thoughts, feelings, and sensations calculated to slow the heart rate. Once the subject learns to recognize the feelings associated with the reduction of heart rate, the instrument is removed and the athlete tries to control the heart rate without it.

Energizing strategies are of two types: team energizing strategies and individual self-energizing strategies. The matching hypothesis was discussed as a reminder of the necessity of matching any sort of intervention with the specific needs and symptoms of the athlete. Indiscriminate use of invervention for either relaxation or activation was discouraged.

As the coach prepares for the season, she recognizes the need to set into motion a number of initiatives designed to keep the team focused and energized for an entire season. Strategies discussed to accomplish this aim included team goal setting, use of pep talks by the coach, the use of bulletin boards and posters, generating publicity and news coverage, generating fan support, precompetition workouts, and effective coach, athlete, and parent interaction.

In addition to mobilizing a team's energy for an entire season, individual athletes need to be able to energize themselves for immediate mobilization. Individual self-energizing strategies designed to accomplish this aim include individual goal setting, liberal use of self-talk and verbal cues, attentional focus, imagery and visualization, and personalized self-activation strategies.

Critical Thought Questions

1. Why would an athlete choose to use an avoidance style of coping as opposed to an approach style? Are these good reasons?

2. Using the two-dimensional coping framework, write three specific coping strategy/style examples that would fit into each quadrant of figure 9.2.

3. List five stressful situations that you have experienced and identify coping strategies that you have used to address these situations. Classify these coping strategies within the two-dimensional conceptual framework for coping.

4. Identify coping strategies you have used in sport that you also use in real-life nonsport situations.

5. How does self-talk differ from the "trash talk" used by many athletes today?

6. Do you think self-talk can really increase self-confidence and performance? Explain and defend your answer.

7. Little evidence exists to suggest that relaxation procedures by themselves enhance athletic performance. Examine this statement and discuss implications for applied sport psychology.

8. Practice your deep breathing skills and explain why you feel deep breathing is effective in helping a person to relax.

9. Of the four methods of relaxation discussed in this chapter, which one do you like the best? Explain why.

10. Each of the relaxation methods discussed in this chapter takes hours and weeks to master. How, then, can these methods be utilized by an athlete who must be able to bring on the relaxation response in a matter of minutes, or even seconds?

11. What is the practical application of biofeedback for a high school football team?

12. Exactly how do you go about matching an intervention with an athlete's maladaptive symptoms?

13. News coverage given by local newspapers and radio talk shows is not always positive. How do you go about protecting athletes from negative news coverage that is demotivating?

14. Develop a brief training manual teaching athletes how to immediately energize themselves in preparation for competition.

Glossary

abdominal breathing Deep breathing, associated with relaxation, that takes place at the level of the abdomen or diaphragm.

affirmation statements Statements that affirm to the athlete that he possesses the skills, abilities, positive attitudes, and beliefs necessary for successful performace.

anxiety/stress spiral The circular effect of anxiety causing poor performance that results in even more anxiety.

approach style of coping The coping preference to address a stressful situation directly.

autogenic training A relaxation training program in which the athlete attends to body feedback.

avoidance style of coping The coping preference to avoid or repress the issues causing distress.

biofeedback A program in which the athlete learns to elicit the relaxation response with the aid of physiological measurement equipment.

bulletin board Vehicle used to visually motivate members of a team by displaying and posting material that the coach feels is for the good of the cause.

chest breathing Shallow breathing, associated with anxiety, that takes place at the level of the chest or thorax.

coping Constantly changing cognitive and behavioral efforts to manage specific external and/or internal demands that are appraised as taking or exceeding the resources of the person.

coping conceptual framework A two-dimensional coping framework for considering coping style and strategy.

coping strategies Ways of alleviating the debilitating effects of the stress response.

coping style An approach to alleviating the debilitating effects of the stress response.

deep breathing Breathing that takes place at the level of the abdomen and diaphragm, as opposed to the chest and thorax.

dispositional hypothesis The hypothesis that athletes have a certain learned or innate way of coping with all stress-related situations.

dynamic hypothesis The hypothesis that athletes' coping responses are dynamic and fluid, changing from situation to situation.

emotion-focused coping strategy Coping strategy in which the individual attempts to alleviate the stress response by regulating emotions.

fan support Getting people who support a team to come to watch them play regardless of their win/loss record.

generalizability of coping skills The notion that coping skills learned in the sporting environment can transfer to nonsport real-life situations.

immediate mobilization The need for an athlete to "turn it on" just before competition in order to be optimally prepared.

individual self-energizing strategies Strategies that the individual uses to induce immediate activation and alertness.

mantra A key phrase or mental device used in transcendental meditation to help the athlete focus attention internally.

matching hypothesis The attempt to develop a closer match between precompetitive affect and psychological adjustment.

meditation A form of relaxation that applies directly to the concepts of selective attention.

mental device A word, phrase, object, or process used to help elicit the relaxation response.

pep talk The practice by the coach or an influential individual of talking to the team just before competition to energize and motivate them.

precompetition workout Not a warm-up session, but a vigorous workout before a competition to energize the team and reduce precompetitive anxiety.

problem-focused coping strategy Coping strategy in which the individual attempts to alleviate the stress response by eliminating the environmental stimulus that is causing the stress.

progressive relaxation A muscle relaxation procedure in which skeletal muscles are systematically tensed and relaxed.

relaxation response Physiological changes that reverse the effect of the sympathetic nervous system.

self-activation Methods developed by successful athletes for energizing themselves on a moment's notice.

self-energizing strategies Strategies calculated to self-energize or activate an athlete immediately before a specific event or situation.

self-talk An effective overt or covert cognitive technique for reinforcing situation-specific self-confidence and ultimately behavior.

self-thought Self-talk statements that are not actually spoken but are mentally framed as thoughts.

stress management The use of various relaxation or arousal management procedures to reduce anxiety.

team energizing strategies Energizing strategies that focus upon the team as a whole and are generally orchestrated by the coach.

transcendental meditation A relaxation procedure that originated in India and features the repetition of a mantra to elicit the relaxation response.

CHAPTER 10

Goal Setting in Sport

KEY TERMS

Action-oriented goal
Behavioral goal
Goal attributes
Goal difficulty
Goal setting
Learning strategies
Long-range goal
Measurable goal
Mobilizing effort
Multiple goal strategy
Needs assessment
Observable goal
Outcome goal
Performance goal
Persistence
Process goal
Realistic goal
Short-range goals
SMART
Specific goal
Timely goal

The headlines from the year 2000 Sydney Olympic Games read, "American Lenny Krayzelburg wins the 100- and 200-meter backstroke." By so doing, Krayzelburg became one of only three men to sweep the backstroke in the Olympic Games. Lenny's dream had begun not in America, but in the Russian Ukraine. At age nine, Lenny practiced nearly six hours a day in hopes of representing his country in the Olympics. When he arrived in the United States in 1989, Lenny was a 13-year-old fish out of water. One of the first things that Lenny's father did was to enroll him with the Team Santa Monica Swim Club. At age 24, Lenny Krayzelburg became the winner of two gold medals and a proud representative of his adopted country (Montville, 2000).

In 2004 Lance Armstrong and his United States Postal Service cycling team made history. Armstrong was the only person in the history of the Tour de France cycle race to win the race six years in a row. In 2005, sponsored by The Discovery Channel, Armstrong gained his seventh victory in a row. Lance Armstrong and his teams are part of this decade's greatest sport dynasties. In the 2004 Tour de France, Armstrong won the prologue and six of the year's 20 stages, and conceded a seventh to a friend. Over a 21-day period (prologue and 20 stages), he put two thousand miles on his legs. Lance Armstrong overcame testicular cancer in 1996 and 1997 to win his first Tour de France in 1999. This is without a doubt one of the greatest sports-related motivational stories in history. Undoubtedly, team and individual goal setting played a major role in this great accomplishment (Murphy, 2004; Price, 2004).

As we shall learn in this chapter, goal setting is about cognition and motivation. By its very nature it is cognitive, because the athlete has to think and plan for the future. It is also motivational in nature, because the very process of setting goals is energizing. Each year of Lance Armstrong's Tour de France victory had to begin with both team and individual goal setting in order to get them on target for another grueling season of training and competition. This chapter on goal setting is placed in this part of the book because of its cognitive and behavioral psychological intervention properties. However, goal setting could also fit well within the motivation part of the text, because of its energizing and motivational properties.

It is also important to point out the similarities and differences between goal orientation, discussed in chapter 6, and goal setting, discussed in this chapter. Goal orientation is about the different ways that athletes think about ability. The task-goal-oriented athlete does not have to defeat an opponent in order to feel successful. She simply has to believe that she tried hard, did her best, and made some improvement—and that's the goal. Conversely, the ego-goal-oriented athlete cannot feel successful unless she has performed better than another person or another team—and that's the goal.

Goal setting, however, focuses on the mechanics of how one can set goals and how those goals can be energizing and motivational. There are, of course, some similarities as well between goal orientation theory and goal setting. For example, in goal setting we might differentiate between outcome and process goals. Because an outcome goal tends to be about winning a match or defeating an opponent, it also tends toward ego involvement. Also, because process goals tend to be about technique and execution, they also tend to be task or mastery oriented. With that differentiation clarified, let us now turn to a discussion of goal setting as an intervention strategy.

It takes a lot of work and dedication to become a world champion in any sport. An accomplishment of this magnitude is realized only through the judicious setting of daily, weekly, and long-term personal goals. **Goal setting** is a theory of *motivation* that effectively energizes athletes to become more productive and effective (Locke & Latham, 1990). Goals set by athletes represent either internal or external motivation, depending on whether or not the goals are internalized and personalized. Simply stated, Locke and Latham's (1985) basic theory is that (a) a linear relationship exists between degree of goal difficulty and performance, and (b) goals that are specific and difficult lead to a higher level of performance than "do your best" goals. In 1990, Locke and Latham reported that 354 out of 393 industrial, organizational, and academically based studies supported their theory. We turn now to a discussion of goal setting as it is applied in the sport and exercise setting. Important topics to be discussed in this chapter include (a) basic types of goals and their effectiveness, (b) reasons goal setting results in improved performance, (c) principles of effective goal setting, (d) a team approach to goal setting, (e) goal management strategies, and (f) common goal busters.

Basic Types of Goals and Their Effectiveness

Three basic types of goals have been identified in the sport psychology literature (Kingston & Hardy,

1997). These three different types of goals are outcome goals, performance goals, and process goals.

Outcome Goals

Outcome goals focus on the outcomes of sporting events and usually involve some sort of interpersonal comparison. A typical outcome goal might be to win a basketball game, place first in a volleyball tournament, defeat an opponent in tennis, or finish the season with a winning record. It is very typical for coaches to speak in terms of the number of wins they hope to have in a particular season.

Performance Goals

Performance goals specify an end product of performance that will be achieved by the athlete relatively independently of other performers and the team. A typical performance goal for an individual athlete might be to strike out seven batters, score twenty-five points in a basketball game, serve five aces in a tennis match, or get fifteen kills in a volleyball game. Intuitively, athletes and coaches should prefer performance goals to outcome goals for two fundamental reasons. First, if performance goals are accomplished, there is a good possibility that outcome goals will also be accomplished. Second, personal satisfaction can be realized from the achievement of performance goals even if outcome goals remain unfulfilled.

A conflict arises, however, if the athlete places the accomplishment of personal performance goals above team outcome goals. Each year in major league baseball, a most valuable player (MVP) is selected from the American and National Leagues. Each year the debate rages as to whether the MVP should be the player with the best personal statistics or the player who was most pivotal in helping his team qualify for postseason play. Near the end of the 2000 regular season, Gary Sheffield of the Los Angeles Dodgers said, "An MVP is who had the best season period. It's not about winning or losing. It's about having a better year than everybody else." Jeff Kent, MVP candidate from the

Professional athletes set specific performance goals for themselves and design their training approach in a way that helps them meet those goals. Courtesy Photolink/ Getty Images.

league-leading San Francisco Giants, countered, "How can you be the most valuable if you didn't help your team get to the playoffs? Isn't that why we play?" (Cannella, 2000, p. 62). This mismatch between team and individual goals is also identified by high school coaches as a coaching frustration (Weinberg, Butt, & Knight, 2001). Team goals focus on team members working together to achieve a common team objective, while individual goals often focus upon individual statistics. A high school basketball player who glories in scoring 25 points per game may do so at the demise of the synergy of the team as a whole.

CONCEPT A multiple goal strategy is most effective in improving performance and psychological skill in athletes.

APPLICATION A multiple goal strategy allows the athlete to set goals in terms of successful outcome, personal performance, and improving technique as an ongoing process. The coach should assist the athlete in keeping these different kinds of goals in perspective as the athlete strives for success and personal improvement.

Process Goals

Process goals focus on specific behaviors exhibited throughout a performance. A typical process goal for an athlete might be to keep the left elbow straight while executing a golf drive, to keep the elbow down and wrist firm in the tennis backhand, or to focus on the spiker and not the ball in volleyball blocking. Each of these behaviors reflects proper and effective technique for executing a specific athletic task. If the athlete is successful in setting and meeting process goals, improved performance and outcome should be the result. It is interesting to note while watching major league baseball that the catcher will frequently remind the pitcher of a particular process goal relative to pitching technique. For example, if the pitcher starts to drop his delivery release point (sidearm delivery), the catcher often mimics the correct overhand throwing action to remind the pitcher of correct technique.

Which Type of Goal Is Best?

Numerous investigations have been conducted contrasting the three different types of goals. Kingston and Hardy (1997) contrasted the effectiveness of performance goals with that of process goals in club golfers relative to their skill improvement and psychological skill development. After a 54-week training period, they observed that both performance and process goals resulted in improved performance, whereas a control group with no goals did not show improvement. In addition, the researchers observed that process goals were superior to performance goals in terms of realizing improvements in anxiety management and selected psychological skills.

Burton, Weinberg, Yukelson, and Weigand (1998) categorized 570 collegiate athletes as either less or more effective in the use of goal setting. The more effective athletes relative to goal setting reported that process goals were more important to them than a combination of performance and outcome goals (product goals). Burton et al. (1998) used the Collegiate Goal Setting in Sport Questionnaire (CGSSQ) as developed by Weinberg, Burton, Yukelson, and Weigand (1993) to measure goals used by collegiate athletes. The CGSSQ measures the frequency and effectiveness of (a) process-related goal setting, (b) product-related goal setting, and (c) goal implementation strategies used by athletes.

Filby, Maynard, and Graydon (1999) assigned college-age soccer players to one of five goal groups based on scores on a soccer wall volley test. The five groups were characterized by (a) no goals (control group), (b) outcome goals only, (c) process goals only, (d) outcome and process goals, and (e) outcome, performance, and process goals combined. After five weeks of training, results showed that the two **multiple goal strategy** groups outperformed the other three groups. Relatively speaking, the group exhibiting the lowest level of improvement was the "outcome only" group. The efficacy of the multiple goal strategy was also supported by Steinberg, Singer, and Murphy (2000).

FIGURE 10.1 | Athlete should focus on a combination of outcome, performance, and process goals.

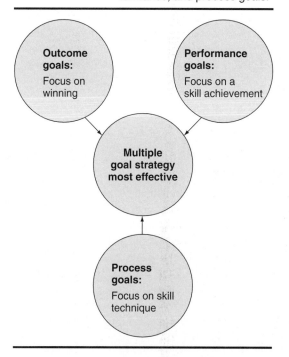

As illustrated in figure 10.1, research supports the position that a multiple goal strategy is best. Used in isolation, outcome goals are probably the least effective, but when used in conjunction with performance and process goals, they are helpful. It would seem that a goal-setting strategy that uses all three types of goals is best for the athlete in terms of psychological development as well as performance improvement. The important thing for the athlete and coach is that they understand clearly the distinctions between the three and use them all effectively.

Reasons Goal Setting Results in Improved Performance

According to Locke, Shaw, Saari, and Latham (1981), there are four basic ways in which goal setting can influence performance. Because it is important for the athlete and the coach to understand why goal setting is effective, these four explanations will be discussed.

Directed Attention

Goal setting causes the athlete to focus her attention upon the task and upon achieving the goal relative to the task. When she has no specific goal, the athlete's attention wanders from one thought to another without any particular direction. Setting a specific goal causes the athlete to focus her attention on that goal and upon the task that is associated with that goal. Think of the wrestler who knows he must try to pin his opponent, but is unsuccessful in getting his opponent into a position that would make this possible. Focusing the athlete's attention on a specific take-down move and practicing it until it is mastered would make it possible for the athlete to achieve his goal.

Effort Mobilization

Once an athlete's attention is directed toward a particular goal, it is necessary for the athlete to put forth the effort necessary to achieve that goal. The very act of increasing or **mobilizing effort** will have a positive effect upon improved performance. Consider the bowler who wishes to consistently bowl a score of around 250. To bowl consistently in this score range, the athlete must be able to follow a strike with another strike, or at least a spare. Goal setting will have the effect of increasing the athlete's effort during practice so that she can accomplish this goal.

Persistence

A third way that goal setting influences performance is through **persistence.** Many athletes can focus their effort and attention on improving a skill for a few minutes or even for a whole practice, but to be successful, an athlete must persist for a long period of time. Persistence is a by-product of effective goal setting. As long as the goal is present and

CONCEPT   Goal setting improves performance by directing attention, increasing effort and persistence, and motivating the athlete to learn new learning strategies.

APPLICATION   Goal setting is one of the best motivational strategies available to the athlete.

The coach and the athlete must learn effective goal-setting techniques. Ineffective goal setting can actually do more harm than good, because it can raise expectations that the athlete cannot realize. In the pages that follow, principles of effective goal setting will be discussed in detail.

the athlete wants to obtain the goal, he will persist in the effort needed to accomplish it. Thirty days after winning the U.S. Open by 15 strokes, Tiger Woods won the British Open by eight strokes. In so doing, he accomplished a career Grand Slam at age 24, two years younger than Jack Nicklaus was when he accomplished it. Woods now holds the record for most strokes under par in the Masters, the U.S. Open, and the British Open. How did he get to be a "physical genius" at such a young age? Here's a clue. He sometimes requires himself to hole one hundred six-foot putts consecutively, using only his right hand during practice (Rushin, 2000). This is persistence, and it requires goal setting to gain that kind of skill and persistence during practice.

Development of New Learning Strategies

Goal setting promotes the development of new **learning strategies.** Without goals for improvement, an athlete is content to get along with the learning strategies and skills that she currently possesses. Setting of new goals not only directs attention, mobilizes effort, and nurtures persistence, but it also forces the athlete to learn new and better ways of accomplishing a skill or task. A post-up player in basketball may be relatively successful in scoring 12 points a game using a drop-step move, but more than one move is necessary if he wants to score 20 points a game. Once a basketball player sets a personal goal to score more points on offense, he must learn new skills and techniques to make this possible.

Principles of Effective Goal Setting

We are now aware that there are three different types of goals and that goal setting improves performance by directing attention, increasing effort and persistence, and motivating athletes to learn new strategies. In the pages that follow we will learn about principles of effective goal setting. Goal setting must be well planned and effective if it is to result in desirable performance results. The principles of effective goal setting are also summarized in table 10.1.

TABLE 10.1 | Principles of Effective Goal Setting

1. Make goals specific, measurable, and observable.
2. Clearly identify time constraints.
3. Use moderately difficult goals; they are superior to either easy or very difficult goals.
4. Write goals down and regularly monitor progress.
5. Use a mix of process, performance, and outcome goals.
6. Use short-range goals to achieve long-range goals.
7. Set team as well as individual performance goals.
8. Set practice as well as competition goals.
9. Make sure goals are internalized by the athlete.
10. Consider personality and individual differences in goal setting.

Make Goals Specific, Measurable, and Observable

It is difficult to determine if a general nonspecific goal has been achieved. If a tennis player sets a general goal to become a more accurate and effective server, how does she know if she has achieved this goal? One source of information could be her win/loss record, but this could be misleading, as the skill of the opponents could have changed. Wins would go up if she played weaker opponents, but this would not be evidence of her improved serving ability. The terms *specific, measurable,* and *observable* are all related to one another. A **specific goal** is one that focuses exactly on the goal to be achieved. For example, "shooting 80 percent accuracy in free-throw shooting" is specific, but "becoming a better basketball player" is not. A **measurable goal** is one that you can quantify, in the sense that you know exactly how close you are to achieving the goal. The general goal "to become a better server in tennis" is not measurable, because you don't know when you have achieved the goal. An **observable goal** is one that you can measure, because you can observe it. For example, the goal "to hit 80 percent of my free throws" is observable as well as measurable, because if I shoot with 75 percent accuracy, I know I have fallen short. Observable performance goals are also referred to as **behavioral** or **action-oriented goals.** Good goals are those that you can measure, and the only way you can measure them is by observing them in behavioral terms. If a goal is specific, measurable, and observable, you will be able to watch the athlete in action and observe whether he is realizing the goal or behavior.

Clearly Identify Time Constraints

In tennis, it does little good for a player to set a goal to serve 60 percent of her first serves into the court if she doesn't specify when she plans on accomplishing this goal. Is this goal to be accomplished by the next major tournament? By the end of the season? By the end of her collegiate career? Stating a long-range goal without specifying the time component of the goal introduces uncertainty into the goal-setting process. Setting time constraint goals that are too short can make a goal seem unreachable and discourage the athlete. Setting time constraint goals that are too distant can also have negative ramifications. This is pointed out in a study reported by Tenenbaum, Bar-Eli, and Yaaron (1999). In this investigation, the sit-up performance of participants who had four, six, or eight weeks to accomplish their assigned goals were compared at four weeks (all groups) and at six weeks (two groups). Participants assigned to the eight-week goal group did not do well at four and six weeks compared to the other groups. It seems that when participants had eight weeks to meet their goals, they took the whole eight weeks to accomplish them. What this research says is that if an athlete can realistically accomplish a goal in thirty days, don't set a goal to accomplish it in sixty days, because the athlete will use all sixty days to realize the task.

A well-stated goal should be **timely** in the sense that it specifies time constraints associated with the goal, but also timely in the sense that it reflects an appropriate amount of time to accomplish the goal. The timeliness of a goal can add to the motivational characteristics of the goal. If the time constraint is too long, the athlete may procrastinate over the achievement of the goal, while if it is too short, the athlete will view it as unrealistic.

Use Moderately Difficult Goals; They Are Superior to Either Easy or Very Difficult Goals

Most of the goal-setting research in sport and exercise has been conducted in this specific area. For maximum performance, Locke and Latham (1990) argued that goals should be so difficult that only 10 percent of individuals can reach them. Research in sport and exercise, however, has failed to support this level of **goal difficulty.** For example, a statistical summary (meta-analysis) of 36 studies conducted in sport and exercise concluded that moderately difficult goals are best (Kyllo & Landers, 1995). Recently, 52 percent of Olympic athletes indicated a preference for moderately difficult goals, whereas only 25 percent preferred very difficult goals (Weinberg, Burton, Yukelson, & Weigand, 2000). Similarly, coaches have expressed frustration with difficult goals because their athletes get discouraged when goals seem unattainable (Weinberg, Butt, & Knight, 2001).

A study by Bar-Eli, Tenenbaum, Pie, Btesh, and Almong (1997) supported this conclusion in a study involving 346 male ninth- and tenth-grade Israeli students from 15 high schools. The students from each school were randomly assigned to one of 15 sit-up treatment conditions. The first five schools participated in the study for four weeks, the next five schools for six weeks, and the last five for eight weeks. Within each group of five schools, there were five goal training conditions: "do," "do your best," "improve by 10 percent" (easy), "improve by 20 percent" (moderately difficult), and "improve by 40 percent" (very difficult). The results showed that the three groups receiving specific goals outperformed the two groups given nonspecific assignments ("do" or "do your best"). Results further showed that the moderately difficult goal group generally outperformed the easy and very difficult groups, although some variability of results occurred as a function of length of training period.

One of the controversies associated with goal difficulty research in sport and exercise has been the problem of controlling for social comparison between members of different training groups. Specifically, participants in the control group who were told "do your best" routinely reported setting goals. This problem was solved in the Bar-Eli et al. (1997) study by using a large sample size and 15 different schools. In this design, participants in one group could not be influenced by members of another group because they belonged to a different school. Therefore, this was a very important study and the reason that it was presented in some detail here.

Goals should be moderately difficult, so that athletes must work hard and extend themselves in order to meet them. At the same time, however,

FIGURE 10.2 | Athletes and coaches must be SMART when setting goals.

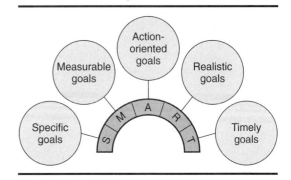

a goal must be **realistic,** in the sense that the athlete must believe that the goal is achievable. If a goal is perceived by an athlete as not being realistic or achievable, she may become discouraged and not try to achieve the goal. The acronym **SMART** has been used by sport psychologists to help athletes remember five important characteristics of well-stated goals that have been discussed in the paragraphs above. Goals should be Specific, Measurable, Action-oriented, Realistic, and Timely (Weinberg & Gould, 1999). The SMART acronym is useful in helping athletes to remember these five important characteristics. The SMART principle is illustrated in figure 10.2.

Write Goals Down and Regularly Monitor Progress

An effective goal is one that you write down and monitor regularly to determine if you are making progress. You must take care to avoid making this a laborious and tedious task. If you have set a goal that you truly want to achieve, then writing it down and knowing how you are doing relative to achieving the goal is of critical importance. An effective goal is not one that you think about and then forget. An effective goal is also not one that you write down, place in a time capsule, and then open up a year later to see if you have accomplished it.

Research shows that coaches do not consistently write down goals (Weinberg, Butt, Knight, & Perritt, 2001).

Individuals striving to gain muscle mass through weight training come to mind. Weight trainers generally are asked to keep a daily log of the amount of weight lifted and the number of repetitions accomplished for each exercise. By recording her goal weight and repetitions for each exercise, the athlete is able to monitor her progress on a daily or weekly basis. Without this sort of recording system, it is unlikely that the athlete could make any sustained progress toward achieving her goals.

Monitoring performance and process goals in a dynamic sport such as tennis or basketball will require assistance from coaches or statisticians to keep track of what occurs during a game or match. It is fairly common for coaches to record player performance statistics in sports such as tennis, basketball, and volleyball, but it is less common for them to monitor process goals. Unless matches and games are videotaped for replay, athletes have no way of knowing on a consistent basis if their process goals, such as maintaining certain body alignments, are being realized.

Effective goal setting usually involves more than the athlete. A case in point is an ecologically valid goal-setting study in which goal-setting effectiveness was observed in four youth speed skaters across an actual competitive season (Wanlin, Hrycarko, Martin, & Mahon, 1997). A multiple baseline design was used in which each athlete received training and monitoring in goal setting across 12 weeks. Each athlete started the goal intervention at different points in time during the 12 weeks. One athlete served as a control and did not receive the goal-setting intervention, while the others started the goal-setting intervention at four, five, and six weeks. Thus all but one athlete had a baseline against which to compare her postintervention performance. Researchers monitored frequency of laps completed in practice, percentage of drills completed in practice, competitive race times recorded during the 12-week study, and off-task

behavior. Results showed an increase in positive practice behaviors and a decrease in negative practice behaviors following introduction of the goal-setting intervention. All three experimental skaters made small improvements in racing times following the goal-setting intervention.

Use a Mix of Process, Performance, and Outcome Goals

As already mentioned in a previous section, a multiple goal strategy will yield the best performance and psychological results. One should never use an outcome goal strategy by itself. Outcome goals (success/failure) serve a useful purpose when used in conjuction with process and performance goals, but by themselves they can lead to a loss of motivation. An athlete has a great deal of personal control over process and performance goals, but not so much over outcome goals. The individual athlete has only a limited amount of control over the outcome of a team sport game such as baseball or soccer. The individual athlete has more control over the outcome of an individual sport contest, but even there personal control is limited by external causes such as skill difficulty. For example, you could run the race of your life, post a personal best on the 5K, and still lose to a faster runner.

Use Short-Range Goals to Achieve Long-Range Goals

If you have ever climbed a high mountain, you will be able to relate to the importance of this principle. When you set out to climb to the top of a mountain peak, your **long-range goal** is to be on top of the mountain looking down within a certain time frame. As you begin the steep climb, however, you almost immediately start making **short-range goals.** For example, you might see a plateau about one hundred yards up and set a goal to get to that point before stopping for a rest. This process continues until you make your last one-hundred-yard short-range goal to reach the top of the mountain before stopping to rest.

If a weight trainer sets a goal to bench press 250 pounds in a single maximum-effort lift, he must start with a short-range goal of, say, benching 200 pounds within two months. As the first short-range goal is reached, he sets another short-range goal of, say, 220 pounds, always keeping the long-range goal in mind. The same thing would apply to a golfer who shoots double-bogey golf but sets a long-range goal to be shooting single-bogey golf within one year's time. Going from double-bogey to single-bogey golf in a single year will require lots of practice and the setting of realistic short-range goals for each practice round and tournament round. The efficacy of setting both short- and long-range goals is supported in the sport psychology literature (Gould, 2001; Bar-Eli, Hartman, & Levy-Kolker, 1994).

Set Team as Well as Individual Performance Goals

Normally, when we think of team goals, we think in terms of outcome goals. For example, we might set a goal for the team to make the playoffs at the end of the season. Performance goals can be set for a group or a team just as they can be set for an individual. This principle is illustrated in a study reported by Johnson, Ostrow, Perna, and Etzel (1997). The five-week bowling performance of 12 bowlers who set individual goals to knock down a certain number of pins was compared with the bowling performance of 12 bowlers who set a team goal to knock down a specific number of pins as a team. The results showed that the group that set goals as a team performed better than the individual-goal group.

Set Practice as Well as Competition Goals

Weinberg, Burke, and Jackson (1997) sampled the goal-setting beliefs and practices of 240 youth tennis players and discovered that they viewed practice goals as being very effective in improving tennis performance. Successful Olympic athletes also value the importance of goal setting for practice

as well as competition (Orlick & Partington, 1988). Coaches recognize the critical importance of effective practices to prepare for competition. How an individual or team performs during practice will be directly correlated with performance in competition. It is also important to recognize that athletes spend much more time practicing their sport than they do actually competing in the sport.

There are a number of ways in which practice goals could help an athlete achieve competitive performance goals. If a basketball player has a competition performance goal to hit 45 percent of her field goal attempts, then she should have the same goal for practice. It makes no sense to practice with no goal in mind relative to individual performance and then expect to achieve competitive performance goals. If I am going to be a good shooter during competition, then I had better be a good shooter in practice as well. Setting practice goals is the way to accomplish competition goals.

There are other kinds of practice goals that will help athletes and teams succeed during competition. These are goals that relate to the work and practice ethic that is present during practice sessions. If you are going to have a good practice, then the athletes must show up on time, ready to play. They must enter into drills with enthusiasm and pay attention to the coaching staff and to the purpose and intent of each practice drill. Athletes must complement each other's good efforts and create an atmosphere that is supportive and fun to take part in. The coach can give practice goals to different athletes to promote team cohesion among players. For example, a player who needs to be more vocal and supportive of teammates during games could be assigned the goal to say something sincere and positive to each teammate during practice.

Munroe-Chandler, Hall, and Weinberg (2004) reported the results of an investigation in which a comparison was made between the types of goals set by 249 athletes representing 18 different sports. Results generally showed similarities between goals set during practice and those set for competition, but some differences were noted as well.

For example, goals set during practice tended to be more subjective (e.g., train effectively, have fun) whereas during competition they were more objective (e.g., win, get a medal or trophy). Mental preparation goals and strategy goals were the most frequently cited goals for both competition and training. Skill improvement and execution goals were used more frequently in training than in competition.

Make Sure Goals Are Internalized by the Athlete

Perhaps one of the most important ingredients of good goal setting is that goals are accepted and internalized by the athlete (Locke, 1991). If an athlete sets her own goals, it is relatively certain that she will internalize them. Conversely, if goals are assigned to the athlete by the coaching staff, it is possible that the athlete will not feel ownership for the goals. Does this mean that the athlete should always set her own goals without involvement from the coaching staff? Not necessarily. It only means that the athlete must accept and internalize the goals she either sets for herself or is assigned by the coach. Expecting athletes to set their own goals is not always the best strategy, because they may not be aware of effective goal-setting principles.

Based on their meta-analysis, Kyllo and Landers (1995) concluded that in sport it is best to let athletes either set their own goals or participate in the goal-setting process. Locke and Latham (1990), however, have argued that participative goals do not necessarily yield better performance results than assigned goals, as long as the leader is supportive and goal instructions are clear. With this background in mind, Fairall and Rodgers (1997) reported an investigation in which 67 collegiate track and field athletes served as participants. The athletes were instructed in principles of effective goal-setting and randomly assigned to one of three goal-setting conditions: athletes set their own goals, goals were set by the coach, and coach and athletes mutually agreed upon goals. Goal-setting

effectiveness was evaluated as a function of measured **goal attributes** (clarity, commitment, influence, certainty, satisfaction, acceptance, and participation). These goal attributes have been identified in the literature as precursors to good performance. Results of the investigation showed that the three goal-setting groups did not differ in terms of measured goal attributes, even though they clearly differed in terms of perceived involvement in the goal-setting process. This led the researchers to conclude that "there is no advantage to participative or self-set goals over assigned goals in terms of goal attributes" (p. 14). Athletes must accept and internalize their goals regardless of who initially wrote the goals down. Athletes must feel as though they are in control (self-determination), but it is not necessary for athletes to set their own goals in order to feel this way.

An interesting twist to this discussion comes from a recent investigation reported by Elston and Ginis (2004). They looked at the difference between self-set versus assigned goals in terms of developing self-efficacy. Based on previous research, they hypothesized that a self-set goal strategy should be superior for a familiar task, but for an unfamiliar task an assigned goal strategy should be superior. Conceivably, the assigned goal strategy would be better for an unfamiliar task, because it instills confidence in the goal recipient to know that an expert believes he can achieve the assigned goal. The unfamiliar task selected for the study was hand grip strength using a hand grip dynamometer. Fifty adults were randomly assigned to either a self-set or an assigned goal condition. At step one, the hand grip strength of all participants was tested and recorded. Following the first strength test, all participants were given bogus feedback that they had achieved hand grip strength of 25 pounds. After the bogus feedback and consistent with the assigned condition, participants either set their own hand strength goal or were assigned the goal of 28 pounds (a 3-pound increase). Following goal selection or assignment, all participants completed a self-efficacy scale relative to their confidence in achieving their goal.

CONCEPT Effective goal-setting practices are a function of being aware of and adhering to the 10 goal-setting principles discussed above and listed in table 10.1.

APPLICATION Most athletes set goals, but very few know how to set effective goals. It is even more challenging to write the goals down in a form that makes them motivational, measurable, and achievable. Coaches should work together and with athletes in learning how to write good goals. Start by reviewing the list of principles outlined in table 10.1. Once the principles are clear and understood by everyone, visually display a short list of poorly written goal statements and ask the athletes to show how each could be improved. From there, get more specific and consider a couple of actual goal statements specific to athletes in the room. See table 10.2 for examples of poor and correctly written goal statements.

TABLE 10.2 | Examples of Improperly and Properly Written Goal Statements for Tennis

Goal Type	Poorly Written Goals	Rewritten and Improved Goals
Process	1. Improve tennis backstroke technique.	1. Execute backstroke with firm wrist and with elbow pointed down.
Performance	2. Improve first-serve effectiveness.	2. During competition, serve no less and no more than 60 percent of first serves into court by end of third tournament.
Outcome	3. Improve win/loss percentage over previous year.	3. Maintain number two ranking on team and win five of seven dual-meet matches prior to playoffs.

Results showed (a) no difference in hand strength at test one, (b) no difference in goals set between groups, (c) no difference in actual hand grip strength at test two, and (d) a significant difference in self-efficacy favoring the assigned group. Thus, consistent with the researchers' expectation, an assigned goal is superior to a self-set goal in terms of developing self-efficacy to achieve a goal on an unfamiliar task. This result appears to be due to the confidence generated when an expert (coach) believes that the goal can be accomplished. This does not alter the need for the participant to internalize goals, but it provides additional insight into the cognition involved in goal setting.

Consider Personality and Individual Differences in Goal Setting

When coaches are involved in the goal-setting process, they should take into consideration personality differences. Lambert, Moore, and Dixon (1999) observed that national-level female gymnasts who exhibited an internal locus of causality disposition performed best when they used a "set your own goals" strategy; in contrast, gymnasts who exhibited an external locus of causality performed best when they used a "coach-set goals" strategy. Likewise, Theodorakis (1996) noted that the psychological characteristics of self-efficacy, satisfaction, and commitment have a direct effect upon goal setting, which in turn has a direct effect upon performance. Finally, Pierce and Burton (1998) reported that a season-long goal-setting program for gymnasts was more effective if the athletes exhibited the personality characteristic of being task oriented as opposed to ego oriented.

These few studies do not provide enough evidence to warrant tailoring goal-setting training stategies on the basis of personality profiles, but they do alert the coach to be aware of individual differences when setting team and individual goals. The failure of a particular goal-setting plan to work with a particular athlete may be due to the personality and psychological characteristics of the athlete, and not the goal-setting strategies employed.

A Team Approach to Setting Goals

Botterill (1983) identified a number of elements that are important in developing a goal-setting system to be used by coaches. Gould (2006) reduced these elements down to three critical components. The three components of a team approach to setting goals are (a) the planning phase, (b) the meeting phase, and (c) the evaluation phase.

The Planning Phase

It would be folly for a coach to stage a goal-setting meeting with her athletes without first doing a needs assessment. In a **needs assessment,** the coaching staff carefully reviews the team as a whole, and each individual, relative to areas of needed improvement. Start with the team as a whole and list the strengths and weaknesses of the team. From the list of weaknesses, you can articulate specific team needs and write them down. From the list of team needs, you may conclude that the team needs to improve in team cohesion (togetherness), physical fitness, and ball handling skills (too many turnovers). From these team needs, you should write down specific goals that state in observable terms if and when team goals are achieved—for example, "when training camp begins, each member of the team will be able to run 3 miles (5K) in less than 24 minutes."

In a similar fashion, the coaching staff considers the strengths and weaknesses of each athlete on the team, one athlete at a time. These could be called "areas of needed improvement" instead of weaknesses. Areas of needed improvement are listed for each athlete on the team. Following this exercise, goals should be written that are specific, measurable, and realistic. They should be written

and planned in a way consistent with the SMART principle and with each of the principles listed in table 10.1. Before the coaching staff approaches the team and individual athletes, they must have done their "homework" and preplanning.

Before moving into the meeting phase, the coach must carefully consider how best to approach the athletes with the needs assessment and goals for the team and individual athletes. Athletes must accept and internalize the goals that coaches give them. This is best accomplished by involving the athletes in the actual goal-setting process. There is no sense in approaching this step from a dictatorial perspective, because if the athlete does not internalize a goal, then it is not his.

In addition to considering how to involve the athletes in the goal-setting process, the coach must plan how to implement the goal-setting process and to monitor it once it is implemented. Who will monitor the team goals? Who will monitor individual athletes' goals? How much of the actual monitoring will be done by the coaching and support staff and how much by the athlete? These questions must be considered during the planning phase.

The Meeting Phase

If the planning phase was carefully considered and implemented, then the meeting phase should go smoothly. The most straightforward component of the meeting phase is the initial meeting, in which team goals can be reflected upon and discussed. This can be a very useful meeting in terms of discussing the previous year's performance and giving a realistic assessment of what to expect for the future. Coaches should educate athletes on the differences between outcome, performance, and process goals. Process and performance goals tell the athletes exactly what they must do as a team to accomplish outcome goals.

In a subsequent meeting, coaches should instruct athletes on the SMART principle and on how to write and put into words their own personal goals. Once they have accomplished this, athletes should be given time to reflect on their personal

FIGURE 10.3 | Sample performance goal-setting form for the sport of volleyball.

<u>Goal-Setting Form for Volleyball</u>

Name _*Jane*_   Position _*Strong side*_   Date _*Sept.*_

Skill	Evaluation +	Evaluation 0	Evaluation −	Specific Need	Specific Goal
Serving	✓				
Serve Reception			✓	*inconsistent passes to setter*	*75% plus passes with no aces by Oct 15th*
Setting	✓				
Spiking			✓	*getting blocked*	*increase angles, 75% in court efficiency by Oct 15th*
Blocking		✓			
Digging		✓			

goals, and then a time should be scheduled for each athlete to meet with the coach. During the one-on-one meeting with the athlete, the coach compares the athlete's goal statements with those written by the coach during the planning phase. Together, coach and athlete mutually agree on goals to be targeted. If time is a major issue, this whole process can be speeded up by having the coach assign individual goals to the athlete and then meet with him briefly to make sure they are acceptable to the athlete. Recall that Fairall and Rodgers (1997) demonstrated that assigned goals are as effective as participatory or self-set goals in terms of realizing selected goal behaviors. Illustrated in figure 10.3 is a goal-setting form that a volleyball player could use for setting personal performance goals.

In addition to setting clear, measurable goals, coaches must implement a plan or strategy to achieve the stated goals. Let's say a runner accepts the goal to run a 5K (3-mile) race in less than 21 minutes before the first competitive meet of the season. An exact plan or strategy must be implemented to give the athlete a reasonable chance to accomplish that goal. If the goal is a difficult one and no plan is in place to accomplish it, the athlete probably will not meet it. In addition to setting goals, coaches must assist athletes in developing a plan to accomplish the goal. In the case of the 5K race, it would be wise to determine exactly how much time must be shaved off the athlete's current running pace, as this will certainly determine strategy. Let's say the runner needs to shave three minutes off his time. This is quite a bit, so a sufficient time frame will be necessary to accomplish it. A series of short-range goals should be set to help break the long-range goal into smaller units. Coach and athlete must decide what daily running schedule would be most beneficial for the athlete. Would it be best to focus on the 5K, or would running some longer training races along with some sprints be helpful? The point is that a detailed strategy must be decided upon if the athlete has any hope at all of achieving a difficult goal. Every goal must have a plan by which to achieve it.

The Evaluation Phase

The evaluation phase of goal setting should take place at the end of the competitive season, but also throughout the season. Goals set by the team and by individuals should be monitored regularly. Monitoring of process and performance goals should take place following each competition, as well as after practice sessions. It is critical to the evaluation component of goal setting that performance statistics be kept on every game and match. Team and individual statistics should be posted after each competition so that athletes can review their own personal goals. If feasible, competition and practices should be videotaped so that process and technique goals can be evaluated. Outcome goals are easier to monitor because they relate to success or failure. Where it is clear that an athlete is falling short of performance goals, the coach should schedule a one-on-one meeting with that athlete, so that they can reevaluate goals in terms of achievability as well as athlete commitment. Without constant monitoring, feedback, and evaluation, the goal-setting process will not be effective.

Common Goal-Setting Pitfalls

Principles listed in table 10.1 identify ways in which goal setting can be made more effective. In a sense, the reverse is also true. Failure to consider the principles of effective goal setting would represent 10 different ways to undermine the goal-setting process. In practice, though, there are several common pitfalls, or reasons goal setting does not result in improved performance. These pitfalls come under the general headings of (a) poorly written goal statements, (b) failure to devise a goal-attainment strategy, (c) failure to follow the goal-attainment strategy, (d) failure to monitor performance progress, and (e) discouragement.

Poorly Written Goal Statements

One common problem for athletes is that their goals are so vague and general that they cannot tell if they are making progress (Weinberg et al., 1997). Violation of the SMART principle in setting goals is the most common reason goals are not met. Among other things, a goal must be specific, measurable, action oriented, realistic, and timely.

Failure to Devise a Goal-Attainment Strategy

A goal without a plan to achieve the goal almost always results in ineffective goal setting. An athlete

CONCEPT Goal setting is an effective motivator of behavior that leads to improved performance, but there are common pitfalls that can interfere with the effectiveness of a goal-setting program.

APPLICATION Two of the most critical pitfalls to effective goal setting relate to the goal-setting plan or strategy designed to achieve a goal. Setting a goal without designing a plan to achieve the goal is a little like making a wish and doing nothing about making the wish come true. Failure to devise a plan to achieve a goal is a major pitfall in goal-setting effectiveness. Related to this is the pitfall of not following the goal strategy or plan once it has been devised. Step one is to set a measurable goal. Step two is to devise a plan to achieve the goal. Step three is to follow the plan.

sets a goal to shoot par golf. Now, exactly what goal strategy plan is set in place to help the athlete accomplish that goal? Without a well-conceived plan to improve drive distance and accuracy, approach shot accuracy, and putting accuracy, it is unlikely the athlete will achieve the goal.

Failure to Follow the Goal-Attainment Strategy

Once a goal-attainment strategy or plan has been decided upon, it is necessary to follow the plan. A man sets a goal to reduce his body fat from 45 percent to 30 percent in 18 months using a scientifically sound program of daily exercise and the restriction of processed foods high in fat, sugar, and salt. Not completely committed to the program, the man fails to lose any weight during the first six months, so he gives up and decides goal setting does not work.

Failure to Monitor Performance Progress

If you are a quarterback in college football, and your goal is to increase pass completion percentage, you won't have to worry about monitoring your progress, because the coach will tell you exactly how many passes you attempted, and how many you caught. This may not be the case, however, in a small high school, or even during practice in college. Failure to monitor measurable and observable progress in sport makes it impossible to tell if goal setting is working.

Discouragement

There are many ways that discouragement can sabotage the effectiveness of goal setting in sport. Here are a few of them:

Goal Difficulty Athletes get discouraged with goal setting when the goal appears too difficult or unrealistic. If performance is being monitored, adjustments in goals can be made. If the goals are too hard and seem impossible to obtain, it makes sense to adjust the goal to make it more reasonable.

Use of Outcome Goals When an athlete sets only outcome goals and does not realize the goals, this can be very discouraging. If your goal was to win seven of ten soccer matches, and you have already lost five games with only five to go, what do you have to work for? Nothing, really. Revising the outcome goals down from 75 percent wins to 25 percent wins might help, but it would be better if you started to focus on achieving performance and process goals. It is never too late to start setting personal performance goals. Maybe you can't win the soccer match, but you can make five defensive tackles per game if you work hard at it.

Too Many Goals Sometimes the coach sets too many goals for the athlete to accomplish. Perhaps it is the athlete who is setting too many goals for herself. Whatever the reason, athletes can get discouraged when they try to accomplish too many things at once. If an athlete is just learning to play the game of tennis, there are numerous areas of needed improvement. The athlete should not try to accomplish too much at once. She should slow down and focus upon one goal at a time. This is called information overload, a topic covered in the chapter on attention.

Summary

Goal setting is a theory of motivation that energizes athletes to become more productive and effective. The three basic types of goals are outcome, performance, and process. Research supports a multiple goal strategy in exercise and sport. Goal setting influences behavior through directed attention, effort mobilization, persistence, and the development of new learning strategies.

Ten principles of effective goal setting were identified and discussed:

1. Make goals specific, measurable, and observable. Observable goals are also referred to as being action oriented and behavioral in nature.
2. Clearly identify time constraints.
3. Use moderately difficult goals; they are superior to either easy or very difficult goals.
4. Write goals down and regularly monitor progress.
5. In setting goals, use a mix of process, performance, and outcome goals.
6. Use short-range goals to assist in achieving long-range goals.
7. Set team as well as individual performance goals.
8. Set goals that relate to practice as well as competition.
9. Make sure goals are internalized and accepted by the athlete.
10. In setting goals, consider personality and individual differences.

An effective team goal-setting system requires an effective planning phase, a productive meeting phase, and an evaluation phase. All three phases are important, but without effective planning, goal setting will suffer. In addition to setting clear, measurable goals, a plan or strategy must be implemented to actually achieve the goals.

Common goal setting pitfalls include (a) poorly written and conceived goal statements, (b) failure to devise a goal-attainment strategy, (c) failure to follow the goal-attainment strategy, (d) failure to monitor performance progress, and (e) discouragement. Discouragement is often associated with goals being too difficult, too many goals, and the inappropriate use of outcome goals.

Critical Thought Questions

1. Locke and associates clearly state that a linear relationship exists between goal difficulty and performance, and that difficult goals lead to a higher level of performance. Yet, research in sport and exercise concludes that moderately difficult goals are superior to very difficult goals in facilitating performance. Discuss this apparent conflict and express your opinion on why differences in research conclusions exist.

2. If you were limited to just one type of goal, which type would you select, and why? Which type would you not select, and why? What is the wisdom and support for the multiple goal strategy concept?

3. Why was the Bar-Eli et al. (1997) study important relative to controlling for the effect of social comparison? What does this investigation show relative to goal difficulty and performance?

4. Should athletes set their own goals or should the coach be involved in this process? What does the research say about this? What are goal attributes? What do you think is the best approach in light of the Fairall and Rodgers (1997) research results?

5. Look at figure 10.3 and see if you can improve on this form. Create separate forms for an individual sport and a team sport that you are familiar with.

Glossary

action-oriented goal A goal that, when achieved, is observable in behavioral terms.

behavioral goal A goal that, when achieved, is observable and action oriented. You can see the athlete perform the goal behavior.

goal attributes The characteristics of effective goals (e.g., clarity, commitment, influence, certainty, satisfaction, acceptance, and participation). These goal attributes are precursors to good performance.

goal difficulty The difficulty associated with accomplishing a goal. For example, a goal can be considered easy, moderately difficult, or very difficult to achieve.

goal setting A theory of motivation that effectively energizes athletes to become more productive and effective through using goals.

learning strategies Effective goal setting encourages development of new ways to accomplish things.

long-range goal A goal that is distal, in the sense that it is going to take a longer time to accomplish. A number of shorter or more proximal goals will need to be achieved before the long-range goal can be realized.

measurable goal A goal whose accomplishment can be determined in a quantitative sense.

mobilizing effort By-product of effective goal setting that suggests increased effort.

multiple goal strategy A strategy in which process, performance, and outcome goals are utilized.

needs assessment A review by coaching staff of the team as a whole as well as individuals, relative to areas of needed improvement.

observable goal A goal in which goal attainment can be observed and monitored in behavioral terms.

outcome goal A goal in which the focus is upon the outcome of a sporting event and usually involves some sort of social comparison.

performance goal An end product that will be achieved by the athlete independently of other performers and of outcome.

persistence Sustained effort over a long period of time; a by-product of effective goal setting.

process goal A goal in which the focus is on a specific behavior exhibited throughout a performance.

realistic goal A goal that is realistic in the sense that the athlete believes that it can be attained.

short-range goals Goals that are achieved along the way toward achieving a long-range goal. Long-range goals are more distal, while short-range goals are more proximal.

SMART Acronym to help athletes remember that goals should be specific, measurable, action oriented, realistic, and timely.

specific goal A goal that focuses exactly on the goal to be achieved.

timely goal A goal that appropriately specifies time constraints associated with its achievement.

CHAPTER 11

Imagery and Hypnosis in Sport

KEY TERMS

Altered state of consciousness
Applied model of imagery use
Attention and arousal set theory
Central control system
Classical dissociation theory
Cognitive-behavioral
  intervention
Cognitive component of skill
Cognitive function of imagery
Cognitive intervention
Descriptionist
Dissociation
External imagery
Four Ws of imagery use
Heterohypnosis
Hidden observer
Hypnosis
Hypnotic induction
Hypnotic responsiveness
Hypnotic state
Hypnotic trait
Hypnotic trance
Imagery
Imagery perspective
Internal imagery
Kinesthetic sensitivity
Mental practice
Motivational function
  of imagery
Neodissociation theory
Neutral hypnosis

Paivio's conceptual model
  of imagery
Pictorialist
Posthypnotic suggestions
Psychoneuromuscular theory
Self-hypnosis
Social-cognitive theory

Social-cognitivist
Stress inoculation training
Stress management training
Subliminal muscle activity
Symbolic learning theory
Visual motor behavior rehearsal
Waking hypnosis

This chapter on imagery and hypnosis in sport is composed of two main sections, one focusing on the use of imagery in sport and the other on the use of hypnosis in sport. As we shall learn, hypnosis is accomplished through the assistance of attention, relaxation, and advanced imagery skills. The following quotation provides an example of perfectly realized and imagery-aided athletic accomplishment:

> And then it happened, just as they'd pictured it. Fully stretched out on his one-arm sequences. Flipping high and free above the bar. The crowd noise building, all eyes riveted, and the final tumbling release that ended with him sticking his landing as firmly as a plug into a socket. Another flawless routine. (Swift, 2004, p. 47)

This quotation describes the emotion associated with Paul Hamm's final performance on the high bar that won him the 2004 Olympic gold medal for best all-around male gymnast. Previous to this performance, Hamm had fallen from the vault, requiring a near-perfect performance on both the parallel bars and the high bar.

Imagery in Sport

Kassi Anderson of Brigham Young University won the 2003 women's 3000-meter steeplechase title at the National Collegiate Athletic Association (NCAA) National Track and Field Championships. In so doing, she set a new NCAA meet record and ran the third-fastest time in U.S. history. After the first 250 meters, she was dead last. Sticking to her preplanned assigned pace and visualizing the race from top to bottom, Kassi followed her coaches' instruction to stay close to the leader. She had been told that if she was close to the leader at the water jump, she was to pass and go. That was her plan as she visualized it, and that is exactly what she did (Reynolds, 2003).

Successful athletes use imagery and visualization to their advantage. Not all athletes are able to verbally describe exactly how they use imagery, but some can. Jack Nicklaus, one of the greatest golfers of all time, not only used imagery, but was able to describe in detail how he used it. The following quotation provides an eloquent description of how this great athlete used imagery prior to every shot:

> I never hit a shot, not even in practice, without having a very sharp, in-focus picture of it in my head. It's like a color movie. First, I "see" the ball where I want it to finish. . . . Then the scene quickly changes and I "see" the ball going there. . . . Then there is sort of a fade-out, and the next scene shows me making the kind of swing that will turn the images into reality. (Nicklaus, 1974, p. 79)

Other great athletes who have commented on the use of imagery in preparing for competition include Michael Jordan in basketball, Chris Evert in tennis, Greg Louganis in diving, Mike Piazza in baseball, and Nancy Kerrigan in figure skating. Clearly, imagery has been useful for great athletes. It is also instructive to hear how figure skaters utilized imagery in a controlled scientific investigation. Garza and Feltz (1998) randomly assigned elite figure skaters into a control condition and two different experimental imagery conditions. One imagery condition used a paper drawing exercise in which skaters traced with a pencil their imagined moves on ice. A second condition did a walk-through on the ice and imagined their skating moves along the way. The control condition simply engaged in stretching. When the post-intervention skating performance of the three groups was compared, no differences were observed between the imagery groups, but significant differences, favoring the imagery groups, were observed between the control group and the imagery groups.

Imagery is a **cognitive intervention** technique that we will discuss in detail in this section. Topics to be discussed include (a) defining imagery, (b) mental practice as a form of imagery, (c) theories of why imagery works, (d) imagery perspective and sensory mode, (e) measurement of imagery, (f) conceptual models for studying imagery, (g) research and the four Ws, (h) developing imagery skills, and (i) cognitive-behavioral interventions using imagery and relaxation.

CONCEPT   When used in conjunction with actual practice, mental practice effectively enhances motor performance. Mental practice by itself is more effective than no practice, and in certain circumstances is as effective as actual practice.

APPLICATION   In order to realize maximum performance, athletes should be taught to mentally practice sports skills in conjunction with actual practice. In addition, mental practice should be used by itself in situations where actual practice is not practical (e.g., waiting in the locker room).

Defining Imagery

Imagery has been defined as "using all the senses to re-create or create an experience in the mind" (Vealey & Greenleaf, 2001, p. 248). An expansion of this brief definition clarifies that (a) an image can be created in the mind in the absence of any external stimuli, (b) an image may involve one or all of the senses, and (c) an image is created from information stored in the sensory register, working memory, or long-term memory.

Block (1981) identified imagery as one of the most important topics in cognitive science. Two general theories have evolved. The first states that when we imagine a scene in our mind's eye, we are scanning an actual image that has somehow formed in our brain. This is not to say that a brain surgeon could find actual physical pictures lodged in our brain, but that the images are as real to us as an image taken from the retina of the eye. This position is held by the so-called **pictorialists.** The second position in that of the descriptionists. The **descriptionist** argues that there is no such thing as a mental image. That is, when we imagine a physical scene in our mind's eye, we are not really seeing an internal image, but the graphic and detailed nature of our language makes it seem so. Our thoughts, as it were, actually manufacture an image so clear that we think we are seeing one.

Regardless of whether the pictorialist or the descriptionist perspective is most accurate, the images seem very real to us. Most everyone has experienced either dreams or daydreams that are so vivid and lifelike that for a moment we truly believe they are real.

Imagery is the language of the brain. In a real sense, the brain cannot tell the difference between an actual physical event and the vivid imagery of the same event (Fisher, 1986). For this reason, imagery can be used by the brain to provide powerful repetition, elaboration, intensification, and preservation of important athletic sequences and skills.

The powerful effect of images and thoughts is highlighted by a study reported by Hale and Whitehouse (1998). They presented skilled soccer players with videos of critical game situations in which either the word "challenge" or the word "pressure" was flashed on the screen. The word "pressure" resulted in an increase in self-reported anxiety and a decrease in self-confidence compared to the presentation of the word "challenge." The images we see influence the emotions we feel, which in turn influence how we perform.

Other terms that have been used as synonyms to imagery include *cognitive and symbolic rehearsal, mental rehearsal, visualization,* and *mental or covert practice.* Some distinction, however, can be made between imagery and mental practice. In the case of learning, imagery is used by the learner in conjunction with physical practice to strengthen the learning pattern. Used in this way, imagery is referred to as mental practice. In the case of performance preparation, imagery is used to prime or prepare the athlete for correct execution of a physical skill. Used in this way, imagery is referred to as mental rehearsal (Rushall & Lippman, 1998). In the following section we will discuss the specific role and function of mental practice in learning.

CONCEPT   The more skillful and experienced an athlete is, the more he will be able to benefit from the use of mental practice.

APPLICATION   To avoid discouraging young athletes from the use of mental practice, make sure that they are familiar enough with the activity to know the difference between a good and a bad performance. An athlete must know what a skill looks like and how it feels in order to effectively mentally practice it.

Mental Practice as a Form of Imagery

The **mental practice** literature is very instructive relative to the general application of imagery to sport. Among other things, the mental practice literature provides evidence that imagery is an effective cognitive process for enhancing learning and performance of motor skills. Excellent literature reviews conclude that mental practice is more effective than no practice, but less effective than physical practice. Mental practice used in a complementary fashion with physical practice often yields the best results (Feltz & Landers, 1983; Grouios, 1992; Hinshaw, 1991). The literature suggests that in addition to physically practicing a sport skill, the athlete should spend a small amount of time rehearsing execution of the skill in her mind. Mental practice can occur prior to actual physical practice (mental rehearsal), or it can occur at a time when physical practice is not possible (e.g., while traveling, in the locker room, while resting). Research with mental practice has also revealed several principles that enhance the effectiveness of mental practice.

Skill Level of the Athlete   An important finding associated with mental practice is that advanced performers benefit from mental practice to a much greater extent than beginners (Feltz & Landers, 1983). Clark (1960) compared the effect of mental practice with that of physical practice in the learning of the Pacific Coast one-hand basketball foul shot. He placed 144 high school boys into physical and mental practice groups on the basis of varsity, junior varsity, or novice experience. All subjects were given a 25-shot pretest before and a 25-shot posttest after 14 days of practice (30 shots per day). Results showed that mental practice was almost as effective as physical practice for the junior varsity and varsity groups, but physical practice was far superior to mental practice for the beginners. Corbin (1967a, 1967b) observed similar results using a wand-juggling task. From the results of these studies, it seems clear that for mental practice to facilitate performance, a certain amount of skill is necessary. In other words, a coach or teacher should not expect mental practice to be effective with athletes who are unskilled in their sports. The more skillful they are, the more useful mental practice will be for them.

Cognitive Component of the Skill   Mental practice is most effective for activities that require some thinking and planning (Hird, Landers, Thomas, & Horan, 1991; Ryan & Simons, 1981). Different sports skills vary as a function of the amount of cognitive processing that is required. A finger maze would be an example of a task that has a large **cognitive component.** The most challenging aspect of learning to move through a finger maze is remembering when to turn left and right. This is something that can be learned in advance, and then the task becomes quite easy. Mental practice should be very helpful in a task of this nature. Mental practice should be less effective in a motor task that has a small cognitive component. A bench press in weight lifting would be an example of a motor skill that would seem to have a small cognitive component. Later, we will learn that imagery

CONCEPT   Mental practice is more effective in enhancing the learning of a motor skill that has a large cognitive component than in enhancing learning of one with a large motor component.

APPLICATION   Mental practice is an important adjunct to the learning of almost all sport skills.

However, it is important to recognize that the beneficial effects of mental practice will be greater for tasks that have a larger cognitive component. This should not discourage the athlete from using mental practice in all sports situations, but it will help to explain why it is more effective in one situation than in another.

CONCEPT   In the case of quality physical practice, more seems to be better, but in the case of quality mental practice, more is not necessarily better.

APPLICATION   There may be an optimal amount of time that an athlete can mentally practice a

physical task in one sitting. Once that amount of time has been exceeded, continuing to mentally practice may yield diminishing returns. An athlete should be encouraged to mentally practice a task until attention fades, and then to turn to other things.

has both a cognitive and a motivational function. It is possible that weight lifting could benefit from the motivational use of imagery, but not from its cognitive use.

Time Factors and Mental Practice   When it comes to mental practice, more is not necessarily better. Using a basketball task, Etnier and Landers (1996) demonstrated that when an athlete holds physical practice constant, mentally practicing for one to three minutes is more beneficial than mentally practicing for five to seven minutes. In this same study it was also demonstrated that mental practice preceding physical practice may be more beneficial than mental practice following physical practice. This gives greater credence to the use of mental rehearsal immediately prior to competition.

Theories of Why Imagery Works

While a great deal of research has been published relative to the effectiveness of imagery and mental practice in sport, sport psychologists know very little about the reasons they are effective or how they work. Why should mentally practicing or imaging a physical task result in improved learning and performance? A number of possible explanations to this basic question have been proposed (Grouios, 1992; Hecker & Kaczor, 1988; Janssen & Sheikh, 1994; Murphy & Jowdy, 1992). For the sake of brevity and simplicity, only three theoretical explanations will be discussed.

Psychoneuromuscular Theory   **Psychoneuromuscular theory** posits that imagery results in subliminal neuromuscular patterns that are identical to the patterns used during actual movement. Even though the imagined event does not result in an overt movement of the musculature, subliminal efferent commands are sent from the brain to the muscles. In a sense, the neuromuscular system is given the opportunity to "practice" a movement pattern without really moving a muscle. A study reported by Jowdy and Harris (1990) confirms that increased electrical activity in the muscles is associated with mental practice and imagery, regardless of the type of imagery used (kinesthetic or visual). Additional research reported by Slade, Landers, and Martin (2002) and Smith and Collins (2004) continued to provide evidence of subliminal electrical activity in the muscles of passive limbs during imagery. However, subliminal activity does not necessarily mirror the electrical activity of the physically involved limb. Nevertheless, it is believed that imagery assists the brain in developing a motor schema for executing a particular motor pattern. Psychoneuromuscular theory is the most plausible explanation for why imagery facilitates physical performance and learning.

Symbolic Learning Theory **Symbolic learning theory** differs from psychoneuromuscular theory in that subliminal electrical activity in the musculature is not required. Mental practice and imagery work because the individual literally plans her actions in advance. Motor sequences, task goals, and alternative solutions are considered cognitively before a physical response is required. The shortstop in softball provides an excellent example of this theory in action. Prior to each pitch to the hitter, the shortstop cognitively reviews in her mind the various possible events and the appropriate response for each event. If there is one out in the eighth inning, the bases are loaded, and the score is tied, the shortstop's play will depend upon the type of ball that is hit to her. By mentally rehearsing the various stimuli and possible responses before each pitch, the shortstop can improve her chances of making the correct play.

Two compelling true stories of what can happen when preplanning or imagery use is not utilized is provided. One example comes from a local boys' high school basketball game and the other from the author's experience of watching a Little League Baseball game. In the basketball example, the boys' basketball team seemed to have the game "in the (proverbial) bag." With 1.2 seconds left in the game, Hickman High School had the ball, a one-point lead, and its star player on the free-throw line to shoot two shots. The first shot was missed, so the Hickman coach instructed the shooter to miss his second shot and pulled the other four players back to the half-court line. There seemed to be no way that Hickman could lose the game, unless the star player tried to get the rebound and fouled an opposing player in the process—which he did! The fouled Rock Bridge player went to the free-throw line and won the game (Baer, 2002).

The second example involved 12-year-old boys in a Little League Baseball game. The game was in the last inning with the home team holding a 2 to 1 lead, two out, and a runner on third base. So, think to yourself: if the ball is hit on the ground, where is the play? Yes, the play is at first base. Every infield player should have been mentally rehearsing the play in the event the ball were hit to him. What happened, though, was that the ball was hit on the ground to the pitcher, who fielded the ball cleanly and threw a strike to home plate in time to easily tag the runner on third base out. But the catcher, who expected the play to be to first, was not even looking at the pitcher or the runner charging from third base; he was looking towards first base as the ball whistled by his head. The runner scored, the game went into extra innings, and the other team eventually won the game.

Attention and Arousal Set Theory **Attention and arousal set theory** combines the cognitive aspects of symbolic learning theory with the physiological aspects of psychoneuromuscular theory. Imagery serves to improve performance in two ways. From a physiological perspective, imagery may help the athlete to adjust his arousal level for optimal performance. From a cognitive perspective, imagery may help the athlete to selectively attend to the task at hand. If the athlete is attending to a task-relevant image, he is less likely to be distracted by irrelevant stimuli.

In the final analysis, the best theory might be eclectic in nature and include elements of all three theories (or more). From a logical perspective, it would seem impractical to exclude any one of these theories in favor of another.

Imagery Perspective and Sensory Mode

There are two factors to take into consideration when discussing the use of imagery by athletes. The first is the perspective from which imagery is practiced, and the second is the sensory mode from which imagery is experienced.

Imagery Perspective There exist two perspectives from which imagery can be applied. The two **imagery perspectives** are internal and external. In **internal imagery,** the athlete imagines herself executing a sport task from within her own body. Shut your eyes and imagine for a moment that you have a basketball in your hand and you are preparing to shoot a free throw. If your perspective at this moment is from within your body looking toward the basket, this is an example of internal imagery. You imagine yourself bouncing the ball a few times, you position yourself for the shot, and you shoot. What do you see? You see your hand releasing the ball and traveling toward the basket. However, you do not see the rest of your body. Internal imagery is very natural for us, because this is the way we actually see the world when we execute a sport skill.

Conversely, external imagery is very unnatural to us. In **external imagery** the athlete imagines herself to be outside of her body watching from a distance. Let's take the basketball free throw example again. Shut your eyes and imagine you are going to shoot a free throw—only this time, imagine that you are outside your body, watching yourself from a distance. You see yourself bounce the ball a few times, position yourself for the shot, and then shoot it. You can see all of

these things. You can see, for example, that your right foot is about six inches in front of your left foot, and you notice that your elbow is pointing toward the basket immediately prior to the release of the ball. External imagery provides an excellent perspective from which to observe skill technique and form.

We might assume that internal imagery is superior to external imagery because it is more natural to us. However, it might be the case that because the internal perspective is the natural state of affairs, external imagery might add something new and unique to our perspective. The uniqueness might actually make external imagery more beneficial from a performance enhancement perspective.

Sensory Mode Earlier we defined imagery as "using all the senses to recreate or create an experience in the mind." Notice that this definition includes the notion that all of the senses are involved in imagery. This would include vision, hearing, smell, taste, and proprioception (feel). Proprioception is a broad term that refers to tactile and kinesthetic input to the brain. **Kinesthetic sensitivity** informs the brain about movements in the joints and in the muscles.

Both internal and external imagery utilize all five of the body's senses, although different sport skills may benefit more from one perspective than from another (Hardy & Callow, 1999). It has generally been believed, however, that internal imagery utilizes kinesthetic sensitivity to a greater degree than external imagery. This conclusion is based on investigations that have demonstrated greater **subliminal muscle activity** in muscles associated with internal as opposed to external imagery (Barr & Hall, 1992; Harris & Robinson, 1986). These findings have led many sport psychologists to conclude that an internal imagery perspective is superior to an external perspective. This conclusion, however, is premature, because research support has been found for both perspectives.

A recent study reported by Hardy and Callow (1999) is of particular interest because it shows strong support for the efficacy of an external

CONCEPT Both internal and external imagery perspectives are effective in enhancing learning, retention, and performance of sport skills. Both perspectives utilize visual and kinesthetic input as well as smell, sound, and taste.

APPLICATION In teaching athletes to use imagery, do not emphasize the use of one imagery perspective at the expense of another; rather, teach the athlete to use both perspectives, as both provide important ways of mentally practicing or rehearsing a motor skill. In learning to use imagery, it is important to try to experience all five senses. Imagining the sound, smell, and taste of peak performance may, in some cases, be more powerful than "feeling" or "seeing" it.

imagery perspective in combination with kinesthetic imagery. Three separate experiments were reported involving three different closed-loop sport tasks in which form was believed to be important. The three closed-loop tasks (closed to environmental influences) included a karate sequence, a floor gymnastics sequence, and an indoor rock-climbing task. Participants were randomly assigned to one of four experimental conditions. The four conditions were combinations of internal and external imagery with or without a kinesthetic focus. Overall, results of the study concluded that an external imagery perspective with a kinesthetic focus is superior for learning and retention of a motor task that requires good form.

Measurement of Imagery

A plethora of questionnaires have been developed and proposed for the measurement of various aspects of imagery. An incomplete list of questionnaires on imagery is provided in table 11.1. The

TABLE 11.1 | An Incomplete List of Imagery Tests Categorized as a Function of Controllability, Style, Use, and Vividness

Imagery Aspect	Questionnaire Name	Source
Controllability	Gordon's Test of Imagery Control (GTIC)	Richardson (1969)
	Group Test of Mental Rotations (GTMR)	Vandenberg & Kuse (1978)
Preferred Style	Individual Differences Questionnaire (IDQ)	Paivio (1971)
	Preferred Imagic Cognitive Style (PICS)	Isaacs (1982)
Imagery Use	Imagery Use Questionnaire (IUQ)	Hall, Rodgers, & Barr (1990)
	Imagery Use Questionnaire for Soccer (IUQ-S)	Salmon, Hall, & Haslam (1994)
	Sport Imagery Questionnaire (SIQ)	Hall, Mack, Paivio, & Hausenblas (1998)
	Exercise Imagery Questionnaire–Aerobic Version (EIQ-AV)	Hausenblas, Hall, Rodgers, & Munroe (1999)
Imagery Vividness	Questionnaire on Mental Imagery (QMI)	Betts (1909)
	Shortened Form of Questionnaire on Mental Imagery (SQMI)	Sheehan (1967)
	Vividness of Visual Imagery Questionnaire (VVIQ)	Marks (1973)
	Movement Imagery Questionnaire (MIQ)	Hall & Pongrac (1983)
	Vividness of Movement Imagery Questionnaire (VMIQ)	Isaac, Mark, & Russell (1986)
	Revised Movement Imagery Questionnaire (MIQ-R)	Hall & Martin (1997)

Gymnasts use imagery to learn complicated floor exercises. Courtesy University of Missouri–Columbia Sports Information.

questionnaires in this list are first categorized as a function of purpose. Within categories, the questionnaires are listed chronologically by publication date.

Imagery *controllability* refers to the amount of personal control an individual has to change and manipulate images. It is believed that greater personal control is related to imagery effectiveness. Imagery *style* reflects individual differences in the way an individual approaches imagery. Imagery *use* reflects how often an athlete uses imagery and for what purpose. Imagery *vividness* rates the clarity, strength, and distinctiveness of images. In conducting research involving imagery, it is often necessary to take into consideration the athlete's imagery ability in terms of controllability and vividness.

Relative to imagery use, research by Weinberg, Butt, Knight, Burke, and Jackson (2003) demonstrated that imagery frequency is highly correlated with the athlete's belief that imagery is effective. With this in mind, it is instructive to note that Weinberg et al. (2003) further observed that (a) athletes use imagery predominantly before competition, (b) male athletes report using it more frequently than female athletes, and (c) pressure situations precipitate more frequent use of imagery.

Conceptual Models for Studying Imagery

Paivio (1985) clarified that imagery has both a cognitive and a motivational function. The **cognitive function of imagery** is the use of mental imagery to experience specific sports skills and to plan strategies in advance of competition. The **motivational function of imagery** is the use of imagery to experience goal attainment, effective coping, and arousal management. One function is primarily cognitive, while the other is primarily motivational. An athlete can use imagery to plan a winning strategy (cognitive function) or to get energized for competition (motivational function).

Paivio's Two-Dimensional Model Paivio further conceptualized the practice of imagery to be either situation-specific or general in nature. Thus, **Paivio's conceptual model of imagery** is two-dimensional in nature. The cognitive function could be either situation-specific or general, and the motivational function could be either situation-specific or general. Utilizing Paivio's two-dimensional model, Hall, Mack, Paivio, and Hausenblas (1998) developed the Sports Imagery Questionnaire (SIQ) for the purpose of measuring how an athlete uses imagery. In the process of developing the SIQ inventory, they discovered that Paivio's model best fits the data if the motivational-general dimension is divided into arousal and mastery components. As revised by Hall, Mack, Paivio, and Hausenblas (1998)

FIGURE 11.1 | Combination of imagery purpose and application yields five different imagery types.

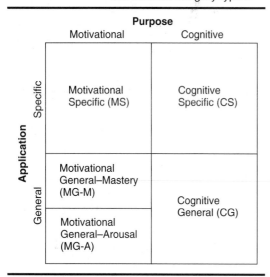

and measured by the SIQ, Paivio's two-dimensional model for imagery use is as illustrated in figure 11.1.

As can be observed in figure 11.1, five different independent types of imagery use are hypothesized. Consistent with Martin, Moritz, and Hall (1999), the five imagery types are these:

1. *Motivational Specific (MS)*   In this type of imagery, the athlete imagines herself in a specific setting that is highly motivating. For example, the athlete might imagine herself making the winning basket in an important basketball game.

2. *Motivational General–Mastery (MG-M)*   In this type of imagery, the athlete imagines himself in a general sport situation exhibiting the ability to remain focused. For example, the athlete might imagine himself thinking positive thoughts every time he comes to bat during an important game.

3. *Motivational General–Arousal (MG-A)*   In this type of imagery, the athlete imagines herself in a general sport situation exhibiting

the ability to control anxiety. For example, the athlete might imagine using deep breathing to stay relaxed during a tennis match.

4. *Cognitive Specific (CS)*   In this type of imagery, the athlete imagines herself correctly executing a specific sport skill during competition. For example, the athlete might imagine chipping a ball onto the green in a golf tournament.

5. *Cognitive General (CG)*   In this type of imagery, the athlete imagines himself reviewing team defensive strategies in volleyball. For example, he might imagine the team shifting the defensive formation to defend against a quick attack from the middle.

As indicated, these five types of imagery use are measured by the different subscales of the SIQ. In completing the SIQ, the athlete is asked to indicate how she uses 30 different verbally described images. In a study reported by Short, Monsma, and Short (2004), athletes were additionally asked to indicate if they used the image for one of five different functions. The five different functions were written to correspond to the five subscales measured by the SIQ. Results of the study showed a strong correlation between the measured subscale and the selected function, providing evidence of test validity. However, the results also showed that different athletes may use the same image for different functions, which underscores the principle of individual differences.

Based on Paivio's basic framework of imagery use and the work of Hall et al. (1998) to develop the five-factor structure of the SIQ, Martin, Moritz, and Hall (1999) proposed an **applied model of imagery use** in sport. The model as depicted in figure 11.2 shows that depending on the sport situation, the type of imagery use selected determines the outcome. In the model, the effect of imagery type on outcome is moderated or determined by imagery ability. The model predicts that the specifics of outcome are dependent upon the

CONCEPT Using Paivio's two-dimensional framework, five different types of imagery can be conceptualized. Each type of imagery can be utilized by the athlete for a specific purpose.

APPLICATION Paivio's framework for conceptualizing the uses and purposes of imagery makes it much easier for the coach to help an athlete use imagery for a specific purpose. Imagery can be used to enhance skill execution or planning, or it can be used to motivate the athlete in an array of specific and general situations.

FIGURE 11.2 | Illustration showing the Martin et al. (1999) applied model of imagery use in sport.

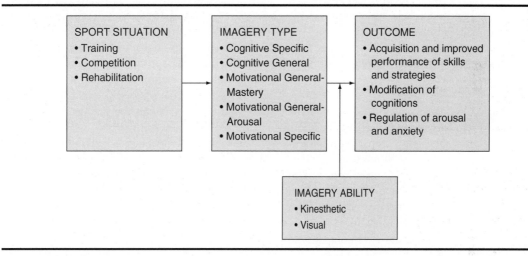

Source: Martin, S. E., Moritz, S. E., & Hall, C. R. (1999). Imagery use in sport: A literature review and applied model. *The Sport Psychologist, 13:* page 248, figure 1. Adapted with permission from Human Kinetics (Champaign, IL).

type of imagery used. For example, the model predicts that in the competitive situation the application of a cognitive specific type of imagery will result in the enhanced performance of a specific skill. Specific outcomes for each type of imagery for each sport situation are predicted by Martin et al. (1999). This is clearly an important advance in our understanding of how imagery works to facilitate performance, cognition, and regulation of arousal and anxiety.

The applied model of imagery use illustrated in figure 11.2 provides researchers with many testable hypotheses. At the present time we don't know the specific links between imagery types and outcomes, but many hypotheses can be formed. The notion that imagery ability moderates (determines) the relationship between imagery use (type) and outcome is also a testable hypothesis. A first step in this direction was an investigation reported by Cregg, Hall, and Nederhof (2005). In this study the imagery use, imagery ability, and performance of 100 Canadian track and field athletes were measured. Results showed that these athletes used motivational general–mastery imagery (MG-M) most often and motivational specific (MS) the least, and that they were more adept at visual than kinesthetic imagery. The specific hypothesis that cognitive specific imagery (CS) would predict track and field performance and that this relationship would be moderated by imagery ability was not supported. While this initial test of the model was not positive, the Martin et al. (1999) model requires further testing. In this particular study the researchers felt that part of the problem was the way in which performance was measured and conceptualized.

Research and the Four Ws

In the following section, recent research that can be categorized under the heading of the four Ws will be discussed. This includes *where* imagery occurs, *when* imagery occurs, *what* is occurring relative to the content of imagery, and *why* or for what purpose imagery occurs.

Where and When Imagery Occurs with Athletes
From Munroe et at. (2000) we know that most imagery takes place either during training or during competition, with most taking place in situations associated with competition. Within training, most imagery takes place during practice, but some also takes place at home or away from the practice field. Relative to competition, imagery takes place before, during, and after competition, with most taking place before competition in the form of mental rehearsal. Adding to this information is the observation that a high correlation exists between off-season and in-season use of imagery, with more highly skilled athletes using imagery the most in both situations (Cummings & Hall, 2002).

Content or Quality of Imagery Use—the What
The content or "what" of imagery use is graphically illustrated in figure 11.3. From this figure we can see the six aspects (column 1) of content as well as the specific divisions of each aspect. Focusing upon type of imagery (5th aspect in column 1), we see that the four types of imagery include visual, kinesthetic, auditory, and olfactory (column 2). We would argue that the sense of taste (gustatory) should be included as a potential

imagery type and that each type of imagery, not just visual imagery, should be considered relative to vividness and perspective (internal, external). Relatively recent research that may be considered under the content of imagery rubric will now be discussed.

Just as we talked about the distinction between intensity and direction of anxiety in chapter 8, we may also talk about the intensity and *direction of imagery* distinction in imagery. Specifically, it has been demonstrated that imagery can be conceptualized or presented in ways that are either facilitative or debilitative for performance (Nordin & Cumming, 2005; Short et al., 2002). Research using golf and dart-throwing tasks has generally shown that debilitative imagery causes a decrement in both self-efficacy and performance. An example of debilitative imagery would be to imagine a putted golf ball approaching the hole on line, but in the last second passing below the cup.

Observing a videotape of oneself performing a motor task is a form of imagery called *self-modeling*. Investigations by Ram and McCullagh (2003) and Smith and Holmes (2004) used volleyball and golf, respectively, to demonstrate this concept. In the Smith and Holmes (2004) study the following four modalities were contrasted: (a) using a written imagery script of successful putting, (b) watching a video of themselves successfully putting, (c) hearing the ball being struck and drop in the hole, and (d) a control condition. Results showed that watching oneself successfully putt the ball into the hole was most effective in terms of postintervention performance.

Using female aerobic exercisers, Wilson, Rodgers, Hall, and Gammage (2003) established a link between imagery use and *self-determination* (autonomy). Imagery use was determined using an instrument that measured imagery as a function of technique, appearance, and energy. Using a variation of the Sport Motivation Scale (SMS), self-determined motivation was measured as a function of external regulation, introjected regulation, identified regulation, and intrinsic motivation

FIGURE 11.3 | Illustration showing the content (the what) of imagery.

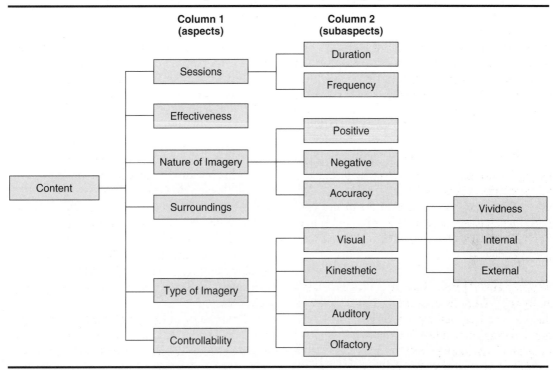

Source: Munroe, K.J., Giacobbi, P.R. Jr., Hall, C., & Weinberg, R. (2000). The four Ws of imagery use: Where, when, why, and what. *The Sport Psychologist, 14:* page 126, figure 1. Adapted with permission from Human Kinetics (Champaign, IL).

(see figure 5.6 in chapter 5). Results show a strong association between autonomous regulation and the uses of imagery. The weakest association was observed to be between external regulation and imagery use. Exercisers who are highly motivated by external rewards (low autonomy) do not use imagery very much for purposes of improving technique, improving appearance, or increasing energy.

Just as a link between imagery use and self-determination has been established, a link or association between imagery and *goal perspective* has also been established. Harwood, Cummings, and Hall (2003) administered the Perceptions of Success Questionnaire (see chapter 6) and the Sport Imagery Questionnaire to 290 young male and female athletes for the purpose of determining their

imagery use and their dispositional goal orientation (e.g., task/goal). Using a statistical technique known as cluster analysis, the athletes were clustered into three distinct goal orientation groups: (a) low task/moderate ego, (b) moderate task/low ego, and (c) high task/high ego. Then, using multivariate procedures, researchers tested the athletes for differences in imagery use among the three clusters. Results of the investigation revealed that athletes who were high in both task and ego goal orientation also exhibited the highest imagery use for all five imagery types (see fig. 11.2).

A study reported by Calmels and Fournier (2001) informs us about the *time component* of imagery. Twelve elite female gymnasts were asked to perform their artistic floor routines physically as well as mentally. Simultaneously, the times to complete the routines were recorded and compared. Results showed that mental movement times were shorter than physical floor exercise routine times.

Imagery Use and Function: The Why   As illustrated in figure 11.2, the expectation is that imagery use leads to certain desirable outcomes. These desired outcomes are the reasons the athlete engages in imagery. That is, the athlete might engage in cognitive imagery to improve technical skill in executing a sport skill (e.g., forehand tennis stroke), or engage in motivational general–arousal to reduce somatic anxiety prior to competition. Current research informs us about the different ways that imagery can influence outcome factors listed in figure 11.2.

Research suggests that facilitative imagery is effective in improving performance in various sport skills (Nordin & Cumming, 2005; Short et al., 2002). Whether or not imagery improves performance is believed to depend on the degree to which it adds additional information to the performer/learner (Cummings & Ste-Marie, 2001). Hardy (1997) said it best this way: "Imagery exerts a beneficial effect on the acquisition and performance of a motor skill only to the extent that the generated images supplement the useful information that would otherwise be available to the performer" (p. 289).

In addition to performance, imagery has been shown to be effective in improving anxiety control, motivation, and confidence in an elite rugby player (Evans, Jones, & Mullen, 2004); imagery vividness of elite female softball players (Calmels, Holmes, Berthoumieux, & Singer, 2004); anxiety control and self-efficacy of novice rock climbers (Jones, Mace, Bray, MacRae, & Stockbridge, 2002); sport confidence of high-level badminton players (Callow, Hardy, & Hall, 2001); and attentional abilities of national-level softball players (Calmels, Berthoumieux & d'Arripe-Longuerville, 2004).

In addition to the cause-and-effect relationships discussed in the previous paragraph, a number of associations have been observed involving imagery use and frequency. Studies reported by Abma, Fry, Yuhua, and Relyea (2002) and Callow and Hardy (2001) showed a strong relationship between different measures of imagery and sport confidence, with the more confident athlete enjoying superior imagery use and ability. Finally, an investigation involving exercisers showed a relationship between imagery use and gender, exercise frequency, and type of exercise (Gammage, Hall, & Rodgers, 2000). Results showed that regardless of gender, frequency of use, or activity type, exercisers used imagery most for improved appearance (cognitive) followed by technique (cognitive) and energy (motivational). In addition, men used imagery more than women, women used appearance imagery more than men, and high-frequency exercisers used all types of imagery more often than low-frequency exercisers. In terms of exercise type, runners used appearance imagery less than weight lifters and aerobic dancers; and weight lifters used technique imagery more than the other exercise types.

Developing Imagery Skills

Detailed practical suggestions for helping athletes to improve and develop imagery skills are provided by Vealey and Greenleaf (2001). Different aspects and characteristics of imagery ability that an athlete might want to develop are found in figure 11.3. Training programs designed to improve and magnify the content of images generally focus upon enhancing controllability and vividness of the images seen. A sample six-step program to enhance imagery ability is provided below:

1. Find a quiet place where you will not be disturbed, assume a comfortable position, and relax completely before beginning. Deep breathing and progressive relaxation are a suggested way to achieve the relaxed state.

2. Practice imagery by visualizing a colored circle that fills the visual field initially and then shrinks to a dot and disappears. Make the circle turn a deep blue. Repeat the process

CONCEPT When considering imagery use for athletes, it is helpful to consider the where, when, what, and why of imagery use.

APPLICATION The where and when of imagery use has to do with the particular situation in which imagery is used. Typically, it is used most often prior to competition. The why of imagery use has to do with whether you are using imagery to motivate or to make cognitive modifications in skill execution or strategy. The what of imagery use has to do with the actual nature and content of the images. When teaching athletes to use imagery, consider the where, when, what, and why of its use.

CONCEPT Imagery ability can be improved with practice. The more effective an athlete is at controlling the vividness and content of mental images, the more effective imagery will be in terms of cognitive restructuring and motivation.

APPLICATION The effective use of imagery is just like any other skill: it must be practiced and refined. Provide the athlete with specific suggestions as to how imagery ability can be improved and with specific suggestions relative to its application.

several times, imagining a different color each time. Relax and enjoy the spontaneous imagery that arises.

3. Create the image of a simple three-dimensional glass. Fill the glass with a colorful liquid; add ice cubes and a straw. Write a descriptive caption underneath the image.

4. Select a variety of scenes and images and develop them with rich detail. Include sport-related images such as a swimming pool, a tennis court, and a beautiful golf course next to the ocean. Practice visualizing people, including strangers, in each of the scenes.

5. Imagine yourself in a sport setting of your choice. First, imagine that you are watching other people perform the skill or sport that you are keenly interested in. Project yourself into the image as if you were one of the performers. Imagine yourself successfully performing the task in the scene. Change the sport setting and repeat the process again.

6. End the session by breathing deeply, opening your eyes, and slowly adjusting to the external environment.

Cognitive-Behavioral Intervention Programs Using Imagery and Relaxation

In this section we will discuss three different cognitive-behavioral intervention programs that link imagery and relaxation together into one comprehensive program. A **cognitive-behavioral intervention** is one that combines a cognitive component, such as images, with a behavioral component, such a relaxation. Research has demonstrated that individualized packaged intervention

CONCEPT   VMBR is an effective intervention program that incorporates principles derived from relaxation training and imagery to reduce anxiety, focus attention, and enhance performance.

APPLICATION   An athlete who suffers from the debilitating effects of anxiety, as well as a nonaffected athlete, can benefit from Visual Motor Behavior Rehearsal.

programs are more effective than nonindividualized programs in which participants select their own strategies. Athletes benefit most from intervention strategies that are designed to fit their needs and are presented in a systematic and organized fashion.

Cognitive-behavioral intervention programs designed for performance enhancement and arousal control have one thing in common: they all include a linkage between relaxation training and imagery. The basic notion is that imagery use is enhanced through relaxation training (Suedfeld & Bruno, 1990).

The three cognitive-behavioral intervention programs to be introduced in this section include Visual Motor Behavior Rehearsal (VMBR), Stress Inoculation Training (SIT), and Stress Management Training (SMT). A summary of the essential components of all three is provided in table 11.2.

While our focus will be upon these three intervention programs, this is not to imply that these are the only programs that are available, or that others are less effective.

Visual Motor Behavior Rehearsal (VMBR)

Visual motor behavior rehearsal (VMBR), originally called visuo-motor behavior rehearsal, was developed by Suinn (1972, 1994) as an adaptation of Wolpe's (1958) desensitization procedures for humans. The process of desensitization was used to help patients to overcome phobias. For example, a patient who feared heights would be desensitized to this phobia through a series of systematic approximations to the fearful stimuli. Although Suinn used VMBR to treat people with depression, he was especially interested in applying the technique to athletes. His particular method of training consisted of (1) relaxing

TABLE 11.2 | Summary of Three Cognitive-Behavioral Intervention Programs That Utilize Imagery and Relaxation

Intervention Program	Characteristic Steps
Visual Motor Behavior Rehearsal (VMBR)	1. Relaxation training for mastery
	2. Practice of imagery in sports-related environment
	3. Sport-specific application of imagery and relaxation
Stress Inoculation Training (SIT)	1. Conceptualization phase
	2. Skills acquisition phase (relaxation, imagery, problem solving, cognitive restructuring)
	3. Inoculation against stress through small manageable steps
Stress Management Training (SMT)	1. Conceptualization of stress phase
	2. Skills acquisition phase (relaxation, imagery, problem solving, cognitive restructuring)
	3. Practice managing strong emotional stress responses

the athlete's body by means of a brief version of Jacobson's progressive relaxation techniques, (2) practicing imagery related to the demands of the athlete's sport, and (3) using imagery to practice a specific skill in a lifelike stressful environment. More recently, Suinn (2000) has referred to VMBR as anxiety management training (AMT).

Basically, VMBR combines relaxation and imagery into one procedure. It also requires the

Football offensive linemen benefit from the cognitive and motivational functions of imagery. Courtesy University of Missouri–Columbia Sports Information.

CONCEPT Similar to VMBR, SIT effectively reduces stress and has been shown to enhance performance of subjects.

APPLICATION The principle of gradually exposing a fearful athlete to situations of progressively greater threat is one that can be readily applied by the practitioner. As the athlete masters the skills of relaxation and imagery, he will be better prepared to cope with situations of increased difficulty.

---

athlete to mentally practice a specific skill under simulated game conditions. Theoretically, this would be better than actual practice, since the practice environment rarely resembles a game situation. Coaches and teachers typically go to great lengths to minimize distractions to their athletes during practice sessions. VMBR teaches the athlete to use relaxation and imagery techniques to create lifelike situations. Going through these stressful experiences mentally should make it easier to deal with the stress of actual competition. Suinn generally recommends the use of internal imagery for VMBR training, but suggests that in addition the athlete should use external imagery to identify performance errors.

Numerous investigations have been reported that demonstrate that VMBR is effective in enhancing athletic performance, as well as in reducing the debilitating effects of overarousal and state anxiety. These include studies involving basketball (Gray & Fernandez, 1990; Kolonay, 1977), karate (Seabourne, Weinberg, & Jackson, 1984), tennis serving (Noel, 1980), pistol shooting (Hall & Hardy, 1991), and archery (Zervas & Kakkos, 1995). In summary, it appears that VMBR training is effective in reducing an athlete's negative affect relative to the sports tasks mentioned above. Furthermore, the potential for VMBR training to improve athletic performance is very good, but its effectiveness depends on the type of task, the skill level of the performer, and the athlete's ability to relax and use imagery.

Stress Inoculation Training (SIT) **Stress inoculation training** (SIT) is a cognitive-behavioral program developed by Meichenbaum (1977, 1985) that incorporates relaxation training, imagery, and other cognitive processes into a single plan. The key element of SIT is the progressive exposure of the athlete to situations of greater and greater stress as a way to inoculate the athlete against the debilitating effects of stress. SIT is composed of three phases. In the *conceptualization phase,* the focus of the sport psychologist is upon establishing a collaborative relationship with the athlete and helping him to better understand the nature of stress and its effect upon emotions and performance. This phase may include interviews, administration of questionnaires, and other strategies to assess the athlete's expectations and goals. During the *skills acquisition phase,* the major objective of the sport psychologist is to help the athlete develop coping skills such as progressive relaxation, cognitive restructuring, imaging, problem solving, and self-instructional training. In the final *application and follow-through phase,* the athlete is encouraged to implement his learned coping skills and responses in day-to-day situations. Small manageable units of stress (whatever distresses the athlete) are introduced to the subject. The athlete is first asked to imagine himself coping with progressively more threatening scenes while in a relaxed state. In this way, the athlete anticipates stressful interactions and practices

CONCEPT Similar to VMBR and SIT, Smith's cognitive-affective SMT program effectively reduces stress and has been shown to enhance performance of athletes.

APPLICATION The principle of helping an athlete to experience competition-like stress through imagery is an effective way to help the athlete overcome real-life competitive stress. The athlete who can visualize herself successfully performing a skill with associated competitive stress is more likely to transfer this ability to a real-life situation.

ways to behave or cope with them. Next, the athlete is introduced to real-life situations in which the level of stress is gradually increased, allowing the athlete to practice his learned coping strategies. In this graded way, the athlete is inoculated against stress.

Threatening situations are presented through imagery, films, role playing, and real-life situations. For example, if the fear of competition is stressful, the athlete is allowed to experience both imagined and real competitive situations. As soon as the athlete is able to cope with a low level of stress, the situation is changed, and a more stressful situation is presented. In this way, the athlete becomes inoculated against progressively increasing levels of stress. Eventually, the athlete's fear of competition is minimized to such a degree that he can cope with it.

Research with SIT in athletic situations has demonstrated its effectiveness in reducing stress and increasing athletic performance in basketball (Hamilton & Fremouw, 1985), gymnastics (Kerr & Leith, 1993), rappelling (Mace & Carroll, 1985), squash (Mace & Carroll, 1986), and cross-country running (Ziegler, Klinzing, & Williamson, 1982), as well as in increasing athletes' pain tolerance (Whitmarsh & Alderman, 1993).

Stress Management Training (SMT) **Stress Management Training** (SMT) is a cognitive-behavioral intervention program developed by Smith (1980) that incorporates relaxation training, imagery, and other cognitive processes. Like Stress Inoculation Training (SIT), SMT is composed of three stages. The significant difference between the two stress management programs is in stage three. SIT emphasizes the ability to manage small incremental changes in stress, while SMT practices managing stress associated with imagined high-stress situations.

In phase one of SMT, the *conceptualization of stress phase,* the athlete is taught to understand the nature of stress generally, and to understand the source of her stress specifically. She learns what causes stress and how to cope with it. During this phase she also learns that she already possesses a number of useful coping strategies for dealing with stress. In phase two, the *skill acquisition phase,* the athlete learns and practices integrated coping responses. The coping responses are based on relaxation, imagery, deep breathing, and other cognitive-behavioral skills. She learns to "trigger" these coping skills through cognitive self-statements. In phase three, the *skill rehearsal phase,* induced affect is used to generate high levels of emotional arousal, which are reduced by the subject through the application of coping responses learned during skill acquisition. In SMT, the athlete is asked to imagine as vividly as possible a relevant stressful situation. Research supports the use of SMT for reducing stress and for enhancing athletic performance (Crocker, 1989).

Hypnosis in Sport

Like imagery, hypnosis is a cognitive-behavioral process that has both a cognitive function and a motivational function. In a cognitive sense, hypnosis is used to restructure the way athletes think about themselves and about the way they execute and learn new sport skills. In a motivational sense, hypnosis is used to modify emotions, reduce anxiety, increase or decrease arousal, and increase effort. In the initial induction phase, hypnotism is physiologically identical to progressive relaxation, autogenic training, and meditation. All of these intervention strategies are associated with reductions in oxygen consumption, respiration rate, and heart rate (Benson et al., 1974; Coleman, 1976). Yet, following the acceptance of a hypnotic suggestion, the hypnotized individual might display heightened physiological characteristics consistent with motivational suggestions given.

Perhaps because it is poorly understood, hypnosis is not a widely utilized intervention strategy in sport. Nideffer (1992) is one of the few sport psychologists who advocate its use on a broad scale. Even then, Nideffer recommends the use of self-hypnosis more often than heterohypnosis. The reasons for this will be discussed in greater detail in later sections of this chapter.

A dated but well-known application of hypnosis took place before the first heavyweight boxing match between Muhammad Ali and Ken Norton in 1973. Norton reportedly hired a professional hypnotist to help him bolster his self-confidence and reduce prematch anxiety. Norton won the match in a stunning upset, effectively calling attention to hypnosis as a viable intervention strategy.

A case study in which hypnosis was used to help an amateur boxer was documented by Heyman (1987). In this chronology, a single-case experimental design was presented in which hypnosis was systematically used as an intervention strategy. The athlete was described as suffering a performance decrement due to anxiety caused by crowd noise. As a result of the controlled and professionally applied use of hypnosis, the athlete was able to show some improvement. While there may be some potential risks associated with the indiscriminate use of hypnosis by an untrained therapist, most concerns about hypnosis are unfounded. It is probably fair to say that hypnosis is more clouded by myths and misconceptions than any other form of psychological intervention.

In the pages that follow, our discussion of hypnosis in sport will focus upon (a) defining hypnosis, (b) theories of hypnosis, (c) the hypnotic trait issue, (d) facts about hypnosis, (e) achieving the hypnotic trance, (f) self-hypnosis, (g) improving effective use of hypnosis, and (h) hypnosis and athletic performance.

Defining Hypnosis

Providing a simple, widely agreed-upon definition of hypnosis is difficult. It appears that you can obtain as many authoritative definitions of hypnotism as there are authorities to give one. Interestingly, though, most, but not all, will contain the word "suggestion" within the definition. The term *hypnosis* comes from Hypnos, the Greek god of sleep (Kalat, 1999), even though it has long been known that hypnosis is not related to sleep. It may, however, be related to sleepwalking (Weitzenhoffer, 2000). Here are a few definitions that have been offered of **hypnosis:**

> "The uncritical acceptance of a suggestion."
> (Ulett & Peterson, 1965, p. 13)
>
> "A procedure wherein changes in sensations, perceptions, thoughts, feelings, or behaviors are suggested." (Kirsch & Lynn, 1995, p. 846)
>
> "An induced condition associated with, not just of, hypersuggestibility, and . . . better described as a suggestibility heightening state." (Weitzenhoffer, 2000, p. 229)
>
> "An induced temporary condition of being, a state, that differs mentally and physiologically from a person's normal state of being." (Weitzenhoffer, 2000, p. 221)

The first three definitions all focus upon the word "suggestion" or "suggestibility." Thus, it is

CONCEPT There is general agreement among psychologists that hypnosis is closely associated with the notion of being responsive to suggestions.

APPLICATION If an athlete is already responsive to suggestions, then other forms of intervention such as relaxation, meditation, and imagery may be just as effective as hypnotism.

---

generally agreed among psychologists that hypnosis is associated with a situation in which suggestions are more readily accepted and acted upon. The last definition, however, elicits a wide number of dissenters as well as advocates. Clearly, psychologists can agree that hypnosis is closely linked with a heightened suggestibility, but are divided on the efficacy of the last definition. It appears that psychologists cannot agree on the notion that hypnosis is an altered state of consciousness, or even on what an altered state of consciousness is. This is to say, however, not that they fall into two polarized camps on the issue, but that they likely fall along a continuum ranging from total acceptance of the altered state of consciousness concept to total dismissal of the notion (Kirsch & Lynn, 1995). In the next section of this chapter we will discuss three specific theories of hypnosis relative to the state issue.

Theories of Hypnosis

Weitzenhoffer (2000) briefly discusses eight different perspectives on the hypnotic state. We will briefly discuss three of these perspectives, or theories. The first two represent extreme positions on the issue of the existence of a hypnotic state, while the third represents a compromise position that has been embraced by many psychologists. The theories to be discussed are (a) social-cognitive theory, (b) hypnosis as an altered state of consciousness, and (c) neodissociation theory.

Social-Cognitive Theory **Social-cognitivists,** led by Sarbin (1989) and Spanos (1991), basically reject the notion of a separate hypnotic state, preferring to look upon hypnosis as an interpersonal

process. Subjects carry out hypnotic behaviors because they have positive attitudes, motivations, and expectations that lead to a willingness to think and imagine using themes suggested by the hypnotist. Therapists who are of the **social-cognitive theory** school of thought believe in the use of hypnotism as a method of increasing a client's willingness to accept suggestions, but they do not believe that this state of uncritical acceptance of suggestions represents an altered state of consciousness.

Hypnosis as an Altered State of Consciousness At the other extreme are psychologists who believe that hypnotized individuals enter into an **altered state of consciousness** known as a trance. It is believed that the trancelike state is different from the normal waking state, and also different from other non-hypnotically-induced states such as daydreaming and relaxation. While in the **hypnotic state** or **trance,** the individual is susceptible to suggestions made by the hypnotist. Those psychologists who espouse the altered state of consciousness viewpoint are generally followers of Erickson (1980).

Neodissociation Theory **Classical dissociation theory** (Prince, 1929) was based on the notion that two tasks can achieve a state or condition of functional independence when one task is performed subconsciously. When functional independence is achieved (dissociation), the performance of the two tasks (one subconsciously) ought to result in less interference than when both are performed consciously. The inability of psychologists to demonstrate this reduction in interference led to a decrease of interest in the theory. Interest in dissociation theory was revived when Hilgard (1973, 1986, 1994) proposed his notion of neodissociation theory. Interestingly, neodissociation theory is described by Kirsch and Lynn (1995) as being close to social-cognitive theory in terms of the altered state notion, while Weitzenhoffer (2000) describes it as being the state theorist's "current favorite hypothesis."

Hilgard (1994) uses **neodissociation theory** to explain hypnosis without suggesting that the hypnotic trance is responsible for the phenomenon associated with hypnosis. Daydreaming and relaxation are considered by many theorists to be examples of the altered state of consciousness that we experience every day. We drive to work each day with our minds focused on anything but the drive, then suddenly arrive at our destination with little recall of the actual drive. This is a form of hypnosis, or what is referred to as **dissociation.**

Hilgard's neodissociation theory is based on two assumptions: (a) there is a **central control system** that performs planning and monitoring functions in the brain; and (b) beneath the central control system there are relatively autonomous subordinate cognitive-behavioral systems (e.g., movement control, perception, memory). In the normal state, the two control systems work in harmony with each other. In the hypnotic trance state, however, the two systems are dissociated from each other. *Hypnotic suggestions are believed to act upon the central control structure, causing it to create a communication barrier that separates a segment of itself from conscious awareness.*

Consider the following ideal situation for studying neodissociation theory. A blind man is hypnotized and a suggestion is given to him that he will not be able to hear sounds. To test this situation, the hypnotist bangs two cymbals together near the spot where the subject is sitting. The resultant sound is loud enough to elicit a startle response in any normal unsuspecting individual, yet in this situation, there is no startle response. This is evidence that the blind man is now also deaf, due to the acceptance of the hypnotic suggestion.

In the next stage of the experiment, the therapist speaks to the "deaf" individual and suggests to him that there exists in his brain a "**hidden observer**" who is able to hear things that he is unable to hear. He then asks the subject to move his finger if he can hear his voice. The subject responds by moving his finger. This entire intriguing situation can be reproduced, under laboratory conditions, in 50 percent of highly hypnotically susceptible subjects (Weitzenhoffer, 2000). The phenomenon of the hidden observer and the separation of the central control structure into two insulated compartments is illustrated in part (b) of figure 11.4. Part (a) of the figure shows the normal coordinated relationship between the central control structure and one subordinate cognitive-behavioral system (perception of hearing). The central control system is completely aware of both input and output to the hearing perception subcontrol system. The two are in perfect coordinated harmony.

Part (b) of figure 11.4 illustrates the phenomenon of hypnosis as explained by neodissociation theory. *In response to a suggestion, the subconscious part of the central control structure attenuates the perception of sound without the knowledge of the conscious part of the central control structure.* Even though the subject does not consciously hear the sound of the cymbals, he is aware of the sounds via the hidden observer. Thus, we have an explanation of how it is that through a hypnotic trance, the unconscious part of the central control system is able to maintain contact with the subordinate control system for hearing perception, while the conscious part is not (except for the hidden observer).

The Hypnotic Trait Issue

The previous discussion on the hypnotic state is independent and unrelated to the notion of the hypnotic trait. A hypnotic state is a situation-specific response to hypnotic suggestions and induction, while the **hypnotic trait** is more of a personality disposition toward **hypnotic responsiveness.** There are at least three principles that

CONCEPT   Some individuals will be more responsive to hypnosis and hypnotic suggestions than others. Through proper preparation, most individuals can benefit from hypnosis, but not all.

APPLICATION   Some athletes will be good candidates for hypnosis, but others will not be. If an athlete wants to try hypnosis as an intervention to help him with some problem such as anxiety, refer him to a therapist who is proficient and skilled in its use.

FIGURE 11.4 | Neodissociation model showing how a hypnotized individual responds to a suggestion.

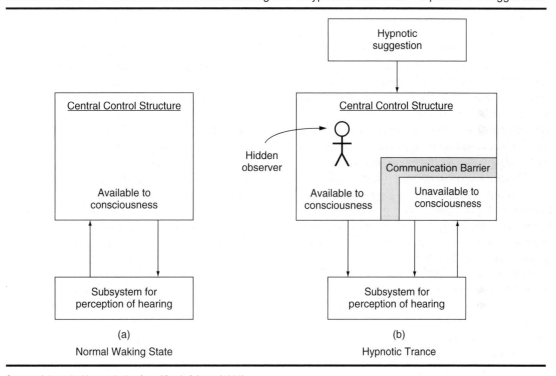

Source: Adapted with permission from Kirsch & Lynn (1998).

can be identified relative to the trait issue (Kirsch & Lynn, 1995):

1. Hypnotic responding does not require any particular skill or abilities. When proper procedures are used, almost anyone can become highly responsive to suggestion.

2. Hypnotic responding requires some stable imaginative inclination or other cognitive abilities. This alone, however, is not sufficient to produce suggested responses. The individual must be sufficiently convinced that she is capable of responding and be motivated to that end.

3. It is likely that responsiveness to the most difficult suggestions, such as amnesia and hallucinations, requires a rare aptitude that cannot be taught.

Facts about Hypnosis and Its Application

Psychologists are divided on what the hypnotic trance is, and on whether there is such a thing as an altered state of consciousness relative to hypnosis, but they are in general agreement about the application of hypnosis (Kirsch & Lynn, 1995).

1. The ability to experience a hypnotic phenomenon does not indicate gullibility or personality weakness.

2. Hypnosis is not the same as sleep, nor is it related to sleep.

3. Hypnotic responsiveness depends more on the efforts and abilities of the individual being hypnotized than on the skill of the therapist.

4. While hypnotized, individuals retain the ability to control their behavior, are aware of their surroundings, and can monitor events outside the framework of suggestions given during hypnosis.

5. Spontaneous amnesia or forgetting is relatively rare following hypnosis.

6. An individual does not need to be hypnotized to be responsive to suggestions.

7. The function of a hypnotic induction is to increase suggestibility to a minor degree.

8. Hypnosis is not a dangerous procedure when practiced by qualified researchers and clinicians.

9. Most hypnotized individuals are not faking compliance to suggestions or merely going along with suggestions to be cooperative.

10. Hypnosis cannot increase the accuracy of memory.

11. Hypnosis does not precipitate a literal re-experiencing of childhood events.

Achieving the Hypnotic Trance

Five phases are associated with inducing the hypnotic trance in a participant. They are preparation of the participant, the induction process, the hypnotic phase, waking up, and the posthypnotic phase.

Preparation of the Participant   When participants are prepared for hypnotism, they must be relieved of any fears and apprehensions they have about hypnotism. Some myths may need to be exposed. For example, participants may be under the impression that they will lose control, that they will be unaware of their surroundings, or that they will lose consciousness. They must have complete trust in the hypnotist and must want to be hypnotized. They also must be told that they will remain in control at all times and will be able to come out of the hypnotic trance if they want to.

Induction Phase   It is during the **hypnotic induction** phase that the hypnotist actually hypnotizes the participant. There are many induction techniques. The best ones are associated with relaxation, attentional focus, and imagery. In fact, the steps involved in eliciting the relaxation response using these techniques are essentially identical to those in hypnosis. The only difference is that the word *hypnosis* is never used in eliciting the relaxation response. It should also be pointed out that in terms of physiological responses, hypnotic induction is identical to the relaxation responses associated with progressive relaxation, transcendental meditation, and autogenic training.

Generally, induction procedures are fairly standard. They are typically composed of a series of suggestions aimed at eliciting the participant's cooperation and directing his attention to thoughts and feelings about being relaxed and peaceful. The selection of an induction technique is generally based on the hypnotist's comfort with it, or her belief that the participant's attentional style or personality is compatible with it. Some of the more common techniques involve fixation on an object, monotonous suggestions ("you feel sleepy"), and imagery. Regardless of which technique is used, the effect is the same. The participant becomes very lethargic, experiences the relaxation response,

Athlete focusing on self-hypnotic suggestions while stretching. Source: © Royalty-Free/Corbis.

and becomes very susceptible to suggestions. The hypnotist can use a number of techniques to help the participant become more responsive to hypnotism. Most of these are associated with relaxing the participant and gaining his confidence. Others include using the word *hypnotism* to define the situation and the manner in which suggestions are given. For example, a good time to suggest to the participant that he is becoming tired is when the hypnotist observes that the participant's eyelids are drooping. The hypnotist must also avoid making suggestions that the participant may fail.

Hypnotic Phase   Once the hypnotic state has been induced, the subject is in **neutral hypnosis.** In this state, physiological responses are identical to those of the relaxation response. The hypnotized participant is generally asked to respond, either in imagination or physically, to suggestions of the hypnotist. Typically, these suggestions are alerting and arousing, and bring about the "alert" trance, or

waking hypnosis. If participants are asked to carry out suggestions while in a trance, they are doing so in the state of waking hypnosis. Participants may, of course, be given suggestions of deep relaxation while in the hypnotic state. Generally, participants will be given suggestions to carry out after they are awake. These are referred to as **posthypnotic suggestions.** Ken Norton was given posthypnotic suggestions for his fight with Muhammad Ali.

Waking Up   The fourth phase of hypnosis is coming out of the trance. Actually, a hypnotized participant can come out of the trance anytime. The only reason participants do not come out on their own is that they don't want to. The relationship between the hypnotist and the participant can be a very pleasant one. When the hypnotist wishes to bring a participant out of a trance, she does so simply by suggesting that the participant wake up on a given signal. For example, the hypnotist

CONCEPT Self-hypnosis, or autohypnosis, can be just as effective as heterohypnosis, and does not place the athlete in a situation of dependence.

APPLICATION If hypnosis skills are taught, self-hypnosis is preferable to heterohypnosis. Self-hypnosis is very similar to autogenic training, meditation, and relaxation.

---

might say, "Okay, when I count to three you will wake up." Occasionally a participant will resist coming out of the trance. If this happens, the participant is taken back into a deep trance and asked why he doesn't want to come out. After a few minutes of discussion and another suggestion to wake up, the participant will generally do so.

Posthypnotic Phase Suggestions given to participants during hypnosis are often designed to influence them during the posthypnotic phase, or after they have come out of the hypnotic trance. Posthypnotic suggestions given to athletes should focus on the way they should feel in certain competitive situations. For example, a baseball player may be told, "when you get into the batter's box, you will find that you feel relaxed and confident." Specific suggestions such as "you'll be able to get a hit almost every time," should be avoided, since failure will tend to undermine the effectiveness of the suggestions.

Self-Hypnosis and Avoiding Negative Suggestions

There are two kinds of hypnosis. The first kind is **heterohypnosis,** and the second is **self-hypnosis,** or autohypnosis. Our discussion up to this point has focused on heterohypnosis, that which is induced by another person, usually a trained therapist or psychologist. Heterohypnosis should be practiced only by skilled professionals. Heterohypnosis is based upon a delicate rapport and trust between the therapist and the client. During periods of hypersuggestibility, the athlete is vulnerable to inadvertent negative suggestions from the

hypnotist. A qualified psychologist will be able to avoid making these kinds of mistakes. Having said this, it is also instructive to understand that heterohypnosis is really an extension of self-hypnosis. In heterohypnosis, the participant is hypnotizing herself, with the assistance of the therapist (Kirsch & Lynn, 1998). Therefore, all hypnosis is really self-hypnosis, and all the benefits associated with heterohypnosis are also available in self-hypnosis.

There are two kinds of self-hypnosis. The first is self-induced, and the second is induced as a posthypnotic suggestion following heterohypnosis. The latter method is easier to achieve. In this method, participants are told during hypnosis that they will be able to hypnotize themselves anytime they wish simply by following some relaxation and attentional focus induction procedures. Because they have already been hypnotized, they know how it feels and they enjoy the feeling. Therefore, it is much easier for them to hypnotize themselves. With each repetition of self-hypnosis, it becomes easier and easier to achieve. What initially begins as relaxation will later become effective hypnosis, as subjects learn to narrow their field of attention.

The phases involved in self-hypnosis are identical to those outlined for hypnosis generally. If a coach or teacher wishes to employ self-hypnosis as an intervention strategy for reducing anxiety and improving concentration and imagery, he should go over these steps with the athlete. First, the athlete must be completely comfortable regarding the use of hypnosis. The athlete should begin with the reminder (suggestion) that he is in complete control and can disengage from the hypnotic trance at any time. The induction procedures are the same as those for heterohypnosis. Some common strategies for induction are to sit in an easy chair and stare at a spot on the wall, imagine a blank screen, or look into a mirror.

Posthypnotic suggestions given during self-hypnosis should always be couched in positive terms, stressing what is to be accomplished rather than dwelling on negative things to be eliminated (Wegner, 1997). For example, the athlete may wish to concentrate on being more positive when she prepares to receive a tennis serve from a tough opponent. A suggestion such as "I will feel relaxed and agile" would be better than "I'm going to hit a winner." The second suggestion contains the seeds of defeat, since you can't always hit a winner. Suggestions such as "I won't feel nervous" are negative, because they call attention only to the problem. The athlete should have specific suggestions already in mind before the hypnotic phase begins. In some cases, the athlete could have the suggestions written on a card that she could read during the hypnotic trance.

In our earlier discussion of positive or facilitative imagery, it was emphasized that imaging a success is positive and leads to an increase in performance as well as an increase in self-efficacy (Nordin & Cumming, 2005; Short et al., 2002). This same research also showed the *devastating negative effect of imaging a failure* (e.g., imaging the putt missing the hole). This concept is further reinforced by research reported by Beilock, Afremow, Rabe, and Carr (2001), in which an attempt to repress a negative thought was found to be counterproductive. The reason negative thought repression is ineffective is that it calls attention to the negative thought that the individual is trying to avoid. It is better to focus completely on positive thoughts and images and to avoid negative images altogether. A case in point is a true story that was shared with the author by a parent. As you reflect on this story, remember the power of suggestion as it relates to self-hypnosis.

> I was standing at the far end of the track with my daughter's coach prior to a state championship hurdling event my daughter was about to run in.

> It had rained the night before and despite attempts to dry the track out with new cinders and soil, there were still a few soft spots on the track. As my daughter came around the track on her final warm-up lap, the coach stopped her and said to her, "There is a soft spot in the track at the far end of the track as you begin your final turn. Be careful as you make your jump in that area." That was it and that is all he said, but I had a sickening feeling as the race began and even more as she rounded the fateful turn. Sure enough, as she hit the soft spot she slipped and missed the hurdle. I never really blamed the coach for calling attention to a negative image, but I also knew instinctively that he had inadvertently planted a negative thought in my daughter's mind. (N. Kaluhiokalani, personal communication, June, 1990)

As I have thought about this story, I have often reflected on what the coach could have done differently. Rather than calling attention to the negative image of a slip, he could have instructed her to take a few practice jumps around the track, including in the affected area. Thus, without his calling attention to a negative outcome to avoid, the athlete could have found out for herself how the turf felt and formed positive images of navigating the course.

Improving the Effectiveness of Hypnosis

Taylor, Horevitz, and Balague (1993) identify five factors that can influence the effectiveness of hypnosis. The first factor is the competence of the professional therapist, or the skill of the athlete if autohypnosis is being employed. The therapist attempting to induce a hypnotic trance or teaching self-hypnosis skills must be well trained in all aspects of hypnosis. Second, the quality of the relationship between therapist and individual being hypnotized is important. The individual must have complete confidence and trust in the therapist. Third, the therapist must do her homework and get to know the person being hypnotized. A failure to have a deep understanding of the athlete's goals

CONCEPT Giving negative suggestions to hypnotized individuals must be guarded against. Positive suggestions may result in a benefit to performance, but negative suggestions almost always are detrimental to performance.

APPLICATION It may seem obvious that one should not give negative suggestions to athletes, whether they are under hypnosis or not. The inexperienced coach or sport psychologist may, however, give negative suggestions without realizing it. For example, telling a hurdler to watch out for soft ground on the first turn of a race may be the equivalent of a negative suggestion, if it is too late for a practice run.

---

and aspirations could be counterproductive. Fourth, effective outcomes require practice of the procedures and instructions given during hypnosis. Considerable effort on the part of the athlete receiving hypnosis is required for best results. Finally, it works best if therapist and athlete both recognize the limitations of hypnosis. Hypnosis will be of little help in overcoming major physical limitations. An athletic injury, for example, needs time to mend.

Hypnosis and Athletic Performance

Is hypnosis effective in facilitating athletic performance? Research on this topic yields a number of basic principles that can be summarized. These important principles are based on extensive reviews and published articles (Baer, 1980; Ito, 1979; Johnson, 1961; Morgan, 1972; Morgan & Brown, 1983; Ulrich, 1973). A list of basic principles gleaned from the literature is provided below, along with some commentary.

1. The more open and susceptible an athlete is to suggestions, the more likely it is that he will benefit from suggestions given to him under hypnosis. This is also the type of individual who is more likely to be hypnotized.

2. Once an individual is hypnotized, the deeper the trance is that she is able to achieve, the more likely it is that suggestions given under hypnosis will be effective.

3. Positive suggestions are effective in facilitating performance, regardless of whether or not the athlete is hypnotized. This principle underscores the importance of uncritical acceptance of suggestions from the teacher or coach. If an athlete will accept positive suggestions uncritically, it makes little difference whether she is hypnotized at the time or not.

4. General arousal techniques are more useful than hypnotic suggestions in enhancing muscular strength and endurance. Hypnosis tends to relax an athlete. Muscular strength and endurance activities require increased levels of arousal and activation, not relaxation.

5. Negative suggestions almost always cause a decrement in performance. This is perhaps the most important principle of all. Negative suggestions given to an athlete under hypnosis are particularly powerful. Negative suggestions given to an athlete at any time can be counterproductive. Often, negative suggestions are given inadvertently.

6. Hypnosis may be able to help a successful athlete, but it cannot make a good performer out of a poor one. A lot of practice, goal setting, and physical ability are required to accomplish this.

If properly used, hypnosis may be effective in enhancing the suggestibility of athletes. The heightened suggestibility of athletes may lead to cognitive or behavioral adjustments that may facilitate performance (Pates, Cummings, & Maynard, 2002; Pates, Cummings, Maynard, & Westbury, 2000; Pates, Maynard, & Westbury, 2001; Pates, Oliver, & Maynard, 2001). Several of the studies reported by Pates and colleagues also show an association between hypnosis intervention and increased Flow. Recall that the concept of Flow was discussed in chapter eight and that it is associated with attentional focus and with a positive mental attitude.

In conclusion, it is important to not overstate the effectiveness of hypnosis in improving athletic performance. Positive suggestions are beneficial to the athlete, regardless of whether the athlete is hypnotized or not. Hypnosis is not effective in enhancing muscular strength and endurance. Finally, a real danger exists in inadvertently giving an athlete a negative suggestion while he is in a state of hypersuggestibility.

Summary

Imagery is the process of using all the senses to recreate or create an experience in the mind. Other terms that have been used as synonyms to imagery include cognitive and symbolic rehearsal, mental rehearsal, visualization, and mental practice. The mental practice literature provides evidence that imagery is an effective cognitive-behavioral process for enhancing learning and performance of motor skills.

Factors that moderate the relationship between imagery use and performance enhancement include the skill level of the athlete and the cognitive component of the skill. The higher the skill level of the athlete and the larger the cognitive component of the skill, the stronger the relationship between imagery and enhanced performance.

Theories of why imagery use enhances learning and performance of sport skills include psychoneuromuscular theory, symbolic learning theory, and attention and arousal set theory. In the final analysis, the best theory might be eclectic in nature and include elements of all three theories.

The process of imagery takes place from both an internal perspective and an external perspective. Regardless of which perspective is used, all of the body's senses are utilized. Recent research suggests that an external perspective with a focus upon kinesthetic sensitivity is most beneficial for performance enhancement.

Fourteen different imagery questionnaires were listed and categorized relative to imagery aspect measured. Questionnaires were categorized relative to the imagery aspects of controllability, preferred style, imagery use, and vividness.

Paivio's conceptual model of imagery includes a cognitive function and a motivational function. Each of these two functions are categorized as being situation-specific or general. The motivational-general dimension of imagery use was further categorized as being mastery- or arousal-related. Thus the five types of imagery use include motivational-specific (MS), motivational general–mastery (MG-M), motivational general–arousal (MG-A), cognitive specific (CS), and cognitive general (CG). The four Ws of imagery use are where, when, what, and why.

Training programs designed to improve and magnify the content of images focus upon enhancing controllability and vividness of the images seen. A sample six-step program designed to enhance imagery ability was presented.

Three cognitive-behavioral intervention programs that include imagery and relaxation were introduced and discussed. These include visual motor behavior rehearsal, stress inoculation training, and stress management training.

Hypnosis is defined as a procedure wherein changes in sensations, perceptions, thoughts, feelings, or behaviors are suggested. Psychologists differ on what is meant by an altered state of consciousness relative to hypnosis. Three different perspectives on the notion of a hypnotic state or trance were discussed. These were the social-cognitivist perspective, the altered state of consciousness perspective, and the neodissociation theory perspective.

A hypnotic state is a situation-specific response to hypnotic suggestions and induction, while the hypnotic trait is more of a personality disposition toward hypnotic responsiveness. Hypnotic responding requires some stable imaginative inclination or cognitive abilities.

Eleven specific facts about hypnosis were listed. Included among these facts were the following: (a) responsiveness to hypnotic suggestions is not a sign of personality weakness, (b) hypnotic responsiveness depends more on the subject being hypnotized than on the hypnotist, (c) an individual does not need to be hypnotized to be responsive to suggestions, and (d) the function of a hypnotic induction is to increase suggestibility to a minor degree.

Five phases are associated with inducing the hypnotic trance in a subject. They are preparation of the subject, the induction process, the hypnotic phase, waking up, and the posthypnotic phase. Hypnotic suggestions and posthypnotic suggestions are given during the hypnotic phase.

Heterohypnosis involves a therapist as well as the subject, whereas self-hypnosis involves only the subject. Heterohypnosis is really an extension of self-hypnosis, because the therapist is only helping the subject hypnotize herself. All the benefits associated with heterohypnosis are also available in self-hypnosis.

Six principles were identified from research on hypnosis and athletic performance. If properly used, hypnosis may be effective in enhancing the suggestibility of athletes. It is important, however, not to overstate the effectiveness of hypnosis in improving athletic performance. Positive suggestions are beneficial to the athlete, regardless of whether the athlete is hypnotized or not.

Critical Thought Questions

1. How might imagery be used to help a fumble-prone running back in football? Devise a plan for accomplishing this goal.

2. Many sport psychologists have suggested that an internal perspective for imagery use is superior to an external perspective. Why do they claim this, and why might they be wrong? What would be your recommendation to an athlete relative to preferred perspective?

3. Provide some specific examples of how imagery could be used to learn team strategies and skill development.

4. Provide some specific examples of how imagery could be used to motivate an athlete to greater arousal and effort.

5. Why do you think psychologists disagree on the existence of and meaning of the hypnotic state or trance?

6. In what ways is hypnosis different from and similar to meditation?

7. If you don't believe in the reality of the hypnotic trance, can you still believe in the efficacy of hypnosis as a means to change sensations, perceptions, thoughts, and behaviors?

8. How do you feel about using hypnosis to assist athletes in anxiety reduction and performance enhancement?

Glossary

altered state of consciousness The notion that while hypnotized, the individual is in a state of consciousness that is different from the normal state of consciousness.

applied model of imagery use A conceptual model that shows causal links between sport situation, imagery use, and outcome as moderated by quality of imagery ability.

attention and arousal set theory Theory combining the cognitive aspects of symbolic learning theory with the physiological aspects of psychoneuromuscular theory to explain the phenomenon of performance enhancement through imagery.

central control system The part of the brain that has overall conscious control of human behavior and thought.

classical dissociation theory The precursor to neodissociation theory as an explanation of the hypnotic state.

cognitive-behavioral intervention An intervention for change that includes a cognitive component, a behavioral component, or both.

cognitive component of skill That part of a motor skill that may be classified as cognitive as opposed to motor.

cognitive function of imagery The use of mental imagery to experience specific sports skills and to plan strategies in advance of competition.

cognitive intervention An intervention, such as imagery, that is cognitive in nature, but may elicit an emotional response.

descriptionist An individual who argues that there is no such thing as a mental image, but that the graphic detail of our language makes it seem so.

dissociation The separation of one's autonomous behavior from conscious awareness.

external imagery Imagery in which the athlete imagines herself executing a sport skill from outside her own body.

four Ws of imagery use Refers to the where, when, why, and what of imagery use.

heterohypnosis Hypnosis utilizing the assistance of a hypnotist or psychologist trained in hypnosis.

hidden observer In neodissociation theory, it is hypothesized that the hypnotized individual has contact with the dissociated part of the brain due to the presence of a "hidden observer."

hypnosis A procedure wherein changes in sensations, perceptions, thoughts, feelings, or behaviors are suggested.

hypnotic induction The process of inducing the hypnotic trance in a subject being hypnotized.

hypnotic responsiveness A desire or willingness to be hypnotized.

hypnotic state A trancelike state associated with hypnosis.

hypnotic trait A personality disposition toward hypnotic responsiveness.

hypnotic trance The state of being hypnotized, or willing to uncritically accept suggestions.

imagery The use of all the senses to re-create or create an experience in the mind.

imagery perspective The perspective from which an athlete imagines herself performing a sport skill.

internal imagery Imagery in which the athlete imagines himself executing a sport task from within his own body.

kinesthetic sensitivity Feedback from the limbs and body parts that informs the brain about movements in the joints and in the muscles. It is one aspect of proprioception.

mental practice The use of imagery and other nonphysical processes to enhance learning and retention of a skill.

motivational function of imagery The use of mental imagery to experience goal attainment, effective coping, and arousal management.

neodissociation theory A hypnotic trance theory based on the notion of a division of consciousness.

neutral hypnosis A phase of hypnosis in which the athlete's physiological responses are identical to those observed in the relaxation response.

Paivio's conceptual model of imagery A two-dimensional model of imagery in which there are two levels of function (cognitive and motivational) and two levels of application (specific and general).

pictorialist Individual who believes that an actual image is being scanned when we visualize a scene.

posthypnotic suggestions Suggestions given during the alert hypnotic trance phase that the subject is to carry out when awake.

psychoneuromuscular theory A theory that purports to explain the phenomenon of performance enhancement through imagery based upon subliminal neuromuscular patterns.

self-hypnosis The process of hypnotizing oneself, without the assistance of a therapist.

social-cognitive theory Relative to hypnosis, the position that hypnosis is best explained as a function of a person's desire to carry out hypnotic behaviors suggested by the hypnotist.

social-cognitivist A person who subscribes to social-cognitive theory on hypnosis.

stress inoculation training A three-phase stress management program in which the goal is to "inoculate" an athlete against stress by guiding the athlete through progressively more stressful situations.

stress management training A stress management program in which the athlete practices stress-coping skills in stressful situations.

subliminal muscle activity Electrical activity in muscles suggesting movement when in fact there is no perceived movement.

symbolic learning theory A theory that purports to explain the phenomenon of performance enhancement through imagery as being based upon advance planning.

visual motor behavior rehearsal A cognitive-behavioral intervention program that uses imagery and relaxation to help athletes deal with stress.

waking hypnosis The stage of hypnosis during which the athlete is asked to carry out suggestions that may be alerting and arousing.

CHAPTER 12

Psychological Skills Training

KEY TERMS

Athlete-centered sport model
Athletic Coping Skills
  Inventory
Between-play routine
Client
Code of ethics
Needs assessment plan
Organizational empowerment
  approach
Ottawa Mental Skills
  Assessment Tool
Performance profiling
Postshot routine
Preshot routine
Psychological intervention
  program
Psychological method
Psychological skill
Psychological Skills Inventory
  for Sports
Psychological skills training
  program
Resonance
Resonance performance model
Self-regulation
Self-regulation model
Test of Performance Strategies

Seconds pour away. Agony. Elvis Grbac screams to his teammates. They scream back. The crowd screams louder. Static rushes through Grbac's helmet. It is fourth down. Two yards to go. Seconds pour away. (Elvis Grbac's baptism of fire against the Denver Broncos—Posnanski, 1998)

It is January of 1998 and the Kansas City Chiefs are trailing the Denver Broncos by four points, fourth down, two yards to go for a first down, 34 seconds left in the game, Denver's 20-yard line, Kansas City has no time-outs remaining. Grbac needs a play. The fans in Kansas City are screaming, "Call a play!" The speaker in Grbac's helmet isn't working. He can't hear the play. He looks to the sideline. The coaches are screaming, "Go for the first down!" Grbac can't hear them. He has to do something, so he calls his own play. The wrong play. He goes for the end zone, but the receiver is double teamed, and the pass is batted down. End of game, Denver wins by four.

In retrospect, we might ask, "Given the circumstances, what could Elvis have done differently?" The obvious answer is that he should have gone for the first down—but who is to know if that would have worked? One thing we do know, however, is that Elvis Grbac was not psychologically prepared to deal with that particular situation. What do you do when time is running out and your helmet speaker doesn't work?

The answer is really pretty simple. The situation that confronted Elvis Grbac on that cold January day was just one of many circumstances that he could have been confronted with. Each potential circumstance and scenario should have been visualized and considered in the calm of a practice facility days or even weeks before the situation occurred. A sport psychologist could have helped Elvis prepare for what confronted him that day. What *do* you do when there is no time left and you have to make the play that makes the difference in the outcome of the game? Isn't that what point guards in basketball, quarterbacks in football, and setters in volleyball are supposed to do? This real-life situation provides an excellent

example of why athletes need the assistance of a sport psychologist.

This chapter on psychological skills training is the culminating chapter on the general topic (Part 4) of cognitive and behavioral interventions in sport and exercise. In previous chapters in part 4, we discussed coping and intervention strategies in sport, goal setting in sport, and imagery and hypnosis in sport. We bring all of these concepts together now in this chapter on psychological skills training. In this chapter we discuss the following eight topics: (a) psychological skill characteristics of the elite athlete, (b) effectiveness of psychological intervention programs, (c) differentiating between skills and methods, (d) measurement of psychological skills, (e) ethics in sport psychology, (f) the sport psychology consultant, (g) a psychological skills training program, and (h) generalization of sport psychology methods to other application domains.

Psychological Skill Characteristics of the Elite Athlete

Studies involving Olympic and/or World Championship athletes provide us with a wealth of information about psychological characteristics of elite athletes (Durand-Bush & Salmela, 2002; Gould, Greenleaf, Chung, & Guinan, 2002; Greenleaf, Gould, & Dieffenbach, 2001). Successful athletes from the 1996 Atlanta Summer Olympics and the 1998 Nagano Winter Olympics had confidence in their ability, were able to make tactical adjustments when necessary, and were prepared for distractions. In addition, elite athletes perceived their coaches to be committed and to have realistic individual and team expectations. Compared to less successful Olympians, the more successful Olympians had a more positive attitude about the Olympics, did not complain as much about housing, and enjoyed good team unity. Durland-Bush and Salmela (2002) studied the psychological development of 10 elite international athletes across their careers. To be included in the study, the athletes had to have won at least two gold medals at Olympic or World Championship games. From a developmental perspective, it was determined that the elite athlete progressed through four stages on his way to becoming an elite athlete. These four stages included a *sampling phase,* in which each athlete engaged in numerous sports and games for pleasure; a *specialization phase,* in which he specialized in one or two sports; an *investment phase,* in which he invested significant time and energy into one sport to become a world champion; and a *maintenance phase,* in which considerable effort and energy were expended to stay on top. Personal characteristics deemed important at the investment phase included self-confidence, intrinsic motivation, and competitiveness. Personal characteristics deemed important at the maintenance phase included all of the above, plus being independent and always striving to learn and improve.

Recent studies that focused on the psychological characteristics of elite youth and collegiate level athletes are also informative (Harwood, Cummings, & Fletcher, 2004; Frey, Laguna, & Ravizza, 2003). Utilizing Division I collegiate baseball and softball athletes, Frey et al. (2003) found that measured psychological skill in both practice and competition was strongly associated with the perception of success. Utilizing 573 male and female young elite athletes (ages 14 to 20) competing in a broad range of sports, Harwood et al. (2004) categorized them as a function of goal orientation and looked for differences in psychological skills. Athletes categorized as being high in both task and ego goal orientation exhibited the highest levels of psychological skills (e.g., imagery use, goal setting, and self-talk).

Some researchers find it useful to look at psychological skill development within the structure of model development (Cleary & Zimmerman, 2001; Kitsantas & Zimmerman, 2002; Newberg, Kimiecik, Durand-Bush, & Doell, 2002). Within their **self-regulation model,** Cleary and Zimmerman define **self-regulation** as "self-generated thoughts, feelings, and behaviors that are planned and cyclically adapted based on performance feedback" (p. 187). The model begins with the *forethought phase* (goal setting, strategy

choice, self-efficacy), proceeds to the *performance phase* (strategy use, self-monitoring, self-instruction, imagery, attention focusing), and finishes with the *self-reflective phase* (self-evaluation, causal attribution, self-satisfaction), which in turn feeds back to the forethought phase. Research involving the self-regulation model shows that more successful athletes exhibit superior regulation skills at each phase of the model.

In a similar vein, Newberg et al. (2002) proposed the **resonance performance model** to explain how athletes become elite athletes. The concept of **resonance** is related to the concepts of Flow, intrinsic motivation, and emotion. Peak performance in any endeavor begins with a dream that is associated with positive feelings and emotions. To achieve the dream, the performer engages in preparation to help her achieve the dream. Preparation comes in the form of physical and psychological skill development. Along the way to achieving the dream, the athlete will be confronted with obstacles. At this point, the athlete must revisit the dream in order to become more motivated and engaged in her preparation. The key to success is that she not be caught in a loop of going back and forth between the obstacle and the preparation (working harder). She must revisit the dream so that she can again experience the positive feelings and emotions associated with the dream.

Finally, we have the **athlete-centered sport model,** which proposes that sport must contribute to the overall development of the athlete physically, psychologically, and socially (Miller & Kerr, 2002). From a psychological skills development perspective, we are always looking for ways to enhance *performance excellence* (observable, measurable athletic outcomes). That is, we want to foster the development of an athlete who can jump farther, swim faster, and generally perform at an elite level. However, from the perspective of the athlete-centered sport model, this goal is shortsighted and imbalanced. While we are striving for performance excellence, we must also be striving at the same time for *personal excellence.* Personal excellence may include performance excellence,

CONCEPT Elite athletes possess psychological skills that make it possible for them to experience unprecedented success on the athletic field. The elite athlete is self-confident, highly motivated, and competitive. The athlete-centered sport model also proposes that attention be given to developing the personal excellence as well as the performance excellence of the athlete.

APPLICATION The elite athlete starts with a dream that, through hard work and dedication,

becomes a reality. It is the sport psychologist and coaches' responsibility to provide the motivational climate that makes it possible to achieve the dream. However, even while records are being broken and performance excellence is being achieved, attention must be given to allowing the athlete to grow and develop as a total well-rounded person. The answer is not always more practice and more dedication. Sometimes the answer is simply encouraging the athlete to practice self-reflection and to develop a feeling of autonomy and personal control over his life.

---

but it also includes all those virtues that make the athlete a better person across a lifetime. As stated by Miller and Kerr (2002), "If high-level sport were delivered in a developmentally appropriate manner, both performance and personal excellence would be possible at the same time" (p. 141).

Effectiveness of Psychological Intervention Programs

A number of literature reviews have been published that verify that planned **psychological intervention programs** are effective in enhancing athletic performance (Greenspan & Feltz, 1989; Vealey, 1994; Weinberg & Comar, 1994). These reviews confirm that of approximately 45 studies reviewed, 38, or 85 percent, have found positive performance effects (Weinberg & Williams, 2006). In addition, as reported below, a number of more recent investigations have supported the effectiveness of psychological interventions.

Of a group of 115 professional tennis players, almost all said that they used some form of psychological strategy to enhance performance. Furthermore, higher-ranked players indicated that they used psychological strategies to a greater degree than lower-ranked players (DeFrancesco & Burke, 1997). In another study, 44 novice adult SCUBA divers were randomly assigned to psychological skill training programs. Compared to a

control group, members of the psychological skill training groups were effective in reducing anxiety, increasing self-confidence, reducing respiration rate, and improving performance (Terry, Mayer, & Howe, 1998). In a third study, male youth baseball players were assigned to either a weight training condition or a mental skills training program for six weeks. The mental training group made significant progress toward maintaining the skills they learned for up to three months postintervention (Grove, Norton, Van Raalte, & Brewer, 1999).

Two single-subject multiple-baseline investigations were reported by Thelwell and Greenless (2001, 2003). In this design, all participants experience a baseline followed by a stagger-start mental skills intervention phase and a postintervention phase. In the single-subject multiple-baseline design, participants start the intervention at different points along a time continuum. If the intervention is effective, a jump in performance should occur for all participants following the intervention. For both investigations, the participants took part in a gymnasium triathlon (rowing, cycling, running) using the single-subject multiple-baseline design. The main difference in the two studies was that competition was included in the later study. For both studies, results showed that a psychological skills training program that included goal setting, relaxation, imagery, and self-talk was effective in improving performance on the endurance tasks.

CONCEPT   Psychological intervention programs are effective in increasing self-confidence, focusing attention, energizing effort, and enhancing athletic performance.

APPLICATION   Sport psychologists and coaches can be confident that a well-conceived and well-administered psychological intervention program will yield desired results. A scientific principle should not be applied until a sufficient research base is developed to justify its application. This appears to be the case relative to psychological skills training. This does not mean, however, that all programs will be effective, because all are not properly conceived and administered.

In a study reported by Mamassis and Doganis (2004), the performance of five elite junior tennis players who received mental skills training and four who did not was contrasted across 25 weeks of tennis competition. Based on self-report measures of postmatch performance and selected psychological skills, the athletes who received the mental training intervention improved in performance and in self-confidence across the 25 weeks of tennis competition, while the control group did not.

Most of the reported studies involve fairly long periods of pre-intervention, intervention, and post-intervention periods of time. Two studies are of interest because they both involved very brief interventions (Arathoon & Malouff, 2004; Miller & Donohue, 2003). In the Miller and Donohue (2003) study, 90 high school long-distance runners completed two "do your best" 1.6-km runs that were separated by a 15-minute time period. Immediately following the initial run, participants were assigned to one of three equal groups in terms of running time and gender. Each group was then randomly assigned to one of three pre-run interventions: (a) listen to motivational and running technique statements, (b) listen to motivational music, or (c) use earphones but with no sound. After the three-minute intervention, the participants completed their second run in heats of five runners. Results showed that compared to the control condition, both motivation intervention groups improved their running performance. In the second study (Arathoon et al., 2004), 68 members of an adult female hockey team completed a positive affect scale 15 minutes before and 15 minutes after a game they subsequently lost. Before they completed the inventory following the game, they were divided into two groups based on their uniform numbers. The 34 members of the experimental condition completed a brief cognitive intervention in which they selected and concentrated on a positive thought for one minute and selected and concentrated on a game-related coping thought for one minute. Results showed that the experimental and control groups were equal in positive affect prior to the game, but the control group suffered a decrement in positive affect following the game, whereas the brief cognitive intervention group did not. These two studies show that even brief interventions are effective in improving performance or in maintaining positive affect following a disappointing loss.

Differentiating between Psychological Skills and Methods

Coaches and athletes often use the terms *psychological skill* and *psychological method* as synonyms, when they actually have different meanings. Vealy (1988) has clarified that **psychological methods,** techniques, or strategies refer to practices that lead to psychological skill. Examples of psychological methods include goal setting, imagery, progressive relaxation, meditation, self-talk, and hypnosis. Each of these psychological methods, when properly learned and applied, lead to enhanced psychological skill. Conversely, **psychological skill** refers to learned or innate characteristics of the athlete that make it possible or even likely that she will succeed in sport. Examples of psychological skill include intrinsic motivation, self-confidence, attentional control, arousal control, anxiety control, and general self-awareness. A case in point is imagery. Imagery is a psychological method or strategy that may be used to develop psychological skill in visualizing correct performance. It is also used in achieving optimal arousal and optimal attentional control. Similarly, goal setting, relaxation training, and thought control are methods used to develop psychological skills that lead to enhanced performance and self-confidence. Approaching a competitive situation with confidence and with the knowledge that the body and mind are prepared for optimal performance is a psychological skill.

Figure 12.1 shows how psychological methods, psychological skills, and performance outcomes relate to each other. The 12 selected psychological skills were identified by Gould, Dieffenbach, and Moffett (2002) as being possessed by 10 U.S. Olympic champions. It is also of interest to note that coaches are not particularly adept at assessing the psychological strengths and weaknesses of their athletes. Overall, Leslie-Toogood and Martin (2003) reported little agreement between volleyball coaches and their athletes, and between track coaches and their athletes, when it comes to assessing the athletes' mental skills.

Measurement of Psychological Skills

Several inventories have been developed that are designed to measure psychological skills used by athletes. Each of the inventories we will mention has demonstrated the ability to distinguish among groups of athletes performing at different levels of skill. Before adopting a specific inventory, the practitioner should become familiar with the reliability, validity, and psychometric properties of the selected inventory.

Psychological Skills Inventory for Sports

The **Psychological Skills Inventory for Sports** (PSIS-5) was developed by Mahoney, Gabriel, and Perkins (1987). The PSIS-5 is a 45-item inventory that measures the psychological skills of anxiety control, concentration, confidence, mental preparation, motivation, and team orientation. While the

FIGURE 12.1 | Illustration showing the relationship between psychological method, psychological skill, and performance outcome.

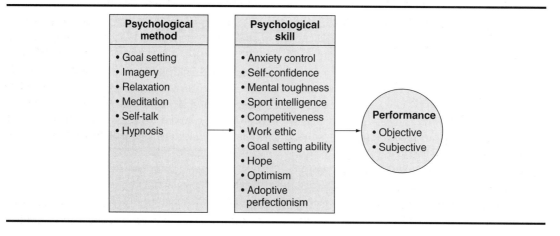

PSIS-5 has exhibited the ability to discriminate among levels of skilled performers, recent research has questioned the underlying structure of the six factors it measures (Chartrand, Jowdy, & Danish, 1992).

Athletic Coping Skills Inventory

The **Athletic Coping Skills Inventory** (ACSI-28) was developed by Smith, Schutz, Smoll, and Ptacek (1995). The ACSI-28 is a 28-item inventory that measures the psychological skills of coping with adversity, peaking under pressure, goal setting/mental preparation, concentration, freedom from worry, confidence and achievement motivation, and coachability. The ACSI-28 is a modest predictor of hitting and pitching performance among professional baseball players (Smith & Christensen, 1995).

Test of Performance Strategies

The **Test of Performance Strategies** (TOPS) was developed by Thomas, Murphy, and Hardy (1999). The TOPS is a 64-item inventory that measures a combination of methods and skills of athletes in strategic situations. Factors measured by the TOPS in the *competitive situation* include self-talk, emotional control, automaticity, goal setting, imagery, activation, negative thinking, and relaxation. Factors measured by the TOPS in the *practice situation* include the same factors used in the competitive situation, with the exception that negative thinking is replaced by attentional control. Thirty-two of the 64 items on the TOPS are related to the competitive situation, while the remaining 32 items are related to the practice situation.

Ottawa Mental Skills Assessment Tool

The **Ottawa Mental Skills Assessment Tool** (OMSAT-3) was developed by Durand-Bush, Salmela, and Green-Demers (2001). The OMSAT-3 is a 48-item inventory that measures 12 mental skill subscales (four items each). These 12 subscales are then further organized into three conceptual

components as follows: *foundation skills* (goal-setting ability, self-confidence, commitment), *psychomotor skills* (stress reactions, fear control, relaxation, activation control), and *cognitive skills* (focusing attention, refocusing attention, imagery ability, mental practice ability, competition planning). Validity testing showed that self-confidence, commitment, stress reaction, focusing, and refocusing were most important in discriminating between elite and less elite athletes.

Ethics in Sport Psychology

As you learned in chapter 1 of this text, the Association for the Advancement of Applied Sport Psychology (AAASP) is the primary organization within the United States and Canada for professionals interested in applied sport psychology. Members of AAASP are bound by a **code of ethics** that governs their interactions with the public and with other professionals. The AAASP Ethics Code is based in large part on the Ethical Principles of the American Psychological Association (1992), and is composed of a preamble, six general principles, and 25 standards (AAASP online, 2005). Readers are referred to the AAASP Web site for details of the ethics code. Here we will only paraphrase the six general principles that govern the conduct of members of AAASP.

Principle 1: Competence

AAASP members maintain a high standard of competence in their work. In this regard, they recognize the boundaries and limitations of their competence. For example, a member trained in exercise and sport science would not attempt to counsel an individual with clinical symptoms of depression. Members are continually upgrading their knowledge and expertise through workshops and inservice training.

Principle 2: Integrity

AAASP members practice and promote integrity in the teaching, science, and practice of applied

CONCEPT   Members of the Association for the Advancement of Applied Sport Psychology (AAASP) are bound by a set of ethical principles and standards that guide their conduct.

APPLICATION   Members of AAASP should read and become familiar with the ethical standards that their association subscribes to. They should also take proactive steps to conduct all of their professional interactions in accordance with these guidelines. In addition, the standards should be made available to individuals who receive professional services from AAASP members.

sport psychology. In this regard, they always present themselves and their credentials accurately and forthrightly. They do not make deceptive or misleading statements about their qualifications, products, fees, research, or services. For example, an AAASP member would not make unsubstantiated claims about a psychological application that she was using.

Principle 3: Professional and Scientific Responsibility

AAASP members take their professional and scientific responsibilities seriously. It is a member's responsibility to protect the reputation of AAASP and the public from members who are deficient in ethical conduct. In this regard, they are concerned about the ethical conduct of members whose ethical conduct is not of the highest level. For example, an AAASP member would take steps to prevent and/or expose unethical conduct in another member.

Principle 4: Respect for People's Rights and Dignity

AAASP members respect the fundamental rights, worth, and dignity of all individuals. An individual's right to confidentiality, privacy, and personal control are respected at all times. In this regard, AAASP members are sensitive to individual differences associated with gender, age, race/ethnicity, national origin, religion, disability, sexual orientation, and socioeconomic status. For example, an AAASP member would not refuse to provide the highest level of consideration to an individual on the basis of the person's gender or race.

Principle 5: Concern for Others' Welfare

AAASP members are personally concerned with and take steps to ensure the personal welfare of individuals they interact with. Conflicts between members or between members and clients are resolved in a manner which minimizes harm and maximizes the concern for the welfare of others. For example, members do not take advantage of differences in power and influence between themselves and others.

Principle 6: Social Responsibility

AAASP members have a responsibility to share their knowledge and research with members of society. In this regard, their responsibility is to contribute to the common good of society and to protect the rights of individuals as they do so. For example, members freely agree to provide workshops that will teach others how to apply principles of human development. They also agree to share their research findings in appropriate scientific settings.

Recently, Etzel, Watson, and Zizzi (2004) conducted a Web-based survey of AAASP members examining their ethical beliefs and behaviors relative to applied sport psychology. The results of this investigation provided relevant information about the beliefs and practices of AAASP members. The survey revealed that females tend to have ethical beliefs and practice ethical behaviors to a greater extent than male members. For example, female members are less willing to socialize with a client or to believe that it is ethical to do so. Relative to background training, the research revealed that members and consultants trained in counseling or clinical psychology express ethical beliefs and exhibit ethical behavior to a greater extent than those trained in physical education and exercise science. For example, the physical education teacher tended not to see anything unethical about serving concurrently as an athlete's teacher and as the athlete's sport psychologist. Last, but not least, certified AAASP consultants tend to have ethical beliefs and exhibit ethical behaviors to a lesser extent than noncertified consultants. For example, the certified consultants were more likely than noncertified consultants to have practiced without supervision or poor consultation.

The Sport Psychology Consultant

In chapter 1, we learned that there are three kinds of sport psychologists: research, educational, and counseling/clinical. These three kinds of sport psychologists, however, are not independent of one another. For example, a person could be a university professor and be involved in research, teaching, and the delivery of counseling psychology services to athletes. Another person could be in private practice, consulting with professional athletes, and teaching a course at a university on sport psychology. A case in point is a young woman named Nicki Moore who was hired by the athletic department at the University of Oklahoma to provide psychological services to athletes and to work on performance enhancement issues. Nicki is both a licensed counseling psychologist and an AAASP Certified Consultant (Thamel, 2004). The point is that there are many different kinds of sport psychologists and many different ways to consult with athletes. The important thing, however, is that there must be a match between professional training and the services delivered by the consultant.

According to Poczwardowski, Sherman, and Ravizza (2004), sport psychology service delivery should be based on a solid philosophical foundation. The consultant's philosophy can serve to provide direction when confronted with unique situations for which there exist no textbook solutions. As illustrated in figure 12.2, the model flows from the stable to the dynamic and from the internal to

FIGURE 12.2 | Illustration showing the hierarchical structure of professional philosophy.

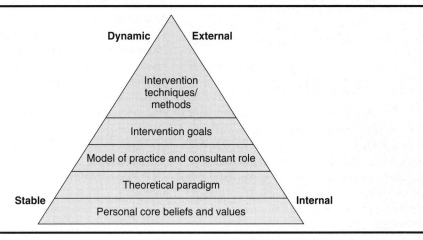

Source: Reproduced with permission of the publisher (Human Kinetics) from Poczwardowski, A., Sherman, C. P., & Ravizza, K. (2004). Professional philosophy in the sport psychology service delivery: Building on theory and practice. *The Sport Psychologist, 18,* 445–463.

the external. The foundation of the model is the *personal core beliefs* and values of the consultant. If the foundation is flawed, nothing that comes after it can be trusted. Built upon the core beliefs are the *theoretical paradigms* that the consultant operates under. Some consultants will base their approach to behavioral change on psychoanalytic theory, while others embrace a social learning approach or a humanistic approach. Built upon the theoretical paradigm embraced by the consultant is the specific *model of practice* (consultant role) favored by the sport psychology consultant. Potential models of practice include (a) the psychological skills training model, (b) the counseling model, (c) the medical model, (d) the interdisciplinary sport science model, and (e) the supervisory consulting model with an integrative approach. In the supervisory consulting model, the consultants work directly with coaches and other professionals within an organization, but do not work directly with athletes. Built upon the selected model of practice are the specific *intervention goals* that are grounded in the philosophical model as a whole. There are as many intervention goals as there are different behavioral issues and problems to deal with. Finally, built upon the intervention goals are the *intervention techniques and methods* selected by the consultants to meet the intervention goals. Every practicing sport psychology consultant should be able to describe and verbalize his professional philosophy as it relates to the services that he provides.

Having established the philosophical foundations of being a sport psychology consultant, it is instructive to see what the literature says about the actual practice of this profession. Dunn and Holt (2003) published the results of a qualitative study involving 27 members of a Canadian collegiate ice hockey team. In this investigation, the athletes were asked about their perception of the delivery of a season-long applied sport psychology program. Results showed that the athletes provided valuable insight relative to logistical issues, multiple roles played by the consultant, and the importance of

Wheelchair athletes can benefit from a psychological skills training program. Source: © Royalty-Free/Corbis.

respect and communication. The athletes appreciated and valued the time spent with the sport psychologist when coaches were not present. They recognized that it was important for the consultant to gain the respect of both the athletes and the coaching staff (multiple roles), and that communication skills were critical.

A study reported by Maniar, Curry, Sommers-Flanagan, and Walsh (2001), revealed that a random sample of 60 collegiate Division I athletes preferred to work with "sport"-titled consultants as opposed to non-sport-titled individuals (e.g., "sport psychologist" versus "psychologist"). They indicated a preference of consulting with their coach, a family member, or a friend before seeking help from a psychologist. Generally, women were found to be more receptive than men to seeking

CONCEPT   The sport psychology consultant must be grounded in terms of a professional philosophy. What are the core values of the sport psychology consultant? How do these core values influence the way that the consultant works with athletes, coaches, and other individuals associated with sport?

APPLICATION   In the examples presented in the text, Robert Rotella and Roberta Seldman both exhibited core values as they described the way in which they consult with athletes. Apply this principle by reviewing the levels shown in figure 12.2 and ask yourself about your own professional philosophy as it relates to sport psychology consulting. This will be a good exercise regardless of whether you are a student, a student/athlete, a coach, or a sport psychology consultant.

help from a sport psychology consultant. Overall, it appears that collegiate athletes are skeptical about working with psychologists of any kind because of the stigma associated with the title. Based on this research, it seems prudent that the sport psychology consultant emphasize her links to sport and to athletics generally before emphasizing her credentials as a psychologist.

Leffingwell, Rider, and Williams (2001) developed three companion inventories designed to help the sport psychologist determine if an athlete or an athletic team is in the proper frame of mind to be helped by a sport psychology consultant. The three inventories measure Stages of Change (SC), Decisional Balance (DB), and Self-Efficacy (SE). The Stages of Change inventory is composed of 32 items that classify the athlete as being in the precontemplative (not ready), contemplative (thinking about it), action (ready), or maintenance (already using) phase relative to being ready to use a sport psychology consultant. The Decisional Balance inventory is composed of 30 items that allow the athlete to weigh the pros and cons of using a consultant. Finally, the Self-Efficacy inventory is composed of 5 items that measure the athlete's belief that a sport psychologist consultant could help him.

It is instructive to hear what successful practicing sport psychologists say about their personal philosophy and approach to working with individual athletes. Robert (Bob) Rotella gave up a position in academia to work full time as a sport psychology consultant to professional golfers (primarily). As a keynote speaker at the 2003 Association for the Advancement of Applied Sport Psychology (AAASP) in Philadelphia, Dr. Rotella revealed what he believed were the three keys to his success (Rotella, 2003). He said that his three goals in working with professional athletes were to (a) get the athletes to play without fear, (b) sell the athletes on themselves, and (c) teach the athletes that they can *choose* to focus on the positive.

At a keynote address at the 2004 AAASP convention held in Minneapolis, Dr. Roberta Seldman (2004) revealed her *person-centered* approach to working with the athlete. The person-centered approach to working with athletes is to focus on the athlete as a total person. She identified three behavioral keys to working with an athlete using the person-centered approach:

1. Listen to the client without being judgmental, without appraisal, and without diagnosis.

2. Be a sensitive, empathetic, concentrated listener.

3. Allow the real person to be seen and heard.

Perhaps the most intriguing part of Dr. Seldman's presentation came when she asked one of her former clients to speak. Allison Wagner, a

CONCEPT   The initial meeting with the athletes sets the stage for the entire psychological skills training program.

APPLICATION   The initial meeting with the athletes must be well planned and organized. The psychological skills training program will be ineffective if this initial meeting does not convince the athletes of the efficacy of psychological skills training. The sport psychologist should be prepared to give concrete examples of how sport psychology can help each athlete achieve peak performance.

former Olympic medal winner in swimming, spoke from the heart about athlete burnout and what it really means to be an elite athlete. Allison's most compelling statement was this: "I didn't need coaches and sport psychologists telling me how to improve my performance—I could do that—I needed someone to see and accept who I really am." She went on to talk about the loneliness of being an elite swimmer and her quest to discover the real person within herself.

Psychological Skills Training Program

A number of psychological skills training programs have been proposed (Boutcher & Rotella, 1987; Gordon, 1990; Orlick, 1986). In addition to these proposed programs, Weinberg and Williams (2006) provide the basic components that they believe should be considered in developing a psychological skills training program. Illustrated in table 12.1 is a proposed **psychological skills training program** (PSTP) that is based upon the literature. The model is composed of seven discrete but related phases that will be discussed in some detail.

Who Is the Client?

The first and most critical thing that must be determined by the sport psychologist is who the client is. If the **client** is the athletic department of a university, then the athletic department defines the nature of the relationship between the sport psychologist and the athlete or coach. If management wishes to be informed of all ongoing aspects of the PSTP, then this is their right. They may, however, wish to waive that right and give the sport psychologist a free hand in working with the athletes. Regardless of what the relationship is, each party involved must be informed of its nature. If the client is the coach, then the coach defines the nature of the relationship between the sport psychologist and the athlete and coach. Finally, if the athlete is the client, then the athlete defines the nature of the relationship between the sport psychologist and the athlete. Furthermore, regardless of the wishes of the coach or management, consultation between athlete and sport psychologist is confidential and privileged when the client is the athlete.

Related to the question of who is the client is the question of who should deliver services to athletes. Recalling our discussion in chapter 1, we remember that the sport psychologist should be certified and qualified to deliver services to athletes. However, what if the team or organization wishes to provide psychological services to its athletes, or they do not have the financial resources to pay for the full-time services of a sport psychologist? To address this need, Smith and Johnson (1990) utilized the **organizational empowerment approach** in working with the Houston Astros' minor league development program. Recognizing that the sport psychologist

TABLE 12.1 | Sample Psychological Skills Training Program (PSTP)

Phase 1: Who Is the Client?

Determine who the client is and develop a working model as to how the PSTP will be delivered.

Phase 2: Initial Meeting with Athletes

The initial meeting is critical in terms of placing an emphasis upon psychological skills training, and getting athletes' and coaches' commitment to the training program.

Phase 3: Education of the Sport Psychologist Relative to Activity

Ideally, the sport psychologist will be an expert on the client's sport from a psychological, biomechanical, physiological, and pedagogical perspective. If not, a period of self-education will be required to help the sport psychologist bridge the gap from being a novice to being fully knowledgeable and conversant about the sport.

Phase 4: Development of a Needs Assessment Plan

In order to develop a needs assessment plan, the sport psychologist must have a working knowledge of athletes' current psychological skills. This can be accomplished only through formal and informal assessment.

1. Interview
2. Performance profiling
3. Observation of athletes during practice and competition
4. Use of objective pencil-and-paper inventories
    - a. CSAI-2R
    - b. SAS
    - c. POMS
    - d. PANAS
    - e. TOPS
    - f. ACSI-28
    - g. 16-PF
    - h. TAIS

Phase 5: Psychological Methods and Strategies to Be Taught

Based on needs assessment, it will become apparent where the athletes are lacking relative to psychological skills. In this phase, a master plan is developed in terms of what, when, and in what sequence psychological methods are to be taught to address psychological skill weaknesses.

Phase 6: Actual Teaching and Learning of Selected Psychological Methods

1. Psychological methods to be taught, practiced, and applied in competition to enhance psychological skills
    - a. Goal setting
    - b. Relaxation
    - c. Self-talk
    - d. Imagery
    - e. Attention skills
    - f. Self-hypnosis
2. Performance routines to be taught, practiced, and applied in competition to enhance psychological skills
    - a. Preshot
    - b. During play
    - c. Postshot

Phase 7: Ongoing and End-of-Season Evaluation of PSTP

For best results, the PSTP must be continually reviewed and evaluated.

cannot be with the athletes all the time, a full-time member of the Houston Astros organization was trained to deliver psychological services to the organization's own athletes. This approach empowers the organization to provide psychological services to its own athletes without the requirement of having a full-time sport psychologist on the staff. The sport psychologist then serves as a consultant to work with members of the organization who have been trained, rather than working directly with the athletes (supervisory consulting model).

CONCEPT An effective psychological skills training program is based on an assessment plan that allows the sport psychologist to identify an athlete's strengths and weaknesses in terms of psychological skill.

APPLICATION There are many potential approaches to ascertaining the psychological skill profile of an athlete. The method that provides the best and most accurate information is the one that should be employed. The particular assessment technique may vary from athlete to athlete. If the athlete has an accurate perception of his psychological strengths and weaknesses, then the performance profiling method should prove effective. It is really the most direct approach, but it requires self-awareness and trust.

Initial Meeting with Athletes

The initial meeting between the sport psychologist and the athletes is pivotal for emphasizing the need for commitment to the PSTP. Coaches and athletes recognize the importance of physical practice and training to prepare for peak performance. Athletes must be equally committed to psychological skills training. A coach who says she is willing to commit 15 minutes at the end of practice to imagery practice and utilization is not committed to psychological skills training. Psychological skills training must be viewed as an equal partner to the practicing of physical skills.

Education of the Sport Psychologist Relative to Activity

Athletes find it easier to relate to a sport psychologist who understands the nuances of the sport that the athletes are trying to excel in. If a sport psychologist cannot relate to an athlete's feelings in a critical game situation, she will have difficulty gaining the confidence of the athlete. What does it really feel like to be on the foul line shooting free throws in the final moments of the game? What muscles are involved in executing a complex gymnastics exercise on the high bar? What are the physiological factors associated with fatigue at the end of a marathon? What is the best way to quickly learn how to execute a backhand drive in tennis? A sport psychologist must be more than a psychologist; she must also be an exercise and sport scientist. It is unrealistic to expect the sport psychologist to be an expert performer in every sport that she serves as a consultant in, but it is realistic to expect the psychologist to be an avid student of the game.

Development of a Needs Assessment Plan

In order to develop a **needs assessment plan,** the sport psychologist must determine the psychological skill strengths and weaknesses of each athlete and of a team as a whole. This is accomplished through a series of interviews and test administrations as indicated below.

Interview An open-ended interview is an important way for the sport psychologist to establish a trusting relationship with the athlete. In this interview, the sport psychologist learns the athlete's attitudes about sport psychology, and his perceptions about psychological strengths and weaknesses.

Performance Profiling Either as an extension of the personal interview or at another time, the athlete is asked to indicate, using her own labels and definitions, what she feels are important psychological skills for success. The athlete then indicates on a scale of 1 to 10 where she feels she falls on that rating scale. The sport psychologist then produces a bar graph that illustrates the skills the athlete selected and the progress being made from week to week. This process has been labeled **performance profiling** (Weinberg & Williams, 2006). Areas of potential psychological skill improvement may include intrinsic motivation, self-awareness, self-esteem, self-confidence, attentional focus, and arousal control.

Observation of Athletes during Practice and Competition

Regardless of an athlete's perception of personal psychological skill, it is informative to observe the athlete during game-like situations to see how he deals with pressure. This will make it possible to affirm the athlete's belief system about psychological skill. If differences exist between observed and perceived psychological skills, then additional interviews might prove beneficial.

Use of Objective Pencil-and-Paper Inventories

Throughout this text we have introduced psychological inventories for assessing anxiety and mood (CSAI-2R, SAS, POMS, PANAS), psychological skill and technique (TOPS, ACSI-28), and personality (16-PF, TAIS). Where appropriate, these inventories should be administered and carefully evaluated relative to other subjectively determined information.

All of the inventories listed above and also listed in table 12.1 are used extensively by practicing sport psychologist consultants and by sport psychologist researchers. It is interesting to note, however, that the instruments most frequently used by sport psychology practitioners are the Profile of Mood States (POMS), the Competitive State Anxiety Inventory–2 (CSAI-2), and the Test of Attentional and Interpersonal Style (TAIS) (O'Connor, 2004). As are all pencil-and-paper tests, all of the inventories listed in table 12.1 are subject to athlete distortion, i.e., "faking good" or "faking bad." In order to minimize the damage caused by an athlete's "faking good" on an inventory, it is often recommended that the short form of the Marlowe-Crowne Social Desirability Scale (MC-SDS) also be administered (Reynolds, 1982). Each of the 13 items on the MC-SDS describes a

socially undesirable yet relatively unlikely behavior. A high score on the MC-SDS is thought to indicate socially desirable responding. If an athlete gets a high score on the MC-SDS, there is a good possibility that she has "faked good" on other companion inventories.

While not mentioned anywhere else in this text and not listed in table 12.1, a Multilevel Classification System for Sport Psychology (MCS-SP) has been proposed (Gardner & Moore, 2004). Much like the Diagnostic and Statistical Manual of Mental Disorders (DSM-IV; American Psychiatric Association, 2000), the MCS-SP proposes to categorize athletes relative to their readiness for psychological skills training. This inventory should be administered and interpreted only by a counseling or clinical sport psychologist. To determine where an athlete fits in the MCS-SP, it is necessary that the athlete go through a three-stage assessment protocol: (a) clinical assessment phase, (b) personal assessment phase, and (c) performance assessment phase. Following the three-phase assessment process, the athlete is classified into one of four performance levels with associated prescribed intervention plans. The four performance level classifications and associated interventions are as follows:

1. *Performance Development*   Psychological skills training (PST) is recommended.

2. *Performance Dysfunction*   Psychological counseling is recommended, with PST as an adjunct.

3. *Performance Impairment*   Psychological counseling and/or psychotherapy are recommended (possibly with medication as an adjunct).

4. *Performance Termination*   Psychological and career counseling are recommended.

Psychological Methods and Strategies to Be Taught

Based on needs assessment in phase 4, it should be clear to the sport psychologist which areas of

Many athletes look to their coach for mental skill training. Courtesy Kansas University Sports Information.

psychological skill the athletes are strong in and which areas they are weak in. It is likely that different athletes will exhibit different profiles relative to their psychological skills. Based on this information, the sport psychologist develops a master plan detailing how to enhance psychological skill through the application of various psychological methods, strategies, and techniques. Timing and sequencing of the delivery of psychological methods are also determined at this time.

Actual Teaching and Learning of Selected Psychological Methods

During this phase, the actual teaching of psychological methods is carried out. Each psychological method is taught with a specific purpose in mind in terms of enhancing psychological skill. For example, if the athlete is lacking in the psychological skill of displaying self-confidence prior to

competition, self-talk, self-hypnosis, and imagery might prove to be particularly effective.

Psychological Methods to Be Taught and Practiced   Throughout this text and especially in this part, of the text, psychological methods effective in enhancing psychological skill and, hence, skilled performance, have been introduced. An incomplete list of potential psychological methods to be taught include goal setting, relaxation, self-talk, imagery, attention skills, and self-hypnosis.

Performance Routines   Performance routines can be categorized as preshot, between-play, or postshot in nature. **Preshot routines** take place immediately preceding the initiation of a shot or play. Preshot routines are most effective in self-paced sports and events that allow time for the athlete to prepare in a stable and predictable manner. Serving in tennis would be a self-paced event, whereas approaching the net for a half-volley would not. As explained by Singer (2002), the preshot routine is a five-step process. These five steps are as follows:

1. *Readying*   In this step, the athlete uses coping skills to create an atmosphere of self-confidence, internal attentional focus, arousal adjustment, and emotional control (may involve repetitive physical actions).

2. *Imaging*   The athlete images a successful outcome.

3. *Focusing attention externally*   Attention is focused on a relevant external cue or thought.

4. *Executing with a quiet mind*   The athlete stays calm and thinks positive thoughts as the skill is executed.

5. *Evaluating*   If time allows, the execution and outcome of the skill, as well as the preshot routine, are evaluated.

Between-play routines take place during breaks in the action of games such as tennis, basketball, volleyball, and baseball. For example, what should baseball outfielders be thinking about or doing during the period of time the catcher is warming up a relief pitcher? One possibility would be to engage in relaxing conversation with teammates or fellow competitors. Another would be to imagine restful scenes on a secluded beach or a walk along a mountain stream.

Postshot routines take place during the period of time immediately following the execution of a skill, or even following a game or match. There is a natural tendency in sport to dwell on the negative aspects of an unsuccessful performance. A planned postshot routine would include a strategy to clear the mind for the next shot or the next match and to save critical analysis for the practice field. A dramatic case in point is the *closer* in baseball. Being a closer in professional baseball is a win/loss situation that can happen in a blink of an eye. Lots of pitchers can save 30 games in a single season, but few can do it across multiple seasons. Trevor Hoffman of the San Diego Padres was an exception. In 2001 he was the only active pitcher to have saved 30 or more games in each of the past six years. For closers, the cruelest, most negative statistic is the *blown save*. This occurs when the closer enters the game in late innings with a lead and loses the game. When Hoffman suffered a blown save, he had a postgame emergency routine to deal with it. "First, while sitting alone in the dugout, he reflects on what just happened; then, even after his worst outings, he goes to the clubhouse and fields questions from the media. . . . Finally, alone, he finds something positive amid the despair. He won't leave the stadium until he is sure the virus is under control" (Verducci, 2001, p. 84).

Research has validated the use of performance routines in sport (Hill & Borden, 1995; Lidor & Singer, 2000; Czech, Ploszay, & Burke, 2004). Examples of preshot, between-play, and postshot routines are provided in table 12.2. To be effective, performance routines must be practiced and must exhibit temporal consistency. This means that the temporal length of the routine must be consistent, and execution of the routine must occur at a consistent time prior to execution of the

CONCEPT   A psychological skills training program that has proven effective for athletes is the NCAA CHAMPS life skills program developed in 1991 and 1994 by the NCAA Foundation. The purpose of the program is to help athletes prepare for life after college as well as for success during college. CHAMPS stands for Challenging Athlete Minds for Personal Success.

APPLICATION   There are many different kinds of PSTP designed to help athletes find success on the athletic field, but programs such as CHAMPS are needed to help athletes succeed as students and to prepare for life after athletics.

TABLE 12.2 | Examples of Performance Routines Used in Sport

Routine	Sport	Situation	Steps
Preshot	Golf	Putting	1. Stand behind the ball and "read" the line of the putt.
			2. Approach the ball and take two practice swings.
			3. Align the putter to the target, set the feet, and take two glances at the hole.
Between-Play	Tennis	Changing Courts	1. Take care of your body and your equipment (water and towel off).
			2. Give your mind some relief (focus on positive thoughts).
			3. Focus on strategy for next game.
Postshot	Volleyball	Passing	1. Clear mind of results of previous pass by yourself or teammate.
			2. Focus on making a perfect pass to the setter.
			3. Use self-talk to remind yourself that you are an excellent passer.

skill. For example, a preshot routine for shooting a basketball free throw should always take about the same amount of time to execute, and be initiated at approximately the same point in time relative to releasing the basketball (Wrisberg & Pein, 1992).

Ongoing and End-of-Season Evaluation of a PSTP

If a psychological skills training program extends across an entire sport season, it is imperative that it be evaluated at the end of the season. If psychological inventories were administered during the needs assessment phase of the program, these same inventories can be administered at the end of the season, noting changes and improvements in variables of importance. Taking into consideration task difficulty, a careful review of performance measures recorded throughout the season will provide helpful information about effectiveness of the PSTP. Finally, open-ended discussions with athletes about the program will provide invaluable information about its effectiveness. In addition to end-of-season evaluations, ongoing evaluation of the program's effectiveness should be obtained at each phase. If an athlete feels uncomfortable about a specific psychological method that she is learning, there is no need to continue it to the end of the program.

CONCEPT Psychological methods found to be effective in the sport domain for enhancing performance excellence as well as personal excellence can be equally effective in business, the arts, music, and the military.

APPLICATION Sport psychologists who are expert in the application of psychological skill training with athletes should also consider generalizing their skills to other performance domains. Just as athletes are interested in improving their psychological skills for purposes of performance enhancement, so are dancers, business executives, performing artists, and military/police officers.

Generalization of Sport Psychology Methods to Other Application Domains

Researchers and practitioners in sport psychology have generated a large literature base that informs good practice. Based on the literature, sport psychologists have learned a great deal about facilitating learning and performance in the sport and exercise domains. Cognitive and behavioral intervention methods introduced in this text for enhancing peak performance in sport can be used in other domains, such as music, the arts, the military, police work, and business, for the same purpose (Gould, 2002a, 2002b). As stated by Gould (2002a), "many AAASP members are transferring what they have learned about facilitating human performance in sport to other domains such as music, the arts, business, and the military" (p. 137).

One of the most fruitful areas for applying principles of positive psychology (Seligman & Csikszentmihalyi, 2000) is the business domain. A case in point is Graham Jones (2002), a sport psychologist, who left academia as a full-time endeavor and formed a business consulting company called Lane 4. Although he still has a part-time appointment as co-Director of the Institute for the Psychology of Elite Performance at the University of Wales, Bangor, his full-time work is as a consultant to business executives. Jones shows links between sport and business in five major areas: (a) organizational issues and similarities, (b) stress and stress management, (c) developing leadership skills, (d) working with high-performance teams, and (e) the need for one-on-one coaching/consultation. He further notes that high-performing business teams learn to create, to unite, and to perform (CUP). The CUP principle in business is equivalent to the sport psychology terms of team building, team work (cohesion), and team effectiveness. In this text, the concepts of team building and team cohesion will be discussed in chapter 15.

Further evidence of the common link between sport and business was provided by Weinberg and McDermott (2002). In this investigation 10 business executives and 10 sport-related leaders were interviewed to discover commonalities. Results of the investigation revealed more similarities than differences between the two groups of leaders relative to principles of organizational stress. Similarly, LeScanff and Taugis (2002) involved 150 French police officers in a psychological training program for purposes of reducing stress. Results showed that, as with athletes, psychological training skills effectively reduce stress in the French police. Finally, Hays (2002) studied similarities and differences between athletes and performing artists (actors, artists, broadcasters, dancers, musicians) relative to four performance issues. The four issues studied were performance enhancement, developmental issues, injury and retirement issues, and eating disorders. While some differences do exist between athletes and performing artists, it was concluded that both groups can benefit from psychological skills training specific to their area of expertise.

Summary

This chapter began with a discussion of the psychological skill characteristics of the elite athlete. The elite athlete possesses psychological skill characteristics that facilitate performance excellence. The athlete-centered sport model proposes that the process of becoming an elite athlete should focus upon personal excellence also, and not just performance excellence. Research was summarized that assures us that psychological intervention programs are effective in enhancing performance and changing behavior. A distinction was made between psychological skills and methods used to achieve psychological skill. *Psychological skill* refers to learned or innate characteristics of the athlete that make it possible for him to succeed in sport. *Psychological methods* refer to practices that lead to psychological skill. Four inventories were identified and explained that measure psychological skill. These were the Psychological Skills Inventory for Sports, the Athletic Coping Skills Inventory, the Test of Performance Strategies, and the Ottawa Mental Skills Assessment Tool.

Members of AAASP are bound by a code of ethics that governs their interactions with the public and with other professionals. The AAASP Ethics Code is based in large part on the Ethical Principles of the American Psychological Association, and is composed of a preamble, six general principles, and 25 standards. Sport psychology delivery should be based on a solid philosophical foundation. The sport psychology consultant's philosophy can serve to provide direction when she is confronted with unique situations for which there exists no textbook solution. A consultant's philosophy should be based on personal core beliefs that provide direction to theoretical paradigms embraced by the consultant.

A sample psychological skills training program (PSTP) composed of seven discrete but related phases was introduced and discussed in detail. The phases included (a) identifying the client, (b) initial meeting with athletes, (c) education of the sport psychologist, (d) needs assessment plan, (e) psychological methods and strategies to be taught, (f) learning of psychological methods, and (g) evaluation. During the learning phase of the PSTP, psychological methods such as goal setting, relaxation, self-talk, imagery, attention skills, and self-hypnosis are taught to athletes. In addition, athletes learn how to develop and use performance routines. Preshot, between-play, and postshot routines are effective in focusing an athlete's attention on appropriate internal and external cues.

The chapter ends with the topic of generalization of sport psychology methods to areas other than sport. Cognitive and behavioral intervention methods introduced in this text for enhancing peak performance in sport can be used in other domains, such as music, the arts, the military, police work, and business, for the same purpose.

Critical Thought Questions

1. Describe the psychological skill characteristics of the elite athlete. How are they different from those of the nonelite athlete?

2. Provide some evidence to support the proposition that psychological intervention programs are effective in facilitating performance excellence.

3. Why do you think it is important to distinguish between psychological methods and psychological skills?

4. How does a sport psychologist develop a viable and ethically sound philosophy of consulting with athletes?

5. Outline and propose your own psychological skills training program. At each step, explain your reasons and rationale.

6. Develop and present in writing proposed preshot routines for batting in baseball/softball, free-throw shooting in basketball, putting in golf, and high jumping in track and field (or, select four sport situations of your choice).

Glossary

Athlete-centered sport model A model that proposes that sport must contribute to the overall development of the athlete physically, psychologically, and socially.

Athletic Coping Skills Inventory An inventory, developed by Smith, Schutz, Smoll, and Ptacek (1995), which assesses psychological skills of athletes.

between-play routine A sequential performance routine that takes place during breaks in the action of an athletic contest.

client The individual or individuals that the sport psychologist contracts with to deliver psychological services.

code of ethics Code that governs how a sport psychologist interacts with the public and with other professionals.

needs assessment plan A plan, based on an assessment of an athlete's psychological skills, that is designed to address the athlete's needs through a psychological skills training program.

organizational empowerment approach Situation in which a member of an organization is trained by a sport psychologist to deliver psychological services to the member's own organization.

Ottawa Mental Skills Assessment Tool A 48-item inventory that measures 12 mental skill subscales.

performance profiling The cooperative development by the sport psychologist and the athlete of a profile showing how the athlete ranks on psychological skills deemed important to the athlete.

postshot routine A performance routine that takes place immediately following the execution of a skill.

preshot routine A performance routine that takes place immediately before the execution of a skill.

psychological intervention program An intervention formalized into a program for improving the psychological skills of athletes.

psychological method A technique or strategy used to enhance psychological skill in an athlete.

psychological skill Learned or innate characteristics of the athlete that make it possible or even likely that she will succeed in sport.

Psychological Skills Inventory for Sports An inventory, developed by Mahoney, Gabriel, and Perkins (1987), which assesses psychological skills of athletes.

psychological skills training program An organized and systemized program that assesses psychological skill and teaches psychological methods designed to enhance psychological skill.

resonance A key element of the resonance performance model that is related to the concepts of Flow, intrinsic motivation, and emotion.

Resonance performance model A model that explains the process by which ordinary athletes become elite athletes.

Self-regulation Self-generated thoughts, feelings, and behaviors that are planned and cyclically adapted based on performance feedback.

Self-regulation model A model that utilizes the concept of self-regulation to explain how psychological skill development takes place.

Test of Performance Strategies An inventory, developed by Thomas, Murphy, and Hardy (1999), which assesses a combination of psychological skills and strategies.

PART 5

Social Psychology of Sport

The first four parts of this book have focused upon the individual. Sport psychology, however, involves more than the individual. It also involves sociological factors that affect the individual. Sport sociology is a discipline that focuses upon social relations, group interactions, and sport-related social phenomena. Because groups are composed of individuals, it is often difficult to determine where psychology ends and sociology begins; hence the need for an area of study called social psychology of sport. While it is beyond the scope of a textbook on sport psychology to provide a comprehensive treatment on the topic of social psychology of sport, it is appropriate that selected topics be addressed. Chapters to be discussed in this part of the text include aggression and violence, social facilitation and self-presentation, and team cohesion. Each of these topics impacts the individual in important ways.

Athlete aggression and fan violence affect the way that society views and values sport. The behavior of an audience has a powerful influence upon the outcome of an athletic contest and upon the behavior of athletes. Team cohesion affects how well athletes work together and the satisfaction that athletes derive from sport. ∞

Aggression and Violence in Sport

KEY TERMS

Aggression
Assertiveness
Bracketed morality
Catharsis effect
Circular effect of aggression
False consensus effect
Fan identification
Frustration-aggression theory
Hostile aggression
Instinct theory
Instrumental aggression
Moral reasoning
Peacemakers
Readiness for aggression
Reformulation of frustration-
    aggression theory
Relational aggression
Social learning theory
Troublemakers

At New York's Shea Stadium during a 1978 Jets-Steelers football game, spectators overpowered a security guard and dropped him over a railing to a concrete walkway 15 feet below. In Toronto, four members of the Philadelphia Flyers hockey team faced maximum penalties of up to three years in prison on assault charges stemming from a wild brawl during the Stanley Cup playoffs of 1975. In the same year, Henry Boucha suffered a severe beating from Dave Forbes during a Boston-Minnesota hockey game, causing Boucha to lose 70 percent of his sight in one eye.

Two athletes strain to maintain their emotional composure. Courtesy University of Missouri–Columbia Sports Information.

In professional basketball, on December 9, 1977, Los Angeles Laker Kermit Washington literally shattered the face of forward Rudy Tomjanovich of the Houston Rockets with a devastating punch. Twenty-five years later, Feinstein (2002) wrote about the devastating effects that the punch had on the lives of both men.

On August 13, 1978, football fans were shocked by the crushing blow Jack Tatum gave receiver Darryl Stingley in an exhibition match between the Oakland Raiders and the New England Patriots. The blow left Stingley a quadriplegic. In 1991, Rob Dibble, pitcher for the Cincinnati Reds major league baseball team, aimed his fastball at base runner Doug Dascenzo as he ran out a successful bunt. During a 1995 Houston Rockets

professional basketball game against the Portland Trailblazers, the Rockets' Vernon Maxwell went into the stands in Portland and slugged an abusive fan. Maxwell was suspended for ten days and fined $20,000.

In December of 1999, Latrell Sprewell, of the Golden State Warriors professional basketball team, grabbed his coach, P. J. Carlesimo, by the throat and choked him for 15 seconds, before players could pull them apart (Taylor, 1997). In May of 1999, Wichita State baseball pitcher Ben Christensen was tossing his warm-up throws while the lead-off hitter for Evansville, Anthony Molina, was standing 30 feet from home plate taking practice swings. Believing that Molina was attempting to "time" his pitches, Christensen threw a fastball at him, hitting him in the left eye, fracturing the eye socket in three places, and leaving his baseball future in doubt. Christensen had been taught by his pitching coach, Brent Kemnitz, that if a batter is standing too close to the plate and timing pitches, you should brush him back. Apparently, 30 feet was too close (Cook & Mravic, 1999).

One of the most repugnant examples of fan violence occurred in 1985 in Europe, where a soccer riot in Brussels left 38 dead and 437 injured after English hooligans attacked panic-stricken Italian fans. The riot occurred prior to the European Cup soccer final in Heysel Stadium in Brussels between Liverpool and Juventus, the soccer team of Turin, Italy. Well-liquored Liverpool hooligans attacked Juventus fans with broken bottles, tin cans, flag sticks, and metal bars. Within minutes, hundreds of Italian fans found themselves pressed against a chain-link fence and a restraining wall. As more bodies pressed against the barriers, they collapsed, pitching hundreds of terrified fans into a hideous pileup in which 31 Italians, 4 Belgians, 2 French, and 1 Briton were killed, most by suffocation. The event has since been referred to as Black Wednesday by shamed residents of Liverpool.

Similarly, more than 40 people were killed and 50 injured at an exhibition soccer match in Johannesburg, South Africa in 1991. Most of the deaths occurred when panicked spectators were crushed against a fence around the field and trampled by fleeing people. Two children were among the dead. Most recently, following a 1996 heavyweight boxing match in New York between Riddick Bowe and Andrew Golota, a confirmed riot ensued. The fight ended after the seventh round as Golota was disqualified for throwing his fourth low blow to Bowe's groin. Thirty-five minutes after the bout, the crowd was ordered to evacuate Madison Square Gardens as riot police rushed in.

Apparently, fan violence does not require the actual presence of competing teams or a filled stadium of people. In Moscow, Russia on June 9, 2002, an outdoor broadcast of a World Cup soccer match outside the Kremlin gates turned into a drunken rampage after the Russian team lost the match 1–0 to Japan. The game was not played in Moscow, but was projected on huge electronic billboards. Only a few hundred spectators were expected, but an estimated eight thousand people showed up. Drinking, hooligans/ruffians, and a lack of sufficient police presence were blamed for the disturbance (Wines, 2002).

Most of the incidences of aggression and violence described in the above paragraphs involved aggression among athletes or violence among fans. In recent years, a number of incidences of aggression and violence have occurred that involve both fans and athletes. One of the most bizarre incidents took place in Detroit, Michigan in a nationally televised professional basketball game between the Detroit Pistons and the Indianapolis Pacers (Wilstein, 2004). It all began in the final minutes of the Pistons' 97–82 victory over the Pacers. It started with Ron Artest's hard foul on Ben Wallace and Wallace's retaliatory shove in the face. It should have ended there, but it didn't. Artest retreated to neutral territory and sprawled out on the scorer's table, only to be showered with a cup of water or beer from a fan in the stands. In a rage, Artest went into the stands to pummel the fan, but got the wrong guy. Before it was over there were numerous Pacer players in the stands fighting with fans. This was all displayed and replayed over and over on national television. In defense of the players, Carr (2004) noted that athletes are not prepared to deal with the psychological stresses associated with fan abuse and misbehavior. He noted that they are paid very well for their athletic skills, not for their coping skills.

Other examples of violence among fans and athletes have been documented (Price, 2003). On April 30, 1993, during a changeover in a professional tennis match between Monica Seles and Magdalena Maleeva, a man reached over a fence and drove a boning knife into Seles's back. Then in September of 2002, in the ninth inning of a baseball game between the Chicago White Sox and the visiting Kansas City Royals, first base coach Tom Gamboa was leaning forward, knees bent, watching intently as Kansas City Royals' centerfielder Michael Tucker popped a bunt into the air. Suddenly, he was attacked from behind and pummeled by two men who knocked him to the ground, landing him on his head and bent neck.

Even more troubling are acts of premeditated violence carried out by athletes and, in some cases, encouraged by coaches. In an unimportant professional ice hockey game, Todd Bertuzzi of the Vancouver Canucks punched the Colorado Avalanche's Steve Moore from behind, leaving him hospitalized with a broken neck, a concussion, and deep facial cuts. The attack was premeditated and in response to an earlier confrontation between Moore and fellow Canuck teammate Markus Nashlund. From that confrontation, Nashlund had been out with a concussion for three games. The interesting thing about professional ice hockey is that the players know when to hold back. During the Stanley Cup playoffs every year, acts of aggression suddenly diminish, because nobody wants to take a penalty that could ruin a season (Vecsey, 2004). Finally, in a college men's basketball game between St. Joseph and Temple, coach John Chaney ordered a "goon" into the game to wreak havoc on opposing players. The inserted player fouled out in only four minutes, leaving one St. Joseph player with a broken arm. Chaney was suspended for the rest of the regular season (Widman, 2005).

CONCEPT   The difference between hostile and instrumental aggression lies in the perceived goal of the aggressor and not in intent.

APPLICATION   Because the intent to harm is present in both forms of aggression, both must be discouraged from an ethical and moral reasoning standpoint.

A number of critical questions come to mind as one contemplates the issue of sport aggression. Does participating in or observing violent sporting events serve as a *catharsis,* or release from aggressive tendencies? Conversely, do these events merely teach and encourage further aggression on and off the playing field? If these two questions can be answered, then is it possible to eliminate aggression and violence from sports? If so, how?

In this chapter, these questions and other critically important issues will be discussed. Topics to be addressed include defining aggression, theories of aggression, the catharsis hypothesis, measurement issues, fan violence, performance issues, situational factors contributing to aggression, and reducing aggression in sport.

Defining Aggression

Two factors must be present in order for a behavior to be labeled **aggression** (Berkowitz, 1993). *First,* the behavior must be aimed at another human being with the goal of inflicting physical harm. *Second,* there must be a reasonable expectation that the attempt to inflict bodily harm will be successful. Consequently, the following behaviors, often mislabeled aggression, are not really examples of aggression:

1. Doing destructive violence to an inanimate object such as a door or a water cooler

2. Unintentionally injuring another person during athletic competition

3. Aggressive behavior in which there is no chance for the intended victim to be injured (e.g., aggressor and victim are separated by bars or by teammates)

Over the years, two basic kinds of aggression have been identified. The first is **hostile aggression.** For individuals engaged in hostile aggression, the primary goal is the injury of another human being. The intent is to make the victim suffer, and the reinforcement is the pain and suffering that is caused. This sort of aggression is always accompanied by anger on the part of the aggressor. A good example of hostile aggression occurs when a baseball pitcher throws a high inside fastball at a batter who has angered him. The clear attempt to injure is present, and the goal is to cause suffering. The outcome of the contest is not a factor to be considered. The goal is to harm, not to win. This kind of aggression is often referred to as *violence.*

The second major kind of aggression is **instrumental aggression.** For individuals engaged in instrumental aggression, the intent to harm another individual is present, but the goal is to realize some external goal such as money, victory, or prestige. The aggressor views the aggressive act as *instrumental* in obtaining the primary goal. A parallel baseball example for instrumental aggression would be one in which the pitcher has been "ordered" by his manager to hit a batter in retaliation for some earlier infraction. The pitcher is not necessarily angry at the batter, but sees hitting the batter as instrumental in achieving the team goal of winning the game. In research involving basketball and ice hockey, aggressive acts were categorized as being instrumental in nature two-thirds of the time. (Kirker, Tenenbaum, & Mattson, 2000).

It must be emphasized that neither type of aggression is acceptable. The aggressor is guilty of purposely inflicting harm with the intent to injure another person. This must be discouraged at all levels of competition, especially the professional level, because young athletes everywhere emulate the pros.

A third category of behavior that is often confused with aggression is **assertiveness,** or assertive behavior. Generally, when coaches encourage their athletes to be more aggressive, what they really want is that they be more assertive. Coaches want their athletes to assert themselves and make their presence felt. Assertiveness involves the use of *legitimate* physical or verbal force to achieve one's purpose. However, there is no intent to harm the opponent. Even if an opponent is harmed as a result of a tackle in soccer, it is not necessarily aggression. It is merely assertive play, as long as it is within the spirit of the agreed-on rules and the intent to harm is not present. Assertiveness requires the expenditure of unusual effort and energy, but if there is no *intent* to harm, then any resultant harm is incidental to the game. Let's go back to our baseball example. If the pitcher throws a high inside fastball, with no intent to hit the batter, this is considered assertive play. The pitcher *must* establish control of the strike zone, or the batter will intimidate the pitcher into throwing either strikes or outside balls.

As can be observed in figure 13.1, an area of ambiguity lies between instrumental aggression, hostile aggression, and assertive behavior. This is to be expected, since at times only the athlete knows whether an "aggressive" act was intended. From a practical standpoint, it is the job of the official to penalize any behavior that is in violation of the rules, regardless of the intent of the violator. However, most sports make provisions for extraordinary penalties if the behavior is deemed to be intentional and/or dangerous. For clarity, let's return to the baseball pitching example. If in the judgment of the umpire a pitcher purposely throws a pitch at a batter with intent to harm, he must be penalized, regardless of why he did it. However, if a batter has his body over the strike zone, he is inviting an assertive pitcher to throw a fastball over the inside part of the plate. If the batter is hit, it is not the fault of the pitcher and it is not an example of sport aggression.

FIGURE 13.1 | Schematic showing the possible difficulties in discriminating among hostile aggression, instrumental aggression, and assertive behavior.

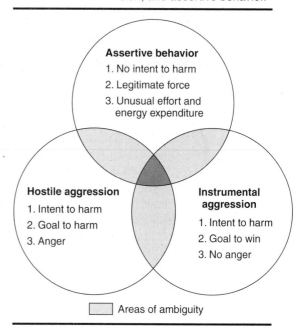

Areas of ambiguity

Source: From J. M. Silva, III, Assertive and aggressive behavior in sport: A definitional clarification. In *Psychology of Motor Behavior and Sport*—1979 by C. H. Nadeau (Ed.). Copyright © 1980 Human Kinetics Publishers, Inc., Champaign, IL. Adapted by permission.

While the hostile versus instrumental aggression dichotomy is useful, it is viewed by some to be too simplistic (Bushman & Anderson, 2000). This is because many aggressive acts have multiple goals and multiple motives. For example, it is feasible that a pitcher might throw at a player to facilitate a goal of winning the game—but he may also be angry at the hitter at the same time. Consequently, as illustrated in figure 13.1, it is not always easy to categorize an act of aggression as being instrumental or hostile. Even the pitcher might have difficulty making the classification, because more than one motivation is involved.

If looks could kill! Is this an example of aggression or assertive behavior?
Source: Courtesy Kansas State University Sports Information.

Also, while most aggression research focuses upon intended physical harm and sometimes intended verbal harm, relational aggression has also been studied. **Relational aggression** is harming others through such things as social ostracism and malicious rumors. Results of an investigation reported by Storch, Werner, and Storch (2003) show that there is a positive correlation between relational aggression and peer rejection for men and women and between relational aggression and alcohol use for women. In addition, a negative correlation was observed between relational aggression and prosocial behavior. Individuals perceived by their peers to be high in relational aggression tended also to be rejected by their peers and to engage in antisocial behavior.

Theories of Aggression

A number of theories have been proposed to explain the phenomenon of aggression. These theories fall into four main categories: instinct theory, social learning theory, Bredemeier's theory of moral reasoning, and Berkowitz's reformulation of the frustration-aggression hypothesis.

Instinct Theory

Instinct theory is based upon the writings of Sigmund Freud and ethologists such as Konrad Lorenz. Freud (1950) viewed aggression as an inborn drive similar to hunger, thirst, and sexual desire. According to Freud, aggression is unavoidable since it is innate, but as with any drive it can

CONCEPT   A relationship exists between an athlete's level of moral and ethical reasoning and her willingness to engage in acts of aggression.

APPLICATION   Coaches and teachers can best control athletes' aggression by appealing to their sense of right and wrong. Athletes must be taught that aggression is just as wrong during an athletic contest as it is in normal everyday life.

be regulated through discharge, or fulfillment. Since humankind is innately aggressive, it benefits society to promote athletic sports and games that provide a socially acceptable outlet for aggression. An important corollary of the biological instinct theory is the notion that aggression results in a purging, or releasing, of the aggression drive. This purging of pent-up aggression is known as catharsis. According to instinct theory, striking an opposing player serves as a catharsis, or release of pent-up aggression.

Social Learning Theory

Social learning theory posits that aggression is a function of learning, and that biological drive and frustration are inadequate explanations of the phenomenon. While the notion of a catharsis is an important component of both biological instinct theory and frustration-aggression theory, it has no place in social learning theory. Acts of aggression serve only to lay the foundation for more aggression, and do not result in a reduction or purging of the drive to be aggressive. Perhaps the leading advocate of social learning theory, relative to aggression, is Bandura (1973). Bandura has argued that aggression has a **circular effect.** That is, one act of aggression leads to further aggression. This pattern will continue until the circle is broken by some type of positive or negative reinforcement. Smith (1980), for instance, argues that violence in ice hockey is due to modeling. Youngsters learn aggression by watching their role models, the professionals, on television or in person. As long as aggression in professional sports is tolerated,

children will continue to have adult models of aggressive behavior.

Support was found for social learning theory in an ice hockey study reported by Sheldon and Aimar (2001). In this investigation, aggressive behaviors were noted 15 seconds before and after successful and unsuccessful behaviors (e.g., score, steal). Results showed that a disproportionate number of successes were preceded by aggression as opposed to no aggression. This outcome suggests that aggression is rewarded by success. Other research supports the proposition that an individual team member's behavior eventually conforms to the normative behavior of the team (Stephens, 2001; Tucker & Parks, 2001). The study by Stephens (2001) specifically showed that likelihood to aggress was predicted by the players' perception of their teams' pro-aggressive norms.

Bredemeier's Theory of Moral Reasoning and Aggression

Based upon Jean Piaget's theory of cognitive development, Bredemeier's theory of **moral reasoning** proposes that an individual's willingness to engage in aggression is related to her stage of moral reasoning (Bredemeier, 1994). Since human aggression is viewed as unethical, Bredemeier reasoned that a relationship should exist between the level of moral reasoning and overt acts of athletic aggression. Contact sport, because it legitimizes acts of aggression, may actually retard a person's moral development. The level of morality necessary for everyday life is often suspended during athletic competition. Bredemeier refers to this suspension of ethical morality as **bracketed morality.** Furthermore, athletic teams create a "moral atmosphere" that may be conducive to the willingness to aggress (Stephen & Bredemeier, 1996; Tucker & Parks, 2001).

In this regard, it should be emphasized that coaches, parents, and society as a whole contribute to the moral atmosphere and the development of moral reasoning in an athlete.

Reformulated Frustration-Aggression Theory

As originally presented by Dollard, Miller, Doob, Mourer, and Sears (1939), **frustration-aggression theory** proposes that aggression is a natural response to frustration, and that the aggressive act provides a catharsis, or purging, of the anger associated with the frustration. Frustration caused by events that are believed to be arbitrary or illegitimate are particularly galling to athletes.

Berkowitz's (1958, 1993) **reformulation of frustration-aggression theory** takes into consideration the observation that frustration does not necessarily result in aggression and proposed that frustration creates a **readiness for aggression.** For aggression to actually occur, certain stimuli associated with aggression must be present. These stimuli are cues that the frustrated person associates with aggression. An example of this phenomenon in animals would be the "red flag" for the enraged and frustrated bull. In the presence of frustration, certain stimuli can serve as "triggers" to release a disposition toward aggression in a frustrated individual (Anderson, Deuser, &

DeNeve, 1995). Negative affect, associated with frustration, is the fundamental spur to the inclination for aggression. Anger is the root of hostile aggression, but depression is another example of negative affect that can trigger an aggressive act. The development of aggressive tendencies is complex, but certainly learning from parents, peers, and other aggressors is a paramount factor. Rewards in the form of incentives and self-gratification play an important role in learning to be an aggresor. Illustrated in figure 13.2 are factors that can influence the strength of the impulse to be an aggressor.

Notwithstanding Berkowitz's reformulation, research does not support the notion that frustration leads to a greater probability of aggression in an athlete. In the sport of ice hockey, incidents of unsuccessful behavior (e.g., failure to score, lost puck) are not followed disproportionately by aggressive behavior (Sheldon & Aimar, 2001).

The Catharsis Effect

Introduced earlier, the **catharsis effect** represents a release of pent-up frustration that makes one feel better. It is a purging of the anger and frustration associated with not being able to accomplish a goal. Venting frustration upon a punching bag or some other inanimate object may serve as a useful catharsis. Venting frustration upon another human being, however, is an unacceptable behavior that is likely to lead to more aggression. Research supports the position that aggression begets more aggression, and that it can become learned behavior. If an act of aggression is precipitated by frustration,

CONCEPT   Sport-related aggression is not cathartic in the sense that it reduces the desire for more aggression. Aggression begets more aggression as the behavior becomes reinforced and learned.

APPLICATION   Aggression on and off the athletic field must be discouraged and penalized as unacceptable behavior. Coaches must take the lead in making sure that an athlete is not rewarded in any way for perpetuating an act of aggression. Aggression is unacceptable in any environmental situation, including the athletic field.

FIGURE 13.2 | Illustration showing factors that can influence the strength of an impulse to commit an act of aggression.

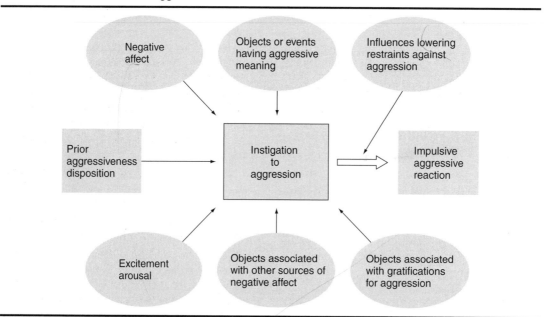

Source: Reproduced with permission from L. Berkowitz (1993). *Aggression: Its causes, consequences, and control.* Philadelphia: Temple University Press (figure 3.6, p. 71).

it may seem to give an immediate cathartic effect, but this feeling of catharsis is quickly followed by feelings of remorse, penalties, and likely escalation of tension and more aggression. *Aggression is not cathartic in the sense that it leads to a reduction in the desire to aggress.* Aggression leads to an increase in aggression as tempers flare and as the behavior becomes learned. This is especially true if aggression is rewarded by fans, by coaches, or by morbid gratification from having inflicted harm on another human being (Russell, 1999).

Measurement of Aggression

A number of inventories have been developed to measure aggressiveness as a personality disposition or trait. Two of these inventories are the Aggression Questionnaire (Buss & Perry, 1992) and

CONCEPT In ice hockey, individuals most likely to take part in fan violence are young males who travel in packs, have a recent history of fighting, like to watch fights, attend hockey games in the hope of seeing fights, react impulsively, and score high on the trait of aggressiveness.

APPLICATION Knowing the physical and mental psychological profile of potential troublemakers should make it possible for sporting event organizers to take precautions that could prevent fan violence. The number one precaution would be for records to be kept, so that those who have a history of fighting can be either closely watched or barred from admission. Fan violence seems to be precipitated primarily by individuals who come to athletic events hoping to see or take part in violence, and who have a recent history of fighting. In ice hockey, troublemakers tend to be young males who travel in packs. However, it would be unfair to assume that all young males in groups are troublemakers.

the Aggression Inventory (Gladue, 1991). Sport-specific inventories include the Athletic Aggression Inventory (Bredemeier, 1978) and the Continuum of Injurious Acts (Bredemeier, 1985). The actual measurement of aggression, however, is much more difficult. Because aggression is defined as the intent to harm another human being, the measurement device must be able to capture this intent. This approach generally requires the use of trained observers using a standardized checklist of some kind, as well as videotaping (Sheldon & Aimar, 2001).

Fan Violence

Most of our discussion in this section has focused upon acts of aggression on the part of sport participants. Unfortunately, however, some of the worst examples of sports aggression and violence occur among the fans watching an athletic contest. This chapter was prefaced with examples of both athlete aggression and fan violence. Intense rivalries, nationalism, and alcohol abuse are major factors contributing to fan violence. Every sports event is attended by individuals who may instigate fan violence. These are individuals who score high in the personality dispositions of anger and physical aggression. These individuals are attracted to violence and fighting among fans, and exhibit a false belief about the willingness of other fans to join in acts of violence. The **false consensus effect** emboldens individuals with a disposition for violence to believe that other fans share their infatuation for fighting and would willingly join them in precipitating an altercation (Russell, 1995; Russell & Arms, 1995).

Research involving ice hockey fans has provided important information about the type of individual who is most likely to take part in fighting and violence (Arms & Russell, 1997; Russell, 1999; Russell & Arms, 1998; Russell & Mustonen, 1998). In carrying out this line of research, trained assistants conducted brief interviews and administered inventories to randomly selected hockey fans during breaks in the action. Results show that the individuals most likely to take part in fan violence are young males who travel in packs, have a recent history of fighting, like to watch fights, attend hockey games in hopes of seeing fights, react impulsively, and score high on the trait of aggressiveness. If a fight were to break out nearby in the stands, 61 percent of the fans interviewed said they would watch, 26 percent said they would try to stop the fight (peacemakers), 7 percent said they would applaud or join in (troublemakers), and the remainder said they would leave the area. **Peacemakers** are not older or of larger stature than other fans; yet, they are willing to risk harm by intervening. **Troublemakers** tend to

CONCEPT   Aggressive play may facilitate performance in some situations and in some sports, but hinder performance in other situations. From an ethical and moral perspective, aggressive (not assertive) play must be severely penalized by referees and umpires, as well as by coaches and team managers. It also must not be subtly promoted by management to boost ticket sales.

APPLICATION   Coaches who want to be successful will not encourage aggression. An unpenalized act of aggression may help a team or individual win an athletic contest now and again, but over the long haul it will be a serious handicap and distraction. A coach's position on acts of aggression must be made perfectly clear. A player who gains an unfair advantage over an opponent through aggressive play must be taken out of the game, even if he is the star player.

be young, small in stature, and have a history of violence and fighting.

Another factor that has been shown to be associated with fan violence is the degree to which fans identify with a sports team. **Fan identification** refers to the psychological connection that individuals have with their team. A study reported by Dimmock and Grove (2005) showed that highly identified professional sport fans feel less control over their behavior at games than moderately identified fans and slightly identified fans.

Effects of Aggression on Performance

Conventional wisdom argues that acts of aggression on the part of an athlete will constitute a distraction and result in a decrement in performance. Not only are aggressive acts on the part of an individual distracting to the individual, but also they are likely to be distracting to the team as a whole. Research shows, for example, that the lower a team is in the standings, the more likely it will be to engage in aggression. An exception to this general observation may be in the sport of ice hockey, where it is often difficult to separate legitimate force (assertiveness) from illegitimate force (aggression). Because hostile aggression is associated with anger and hence with an increase in physiological arousal, it is possible that for some individuals an increase in anger may produce a

level of physiological arousal conducive to best performance. Conversely, it may produce a level of arousal that is above an athlete's zone of optimal functioning.

While aggression among athletes must be strongly discouraged for moral and ethical reasons, it is difficult to conclude that aggression isn't rewarded in sports such as ice hockey. As previously reported, Sheldon and Aimar (2001) showed that in ice hockey a disproportionate number of successes are preceded by aggression on the part of players. This suggests that aggressive play is leading directly to successful performance.

Situational Factors in a Sport Setting

Much of the research in sport-related aggression has dealt with situation-specific factors. Factors associated with the occurrence of aggression in sport-specific situations are as follows:

1. *Environmental temperature*   Using archival data from major league baseball games played during the 1986, 1987, and 1988 seasons, Reifman, Larrick, and Fein (1991) observed a linear relationship between hit batters and environmental temperature. The data suggest that higher temperatures lead major league pitchers to become more aggressive in pitching to batters.

CONCEPT   Acts of aggression occur more frequently among losing teams, during games with high point differentials, and after the first quarter of play.

APPLICATION   Athletes who have a history of aggression should be closely monitored during these situations.

2. *Perception of victim's intent*   If athletes perceive that an opponent's intent is to inflict harm, they are more likely to respond with aggression against the opponent. This means that perception of an opponent's aggressive intentions may be more salient than such things as defeat and competition. When basketball players perceive that their opponents' rough play is intentional and designed to inflict harm, they are more likely to respond with aggression than if they perceive that the roughness is incidental. A study by Harrell (1980) using male high school basketball players demonstrated this point. The most significant factor in predicting player aggression was the amount of aggression directed against the subject. The athlete who perceives that an opponent is trying to inflict harm will respond in the same way (Stephens, 2000).

3. *Fear of retaliation*   To some degree, the fear of retaliation on the part of the individual who is the target of aggression can inhibit another player from initiating that aggression. A basketball player is a little less likely to elbow her opponent in the ribs if she fears similar treatment from the opponent. This sort of respect for an opponent's ability to "give as good as she gets," however, can quickly escalate into open aggression and counteraggression (Knott & Drost, 1972).

4. *Structure of the game*   Two of the earliest studies of game variables and aggression were conducted by Volkamer (1972) with soccer and Wankel (1972) with ice hockey. These studies were quickly followed by investigations by Lefebvre and Passer (1974) with soccer, Cullen and Cullen (1975) with ice hockey, Martin (1976) with basketball and wrestling, Russell and Drewery (1976) with soccer, and Engelhardt (1995) with ice hockey. Following is a summary of the findings with respect to game variables:

a. *Point differential*   More aggressive penalties occur as the game score differential increases. When teams are tied or the scores are close, aggression is at a minimum. The penalty for aggression in a critical game situation is so high that players, coaches, and managers go out of their way to avoid it.

b. *Playing at home or away*   Whether home or visiting teams display more aggressive behavior may depend on the nature of the aggression and the type of game involved. Soccer teams tend to be more aggressive when playing away from home, whereas aggression is almost equal for home and visiting ice hockey teams.

c. *Outcome of participation*   Consistent with the frustration-aggression hypothesis, members of losing teams are observed to be more aggressive than members of winning teams.

d. *League standings*   The lower a team is in the standings, the more its members engage in aggression. The lowest incidence of aggression occurs with teams in first place.

e. *Periods of play*   As a general rule, acts of aggression increase as the game proceeds. Clearly, the lowest number of acts of aggression occurs during the first period of play. This finding may be related to point differential.

5. *Rivalry, familiarity, and frequency of play*
Intradivisional play in professional ice hockey is associated with significantly more incidents of aggression among players than interdivisional play (Widmeyer & McGuire, 1997). Intradivisional play features frequent competition among teams that are geographically close to each other (cities) and that have intense rivalries. Conversely, interdivisional play features less frequent competition among teams that are often from different geographical areas. In interdivisional play, the rivalries are less intense and the players are less familiar with one another. As players become more familiar with one another due to frequency of play, and as the rivalries become more intense due to geographical location, aggression becomes more frequent.

6. *Goal orientation*   Elite youth ice hockey players exhibiting high levels of ego goal orientation (focus on social comparison and winning) are more likely to view aggressive acts in ice hockey as legitimate and part of the game. A respect for rules and officials declines as the ego orientation of the athlete increases. Conversely, high task goal orientation is associated with higher levels of sportspersonship (Dunn & Dunn, 1999; Rascle, Coulomb-Cabagno, & Delsarte, 2005; Stephens, 2001).

7. *Athlete and sport differences*   Research confirms that more aggression occurs in men's ice hockey than in men's basketball. In a study reported by Kirker et al. (2000), two highly skilled men's basketball games and two skilled ice hockey games were filmed and studied. Of 105 observed acts of aggression, 66 occurred in ice hockey and only 39 in basketball. In addition, 65 were physical in nature, whereas 40 were verbal in nature. Results further showed that (a) ice hockey is a more violent game than basketball, (b) aggression is more accepted in ice hockey than basketball, (c) aggressive acts tended to be both preceded and followed by physical and verbal aggressive behavior, (d) most aggression is instrumental as opposed to hostile in nature, and (e) verbal abuse of referees was the most common aggressive behavior (this by basketball players). Research also shows that despite suggestions to the contrary from the media and some academics, athletes do not have a greater propensity than nonathletes to commit sexual assault, or to commit off-field aggressive acts. The research, however, does show that physical size is a predictor of hostile aggression (Lemieux, McKelvie, & Stout, 2002; Smith & Stewart, 2003).

Reducing Aggression in Sport

Aggression in sport can be curtailed, or at least minimized, if all concerned are interested in doing so. The sad part is that some of the most influential people actually promote rather than discourage violence because they believe it sells tickets. As long as this attitude is allowed to continue, there is little hope of solving the problem. If it is allowed to continue on the professional level, it will continue to be promoted at the lower skill levels. Athletes in the youth leagues emulate their heroes on the collegiate and professional levels. They watch their sport heroes receive awards, applause, money, and adulation for behavior that borders on open aggression, and they want to become like them.

Research shows that angry feelings and angry behavior, the precursor to hostile aggression, can be modified through anger awareness training and role playing (Brunelle, Janelle, & Tennant, 1999). Athletes can learn to control their feelings of hostility and anger. Role playing is particularly effective in reducing an athlete's angry feelings and behavior. The effects of anger management training and role playing persist after training ceases. In the two sections that follow, specific suggestions are given as to how aggression by athletes and violence by fans can be reduced or eliminated. These suggestions are based upon the literature generally, but also upon an important position paper endorsed by the International Society of Sport Psychology (Tenenbaum, Stewart, Singer, & Duda, 1997).

Curtailing Aggression and Violence by Athletes

1. Young athletes must be provided with models of nonaggressive but effective assertive behavior.

2. Athletes who engage in aggressive acts must be severely penalized.

3. The penalty or punishment that an athlete receives for an act of aggression must be of greater punitive value than the potential reinforcement received for committing the act. On balance, it must be demonstrated that aggression does not pay.

4. Coaches who encourage or even allow their athletes to engage in aggressive behavior should be fined, censored, and/or suspended from their coaching duties.

5. External stimuli or cues capable of evoking hostile aggression on the field of play should be removed. An example of an aggressive cue might be the antics of an overly zealous fan displaying an inflammatory sign.

6. Coaches and referees should be encouraged to attend in-service training workshops on dealing with aggression on the part of players.

7. In addition to receiving punishment for acts of aggression, athletes should receive rewards and praise for showing restraint and patience in emotionally charged situations.

8. Strategies and coping skills designed to curtail acts of aggression should be practiced.

9. Social interaction between members of opposing teams should be encouraged by coaches and managers during the days leading up to a contest.

Curtailing Aggression and Violence by Fans

1. Potential troublemakers should be closely supervised. Fans with a history of violence and fighting should be identified and denied admission.

2. The sale, distribution, and use of alcoholic beverages at sporting events should be limited and controlled.

3. Athletic events should be promoted and encouraged as family affairs. The best way to do this is to promise a family-like environment and to provide financial incentives for family attendance.

4. The media should promote responsible behavior on the part of the fans by not glamorizing acts of aggression on the field of play and by not promoting a sense of friction or dislike between the players and fans of the two competing teams.

5. As with athletes and coaches, fan aggression must be swiftly and severely punished.

Summary

Two factors must be present in order for a behavior to be labeled aggression. First, the behavior must be aimed at another human being with the goal of inflicting physical harm. Second, there must be a reasonable expectation that the attempt to inflict harm will be successful. There are two kinds of aggression, hostile and instrumental. In hostile aggression the goal is to harm, while in instrumental aggression the goal is to obtain some external goal, such as victory. Assertiveness is not aggression, but because legitimate physical force is often used, it is often confused with aggression

Theories of aggression discussed include instinct theory, social learning theory, moral reasoning theory, and reformulated frustration-aggression theory. Instinct theory posits that aggression is a catharsis that results in a reduced drive to aggress. Social learning theory posits that aggression is a learned behavior that does not result in a catharsis. Bredemeier's theory of moral reasoning links an individual's degree of moral reasoning with the willingness to aggress. Berkowitz's reformulation of frustration-aggression theory focuses upon the notion that frustration results in a readiness to aggress, but not necessarily in aggression.

Individuals likely to precipitate fan violence tend to be young males who travel in packs, have a recent history of fighting, like to watch fights, are impulsive, and score high on the trait of aggressiveness. In every incident of fan violence there will be onlookers, peacemakers, and troublemakers. The onlookers are likely to constitute the clear majority of the fans, while approximately 26 percent say they would try to stop the fight (peacemakers), and 7 percent would join in or encourage others to join in the violence (troublemakers).

Research has demonstrated that there are certain situational factors that are associated with aggression on the part of athletes. A knowledge of these situational factors is likely to help reduce aggression in sport. Recommendations are given for reducing aggression among athletes and reducing fan violence.

Critical Thought Questions

1. The discussion in this chapter has focused upon aggression and physical harm. How could the operational definition of aggression be revised to include psychological harm?

2. Which theory of aggression do you think provides the best explanation of aggressive behavior in sport? Explain.

3. Discuss the concept of catharsis relative to instinct theory, frustration-aggression theory, and social learning theory.

4. Can a researcher differentiate between aggressive behavior and assertive behavior when using archival data? Explain.

5. Add to the list of strategies for curtailing aggression among athletes and violence among fans.

6. Why do you think that there is a general belief that athletes are more likely to commit acts of aggression than non-athletes? What can be done to dispel this myth?

Glossary

aggression A sequence of behaviors in which the goal is to injure another person.

assertiveness The expenditure of unusual effort and energy to achieve an external goal.

bracketed morality The suspension of ethics, or morality, during athletic competition.

catharsis effect The purging of anger and frustration associated with not being able to accomplish a goal.

circular effect of aggression The pattern in which one act of aggression leads to further aggression.

false consensus effect The belief on the part of some violence-prone fans that others share their infatuation for fighting and would willingly join them in precipitating an altercation.

fan identification The psychological connection or identification that individuals have with their teams.

frustration-aggression theory As originally conceived by Dollard et al. (1939), the theory that frustration always results in aggression.

hostile aggression Aggression against another human being with the intent to harm; the reinforcement or goal is to inflict pain and suffering on the victim. It is always accompanied by anger.

instinct theory The theory that human aggression is an innate biological drive that cannot be eliminated, but must be controlled through catharsis for the good of humankind.

instrumental aggression Aggression against another human being with the intent to harm; the reinforcement is to obtain some external goal, such as victory or prestige.

moral reasoning An individual's capacity to understand and embrace standards of moral behavior. Bredemeier asserts that an individual's

willingness to engage in aggression is related to her stage of moral reasoning.

peacemakers Those who try to make peace when a riot occurs. Peacemakers are contrasted with those who watch and those who incite.

readiness for aggression According to Berkowitz, the condition of being primed for aggression because of frustration. Aggression does not occur unless an aggressive cue is presented to the frustrated person.

reformulation of frustration-aggression theory Berkowitz's theory that frustration does not necessarily result in an aggressive response, but does result in a readiness for aggression.

relational aggression Harming others through such things as social ostracism and malicious rumors.

social learning theory Relative to aggression, a theory that posits that aggression is a function of learning, and that biological drive and frustration are inadequate explanations for aggression.

troublemakers Those who incite and take part in a riot. Troublemakers are contrasted with those who watch and those who try to make peace.

Audience and Self-Presentation Effects in Sport

KEY TERMS

Archival data
Audience density
Away court disadvantage
Dysfunctional assertive
 behavior
Functional assertive
 behavior
Home advantage
Home disadvantage
Hostile crowd
Impression construction
Impression management
Impression motivation
Interactive audience
Moderating variable
Self-attention
Self-handicapping
Self-presentation
Social facilitation
Zajonc's model

When the crowd gives to the athlete, the athlete gives back to the crowd. (Dan O'Brian, U.S.A., 1996 Olympic Decathlon Champion; O'Brian & Sloan, 1999).

Perhaps no social-psychological effect is more important to athletic performance and outcome than the audience, or spectator, effect. The evidence is clear, for example, that there is significant advantage to playing at home in baseball, football, basketball, ice hockey, and soccer. The perception of a home court advantage is especially evident in men's collegiate basketball and professional soccer. Many basketball conferences have adopted the policy of sending the winners of their postseason tournaments to the NCAA tournament. Thus, the conference championship has in many cases been reduced to a scramble for a home court advantage in the first round of the conference postseason tournament.

In professional sports, two well-publicized examples of the home court advantage may be cited. Sports writers have coined the phrase "Celtic Mystique," when referring to the win-loss record of the Boston Celtics basketball franchise when playing at Boston Gardens. Prior to losing game number four to the Los Angeles Lakers in the 1987 NBA championship series, the Celtics had won 94 of their previous 97 games in "friendly" Boston Gardens. The 1987 World champion Minnesota Twins baseball team won 70 percent of its regular-season home games. In addition, the Twins won all their postseason home games when they defeated the heavily favored Detroit Tigers for the American League Pennant, as well as all their home games against the St. Louis Cardinals in the World Series.

While many variables may help create the home court or home field advantage, none seem to be as important as the presence of a supportive audience. Determining how and why an audience presence affects athletic performance is the focus of this chapter. Major topics to be discussed in this chapter include social facilitation, effects of an interactive audience on performance, and self-presentation effects in sport.

Social Facilitation

Social facilitation research is based on the notion that the presence of an audience of one or more spectators can facilitate performance. This is an appealing concept, since almost everyone has experienced the desire to perform better when friends, family, or members of the opposite gender are watching.

Research in the area of social facilitation was significantly influenced by the work of Robert Zajonc (pronounced "science"). Zajonc's classic paper on the topic remains the single most critical factor in the development of social facilitation as a field of inquiry (Zajonc, 1965). Based upon drive theory (see chapter 8), **Zajonc's model** proposed that the presence of an audience has the effect of increasing arousal (drive) in performing subjects. Since increased arousal facilitates the elicitation of the dominant response, the presence of an audience will enhance the performance of a skilled individual while causing a decrement in the performance of an unskilled individual. This concept is illustrated in figure 14.1 for athletic competition.

While Zajonc's model generated hundreds of research investigations, it suffered a fatal flaw from the perspective of sport psychology research. Social facilitation was defined as "consequences upon behavior which derive from the sheer presence of other individuals" (Zajonc, 1965, p. 269). To test the model, researchers were obligated to focus on the "sheer presence" of an audience with no interaction between the performer and the audience. Since this situation *rarely* occurs in competitive athletics, the research generated from testing the model is not easily applied to sport. Therefore, the balance of this section will be devoted to research in which an interactive relationship between participants and spectators is assumed. For a review of social facilitation research, the reader is referred to Cox (1990).

CONCEPT   The presence of a supportive and emotionally arousing crowd translates into a home court advantage in many situations.

APPLICATION   Since the home court advantage is a function of fan support, it is important to capitalize on this advantage by filling the stadium or fieldhouse. Additionally, the band, the cheering squad, and publicity should be used to generate excitement and enthusiasm.

FIGURE 14.1 | Drive theory prediction of the influence of a crowd on the performance of athletes of differing skill levels.

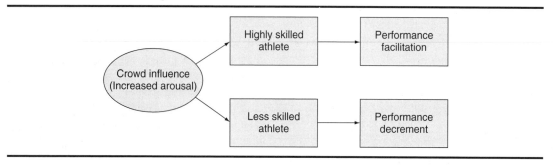

Effects of an Interactive Audience on Performance

Perhaps the most interesting topic associated with the **interactive audience** is that of the **home advantage.** The fact that the home advantage exists in such team sports as basketball, baseball, football, ice hockey, and soccer is well documented (Bray, 1999; Bray, Law, & Foyle, 2003; Brown, Van Raalte, & Brewer, 2002). In addition to the concept of a home court advantage in traditional team sports, we also have evidence of a home country advantage relative to the Olympics (Leonard, 1989) and to individual sports (Bray & Carron, 1993). Some authors have argued that the home advantage could be due to factors other than the audience, such as jet lag, travel fatigue, sleeping conditions, changed eating habits, unfamiliarity with local playing conditions, and referee bias. While it would be difficult to rule all of these factors out, researchers have shown that the negative effects of travel (Courneya & Carron, 1991) and lack of facility familiarity (Moore & Brylinski, 1995) are insufficient explanations for poor performance on the part of visiting teams. In the pages that follow, we will focus upon the most viable explanation for the home court advantage: the presence of a supportive and interactive audience.

Why Is There a Home Court Advantage?

The most plausible explanation for the home advantage in sport is the presence of a supportive and interactive audience. But how does this work? Does the audience energize the home team, or does it inhibit the performance of the visiting team? The best available answers for these questions come from two separate investigations.

The first investigation of interest, reported by Varca (1980), involved collegiate men's basketball games played during the 1977–78 season in the Southeastern Conference. Varca tested the hypothesis that the home court advantage was attributable to more functional assertive play on the part of the

CONCEPT Winning on the road can be enhanced by understanding the nature of the home court advantage.

APPLICATION When playing away from home, it is important that the coach develop a careful game plan and stay with it. The game plan should emphasize patience on offense, tactics to keep the crowd calm, and careful avoidance of penalties and fouls.

CONCEPT Playing before a supportive but expectant audience can increase the cost of not winning, thereby leading to self-attention and "pressing" on the part of an athlete or a team.

APPLICATION There are lots of examples of the self-attention effect in sport. It often happens when a new player replaces a popular home-town favorite on the team roster. Expectations are high and the player tries too hard to please the crowd. A sport psychologist or informed coach can help an athlete in this situation by teaching him patience and by building the athlete's self-confidence.

---

home team and more dysfunctional assertive play on the part of the visiting team. Increased arousal caused by the supportive crowd was believed to facilitate assertive play. In Varca's terminology, **functional assertive behavior** in basketball included superior performance in the skills of rebounding, steals, and blocked shots, while **dysfunctional assertive behavior** was limited to personal fouls, a behavior believed to inhibit performance. As predicted by Varca's hypothesis, significant differences were noted between home and away teams on the functionally assertive skills of stealing, blocking shots, and rebounding. The home teams enjoyed a superiority in these three important skills. Additionally, the visiting teams had significantly more fouls than the home teams. Varca's research is very helpful in explaining why the presence of a roaring crowd could facilitate the home team's performance, but inhibit that of the visiting team. The skills involved in rebounding, stealing, and blocking shots are closely associated with

strength and speed. These are the kinds of skills that are facilitated by very high arousal. While trying to negate the functional assertive behavior of the home team, the visiting team gets whistled for personal fouls. This causes increased frustration, and more dysfunctional behavior results.

The second study of interest was reported by Silva and Andrew (1987). Based on previous research, the investigators knew that the home team won more games than did the visiting team in collegiate basketball. They hypothesized, however, that the advantage favoring the home team was due not to increased performance caused by a supportive audience, but to inferior performance on the part of the visiting team—sort of an **away court disadvantage,** as opposed to a home court advantage. **Archival data** from 418 men's collegiate basketball games played in the Atlantic Coast Conference from 1971 to 1981 were utilized in the investigation. The unique aspect of this investigation was that performance of players during actual competition was compared with a pregame standard of good performance provided by coaches. While home teams did exhibit superior game statistics when compared to visiting teams, this occurred not because the home teams exhibited game statistics better than expected, but because the visiting teams exhibited game statistics worse than expected.

When Is the Home Court/Field a Disadvantage?

Is playing at home always an advantage, or can it sometimes be a disadvantage? For a number of reasons, playing at home can create a **home disadvantage.** One reason might be that the fans expect you to win at home; this can result in additional pressure to play well. A second reason might be that playing before a very vocal and supportive audience can raise arousal to a level that results in a decrement of performance.

> Sometimes, playing at home in the postseason isn't an advantage. You get so charged up that you lose focus of what you have to do.
>
> (Joe Torre, New York Yankees manager; Walker, 1996.)

A case in point is the above observation by Joe Torre, manager of the New York Yankees baseball team, following the loss of the first two games of the 1996 World Series while playing at home. The Yankees went on to win the series in six games. In this series the Atlanta Braves lost three straight games at home as well. According to Baumeister and Steinhilber (1984), this is the heightened self-attention, or self-awareness, effect that plagues home teams during important home games. The presence of a supportive audience may have the effect of increasing the cost of not winning when you are expected to. The athlete or athletes begin to "press," which interferes with the execution of skillful play (Wright, Voyer, Wright, & Roney, 1995).

Butler and Baumeister (1998) asserted that for self-attention reasons, participants may adopt a cautious performance style that, in the presence of a supportive audience, may lead to suboptimal performance (e.g., trying too hard to please the hometown fans in a critical game situation). Law, Masters, Bray, Eves, and Bardswell (2003), however, demonstrated that this effect would occur only if the athletes possessed explicit knowledge as opposed to conceptual knowledge of how to perform a skill. For example, a tennis player who possessed only a conceptual understanding of how to hit a topspin tennis drive should not suffer a performance decrement in the presence of a supportive audience. Conversely, a tennis player who possessed detailed technical knowledge (explicit knowledge) of how to hit a topspin tennis drive may suffer a performance decrement in the presence of a supportive audience. This takes us back to our study of attention in chapter 7, where we learned about the debilitative performance effects of disrupting the automatic nature of a motor task. Due to self-attention, the supportive crowd causes the athlete to resort back to attending to the explicit-knowledge details of executing a motor skill.

Audience Characteristics

Having determined that a home advantage usually exists in sport and that this advantage is related to the presence of a supportive and interactive audience, we should now examine characteristics of the audience. Do certain audience characteristics lead to a greater home advantage? This question will be discussed in the following paragraphs.

Crowd Size, Intimacy, and Density   There is evidence in professional baseball that crowd size makes a difference. Schwartz and Barsky (1977), for example, demonstrated that audience size is related to performance in baseball. The winning percentage of home teams increased as the size of the crowd increased. This effect is most pronounced when first-division home teams play visiting teams from the second division (those with fewer wins). Also based upon the Schwartz and Barsky data is the observation that sports such as basketball and ice hockey enjoy a greater home advantage than baseball and football. Since baseball and football

CONCEPT A supportive audience is important for the home team. However, the home team should make sure that the mood of an audience does not turn ugly and hostile.

APPLICATION It is unethical and unsportsmanlike to promote fan hostility in support of the home team. Coaches, managers, and team officials are morally obligated to avoid such a situation.

normally accommodate a far greater number of fans than basketball and/or ice hockey, factors such as audience density and audience intimacy may be more important than size for creating the home court advantage (Agnew & Carron, 1994). **Audience density** and audience intimacy are related to how tightly packed together the fans are and how close they are to the field of play. Successful teams that opt to move out of smaller, more intimate facilities into larger ones often do so at the expense of crowd density and intimacy.

Crowd Hostility It is generally understood that a supportive and friendly crowd will help the home team. What is the effect, however, of a seemingly **hostile crowd** on player performance? Research by Greer (1983) demonstrated that sustained hostile spectator protests have a clearly negative impact on the visiting team. Home basketball games of two Division I basketball teams were monitored and studied. Observations of sustained spectator protest were identified and studied relative to subsequent skill performance. Following episodes of sustained fan protest (usually directed at officials), the performance of athletes was monitored for five minutes of running game time. The results of the research showed a slight improvement in the performance of the home team, paralleled by a more significant and pronounced decline in performance of the visiting team following spectator protest.

Arie Selinger, former head coach of the U.S. women's national volleyball team, can attest to the devastating effect of a hostile audience (Steers, 1982). Arie took his heavily favored women's team to Peru in 1982 to compete in the World Championships. Everything went according to plan until the U.S. team played Peru. That was when the

crowd took over. For two hours, it was impossible for players, coach, or officials to communicate verbally. The highly unsportsmanlike fans were armed with whistles and noisemakers. Each time a U.S. player went back to serve, the noise was deafening. "The sound came down like thunder. You could feel the vibrations. You're totally disoriented. It's a terrible experience," said Coach Selinger. A father of one of the athletes summed it up this way: "The team prepared for nine months to win the World Championships and they were beaten by a wireless microphone and fifteen thousand plastic whistles."

Sometimes it is not necessarily the entire crowd that is hostile, but a small and highly vocal section of the crowd. A case in point is the "Antlers," a rowdy, raucous, almost-anything-goes men's basketball student jeering section composed of University of Missouri–Columbia undergraduates wearing black T-shirts, goofy hats, and painted faces. The antics of the "Antlers" are at times so offensive that they have to be censured by university administrators (Fallstrom, 1993).

Home Court Advantage and Team Quality

From the previous discussions we understand that the home team usually enjoys a home court or field advantage. At least, we know that the home team wins more often than the visiting team. This advantage is more noticeable in basketball and ice hockey (63 percent) compared to football (60 percent) and baseball (53 percent), but it is a consistent observation on most levels of play. What these statistics do not reveal, however, is the effect of team quality on home court advantage. Bray (1999) studied archival data from the National

The "Antlers" provide raucous and sometimes rowdy support for the home team. Source: Courtesy University of Missouri–Columbia Sports Information.

Hockey League (NHL) across nearly 20 years, and over thirty thousand games. For most of the designated period of time, 26 teams were involved in an 80-game schedule (40 at home, 40 away). By grouping teams as a function of winning percentages, Bray was able to report that the home winning percentages of low-, average-, and high-quality teams were 32 percent, 52 percent, and 70 percent, respectively. Conversely, away winning percentages of low-, average-, and high-quality teams were 17 percent, 35 percent, and 52 percent, respectively. It is an advantage to play at home in the NHL, but the chances of winning at home are far greater for high-quality teams as opposed to lower-quality teams.

Madrigal and James (1999) conducted a similar investigation involving archival data from 10 years of women's Big Ten basketball (1,800 games). Their analysis showed that over the ten-year period, the home teams won 61 percent of the contests. When the percentage of games won by home teams was considered as a function of team quality, strong teams defeated other strong teams, moderately strong teams, and weak teams at home 70 percent, 86 percent, and 95 percent of the time, respectively. High-quality teams performed better at home than away in terms of field goal percentages, steals, and fouls, when they played the same opponent in the same season. Conversely, for low-quality teams, the opposite was observed; they

CONCEPT Team quality is a more powerful predictor of whether or not a team will win a contest
than where the game is being played. When two
teams of equal quality play each other, the home
team should have the advantage.

APPLICATION Teams and coaches should
worry less about whether they are playing at
home or away and focus more on team quality.
The stronger and better team should have the

advantage regardless of whether the game is at
home or away. In those cases where teams are of
equal quality, the home court or field advantage
can have a powerful effect upon the outcome of
the game. Regardless of where a game is being
played, a quality team should always enter a
contest believing they are the best team and that
they will win if they play as well as they should.
The focus should be upon execution and quality
of play and not upon the crowd or the facility.

---

performed better away than at home on these same
skills. Factors that contributed most to the home
team advantage, after controlling for team quality,
were crowd density, rebounds, steals, and field goal
shooting percentage.

From these two investigations, involving two
different team sports, it seems clear that team
quality is a **moderating variable** that determines
the strength of the relationship between playing at
home and winning percentage. Winning at home
occurs more often for high-quality teams than for
low-quality teams.

Players' Perceptions of Home Court Advantage

The majority of research on home court advantage
has been generated using archival data. Seldom
have athletes been asked in a systematic way about
their perception of the phenomenon. Bray and
Widmeyer (2000) asked 40 collegiate female
basketball players about their perceptions of the
home court advantage. The athletes indicated that
they believed there was a home court advantage in
their league, and that about 61 percent of the games
were won by the home team. They further indicated
that they felt that home court familiarity and crowd
support were the primary factors determining the
home court advantage. Athletes indicated that they
believed that travel considerations were of borderline importance, and that special "house rules"

associated with the building they played in were of
no consequence. Finally, athletes believed that they
were more self-confident when they played at
home than when they played away.

Self-Presentation Effects in Sport

Earlier in this chapter we introduced Zajonc's
model of social facilitation, which proposes that the
arousal associated with the presence of an audience
could either facilitate or inhibit the performance of
an athlete. We further learned that the tenets of
Zajonc's model are grounded in drive theory. However, these same relationships can be explained
through a principle of social psychology called
self-presentation. "Self-presentation, also called
impression management, refers to the processes
by which people monitor and control how they are
perceived by other people" (Leary, 1992, p. 339).
As explained by Leary and Kowalski (1990),
impression management or self-presentation has
two components. The first component of impression management is impression motivation, while
the second is impression construction. **Impression
motivation** involves the process that causes a
person to be concerned about how she is perceived
by others and her attempts to regulate other people's impression of her. **Impression construction**
deals with the types of images a person wants to
construct for people to see. This two-component
model of impression management is the theoretical

FIGURE 14.2 | Self-presentation in sport may be manifested as a function of social facilitation, self-attention, or self-handicapping.

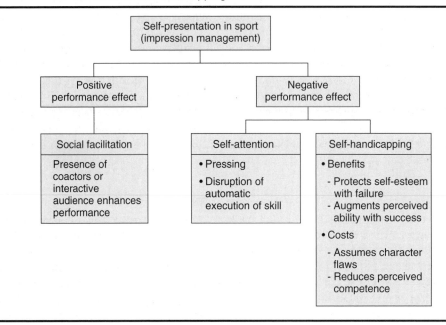

foundation of the Self-Presentation in Exercise Questionnaire (SPEQ) that will be introduced in chapter 16, on exercise psychology.

As illustrated in figure 14.2, an athlete's efforts to regulate other people's (the audience's) impression of him can result in either a positive performance effect or a negative performance effect. In the case of a positive performance effect, it is impression motivation and not physiological arousal that causes an increase in performance (Carron, Burke, & Prapavessis, 2004). Conversely, if efforts to regulate people's image do not go well, a decrement in performance could result. We introduced this earlier in this chapter when we were talking about the home field/court disadvantage. While playing at home, the athlete may try too hard to impress the home team crowd. Pressing results in **self-attention,** which tends to disrupt the automatic execution of a motor task. This causes the athlete to fall back into attending to the details of the execution of a motor task.

As can be seen in figure 14.2, there is another way that impression management associated with self-presentation can lead to a decrement in performance. This is through **self-handicapping.** Self-handicapping is a form of self-presentation because the athlete is attempting to regulate the impression that other people have of her. As stated by Leary (1992), "research has demonstrated that self-handicapping has a strong self-presentational component. People are more likely to self-handicap when others will be aware of their handicaps, suggesting that people erect such handicaps, in part, to protect their social images in the face of failure" (p. 346). In this regard, self-handicapping is related to attribution theory, as it has to do with predetermining a cause (Hausenblas, Brewer, & Van Raalte, 2004; Prapavessis, Grove, & Eklund, 2004). In self-handicapping individuals make preplanned proactive use of effort reduction and performance excuses in order to protect their self-esteem from potential negative feedback within a

CONCEPT   Efforts to regulate impressions that other people have of you may result in self-handicapping. Self-handicapping involves the attempt on the part of the athlete to protect the athlete against a loss of self-esteem by establishing an a priori excuse for performing poorly. Self-handicapping is related to low task and high ego orientation, and to the perception of a competitive environment.

APPLICATION   The use of self-handicapping to attempt to regulate the impressions that others

have of us is a common practice. It is a practice, however, that should be discouraged, because it is misleading and because it could result in other people not believing us or discounting our precompetitive attributions for failure. While self-handicapping does not necessarily result in a decrement in performance, it is manipulative and it creates an expectation of failure. Take a positive approach with the athlete: teach her to "think positive" and to try her best at all times.

social evaluative setting. For example, a tennis player fearing that she is going to be defeated by a superior player in a weekend tournament misses three days of practice during the week leading up to the match. This makes it possible for the athlete to make the argument to herself and to those she hopes to influence that her poor performance was due to lack of practice, and not to lack of ability or skill. If an athlete is effective in self-handicapping, he can look good if he performs poorly because of the pre-established cause, but also look great if he succeeds in the face of so many obstacles. Thus, the benefit of effective self-handicapping is to protect self-esteem after failure and to augment perceptions of ability after success. However, there are potential costs associated with ineffective self-handicapping. If the athlete is not convincing, or the audience does not believe the athlete's predetermined explanations for failure, others may come to perceive that the athlete suffers from a character flaw (Prapavessis et al., 2004).

A number of investigations have linked self-handicapping with goal perspective theory (Ommundsen, 2001, 2004; Ryska, Zenong, & Boyd, 1999). In all of these investigations, athletes who score high in the disposition to self-handicap also score low in dispositional task goal orientation. Athletes who practice self-handicapping are less likely to value hard work, effort, and long-term dedication to learning a task. The disposition to

self-handicap may be measured using the Self-Handicapping Scale (Jones & Rhodewalt, 1982).

Recent research has also linked self-presentation in sport to reduced athletic identity and to positive and negative health behaviors. A study reported by Grove, Fish, and Eklund (2004) measured athletic identity one week before, shortly after, and two weeks after announcing the selection of a young female athlete all-star team. Those young women who did not make the team suffered an immediate reduction in perceived athlete identity. The researchers reasoned that the drop in athletic identity may have been an example of impression management. The unsuccessful athletes expressed themselves as being less identified with athletics in order to protect their self-image.

Ginnis and Leary (2004) observed that both good and bad health behaviors may be directly related to self-presentational attempts to practice impression management. For example, a young man who risks his life by diving off a cliff into dangerous water for the purpose of impressing his girlfriend is engaging in a health-damaging behavior. Similarly, a young man who drives his car too fast in an attempt to impress his friends is also engaging in health-damaging behavior. Conversely, a young woman may take up a regular exercise program to impress her boyfriend. This would be an example of using impression management to facilitate a healthy behavior.

Summary

Zajonc's model and social facilitation research were based on the notion that the presence of an audience of one or more spectators can facilitate performance. Because Zajonc's model was based on the effect that the "sheer presence" of an audience had on performance, interactive audiences were ruled out. Because athletic competition almost always involves an interaction between athletes and spectators, Zajonc's model cannot be easily applied to sport. Therefore, the focus of this chapter was upon the effects of interactive audiences on performance.

It is well documented that the home team wins most athletic contests, but less is known about the reasons for this advantage. Research was reviewed that suggests that an audience generates functional assertive behavior in home team athletes and dysfunctional assertive behavior in visiting team athletes. Research also suggests that the home court advantage may be more of an away court disadvantage, because visiting team athletes often play below their normal level of play.

Some athletes perform better away than they do at home. This is known as the home court disadvantage. It is believed that this occurs when athletes try too hard to please the hometown fans and begin to "press." This is the self-attention effect, which interferes with skillful play.

While the size of the crowd may be an important predictor of team performance, the density of the crowd and crowd intimacy are even more important. Related to the density of the crowd is the mood of the audience. A hostile and protesting crowd can have a particularly negative effect on the visiting team. Team quality seems to moderate the relationship between playing site and team performance. The home court advantage is much stronger for high-quality teams than for lower-quality teams.

Self-presentation refers to the processes by which athletes monitor and control how they are perceived by other people. Self-presentation is also called impression management, and is composed of impression motivation and impression construction. When an athlete is successful in regulating how others perceive him, social facilitation is the end result. When he is unsuccessful, the end result is self-attention. Self-handicapping is a form of self-attention, because the athlete is attempting to regulate the impression that other people have of him.

Critical Thought Questions

1. How can the home team best take advantage of the home court advantage when playing a team of equal quality and ability? Devise a game plan in your favorite team sport.

2. How can the visiting team best prepare for an away contest when playing a team of equal quality and ability? Devise a game plan in your favorite team sport.

3. As a sport psychologist, how would you suggest working with an athlete who suffers from self-attention in front of the home crowd?

4. Imagine coaching a basketball team (or sport team of your choice) in front of an abusive and hostile crowd. Consider the fact that you will not be able to communicate with your athletes without shouting. Devise a game strategy for this situation.

5. Discuss self-handicapping as a strategy for regulating the impression that other people have for an athlete. Give specific examples in yourself and in athletes you have observed who have used self-handicapping to regulate other people's impression. Discuss the pros and cons of self-handicapping.

Glossary

archival data Data that have been saved from earlier games. Generally, official records from collegiate and professional team games are kept for many years.

audience density How crowded an audience is; how close to and intimate with the players the audience is.

away court disadvantage The notion that teams win more often at home not because of a home court advantage, but because of an away court disadvantage for the visiting team.

dysfunctional assertive behavior Aggressive or assertive behavior, such as fouling, that interferes with successful performance.

functional assertive behavior Aggressive or assertive behavior, such as rebounding, stealing, and shot blocking in basketball, that facilitates successful performance.

home advantage The notion that playing an athletic contest at home is an advantage.

home disadvantage The idea that if athletes try too hard to please an expectant audience, playing at home may actually be a disadvantage.

hostile crowd An audience that is hostile and threatening to the visiting team in a sustained and noisy way.

impression construction The process of constructing images of oneself for other people to see.

impression management The process by which people monitor and control how they are perceived by other people.

impression motivation A personal concern about how she is perceived by others and her attempts to regulate other people's impression of her.

interactive audience An audience or crowd that interacts in various ways with the athletes. Usually the interaction is visual and auditory.

moderating variable A variable, such as team quality, that determines how two other variables relate to each other.

self-attention The tendency of an athlete to "press," or try too hard to please the crowd, when playing in front of an expectant home crowd.

self-handicapping A form of self-presentation in which people make preplanned proactive use of effort reduction and performance excuses in order to protect self-esteem.

self-presentation The process by which people monitor and control how they are perceived by other people.

social facilitation The benefits or detriments associated with the presence of a noninteractive audience.

Zajonc's model A model of social facilitation based upon drive theory.

Team Cohesion in Sport

KEY TERMS

Coactive sports
Conceptual model of team
  cohesion
Consequences of team cohesion
Determinants of team cohesion
Direct intervention approach
Direct measurement approach
Direction of causality
Group Environment
  Questionnaire
Indirect intervention approach
Indirect measurement approach
Interactive sports
Personal satisfaction
Social cohesion
Task cohesion
Team building
Team cohesion

Intuitively, athletes, coaches, and sport enthusiasts understand that there is more to athletic success than the collective individual skills of the members of a team. Sport psychologists refer to this extra team ingredient as *group* or *team cohesion*. Athletes have described the presence or absence of team cohesion in interesting ways.

Naturally there are going to be some ups and downs, particularly if you have individuals trying to achieve at a high level. But when we stepped in between the lines, we knew what we were capable of doing. When a pressure situation presented itself, we were plugged into one another as a cohesive unit. That's why we were able to come back so often and win so many close games. And that's why we were able to beat more talented teams.

(Michael Jordan, Chicago Bulls;
Jordan, 1994, p. 23.)

We've got a funny chemistry here. It's a strange mixture of guys. They're all good guys; I don't have any personal problems with any of them. They are guys who have great talent and good dispositions, but the mix—something's not there. I can't really explain it other than it's a strange chemistry.

(Rob Murphy, Cincinnati Reds;
Kay, 1988, p. 15.)

The first quotation was by Michael Jordan, arguably the best professional basketball player in the history of the game, describing how the Chicago Bulls played together as a cohesive unit to defeat more talented teams. The second quotation was by Rob Murphy, a relief pitcher on the 1988 Cincinnati Reds major league baseball team. After being picked to win the National League West in 1988, the Reds suffered a lackluster season. Murphy made his comment in an effort to explain how the talent-laden Reds could have performed so poorly on the field. He attributed it to a "strange chemistry," or what was likely a lack of team cohesion among the players.

The sports pages of local newspapers are full of examples of talented teams that failed to live up to expectations, or less talented teams that performed far above expectations. In sport, it is a well-established principle that a group of individuals working together is far more effective than the same individuals working independently of one another. On a basketball team, there may be several individuals capable of scoring 20 or more points a game. However, in the interest of team success, the coach may require that one or more of these athletes assume nonscoring roles. For example, a point guard has the primary responsibility of setting up plays and getting the offense started, while the power forward must "crash" the boards and get offensive and defensive rebounds. Athletes who play these specialized roles rarely score as many points as shooting guards or forwards. Yet, out of the desire to be "team players," these athletes

accept less glamorous roles for the common good of the team. Thus, as a group or team evolves, a certain structure develops. This structure varies from group to group and situation to situation, but it is critical for team success.

When the Pistons won, I thought there might be hope yet for the National Basketball Association. A group of virtual unknowns who played together as a team beat a more talented team built around four superstars. How old-school can you get? There's an art to putting together a team that can compete with any other team. It isn't just a matter of having talent at each position, or matching up with other teams position by position. The players have to be able to play the game, to want to play together, to be willing to pick one another up and to be capable of making intelligent decisions.

(Oscar Robertson (2004) commenting on the Detroit Pistons' defeat of the Los Angeles Lakers in the 2004 NBA Championship series.)

Not only do members of successful teams have the ability to work together (teamwork), they also enjoy a certain attraction to one another. In this respect, it seems logical that teams composed of members who like each other and enjoy playing together will somehow be more successful than teams lacking this quality. In 1979, the Pittsburgh Pirates won the World Series. Their theme was "We Are Family," suggesting that they owed their success to this ability to get along and work together for a common goal. Ironically, the Oakland Athletics of the early 1970s and the New York Yankees in 1978 also enjoyed World Series success, but with well-publicized disharmony within their ranks.

As a social psychological topic, team cohesion ranks as a very important factor for enhancing team performance and feelings of satisfaction among members. It has evolved as a complex concept that requires study and additional research before it can be fully understood and appreciated. In the following sections, team cohesion will be discussed in terms of its defining characteristics, a conceptual model, its measurement, its determinants, its consequences, and its development.

CONCEPT   Team cohesion is a multidimensional construct that includes both task and social cohesion.

APPLICATION   When considering the development of team cohesion among members of a team, it is important that the coach differentiate between task and social cohesion. These two types of cohesion can be developed simultaneously in a team, or they can be developed independently of each other. It is possible to see an athletic team develop a high degree of social cohesion, yet not enjoy athletic success due to poor task cohesion.

Defining Characteristics of Team Cohesion

Albert Carron, a prominent sport social psychologist, defined group cohesion as "a dynamic process which is reflected in the tendency for a group to stick together and remain united in the pursuit of goals and objectives" (Carron, 1982, p. 124). Because an athletic team is a group, Carron's definition of group cohesion applies equally well as a definition for **team cohesion.** Intuitively, we know that team cohesion is the elusive ingredient that changes a disorganized collection of individuals into a team.

Fundamental to the study of team cohesion is the understanding of group dynamics. Members of a team or group begin to interact with each other the moment the group is first formed. Once a group is formed, it ceases to interact with outside forces in the same manner that a collection of individuals would. The team becomes an entity in and of itself. From a Gestalt perspective, the whole (group or team) is greater than the sum of its parts.

Over the past 20 years, research on team cohesion has made it clear that one must understand two basic concepts in order to understand the relationship between cohesion and team behavior. The first is the distinction between task and social cohesion, and the second is the distinction between direct and indirect measurement of cohesion.

Task and Social Cohesion

Task and social cohesion are two independent components of team cohesion. Failure to discriminate between the two can result and has resulted in hopelessly confusing results relative to the relationship between athletic performance and team cohesion. **Task cohesion** is the degree to which members of a team work together to achieve a specific and identifiable goal. We see task cohesion on display when a baseball team turns a double play, executes a hit-and-run, or completes a double steal. We see task cohesion on display when a basketball team runs a motion offense or sets up a full-court zone defense. We see task cohesion on display when a volleyball team executes the multiple-attack offense, or defends against the same.

Social cohesion is the degree to which the members of a team like each other and enjoy personal satisfaction from being members of the team. The independence of task cohesion and social cohesion was easily observed in the example of the world champion New York Yankees baseball team of 1978. This was a team that could turn the double play, hit the cut-off man, advance runners, and work together on the field of play better than any other team in baseball. Yet, this was also a team whose members did not like one another. Team members fought with each other, cliques were formed, and angry words were exchanged both privately and through the media.

If a study had been conducted on the 1978 Yankees to relate task cohesion and team performance, a very high and positive relationship would have been observed. Yet, if a study had been conducted to relate social cohesion and team performance, a very strong negative relationship would have been observed. If care were not taken to distinguish between the two different kinds of team cohesion in this example, confusing results would have been obtained. Such has been the case with numerous early studies on the topic of team cohesion and athlete behavior.

The Los Angeles Lakers of the National Basketball Association (NBA) provide a recent example of this paradoxical relationship. Before the break-up of the team in 2004, the tandem of Shaquille O'Neal and Kobe Bryant was instrumental in leading the L.A. Lakers to three NBA championships in five years. This feat was accomplished even though these two great athletes did not like each other (Broussard, 2004).

Direct and Indirect Measurement of Cohesion

Just as many early studies failed to differentiate between task and social cohesion, many also failed to differentiate between the two basic approaches to measuring team cohesion (Carron, 1980; Cox, 1985). The **indirect measurement approach** to assessing team cohesion tries to get at team cohesion by asking each team member how she feels about every other member of the team on some basic question (e.g., How much do you like the different members on your team?). Summed scores from team members would represent a measurement of team cohesion. The **direct measurement approach** to assessing team cohesion is direct in the sense that players are asked to indicate how much they like playing for the team (individual attraction) and how well they feel the team functions as a unit (group integration). Research using the indirect approach has generally failed to find a meaningful relationship between team cohesion and team or individual behavior. As with task and social cohesion, it is of critical importance that the approach to measuring team cohesion be reported, as results could vary greatly as a function of the approach. The indirect approach to measuring team cohesion is very rare in sport psychology research today.

A Conceptual Model of Team Cohesion

Building upon the distinction between task and social cohesion and focusing upon the direct measurement approach, Widmeyer, Brawley, and Carron (1985) developed the **conceptual model of team cohesion.** As illustrated in figure 15.1, the conceptual model is based on an interaction between the athlete's group orientation (social versus task) and the athlete's perception of the team. Task and social cohesion are relatively easy concepts to understand, given our discussion on their distinction. Conversely, perception of team is not quite so easy to understand. When an athlete conceptualizes team cohesion, is he thinking about the team as a collective whole (including himself), or is he thinking about his individual attraction to the team (he likes the style of play) and his individual

FIGURE 15.1 | Widmeyer, Brawley, and Carron's conceptual model of team cohesion.

| | Athlete's perception of team | |
	Group integration	Individual attraction
Group orientation — Social	Bonding to the team as a whole to satisfy social needs (GI-S)	Attraction to team and team members to satisfy social needs (ATG-S)
Group orientation — Task	Bonding to the team as a whole to satisfy task completion needs (GI-T)	Attraction to team and team members to satisfy task completion needs (ATG-T)

CONCEPT   The conceptual approach to looking at team cohesion takes into consideration task and social cohesion as well as the athletes' perceptions of the team.

APPLICATION   The conceptual model takes into consideration the multidimensional nature of team cohesion. If the coach looks at team cohesion from a multidimensional perspective, it will be easier to understand the positive influence of team cohesion on athletic behavior. Social cohesion is different from task cohesion, and individual attraction to the group is different from group integration.

---

attraction to team members (they are good friends)? If he is thinking of the team as a unit, this is called group integration (GI). If he is thinking about his attraction to the team or to individual members, this is called individual attraction, or attraction to group (ATG). The combination of the two kinds of group orientation and two kinds of perception yields four different dimensions of team cohesion:

1. Group integration–social (GI-S)
2. Group integration–task (GI-T)
3. Individual attraction to the group–social (ATG-S)
4. Individual attraction to the group–task (ATG-T)

Measurement of Team Cohesion

A number of inventories have been developed for measuring team cohesion in sport. An incomplete list of inventories includes the Sports Cohesiveness Questionnaire (SCQ; Martens & Peterson, 1971); the Team Cohesion Questionnaire (TCQ; Gruber & Gray, 1981); the Sport Cohesion Instrument (SCI; Yukelson, Weinberg, & Jackson, 1984); the Group Environment Questionnaire (GEQ; Widmeyer, Brawley, & Carron, 1985); and the Team Psychology Questionnaire (TPQ: Partington & Shangi, 1992).

Of these five inventories, the **Group Environment Questionnaire** (GEQ) has been sport psychologists' primary inventory of choice over the last 15 years. The GEQ is composed of 18 items that measure the four team cohesion dimensions as illustrated in figure 15.1. Based upon the conceptual model of team cohesion, the GEQ devotes four items to measuring the GI-S dimension, five to the GI-T dimension, five to the ATG-S dimension, and four to the ATG-T dimension. Each item is anchored to an eight-point Likert Scale (1 = strongly disagree, 8 = strongly agree). Studies by Carron and Spink (1992) and Li and Harmer (1996) confirmed the four-dimension factor structure of the GEQ, while an important study by Schutz, Eom, Smoll, and Smith (1994) failed to confirm its factor structure. The Schutz et al. (1994) investigation did not call into question the four-factor conceptual model of team cohesion, but it did call into question the ability of the GEQ to accurately measure these four factors. Notwithstanding the results of this investigation, the GEQ has continued to be used extensively by researchers and practitioners. Recently, a French version of the GEQ has been developed (Heuzé & Fontayne, 2002).

Determinants of Team Cohesion

Carron (1982) proposed a sport-specific framework for studying team cohesion determinants and consequences. As illustrated in figure 15.2, the basic conceptual framework is composed of four classes of determinants and two classes of consequences. The basic notion is that there are certain factors that lead to or determine team cohesion, and certain consequences associated with having or not having team cohesion. In this section we

FIGURE 15.2 | Illustration showing determinants and consequences of team cohesion.

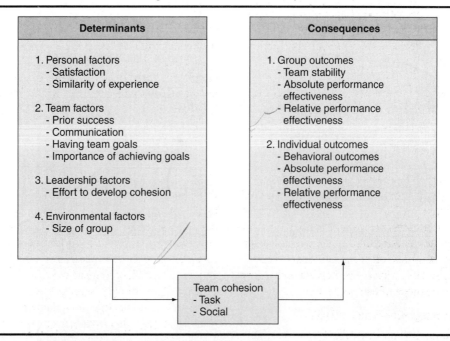

Source: From Carron, A. V. (1982). "Cohesiveness in sport groups: Interpretations and considerations." *Journal of Sport Psychology,* *4*(2), 131. Copyright 1982 by Human Kinetics Publishers. Adapted by permission.

will focus attention upon the **determinants of team cohesion;** in the following section, upon the consequences of team cohesion.

In an important study reported by Widmeyer and Williams (1991), factors that determine team cohesion among female collegiate NCAA Division I golfers were investigated and reported. In this investigation, team cohesion was measured using the multidimensional GEQ. The results of this investigation revealed that each specific determinant shown in figure 15.2 was predictive of some aspect of team cohesion. The strongest predictor of team cohesion, however, was **personal satisfaction.** For intercollegiate golfers, the best way to develop team cohesion is by cultivating a personal feeling of satisfaction toward the team and team members.

Widmeyer and Williams' research is a benchmark study because it systematically studied the relationship between Carron's (1982) taxonomy of team cohesion determinants and team cohesion among intercollegiate golfers. Whether the specific findings of Widmeyer and Williams can be generalized to team sports such as volleyball, basketball, and football remains to be seen. Is personal satisfaction with the team as a whole and members generally as strong a predictor of team cohesion in basketball as it is in golf? This is an important research question, since team cohesion is generally believed to be of greater consequence in team sports than in individual sports.

Although the Widmeyer and Williams study was the most comprehensive investigation to date dealing with determinants of team cohesion, other studies have focused upon specific antecedents. For example, team stability as an antecedent of team cohesion has been studied by Donnelly, Carron, and Chelladurai (1978), with the general

A tremendous amount of task cohesion and coordinated play is required to execute the "multiple attack" in volleyball. Courtesy Ball State University Sports Information.

finding that team stability fosters cohesion. Similarly, research by Widmeyer, Brawley, and Carron (1990) suggests that team cohesion decreases as team or group size increases.

Communication among members of an interactive team is an important determinant of team cohesion (Eccles & Tenenbaum, 2004; Wickwire, Bloom & Loughead, 2004). As you will recall, effective communication was identified in chapter 3 as an important characteristic of successful leaders. Here we focus upon the athletes and upon the ways effective communication leads to cohesion

CONCEPT The feeling of personal satisfaction with the team as a whole and members generally is the strongest predictor of team cohesion in intercollegiate golf.

APPLICATION Other determinants of team cohesion, such as team success, group size, and interpersonal communication, are of small consequence in developing team cohesion compared to personal satisfaction. Golf coaches who value team cohesion should focus on developing a feeling of satisfaction among team members.

CONCEPT Team cohesion is related to size and stability of a team or group.

APPLICATION It is difficult to maintain team cohesion in teams or groups that are constantly changing and increasing in size. Coaches and leaders who wish to increase cohesion among members must avoid constant turnover and keep groups or subgroups relatively small.

among members, which leads to performance effectiveness. Wickwire et al. (2004) reported results of a qualitative investigation in which the athlete-athlete dyad in male international-level beach volleyball was studied. Of interest were identified factors and elements of the dyad that characterize the effective elite doubles volleyball team. Like doubles in tennis, doubles in sand volleyball requires superb athleticism and teamwork in order to be successful. Factors that emerged as being critical to good teamwork included mental strength, physical skill and strength, time with partner, personality traits, interpersonal development, and the ability to communicate verbally and nonverbally during play. The athletes identified communication and player cohesion as being codependent and equally important. One important component of team cohesion is shared knowledge, and the way that knowledge is shared is through communication (Eccles & Tenenbaum, 2004).

Consequences of Team Cohesion

Athletic Performance

Most research on **consequences of team cohesion** has focused upon performance. The primary question that has been asked is to what degree team cohesion leads to improved team or individual performance. This basic question is also reflected in figure 15.2, where performance is described in terms of individual and group outcomes. Absolute and relative performance effectiveness refer to the difference between winning or losing a contest, as opposed to performing better or worse than the last time. Having a team's performance reduced to a slash in the win or loss column is an absolute measure of performance effectiveness, whereas comparing a team's performance to how well it performed in the last outing is a relative measure of performance effectiveness. A similar dichotomy can be developed for the performance of individual sport athletes. From an absolute performance perspective, a golfer may not have won a golf tournament, but from a relative perspective, she may have improved her score significantly.

Research has consistently shown that a significant relationship exists between team cohesion and athletic performance (Carron & Dennis, 1998; Carron, Coleman, Wheeler, & Stevens, 2002; Grieve, Whelan, & Meyers, 2000; Lowther & Lane, 2002; Mullen & Cooper, 1994; Widmeyer, Carron, & Brawley, 1993). This observed relationship is much stronger when task cohesion as opposed to social cohesion is involved, and when interactive as opposed to coactive sports are involved. **Interactive sports** are those team sports, such as volleyball, basketball, and football, that require members of the team to interact with one another. **Coactive sports** are those activities, such as bowling, archery, and riflery, that do not require members of the team to interact with each other for team success.

A meta-analysis published by Carron et al. (2002) is very supportive of the cohesion-performance relationship. This is a very important study, as it shows the strength of the relationship between team cohesion and athletic performance in numerous situations and conditions from 1967 to 2000. For example, it shows relationships using all reported studies, as well as those that used only the Group Environment Questionnaire (GEQ). When the GEQ was used, the results show (a) a much stronger relationship between cohesion and performance for men compared to women, (b) a slightly stronger relationship for task cohesion compared to social cohesion, and (c) a much stronger relationship for subjective as opposed to objective measures of performance. It is generally believed that a stronger relationship exists between team cohesion and performance for interactive sports compared to coactive sports, but this is not entirely clear in the meta-analysis. The average effect size (measure of strength of relationship) is actually larger for coactive teams compared to interactive teams. It is likely,

however, that this is due to the small number of studies that looked at coactive teams.

An ethnographic study reported by Holt and Sparkes (2001) is interesting because 13 members of a male soccer team were studied across an entire season. The focus of this investigation was not upon performance but upon factors that are believed to lead to team cohesion. Specifically, the results of the study showed that the athletes improved across the course of the eight-month season in role acceptance, clear and meaningful personal goals, unselfishness, willingness to sacrifice for the team, and use of positive communication. These are all factors that are believed to contribute to team cohesion.

It is often difficult to find a measurable relationship between team cohesion and objective performance. This was generally true with a study reported by Bray and Whaley (2001) with high school basketball teams in terms of three of four subscales measured by the GEQ. However, it was interesting to note that the one significant relationship was between social cohesion and objective individual performance. It was further demonstrated that expended effort mediated the relationship. In other words, social cohesion leads to individuals' trying harder, which leads to increased basketball performance. So, even though social cohesion may not have a direct effect on improved performance, it may have an indirect effect through expended effort.

In the sections that follow, other consequences of team cohesion will be discussed. These include direction of causality for the cohesion-performance relationship, improving group self-efficacy, predicting future participation, homogeneity among starters and nonstarters, disruptive effects of self-handicapping, and team momentum.

Direction of Causality for the Cohesion-Performance Relationship

As was briefly mentioned above, numerous investigations have verified that a significant and positive relationship exists between direct measures of

CONCEPT Interactive sport teams, such as soccer, volleyball, and basketball, that enjoy high levels of task cohesion are more likely to experience performance success than equally skilled teams that are low in task cohesion.

APPLICATION It is especially important for interactive teams to work hard to develop task cohesion among members of the team. Coaches should also encourage the development of social cohesion on interactive teams and both task and social cohesion on coactive teams, but these things are less critical to team success than task cohesion is for interactive teams. Coaches should use the GEQ or some other team cohesion measurement instrument of choice to monitor task and social cohesion of interactive team members.

---

team cohesion and performance in both individual and team sports. The issue of **direction of causality,** however, has been a difficult issue to resolve. Does team cohesion lead to or cause successful performance, or does successful performance lead to or cause high team cohesion? As you might guess, this is not a good "either/or" question. It is likely that high team cohesion leads to high performance, but it is also likely that successful performance leads to perceptions of team cohesion. The critical issue is which direction is the most dominant. We would like to think that the direction from team cohesion to successful performance is most dominant. Almost all athletes, however, have experienced the "halo effect" of success. When your team is winning, it is a lot easier to feel at one with your team and with your teammates.

> It was an easy season for me. . . . I'm a lot more comfortable right now . . . when you're winning everybody loves you. (Wesley Stokes, former University of Missouri–Columbia basketball player; Thompson, 2002)

The direction of the relationship between team cohesion and athletic performance has been a subject of discussion and academic debate for over 25 years. Initially, it was assumed that team cohesion leads to improved performance, but then a number of well-controlled studies started to suggest just the opposite, that performance leads to cohesion. Based upon the Carron et al. (2002) meta-analysis, it seems safe to say that a moderately

FIGURE 15.3 | Team cohesion leads to increased team performance, but increased team performance also leads to an increase in team cohesion.

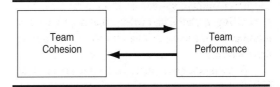

strong relationship exists between team cohesion and athletic performance regardless of direction of relationship, with the strongest relationships being observed when the two are measured concurrently. This relationship is illustrated in figure 15.3. It should be no surprise to anyone, however, that winning an athletic contest would lead to perceptions of increased cohesion among members and that losing a contest would lead to perceptions of reduced team cohesion (Boone, Beitel, & Kuhlman, 1997; Kozub & Button, 2000; Matheson, Mathes, & Murray, 1997).

Improving Group Self-Efficacy

The importance of individual self-efficacy in developing self-confidence and in skilled performance was introduced in chapter 5. Research by Kim and Sugiyama (1992) likewise points to the importance of group or team self-efficacy in helping teams

CONCEPT   The winning, and even more, the losing, of an athletic contest have a strong effect upon an athlete's perceived team cohesion. This effect may even be stronger than the effect that precompetitive team cohesion has upon team performance, but it in no way minimizes the importance of developing team cohesion in sport teams. Team cohesion, especially task cohesion, leads to improved performance of interactive team sports.

APPLICATION   It is useful to understand that winning or losing can influence perceived team cohesion, but the coach must not allow this information to reduce his efforts to develop team cohesion among members of an athletic team. Team cohesion does lead to improved performance of teams that are required to work together to achieve a common goal.

believe that they will be successful. Teams that have developed high levels of team cohesion tend to exhibit high levels of group efficacy as well. This effect is stronger for task cohesion than for social cohesion (Kozub & McDonnell, 2000).

Predicting Future Participation

For young athletes especially, it is important that the sport experience lead to the expectation of continued participation. Sport participants who exhibit high levels of social cohesion also exhibit high scores in the expectation that they will participate in sport during the following season. Thus, social cohesion is a predictor of the intention to continue sport involvement (Spink, 1995). This prediction is undoubtedly related to the further observation that high levels of team cohesion are related to lowered state anxiety (Prapavessis & Carron, 1996). Consistent with the McClelland-Atkinson model of motivation, individuals low in state anxiety are more likely to continue sports participation.

Homogeneity of Team Cohesion

It is not enough that starters alone exhibit high levels of team cohesion. Research indicates that homogeneity of team cohesion among both starters and nonstarters is an important predictor of successful team performance. Spink (1992) showed that successful volleyball teams are characterized by high levels of team cohesion on the part of both starters and nonstarters. Conversely, less successful

teams are characterized by a lack of homogeneity (agreement) in team cohesion between starters and nonstarters. This observation suggests that the coach must develop high team cohesion among all the members of a team, and not just the starters.

Moderator of the Disruptive Effects of Self-Handicapping

Introduced in chapter 14, self-handicapping represents the strategies athletes use to proactively protect their self-esteem by creating excuses for their performance in forthcoming events through adopting or advocating impediments for success. Typical excuses might include missing practice due to injury or illness, partying and loss of sleep, school commitments or distractions, and family commitments or distractions. If success follows, the athlete or athletes can always internalize (take credit for) the victory, but if failure follows, they will have numerous external explanations as to why they have failed. This behavior causes disruption in the athlete's preparation for competition, and is therefore referred to as *self-handicapping*. Research (Carron, Prapavessis, & Grove, 1994; Hausenblas & Carron, 1996) indicates that team cohesion has a moderating effect on the trait of self-handicapping. Athletes high on the trait of self-handicapping rated the severity of disruption associated with it as low when team cohesion was low, but high when team cohesion was high. There is something about being a member of a cohesive group that makes athletes sensitive to disruptions associated with self-handicapping.

CONCEPT   In addition to increased athletic performance, there are numerous other positive consequences associated with increased team cohesion. These include collective self-efficacy, sports retention, sensitivity to disruptive effects of self-handicapping, psychological momentum, and mood.

APPLICATION   Even if increased team performance is not a direct result of a coach's efforts to increase team cohesion, there are many other positive consequences associated with enhanced team cohesion. Coaches should work to increase the task and social cohesion among members of athletic teams.

Development of social cohesion is an important goal for an athletic team. Courtesy University of Missouri–Columbia Sports Information.

Effects of Team Cohesion on Psychological Momentum

Research by Eisler and Spink (1998) demonstrated, using high school volleyball players, that a high level of task cohesion is associated with perceived psychological momentum. As a psychological construct, perceived momentum was introduced in chapter 5. Here we learn that teams that enjoy a high level of task cohesion are more likely to enjoy the benefits of psychological momentum. There are times in an athletic contest at which the momentum seems to be in one's favor. For teams that are high in task cohesion, this perception of psychological momentum is likely to be more pronounced. Thus, we have another positive consequence of team cohesion.

Mood and Emotion

Athletes who belong to a cohesive team enjoy increased levels of positive mood, particularly in terms of vigor. Lowther and Lane (2002) observed that pregame measures of team cohesion are positively related to pregame measures of positive mood in male soccer players. Research also shows an association between task cohesion and directional state anxiety. Eys, Hardy, Carron, and Beauchamp (2003) measured competitive state anxiety in young athletes (soccer, rugby, field hockey) prior to a contest and task cohesion after the same contest. Using directional anxiety scores, the athletes were divided into two extreme groups, classified as viewing anxiety as being facilitative or debilitative to performance. The researchers then attempted to correctly classify the athletes as being facilitative or debilitative as a function of post game task cohesion measures. Results showed that athletes who perceived their anxiety to be facilitative to good performance tended to have higher task cohesion scores. Conversely, athletes who perceived their anxiety to be debilitative to good performance tended to be low in task cohesion.

Developing Team Cohesion

Given that team cohesion is an important characteristic of successful teams, how can it best be developed? In this section we will address that important question in three different ways. First, we will discuss the development of team cohesion as a process. Second, we will discuss team building as a way to develop team cohesiveness among team members. Finally, we will identify specific interventions calculated to enhance team cohesion.

Team Cohesion as a Process

Very early, Tuckman (1965) described four basic stages that a team must pass through in order to emerge as a cohesive unit. These four stages include forming, storming, norming, and performing. In the *forming* stage, the athletes experience the excitement of new relationships and getting together with teammates for a common goal or cause. In the *storming* stage, the athletes struggle with the frustrations of trying to learn a new team system and of getting acquainted with teammates with whom they may have little in common. During the *norming* stage, members of the team start agreeing upon common goals and establishing what the norms of acceptable and good performance are. Finally, during the *performing* stage, the team is ready to perform as a cohesive unit. As we look at these four stages of development, it should be clear that team cohesion should be at its lowest during the forming and storming stages. For this reason, if team cohesion is measured during one of these two early stages, one should expect it to be very low. This would be consistent with measuring team cohesion during spring training or some other preseason period of time. If you want to study the relationship between team cohesion and team performance, you should not assess team cohesion during the forming or the storming stage. The best time to measure team cohesion would be during the norming or the performing stage. If team cohesion were low during the performing stage, this could indicate that the team had not progressed as it should, and in reality might not be in the performing stage. Team building is a process that should be helpful for a team to emerge from Tuckman's four stages as a cohesive unit (Bloom, Stevens, & Wickwire, 2003).

Team Building

Team building is described by Newman (1984, p. 27) as a process to "promote an increased sense of unity and cohesiveness and enable the team to function together more smoothly and effectively."

Thus, team building is a process that should lead to cohesiveness among members of a team. In this regard, the entire March issue of volume 9 (1997) of the *Journal of Applied Sport Psychology* was devoted to the topic of team building. From this edition we learn that there are numerous approaches to team building. Here we will discuss three of these approaches. However, it is important first to point out that team building is supported by research. Using a physical challenges approach to team building, Ebbeck and Gibbons (1998) demonstrated that sixth- and seventh-grade physical education students could increase their perceived global self-worth, athletic competence, physical appearance, social acceptance, scholastic competence, and behavioral conduct.

Yukelson (1997) proposed a team building approach that he referred to as a direct intervention approach. In the **direct intervention approach,** the sport psychologist works directly with athletes and employees to empower them, through a series of educational seminars and experiences, to develop a shared vision, unity of purpose, collaborative teamwork, individual and mutual accountability, team identity, team cohesiveness, open and honest communication, and trust at all levels. Dunn and Holt (200) reported on the effectiveness of a personal approach to team b in nature. Results s in confidence, trust, teammates.

Carron, Spink, a a team building appr indirect intervention **vention approach,** coaches and manage their athletes and e building approach is three stages occur fourth involves the application of tions learned in the workshop. The four stages of this program include the introductory phase, the conceptual phase, the practical phase, and the intervention phase. During the *introductory phase,* the coaches learn about the general benefits of group cohesion. During the *conceptual phase,* the coaches learn to conceptualize team cohesion as a direct result of the distinctiveness of the group environment, role clarity, conformity to group norms, cooperation, goal setting, and team sacrifices.

Finally, Smith and Smoll's (1997a) Coach Effectiveness Training Program (CET) is identified as an excellent team-building program. Recall that the CET program was first introduced in chapter 3, when we discussed leadership in sport. The purpose of the CET program is to teach coaches how to develop teams that have a positive team climate and to develop athletes who experience true satisfaction and feel interpersonal attraction to the team and team members. Thus, the CET program is an indirect team building program, in that the coach learns how to deliver the program to her own athletes.

Specific Interventions Designed to Enhance Team Cohesion

In the process of team building, specific interventions are learned that, if applied, will lead to increased team cohesion among team members. Ten specific interventions and strategies for developing listed below:

player with the responsibilities ayers. This can be accomplished by allowing players to play other ng practices. This will give ciation for the importance of ayers. For example, a spiker who complains of poor setting en the chance to set once in a

r teacher, take the time to learn rsonal about each athlete on the le will come to appreciate and cooperate with those who know little things about them, such as a girlfriend's name, a birthday, or a special hobby.

3. *Develop pride within the subunits of large teams.* For example, in football, the various special teams need to feel important to the team and take pride in their accomplishments. For smaller units such as basketball teams, this may not be so critical. However, the team as a whole should develop pride in its accomplishments.

4. *Develop a feeling of "ownership" among the players.* Individual players need to feel that the team is *their* team and not the coach's team. This is accomplished by helping players become involved in decisions that affect the team and them personally. Individual players need to feel that their voice will be heard.

5. *Set team goals and take pride in accomplishments.* Individuals and teams as a whole must have a sense of direction. Challenging but obtainable goals should be set throughout the season. When these goals are reached, players should collectively be encouraged to take pride in their accomplishments and then set more goals.

6. *Make sure that each player on the team learns his role and comes to believe it is important.* In basketball, only five players can be on the floor at one time. The process of keeping the other seven players happy and believing that they too are important is one of the great challenges of teaching and coaching. Each player on the team has a unique role. If players do not feel this, they will not feel they are part of the team, which will detract from team unity.

7. *Do not demand or even expect complete social tranquility.* While it is not conducive to team cohesion to allow interpersonal conflicts to disrupt team unity, it is equally unrealistic to expect interpersonal conflicts to be completely absent. Anytime individuals are brought together in a group, there is potential for conflict. The complete elimination of any friction may actually suggest a complete lack of interest in group goals.

8. *Since cliques characteristically work in opposition to the task goals of a team, avoid their formation.* Cliques often form as a result of (1) constant losing, (2) players' needs not being met, (3) players not getting adequate opportunities to play, and (4) coaches who promote the development of cliques through the use of "scapegoats" or personal prejudice.

9. *Develop team drills and lead-up games that encourage member cooperation.* Many drills are designed solely for the purpose of skill development. Many other drills must be developed that teach athletes the importance of reliance upon teammates. For example, in basketball, drills that emphasize the importance of teammate assists could be emphasized.

10. *Highlight areas of team success, even when the team loses a game or match.* Since we know from the literature that performance affects feelings of satisfaction and cohesion, the coach must capitalize on this. If a volleyball team played good team defense in a losing effort, point this out to them.

Summary

Group or team cohesion is defined by Carron as "a dynamic process which is reflected in the tendency for a group to stick together and remain united in the pursuit of goals and objectives." Task and social cohesion are two independent components of team cohesion. Task cohesion reflects the degree to which members work together to achieve a specific goal. Social cohesion reflects the degree to which members of a team like each other and enjoy being members of the team. Both a direct and an indirect approach have been used to measure team cohesion.

The conceptual model of team cohesion is based upon an interaction between the athlete's group orientation (social versus task) and the athlete's perception of the team in terms of individual attraction and group integration. The Group Environment Questionnaire measures four team cohesion dimensions and is based upon the conceptual model of team cohesion.

Determinants of team cohesion include personal satisfaction, team factors, leadership factors, and size of group. Consequences of team cohesion include team stability, behavioral outcomes, and absolute and relative performance effectiveness.

Relative to team and individual performance, research has consistently shown that task cohesion leads to enhanced performance in interactive teams. Based upon the Carron et al. (2002) meta-analysis, it seems safe to say that a moderately strong relationship exists between team cohesion and athletic

performance regardless of direction of relationship, with the strongest relationships being observed when the two are measured concurrently.

In addition to increased athletic performance, there are numerous other positive consequences associated with increased team cohesion. These include collective self-efficacy, sports retention, sensitivity to the disruptive effects of self-handicapping, psychological momentum, and positive mood.

The development of team cohesion may be characterized as a process that passes through the four stages of forming, storming, norming, and performing. Team building is described by Newman as a process to "promote an increased sense of unity and cohesiveness and enable the team to function together more smoothly and effectively." Direct and indirect team-building intervention approaches were discussed. Finally, 10 specific interventions were identified that are instrumental in developing team cohesion in athletic teams.

Critical Thought Questions

1. When discussing team cohesion, why is it so critical to differentiate between task and social cohesion?

2. Why is the conceptual model of team cohesion so important to our understanding of this psychological construct?

3. Discuss the determinants of team cohesion illustrated in figure 15.2 relative to the

10 interventions for developing team cohesion. Are there similarities? Should there be?

4. Discuss the issue of direction of causality between team cohesion and athletic performance. Why is this an important concept to understand?

Glossary

coactive sports Activities, such as bowling, archery, and riflery, that do not require members of a team to interact with one another for team success.

conceptual model of team cohesion A model of team cohesion that is based on an interaction

between an athlete's group orientation and the athlete's perception of the team.

consequences of team cohesion Outcomes derived from team cohesion.

determinants of team cohesion Factors that cause or determine team cohesion.

direct intervention approach The accomplishment of team building by working directly with the members of a team or group.

direct measurement approach A team cohesion measurement approach that assesses team cohesion by directly asking team members how much they like playing for the team and how well they feel the team functions as a unit.

direction of causality The issue of whether team cohesion causes an improvement in performance or a good performance causes an increase in team cohesion.

Group Environment Questionnaire A team cohesion measurement instrument designed to measure four dimensions of team cohesion.

indirect intervention approach The accomplishment of team building by teaching coaches and managers how to conduct team building with their athletes and employees.

indirect measurement approach A team cohesion measurement approach that assesses team cohesion by asking each team member how she feels about every other member of the team on some basic question.

interactive sports Team sports, such as volleyball, basketball, and football, that require members of a team to interact with one another.

personal satisfaction The contentment or enjoyment an individual derives from being a member of a sports team.

social cohesion The degree to which the members of a team like each other and enjoy personal satisfaction from being members of the team.

task cohesion The degree to which members of a team work together to achieve a specific and identifiable goal.

team building A process used to promote an increased sense of unity and cohesiveness and to enable a team to function together more smoothly and effectively.

team cohesion A dynamic process that is reflected in the tendency for a group or team to stick together and remain united in the pursuit of goals and objectives.

PART 6

Psychobiology of Sport and Exercise

Chapters 13 through 15 (part 5) of this text dealt with several social psychology topics. In a similar fashion, the present part of the text deals with issues that combine psychology with biology. Just as social psychology of sport is viewed as a subset of sport psychology, so also is psychobiology of sport and exercise viewed as a subset of sport psychology. Each of these subset areas could easily be expanded into a separate content area of its own. However, for the purposes of this book, these areas are treated as subsets within the larger discipline of sport psychology. If a university or college curriculum offers a separate course in psychobiology of sport and exercise, this section could serve as an introduction to that course. However, if a separate course is not available, this part of the book will be invaluable to the sport psychology student. The psychobiological issues to be discussed in this part of the text are included in the following four separate chapters: exercise psychology (chapter 16), overtraining and burnout (chapter 17), psychology of athletic injuries (chapter 18), and drug abuse in sport and exercise (chapter 19). ∞

Exercise Psychology

KEY TERMS

Acquired immune deficiency
  syndrome (AIDS)
Activity anorexia
Acute exercise
Aerobic exercise
Amine hypothesis
Anaerobic exercise
Anorexia analogue
  hypothesis
Anorexia nervosa
Body image
Bulimia nervosa
Cardiovascular fitness
  hypothesis
Chronic exercise
Cognitive behavioral
  hypothesis
Delayed anxiolytic effect
Distraction hypothesis
Endorphin hypothesis
Exercise addiction
Exercise adherence
Exercise determinants
Exercise self-efficacy
Exercise self-presentation
  efficacy
Exercise self-schemata
Human immunodeficiency
  virus (HIV)
Immune system functioning

Life stress
Mediator variable
Moderator variable
Muscle dysmorphia
Natural history of exercise
Obligatory runner
"P" factor
Physical self-concept
Processes of change
Resistance exercise

Self-schemata
Social interaction hypothesis
Social physique anxiety
Stress inoculation
Subclinical eating disorders
Super-adherer
Theory of planned behavior
Theory of reasoned action
Transtheoretical model

Documentation of the physiological benefits of regular exercise has led to the inclusion of "lack of exercise" by the American Heart Association (1999) as a fourth risk factor for heart disease that can be modified or controlled by the individual. The other three risk factors are smoking, high blood pressure, and elevated cholesterol. Among other things, regular physical exercise helps lower cholesterol, decreases the percentage of body fat, mediates the effects of diabetes, reduces weight, and lowers blood pressure (Paffenbarger, 1994; Pate et al., 1995).

As stated by the President's Council on Physical Fitness & Sports (Staff, 1992), "if exercise could be packed into a pill, it would be the single most widely prescribed and beneficial medicine in the nation" (p. 5). But notwithstanding the documented physiological benefits of regular physical exercise, Dishman (2001) reports that (a) only 8 to 20 percent of the U.S. population regularly participate in vigorous physical activity; (b) 30 to 59 percent of the U.S. population have relatively sedentary lifestyles; and (c) 50 percent of the individuals who start regular physical activity programs drop out within six months.

Specific topics to be treated in this chapter include (a) psychological benefits of exercise, (b) theoretical explanations for exercise benefits, (c) exercise adherence and determinants, (d) theories of exercise behavior, (e) fitness as a moderator of life stress, (f) the immune system, cancer, HIV, and exercise, (g) social physique anxiety, (h) exercise addiction, and (i) eating disorders.

Psychological Benefits of Exercise

A large body of literature has been amassed that supports the position that regular exercise leads to improved psychological affect. Improved psychological affect is manifested in the form of a reduction in negative affect (e.g., anxiety and depression) and an increase in positive affect (e.g., self-efficacy, vigor, well-being). These consistent findings have led many mental health care professionals to prescribe exercise as a treatment for selected mental health symptoms. Exercise in many cases is as effective as psychotherapy and antidepressant drugs in treating emotional disorders (Babyak et al., 1999, 2000; Nicoloff & Schwenk, 1995).

These conclusions are supported by several narrative reviews and meta-analyses (Craft & Landers, 1998; Biddle, 1995; LaFontaine, DiLorenzo, Frensch, Stucky-Ropp, Bargman, & McDonald, 1992; Leith & Taylor, 1990; Long & Van Stavel, 1995; North, McCullagh, & Tran, 1990; Petruzzelo, Landers, Hatfield, Kubitz, & Salazar, 1991), as well as recently reported research (e.g., Bixby, Spalding, & Hatfield, 2000; Cox, Thomas, Hinton, & Donahue, 2004; Focht & Koltyn, 1999; Hale, Koch, & Raglin, 2000; Lochbaum, Karoly, & Landers, 2004; Van Landuyt, Ekkekakis, Hall, & Petruzzello, 2000).

Studies cited to support the relationship between exercise and psychological affect benefits have used both acute and chronic exercise. **Acute exercise** refers to exercise that is of short duration (e.g., 30 minutes), while **chronic exercise** refers to long-term exercise (e.g., 12 months). Studies have also tended to focus upon either aerobic or resistance exercise. Many studies feature acute aerobic exercise in which intensity is manipulated. This is usually accomplished on a treadmill (jogging) or a stationary cycle. While individual differences often prevail (Van Landuyt et al., 2000), it is generally believed that best psychological benefits are derived using a moderate intensity of exercise as opposed to a very low or a very high intensity. Research by Cox et al. (2004), however, provides convincing evidence through a well-controlled investigation that a bout of relatively intense exercise is superior to a moderate bout of aerobic exercise in terms of reducing state anxiety.

Aerobic exercise refers to exercise that is accomplished at an exercise intensity that allows for the intake of sufficient oxygen to maintain continuous exercise. This is opposed to **anaerobic exercise,** in which the exerciser does not get enough

| 16.1 | CONCEPT & APPLICATION |

CONCEPT   While an acute bout of exercise can result in a measurable reduction in negative mood state, chronic exercise habits are required to maintain these psychological benefits.

APPLICATION   In a sense, a single bout of exercise is like a single dose of medication. If the medication, or in this case exercise, is to be of long-term benefit, it must be maintained over a sufficiently long period of time.

| 16.2 | CONCEPT & APPLICATION |

CONCEPT   A relatively large body of literature supports the position that regular exercise (generally, aerobic exercise) is associated with improved psychological affect.

APPLICATION   The importance of this scientific finding should not be underestimated. Not only can regular exercise improve cardiovascular fitness, but it is also believed to have a beneficial effect upon the psychological mood state of mentally healthy individuals.

oxygen to maintain continuous exercise. Anaerobic exercise requires the athlete to breathe hard following exercise in order to replenish stored energy. After a bout of anaerobic exercise, the athlete will need a period of time to "catch her breath." This is not generally necessary with aerobic exercise.

While most research has focused upon acute aerobic or chronic aerobic exercise (usually running or cycling), many studies have focused upon resistance exercise. **Resistance exercise** usually involves the use of weights or weight training to provide resistance to the muscles. Like acute aerobic exercise, resistance exercise is also associated with beneficial psychological effects (Bartholomew, 1999; Bartholomew, Moore, Todd, Todd, & Elrod, 2001; Focht & Koltyn, 1999). Sixty minutes of cross-training, or training that includes both acute aerobic exercise and resistance training, has also been shown to be effective in reducing anxiety (Hale, Koch, & Raglin, 2000). In many cases an

acute bout of aerobic or resistance exercise will not result in an immediate decrease in anxiety, but it will result in an anxiety decrease following a delay of 30 to 90 minutes. In the case of anxiety, this is known as the **delayed anxiolytic effect** of acute exercise (Cox, Thomas, & Davis, 2000). This effect may be due to either the intensity of the exercise or the arousal component of anxiety (Ekkekakis, Hall, & Petruzzello, 1999).

In addition to improving psychological mood, research links acute and chronic aerobic exercise with improved cognitive functioning (Tomorowski & Ellis, 1986). Animal research (Cotman & Engesser-Cesar, 2002) suggests that the brain can produce molecules that nourish neurons and ensure overall brain health. Such molecules do exist; they fall into a clan of proteins called growth factors, or neurotrophic factors. One neurotrophic factor, brain-derived neurotrophic factor (BDNF), is capable of mediating the beneficial effects of exercise to the brain. Research shows that exercise

CONCEPT   The psychological benefits of regular physical activity are more pronounced for mentally ill individuals than for normal, mentally healthy individuals.

APPLICATION   Regular, supervised physical activity is an important adjunct treatment for individuals suffering from anxiety, depression, schizophrenia, and other emotional disorders. Hospitalized individuals would benefit significantly from organized daily physical activity appropriate to their environments.

increases the presence of BDNF in the brains of laboratory-exercised animals. Utilizing the human model, Miller (2000) studied the behavior and academic performance of fourth-grade students following and during a six-week, 10-minute-a-day walking intervention. Results showed improved behavior compared to that of a control group, and academic performance equal to that of the control group—even though the control group enjoyed an extra 10 minutes of class time each day.

Special Populations

Discussion to this point has focused upon the benefits of regular exercise for normal, healthy individuals. As we have seen, the evidence supporting the beneficial psychological effects of regular aerobic exercise is substantial. We turn our attention now to the beneficial psychological effects of regular physical activity on special populations of people.

Clinical Patients   The benefits of regular physical activity are even greater for individuals suffering from psychological disorders than for normal individuals (North et al., 1990; Petruzzelo et al., 1991). This effect was clearly documented for clinical depression by Craft and Landers (1998). Using a meta-analysis procedure, Craft and Landers observed that (a) both aerobic and nonaerobic exercise were effective in reducing clinical depression, (b) more depressed individuals benefited more from exercise, (c) exercise was as beneficial as psychotherapy and drug therapy for reducing

depression, and (d) long-term exercise programs were more effective than short-term programs for reducing depression in the clinically ill. Similar findings were reported for anxiety reduction (Petruzzello et al., 1991). In addition to treating depression and anxiety, exercise is an effective treatment for clinical patients suffering from schizophrenia. Faulkner and Sparkes (1999) documented the effects of a 10-week exercise program on three hospitalized individuals suffering from chronic schizophrenia. Results of the exercise program showed psychological improvements in the form of reduced auditory hallucinations and better sleep patterns. In another investigation, Martinsen, Raglin, Hoffart, and Friis (1998) demonstrated that patients suffering from severe panic disorder could safely undergo vigorous exercise without suffering panic attacks.

Finally, Bodin and Martinsen (2004) observed an increase in positive mood and self-efficacy for clinically depressed individuals participating in martial arts. Similar changes were not observed for exercise on the stationary bike. The researchers hypothesized that improvement in self-efficacy may have been necessary for an increase in positive mood to take place.

Children and the Elderly   Research has also shown the beneficial effects of exercise on children and older adults. Children's exercise behaviors are greatly influenced by their parents' attitudes and behaviors regarding exercise (Davidson, Cutting, & Birch, 2003). Factors that can influence a child's decision to be physically active include parents' beliefs, the children's perception of their own competence, and, to some extent, their goal orientation. A task, or mastery, orientation is a fairly strong predictor of exercise behavior in children (Brustad, 1996a; Kimiecik, Horn, & Shurin, 1996). Using 933 children as participants, Tomson, Pangrazi, Friedman, and Hutchison (2003) reported an inverse relationship between physical and health-related fitness and depression. Being physically fit and involved in fitness and sport activities serve as an antidepressant in children.

Regarding exercise and the elderly, research shows that participation in aerobic exercise selectively preserves some cognitive functioning that normally declines with age. So, for the elderly, there is not only the benefit of improved fitness and improved psychological affect associated with exercise, but also the prospect of slowing the decline of some cognitive functions. Exercise in the elderly is associated with the preservation of certain aspects of memory and spatial relationships (Shay & Roth, 1992). Finally, older adults (aged 60 to 77) participating in a six-month progressive resistance exercise program experienced reductions in confusion, tension, and anger (McLafferty, Hunter, Wetzstein, & Bamman, 2000).

In addition to enhancing or maintaining cognition in the elderly, exercise serves to have a beneficial effect on psychological mood, as it does with children and adults (Arent, Landers, & Etnier, 2000). McAuley et al. (2000) observed that older adults showed in increase in psychological well-being as a result of a six-month walking, toning, and stretching program. They also reported, however, that this beneficial effect of exercise eroded if participants did not continue to exercise during the six-months following the intervention. This result underscores the importance of chronic exercise habits in the elderly. Not only must the elderly continue to exercise to enjoy the psychological benefits, but they also must exercise at an intensity that leads to perspiring and heavy breathing (Lampinen, Heikkinen, & Ruoppila, 2000). While children, adults, and older adults must exercise

regularly in order to enjoy the psychological benefits, it is of interest to note that young adults, adults, and older adults differ in their motivation for chronic exercise (Cambell, MacAuley, Mc-Crum, & Evans, 2001). The top five reasons that adults and young adults, ages 16–44, give for exercise are these: (a) to feel in good physical shape, (b) to improve and maintain health, (c) to be mentally alert, (d) to have fun, and (e) to get out of doors. The top five reasons that older adults, ages 45–74, give for exercise are these: (a) to be mentally alert, (b) to feel in good physical shape, (c) to get out of doors, (d) to feel independent, and (e) to relax and forget cares.

Disabled Individuals   Finally, it is important to mention that the beneficial psychological effects of regular exercise extend to physically challenged individuals as well. For example, when compared to wheelchair nonsport participants, wheelchair sport participants have been observed to enjoy increased psychological benefits associated with regular physical activity (Cardinal, Kosma, & McCubbin, 2004).

Moderating Variables

From our discussion in this section, it should be clear that regular physical activity can have a beneficial psychological effect on individuals, regardless of their circumstances. In addition, research suggests that there are a number of variables that may moderate or facilitate the effectiveness of regular exercise on mental well-being.

Time of Day   Research suggests that time of day is not an important factor relative to psychological benefits derived from exercise. You get just as much affective benefit from running in the morning as from doing so at midday or in the evening (O'Connor & Davis, 1992). Furthermore, from a psychological perspective, it makes no difference if you exercise to exhaustion in the morning as compared to the evening (Koltyn, Lynch, & Hill, 1998).

CONCEPT   The psychological benefits of exercise extend to all individuals, regardless of age or degree of physical challenge.

APPLICATION   We must not lose sight of the need to extend opportunities to be physically active to all populations of people. Children are in particular need, because it is at a young age that exercise behaviors for a lifetime are established. Older adults are also in particular need because of the challenges of growing older. Physical activity can lessen or buffer the debilitating effects of aging, both physiological and psychological. Physically challenged individuals are in need as well, because it is often incorrectly assumed that they are incapable of meaningful physical activity.

Mode of Exercise   The psychological benefits of acute aerobic exercise appear to be the same, regardless of the mode of exercise. For example, Cox, Thomas, and Davis (2000) observed no difference in anxiety between treadmill and stepper exercisers following a 30-minute bout of exercise. However, research shows that mode of exercise does make a difference in terms of energy expenditure. Moyna et al. (2001) exercised participants at three different levels of perceived exertion (light, somewhat hard, hard) on six different exercise machines. Results showed that energy expenditure at each level of exertion was higher for men on the treadmill and ski simulator, and for women on the treadmill, ski simulator, and rowing ergometer, compared to the three other modes.

Music   Research suggests that listening to music during exercise can increase positive affect in the exerciser. Not only does listening to music during exercise enhance the beneficial effects of exercise, but it also reduces perceived exertion. At this time we can only speculate as to the effect that different kinds of music may have upon this observation (Boutcher & Trenske, 1990).

Attentional Strategy   Relative to attentional strategy, there is evidence that a dissociative (external) attentional strategy may result in greater psychological benefit (Masters & Ogles, 1998b). Runners who are asked to listen to their own heart rates during exercise (internal focus) exhibit greater emotional stress than runners who dissociate during exercise (Harte & Eifert, 1995).

Social Environment and Self-Efficacy   The social environment associated with exercise has an effect upon psychological benefits of exercise. In a study reported by Turner, Rejeski, and Brawley (1997), ballet students were randomly assigned to either a socially enriched learning environment or a socially bland environment. In the socially enriched environment, the students were treated to socially supportive interactions with the instructor and with members of the class. Results show increased benefits for the socially enriched environment in the form of revitalization and self-efficacy. Similarly, McAuley, Blissmer, Katula, Duncan, and Mihalko (2000) observed increases in self-esteem and self-efficacy in older adults who participated in walking or stretching/toning classes.

Theoretical Explanations for the Relationship between Exercise and Improved Mental Health

Many hypotheses have been proposed to explain why exercise is associated with improved mental health. A number of these hypotheses will be reviewed and discussed in the following paragraphs. The first three explanations are considered to be psychological in nature, while the remaining three are physiological in nature (North et al., 1990). While it is tempting to subscribe to one hypothesis at the expense of the others, it is likely that the ultimate explanation is eclectic and multidimensional in nature.

Cognitive Behavioral Hypothesis

The basic premise of the **cognitive behavioral hypothesis** is that exercise encourages and generates positive thoughts and feelings that serve to counteract negative mood states such as depression, anxiety, and confusion (North et al., 1990; Simons, Epstein, McGowan, Kupfer, & Robertson, 1985). This theoretical explanation parallels Bandura's theory of self-efficacy, discussed in chapter 5. According to Bandura (1997), when individuals master tasks they perceive to be difficult, they experience an increase in self-efficacy. Exercise is perceived by nonexercisers as a difficult task. When the nonexerciser succeeds in becoming a regular exerciser, she experiences a feeling of accomplishment and self-efficacy. An increase in self-efficacy is helpful in breaking the downward spiral of negative affect associated with depression, anxiety, and other negative mood states.

Social Interaction Hypothesis

The basic premise of the **social interaction hypothesis** is that the social interaction associated with exercising with friends and colleagues is pleasurable and has the net effect of improving mental health (North et al., 1990). While the social interaction hypothesis provides a partial explanation for the psychological benefits of exercise, it does not provide an acceptable complete explanation. Evidence of the psychological benefits of regular exercise abounds, whether the exercising is done in groups or alone. The North et al. (1990) meta-analysis, for example, confirmed that exercising alone and at home results in greater reductions in depression than exercising at other locations (usually with others).

Distraction Hypothesis

The basic premise of the **distraction hypothesis** is that exercise affords an opportunity for individuals to be distracted from their worries and frustrations. Support for this hypothesis comes from Alfermann and Stoll (2000) and from Bahrke and Morgan (1978). Bahrke and Morgan (1978) observed that acute doses of meditation and quiet rest were as effective as exercise in reducing anxiety. The North et al. (1990) meta-analysis, however, concluded that chronic exercise is a more powerful and effective treatment for reducing negative mood than relaxation or other distracting but enjoyable activities. It may be that distraction provides a viable explanation for short-term reduction in depression and anxiety, but not for long-term reduction.

Cardiovascular Fitness Hypothesis

The basic premise of the **cardiovascular fitness hypothesis** is that improved mood state is associated with improved cardiovascular fitness (Morgan, 1969). The cardiovascular fitness hypothesis, however, is not generally supported by the literature (Emery & Blumenthal, 1988; North et al., 1990). The results of the North et al. (1990) meta-analysis suggest that the initial psychological benefits of chronic exercise occur during the first few weeks, before subjects experience substantial changes in cardiovascular fitness.

Amine Hypothesis

The basic premise of the **amine hypothesis** is that increased secretion of chemicals that serve as neurotransmitters is related to improved mental health. Neurotransmitters serve to transmit signals from nerve to nerve and from nerve to muscle. Studies have shown that depressed individuals often suffer a decrement in the secretion of various amines, such as norepinephrine, serotonin, and dopamine (Fawcett, Mass, &

CONCEPT At least six plausible explanations exist for the relationship between improved mood and exercise. By itself, not one of the hypotheses provides a complete and satisfying explanation as to why exercise improves mental health.

APPLICATION The absence of a definitive explanation for the positive relationship between exercise and improved mood should not lessen the importance of the association. Exercise should be encouraged as a valid treatment for depression, anxiety, anger, and other psychological maladies. Nonexercisers, however, should consult their physician before beginning strenuous exercise programs.

Dekirmenjiar, 1972; Morgan, 1985; North et al., 1990), and that exercised rats experience an increase in brain norepinephrine (Brown & Van Huss, 1973). Theoretically, exercise stimulates the production of neurotransmitters that in turn have a positive effect upon psychological mood.

Endorphin Hypothesis

The **endorphin hypothesis** postulates that exercise is associated with brain production of chemicals that have a "morphine-like" effect on the exerciser (pain reduction and general euphoria).

Athlete enjoying the benefits of exercise and competiton.
Source: © Royalty-Free/Corbis.

This effect has been referred to, in popular literature, as the "runner's high." The general euphoria produced by the endorphins serves to reduce the levels of depression, anxiety, confusion, and other negative mood states. While this is an appealing concept, the evidence in support of the theory is meager. Human studies by Farrell, Gustafson, Garthwaite, Kalkhoff, Cowley, and Morgan (1986) and by Kraemer, Dzewaltowski, Blair, Rinehardt, and Castracane (1990) have failed to support a role for endorphins in the exercise and mood state relationship. Kraemer et al. (1990), for example, observed a decrease in blood plasma endorphins with an increase in positive mood. While endorphin release into the bloodstream may be associated with mood changes, there are many other physiological transmitter systems involved (Hoffman, 1997).

Exercise Adherence and Determinants

The basic premise of this chapter is that exercise is associated with positive psychological and physiological benefits. The previous sections have reinforced the reality of this strong relationship. In contrast with these positive research findings is the grim reminder that 58 percent of the American population is sedentary, 10 to 25 percent of Americans suffer from mild to moderate depression and anxiety, and 50 percent of the people who start a structured exercise program drop out within the first six months (LaFontaine et al., 1992). With these facts in mind, it becomes clear that another important aspect of exercise psychology is to determine what motivates individuals to start exercising, what motivates them to adhere to an exercise program, and what motivates them to try again after failing the first (or second) time.

A structural model proposed by Sallis and Hovell (1990) provides a framework for studying what these authors call the **natural history of exercise.** The natural history of exercise model, as illustrated in figure 16.1, proposes a framework for studying the *determinants* of exercise behavior.

As depicted in figure 16.1, the determinants of exercise behavior focus upon the three *transitions*

FIGURE 16.1 | Four major phases of the natural history of exercise. Transitions denoted by T_1, T_2, and T_3.

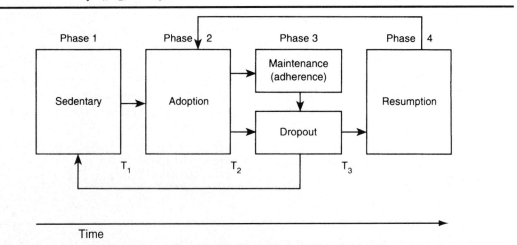

Source: Adapted with permission from Sallis, J. F., & Hovell, M. F. (1990). Determinants of exercise behavior. In Pandolfi, K. B., & Holloszy, J. O. (Eds.), *Exercise and Sport Sciences Reviews, 18,* 307–330. Copyright 1990 by Lippincott, Williams & Wilkins, Baltimore.

between the sedentary phase, the adoption phase, the maintenance or dropout phase, and the resumption phase. Research that has been or should be conducted on exercise determinants examines the *three transitions* between the *four phases* of the natural history of exercise.

Transition from Sedentary State to Exercise Adoption

Exercise determinants that motivate individuals to make the transition from a sedentary lifestyle to regular exercise are largely unknown. An exception to this general observation is a study reported by Sallis, Haskell, Fortmann, Vranizan, Taylor, and Solomon (1986). In this investigation, 1,400 adults were initially assessed with a battery of potential determinants. One year later these potential determinants were compared with exercise behaviors. As a result of these comparisons, several predictors of vigorous physical exercise were identified. Based on this investigation, individuals likely to adopt a vigorous exercise lifestyle exhibit the following characteristics:

1. Confidence they can succeed at a vigorous exercise program (exercise self-efficacy).

2. Knowledge about what constitutes a healthy lifestyle.

3. Knowledge about the importance and value of regular exercise.

4. The perception that they enjoy a high level of self-control.

5. Good attitudes about the value and importance of regular exercise.

6. Initial condition of not being overweight or obese.

The importance of self-efficacy as a determinant of exercise behavior has been documented (McAuley & Blissmer, 2000). Highly efficacious individuals experience lower perceptions of effort expenditure during exercise, and report positive affect associated with vigorous exercise.

In addition to the Sallis et al. (1986) research and McAuley and Blissmer's (2000) observations relative to self-efficacy, several other recent lines of research have increased our understanding of determinants of exercise behavior. These include environmental factors, assessibility of exercise equipment, and parental beliefs. In terms of the *environment,* Sallis, Johnson, Calfas, Caparosa, and Nichols (1997) observed that walking and vigorous exercise behavior were not predicted by any aspect of the environment measured, while strength exercise was predicted by the assessibility of home equipment. Strength exercise was also correlated with socioeconomic status. These findings suggest that the strongest environmental determinant of physical activity is having strength training equipment in the home, which is related to the ability to purchase the equipment. Environmental factors such as convenient nearby exercise facilities and neighborhood environment (e.g., character and safety) were not predictors of exercise behavior.

Related to the findings of the study by Sallis et al. (1997) was an investigation by Raynor, Coleman, and Epstein (1998) on exercise equipment accessibility. In this study, undergraduates were exposed to varying conditions in which interesting sedentary activities (e.g., newspapers, crossword puzzles, and music) and exercise equipment (stationary bicycle, resistance training equipment) were placed at varying proximity to the students. Results showed that most free-choice exercising took place when exercise equipment was nearby (accessible) and sedentary activities were far away. When sedentary activities were easily accessible, students did not exercise very much. These results suggest that accessibility and nearness of exercise equipment are strong predictors of exercise behavior.

It has often been hypothesized that parental involvement in vigorous physical activity would be a strong determinant of the exercise behavior of their children. Interestingly, this logical hypothesis has not been supported. What does predict vigorous physical activity in children is *parental beliefs* about the value and importance of vigorous physical activity (Kimiecik & Horn, 1998). Apparently, many parents who are not physically active have strong feelings about the value of vigorous physical activity, and this influences their children's exercise behaviors. Related to this finding is the observation that a mother's task goal orientation is also predictive of her child's exercise behavior.

Transition from Adoption to Maintenance or Dropout Status

The statistics that only 30 percent of all adult North Americans exercise regularly, and that 50 percent of all adults who begin an exercise program drop out within six months, are alarming (Dishman, 2001). The positive psychological and physiological benefits associated with regular physical activity cannot be realized in the absence of exercise. Most of the research that has been conducted on exercise determinants has focused upon the transition from adoption to maintenance (T_2 in figure 16.1). This area of research is referred to as **exercise adherence**, or the degree to which exercisers adhere to their exercise programs. Excellent reviews of exercise adherence research have been provided by Carron, Hausenblas, and Mack (1996); Dishman (1987); and Sallis and Hovell (1990).

More recent reviews and investigations have continued to add to the body of knowledge relative to exercise adherence. These studies have sharpened our understanding of how such factors as group cohesion, equipment accessibility, self-efficacy, intrinsic motivation, and social physique anxiety determine or are predictive of exercise adherence. In group exercise programs, *group cohesion* developed among the members of the exercise group increases exercise adherence (Estabrooks, 2000). Placing a treadmill in the home (*accessibility*) of obese female exercisers increases the likelihood that they will adhere to their exercise program (Jakicic, Winters, Lang, & Wing, 1999; Oman & King, 2000). A recent narrative review shows the importance of *exercise self-efficacy* in predicting exercise adherence. Exercisers who believe they can succeed at a regular exercise program do succeed (McAuley and Blissmer, 2000). Physical activity participants who initially exhibit a high level of *intrinsic motivation* as opposed to extrinsic motivation are better adherers than those low in intrinsic motivation (Ryan, Frederick, Lepes, Rubio, & Sheldon, 1997). Age is a moderator of the relationship between *social physique anxiety* and exercise adherence. Younger obese women who are high in social physique anxiety tend to be exercise program dropouts, whereas older women high in the construct are less likely to drop out (Treasure, Lox, & Lawton, 1998). Social physique anxiety will be discussed in greater detail in a later section of this chapter. A summary of determinants of exercise adherence and nonadherence is provided in table 16.1.

TABLE 16.1 | Primary Determinants of Adherence and Nonadherence to Vigorous Exercise Programs

A. Determinants of Exercise Adherence

1. Available time
2. Behavioral coping skills
3. Equipment and facility accessibility
4. Exercise self-efficacy
5. Group cohesion
6. High risk of heart disease
7. Intrinsic motivation
8. Personal perception of good health
9. Social support

B. Determinants of Exercise Nonadherence

1. Being a blue-collar worker
2. Being overweight or obese
3. Mood state disturbances relative to exercise
4. Physical discomfort during exercise
5. Being a smoker
6. Social physique anxiety

CONCEPT An incomplete list of determinants of both exercise adherence and nonadherence has been identified through research.

APPLICATION Once an individual has committed to a vigorous long-term program, it is the responsibility of the exercise psychologist and fitness leader to help him maintain a lifelong commitment to regular exercise. Knowledge of the determinants of exercise adherence and non-adherence should be used to anticipate potential dropouts. Planned intervention strategies should be applied, when needed, to maintain motivation and commitment.

It is of interest to note that Morgan (2000) addressed the American College of Sports Medicine during its national convention and called for a paradigm shift relative to addressing exercise adherence. Instead of focusing upon such topics as mode, intensity, frequency, and duration to achieve maximum benefits of exercise, the focus should be upon the "P" factor. The **"P" factor** in Morgan's terminology refers to "purpose." In order for physical activity to be meaningful, it must have a purpose. The purpose must be more meaningful and immediate than wanting to be physically fit or lose weight. Examples of having a purpose include buying a dog and taking the dog for a 30-minute walk every day; walking or riding your bike to work to save gas and the environment; and parking a distance from the grocery store, so that a walk is required.

Research continues to reinforce the importance of good weather, personal convenience, and a paucity of debilitating stressful life events on exercise adherence (Oman & King, 2000; Salmon, Owen, Crawford, Bauman, & Sallis, 2003). Some factors that might make it more conducive to continue exercising include variability, frequency, and intensity of exercise (Glaros & Janelle, 2001; Perri et al., 2002). Adherence levels of previously sedentary individuals can be increased by varying exercise mode so that it does not get boring; by increasing the frequency of exercise bouts during a week from, say, two to three days a week to five to seven days a week; and by maintaining moderate- as opposed to high-intensity exercise bouts. Research shows that an open as opposed to a closed-loop feedback system is preferred in getting children ages 8 to 12 to exercise (Roemmich, Gurgol, & Epstein, 2004). Children lose interest in exercising when TV time is tied directly to exercise (e.g., the TV switches off when exercise stops). Children respond better if "activity counts" are recorded and TV rewards come later. Research also shows that exercise imagery is positively associated with exercise motivation, self-efficacy, and exercise frequency (Giacobbi, Hausenblas, Fallon, & Hall, 2003). Exercisers use imagery to increase energy, improve appearance, and improve exercise technique. It is also believed that imagery use increases self-efficacy, which in turn has a direct effect on exercise participation.

Transition from Dropout Status to Exercise Resumption

As stated by Sallis and Hovell (1990), the transition from being an exercise dropout to resuming a vigorous exercise program has been completely ignored by researchers and theorists. This is an important part of the exercise psychology literature that must be addressed. Statistics are not available on the percentage of people who drop out of an exercise program and then get started again. Is it harder to resume an exercise program after once dropping out, or is it harder to start initially? Do people who resume their exercise programs after dropping out tend to be good adherers, or do they tend to drop out again? Are the determinants for exercise maintenance the same as those for exercise resumption, or is there a separate set of determinants? These questions and others need to be addressed by exercise psychologists.

Theories of Exercise Behavior

Psychological models of human behavior have been applied to the exercise setting in an attempt to explain why people don't exercise, why they start to exercise, why they do or do not continue to exercise, and why they start exercising again if they stop. These models include (a) the theory of reasoned action, (b) the theory of planned behavior, (c) the transtheoretical model of stages of change, (d) social cognitive theory, and (e) exercise self-schemata theory. Each of these theories will now be briefly discussed.

The Theory of Reasoned Action

Originated by Ajzen and Fishbein (1977), the **theory of reasoned action** proposes that the main precursor of a behavior such as exercise is the individual's *intention* to perform the behavior. The intention to perform the behavior is determined by the individual's *attitude* toward the behavior as well as *social norms* or social pressure to perform the behavior. Research by Estabrooks and Courneya (1997) has demonstrated the effectiveness of the theory of reasoned action in exercise settings. While the theory of reasoned action is a viable model for predicting exercise behavior, research has demonstrated that its predictive power is increased when personal control is added to the model (Yannis, 1994). This observation led to the development of the theory of planned behavior.

The Theory of Planned Behavior

Originated by Ajzen (1985), the **theory of planned behavior** is an extension of the theory of reasoned action (Godin, 1994). The *intention* to perform a behavior is fundamental to the theory. Intention is determined by the individual's *attitude*

toward the behavior and *social norms*. The difference between the two theories is the addition of perceived *behavioral control* to the original model. An individual will maintain or initiate an exercise program if his intention is firm and he feels in control. Intention is in turn a function of his attitude toward exercise and perceived social norms. The expanded Theory of Planned Behavior (TPB) is illustrated in figure 16.2. In this figure, the original TPB is shown as solid-line boxes and solid-path arrows leading from one box to another. The box originally labeled *social norms* in the model is replaced by the box labeled *social support*. Researchers originally thought that these two terms were synonymous, but research reported by Rhodes, Jones, and Courneya (2002) demonstrated that social support is a stronger predictor of exercise intention than social norms. Therefore, in figure 16.2, social support instead of social norms leads to intention to exercise. In the model, intention to exercise completely mediates the effects of both exercise attitude and social support on exercise behavior. Self-efficacy and perceived behavioral control have both a direct and an indirect effect upon exercise behavior. That is, intention to exercise is a partial mediator of the effects of self-efficacy and perceived control on exercise behavior. As you can see from the TPB model, a **mediator variable** mediates or conveys the effect of one variable on another.

In figure 16.2, self-efficacy is shown in a dashed-line box and with a dashed line leading to intention to exercise and exercise behavior. This is so because this variable was not originally included as part of the TPB, but is included here to reflect research reported by Hagger, Chatzisarantis, and Biddle (2002). Also included in figure 16.2, and shown with dashed lines, is the effect of personality factors upon exercise behavior. According to research reported by Rhodes, Courneya, and Hayduk (2002), the personality factors of neuroticism, extraversion, and conscientiousness moderate the relationships between both attitude and social support and the intention to exercise, and

FIGURE 16.2 | Schematic representation of the original theory of planned behavior (solid lines) and the expanded model of the theory (dashed lines).

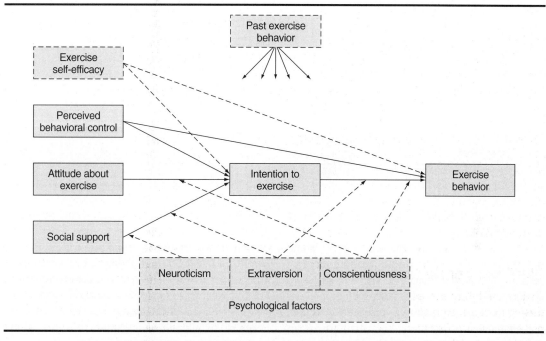

between the intention to exercise and exercise behavior. A **moderator variable** is one that determines the nature of the relationship between two other variables. For example, being highly conscientious will strengthen the effect of intention to exercise on exercise behavior, whereas a lack of conscientiousness will weaken that relationship. Finally, the inclusion of the dashed-line box for *past behavior* is based on research reported by Hagger et al. (2002), which shows that past exercise behavior has a direct effect upon every variable in the model. Arrows are not shown between past exercise behavior and the other variables in order to avoid unnecessarily complicating the model.

Research has demonstrated general support for the theory of planned behavior in predicting exercise behavior (Mummery & Wankel, 1999; Wankel & Mummery, 1993). It has been suggested,

however, that expectation to exercise is a stronger predictor of exercise behavior than intention. These two terms are virtually identical, but it is believed that expectation to exercise takes into consideration noncognitive habits and perceived capabilities to a greater degree than intention does (Courneya & McAuley, 1994). Strong support for the theory of planned behavior is provided through a meta-analysis reported by Hausenblas, Carron, and Mack (1997).

The Transtheoretical Model

The *transtheoretical model* was originally proposed as a stage theory of behavioral change by Prochaska and DiClemete (1986). Prochaska and Marcus (1994) provide an insightful explanation as to how the model is applied to exercise. According to the **transtheoretical model,** individuals

FIGURE 16.3 | The transtheoretical model, showing stages of change and processes of change that interact to bring about improved exercise behavior.

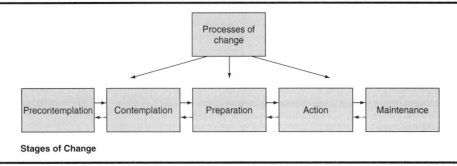

pass through five dynamic stages in adopting healthy long-term exercise behavior. The stages are dynamic because individuals may move in and out of the several stages before reaching the final stage, which is also dynamic. The five stages of change, illustrated in figure 16.3, include precontemplation, contemplation, preparation, action, and maintenance. Interventions called **processes of change** may be utilized to help exercisers move along the continuum from one stage to the next. It is important to know which stage an individual is in, because some interventions work better in one stage than in another. In applying the model, the exercise leader assesses the stage that the exerciser is in and then selectively applies a process of change intervention designed to help him move to the next level (Gorely & Gordon, 1995; Marcus & Simkin, 1994). Processes of change interact with the various stages of the transtheoretical model to bring about successful change in exercise behavior.

Marcus, Rossi, Selby, Niaura and Abrams (1992) developed the 39-item Processes of Change Questionnaire (PCQ) to help behavioral psychologists to measure 10 different processes of change that may facilitate moving along the stages-of-change model. The 10 identified processes of change include five cognitive processes and five behavioral processes. Results of this investigation showed that cognitive processes are more effective in the pre-action phases (precontemplation,

contemplation, and preparation), while the behavioral processes are most effective in the action and maintenance phases (Plotnikoff, Hotz, Berkett and Courneya (2001). Reading information about the values of exercise would be an example of a cognitive process to motivate a person to exercise. Utilizing social relationships to help people to exercise would be an example of a behavioral process to motivate a person to exercise.

Different approaches and inventories have been developed to determine the stage of change that an exerciser or prospective exerciser is in. A case in point is the Stage of Exercise Scale (SES) developed by Cardinal (1995) and illustrated in figure 16.4. In practice, the individual completes the SES, which allows the practitioner to categorize her as being in one of five stages. In figure 16.4, if the individual circled number 2, this would place her in the preparation phase. Once it has been established which stage of change the individual is in, then the exercise leader applies interventions or processes of change to help the individual move to the next stage. For example, if an individual were in the contemplation phase, a discussion with the exercise leader about how exercise might fit into the contemplator's day might prove beneficial. If an individual were in the action phase, then seeking social support would be an intervention that might help move the exerciser into the maintenance phase (Dunn & Blair, 1997).

FIGURE 16.4 | Stage of Exercise Scale.

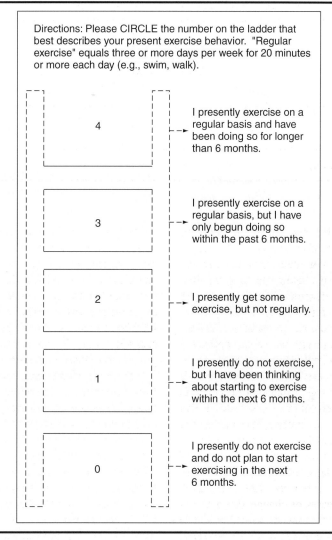

Directions: Please CIRCLE the number on the ladder that best describes your present exercise behavior. "Regular exercise" equals three or more days per week for 20 minutes or more each day (e.g., swim, walk).

4 — I presently exercise on a regular basis and have been doing so for longer than 6 months.

3 — I presently exercise on a regular basis, but I have only begun doing so within the past 6 months.

2 — I presently get some exercise, but not regularly.

1 — I presently do not exercise, but I have been thinking about starting to exercise within the next 6 months.

0 — I presently do not exercise and do not plan to start exercising in the next 6 months.

Source: Reproduced with permission from Cardinal, B. J. (1995). The stages of exercise scale and stages of exercise behavior in female adults. *Journal of Sports Medicine and Physical Fitness, 35,* 87–92.

In the full model, in addition to processes of change, other factors interact with the stages of change to bring about a change in behavior. These include self-efficacy, perception of gains and losses, and a set of psychological obstacles that may need to be addressed (Prochaska & Velicer, 1997). In general, the research has supported the transtheoretical model as a means to enhance exercise behavior (Armstrong, Sallis, Hovell, & Hofstetter, 1993; Cardinal, 1997; Courneya, 1995; Marcus, Eaton, Rossi, & Harlow, 1994). Support for the transtheoretical model has extended to muscular fitness as well as aerobic fitness (Cardinal & Kosma, 2004; Van Vorst, Buckworth, & Mattern,

2002), to different cultures (Cardinal, Tuominen, & Rintala, 2004), and to adolescent as well as adult samples (Lee, Nigg, DiClemente, & Courneya, 2001).

Recently, research has effectively linked self-determination theory with the transtheoretical or stages-of-change model. Recall from chapter 5 and figure 5.6 that motivation can be conceptualized along a self-determination continuum that goes from external to internal regulation, and that there are four levels of ascending extrinsic motivation (external, introjected, identified, integrated). Together, external and introjected external regulation are considered to be controlling in nature, while identified regulation, integrated regulation, and intrinsic motivation are considered to be autonomous in nature. For the purposes of measuring degree of self-determination, Mullan, Markland, and Ingledew (1997) developed the 15-item Behavioral Regulation Exercise Questionnaire (BREQ). The BREQ measures the degree of external regulation, introjected regulation, identified regulation, and intrinsic motivation. Wilson, Rodgers, Fraser, and Murray (2004) utilized the BREQ to study the relationship between self-determination and exercise behavior. Results showed a strong predictive relationship between the BREQ subscales and actual exercise behavior. Identified regulation and intrinsic motivation were the strongest predictors of exercise behavior/intention for both men and women. Using a sample of African American women, Landry and Solmon (2004) studied the relationship between self-determination, as measured by the BREQ, and stages of change, as measured by the Stage of Exercise Scale. Results of the investigation showed that introjected regulation, identified regulation, and intrinsic motivation are the strongest predictors of stage of change. Important findings included the following:

1. Strategies that rely on coercion are unlikely to have any effect on African American women's decisions to exercise.

2. Reinforcing forms of self-motivation and a sense of autonomy are likely to be most effective in encouraging women to choose to be active.

3. Rewards and threats are poor motivators when it comes to being physically active.

4. Strategies reinforcing higher levels of self-regulation are more likely to foster long-term adherence to an exercise program.

Social Cognitive Theory

As proposed by Bandura (1997), *social cognitive theory* provides a viable way to explain exercise behavior. Individuals who are dissatisfied with their current exercise behavior, who exhibit high levels of **exercise self-efficacy,** and who set exercise goals are generally able to achieve their goals. Exercise self-efficacy is a powerful predictor of exercise behavior. Individuals who believe in themselves and believe that they can be successful at maintaining an exercise program generally are successful (DuCharme & Brawley, 1995; Maddison & Prapavessis, 2004; McAuley & Blissmer, 2000).

While social cognitive theory has been presented here as a stand-alone theory of exercise behavior, tenets of the theory are best incorporated into other theories. For example, self-efficacy is included as an important component of the theory of planned behavior and the transtheoretical model. Current theory suggests that best results may be obtained by applying components of several theories into the same strategies for improving exercise behavior in sedentary individuals (Brawley, 1993; Dishman & Buckworth, 1996).

Exercise Self-Schemata Theory

The notion of self-schemata to explain perception, inference, and memory was introduced by Markus (1977). According to Markus, **self-schemata** "are cognitive generalizations about the self, derived

from past experience, that organize and guide the
processing of self-related information contained
in the individual's social experiences" (p. 64).
Kendzierski (1988) was the first to apply the
notion of self-schemata to behavior, and specifically to exercise behavior. Kendzierski (1988)
developed specific questionnaire items that made it
possible to categorize an individual as having an
exercise schema or a *nonexercise schema.* Individuals who could not be classified into one of these
two categories were labeled *aschematic.* By obtaining exercise intention and behavior information, it
was possible to demonstrate that individuals with
an exercise schema were much more likely to
exercise than those who had a nonexercise schema
or who were aschematic. Based on these findings,
Kendzierski concluded that interventions could
be developed to help individuals who were aschematic or had nonexercise schemata to become
more exercise schematic.

Additional research with **exercise self-
schemata** revealed that exercise-schematic individuals process exercise-related information more
quickly and report more instances of past exercise
behavior and future intent than nonexercise-
schematic individuals (Kendzierski, 1990). When
applied to dieting behavior, it was observed that
diet self-schemata moderated the relationship
between actual dieting and the intent to diet. When
the diet schema was present, a person's intent to

diet translated to actual dieting more often than
when the diet schema was not present (Kendzierski
& Whitaker, 1997). Similarly, Kendzierski, Furr,
Schiavoni (1998) found evidence of self-schemata
in weightlifters and basketball players, showing
that the self-schemata concept applies to physical
activity generally, and not just to exercise. Exercise-schematic individuals tend to give unstable attributions to exercise lapses, whereas nonexercise-
schematic individuals give more stable attributions
(Kendzierski & Sheffield, 2000; Kendzierski,
Sheffield, & Morganstein, 2002). Thus, nonexer-
cise-schematic exercisers see lapses as somewhat
permanent, whereas exercise-schematic individuals see them as only temporary.

According to exercise self-schemata theory,
the way to get people to exercise initially and
to continue to exercise once they start (adherence)
is to help them to develop the cognitive self-
schemata for exercising. As explained by
Kendzierski (2004), factors that are necessary for
the development of an exercise self-schema include enjoyment of the exercise, wanting to exercise, trying to exercise, a commitment to exercise,
and the ability to exercise. These same factors
would be necessary for the development of a
self-schema for any desirable activity. The relationships among the factors necessary for developing exercise self-schemata are illustrated in
figure 16.5.

CONCEPT A person possessing an exercise self-schema is much more likely to maintain a chronic exercise program than a person who possesses a nonexercise self-schema.

APPLICATION The goal is to help individuals to develop exercise self-schemata. An exercise schema is really just a way of thinking about things. It is a cognitive generalization about how you want to live your life. As illustrated in figure 16.5, exercise must first be viewed as something you enjoy and want to try. In addition to wanting to exercise, you must take the next step by actually getting out and exercising. Trying to exercise and being successful lead to a commitment to continue and a belief in your own ability to exercise. Commitment and perceived ability lead to the development of the exercise self-schema.

FIGURE 16.5 | Structural model showing the relationships among factor that lead to development of exercise self-schemata.

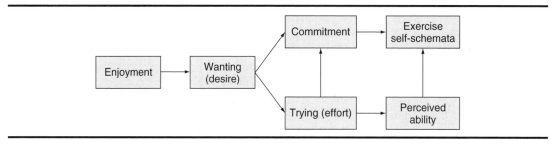

Fitness as a Moderator of Life Stress

Given the positive relationship between exercise and improved mental health, it follows that physical fitness should serve as a buffer against life stress. The ability of individuals to insulate, protect, or inoculate themselves against the stresses of life through regular exercise is called **stress inoculation.** Research shows that the psychological benefits associated with regular exercise do not normally require an increase in physical fitness (Rejeski, Brawley, & Schumaker, 1996). Aerobic fitness, however, does appear to be a necessary precursor to the stress inoculation effect. Aerobically fit individuals appear to be inoculated against stress, illness, and the general hassles of life to a greater extent than less aerobically fit individuals. Children and adults who engage in healthy behavior that leads to physical fitness can insulate themselves from various physical and psychological health problems throughout their lives (Kubitz & Landers, 1993). While the exact mechanisms involved in stress inoculation are not known, it is believed that they may involve a complex pattern of central and autonomic nervous system adaptations.

Life stress represents an accumulation of the daily hassles and challenges of living out our lives. Individuals who exercise regularly and maintain a high level of physical fitness should be less susceptible to the negative effects of life stress. Evidence for this hypothesis has been provided by Brown (1991) and by others. The investigation by Brown is of special interest, because objective measures of physical fitness and illness were assessed. Brown studied the relationship between level of physical fitness, as measured by the bicycle ergometer; life stress, as measured by

FIGURE 16.6 | Level of physical fitness moderates the relationship between life stress and illness.

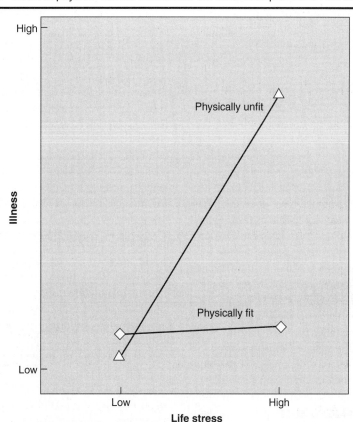

Source: Adapted with permission from Brown, J. D. (1991). Staying fit and staying well: Physical fitness as a moderator of life stress. *Journal of Personality and Social Psychology, 60,* 555–561. Copyright 1991 by the American Psychological Association.

the Life Experience Survey; and number of visits to the university health center. As illustrated in figure 16.6, the results of the investigation show an interactive relationship between life stress, physical fitness, and number of visits to the health center (illness). Being physically fit serves to inoculate the individual against illness during periods of high stress. Conversely, physically unfit individuals appear to be unprotected against high stress.

Tangentially related to the life stress issue is the observation that exercise leading to physical fitness is an effective treatment to reduce high blood pressure. Martin and Calfas (1989) provided a review of 17 uncontrolled or partially controlled studies and 13 controlled studies. The results of this review suggest that exercise is an effective nonpharmacologic treatment for hypertension. Chronic aerobic exercise produces a reduction in blood pressure that is independent of weight loss or diet.

Given the promising buffer effect that exercise has upon life stress, one wonders why more people do not take advantage of it. One possible explanation could be lack of knowledge about the beneficial stress inoculation effects of exercise. Another

CONCEPT Physical fitness is a buffer of life stress, reduces hypertension, and is associated with fewer visits to the doctor.

APPLICATION Time spent exercising is not wasted time. Because we live in a fast-paced, stressful world, steps must be taken to buffer daily stress. Individuals must be encouraged to place daily vigorous exercise at the top of their priority lists.

partial explanation might be the personalities of individuals who either choose or do not choose to exercise. Research suggests that individuals who regularly engage in exercise have distinctive personality characteristics. For example, Hartung and Farge (1977) reported that exercisers exhibit a profile of increased reserve, intelligence, seriousness, imagination, forthrightness, and self-sufficiency when compared with nonexercisers. More recently, Schnurr, Vaillant, and Vaillant (1990) addressed the question of whether personality in young adulthood predicts exercise in later midlife. Male Caucasian Harvard graduates from the classes of 1942 to 1944 were traced to determine if personality characteristics measured in college were predictive of exercise habits later in life. As part of the Harvard longitudinal study begun in 1938, personality was assessed by two psychologists who used a review of 20 hours of interview transcripts. In college, hours and type of daily and weekly exercise were recorded. As part of the follow-up, subjects were asked about the amount and type of exercise they had engaged in since age 55. Results of the investigation showed that personality characteristics of vitality, integration, lack of anxiety, and lack of shyness during college were predictive of frequent exercise behavior later in life.

The Immune System, Cancer, HIV, and Exercise

In recent years research has linked two of the great plagues of our time (cancer and HIV) to exercise and its effect on the immune system. While exercise has generally been linked to benefits, in cases of excess it can have negative consequences. It is like a two-edged sword: it cuts both ways. If applied in moderation it can have beneficial effects, but if applied in excess it can have negative effects.

Exercise and Cancer

Moderate exercise applied on a regular basis is associated with both psychological and biological benefits. Moderate exercise is linked to a lowered incidence of colon and breast cancer. Young women who regularly participate in physical exercise activities during their reproductive years have a reduced risk of breast cancer. Individuals who have cancer, but who exercise regularly, may benefit from improved psychological well-being, preservation of lean tissue, and enhanced immune systems (Bernstein, Henderson, Hanisch, Sullivan-Halley, & Ross, 1994; Courneya, 2001; Courneya, Wackey, & Jones, 2000; Lee, 1995; Sternfeld, 1992).

Exercise and the Immune System

Research clearly suggests that exercising in moderation leads to improved psychological mood and enhanced **immune system functioning** (Mackinnon, 1994; Nieman, 2001; Shephard, Rhind, & Shek, 1995; Shephard & Shek, 1994). Conversely, it is widely believed that chronic intense and stressful exercise may result in mood disturbance and in suppression of the immune system (Rowbottom & Green, 2000). Research indicates, however, that acute bouts of intense exercise are not associated with a reduction in immune system functioning as long as the exercise is within a range recommended by the American College of

CONCEPT Immune function is stimulated by moderate exercise but possibly suppressed by overly intense exercise. It appears that there exists an optimal level of regular physical activity conducive to the resistance to illness.

APPLICATION It is critical that coaches and exercise leaders recognize and understand the delicate balance between the beneficial effects of moderate exercise and the detrimental effects of overly intense exercise. When the integrity of the immune system is involved, the coach must be very sensitive to this balance. The most immediate concern is reduced immune system response and upper respiratory infection in the form of the cold virus and influenza. These illnesses weaken athletes and make them more susceptible to other diseases.

FIGURE 16.7 | Illustration showing the effect of moderate and high exercise workloads on the integrity of the immune system.

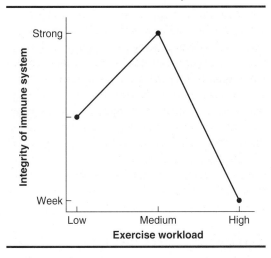

Sports Medicine (Rowbottom & Green, 2000). Chronic intense exercise and acute exercise that goes beyond recommended intensities may result in a reduction in immune system functioning (Mackinnon, 2000). There is growing evidence that for several hours following heavy sustained exertion, the immune system is suppressed (Nieman, 2000; Nieman, Kernodle, Henson, Sonnenfeld, & Marton, 2000). Athletes who do experience transient or chronic immune system suppression seem to be most susceptible to upper respiratory tract infection. It is believed that the immune system is stimulated and strengthened by moderately intense exercise, but suppressed by overly intense exercise. It appears that there exists an optimal level of regular physical activity conducive to the resistance to illness. Apparently, you can have too much of a good thing.

Our current level of understanding about the positive effects of exercise on the immune system is summarized in an excellent position statement written by the President's Council on Physical Fitness and Sports (2001). As illustrated in figure 16.7, by far "the most important finding that has emerged from exercise immunology studies is that positive immune changes take place during each bout of moderate physical activity" (p. 6).

Exercise and the Human Immunodeficiency Virus

Magic Johnson's brief return to professional basketball and his participation in the 1992 Summer Olympics in Barcelona, Spain, after contracting the **human immunodeficiency virus (HIV)**, led to speculation as to the possible negative side effects of vigorous physical activity to his physical and psychological health. Since it is widely believed by the medical profession that the presence of the HIV ultimately leads to **acquired immune deficiency syndrome (AIDS)**, there was cause for concern (Cinelli, Sankaran, McConatha, & Carson, 1992). Evidence reported by Ironson, LaPerriere, Antoni, Klimas, Fletcher, and Schneiderman (1990) indicates that when asymptomatic gay

CONCEPT   The evidence suggests that asymptomatic HIV–positive individuals can enjoy the positive psychological and physiological benefits of chronic exercise without suppressing already compromised immune systems.

APPLICATION   Under the supervision of a physician, asymptomatic HIV–positive individuals should be encouraged to engage in an aerobic exercise program designed to improve cardiovascular fitness and reduce the debilitating effects of anxiety and depression.

males are informed of their *HIV-positive status,* they display a significant increase in anxiety and other distress scores. Furthermore, evidence has been accrued that links affective factors, such as depression and anxiety, with accelerated HIV infection (Ironson et al., 1990). Goodkin (1988) further suggests that increased anxiety and depression should be viewed as risk factors facilitating the development of AIDS. Because exercise has been positively linked with decreased anxiety and depression, it follows that chronic exercise should be effective in retarding the negative progression and effects of HIV.

Since 1990, at least six investigations have been reported that have a bearing on the question of exercise among HIV-positive individuals. A study by LaPerriere et al. (1990) demonstrated the buffering or protective effect that aerobic exercise had upon gay men who were informed of their HIV-positive status. Gay males were assigned to either a five-week exercise condition or a control condition. After completion of the exercise period, all subjects were informed of their HIV status. HIV-positive controls but not HIV-positive exercisers experienced mood disturbances and suppressed immune system functioning.

A study by Rigsby, Dishman, Jackson, MaClean, and Raven (1992) assigned HIV-positive men to either a 12-week aerobic exercise program or a counseling control group to see if exercise would further compromise an already weakened immune system. Results revealed that exercisers improved their strength and endurance without suppressing their immune systems, as evidenced by counting of leukocytes and lymphocytes.

While the previous two investigations focused upon immune system response to aerobic exercise, a study by Lox, McAuley, and Tucker (1995) focused upon psychological response to aerobic exercise on the part of HIV-infected men. Thirty-three HIV-infected men were randomly assigned to an aerobic exercise treatment, a resistance weight-training treatment, or a stretching/flexibility control treatment for a period of 12 weeks. Results of the research indicated that aerobic exercise and weight training enhanced physical self-efficacy, positive and negative mood, and satisfaction with life. The control participants suffered declines in these three psychological measures. These results suggest that moderate exercise is an effective complementary therapy for treating psychological manifestations associated with HIV infection.

An investigation by Stringer, Berezovskaya, O'Brian, Beck, and Casaburi (1998) demonstrated that a six-week exercise training program of moderate to high intensity would not compromise immune system indices of HIV-positive subjects. Compared to a control group of HIV-positive men, the moderate exercise group improved aerobic functioning, improved on quality-of-life indices (hope, desire to live), and improved on one measure of immune system functioning. Compared to the control group, the high-intensity exercise group also improved aerobic functioning and quality-of-life indicators, with no change in immune system functioning.

A study by Wagner, Rabkin, and Rabkin (1998) demonstrated that 12 weeks of resistance exercise was an effective adjunct to testosterone treatment for slowing physical wasting symptoms in HIV-positive men with AIDS. Both exercisers and controls were given testosterone, but only the exercisers improved in psychological mood, lean body mass, strength, and nutritional status.

Finally, a recent study by Rojas, Schlicht, and Hautzinger (2003) confirms the findings of the previously cited investigations. In this study a sample of HIV-positive men and women were assigned to a 16-week moderate exercise group or a 16-week nonexercise control group. Results of the study revealed no differences between groups in terms of immune system functioning, but significant improvement in quality of life, psychological well-being, and cardiopulmonary fitness of the exercise participants. Consistent with previous research, it appears that moderate exercise enhances the health-related quality of life of HIV-positive individuals.

Social Physique Anxiety, Physical Self-Concept, and Body Image

Social physique anxiety, physical self-concept, and body image are all constructs that describe how an individual feels about her physical appearance. While these constructs are not identical to one another, they are correlated, and are predictive of exercise behavior. A high score on social physique anxiety and low scores on physical self-concept and body image are predictive of a low level of exercise behavior. Individuals who are anxious about their bodies, have low physical self-concepts, and have low body images have a hard time getting motivated to exercise. This is a sad situation, because it is these individuals who would benefit most from physical activity.

Social Physique Anxiety

Social physique anxiety is the anxiety that people experience when they perceive that other people evaluate their physiques negatively. They may feel that others evaluate them as too thin, or too heavy, or too fat, and so on. Because of our previous discussion about self-presentation concerns in sport

(chap. 14), you will recognize social physique anxiety as a special case of self-presentation in exercise situations (Hausenblas et al., 2004). Recall that self-presentation was defined as all of the processes that people go through to try to control how they are perceived by other people. Individuals who perceive that they are ineffective in conveying the image that they are healthy, physically fit, and physically attractive experience an increase in social physique anxiety. Thus, in exercise situations negative self-presentational concerns and social physique anxiety are the same things.

In the exercise and fitness environment, **exercise self-presentation efficacy** has been conceptualized as a person's confidence in his ability to create the public impression of himself as being physically fit, coordinated, and physically attractive (Fleming & Ginis, 2004). The Self-Presentation in Exercise Questionnaire (SPEQ) was developed by Conroy, Motl, and Hall (1998, 2000) to measure the exercise self-presentation efficacy construct. The 8-item SPEQ is composed of two factors that measure exercise impression and exercise motivation (Gammage, Hall, Prapavessis, Maddison, Haase, & Martin, 2004). A high score on the SPEQ subscales would indicate that the exerciser enjoys confidence in her ability to convey an image of fitness and attractiveness, while a low score would be highly correlated with social physique anxiety.

In a study reported by Gammage, Ginis, and Hall (2004), exercise self-presentation efficacy was manipulated by placing female exercisers in either a stressful environment where they wore form-fitting clothing, exercised in a room with mirrors, windows, video cameras, and a male video operator; or an environment of loose-fitting clothing, no mirrors, blocked windows, and a female camera operator. As predicted, this manipulation resulted in higher social physique anxiety for the women placed in the stressful environment. In a second study (Fleming & Ginis, 2004), female undergraduates were asked to complete an exercise self-presentation efficacy questionnaire before and after viewing either a perfect-looking female exercise model or a normal-looking exercise model. Results showed that the women who viewed the "perfect model" video suffered a significant reduction in self-presentation efficacy.

In an attempt to quantify the degree to which people experience social physique anxiety, Hart, Leary, and Rejeski (1989) developed the 12-item Social Physique Anxiety Scale (SPAS). Later, Martin, Rejeski, Leary, McAuley, and Bane (1997) refined the 9-item version of the same scale. Research with the SPAS has confirmed that women who score high on the SPAS may at times be reticent about starting an exercise program where other people will be present. It has also been demonstrated that women who score high on the SPAS adopt exercise programs for different reasons than women who score low on the SPAS. The higher social physique anxiety is, the more likely it is that women will choose to exercise for reasons associated with weight reduction, body tone, and improved physical attractiveness (Eklund & Crawford, 1994; Lantz, Hardy, & Ainsworth, 1997; Martin & Mack, 1996).

Recent research shows a number of interesting relationships relative to social physique anxiety. Research in general shows a reduction in anxiety for men and women following a 20- to 30-minute bout of moderate-intensity aerobic exercise (Van Landuyt et al., 2000). This expected outcome, however, is not observed with high-SPA women when they exercise in a naturalistic exercise setting with mirrors and other people watching (Focht & Hausenblas, 2003, 2004). Female exercisers are very sensitive to the sex of individuals who might be watching them exercise. Social physique anxiety increases in women as they imagine exercising in front of other women, a mixed group, and men, in that order (Kruisselbrink, Dodge, Swanburg, & MacLeod, 2004). Social physique anxiety in women is related to their perceptions of body shape, body size, and appearance (Sabiston, Crocker, & Munroe-Chandler, 2005). Research by Russell (2002) and Russell and Cox (2003) shows that body dissatisfaction and self-esteem are related to social physique anxiety in

men as well as women; and that weight discrepancy (actual weight minus ideal weight) is considered to be a precursor or antecedent to social physique anxiety.

Physical Self-Concept

Physical self-concept is the perception that people have about themselves relative to the physical self. Physical self-concept is closely tied to the notion that an individual's feeling of self-worth and self-esteem is related to how he perceives himself within his body. Physical self-concept is measured by the Physical Self-Perception Profile (PSPP; Fox & Corbin, 1989). The PSPP measures perceived body attractiveness, along with perceptions about physical competence, physical strength, and physical conditioning. The PSPP is the foundation of what has come to be referred to as the Fox (1990) Hierarchical Model of Physical Self-Concept. This model leads to the prediction that positive physical self-concept contributes to the development of global self-esteem. Individuals who enjoy a high level of positive physical self-concept are likely to enter into competitive situations and to feel good about exercising in the presence of other people (Crawford & Eklund, 1994; Hayes, Crocker, & Kowalski, 1999). In an investigation reported by Kowalski, Crocker, and Kowalski (2001), it was shown that the physical conditioning component of the PSPP predicts physical activity. The study also hypothesized that social physique anxiety would moderate the relationship between physical self-concept and physical self-concept, but this was not confirmed.

The PSPP as developed by Fox and Corbin (1989) is not the only inventory designed to measure physical self-concept. Marsh, Richards, Johnson, Roche, and Tremayne (1994) developed the Physical Self-Description Questionnaire (PSDQ). Composed of 70 items, the PSDQ measures nine specific components of physical self-concept and two additional components of global physical self-concept (physical self-concept, self-esteem). The nine specific components measured by the PSDQ include physical activity, appearance, body fat, coordination, endurance/fitness, flexibility, health, sport competence and strength. Subsequent investigations reported on the construct, convergent, and discriminant validity of the PSDQ (Dunton, Jamner, & Cooper, 2003; Marsh, Asci, & Tomas, 2002).

Body Image

Body image refers to the images or pictures people have about their bodies. The image that a person has about her own body can be quite different from the one that other people have of her. For example, an individual suffering from anorexia nervosa may in fact be very thin, but may picture herself as being fat and heavy. Body image may be measured using the Multidimensional Body-Self Relations Questionnaire (MBSRQ; Cash, 1994). The MBSRQ is a 69-item inventory that measures *satisfaction* with body appearance, fitness, and health, as well as *orientation* with body appearance, fitness, and health. Research shows that physically active people have better body images than physically inactive people (Loland, 1998). In addition, marathon runners have a greater health/fitness orientation than a normative sample, yet are less preoccupied with body appearance (Huddy & Cash, 1997).

A meta-analysis conducted by Hausenblas and Downs (2001) confirmed that male and female athletes have a more positive concept of their body image than non-athletes. Hausenblas and Downs (2001) also reported that from 1973 to 1997, body dissatisfaction for women increased from 23 percent to 56 percent, and that for men it increased from 15 percent to 43 percent. These are startling statistics, but the good news is that something can be done about it. For example, Depcik and Williams (2004) reported that in a study of body-image-disturbed women, those who participated in a 13-week program of weight training effectively improved their body image, while those in the control groups saw no improvement. In general, male athletes tend to view their own body image as being less muscular than the ideal, and less muscular than what they think women like (Raudenbush & Meyer, 2003).

Exercise Addiction

Exercise addiction is generally defined as a psychophysiological dependence on a regular regimen of exercise. The normal benefits associated with regular exercise at a moderate intensity are lost for the exercise-addicted individual. Failure to exercise according to schedule results in a mood state disturbance in the addicted individual. From an attributional perspective, the addicted exerciser is controlled by the activity, as opposed to the activity's being controlled by the exerciser. Compared to nonaddicted exercisers, addicted exercisers report being more restless and stressed out prior to

CONCEPT Exercise addiction is associated with depression and anxiety in response to missing a regular exercise session. Additionally, individuals suffering from exercise addiction risk more serious injury or illness by refusing to take a day off in the face of sickness or an exercise-related injury.

APPLICATION It is not consistent with a wellness lifestyle to allow an exercise addiction to control a person's behavior. Steps should be taken to assist an individual who suffers from exercise addiction to take control of her own exercise behavior. Alternative forms of recreational activity should be used to replace addictive exercise behaviors when they become controlling.

an exercise bout. They also experience a higher degree of depression, anxiety, and general discomfort when they miss a scheduled workout. An important characteristic of the exercise addict is that he will generally insist on exercising in the face of physical pain or injury (Anshel, 1991). The **super-adherer** is generally believed to be addicted to exercise. The super-adherer is an exerciser who participates in and constantly trains for endurance events that require significant long-term effort and commitment. Often, these endurance events are "super-events" ranging from 50 to 100 miles at a time in length. The Running Addiction Scale (RAS) was developed by Chapman and Castro (1990) to measure exercise addiction. Another term used to describe the addicted exerciser is **obligatory runner.** Male runners are categorized as obligatory runners to a greater extent than female runners. Obligatory runners are highly motivated to exercise, and when they can't, they experience abnormal feelings of anxiety and psychological discontent (Conboy, 1994; Ogles, Masters, & Richardson, 1995).

Eating Disorders and Physical Activity

The table is set, and I can smell the turkey cooking. My stomach turns in disgust. My family huddles around the television to watch Macy's Thanksgiving Day Parade. The day seems ideal.

I wait in anticipation for my worst fear, the meal. I do not want to gain weight. I have anorexia. (Von Rein, 2001, p. 04)

Actual clinically diagnosed eating disorders are relatively rare among athletes and physical activity enthusiasts. Much more prevalent are a whole array of unhealthy subclinical eating disorders. We will discuss both in this section. Perhaps the most well-known example of a clinically diagnosed sport-related eating disorder was the case of former U.S. Olympic gymnast Christy Henrich (Beals, 2000). Christy died in 1994 at the age of 22 from an eight-year struggle with anorexia nervosa, effectively calling the nation's attention to the dangers of clinically diagnosed eating disorders. In a non-sport-related example, the following quotation by Samantha Skinner describes Erin Anderson's battle with bulimia nervosa. Growing up, Erin was called "skinny." As she grew up, her drive for perfection and size "0", influenced by Western culture and glamorous magazines, drove her into an eating disorder.

Erin did not binge and purge as many bulimics do. She did not eat whole pizzas or tubs of ice cream and then throw up. Instead she would make herself sick after only a normal meal or snack. The number of times she threw up ranged from once a day or not at all to three or four times a day. Looking in the mirror or flipping through the newly delivered magazines might make her want to be sick, but stress or sadness could send her to the bathroom just as quickly. Sometimes, even if she wasn't hungry, she would eat just to throw up. Like a cigarette calms a smoker, vomiting calmed Erin. It made everything go away (Skinner, 2000, p. 9).

The balance of this section will be devoted to three areas of discussion. First, an explanation of the most severe cases of clinically diagnosed eating disorders will be presented. Second, clinical and subclinical eating disorders among athletes will be discussed. Finally, we will conclude with a discussion of eating disorders as they relate to unhealthy physical activity behaviors.

Clinically Diagnosed Eating Disorders

The two most severe clinically diagnosed or pathogenic eating disorders are anorexia nervosa and bulimia nervosa. Individuals suffering from one of these two disorders are suffering from a clinically diagnosed mental illness as defined by the *Diagnostic and Statistical Manual of Mental Disorders* (DSM; American Psychiatric Association, 1994). A very small percentage of girls and women in North America suffer from pathogenic eating disorders. The incidence of clinically diagnosed eating disorders among female athletes is also low, estimated to be about 4 percent (Petrie & Stoever, 1993), although estimates vary depending on sample and measurement techniques used. The Questionnaire for Eating Disorder Diagnosis (Q-EDD; Mintz, O'Holloran, Mulholland, & Schneider, 1997) is an instrument that operationalizes the DSM-IV criteria for eating disorders. The Q-EDD has been used in eating disorder research involving an athletic sample (Sanford-Martens et al., 2005).

Anorexia Nervosa   In order for individuals to be diagnosed with **anorexia nervosa,** they must exhibit the following symptoms: (a) severe weight loss, (b) refusal to maintain normal body weight, (c) intense fear of gaining weight or becoming fat, (d) severe body image disturbance, and (e) absence of three or more consecutive menstrual cycles

(amenorrhea). Anorexics eat very little food, and when they do eat they tend to "play" with their food and take tiny bites, chewing each bite a given number of times. They are proud of their rigid control, fear others will force them to eat, and dress in loose, layered clothing to hide their thinness. To burn off fat and calories, anorexics often become hyperactive, exercising excessively (Yancey, 1999). Treatment and recovery from anorexia nervosa require professional help. The diagnosed anorexic cannot overcome this mental illness herself.

Bulimia Nervosa   In order for individuals to be diagnosed with **bulimia nervosa,** they must exhibit the following symptoms: (a) binge eating followed by purging at least twice per week for three months, (b) loss of self-control, (c) severe body image disturbance. Bulimics are preoccupied with food and weight, fear getting fat, and exhibit chaotic eating behaviors. Unlike anorexics, bulimics turn to food, rather than away from it, to cope with emotional problems. Purging may come in the form of laxatives, diuretics, enemas, and/or self-induced vomiting. Eating binges are followed by periods in which bulimics may fast, exercise too much, or turn to vomiting. Physical symptoms associated with vomiting may include finger calluses, sore throat, feeling of bloating, stomach alkalosis, and chemical imbalance (Yancey, 1999). As with anorexia nervosa, treatment and recovery from bulimia nervosa require professional help.

Eating Disorders Not Otherwise Specified (EDNOS)   The DSM also lists eating disorders that contain some but not all of the criteria associated with anorexia and bulimia. These include the EDNOS category as well as a category titled *anorexia athletica,* which describes fear of obesity among female athletes. All of these disorders that fail to meet the standards to be classified as anorexic or bulimic have been labeled **subclinical eating disorders** (Beals, 2000). It is the subclinical eating disorders that are of greatest concern for female athletes participating in sports that encourage low body weight and thinness. Subclinical

TABLE 16.2 | Pathogenic Weight Control Behaviors and Health Consequences

Behavior	Health Consequence
Diet Pills	Heightened anxiety, rapid heart rate, poor concentration, insomnia, dehydration
Diuretics	Dehydration, electrolyte imbalance, little fat loss, weight loss quickly regained
Excessive Exercise	Menstrual dysfunction in females, fatigue, increased risk of overuse injuries, hunger following exercise
Fasting/Starvation	Loss of lean body mass and bone density, poor physical and cognitive performance, poor nutrition
Fat-Free Diets	Difficulty of maintaining weight loss and possible lack in essential vitamins, nutrients, and fatty acids
Laxatives/Enemas	Dehydration, electrolyte imbalance, constipation, cathartic colon
Saunas	Dehydration and electrolyte imbalance, no permanent weight loss
Self-Induced Vomiting	Dehydration, electrolyte imbalance, gastrointestinal problems, stomach ulcers, erosion of tooth enamel

Source: Adapted from Beals, 2000.

eating disorders are far more prevalent among female athletes than anorexia nervosa or bulimia nervosa.

Subclinical and Clinical Eating Disorders among Athletes

Males and females involved in activities that link leanness to success are often pressured to be thin. This is especially true of female athletes involved in gymnastics, dancers, and models. In an effort to be thin and to meet their coaches' expectations, athletes may turn to a number of questionable eating and exercise behaviors that may compromise their health. In most cases, desire to be thin does not result in clinically diagnosed anorexia or bulimia. However, subclinical eating disorders have been reported in anywhere from 1 to 62 percent of female athletes (American College of Sports Medicine, 1997). At some point, if left unchecked, subclinical eating disorders may result in dysfunctional social interaction, decreased physical performance, reduced physical health, and, in some cases, anorexia or bulimia. Ways in which athletes suffering from subclinical eating disorders attempt to lose weight and become thin include the following: fasting/starvation, diet pills, diuretics, laxatives/

enemas, vomiting, fat-free diets, saunas, and excessive exercise. These pathogenic health weight control behaviors along with potential negative consequences are listed in table 16.2.

A meta-analysis conducted by Hausenblas & Carron (1999) provides an excellent summary of clinical and subclinical eating disorders among athletes. The analysis involved 92 studies, 560 effect sizes, and 10,878 athletes and non-athletes. Results of this meta-analysis are summarized as follows:

1. Athletes report more eating disorder symptoms than non-athletes.

2. Athletes competing in aesthetic sports (e.g., gymnastics, dance, diving) report more eating disorders than those in nonaesthetic sports.

3. Athletes do not have a greater drive for thinness than non-athletes.

Notwithstanding these results, research published after 1999 continues to provide important insights into the relationship between sport and eating disorders (Anshel, 2004; DiBartolo & Shaffer, 2002; Hausenblas & Carron, 2000). Of particular interest are three other studies, reported

CONCEPT The incidence of anorexia nervosa and bulimia nervosa among female athletes and females generally is of serious concern. Of even greater concern, however, is the very high rate of eating disturbances among female athletes that are not diagnosed as pathogenic. These tend to go untreated and unnoticed.

APPLICATION Eating disturbances of any kind should be of concern to athletes, coaches, and professionals associated with women's sports. Unhealthy behaviors such as fasting, dieting, and the taking of weight-control drugs are particularly dangerous to young women engaging in demanding training schedules. Athletes are under tremendous pressure to excel at their sports. When they come to believe that losing weight and becoming thin will help them perform better, they become particularly vulnerable to pathogenic eating disorders such as anorexia or bulimia. Extraordinary steps should be taken to educate female athletes about the danger of unhealthy eating behaviors. While we must be similarly concerned about eating disorders among boys and young men, they are far less prevalent in sport and in our society today.

by Davis and Strachan (2001), Hausenblas and McNally (2004), and Madison and Ruma (2003).

In the Davis and Strachan (2001) investigation, 144 female hospital patients diagnosed with eating disorders were identified. Twenty-five percent of the patients were classified as athletes and the rest were classified as non-athletes. In comparing these two groups, it was found that they did not differ in terms of an array of personality-related measures (obsessive-compulsive disorder, narcissism, neurotic perfectionism, borderline personality, and emotional distress), but did differ in some aspects measured by the Eating Disorder Inventory (EDI; Garner & Olmsted, 1984). In particular, athletes tended to score a little higher in maturity fears and perfectionism, but a little lower in bulimia.

As it relates to eating disorders, there is a theory that suggests that there is an association between severity of symptoms and increased weekly exercise (the more severe the symptoms, the more the individual exercises). This theory was tested by Madison and Ruma (2003) using 110 adolescents suffering from various eating disorders. They categorized the participants as being athletes, casual athletes, and non-athletes, and manipulated the amount of weekly exercise. The results showed that the theory was supported for non-athletes, but not for athletes. Exercise has a different meaning for athletes suffering from eating disorders. The researchers concluded that one should not necessarily restrict exercise in athletes suffering from eating disorders. In a similar fashion, Hausenblas and McNally (2004) found that track and field athletes may be protected from eating disorders and the drive for thinness because of their high caloric output and the fact that they are already thin.

Eating Disorders and Unhealthy Exercise Behavior

In some cases eating disorders have been linked to potentially unhealthy exercise behavior. In this subsection we briefly discuss some of those behaviors and relationships.

Anorexia Analogue Hypothesis Yates (1987, 1991) hypothesized that male obligatory runners and anorexic females share common personality characteristics and a common drive for thinness, which they obtain through excessive exercise. Yates referred to this as the **anorexia analogue hypothesis,** while Dess (2000) referred to it as **activity anorexia.** According to the anorexia analogue hypothesis, obligatory runners use running to control their body weight. As they continue to run and diet to reduce body fat, they are following the anorexia nervosa format. The need to have absolute control over the body is similar to that found in the anorexic. Further, Yates argued, obligatory runners and anorexics have similar family backgrounds, socioeconomic status, personality characteristics, tolerance of pain, and quest for asceticism. Research reported by Coen and Ogles (1993); Parker, Lambert, and Burlington (1994); and Matherson and Crawford-Wright (2000) provided only partial support for this hypothesis. Male obligatory runners and eating-disordered females share a number of personality characteristics, but they do not seem to share the same psychological disturbances.

In a similar vein, researchers have wondered if female aerobics instructors were at risk for developing eating disorders and an obsessive attitude toward exercise. Martin and Hausenblas (1998) measured the eating disorder behavior and exercise attitudes of 286 female aerobics instructors. Results of the investigation showed the aerobics instructors to be good role models. They did not exhibit unhealthy eating behaviors or unhealthy pathological attitudes about excessive exercise.

Muscle Dysmorphia   Male weightlifters suffering from muscle dysmorphia differ from normal weightlifters on many measures, including body dissatisfaction, eating disorders, anabolic steroid use, and mood disturbance. **Muscle dysmorphia** is defined as an individual's preoccupation with the notion that he is not sufficiently muscular. Because of its similarity to anorexia nervosa, this disorder has been called *reverse anorexia nervosa.* The unrealistic pursuit of thinness in anorexics shows parallels to the unrealistic pursuit of "bigness" in muscle-dysmorphic individuals. As demonstrated by Olivardia and Pope (2000), individuals classified as being muscle dysmorphic think constantly about their muscularity and have little control over compulsive weightlifting and dietary regimens.

Wrestlers Making Weight   The adverse physiological effects of rapid weight loss or "cutting" in preparation for competition are well documented in the literature. Rapid weight loss through behaviors listed in table 16.2 results in decreased plasma volume, dehydration, and hypoglycemia. Research reported by Choma, Sforzo, and Keller (1998) demonstrated that this unhealthy practice also results in a cognitive functioning decrement. Cognitive decrements were noted primarily in short-term memory and digit span recall. Mood state disturbances were also noted. Landers, Arent, and Lutz (2001) confirmed that rapid weight loss results in a mood disturbance prior to weigh-in, but did not observe a decrement in cognitive functioning compared to a control group. Rapid weight loss appears to offer no documented reward or advantage, only potential disadvantages.

Summary

Topics discussed in this chapter included (a) psychological benefits of exercise; (b) theoretical explanations for benefits; (c) exercise adherence and determinants; (d) theories of exercise behavior; (e) fitness as a moderator of life stress; (f) the immune system, cancer, HIV, and exercise; (g) social physique anxiety; (h) exercise addiction; and (i) eating disorders.

A large body of literature has been amassed that supports the position that regular exercise leads to improved psychological affect. Improved psychological affect is manifested in the form of a reduction in negative affect and an increase in positive affect. These consistent findings have led many mental health care professionals to prescribe exercise as a treatment for selected mental health symptoms. Exercise in many cases is as effective as psychotherapy and antidepressant drugs in treating emotional disorders.

Six specific theoretical explanations for the beneficial effects of exercise on mental health were discussed. These included (a) the cognitive behavioral hypothesis, (b) the social interaction hypothesis, (c) the distraction hypothesis, (d) the cardiovascular fitness hypothesis, (e) the amine hypothesis, and (f) the endorphin hypothesis.

Exercise adherence and determinants were discussed within the framework of the natural history of exercise model. The important transitions in the model included (a) going from the sedentary state to adoption of exercise, (b) going from adoption to maintenance or dropout status, and (c) resumption of exercise following dropout. Most research has been conducted relative to the second transition, involving exercise maintenance or dropout. Factors that determine exercise adherence include available time, behavioral coping skills, equipment accessibility, self-efficacy, group cohesion, heart disease risk, intrinsic motivation, good health, and social support.

Several theories of behavior that explain why people don't exercise, why they start to exercise, why they do or do not continue to exercise, and why they start exercising again if they stop were discussed. Models included in this discussion were (a) the theory of reasoned action, (b) the theory of planned behavior, (c) the transtheoretical model of stages of change, (d) social cognitive theory, and (e) exercise self-schemata theory.

Fitness was discussed as a moderator of life stress. The ability of individuals to insulate, protect, or inoculate themselves against the stresses of life through regular exercise is called stress inoculation. Being physically fit serves to inoculate the individual against illness during periods of high stress. Conversely, physically unfit individuals appear to be unprotected against high stress.

Important connections between exercise and the immune system, the human immunodeficiency virus, and cancer were discussed. While too much exercise can compromise the responsiveness of the immune system, moderate exercise is viewed as a possible moderator of HIV and cancer. Finally, the interactive relationships between exercise addiction, social physique anxiety, and the incidence of eating disorders were explored.

Critical Thought Questions

1. Are there alternative explanations for the positive effects of exercise on mental health? Discuss some of these explanations and their viability.

2. Following an acute bout of exercise, a decrease in anxiety below baseline does not occur until 30 minutes or even 60 minutes after the cessation of exercise. Can you think of plausible explanations for the delayed anxiolytic effect?

3. Relatively speaking, why do mentally ill individuals benefit more from exercise than mentally healthy individuals?

4. Six different explanations were given for why exercise has a positive effect on affect. Which explanation do you think is most viable? Compose your own eclectic theory based on these explanations.

5. Discuss specific ways that the "P" factor could be implemented to help people maintain an active lifestyle. Be creative.

6. Based on the literature, would you recommend an exercise program for an individual who had the HIV virus? What sort of program would you recommend? How about if the person had AIDS symptoms?

7. What is the relationship between social physique anxiety and exercise self-presentation efficacy? How is social physique anxiety counterproductive to a physically active lifestyle?

8. Why are subclinical eating disorders more of a threat to the athlete than actual clinical eating disorders? Discuss the relationship between type of sport and incidence of eating disorders.

Glossary

acquired immune deficiency syndrome (AIDS) Caused by the human immunodeficiency virus, the inability of the human immune system to combat disease.

activity anorexia An unhealthy approach to exercise (see anorexia analogue hypothesis).

acute exercise Short-duration, isolated bouts of exercise lasting approximately 30 minutes.

aerobic exercise Continuous and rhythmic exercise in which a sufficient supply of oxygen is available to the exerciser.

amine hypothesis The hypothesis that increased secretion of neurotransmitters associated with exercise is responsible for improved mental health.

anaerobic exercise High-intensity and short-duration exercise requiring a period of recovery to replenish stored energy.

anorexia analogue hypothesis The hypothesis that anorexics and obligatory runners share a common core of personality characteristics.

anorexia nervosa A pathogenic eating disorder characterized by bizarre dieting behaviors and rapid weight loss.

body image The image or picture that a person has about her body.

bulimia nervosa A pathogenic eating disorder characterized by binge eating and vomiting to remain thin.

cardiovascular fitness hypothesis The hypothesis that improved mental health associated with exercise is due to improved cardiovascular fitness.

chronic exercise A daily or regular exercise program across a long period of time.

cognitive behavioral hypothesis The hypothesis that exercise encourages and generates positive thoughts and feelings that serve to counteract negative mood states.

delayed anxiolytic effect The phenomenon that beneficial reduction in anxiety does not manifest itself until sometime following an acute bout of exercise.

distraction hypothesis The hypothesis that exercise affords the individual an opportunity to be distracted from worries and frustrations.

endorphin hypothesis The hypothesis that exercise is associated with brain production of chemicals that have a "morphine-like" effect on the exerciser.

exercise addiction Psychophysiological dependence on a regular regimen of exercise.

exercise adherence The process of adhering to or complying with a prescribed exercise program.

exercise determinants Factors that motivate a person to make a transition from a sedentary lifestyle to regular physical activity.

exercise self-efficacy Confidence that one can initiate and/or maintain a personal exercise program.

exercise self-presentation efficacy A person's confidence in his ability to create the public impression of himself as being physically fit, coordinated, and physically active.

exercise self-schemata Self-schemata that focus upon exercise and exercise-related experiences.

human immunodeficiency virus (HIV) A communicable virus that leads to the weakening of the human immune system.

immune system functioning The degree to which the immune system is working to fight off disease and illness.

life stress Positive and negative stress associated with living.

mediator variable Variable that mediates the effect of one variable on another.

moderator variable Variable that determines the nature of the relationship between two other variables.

muscle dysmorphia An individual's preoccupation with the notion that he is not sufficiently muscular.

natural history of exercise A framework for studying the determinants of exercise behavior.

obligatory runner A runner who is addicted to exercise (see exercise addiction).

"P" factor Relative to exercise adherence, the possession of a purpose for exercising.

physical self-concept The perception people have about themselves relative to the physical self.

processes of change Interventions used in the transtheoretical model to move from one stage of exercise to another.

resistance exercise Exercise such as weightlifting, in which resistance can be increased by adding weight.

self-schemata Cognitive generalizations about the self, derived from past experience, that organize and guide the processing of information contained in the individual's social experiences.

social interaction hypothesis The hypothesis that improved mental health associated with exercise is due to social interaction with friends and colleagues who are also exercising.

social physique anxiety Anxiety that people experience when they perceive that other people evaluate their physiques negatively.

stress inoculation The ability of individuals to insulate, protect, or inoculate themselves against the stresses of life through regular exercise.

subclinical eating disorders Eating disorders that fail to meet the clinical standards required to be classified as anorexic or bulimic.

super-adherer An exerciser who participates in and constantly trains for endurance events that require significant long-term effort and commitment.

theory of planned behavior A theory of exercise behavior that suggests that intention is caused by attitude, subjective norm, and perceived behavioral control, and that intention leads to exercise behavior.

theory of reasoned action A theory of exercise behavior that suggests that intention is caused by attitude and subjective norm, and that intention leads to exercise behavior.

transtheoretical model A stage theory of behavioral change. When applied to exercise, the model proposes that individuals pass through five dynamic stages in adopting healthy long-term exercise behavior.

Burnout in Athletes

KEY TERMS

Alternative identity
Burnout in sport and
    exercise
Career termination
Cognitive-affective model
    of burnout
Empowerment model
    of burnout
Entrapment
Investment model of
    burnout
Mood disturbance
Negative adaptation to
    training stress
Overreaching
Overtraining
Positive adaptation to
    training stress
Staleness
Training stress
Training stress model
    of burnout
Training stress syndrome

Much of the previous chapter, on exercise psychology, was devoted to the positive benefits associated with regular moderate exercise. It should be clear from this discussion that exercise in moderation yields powerful beneficial psychological and physiological effects. Near the end of that chapter, however, we touched briefly upon the negative effects of too much exercise, to the point of its becoming an obsession. Too much exercise can result in a reduction in the effectiveness of the immune system to fight disease and an increase in negative psychological mood. In a very practical way, exercise can be considered along a continuum from not enough exercise to too much exercise. Negative psychological and biological outcomes are associated with too little and too much exercise. Overtraining in athletes represents a paradox, because many of the benefits associated with exercise are reversed in the athlete who trains too much. For the athlete, the question of how much is too much is a complex one. Athletes are continually challenging the delicate balance between training and overtraining, since high levels of training are required for success in sport.

> When I was sixteen, I was swimming worse than when thirteen, and I felt like I was never going to come out of it. I really wasn't enjoying the sport anymore because I was doing so poorly, and that time was really tough. . . . I'd done it for over ten years, and it's hard to give up something after that long. I kept thinking, 'Maybe it will turn around, maybe things will get better.' . . . I guess I realized that you have to make it fun. If you're so serious about it all the time and it starts going bad, then it's really going to destroy you.
>
> (Leslie Hoh, University of Missouri–Columbia swimmer)

As quoted by Quitmeir (2000, p. B1), the above statement reflects Leslie Hoh's struggle to remain in swimming and to be invited to compete in the year 2000 Olympic trials. Leslie's story of her love-hate relationship with swimming and near burnout is similar to those of many other young athletes. The purpose of this chapter is to help the reader understand what burnout is, what causes it, and how it can be prevented. To accomplish our purpose, the chapter will be divided into four sections, which include (a) defining burnout and other terms, (b) models of burnout, (c) symptoms and interventions for burnout, (d) recommendations for athletes, coaches, and parents, (e) burnout in coaches, and (f) career termination among athletes.

Defining Burnout and Other Related Terms

As defined by Raedeke and Smith (2001, p. 283), **burnout in sport and exercise** is "a psychological syndrome of emotional/physical exhaustion, reduced sense of accomplishment, and sport devaluation." As can be observed, the focus of this particular definition of burnout is upon physical and mental exhaustion, reduced interest in sport, and reduced performance. In discussing burnout in sport, authors typically use words and terms that are believed to be precursors to burnout. Common terms include *overtraining, overreaching, staleness,* and *withdrawal.*

Overtraining and Overreaching

Not to be confused with the physiological principle of *training overload,* **overtraining** implies that the athlete trains beyond the level that is ideal for maximum benefit. Overtraining is maladaptive behavior that may lead to staleness and burnout. **Overreaching** is a form of short-term overtraining that is a part of normal training. Overreaching, for short periods of time, is synonymous with training overload and progressive resistance. Overreaching that extends for long periods of time at high intensities eventually becomes overtraining (Lehmann, Lormes, Optiz-Gress, Steinacker, Netzer, Foster, & Gastmann, 1997).

Staleness

In a stress model, staleness and overtraining are believed to work together to bring about the condition of athlete burnout. As a result of training, an athlete makes rapid gains in achieving specific training goals. Often, the athlete will experience a *plateau* in performance that is difficult to overcome. For example, a weight lifter might reach a plateau where he cannot get past five repetitions at 250 pounds (bench press). After remaining at this plateau for three weeks, the athlete begins to experience a feeling of **staleness,** which is the initial

CONCEPT   How an athlete adapts to training stress may ultimately determine whether he will have a positive training experience or suffer staleness, overtraining, and burnout.

APPLICATION   Athletes will make a positive adaptation to training stress if they are taught to recognize the signs of negative adaptation and are given the opportunity to cope. Relentless demands from coaches, parents, and teammates will interfere with the athlete's ability to cope.

failure of the body to adapt to training. In an effort to break through the physical or psychological plateau, the athlete initiates a period of overtraining that could result in burnout. The same scenario may be applied to sports of all varieties.

Models of Burnout

Our best understanding of the concept of burnout comes from an investigation of different models of burnout. Burnout is a multidimensional phenomenon that may have many different causes. These causes are clarified through the presentation of the different models. In this section, we consider three different models of burnout: the stress model, the investment model, and the sociologically based empowerment model. Two different stress models will be presented, along with a single example of an investment model and a sociological model.

Stress Models of Burnout in Sport

Stress as the cause of burnout is the focal point of the two models to be presented in this section. These two models of burnout are Silva's (1990) training stress model, and Smith's (1986) cognitive-affective model of stress and burnout.

Silva's Training Stress Model   As illustrated in figure 17.1, the **training stress model of burnout** is based on the notion that **training stress** is necessary for improvements in performance to be made. If a **positive adaptation to training stress** takes place, the athlete will respond with a

training gain. If a **negative adaptation to training stress** takes place, the athlete will experience a lag in training gain, which will be interpreted as staleness. The combination of staleness, overtraining,

FIGURE 17.1 | Negative and positive adaptation to training stress.

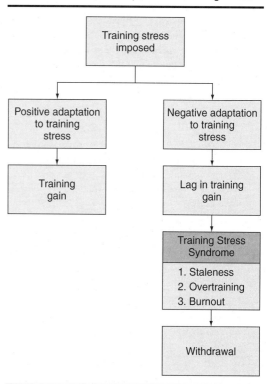

Source: Adapted with permission from Silva, J. M., III (1990). An analysis of the training stress syndrome in competitive athletics. *Journal of Applied Sport Psychology, 2,* 5–20.

FIGURE 17.2 | Smith's cognitive affective model of stress and burnout.

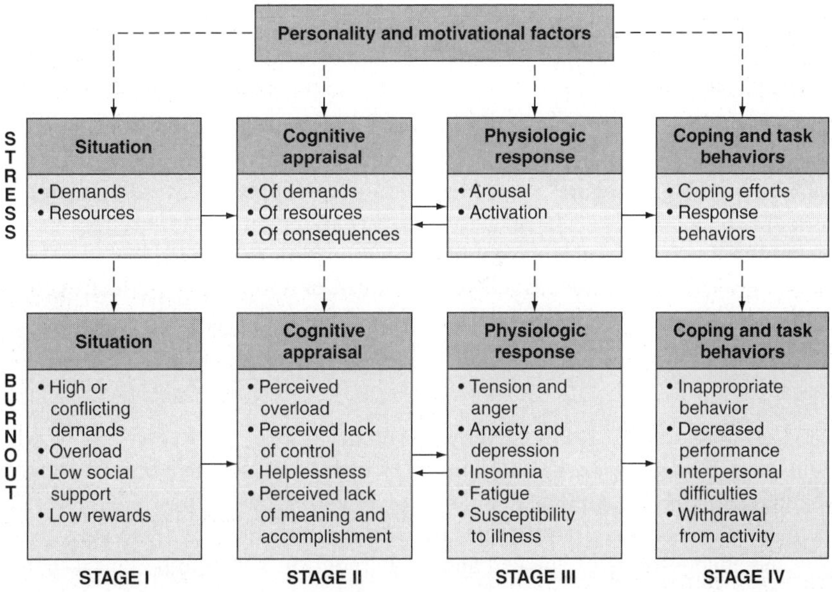

Source: Smith, R.E. (1986). Toward a negative-affective model of athletic burnout. *Journal of Sport Psychology, 8:* 40, figure 1. Adapted with permission from Human Kinetics (Champaign, IL).

and burnout is referred to by Silva as the **training stress syndrome.** If the training stress syndrome is not reversed through rest or some other creative intervention, the end result will be withdrawal from sport (sport dropout).

Smith's Cognitive-Affective Model of Stress and Burnout
Smith's (1986) **cognitive-affective model of burnout** is a four-stage model that parallels stages of the stress process first introduced in chapter 8. The details of Smith's stress and burnout model are illustrated in figure 17.2. From the illustration it should be clear than an athlete's personality and level of motivation interact with all four stages. The situational, cognitive, physiologic, and behavioral components of the *general* stress process are paralleled by the situation-specific components of the burnout process.

In the first stage of the model, the athlete is confronted with objective demands that are beyond her ability to address. These demands are presented in the form of pressure to win, excessive practice and training time, and perhaps a low return on her time investment (lack of playing time). In stage two, a cognitive appraisal is made of the objective demands being placed on the athlete. The cognitive appraisal results in a threat to the athlete in the form of perceived overload, lack of control, feelings of helplessness, and lack of meaning. In stage three, perceived threat, as a consequence of cognitive appraisal, results in a physiologic response manifested in the form of anxiety/tension, depression, insomnia, fatigue, and/or susceptibility to illness. Finally, in stage four, the athlete responds with some sort of coping behavior or response, such as inappropriate behavior, decreased performance, interpersonal

CONCEPT According to Smith's affective-cognitive model, burnout parallels stress, in that burnout is viewed as a process resulting from the inability of the athlete to cope with high levels of stress.

APPLICATION The problem begins when the athlete perceives that the demands of the situation are greater than his ability to cope. The perception that he cannot cope with the demands of the situation leads to painful cognitive conclusions and physiological responses. Unresolved stress only becomes worse as the athlete becomes tired, depressed, and fatigued. Finally, in stage four, the athlete withdraws from sport as a way to reduce stress. In this sense, withdrawal from sport is a form of coping. To avoid burnout and sport withdrawal, the athlete must either change the objective situation, change the way he thinks about stress, or develop more effective coping skills.

difficulties, and/or withdrawal from activity. Thus, *burnout is viewed as a response to chronic stress.* It is characterized by psychological, emotional, and perhaps physical withdrawal from a sport or activity the athlete formerly pursued and enjoyed.

From a stress model perspective, overtraining stress leads to athlete burnout. The question, however, is this: how do the internal coping skills of the athlete and social support from family and friends influence the relationship between overtraining stress and burnout? As illustrated in figure 17.3, there are two viable answers to this question. In model (a), coping resources and social support moderate the relationship between overtraining stress and athlete burnout. If coping resources and social support are high, athlete burnout should not occur. Conversely, if coping resources and social support are low, athlete burnout may occur. In model (b), overtraining stress mediates the relationship between coping resources/social support and athlete burnout. That is, coping resources and social support influence overtraining stress, which in turn affects the occurrence of athlete burnout. If coping resources and social support are high, overtraining stress is reduced, thereby having little negative effect on burnout. Research reported by Raedeke and Smith (2004), using a large sample of age-group swimmers, suggests greater support for the stress mediating

model (model b). Regardless of which model is adopted, it is clear that coping resources of the athlete and social support play an important role in determining the effect that stress has upon athlete burnout. It is also important to note that it is not just sport-related stress that brings about athlete burnout. Non-sport-related stress adds to overtraining stress to bring about athlete burnout. Stress associated with school, work, family, and friends can add to the overtraining stress experienced by the athlete (Meehan, Bull, Wood, and James, 2004).

Investment Model of Burnout

Various versions of the **investment model of burnout** have been proposed for sport (Raedeke, 1997; Raedeke et al., 2000; Schmidt & Stein, 1991; Weiss & Weiss, 2003). In its simplest form it can be viewed as an imbalance between the costs and benefits associated with athletic participation (Van Yperen, 1997). In its more complete form, it is conceptualized as being a function of five determinants of commitment to sport involvement. How the athlete evaluates these five determinants will determine whether his commitment is based upon *enjoyment* or *entrapment*. If sport commitment is based upon enjoyment, the athlete will participate enthusiastically. If sport commitment is based upon **entrapment,** it is only a matter of time

FIGURE 17.3 | Illustration showing how social support and coping resources interact with overtraining stress to produce athlete burnout. In model (a), coping resources and social support serve as moderators, while in model (b) they influence overtraining stress, which in turn leads to athlete burnout.

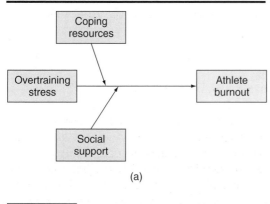

(a)

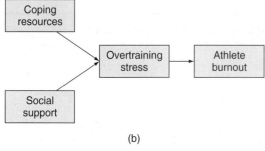

(b)

Commitment Due to Enjoyment   In terms of the determinants of commitment, it is easy to see why athletes who fit the enjoyment profile continue their sport involvement. The rewards of participation are high and the costs are low. For whatever reason, the athlete finds the sport experience to be very rewarding relative to the sacrifices in energy and time that go into it (costs). Athletes who start in sport when they are young and stay with it through young adulthood invest a significant part of their lives in sport. High investment is worth it because of the favorable reward/cost ratio and because of the satisfaction that participation gives them. Because of high investment in sport, the athlete has not cultivated alternative things to invest his time in. This, however, is not viewed as negative because it was his choice (self-determination).

Commitment Due to Entrapment   As you compare enjoyment with entrapment in the model, you notice that they are exact opposites in terms of rewards, costs, and satisfaction, yet identical in terms of investment and alternatives. It is the similarity that keeps the athlete involved despite low satisfaction and a poor reward/cost benefit ratio. This is an athlete who is not enjoying the sport experience. Practice is not fun, competition is not fun, and it all feels like drudgery. Yet, the athlete persists and remains committed. Because investments are high and alternatives are low, she remains involved. After investing huge amounts of time and energy into her sport across many years, it is difficult to give it up. It is for this reason that the model is named the investment model. The second reason that the athlete continues her sport involvement in the face of entrapment is the feeling that she has few alternatives. Because of many years of commitment to sport, the athlete has not developed other viable interests.

The unhealthy situation of sport commitment due to entrapment cannot last for very long, because the athlete begins to experience burnout. If the athlete is unable to cope with burnout and its

before burnout sets in and the athlete withdraws from sport. The investment model is illustrated in figure 17.4.

As can be observed in figure 17.4, the determinants of commitment in the investment model are rewards, costs, satisfaction, investments, and alternatives. The difference between commitment due to enjoyment and commitment due to entrapment depends upon the values given to each of the determinants of commitment. The model takes its name from the investment determinant.

FIGURE 17.4 | Investment model of burnout in sport.

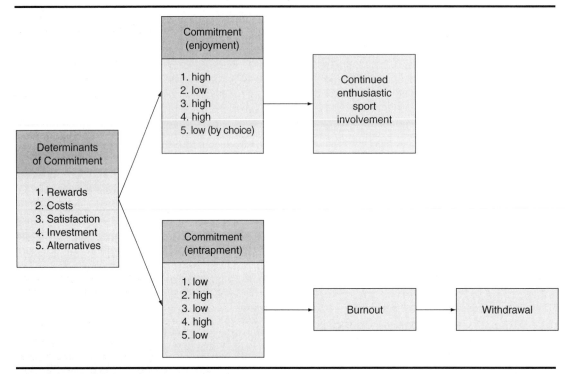

symptoms, he will withdrawal from sport in spite of high investment and low alternatives. Over time the athlete will develop other attractive alternatives and begin to invest less time in sport, making it easier to withdraw.

Empowerment Model of Burnout

Coakley's (1992) **empowerment model of burnout** is based on the notion that burnout in sport is a social problem caused by an overly controlling and constraining social structure. Coakley does not deny the existence of stress in a young athlete's life, but asserts that it is only a symptom of burnout and not the cause. In Coakley's model, burnout is defined as

> a social phenomenon grounded in a set of social relations through which young athletes become disempowered to the point of realizing that sport participation has become a developmental

Stress associated with sport involvement can result in burnout. Source: © Royalty-Free/Corbis.

CONCEPT   An athlete's perception of the conditions associated with sports training and involvement will determine the nature of her commitment and possible withdrawal.

APPLICATION   For an athlete to enjoy her commitment to sport, she must perceive the rewards to be high and the stress-induced costs to be low. In addition, perceived satisfaction and investment must remain high, while attractive alternatives to continued involvement must be viewed as low. It is unrealistic to expect an athlete to remain happily committed to her sport activity if these conditions are not present.

CONCEPT   The empowerment model of burnout provides a sociological explanation for burnout and withdrawal from sport. Burnout occurs as athletes seek to develop identities separate from sport and to have more personal control over their lives. Failure to realize these desires may cause an athlete to experience burnout and to withdraw from sport.

APPLICATION   The issues raised by Coakley in the empowerment model of burnout remind us of issues raised in chapter 5 about youth sports. If the sport experience is so constraining that an athlete cannot develop an alternate identity and feel control over her life, then the sport experience needs to be restructured. Coaches, parents, and organizers of youth sport programs must work hard to make the sport experience one that is not so constraining that athletes are forced to leave in order to realize fundamental needs of autonomy and self-identity.

dead-end for them and that they no longer have any meaningful control over important parts of their lives (pp. 272–73).

Coakley argues that stress models of burnout focus exclusively upon the individual and do not consider the possibility that the burnout could be caused by the social organization of sport. Under the stress model, when an athlete experiences burnout, one treatment is to teach him coping skills; this suggests that the problem lies within the athlete and not the social institution of sport.

Young athletes who participate in high-performance sports usually start at a young age and are expected to continue on to adulthood. During this period of time they are highly controlled by the social organization and are not given opportunities to develop identities separate from sport. Coakley's contention is that at some point a young person's desire for an **alternative identity** and personal control over his life (autonomy) forces him to leave sport. This is a painful experience involving stress-like symptoms that we have come to associate with burnout. In a sense, the athlete is "empowered," or liberated, by her decision to withdraw from sport. Burnout from sport could be eliminated by restructuring the social organization of high-performance sport. In summary, Coakley

FIGURE 17.5 │ Empowerment model of burnout and withdrawal from sport.

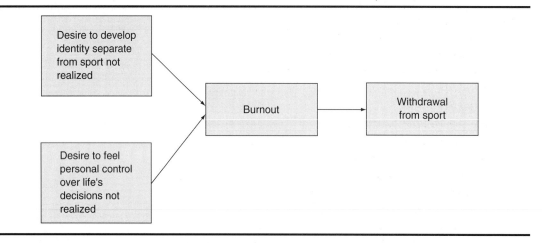

states that burnout in sport occurs in connection with two conditions:

1. When the sport experience is so constraining that the young person is unable to develop a desirable alternate identity, the athlete seeks to liberate himself from sport.

2. When the social organization of sport is so structured that the athlete comes to believe that he has no control over his life, the athlete seeks to liberate himself from sport.

Coakley's empowerment model is illustrated in figure 17.5. The craving for an alternative identity and the craving for personal control are powerful needs in young people. If the sport experience restricts the athlete from realizing these needs, burnout may occur. The reader will recognize that personal control, autonomy, and self-determination are fundamental components of intrinsic motivation. When an athlete comes to believe that she no longer has control over an activity, she loses intrinsic motivation for the activity (chapter 5).

Recognizing that not every young person suffers burnout from sport, Coakey suggests that certain individuals would be less likely to burn out. These would include (a) athletes from backgrounds in which life chances are so limited that they cannot conceive of an attractive alternative identity separate from sport; (b) athletes who, because of sport involvement, have ready access to many opportunities not available to others; and (c) athletes who have been heavily rewarded for success in sport and are so tightly controlled because of that success that they are unaware of attractive alternatives.

Symptoms of Burnout and Interventions

Researchers have addressed and identified physiological and psychological symptoms associated with burnout in athletes. As summarized in table 17.1, the athlete experiences a reversal of many of the physiological benefits associated with exercise, suffers from a loss of appetite and libido, gets more colds and respiratory infections, loses weight, loses sleep, becomes irritable or depressed, experiences feelings of exhaustion, suffers a loss of self-esteem, and experiences a negative change in interpersonal interactions. While athletes experiencing burnout have many common characteristics, it is also well to remember that individual athletes often exhibit very different symptoms (Gould, Tuffey, Udry, & Loehr, 1997).

TABLE 17.1 | Physiological and Psychological Symptoms of Burnout

Physiological Symptoms

1. Increased resting and exercise heart rate
2. Increased resting systolic blood pressure
3. Increased muscle soreness and chronic muscle fatigue
4. Increased presence of biochemical indicators of stress in the blood
5. Increased sleep loss
6. Increased colds and respiratory infections
7. Decreased body weight
8. Decreased maximal aerobic power
9. Decreased muscle glycogen
10. Decreased libido and appetite

Psychological Symptoms

1. Increased mood disturbances
2. Increased perception of physical, mental, and emotional exhaustion
3. Decreased self-esteem
4. Negative change in the quality of personal interaction with others (cynicism, lack of feeling, impersonal relating)
5. Negative cumulative reaction to chronic everyday stress as opposed to acute doses of stress

Measurement of Burnout and Coping Strategies

Burnout can be identified through symptoms listed in table 17.1 and through the administration of the Maslach Burnout Inventory (MBI; Maslach & Jackson, 1986), the Eades Athletic Burnout Inventory (EABI; Eades, 1991), or the Athlete Burnout Questionnaire (ABQ; Raedeke & Smith, 2001). The Athlete Burnout Questionnaire is composed of 15 items that measure the following three aspects of athlete burnout: (a) emotional and physical exhaustion, (b) reduced sense of accomplishment, and (c) sport devaluation. These same three aspects of athlete burnout were also identified in a qualitative study reported by Raedeke, Lunney, and Venables (2002). The research that led to the development of the ABQ also was the inspiration for the definition of athlete burnout that appears at the beginning of this chapter.

When symptoms of burnout are identified, steps must be taken to reverse debilitating effects of the symptoms as soon as possible. Of importance in heading off or reversing burnout are the coping strategies possessed by athletes. In this regard, the COPE instrument (Carver, Scheier, & Weintraub, 1989) and the modified COPE instrument (MCOPE; Crocker & Graham, 1995) have been developed and tested (Eklund, Grove, & Heard, 1998) for the purpose of measuring coping strategies of athletes suffering from a slump in performance (staleness).

Measurement of Mood States

Measurement of mood using the Profile of Mood States (POMS) was first introduced in chapter 2 as it related to athletic performance. Here we suggest the use of the POMS as a way of monitoring mood states associated with burnout. **Mood disturbance** is one of the indicators of overtraining in sport. For example, biopsies of exercised muscles demonstrate a connection between diminished muscle glycogen and increased mood disturbance

CONCEPT Many things, such as fatigue, performance decline, and proneness to infection, may signal overtraining in an athlete, but monitoring of mood states is one of the simplest and most effective ways to get an early warning of overtraining.

APPLICATION Mood states can be easily measured and monitored using the Profile of Mood States (POMS) or some variation of it. The important thing is to establish a baseline from which to work. The baseline represents the athlete's normal healthy level of mood. It is from this baseline, which will differ for each athlete, that a determination of mood disturbance is made. A 50 percent increase in total mood is recommended as a criterion for concern. When using the POMS, total mood is determined by summing the five negative mood states and subtracting the score for vigor (see figure 2.3). Since this value may be less than zero, always add a constant of 100 to each total mood score.

(Puffer & McShane, 1992). Berglund and Safstrom (1994) effectively used the POMS to monitor mood states of Swedish canoeists during a three-month period leading up to the Barcelona Olympics. In this study they operationally defined mood disturbance as an increase in total mood to a level 50 percent above an established baseline. When the criterion of 50 percent was passed, intervention was applied in the form of reduced or altered training. Mood disturbance has been repeatedly observed in swimmers and distance runners, but it also occurs with basketball and other nonendurance sports (Raglin, Eksten, & Garl, 1995; Raglin, Koceja, Stager, & Harms, 1996).

Given the important connection between overtraining and mood disturbance, it follows that (a) mood should be monitored, and (b) interventions should be applied in the form of reduced or altered training schedules when mood disturbance rises above a predetermined level (Hooper & Mackinnon, 1995). Notwithstanding this strong and very valid recommendation, it must be pointed out that it is often very difficult to observe a mood disturbance in situations of short-duration overtraining. Research does show that chronic high-intensity exercise results in a mood disturbance (Berger, Mott, Butki, Martin, Wilkinson, & Owen, 1999), but this is not necessarily the case in short-duration overtraining. For example, high-intensity training of competitive cyclists was monitored over a six-week period without a noticeable fluctuation in mood (Martin, Andersen, & Gates, 2000). Similar results were obtained by Berger et al. (1999) in a study involving three weeks of intense cycling. In another study involving swimmers, the mood states of swimmers were monitored across an entire season (Hooper, MacKinnon, & Hanzahan, 1997). Of the 14 athletes studied, three were identified as exhibiting the depressed performance characteristics of the stale athlete. Based on monitored POMS scores, however, these three stale athletes could not be distinguished from the other 11 athletes. These results lead to the conclusion that intense training is not necessarily a precursor for elevated mood states. When a mood disturbance is observed, however, this is cause for concern.

While the Profile of Mood States (POMS) has been the instrument of choice for measuring mood disturbance in athletes, it is not the only inventory available. Developed by Kellman, Altenburg, Lormes, and Steinacker (2001), the Recovery-Stress Questionnaire for Athletes (RESTQ-Sport; Kellman & Kallus, 2001) is a viable alternative to the POMS. Composed of 77 items, the RESTQ-Sport measures nine recovery-related subscales and 10 stress-related subscales.

CONCEPT   A completely linear relationship does not exist between increased training and enhanced strength, endurance, and performance.

APPLICATION   The mistaken belief that "more is better" when it comes to sports training may lead to staleness, overtraining, and burnout. Coaches and trainers must carefully monitor their training regimens to assure that their efforts actually result in increased performance and positive affect.

Recommended Intervention

Fender (1989) proposed three intervention steps for addressing burnout in athletes:

1. The first and primary step in addressing burnout is self-awareness. The athlete must first recognize he is suffering from burnout and communicate his difficulties to a sympathetic parent, coach, or sport psychologist.

2. The second step is to take time off from the offending activity. If symptoms are identified early, taking a few days off from practice might be all that is necessary. If burnout has progressed to the point of withdrawal, however, total rest and relaxation might be necessary for the athlete's well-being.

3. In the final and third step, relaxation strategies as identified in chapter 9 of the text may be beneficial as coping strategies for reversing the debilitating effects of stress and burnout.

In summary, recall that according to Silva (1990), the three phases of negative stress syndrome are staleness, overtraining, and burnout. With this in mind, it follows that the best way to address the debilitating effects of burnout is to intervene while the athlete is still in the staleness stage. The wise and experienced coach will recognize the signs of staleness and overtraining before they escalate to burnout. If each athlete is treated as a valued individual, little justification exists for a coach or leader to allow the negative stress syndrome to progress to the final stage of burnout and withdrawal. However, self-inflicted burnout and withdrawal are also possibilities.

Recommendations for Athletes, Coaches, and Parents

Few empirical studies of burnout have been conducted. An exception to this observation is a pair of studies reported by Gould, Udry, Tuffey, and Loehr (1996); and Gould, Tuffey, Udry, and Loehr (1996). These investigations involved the study of burnout in 30 junior tennis burnouts and 32 non-burnout comparison tennis players who were similar in age, playing experience, and sex. In the first study (1996), the burned-out and non-burned-out junior tennis players were compared on a number of quantitative measures. In the second study (1996), a qualitative analysis was conducted on 10 tennis players identified quantitatively in the first study as being most burned out. While a number of interesting results came out of these studies, two were of great importance. The first was that from a demographic, psychological, personal, and behavioral perspective, it was possible to differentiate between the two groups of athletes. The burned-out tennis players, in contrast to comparison players, exhibited higher burnout scores, were lower in motivation, were more withdrawn, were less likely to use coping strategies, and differed on a variety of perfectionism subscales (e.g., showed greater concern over mistakes). The second result of import was that through the qualitative analyses, recommendations were given to players, coaches, and parents as to how to avoid burnout in junior tennis.

TABLE 17.2 | Recommendations (Advice) Given to Players, Coaches, and Parents on How to Avoid Burnout in Junior Tennis Players

Target Population	Recommendations
Player	1. Play for your own reasons.
	2. Balance tennis with other things in your life.
	3. If it is not fun, then don't play.
	4. Try to make practice and games fun.
	5. Relax and take time off occasionally.
Coach	1. Cultivate personal involvement with player.
	2. Establish two-way communication with athlete.
	3. Solicit and utilize player input.
	4. Work to understand player feelings and perspective.
Parent	1. Recognize the optimal amount of "pushing" needed.
	2. Back off and lessen involvement.
	3. Reduce importance of winning.
	4. Show support and empathy for child's efforts.
	5. Don't coach if not the coach, and separate roles if you are the coach.
	6. Solicit child's input.

Gould et al., 1996

These recommendations are shown in tabular form in table 17.2. These recommendations are of particular importance for parents and coaches, because evidence exists that these individuals are often perceived by the athlete as contributing to stress that leads to burnout (Udry, Gould, Bridges, & Tuffey, 1997).

Burnout in Coaches

In addition to studying burnout in athletes, researchers have studied burnout in coaches. In this regard, Vealey, Armstrong, Comar, and Greenleaf (1998) reported the results of an investigation that indicates that burnout in coaches is linked to burnout in athletes. According to the Vealey model, coach burnout has a direct effect upon the athlete's perception of the coach's behavior, which in turn is a predictor of athlete burnout. Conceivably, this finding would fit into stages one and two of Smith's cognitive-affective model of burnout (fig. 17.2). Consistent with Vealey et al. (1998),

Price and Weiss (2000) observed that soccer coaches experiencing emotional exhaustion were perceived by their athletes as providing less training instruction and less social support. Soccer coaches who were perceived by their athletes as being autocratic, providing inadequate instruction, little social support, and little positive feedback were associated with athletes who experienced high levels of anxiety and burnout and low levels of enjoyment and perceived competence. Coaches' burnout negatively affects the athletes' perception of the coaches' behavior, which in turn has a negative effect on athlete behavior.

Researchers have also looked at coach burnout from the perspective of the investment or commitment model (Raedeke, 2004; Raedeke, Granzyk, & Warren, 2000; Raedeke, Warren, & Granzyk, 2002). According to Raedeke et al. (2002), which involved 469 age-group swim coaches, the strongest predictors of commitment in coaching are perceived satisfaction with coaching and perceived investments. Perceived benefits and costs associated with

CONCEPT Perceived investment in the coaching profession and satisfaction with the coaching experience are what keeps coaches coaching. When a coach begins to experience burnout, this affects the athletes' perception of the coach and has a negative effect on the athletes' enjoyment of the athletic experience. Thus, it appears that athlete burnout is connected in many ways to the behavior of the coach. You cannot blame athlete burnout on the coach, but there is a connection between coach behavior and athlete behavior.

APPLICATION Costs and benefits associated with the coaching experience have a direct effect on

coach satisfaction; this, in turn, has a direct effect on commitment. Secondary school coaches must be paid commensurate with the amount of time that they devote to coaching. When practice time, travel time, and competition time are all figured into the equation, secondary school coaches are paid well below minimum wage. School administrators can also help by protecting coaches from abusive parents who demand more from the coach than is possible to give. Administrators would be well advised to study the investment/commitment model in trying to understand why it is so hard to keep good coaches coaching.

coaching have an indirect effect on commitment through perceived coach satisfaction. Alternative options and social constraints were shown to be weak predictors of coach commitment.

Career Termination among Athletes

> Athletic participation is characterized by glorious peaks and debilitating valleys. The range of events and emotions experienced by athletes seems to be extreme compared to the normal population. Perhaps the most significant and potentially traumatic experience encountered by athletes is career termination. (Tayor & Olgilvie, 2001, p. 672)

Retirement or termination from athletic involvement is often sudden and unexpected. In many ways, it is related to the concept of athlete burnout that has been developed in this chapter. Consider the high school junior who plans on playing college basketball, but is cut from his team before he even gets to the senior year. Consider the college quarterback who aspires to play professional football, but is not drafted by any professional team. Consider the professional football player who plays five

years and then sustains a career-ending injury. The list goes on. In many cases, even when retirement is planned, the athlete is unprepared for the sudden change in lifestyle. Because sport psychologists are not routinely employed by all collegiate athletic departments and professional sport teams, there is often no one available to help athletes face a sudden or even planned termination of the athletic experience. This is true also of athlete and coach burnout.

While there has been much written about career termination and transition in sport, we owe much of our conceptual understanding of career termination to Jim Taylor and Bruce Ogilvie (Ogilvie & Taylor, 1993; Taylor & Ogilvie, 1994, 2001). As illustrated in figure 17.6, Taylor and Ogilvie (1994, 2001) proposed the conceptual model of career termination. The conceptual model of athletic **career termination** acknowledges that there are multiple reasons for career termination (age, deselection, injury, free choice). The interaction between a wide range of psychological, social, financial, and occupational factors and available coping skills will determine the quality of the adaptation to career termination. If adaptation to career termination is smooth and well managed, the result will be a healthy career transition. Alternatively, if career termination and transition

FIGURE 17.6 | The conceptual model of career termination as proposed by Taylor and Ogilvie
(1994, 2001).

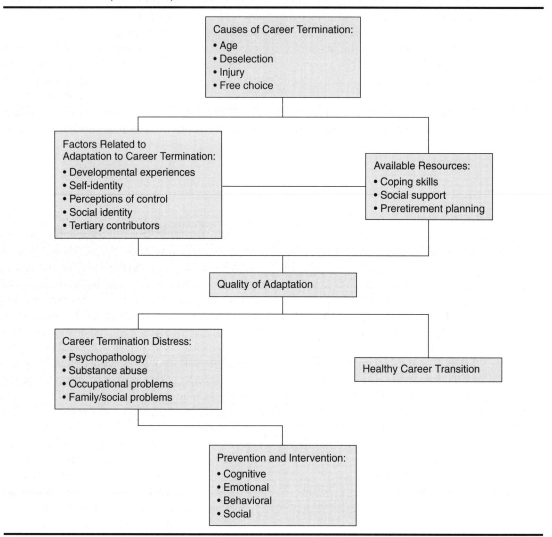

Source: From Taylor, J., & Ogilvie, B. (1994). A conceptual model of adaptation to retirement among athletes. *Journal of Applied Sport Psychology, 6,* 1–20. Reproduced with permission of the publisher (Taylor & Francis).

are not smooth and well managed, the result can be distress, anger, and frustration. As illustrated in figure 17.6, failure to experience a quality adaptation to career termination can result in psychopathology, substance abuse, occupational problems, and family and social problems. If an unhealthy career transition and termination take place, the former athlete may need professional help to overcome cognitive, emotional, behavioral, and social challenges.

CONCEPT Unplanned and sudden termination from sport and athletics can place unusual stress on the athlete. Termination from competitive sport involvement includes a number of unique experiences and challenges that the athlete is unprepared for.

APPLICATION There is no substitute for early planning for sport termination and career transi-

tion. Competitive sport involvement is a young man or woman's experience that is usually destined to come to an end sooner than hoped. Every organization that promotes competitive sports, from high school through college, and up to the professional level, is morally obligated to provide career transition training for its athletes. This training should begin with the high school counselor who can talk to the athlete about life after sport.

Summary

Burnout in sport and exercise is defined as "a psychological syndrome of emotional/physical exhaustion, reduced sense of accomplishment, and sport devaluation." Models that purport to explain the burnout phenomenon in sport include the training stress model, the cognitive-affective model, the investment model, and the empowerment model.

Silva's training stress model of burnout is based on the notion that training stress is necessary for improvements in performance to be made. If a positive adaptation to training stress takes place, the athlete will respond with a training gain. If a negative adaptation to training stress takes place, the athlete will experience a lag in training gain, which will be interpreted as staleness. The combination of staleness, overtraining, and burnout is referred to by Silva as the training stress syndrome.

Smith's cognitive-affective model of burnout is a four-stage model that parallels stages of the stress process. The situational, cognitive, physiologic, and behavioral components of the general stress process are paralleled by the situation-specific components of the burnout process. Burnout is viewed as a response to chronic stress characterized by psychological, emotional, and perhaps physical withdrawal from a sport or activity the athlete formerly pursued and enjoyed.

The investment model of burnout is conceptualized as being a function of five determinants of commitment to sport involvement (rewards, costs, satisfaction, investment, alternatives). How the athlete conceptualizes these five determinants will determine whether commitment is based upon *enjoyment* or *entrapment*. If sport commitment is based upon enjoyment, the athlete will participate enthusiastically. If sport commitment is based upon entrapment, it is only a matter of time before burnout sets in and the athlete withdraws from sport.

Coakley's empowerment model is based on the notion that burnout in sport is a social problem caused by an overly controlling and constraining social structure. The craving for an alternative identity and the craving for personal control are powerful needs in young people. If the sport experience restricts the athlete from realizing these needs, burnout may occur.

Physiological and psychological symptoms of burnout were identified. It was suggested that the Profile of Mood States or the Recovery-Stress Questionnaire for Athletes be used to monitor mood in athletes participating in intense training. When a mood disturbance is discovered, corrective steps should be taken. One important corrective step is to rest the athlete and reduce training load for a period of time. In severe cases of burnout, relaxation procedures should be applied to reverse the debilitating effects of stress. The chapter concluded with recommendations for athletes, parents, and coaches; a discussion of burnout in coaches; and a discussion of career termination among athletes.

Critical Thought Questions

1. Which of the four theories of burnout discussed in this chapter do you feel most comfortable with? Why?

2. Would you feel more comfortable with an eclectic model? If so, describe your eclectic model as you visualize it.

3. How do you feel about Coakley's empowerment model of burnout? Do you think it provides a reasonable explanation for the phenomenon of burnout? Why or why not?

4. In which kinds of sports do you think burnout is most likely to occur? Why?

5. What is the nature of the relationship between athlete burnout and burnout in coaches?

6. Discuss the important concept of career termination among athletes. Apply the conceptual model of career termination to some real-world examples that you can think of.

Glossary

alternative identity An identity that an athlete can establish separate from sport.

burnout in sport and exercise A syndrome of physical/emotional exhaustion, sport devaluation, and reduced athletic accomplishment.

career termination Often called career retirement, the term describes the process that athletes go through when their playing days come to an end.

cognitive-affective model of burnout A four-stage model of burnout that parallels the stress process.

empowerment model of burnout A model of burnout based on the notion that burnout in sport is a social problem caused by an overly controlling and constraining social structure.

entrapment Condition in which an athlete's continuation of her sport involvement is based on the wrong reasons.

investment model of burnout A model of burnout based on the notion that five determinants of sport commitment determine whether an athlete's sport involvement will be based upon enjoyment or entrapment. Personal investment is one of the determinants.

mood disturbance An indicator of overtraining in sport.

negative adaptation to training stress An athlete's response of experiencing a lag in training gain when confronted with training stress.

overreaching Short-term overtraining that is part of normal training.

overtraining Training beyond the level that is ideal for maximum benefit.

positive adaptation to training stress An athlete's response of achieving a training gain when confronted with training stress.

staleness Initial failure of the body to adapt to training stress.

training stress The stress associated with training in sport and exercise.

training stress model of burnout A model of burnout based on the notion that training stress is necessary for improvements in performance to be realized.

training stress syndrome The occurrence of overtraining, staleness, and burnout in response to a lag in training gain.

CHAPTER 18

The Psychology
of Athletic Injuries

KEY TERMS

Acute pain
Adherence to injury
  rehabilitation
Behavioral response
Benign pain
Chronic pain
Cognitive appraisal
Coping behavior
Distributed approach
Emotional response
Harmful pain
Injury pain
Injury rehabilitation
  interventions
Integrated sport injury model
Nonpharmacological
  pain-focusing techniques
Nonpharmacological
  pain-reduction techniques
Pain catastrophizing
Pain tolerance
Performance pain
Personal factors
Psychological response
  to injury
Rehabilitation rehearsal
Situational factors

Specialist approach
Stress and injury model
Stress response

My knee's shot. My knee's shot. There goes my career. It's over. I'm through.

(Keith Millard,
Minnesota Vikings' defensive tackle)

The above words by an injured National Football League player reveal the anguish and frustration associated with an athletic injury. As explained by sports writer Jill Lieber (1991, p. 37), Millard sustained his season-ending injury while rushing the Tampa Bay quarterback. Following his injury, and while agonizing over his misfortune, the 6-foot-5-inch, 265-pound football player put his head in his hands and sobbed.

Physical factors such as overtraining, equipment failure, and poor playing conditions are believed to be the major factors contributing to athletic injuries. Evidence is mounting, however, to suggest that psychological factors play an important role in the incidence, prevention, and rehabilitation of athletic injuries. An athlete trains his body and mind for optimal athletic performance, only to have it all come to a halt with an injury. Athletes and athletic teams enter each season with high hopes. Oftentimes, season results are determined not by which team is the best at the beginning of the season, but by which team suffers the fewest injuries during the course of the season. For the athlete who has her self-image tied to her performance on the athletic field, a season-ending or partial-season-ending injury can leave the athlete emotionally crippled. It is at this point that the sport injury rehabilitation personnel take over and the journey to full recovery begins. To be successful, the rehabilitation process must take into consideration both physical and psychological training and preparation.

In addressing the important subject of the psychology of athletic injuries, three main chapter sections have been prepared. These include (a) psychological predictors of athletic injuries, (b) athlete response to injury and rehabilitation, and (c) other considerations.

Psychological Predictors of Athletic Injury

It stands to reason that if researchers can identify psychological factors associated with the occurrence of injuries, steps can be taken to reduce the number and severity of those that do occur. A model for explaining the interactive relationship between athletic injury and such psychological factors as personality, life stress, coping resources, the stress response, and potential interventions was proposed by Andersen and Williams (1988) and revised by Williams and Andersen (1998). The Williams and Andersen (1998) **stress and injury model** is illustrated in figure 18.1. The key element of the model is the **stress response.** The stress response in this model is similar to the stress process illustrated in figure 8.1 of chapter 8. A potentially stressful athletic situation requires the athlete to complete a cognitive appraisal of the task's *associated demands,* the athlete's *coping resources,* and the *consequences.* If, in the athlete's judgment, the situational demands exceed the personal resources needed to address the situation, the stress response will be significant. Conversely, if the athlete's perceived resources outweigh the demands, the stress response will be minimal. The elicitation of the stress response represents a perceived imbalance between the athlete's resources to cope with the demands of the situation and the actual demands. The elicitation of the stress response evokes selected physiological and attentional changes in the athlete. These changes include *increased muscle tension, narrowing of the visual field,* and *increased distractibility.* Each change is believed to enhance the chances of the athlete's sustaining an athletic injury (Williams, Tonymon, & Andersen, 1991). In addition to an imbalance between demands and resources, perceived consequences of the athletic situation can lead to the elicitation of the stress response. In essence, any cognitive appraisal that leads to the stress response puts the athlete at risk for injury. Factors that impact the stress response include

CONCEPT An athlete's perceived inability to respond to the demands of a potentially stressful athletic situation results in the stress response. The stress response in turn gives rise to increased muscle tension, narrowing of the visual field, and attentional distractibility.

APPLICATION Once the athlete experiences the stress response, she is in a situation of heightened risk for injury. Every effort must be used to prevent this situation from developing in the first place.

FIGURE 18.1 | Revised version of the stress and injury model.

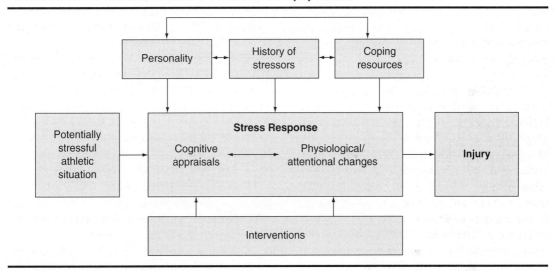

Source: Reproduced with permission from Williams, J. M., & Andersen, M. B. (1998). Psychosocial antecedents of sport injury: Review and critique of the stress and injury model. *Journal of Applied Sport Psychology, 10,* 5–25.

personality of the athlete, history of stressors, coping resources, and potential interventions.

To reiterate, the key element of the model illustrated in figure 18.1 is the stress response. Whether or not psychological factors will contribute significantly to injury depends on the balance between an athlete's perceived ability to address a potentially threatening situation and the demands and consequences associated with the situation. If the situation results in a perceived imbalance (threat), the athlete will respond with increased muscle tension and inappropriately narrowed attention. It is the narrowed attention, attentional distractibility, and muscle tension that lead

to a situation of increased vulnerability. As predicted by the model, athletes who score high on the ability to focus on a task experience fewer acute and chronic athletic injuries during the course of a season (Williams, Hogan, & Andersen, 1993).

As can be observed in figure 18.1, in addition to the key element of adjusting to the stress response, four other factors moderate the relationship between a potentially stressful athletic situation and an injury. These four factors include personality of the athlete, history of stressors, coping resources available to the athlete, and interventions. Each of these four factors will be briefly discussed.

Personality Factors

Personality factors that might have an effect upon how the athlete responds to a stressful athletic situation include hardiness, locus of control, sense of coherence, competitive trait anxiety, and intrinsic motivation. As can be observed in figure 18.1, personality factors affect the stress response directly, as well as indirectly, through the history of stressors and coping resources. They are not directly related to the incidence of athletic injuries, but are directly and indirectly related to how the athlete reacts to the stress response, which in turn directly predicts athletic injury (Williams & Andersen, 1998).

History of Stressors

Factors incorporated under the category of history of stressors include stressful life events, daily hassles, and previous injuries. Taken together, these factors are believed to have an interactive effect upon the stress response leading to athletic injury.

Life Stress and Daily Hassles   As previously illustrated in figure 16.6, life stress is related to the incidence of illness. This relationship between stressful life events and increased illness is extended to the athletic domain. Life stress and daily hassles tend to undermine the ability of the athlete to effectively address the stress response and associated physiological and attentional consequences that may lead to injury vulnerability (Hanson, McCullagh, & Tonymon, 1992). *Positive life stress* includes such events as studying for examinations, developing social relationships, and raising a family. *Negative life stress* includes such events as divorce, death in the family, and loss of job. The more life stress the athlete experiences, the greater is the incidence and severity of athletic injury (Patterson, Smith, Everett, & Ptacek, 1998).

Previous Injury   How an athlete adjusts to a previous injury will determine its impact on the stress response to a potentially stressful athletic situation. Athletes who are worried about the recurrence of an injury, or about whether or not they have fully recovered from a previous injury, are vulnerable to further injury. This is the case because they will tend to be distracted and inappropriately focused during competition. As indicated in figure 18.1, negative appraisal may result if an athlete is psychologically unprepared to return to competition after sustaining an injury. Negative cognitive appraisal will almost certainly occur if an athlete is psychologically unprepared to return to competition. Intuitively, previous injury is an important factor to consider in the relationship between past history and the prediction of future injury or reinjury. Conversely, learning from the mistakes associated with past injuries can lower the probability of future injuries. In this regard, Rose and Jevne (1993) argue that there are *lessons* to be learned from past injuries, and that if these lessons are appropriately applied, they can result in a reduction in future injuries. Macchi and Crossman (1996) report that as a result of an injury sustained in ballet, many dancers learn to use correct technique, stretch more, and modify exercises that may lead to injury.

What if the injury an athlete sustains results in the end of his career? In this case we are not talking about the relationship between a previous injury and vulnerability for a future injury, but about the psychological well-being of the athlete. Some research has suggested that a career-ending injury results in decrement in self-esteem and life satisfaction. More recent research, however, has concluded that a decrease in life satisfaction results only if the individual suffering the career-ending injury had strong aspirations regarding a future career in professional sports (Kleiber & Brock, 1992).

Coping Resources

Coping resources available to the athlete include general coping behavior, social support, stress management techniques, attentional strategy, and prescribed or self-prescribed medication. Collectively, these factors are believed to have an interactive effect on whether or not the athlete will experience the stress response.

Coping Behaviors   Any behavior that assists an individual in dealing with a stressful situation is considered to be a **coping behavior.** The use of coping strategies or behaviors to address high-stress situations was discussed in detail in chapter 9. Coping behaviors are highly individualistic and varied in nature. Well-developed general coping behaviors have been linked with the reduced incidence of athletic injuries in several research investigations. Hanson et al. (1992), for example, reported that coping resources are associated with reduced severity and frequency of track and field athlete injuries. The stress response might not occur in athletes who perceive they have coping skills sufficient to deal with stress associated with the athletic experience.

Further support for the notion that athletic injury can be predicted by life stress, coping behaviors, and their interaction is provided by Wiechman, Smith, Smoll, and Ptacek (2000). In an initial regression analysis involving 352 high school athletes, the researchers did not observe a relationship between life stress and coping behaviors with the incidence of athletic injury. However, a different result was obtained when athletes who scored high in social desirability were removed from the data set. Recall from chapter 12 that social desirability is the tendency to "fake good" on a pencil and paper test. When these observations were removed from the data set, life stress and coping behavior of high school athletes were observed to be reliable predictors of the incidence of athletic injury.

Social Support   Social support is one of the important coping resources available to athletes to reduce the debilitating effect of the stress response (Petrie, 1993). Individuals and groups that provide social support for the athlete include parents, friends, coach, teammates, fraternity/sorority, clubs, and religious groups. In a study reported by Smith, Smoll, and Ptacek (1990), twenty different

individuals or groups were identified that might provide social support to the athlete. Not only is social support an effective coping mechanism in its own right, it is also a powerful moderator between life stress and the incidence of athletic injury. When social support is either absent or negative, a strong association is observed between life stress and athletic injury. Conversely, when social support is present, the relationship between life stress and athletic injury is negligible (Patterson et al., 1998; Smith et al., 1990).

As we shall learn in this chapter, social support is important for both injury prevention and injury rehabilitation. Bianco (2001) and Bianco and Eklund (2001) provided researchers and practitioners with background information about the complexities of social support construct. For example, they clarified that social support is of three interrelated but different types: emotional, informational, and tangible. *Emotional support* involves such things as listening, emotional comfort, and emotional challenge. *Informational support* involves reality confirmation, task appreciation, and task challenge (e.g., expressing appreciation for hard work and challenging/motivating for even greater accomplishments). Finally, *tangible support* involves providing actual material and personal assistance.

Stress Management   Many athletes utilize stress management and cognitive intervention techniques as coping strategies for controlling the stress response. Often these same techniques are used by the athletes as arousal control strategies to buffer the effects of the stress response once it has developed. Research has demonstrated that effective reduction in the stress response is associated with a reduction in the number and severity of injuries sustained by athletes (Davis, 1991; Kerr & Goss, 1996).

Attentional Strategy   A coping resource available to distance runners is attentional strategy. As we learned in chapter 7, distance runners use some combination of associative and dissociative

CONCEPT   Factors that determine whether or not an athlete will experience the stress response include the athlete's personality, history of stress, and coping resources.

APPLICATION   From a psychological perspective, knowledge about these three factors may be useful in helping the athlete reduce the probability of injury. Understanding the person's personality and stress history will help the coach identify at-risk individuals. Assisting the athlete in developing coping skills and supportive social relationships will help her deal effectively with a potentially stressful environment.

strategies when they run. The associative strategy is related to internal monitoring of their body and greater effort. Runners who use the associative strategy are highly motivated, are driven, and seek high performance. Dissociative runners get more enjoyment out of their runs and are less motivated to high performance. Research shows that the dissociative strategy of running is associated with lower incidence of injury (Masters & Ogles, 1998b). Greater reliance upon a dissociative strategy is a coping strategy that could protect the athlete from muscle and bone injury.

Medication   Drugs are used by athletes for various legitimate and illegitimate reasons, including performance enhancement, recreation, injury treatment, and pain management. Many drugs have the ability to influence the stress response, and thus the probability of injury. For example, animal and human research suggests that the side effects of anabolic steroids may include aggression, depression, anxiety, and social withdrawal. All these psychological effects have the potential to reduce the coping resources of the athlete (Gregg & Rejeski, 1990).

Interventions

Part 4 (chapters 9–12) of this book was dedicated to arousal control techniques and cognitive interventions that may be utilized to enhance athletic performance, as well as to inhibit the development of the stress response. As illustrated in figure 18.1, these interventions play an important role in determining whether or not a potentially stressful athletic situation will lead to conditions conducive to athletic injury. The stress and injury model, as displayed in figure 18.1, suggests a two-pronged approach for interventions to prevent injuries caused by high stress. One set of interventions seeks to *change the cognitive appraisal* of potentially stressful events, while the second seeks to *modify the physiological/attentional aspects* of the stress response.

Cognitive appraisal might be changed by re-thinking how one plans to address a particularly stressful situation. Physiological/attentional aspects might be modified through progressive relaxation and imagery (Williams & Andersen, 1998). Evidence supporting the position that pre-injury interventions can reduce the number and severity of athletic injuries has been documented by empirical studies (Davis, 1991; Kerr & Goss, 1996; May & Brown, 1989; Schomer, 1990). The fundamental goal of pre-injury intervention is to identify the subjective cost of injury, while teaching and strengthening coping resources (Cupal, 1998).

Psychological Response to Injury and Rehabilitation

Factors associated with an athlete's psychological response to injury and follow-up rehabilitation occur after the injury has occurred. In order to

CONCEPT Moderated by athlete personality, history of stressors, and coping resources, the presence of a challenging situation sets up the possibility that the stress response will be elicited. Before or while the stress response is being elicited, the athlete has one last chance to modify the debilitating effect of the stress response; and that is through cognitive and behavioral interventions. These two categories of intervention come in the form of cognitive reappraisal and arousal adjustment.

APPLICATION Strategies designed to teach the athlete how to change cognitive appraisal and modify stress through arousal control must be learned prior to the onset of the stress response. Using cognitive-behavioral interventions for the purpose of reducing the chances of sustaining a serious injury has far-reaching consequences. It makes the time investment necessary to learn how to apply cognitive-behavioral interventions well worth the athlete's time and energy. Injury is a major impediment to optimal athletic performance.

understand the complexities of what occurs following injury, a comprehensive model is needed. In response to this need, an *integrated model of psychological response to injury and rehabilitation* was developed (Wiese-Bjornstal, Smith, & LaMott, 1995; Wiese-Bjornstal, Smith, Shaffer, & Morrey, 1998). A recent version of the integrated model is illustrated in figure 18.2. The top part of the integrated model is an abbreviated version of the stress and injury model (figure 18.1). The main panel of the **integrated sport injury model** focuses upon the athlete's response to sport injury and the rehabilitation process. In the integrated model, the moderators of the stress response are also moderators of the response to sport injury and the rehabilitation process (personality, history of stressors, coping resources, and interventions).

The main panel of the integrated model is composed of *cognitive appraisal, emotional response,* and *behavioral response.* These are the three main components of the integrated model that we will consider. Together, cognitive appraisal and emotional response will be considered under the general heading of *psychological response to injury.* Behavioral response relates primarily to the rehabilitation process. *Personal factors* and *situational factors* serve as a background to the entire

response to the sport injury and rehabilitation process. Notice that these two factors have their initial impact upon cognitive appraisal of the sports injury.

The core of the model (arrows) illustrates the dynamic nature of the recovery process. The predominant path followed is in a clockwise direction (wide arrows) to full recovery. In the full recovery path, cognitive appraisal affects emotional response, which in turn affects behavior, which in turn affects cognitive appraisal again. Slippage or nonadherence to the rehabilitation process is also possible, and is reflected by the narrower arrows moving in a counterclockwise direction.

Before we begin a more detailed discussion of the major components of the integrated model, two studies that relate to the full span of the process from injury to recovery are of interest. Utilizing elite skiers, Bianco, Malo, and Orlick (1999) used the interview method to track sick or injured athletes through three phases. These three phases were (a) the injury/illness phase, (b) the rehabilitation and recovery phase, and (c) the return to full activity phase. Two decision points were identified through these three phases. The first decision point represented the often difficult decision to stop training in order to receive treatment. A broken leg

FIGURE 18.2 | Integrated model of psychological response to the sport injury and rehabilitation process.

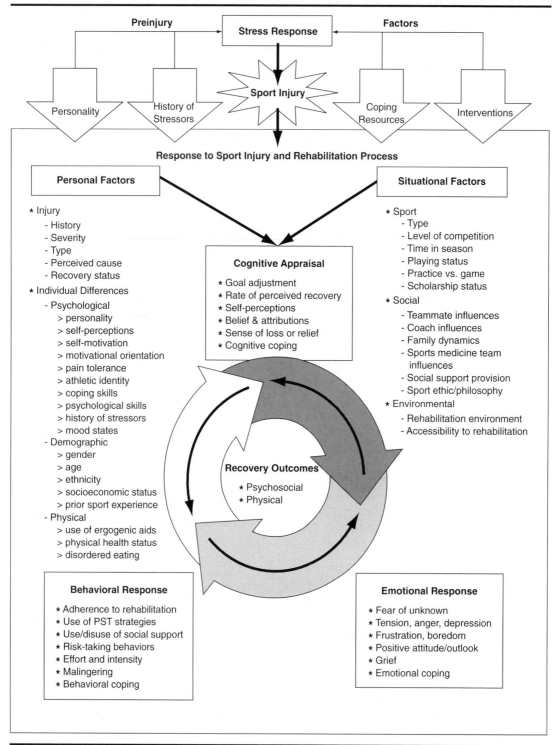

Source: Reproduced with permission from Wiese-Bjornstal, D. M., Smith, A. M., Shaffer, S. M., & Morrey, M. A. (1998). An integrated model of response to sport injury: Psychological and sociological dynamics. *Journal of Applied Sport Psychology, 10,* 46–70.

CONCEPT Cognitive appraisal at the time of an athletic injury is a predictor of emotional response. Self-esteem, self-worth, self-confidence, and self-efficacy may be reduced as a result of an injury, but the reduction depends on the specific nature of the measure (e.g., self-efficacy for what?). Interventions designed to enhance self-esteem, self-worth, self-confidence, and self-efficacy following injury are effective.

APPLICATION Cognitive appraisals made by the athlete influence his emotional responses, which in turn influence rehabilitation. For this reason, it is important that interventions be applied at the time of injury to bolster the injured athlete's self-esteem, self-worth, self-confidence, and self-efficacy.

or arm would of course require the athlete to stop training immediately, but many injuries and illnesses are of the nature that the athlete "trains through the pain" in order to avoid losing training and competition time. Thus, the decision to stop training in order to receive treatment was often a very difficult and emotionally charged decision. The second decision point occurred after rehabilitation, when the athlete had to decide when to return to full activity. This was also a difficult and emotional decision, because the skiers were concerned about reinjury and loss of skill due to the layoff.

In the second study, Quinn and Fallon (1999) tracked 136 elite athletes across four phases of the rehabilitation process. In order to be included in the study, the athlete must have had an estimated recovery time of at least four weeks. The estimated time of recovery was divided by three to give three time periods and four measurement points. For example, if the estimated recovery period was nine weeks, then each of three time periods was three weeks in length. Psychological assessments were taken when the injury occurred (baseline) and after each of three time periods, for a total of four administrations. Measurements included medical response (e.g., strength, range of motion), mood states, recovery self-efficacy, coping skills, self-motivation, sport confidence, and physical functioning. Results showed a linear improvement over time in terms of medical response, mood

states, and self-motivation. Little change in recovery self-efficacy or coping skills was observed across recovery. Confidence in being successful again in sport decreased initially from baseline, but increased back to baseline following the final time period.

Psychological Response to Injury

The **psychological response to injury** includes both cognitive appraisal and emotional response. When an injury occurs, the athlete cognitively appraises the situation while at the same time exhibiting emotional responses.

Cognitive Appraisal Factors associated with **cognitive appraisal** include (a) the need to adjust performance goals, (b) an estimate of recovery time, (c) evaluation of perceived self-worth and self-confidence, (d) appraisal of beliefs about attributions, (e) sense of loss, and (f) appraisal of coping skills. Cognitive appraisal of these factors helps determine the athlete's emotional response to injury, as well as her behavioral response. For example, Daly, Brewer, Van Raalte, Petitpas, and Sklar (1995) found that athletes' cognitive appraisals were correlated with total mood disturbance (emotional response). Most research in cognitive appraisal has focused upon the athlete's perception of self-esteem and self-worth following a serious sport injury. Perceptions of self-worth and self-esteem tend to be lower in the injured athlete than in the noninjured athlete (Brewer, 1993; Chan & Grossman, 1988; Connelly, 1991; McGowan, Pierce, Williams, & Eastman, 1994).

Researchers have also studied self-confidence and self-efficacy in injured athletes. As would be expected, self-confidence and self-efficacy decline as a result of sports injury (Connelly, 1991), but increase in response to intervention (Flint, 1991). Self-efficacy about adhering to a rehabilitation program is just as strong at the time of injury as it is during rehabilitation (Quinn & Fallon, 1999). Self-confidence about sport performance declines following an injury, but recovers by the end of the rehabilitation phase (Quinn & Fallon, 1999).

Emotional Response   As illustrated in figure 18.2, factors associated with **emotional response** following injury include (a) fear of the unknown, (b) feelings of tension, anger, and depression, (c) frustration and boredom associated with being injured, (d) positive/negative attitude, (e) grief associated with an injury, and (f) emotional coping skills. These factors parallel very closely the stress and frustration expressed by 21 U.S. alpine and freestyle ski team members who suffered season-ending injuries (Gould, Udry, Bridges, & Beck, 1997). Frustrations expressed by these elite athletes included shattered hopes and dreams, fear of reinjury, isolation, others' recovery expectations, physical inactivity, concern about future poor performance, uncertainty of medical diagnosis, instability of sponsorship, and missed non-skiing opportunities. Given this list of frustrations, it is understandable that mood disturbances accompany season- or career-ending injuries. According to Smith (1996), raw mood state scores (POMS) exceeding 35 for depression, 25 for tension, and 20 for anger are cause for concern and deserve attention. Injured athletes who were reported to have attempted suicide all had depression scores greater than 40 (Smith & Milliner, 1994). Following injury, it is recommended that the

POMS inventory be administered, as well as the Emotional Responses of Athletes to Injury Questionnaire (ERAIQ; Smith, 1996; Smith, Scott, & Wiese, 1990). The ERAIQ parallels and measures many aspects of the integrated model illustrated in figure 18.2.

LaMott (1994) and Morrey (1997) monitored mood state across three and six months. Their research showed negative affect to be very high immediately following a knee injury, but to decrease gradually over time. Similarly, Quinn and Fallon (1999) observed linear decreases in negative mood across 4- to 99-week recovery periods of 136 elite athletes. However, they also observed significant quadratic and cubic trends, suggesting that patterns of change were not constant across time. From these investigations we learn that injury is associated with mood disturbance, and that mood improves with time across a successful recovery period. The mood improvements, however, are not necessarily smooth and consistent.

Wiese-Bjornstal et al. (1998) summarized 19 studies associated with emotional responses of injured athletes. From this review we learn that while some athletes experience clinical levels (professional care needed) of mood disturbance, most experience only normal to mild manifestations. Competitive athletes experience higher levels of negative affect associated with injury than do recreational athletes, but in turn competitive athletes recover more quickly. As suggested by Morrey (1997), it is possible that the higher levels of mood disturbance associated with injury might actually facilitate a faster recovery period. Perhaps the extreme frustration and associated mood disturbance in the competitive athlete motivate the athlete during the long and arduous rehabilitation process (Tracey, 2003).

As a way of providing emotional support to injured athletes, Gutkind (2004) has proposed the application of solution-focused brief counseling (SFBC) techniques as an intervention. The cornerstone of the SFBC method is the use of the "miracle question" once the athlete has identified the

CONCEPT Athletic injury is associated with mild to severe mood disturbance. The degree of mood disturbance is believed to be associated with severity of injury as well as with cognitive appraisal.

APPLICATION Psychological mood of injured athletes should be measured at the time of injury and monitored thereafter using the Profile of Mood States or some other short inventory. Psychological mood at the time of the injury will help the sport-injury rehabilitation personnel (SIRP) determine the degree of mood disturbance and to implement appropriate interventions to reduce the debilitating effect of negative affect. It is expected that negative mood will dissipate as the road to full recovery proceeds, but fluctuations should be anticipated.

problem, or the reason she is seeking professional help (O'Connell, 1998). The miracle question is this:

> "Imagine when you go to sleep at night a miracle happens and the problems we've been talking about disappear. As you were asleep, you did not know the miracle had happened. When you wake up what would be the first signs for you that a miracle had happened?" (O'Connell, 1998, p. 50)

As explained by Gutkind (2004), the question enables the client (athlete) to generate a detailed picture of what the solution to the problem looks like. This gives the athlete and the counseling sport psychologist a goal to work on together.

Finally, a study reported by Green and Weinberg (2001) shows that an injured athlete's satisfaction with his social support network is related to mood disturbance measured within two days of the first visit to the sports medicine clinic. Increased satisfaction with social support network leads to lower levels of mood disturbance.

Rehabilitation and the Behavioral Response to Injury

The third factor leading to injury recovery, and associated with cognitive and emotional response, is the **behavioral response** of the athlete to injury. Factors associated with behavioral response to injury include (a) adherence to rehabilitation, (b) use of psychological skill training strategies, (c) use of social support, (d) risk-taking behavior, (e) effort and intensity, (f) malingering, and (g) behavioral coping. The primary focus of research in the area of behavioral response to injury has been upon adherence to injury rehabilitation, coping and intervention, and pain management. These three focus areas will be discussed in the following paragraphs.

Adherence to Injury Rehabilitation Several theories have been proposed to explain **adherence to injury rehabilitation** (Brewer, 1998). According to *personal investment theory* (Maehr & Braskamp, 1986), motivation to adhere to rehabilitation is thought to be based upon personal incentives, beliefs about self, and perceived options. Another approach, *protection motivation theory* (Maddux & Rogers, 1983), posits that the motivation to adhere is thought to be related to a person's desire for a healthy recovery. Finally, *cognitive appraisal theory* holds that adherence to rehabilitation is related to cognitive and emotional responses to injury, as illustrated in figure 18.2 (Wiese-Bjornstal et al. 1998).

In order for an injury rehabilitation program to be successful, it is believed that the athlete must adhere to the program. Thus, adherence to sport injury rehabilitation programs has emerged as a very important area of study. Adherence to a rehabilitation program is often measured as a function of attendance or through the administration of the Sport Injury Rehabilitation Adherence Scale (SIRAS; Brewer, et al., 2000). According to Brewer (1998), typical behaviors associated with adherence to injury rehabilitation include the following:

1. Compliance with instructions to restrict physical activity

2. Faithful completion of home rehabilitation exercises

3. Faithful completion of home cryotherapy or injury icing schedule

4. Compliance with medical prescriptions (e.g., painkillers)

5. Consistent and enthusiastic participation in clinic-based rehabilitation and exercise programs

Predictors of injury rehabilitation adherence are identified in figure 18.2 as personal factors and situational factors. *Personal factors* represent relatively stable characteristics of the injured athlete, while *situational factors* represent the social and physical environment. Various aspects of these two factors interact to influence the entire rehabilitation process, including adherence (Brewer, 1998). Self-motivation is the personal factor most consistently related to adherence. Other **personal factors** related to adherence include pain tolerance, tough-mindedness (e.g., self-assurance, assertiveness, independence), and goal perspective. A task or mastery goal orientation is associated with better adherence, as is a mastery-oriented climate (Gilbourne & Taylor, 1998; Magyar & Duda, 2000). Based on research, it is predicted that injured athletes who are self-motivated, are tolerant of pain, are tough-minded, and exhibit a mastery goal orientation will be good adherers to an injury rehabilitation program.

As indicated earlier, protection motivation theory hypothesizes that the motivation to adhere is thought to be related to a person's desire for a healthy recovery. Brewer, et al. (2003) reported the results of an investigation designed to test this theory. In so doing, they correlated adherence as measured by the SIRAS with beliefs about health behavior. Beliefs or perceptions about health behavior were measured using the Sports Injury Rehabilitation Beliefs Scale (SIRBS; Taylor & May, 1996). The SIRBS measures perceived *severity* of injury, perceived *susceptibility* to injury, perceived *treatment self-efficacy,* and perceived *self-efficacy* to perform prescribed health behaviors. Results of the investigation showed strong association between measures of adherence to rehabilitation and beliefs about performing health behaviors.

Situational factors most closely related to adherence include (a) belief in the efficacy of treatment procedures, (b) comfort of the rehabilitation clinical environment, (c) convenience of rehabilitation program scheduling, (d) the exertion put forth during rehabilitation exercises, and (e) social support for the rehabilitation program (Brewer, 1998). Best results for adherence will occur when the athlete believes in the efficacy of the rehabilitation program, the rehabilitation program is comfortable and conveniently scheduled, the athlete works hard at the exercises, and the athlete receives positive social support from family, friends, and health care professionals (Brewer, 1998).

As illustrated in figure 18.2, both personal and situational factors affect cognitive appraisal, which in turn influences adherence to an injury rehabilitation program. Within cognitive appraisal, goal setting and goal adjustment play a role in the injury rehabilitation process. This expectation, relative to goal setting, is supported by research reported by Evans and Hardy (2002a, 2002b). Seventy-seven injured athletes were randomly assigned to one of three rehabilitation treatment interventions: (a) goal setting, (b) social support, and (c) control. Results showed a superiority of the goal-setting intervention compared to those of the other two groups in terms of adherence to an injury rehabilitation program. Over time, however, all three groups showed improvement in program investment and treatment self-confidence.

CONCEPT   Personal factors and situational factors, as well as their interaction, are predictive of adherence to injury rehabilitation.

APPLICATION   The ideal rehabilitation situation will involve athletes possessing desirable personality characteristics, and an environment that is both comfortable and convenient. The reality, however, is that most circumstances will not be ideal in terms of both personal and situational factors. It is the responsibility of the sport injury rehabilitation personnel to make the best of every situation and to be aware of both personal and situation factors. Where appropriate, cognitive-behavioral interventions should be implemented in order to improve the fit between personal and situational factors.

An injured athlete enjoys the encouragement and support of friends. Courtesy Ball State University Sports Information.

Coping, Social Support, and Interventions

Coping skills possessed by the athlete, availability of positive social support, and cognitive-behavioral interventions (applied by others or the athlete) are all effective in enhancing adherence to injury rehabilitation programs (Cupal, 1998; Udry, 1997). Injured U.S. ski team members who were able to recover to pre-injury rankings reported using the following coping strategies more than unsuccessful skiers: (a) management of emotions and thoughts, (b) use of visualization and mental skills, (c) being patient and "taking it slow" (Gould, Udry, Bridges, & Beck, 1997). Russell (2000) recommended the use of rehabilitation rehearsal as a coping device using imagery.

Rehabilitation rehearsal is defined as "the conscious use of mental imagery for the purpose of effective coping with injury rehabilitation" (p. 43). Rehabilitation rehearsal can be used at any time during the rehabilitation process to help the athlete get through challenging periods. In one application, the athlete introduces anticipated problems into a rehearsal scenario. The athlete imagines herself coping with a difficult adherence problem and visualizes herself producing a positive outcome. Cupal (1998) reviewed 13 studies that document the beneficial effects of rehabilitation intervention.

Injury rehabilitation interventions typically include guided imagery, relaxation, stress inoculation, goal setting, and biofeedback. Cognitive-behavioral interventions that may be applied to injury rehabilitation and adherence were discussed in detail in part 4 of the text. The student is encouraged to review the chapters included in that part of the book. Wagman and Khelifa (1996) have identified 13 different psychological interventions that may prove beneficial to a successful injury rehabilitation program. They are as follows:

1. *Career Adjustment Techniques:* receiving individual or group counseling

2. *Cognitive Restructuring:* rethinking cognitive thought processes

3. *Concentration Skills:* practicing attentional focusing

4. *Confidence Training:* learning that being confident is a choice

5. *Coping Rehearsal:* using coping videotape

6. *Imagery:* using imagery to visualize healing and pain management

7. *Motivation:* practicing goal setting and other motivational methods

8. *Panic Mitigation:* reassuring with positive, hopeful thoughts

9. *Positive Self-Talk:* learning positive self-affirmation statements or thoughts

10. *Rational Emotive Therapy:* rethinking irrational thought processes

11. *Relaxation Skills:* practicing various progressive relaxation methods

12. *Systematic Desensitization:* gradually overcoming fear

13. *Thought Stoppage:* replacing negative thoughts with positive thoughts

Pain Management   Pain tolerance is a personality characteristic that has an important impact upon cognitive appraisal, emotional response, and adherence to rehabilitation. Individuals with a low tolerance to pain may have a more difficult time going through the three stages of the sport injury recovery process. Pain is a subjective experience that cannot be directly measured or felt by another individual (hence the falseness of the cliché, "I feel your pain"). There are different ways of categorizing pain as it relates to the athletic experience (Taylor & Taylor, 1998). Performance pain can be differentiated from injury pain. **Performance pain** is controlled by the athlete and is associated with improved performance and a sense of accomplishment. Conversely, **injury pain** is not controlled by the athlete and may be of either the acute or the chronic variety. **Acute pain** is due to a trauma to the body and is intense and short in duration. Conversely, **chronic pain** is long lasting, is uncontrollable, continues long after the initial injury, and is very complex in its origin. Pain can also be categorized as benign or harmful. **Benign pain** is generally short in duration and is not associated with swelling and soreness. Conversely, **harmful pain** is present before and after exertion and is associated with swelling, tenderness, and prolonged soreness. The different ways of conceptualizing and categorizing pain are illustrated in figure 18.3. It is important that the athlete be aware of the type of pain he is experiencing (Taylor & Taylor, 1998). An indirect assessment of pain can be made using the Ratings of Perceived Discomfort scale (RPD; Thorn & Williams, 1989).

Pain associated with an athletic injury is managed through a combination of pharmacological (prescription drug) and nonpharmacological approaches. Pharmacological pain management

FIGURE 18.3 | Ways of categorizing pain in sport and exercise.

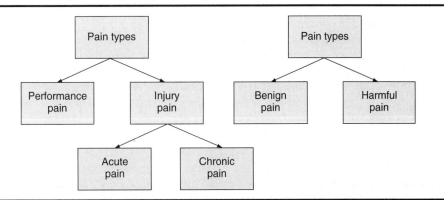

strategies are often needed short term, but there is always a concern of dependency and masking of important body information. Nonpharmacological pain management strategies are classified as being of the pain-reduction or the pain-focusing variety (Heil, 1993).

Nonpharmacological pain-reduction techniques that can be applied during rehabilitation include deep breathing, muscle relaxation, meditation, and therapeutic massage (Taylor & Taylor, 1998). **Nonpharmacological pain-focusing techniques** utilize association and dissociation attentional strategies to manage pain. Dissociation is used to direct the injured athlete's attention away from pain and is believed to be most effective in acute pain. In the case of association, the injured athlete's attention is internalized and focused on the pain. Focusing internally upon the emotional and informational aspects of pain seems to be most beneficial with chronic pain. Association heightens body awareness, cultivates a sense of emotional detachment, and increases the athlete's perception of control over the pain (Taylor & Taylor, 1998).

Pain catastrophizing is the degree to which individuals focus on pain, exaggerate the threat of pain to their well-being, and perceive themselves as unable to cope effectively with pain (Sullivan, Tripp, Rodgers, & Stanish, 2000). Catastrophizing is measured by the 13-item Pain Catastrophizing

Scale (PCS; Sullivan, Bishop, & Pivik, 1995). Consistent with the general definition of catastrophizing, the PCS measures the three conceptually integrated subscales of rumination, magnification, and helplessness. High scores on the PCS subscales would indicate a psychological inability to cope well with pain. Using a sample of male and female collegiate athletes and sedentary nonathletes, Sullivan et al. (2000) studied the relationship between pain tolerance, catastrophizing, group membership, and sex. Pain tolerance was measured by immersing a participant's arm in a cold pressor apparatus for 60 seconds (2° to 4° Celsius) and obtaining a rating of pain on a scale from 0 to 10. Results showed that men tolerate pain better (had lower pain ratings) than women and athletes tolerate pain better than sedentary individuals. Similar results were obtained for measures of catastrophizing, with women and sedentary individuals scoring higher on the PCS subscales and total score. Correlation between pain rating scores and total PCS scores was higher for sedentary individuals ($r = .43$) than it was for athletes ($r = .30$). Finally, it was demonstrated statistically that PCS mediates the relationship between sex of participant (male/female) and pain tolerance, but it does not mediate the relationship between group membership (athlete/sedentary) and pain tolerance. In the case of gender, the sex of the participant

FIGURE 18.4 | Path diagram showing how pain catastrophizing interacts with group membership (athlete/nonathlete), sex of participant, and pain perception.

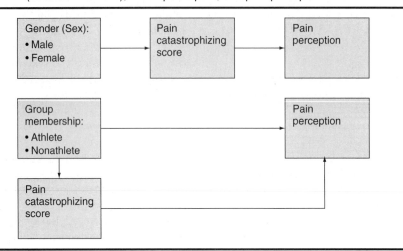

predicts pain catastrophizing (PCS), which in turn predicts pain tolerance; but in the case of group membership, being an athlete or sedentary individual has a direct effect on pain tolerance, as does PCS. These mediating relationships are illustrated in figure 18.4.

Other Considerations

Other factors that will be briefly discussed include (a) providing sport injury rehabilitation personnel with psychological expertise, (b) the impact of injury upon retirement satisfaction, and (c) benefits associated with sustaining and recovering from an athletic injury.

Providing Sport Injury Rehabilitation Personnel with Psychological Expertise

There are two basic approaches to providing sport injury rehabilitation personnel (SIRP) with knowledge and skill relative to the psychology of athletic injuries: the distributed approach and the specialist approach. In the **distributed approach,** the goal is to make sure that all SIRP receive training in

sport psychology applications. SIRP who would require training in sport psychology would include (a) sport physiotherapists, (b) physical therapists, (c) athletic trainers, and (d) sport physicians. According to Gordon, Potter, and Ford (1998), a prospective SIRP should do the following things in the course of a psychoeducational curriculum:

1. Learn to recognize the limitations of his own expertise
2. Listen to and be tested on lectures of psychological aspects of sport injuries
3. Attend lectures and workshops on applied psychological skills
4. Learn about coping behaviors, recognize psychological distress, and learn how to deal with poor psychological response to injury
5. Learn how to deal with athletes who experience long-term injury, career-ending injury, or permanent disability
6. Learn how to recognize if an athlete is malingering relative to rehabilitation

A second approach to providing a SIRP team with psychological expertise is to employ a

CONCEPT Athletes who suffer career-ending injuries and have a strong athletic identification are particularly susceptible to personal adjustment problems.

APPLICATION Athletes who suffer career-ending injuries should be provided with psycho-logical counseling to help them deal with the psychological trauma of having their athletic careers ended so quickly and completely. This is particularly true for athletes who identify strongly with the athletic culture and environment. Athletic identity can easily be assessed with the Athletic Identity Measurement Scale.

full-time sport psychologist. In the **specialist approach,** the SIRP team hires a sport psychologist to work with injured athletes requiring psychological services. While this second approach seems ideal, it presents challenges (Petitpas, 1998). Only about 5 to 13 percent of injured athletes are expected to display psychological distress that requires the services of a psychologist. Unless a sports medicine clinic were very large, it would be difficult to keep a full-time psychologist busy. Therefore, in order to gain entrance into the typical sports medicine clinic, the sport psychologist would have to convince the clinic that her services were cost effective and necessary. Possessing multiple skills and licensures (e.g., in athletic training, counseling, exercise physiology, research) is a good way to demonstrate added value.

The Impact of Athletic Injury upon Retirement Satisfaction

> As they limp into the sunset, retired NFL [football] players struggle with the game's grim legacy: a lifetime of disability and pain (Nack, 2001, p. 60).

Athletes who retire early from sport may suffer adjustment problems. Typical reasons for early retirement from sport include injury, the inability to compete at the next level, and personal choice. Among early retirees, athletic identity is related to retirement difficulty, perception of a vague future, and low life satisfaction. Strong relationships exist between athletic identity and retirement difficulty and between athletic identity and perception of a vague future when early retirement is caused by an athletic injury (Webb, Nasco, Riley, & Headrick, 1998). Athletic identity is typically measured using the Athletic Identity Measurement Scale (AIMS; Brewer, Van Raalte, & Linder, 1993).

Benefits Associated with Sustaining and Recovering from an Athletic Injury

While it is generally assumed that nothing good comes from an athletic injury, this may not be entirely true. Evidence suggests that successful recovery from an athletic injury is associated with several benefits. Twenty-one U.S. ski team members who sustained and recovered from season-ending injuries were asked to identify benefits associated with being injured (Udry et al., 1997a). Seventeen of the athletes identified *personal growth* benefits associated with sustaining and recovering from an athletic injury. Relative to personal growth, athletes felt they had gained perspective, experienced personality development, developed non-skiing aspects of their lives, and learned better time management skills. Seventeen of the athletes identified *psychologically based performance enhancement* benefits. Relative to the enhancement of psychological skills, the athletes felt they had experienced an increase in self-efficacy, mental toughness, personal motivation, and had learned to be more realistic in their performance expectations. Finally, 10 of the athletes identified

CONCEPT A truly successful rehabilitation from an athletic injury is associated with benefits related to personal growth, psychological skill, physical health, and skill improvement.

APPLICATION Experiencing an athletic injury is a traumatic experience for an athlete. Yet, once the decision is made to enter the rehabilitation process with optimism and determination, unexpected benefits may be realized. It is the responsibility of the sport injury rehabilitation personnel to provide the expertise and climate that will enhance the realization of positive benefits.

physical and technical development benefits associated with the injury/recovery experience. They felt their general health was improved and that they had learned to ski technically better and more intelligently as a result of the injury and recovery process.

Summary

In addressing the important subject of the psychology of athletic injuries, three main chapter sections were discussed. These were (a) psychological predictors of athletic injuries, (b) athlete response to injury and rehabilitation, and (c) other considerations.

The discussion of psychological predictors of athletic injuries focused upon Williams and Andersen's (1998) stress and injury model. The elicitation of the stress response represents a perceived imbalance between the athlete's resources to cope with the demands of the situation and the actual demands. The stress response evokes physiological and attentional changes in the athlete that enhance chances of an athletic injury. Moderators of the stress response include personality factors, history of stressors, coping resources, and psychological interventions.

Factors associated with an athlete's psychological response to injury and follow-up rehabilitation occur after the injury has occurred. In order to understand the complexities of what occurs following injury, a comprehensive model is needed. In response to this need, the Wiese-Bjornstal, Smith, Shaffer, and Morrey (1998) integrated sport injury model was introduced and discussed. Response to sport injury and the rehabilitation process was discussed as a function of cognitive appraisal, emotional response, and behavioral response. Factors associated with behavioral response to injury include (a) adherence to rehabilitation, (b) use of psychological skill training strategies, (c) use of social support, (d) risk-taking behavior, (e) effort and intensity, (f) malingering, and (g) behavioral coping. Coping skills possessed by the athlete, availability of positive social support, and cognitive-behavioral interventions (applied by others or the athlete) are all effective in enhancing adherence to injury rehabilitation programs.

Predictors of cognitive appraisal, emotional response, and injury rehabilitation include personal and situational factors. Individuals with a low tolerance to pain may have a more difficult time going through the three stages of the sport injury recovery process. Pain associated with an athletic injury is managed through a combination of pharmacological (prescription drug) and non-pharmacological approaches.

Either the distributed or the specialist approach is utilized to provide sport psychology expertise on the sport injury rehabilitation person- nel team. If a full-time sport psychologist is hired, it is likely that the individual will need to possess multiple skills and licensures in order to justify a full-time position.

Athletes who suffer career-ending injuries should be provided with psychological counseling to help them deal with the psychological trauma of having their athletic careers ended so quickly and completely. This is particularly true for athletes who identify strongly with the athletic culture and environment.

While it is generally assumed that nothing good comes from an athletic injury, this may not be entirely true. Evidence suggests that successful recovery from an athletic injury is associated with benefits associated with personal growth, psychological skill, and physical and technical development.

Critical Thought Questions

1. Research links personality of the athlete, his- tory of stressors, and coping mechanisms with athletic injury. The Williams and Andersen stress injury model provides one way of conceptualizing the actual mecha- nism, or connection between these factors and injury. See if you can think of an alter- nate plausible explanation as to how these connections can be made. Provide a written description of your model.

2. Now that you have studied the integrated sport injury rehabilitation model, do you think it provides an adequate explanation of the complexities of the rehabilitation process? How would you suggest that the model be revised?

3. Develop a detailed nonpharmacological plan for pain reduction in the injured athlete.

4. Why do you think different athletes have different tolerances to pain?

5. What is meant by pain catastrophizing? How does it relate to pain perception, sex, or whether a person is an athlete or not?

6. Is having a strong athletic identity good or bad relative to early retirement from sport? Justify your answer.

Glossary

acute pain Pain caused by a trauma to the body that is intense, but of short duration.

adherence to injury rehabilitation The degree to which an athlete follows an athletic rehabilita- tion program.

behavioral response The way an athlete behaves following cognitive and emotional response to injury. Generally interpreted to mean the way the athlete responds to rehabilitation.

benign pain Pain that is short in duration and not associated with swelling and soreness.

chronic pain Long-lasting, uncontrollable pain that continues long after the initial injury.

cognitive appraisal The way an athlete thinks about a demanding situation leading to the stress response, as well as about an actual injury. It is moderated by both personality and situational factors.

coping behavior A behavior that assists an individual in dealing with a stressful situation.

distributed approach Situation in which sport psychology knowledge and skill are distributed among the sport injury rehabilitation personnel.

emotional response The way an athlete responds in emotional ways to an athletic injury.

harmful pain Pain that occurs before and after exertion, and is associated with swelling, tenderness, and prolonged soreness.

injury pain Pain that is not controlled by the athlete and that occurs as a result of an injury, as opposed to performance.

injury rehabilitation interventions Interventions, such as guided imagery, relaxation, stress inoculation, goal setting, and biofeedback, designed to facilitate the rehabilitation process.

integrated sport injury model A sport injury model that integrates antecedents of injury, cognitive appraisal of injury, emotional response to injury, and behavioral response to injury into a comprehensive injury rehabilitation model.

nonpharmacological pain-focusing techniques The use of either association or dissociation attentional strategies to manage pain.

nonpharmacological pain-reduction techniques Pain reduction techniques, such as deep breathing, muscle relaxation, meditation, and massage, applied during injury rehabilitation.

pain catastrophizing The degree to which individuals focus on pain, exaggerate the threat of pain to their well-being, and perceive themselves as unable to cope effectively with pain.

pain tolerance A personality characteristic to tolerate or endure pain.

performance pain Pain controlled by the athlete during performance.

personal factors Personality characteristics of the athlete that influence the rehabilitation process, beginning with cognitive appraisal.

psychological response to injury In the integrated sport injury model, an athlete's response to injury that comprises both cognitive appraisal and the emotional response.

rehabilitation rehearsal The conscious use of mental imagery for the purpose of effective rehabilitation.

situational factors Sport, social, and environmental factors that influence injury rehabilitation, beginning with cognitive appraisal.

specialist approach Situation in which a sports medicine clinic hires a sport psychologist to work with sport injury rehabilitation team personnel relative to psychological applications.

stress and injury model A model developed by Williams and Andersen (1998) to explain what causes the stress process, what moderates the stress process, and how it is related to athletic injury.

stress response The manifestation of distress or state anxiety in response to a demanding or threatening situation.

CHAPTER 19

Drug Abuse in Sport and Exercise

KEY TERMS

Anabolic-androgenic steroids
Anabolic effect
Anabolic steroids
Androgenic effect
Androstenedione
Behavioral technique
Cognitive technique
Creatine
Deterrence theory
Endogenous testosterone
Exogenous testosterone
Phosphocreatine
Psychological expectancy effect
Religiosity

While of little scientific value, anecdotal evidence of drug abuse by high-profile athletes heightens our awareness of this problem. Ben Johnson, a Canadian world record holder in the 100 meters, tested positive for anabolic steroids following his gold medal race in the 1988 Seoul Olympics. He had set a new world record of 9.79 seconds, beating his old world record of 9.83 by .04 seconds. The International Olympic Committee (IOC) declared Johnson's race null and void, stripped him of his gold medal, and awarded it to Carl Lewis of the United States (Johnson & Moore, 1988).

Lyle Alzado, a former National Football League (NFL) star, admitted to using anabolic steroids and human growth hormone for purposes of performance enhancement and blamed his drug abuse for a brain lymphoma (cancer) that a short time later would result in his death (Alzado, 1991). Alzado gave personal testimony to the incredible mood swings that he said made him mean, aggressive, and violent both on and off the field of play. In his dying words, he exclaimed, "It was addicting, mentally addicting. I just didn't feel strong unless I was taking them" (p. 24).

Tom Gugliotta, of the Phoenix Suns basketball club, suffered an adverse reaction from taking the supplement furanone dihydro to help him sleep. Gugliotta suffered a postgame seizure that caused him to temporarily stop breathing and to lose consciousness for several hours. Furanone dihydro has been marketed not only as a sleeping aid, but also as a sex enhancer and muscle builder (MacMullan, 2000).

High-profile baseball players Barry Bonds, Mark McGwire, and Sammy Sosa thrilled the nation with home run feats in 1998 and 2001. Mark McGwire and Sammy Sosa hit 70 and 66 home runs in 1998, to break Roger Maris's long-standing record of 61 home runs in the 1961 season. Shortly after that, Barry Bonds hit 73 home runs in the 2001 season, to break McGwire's record of 70 hits in a single season. How can this be? Maris's record of 61 home runs held for 37 years, yet it was broken three times in a span of three years.

Unfortunately, the accomplishments of these three great home run hitters have been tainted by the possibility of anabolic steroid use (Dohrmann, 2004; Smith, 2005).

Such behavior and the accompanying consequences and publicity create a negative climate for competitive sports. As stated by Longman (2003), a corrosive atmosphere persists in sports from football to cycling and table tennis. High profile athletes perform under constant suspicion and parents wonder if their own children will have to use drugs to compete. Records are perceived as tainted and fans watch events wondering if the results are valid.

In chapter 16 we learned of athletes who have succumbed to eating disorders for purposes of performance enhancement. We have also learned of athletes who overtrain and experience burnout in an effort to perform at a level higher than that of their competitors. Similarly, in this chapter we learn of athletes who turn to the use of drugs in an effort to gain an unfair advantage over their competitors.

There appear to be three fundamental problems associated with the use of drugs to enhance athletic performance (Anshel, 2006). The first problem has to do with *ethics*. Because drug use for purposes of performance enhancement is illegal, it is ethically wrong to take them in an effort to obtain an unfair advantage over the opposition. Amateur and professional sport organizations publish and continually revise their own list of banned substances. In addition, the United States Olympic Committee (USOC) and the International Olympic Committee (IOC) publish updated lists of banned substances (M. H. Williams, 1998). The second problem has to do with the potentially *addictive properties* of drugs. Once an athlete starts taking a drug for performance enhancement purposes, it may be difficult for her to stop taking them later on. Drugs may be physically and/or psychologically addictive. A third problem is related to the potentially *lethal effects* of drugs on the health and well-being of athletes. While it is often difficult to prove that the abuse of a drug led to the death or serious illness of an athlete, it is difficult to ignore the "gut-wrenching" testimonials of victims such as Lyle Alzado.

In this chapter on drug abuse, we will (a) address the hoped-for benefits and negative consequences of certain banned substances, (b) summarize a position statement of the National Strength and Conditioning Association (NSCA), and (c) conclude with some suggestions for combating drug abuse.

Psychophysiological Effects of Certain Banned Substances

Each of the drugs or banned substances that will be mentioned in this brief review has both a hoped-for benefit (the reason it is taken by the athlete) and a negative consequence. In some cases the negative consequences are well documented, but in other cases, due to limitations of research, they are not. We will first address the use and abuse of anabolic steroids because of their widespread use by athletes seeking greater size, aggressiveness, and strength.

Anabolic-Androgenic Steroids

Anabolic steroids are hormones that stimulate protein anabolism in the body. Athletes ingest anabolic steroids because they believe that they are responsible for alterations in body composition that result in greater size, strength, and power. What we call **anabolic steroids** are a group of synthetic derivatives of the male hormone testosterone that have been modified so that their presence in the bloodstream is prolonged. They have both an **anabolic effect** (increasing muscular strength and size) and an **androgenic effect** (masculinizing effect) on the user. Consequently, what we commonly refer to as anabolic steroids are really **anabolic-androgenic steroids** that are synthetically derived to increase muscle mass while at the same time minimizing the masculinizing, or androgenic, effect.

The term **exogenous testosterone** refers to the administration of an anabolic steroid to mimic the effects of testosterone in the body. Conversely, the term **endogenous testosterone** refers to the naturally occurring levels of testosterone in the body (Bahrke, Yesalis, & Wright, 1996). The food supplement **androstenedione** (pronounced andro-steen-dee-own) is a direct precursor hormone to the production of endogenous testosterone in the body.

Biological Effects of Anabolic Steroid Use
Research clearly shows that anabolic steroid use is associated with increased body weight and mass, altered body composition, increased muscle size and strength, increased blood volume, and increased number of red blood cells (Stone, 1993). Suspected negative physiological consequences associated with anabolic steroid use include increased risk of heart disease, certain cancers, and undesirable sex-specific effects. For men, undesirable sex effects *may* include shrinking testes, hair loss, enlarged breasts, and possible sterility. For women, undesirable sex effects *may* include shrinking breasts and uterus, enlarged clitoris, irregular menstruation, increased facial and body hair, and a deepening voice (Is it safe, 2000).

Perhaps the most extreme example of the effect of anabolic steroids on women is the case of Heidi Krieger (Longman, 2004). Heidi, a victim of a state-sponsored attempt to build a country of 16 million into a sports power rivaling the United States and the former Soviet Union, began taking the anabolic steroid Oral-Turinabol when she was 16 years of age. She was told by her East German coaches that the round blue pill that she was told to take was a vitamin pill that would increase strength. At age 16 she threw the shot put just over 46 feet; three years later, weighing 200 pounds, she threw the shot 65 feet, 6 inches at the 1986 European women's shot put championship. Confused as a teenager about her sexual identity, she later had a sex change operation and became known as Andreas.

Athletes are taught superior skills as an alternative to drug use.
Courtesy University of Missouri–Columbia Sports Information.

Psychological Effects of Anabolic Steroid Use   From the standpoint of increased size and muscle mass, it is relatively clear what the biological effects of anabolic steroid use are, but it is far less clear what the psychological effects are. We do know that *endogenous testosterone levels* in animals and humans are linked to aggressive behavior. The higher the serum level of naturally occurring testosterone in the body, the higher the level of aggression. Ingesting moderate levels of *exogenous anabolic steroids* does not seem to result in

overt aggressive behavior in humans, but ingestion of high levels does (Bahrke et al., 1996). Assuming that most users of anabolic steroids ingest them at moderate levels, there should be relatively few reported cases of deviant psychological behavior and aggression. Indeed, Bahrke et al. write that "it is interesting to note that with a million or more steroid users in the U.S., only a small percentage of users appear to experience mental disturbances which result in clinical treatment" (p. 387). Bahrke et al. (1996) further lament that there may be many

CONCEPT Anabolic steroid use is associated with increased body weight and mass, altered body composition, increased muscle size and strength, increased blood volume, and an increased number of red blood cells.

APPLICATION From purely a strength and muscle mass perspective, it seems clear that anabolic steroid use should lead to an unfair advantage in certain sport tasks involving strength and power.

Examples might include weight lifting, body building, track and field, swimming, and American football. Gains in performance due to increased strength and muscle mass may be of small long-term consequence, however, compared to negative health effects. Athletes seeking fame and fortune may come to believe that the risk is worth it, but coaches and sports medicine personnel must take extraordinary steps to teach athletes the dangers and risks associated with the use of anabolic steroids.

CONCEPT While extremely high levels of anabolic steroid use are linked to aggressive behavior, the cause-and-effect link between moderate levels of anabolic steroid use and deviant psychological behavior has not been established. Even when links have been observed, they are obscured by confounding psychosocial factors.

APPLICATION It is counterproductive to cry "wolf" when there is no "wolf." Trying to convince athletes that they should not use anabolic steroids because of negative benefits or negative feelings is in conflict with the literature and in conflict with what they hear from other athletes. A better approach is to appeal to the athlete's sense of fairness and desire to accomplish great things without the aid of drugs and supplements.

beneficial medical effects associated with anabolic steroid use, but they remain unstudied because of the paranoia of the media and hysterical unsubstantiated references.

The scientific link between anabolic steroid use and deviant psychological behavior is a weak one. Sharp and Collins (1998) note that there is a growing body of literature that links anabolic steroid use with aggressive behavior, but that the causal connections are weak. They point out that there are numerous psychosocial factors that likely interact with anabolic steroid use to bring about aggressive behavior. These psychosocial factors

include (a) social mediation, (b) expectancy effects, and (c) the power of group conformity. Athletes read the newspapers and popular magazines. They know how they are supposed to behave in response to anabolic steroid use.

Olrich and Ewing (1999) conducted in-depth interviews of 10 body builders or weight lifters who were using or had used anabolic steroids. These athletes started using anabolic steroids out of curiosity and a desire to make strength improvements. Five lifters indicated that they started using steroids in the face of strong internal conflict, and one athlete did so even though he believed it would result in cancer. Nine of the ten athletes described their experience with anabolic steroids in a positive light, but did indicate a perception of psychological dependence. None reported horrific negative side effects associated with their use of the drug. The users reported enhanced physical functioning (energy, libido, muscle mass); enhanced psychological functioning (alertness, aggressiveness, confidence); enhanced social recognition and acceptance (peer recognition, sexual attraction); and enhanced vocational functioning (alertness, confidence, effectiveness). One lifter did complain of joint pains, fluid retention, a bloated feeling, muscle strains and tears, and *extreme guilt*. Overall, the researchers concluded that you cannot deter anabolic steroid use by claiming negative short-term benefits or feelings, although they noted that the long-term effects are unknown.

There seems to be no question that anabolic steroid use is associated with increased muscle mass and body size, but it is less clear that their use leads to an increase in performance. Stated another way, it may be that increases in performance may be due to the **psychological expectancy effect,** and only indirectly to anabolic steroid use. This possibility is reinforced by an investigation reported by Maganaris, Collins, and Sharp (2000). Eleven national-level power lifters (bench, dead lift, squat) took two pills immediately before an experimental trial in which they completed a one maximum repetition (1RM) on all three lifts. The lifters believed that the pills contained an anabolic steroid that would have an immediate action on their strength, when in fact the pills contained saccharin. All 11 lifters improved their lifts above baseline. They were given two more pills for the following week's training. Seven days later, they again completed a second 1RM lifting trial on all three lifts. Five of the lifters were informed in confidence, just before they made their lifts, that the pills they had been taking contained saccharine. The six lifters who thought they were taking pills containing an anabolic steroid again posted lifts above baseline. The other five lifters did not perform above baseline, and in fact, dropped

significantly below baseline. This is the psychological expectancy effect.

The long-term effects of anabolic steroid use are unknown. Many sport psychologists believe that long-term use of this drug will lead to poor health. Organs that are particularly susceptible to negative consequences of anabolic steroid abuse are those, such as the kidneys and liver, that are responsible for the transport, metabolism, and detoxification of the drug. Since the liver serves a central role in the metabolism of drugs, it is not surprising that it is frequently damaged by drug use and abuse. If a drug has a negative effect upon even one part of the body, the function of the entire body can suffer (Stone, 1993).

Reversing the Trend towards Steroid Abuse

In 2003 the American College of Sports Medicine (ACSM) condemned the use of steroids to enhance body size and strength and further condemned the development and use of new *designer steroids* developed to avoid detection in drug tests (ACSM, 2003). The most recent designer drug is Tetrahydrogestrinone (THG), pronounced "tetra-hydro-gest-re-own." In its news release, the ACSM also appealed to "clean" athletes to publicly deplore the use of steroids among their teammates and peers.

As a result of the recent outrage over the apparent use of anabolic steroids by such famous major league baseball (MLB) players as Jose Canseco, Mark McGwire, Sammy Sosa, and Barry Bonds, MLB was forced to establish a tougher policy on steroid use (Kepner, 2005). The new rules require mandatory unannounced testing of all MLB players once a year and unlimited random testing throughout the season and off-season. As of November 15, 2005, MLB players and owners agreed to tougher penalties for steroid use (Blum & Fendrick, 2005). The penalty for the first failed test will be a 50 game suspension, 100 games for the second, while for the third it will be a lifetime ban. Hopefully, other professional sports and leagues will adopt these harsher penalties. To the baseball purist, Roger Maris' 61 home runs in a single season look pretty good right now. Tellingly, the following

CONCEPT Athletes who take anabolic steroids expect to be stronger, expect to perform better, and expect to be aggressive and more confident. Superior performance associated with anabolic steroid use may be due to the effects of taking the drug, but it also may be due to the psychological expectancy effect or some combination of the two, as well as other psychosocial factors.

APPLICATION The relationship between anabolic steroid use and improved performance and mood is a very complex one. Coaches and sports medicine personnel must be completely honest and truthful with athletes regarding the use of anabolic steroids. The bottom line, however, is that their use is illegal, and athletes must not get mixed signals from their coaches in this regard.

statement was made by Jose Canseco on CBS's *60 Minutes* (Steroids made baseball possible, 2005):

> I don't recommend steroids for everyone and I don't recommend growth hormones for everyone, but for certain individuals, I truly believe, because I've experimented with it for so many years, that it can make an average athlete a super athlete. It can make a super athlete incredible. Just legendary.

Later in this chapter we talk more about combating drug abuse, but for now it seems apparent that neither professional sports nor society as a whole is prepared to make the penalty for anabolic steroid use severe enough to prevent its use. If being caught using anabolic steroids meant that you were banned from professional sport for two years on the first infraction, as is the case with Olympic sports (Kepner, 2005), far fewer athletes would risk being caught.

Stimulants

Stimulants, such as amphetamines and cocaine, increase the rate and work capacity of the central nervous system, respiratory system, and heart. The neural-stimulating and cardiac-stimulating effects of these drugs can provide a physiological advantage to the athlete by inhibiting mental and physical fatigue. The illegal and unethical use of stimulants may result in performance enhancement, but not without some danger to the athlete. These drugs are physically and/or psychologically addicting and their use may lead to serious health problems.

The danger of stimulants is illustrated in the death of Steve Bechler, a former pitcher for the Baltimore Orioles professional baseball team (Olney, 2003). Belcher died of apparent heart failure during spring training in 2003. He had been taking the weight loss drug Xenadrine, which contains Ephedra, a stimulant banned by the NCAA and the NFL. As stated by Dr. John Lombardo, medical advisor for the National Football League, "The heart of someone in poor condition is forced to work hard, and if that person is taking a stimulant, there is additional stress on the heart."

Depressants

Depressants, such as barbiturates, sedative-hypnotics, and alcohol, are designed to relieve tension, depression, and anxiety in the athlete. Theoretically, this could help the fearful and anxious athlete by providing a steadying effect. These drugs, however, do not always have the desired effect on the athlete. Depressants may actually have the effect of reducing inhibition, reducing judgment, and heightening risk-taking behavior, which may in turn result in poor as opposed to superior performance. These drugs are also highly addictive, making it difficult to quit using them without severe withdrawal symptoms. As with all drugs, their abuse may lead to serious health consequences due to damage to organs responsible for metabolizing them.

Other Banned Drugs

Other drugs that have been banned by the International Olympic Committee (IOC) include diuretics, hallucinogens, and beta-adrenergic blockers. *Diuretics* are sometimes used by wrestlers, jockeys, and boxers to artificially induce an acute reduction in body weight through fluid elimination via the urine. Negative effects of diuretics may include nausea, heat stroke, blood clotting, reduced blood volume, and muscle cramps. The primary purpose of hallucinogens is to alter the perception of incoming stimuli. Because *hallucinogens* inhibit response and decision time as well as attentional focus, they tend to inhibit athletic performance instead of facilitating it. *Beta-adrenergic blockers* are used to steady and slow the heart rate, which may decrease anxiety/tension and indirectly enhance athletic performance.

Creatine Use by Athletes

While creatine is not a substance currently banned by the International Olympic Committee, it is a food supplement extensively used by athletes seeking enhanced performance. Creatine use has been on the rise since the early 1990s; along with androstenedione, creatine gained some notoriety because of its alleged use by Sammy Sosa and Mark McGwire during the 1999 baseball season. **Creatine** is a naturally occurring energy-producing substance that is synthesized from amino acids in the human body. It is also consumed in the diet through the consumption of animal products. Creatine, in the form of **phosphocreatine,** serves as an energy buffer (shield) during periods of intense exercise. Creatine use is associated with an increase in body mass that is generally attributed to increased water retention.

The majority of the evidence indicates that creatine supplementation has a beneficial effect on acute, repetitive bursts of intense exercise, but little beneficial effect upon distance or aerobic exercise. Anecdotal evidence suggests that short-term adverse reactions to creatine use include gastrointestinal distress, nausea, and muscle cramping. Long-term negative effects on the liver, kidneys, and brain are only beginning to be investigated. Kreider et al. (2001) reported no negative side effects associated with 21 months of creatine use by collegiate football players. However, Keys et al. (2001) reported that 10 months of creatine supplementaion yielded evidence of liver damage and chronic hepatitis in mice. No negative psychological effects have been reported (Volek, 1999; M. H. Williams, 1998; Williams, Anderson, & Winett, 2004).

Athletes and Dietary Supplements

Dietary supplements are often recommended by various promoters as safe alternatives to drugs. Starting in high school, some of the drugs that athletes take are labeled dietary supplements, as if they are innocuous and beneficial for their health. To further confuse the issue, selected dietary supplements are banned by some professional organizations but not others. Tellingly, Frank Uryasz, President of the National Center for Drug Free Sport was quoted as making the following statement about dietary supplements and sport (Wertheim, 2003, p. 73):

> What kids—especially those health conscious and interested in sports—don't want to supplement their diet? But the notion is a joke. No one is going to suffer because of an ephedra or creatine deficiency. We need to call these things what they are: drugs.

On a positive note, there has been some evidence that odor may be effective in enhancing athletic performance. Research reported by Raudenbush, Corley, and Eppich (2001) showed that placing two drops of peppermint oil under the nose in an adhesive strip increases performance on selected physical tasks. Control participants got adhesive strips without peppermint oil, while experimental participants got the adhesive strips containing peppermint oil. In tests, the experimental participants outperformed the control participants in push-ups to exhaustion, the 400 meter run, and a hand grip dynamometer task.

Position Statement of the NSCA

Athletes competing in the sport of weight/power lifting have received more publicity for abusing drugs (particularly anabolic steroids) than any other group of athletes. In a sense this publicity has tarnished the reputation of this sport and profession. In an effort to protect the image of the sport, and the athletes who compete fairly in the sport, the National Strength and Conditioning Association (NSCA) published a position statement in opposition to the use of drugs in general and anabolic steroids in particular (NSCA, 1993). The position statement is based upon a comprehensive survey and analysis of the scientific literature dealing with the effects of anabolic steroids on athletic performance. In the paragraphs that follow, the 10 statements that make up the NSCA Position Statement of 1993 have been paraphrased.

1. The use of anabolic-androgenic steroids (AAS) by athletes is illegal and punishable by law. Coaches or NSCA members who promote the use of AAS risk NSCA censure with potential legal penalties.

2. Strength and conditioning professionals must not condone the use of AAS. There is no compromise on this issue.

3. Competitive advantages may be derived from the use of AAS by users. These advantages may come in the form of increased lean body mass, decreased body fat, and increased strength and power, which may result in enhanced performance.

4. Those who use AAS face increased health risks, which can include liver disease, adverse effects on blood lipids, stroke and/or myocardial infarction, temporary infertility, and unwanted masculinization. Psychological aberrations are possible.

5. Both the risks and the benefits of AAS have been exaggerated by the lay press and general public, resulting in confusion and misinformation. The NSCA encourages full disclosure of known risks and benefits associated with AAS use.

6. Scientific investigations are encouraged that study the prevalence of AAS use in scholastic, collegiate, and professional athletes. Studies investigating the short- and long-term health risks associated with AAS use are also encouraged.

7. In order for drug testing to be a deterrent to AAS usage, it should be equally applied to all sports and levels of athletics.

8. A win-at-all-costs philosophy creates enormous pressure on athletes. Society in general and individuals who are supportive of athletics must work to change the philosophy that an athlete must win in order to be successful.

9. It is the aim of the NSCA to discourage AAS use and promote athletic performance that is based upon proper training methods and fair play.

10. The NSCA denounces the use of AAS for the purpose of performance enhancement.

Combating Drug Abuse in Sport

Better and more accurate research is needed relative to the use and abuse of drugs among scholastic, collegiate, and professional athletes. Underreporting is a serious limitation of research involving drug use among athletes. It is even more difficult to get accurate information from athletes about their coach's direct or indirect role in encouraging drug use for purposes of performance enhancement. Accurate data must be collected in a manner that would make it impossible to detect the name of the athlete reporting a result or the name of a coach associated with a particular athlete. This can only be accomplished if two conditions exist. First, data must be truly anonymous and untraceable, even in the face of a court subpoena. Second, the athletes filling out the questionnaires must *believe* that the data are truly anonymous and untraceable, even in the face of a court subpoena.

Two basic approaches to combating drug use in sport are mentioned by Anshel (2006). These are the use of cognitive techniques and the use of behavioral techniques. *Cognitive techniques* utilize intellectual and psychological methods to influence behavior and attitude. Conversely, *behavioral techniques* shape the athlete's environment in ways that will elicit desirable responses and behaviors from the athlete.

Cognitive Techniques

Using **cognitive techniques,** the coach utilizes support groups among the players to encourage drug abstinence. The coach shows concern for athletes, sets limits on unacceptable behavior, develops team policy, and teaches athletes specific coping skills to deal with the pressure to excel. The coach must be aware of each athlete's mental status, both in and out of the sport environment. Coaches can also help athletes by making them feel part of the team and by seeking their input on important team decisions.

As a cognitive strategy to reduce drug abuse among athletes, Strelan and Boeckmann (2003) proposed the Drugs in Sport Deterrence Model (DSDM) to study athlete decision making and to provide structure for research aimed at minimizing drug use by athletes. **Deterrence theory** is a theoretical approach to understanding compliance with the law (Paternoster, 1987). It is based on a cost/benefit analysis of likely consequences of a behavior. An athlete's decision to use most banned substances requires time, reflection, and planning. As illustrated in figure 19.1, the DSDM has three components: (a) the costs of a decision to use drugs (deterrents), (b) the benefits associated with using drugs, and (c) the situational factors that may impact the cost-benefit analysis. According to Strelan and Boeckmann (2003), the solution to minimizing drug use by athletes is in systematically studying the DSDM model and determining the deterrents (costs) on which to focus society's interest. For example, self-imposed sanctions may ultimately be most effective, because morality research shows that the more ingrained an ethical belief is, the more likely it is to be adhered to. If young athletes came to believe that drug use in sport is immoral and unfair, this would be a great deterrent.

Behavioral Techniques

The vast majority of athletes take drugs for the purpose of performance enhancement. Therefore, the focus of **behavioral techniques** should be upon teaching athletes alternative ways to enhance performance that do not include the use of drugs. These alternative methods to increased performance include teaching motor skills and strategies that lead to increased performance. Coaches do not always spend much time in practice helping individual athletes improve their personal skills. They may instead run scrimmages in which individual skills are largely overlooked and assumed to already exist. Other behavioral techniques that are effective include peer involvement in drug education and drug prevention efforts. Young athletes are much more likely to take advice from an admired peer than from an adult. In fact, many athletes get involved in the use of drugs because they have listened to an admired peer who was not setting a good example. In setting up a drug-free environment, the coach may want to introduce mandatory drug testing, a clear course of action when drug abuse is detected, and interesting activities to engage athletes during free time. Athletes are much less likely to take drugs for the purpose of performance enhancement if they fear detection through mandatory drug testing.

Finally, research reported by Storch, Storch, Kovacs, Okun, and Welsh (2003) suggests that athletes scoring high in intrinsic **religiosity** may be less prone to use alcohol, marijuana, and other recreational and illicit drugs. This finding provides an additional behavioral approach to discouraging drug use by athletes.

FIGURE 19.1 | The Drugs in Sport Deterrence Model (DSDM) as proposed by Strelan, P., & Boeckmann, R.J. (2003).

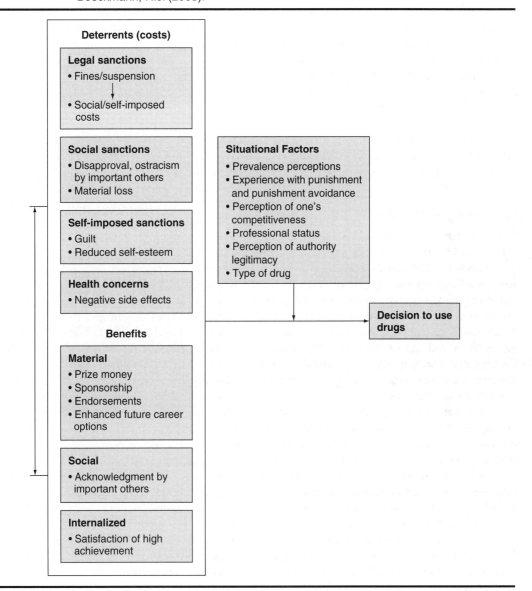

Source: A new model for understanding performance-enhancing drug use by elite athletes. *Journal of Applied Sport Psychology, 15* (2), 176–83. Reproduced with permission of Taylor and Francis.

CONCEPT   Athletes are under tremendous pressure from coaches, parents, peers, and themselves to exhibit superior athletic performance. It does not seem to be enough to do your best anymore; you must be better than everyone else. Since this is an unrealistic expectation, it is not too surprising that some athletes turn to "performance-enhancing" drugs.

APPLICATION   It is the personal responsibility of all coaches and parents to make sure that no athlete they are associated with feels the pressure to excel to such a degree that she would resort to "performance-enhancing" drugs to accomplish this. Coaches, teachers, and athletes must "buy into" the notion of task, or mastery, goal orientation, as opposed to ego orientation. Athletics should be about becoming the best that you can become, but not necessarily about being better than everyone else. Mandatory drug testing can serve as a deterrent to athletes prone to using drugs for purposes of performance enhancement, but it cannot address the deeper issue of why an athlete would resort to such illegal behavior in the first place.

Summary

In this chapter on drug abuse, we (a) addressed the hoped-for benefits and negative consequences of certain banned substances, (b) summarized a position statement of the National Strength and Conditioning Association (NSCA), and (c) concluded with some suggestions for combating drug abuse.

The psychophysiological effects of anabolic steroids, stimulants, depressants, creatine, and other substances were discussed, with a primary emphasis upon anabolic-androgenic steroids. Anabolic steroids are a group of synthetic derivatives of the male hormone testosterone that have been modified so that their presence in the bloodstream is prolonged. They have the anabolic effect of increasing muscular strength and size, and an androgenic masculinization effect. While extremely high levels of anabolic steroid use are linked to aggressive behavior, the cause-and-effect link between moderate levels of anabolic steroid use and deviant psychological behavior has not been established. Even when links have been observed, they are obscured by confounding psychosocial factors.

Creatine is a naturally occurring energy-producing substance that is synthesized from amino acids in the human body. It is also consumed in the diet through the consumption of animal products. The majority of the evidence indicates that creatine supplementation has a beneficial effect on acute, repetitive bursts of intense exercise, but little beneficial effect upon distance or aerobic exercise.

Two basic approaches to combating drug use in sport were mentioned. These are the use of cognitive techniques and the use of behavioral techniques. *Cognitive techniques* utilize intellectual and psychological methods to influence behavior and attitude. Conversely, *behavioral techniques* shape the athlete's environment in ways that will elicit desirable responses and behaviors from the athlete.

Critical Thought Questions

1. Discuss the psychology of illegal drug use by athletes. Why do they use illegal drugs when they know it is cheating and they know there are health risks?

2. Discuss the biological and psychological effects of anabolic steroid use.

3. Describe an educational program you would recommend that would discourage drug use by athletes.

4. Discuss the Drugs in Sport Deterrence Model as a way of studying drug use among athletes.

Glossary

anabolic-androgenic steroids Synthetically derived hormones that have both an anabolic effect (increase in muscular size and strength) and an androgenic (masculinizing) effect.

anabolic effect The effect of increasing muscle mass and body size. Used in reference to anabolic steroids.

anabolic steroids Synthetically derived hormones that have both an anabolic effect (increase in muscular size and strength) and an androgenic (masculinizing) effect. Same as anabolic-androgenic steroids (shortened for convenience).

androgenic effect The effect of masculinization. Used in reference to anabolic steroids.

androstenedione A precursor hormone to the production of endogenous testosterone in the body.

behavioral technique An approach used to combat drug use in sport that is based upon teaching athletes alternative ways to maximize athletic performance.

cognitive technique An approach used to combat drug use in sport that is based upon teaching athletes how to avoid drugs and to resist peer pressure.

creatine A naturally occurring energy-producing substance that is synthesized from amino acids in the human body.

deterrence theory As used in the Drugs in Sport Deterrence Model (DSDM), it is a theory that helps explain cognitive decisions made by athletes.

endogenous testosterone Naturally occurring levels of testosterone in the body.

exogenous testosterone An anabolic steroid that is administered to mimic the effects of testosterone in the body.

phosphocreatine A form of creatine that serves as an energy buffer (shield) during periods of intense exercise.

psychological expectancy effect The expectation of athletes that they will get stronger and more aggressive when they take anabolic steroids.

religiosity The tendency for individuals to be religious and to allow religious beliefs to affect behavior.

References

A

AAASP online (2000). *Ethical standards.* Official Web site of the Association for the Advancement of Applied Sport Psychology (http://www.aaaspsonline.org/ethics.html).

Abma, C. L., Fry, M. D., Yuhua, L., & Relaye, G. (2002). Differences in imagery content and imagery ability between high and low confident track and field athletes. *Journal of Applied Sport Psychology, 14,* 67–75.

Adams, R. M. (1995). Momentum in the performance of professional tournament pocket billiards players. *International Journal of Sport Psychology, 26,* 580–587.

Agnew, G. A., & Carron, A. V. (1994). Crowd effects and the home advantage. *International Journal of Sport Psychology, 25,* 53–62.

Aguglia, E., & Sapienza, S. (1984). Locus of control according to Rotter's S.R.I. in volleyball players. *International Journal of Sport Psychology, 15,* 250–258.

Ajzen, I. (1985). From intention to actions: A theory of planned behavior. In J. Kuhl & J. Beckman (Eds.), *Action-control: From cognition to behavior* (pp. 11–39). Heidelberg: Springer.

Ajzen, I., & Fishbein, M. (1977). Attitude-behavior relations: A theoretical analysis and review of empirical research. *Psychology Bulletin, 84,* 888–918.

Albrecht, R. R., & Feltz, D. L. (1987). Generality and specificity of attention related to competitive anxiety and sport performance. *Journal of Sport Psychology, 9,* 231–248.

Alexander, R. (July 5, 1999). Sampras overwhelms Agassi for the men's title. *Columbia Missourian, 253,* B1.

Alferman, D., & Stoll, O. (2000). Effects of physical exercise on self-concept and well being. *International Journal of Sport Psychology, 30,* 47–65.

Allen, J. B., & Howe, B. L. (1998). Player ability, coach feedback, and female adolescent athletes' perceived competence and satisfaction. *Journal of Sport & Exercise Psychology, 20,* 280–299.

Alzado, L. (July 8, 1991). I'm sick and I'm scared. *Sports Illustrated, 75,* 21–24, 27.

American College of Sports Medicine (1997). The female athlete triad: Disordered eating, amenorrhea, and osteoporosis. *Medicine & Science in Sport & Exercise, 29,* i–ix.

American College of Sports Medicine (Oct. 23, 2003). Steroids threaten health of athletes and integrity of sports performances. *American College of Sports Medicine News Release.*

American Heart Association (1999). *2000 heart and stroke statistical update.* Dallas, TX: American Heart Association.

American Psychiatric Association. (1994). *Diagnostic and statistical manual of mental disorders.* 4th ed. Washington, DC: American Psychiatric Association.

American Psychiatric Association (2000). *Diagnostic and statistical manual of mental disorders* (4th ed.). Washington, DC: Author.

Amiot, C. E., Gaudreau, P., & Blanchard, C. M. (2004). Self-determination, coping, and goal attainment in sport. *Journal of Sport and Exercise Psychology, 26,* 396–411.

Amorose, A. J. (2003). Reflected appraisals and perceived importance of significant others' appraisals as predictors of college athletes' self-perceptions of competence. *Research Quarterly for Exercise and Sport, 74,* 60–71.

Amorose, A. J., & Horn, T. S. (2000). Intrinsic motivation: Relationships with collegiate athletes' gender, scholarship status, and perceptions of their coaches' behavior. *Journal of Sport & Exercise Psychology, 22,* 63–84.

Amorose, A. J., & Horn, T. S. (2001). Pre- to post-season changes in the intrinsic motivation of first year college athletes: Relationships with coaching behavior and scholarship status. *Journal of Applied Sport Psychology, 13,* 355–373.

Amorose, A. J., & Weiss, M. R. (1998). Coaching feedback as a source of information about perceptions of ability: A developmental examination. *Journal of Sport & Exercise Psychology, 20,* 395–420.

Amos, C. (1992). Achievement goals, motivational climate, and motivational processes. In G. C. Roberts (Ed.), *Motivation in sport and exercise* (pp. 161–176). Champaign, IL: Human Kinetics.

Andersen, M. B., & Williams, J. M. (1988). A model of stress and athletic injury: Prediction and prevention. *Journal of Sport and Exercise Psychology, 10*(3), 294–306.

Anderson, C. A., Deuser, W. E., & DeNeve, K. M. (1995). Hot temperatures, hostile affect, hostile cognition, and arousal: Tests of a general model of affective aggression. *Personality and Social Psychological Bulletin, 21,* 434–448.

Anderson, M. B., Williams, J. M., Aldridge, T., & Taylor, J. (1997). Tracking the training and careers of graduates of advanced degree programs in sport psychology, 1989–1994. *The Sport Psychologist, 11,* 326–344.

Annesi, J. J. (1997). Three-dimensional state anxiety recall: Implications for individual zone of optimal functioning research and application. *The Sport Psychologist, 11,* 43–52.

Annesi, J. J. (1998). Application of the individual zones of the optimal functioning model for the multimodal treatment of precompetitive anxiety. *The Sport Psychologist, 12,* 300–316.

Anshel, M. H. (1991). A psycho-behavioral analysis of addicted versus non-addicted male and female exercisers. *Journal of Sport Behavior, 14*(2), 145–154.

Anshel, M. H. (1993). Against the certification of sport psychology consultants: A response to Zaichkowsky and Perna. *The Sport Psychologist, 7,* 344–353.

Anshel, M. H. (1998). Drug abuse in sport: Causes and cures. In J. M. Williams (Ed.), *Applied Sport Psychology: Personal growth to peak performance* (pp. 372–397). Mountain View, CA: Mayfield.

Anshel, M. H. (2004). Sources of disordered eating patterns between ballet dancers and non-dancers *Journal of Sport Behavior, 27,* 115–133.

Anshel, M. H. (2006). Drug abuse in sport: Causes and cures. In J. M. Williams (Ed.), *Applied Sport Psychology: Personal growth to peak performance* (pp. 505–540). St. Louis, MO: McGraw-Hill.

Anshel, M. H., Jamieson, J., & Raviu, S. (2001). Cognitive appraisals and coping strategies following acute stress among skilled competitive male and female athletes. *Journal of Sport Behavior, 24,* 128–143.

Anshel, M. H., Williams, L. R. T., & Hodge, K. (1997). Cross-cultural and gender differences on coping style in sport. *International Journal of Sport Psychology, 28,* 141–156.

Apter, M. J. (1982). *The experience of motivation: The theory of psychological reversals.* London: Academic Press.

Apter, M. J. (1984). Reversal theory and personality: A review. *Journal of Research in Personality, 18,* 265–288.

Arathoon, S. M., & Malouff, J. M. (2004). The effectiveness of a brief cognitive intervention to help athletes cope with competitive loss. *Journal of Sport Behavior, 27*, 213–229.

Arent, S. M., & Landers, D. M. (2003). Arousal, anxiety, and performance: A reexamination of the Inverted-U hypothesis. *Research Quarterly for Sport and Exercise, 74*, 436–444.

Arent, S. M., Landers, D. M., & Etnier, J. L. (2000). The effects of exercise on mood in older adults: A meta-analytic review. *Journal of Aging and Physical Activity, 8*, 407–430.

Arms, R. L., & Russell, G. W. (1997). Impulsivity, fight history and camaraderie as predictors of a willingness to escalate a disturbance. *Current Psychology: Research & Reviews, 15*, 279–285.

Armstrong, C. A., Sallis, J. F., Hovell, M. F., & Hofstetter, C. R. (1993). Stages of change, self-efficacy, and the adoption of vigorous exercise: A prospective analysis. *Journal of Sport & Exercise Psychology, 15*, 390–402.

Arripe-Longueville, F., Saury, J., Fournier, J., & Durand, M. (2001). Coach-athlete interaction during elite archery competitions: An application of methodological frameworks used in ergonomics research to sport psychology. *Journal of Applied Sport Psychology, 13*, 275–299.

Asken, M. J. (1991). The challenge of the physically challenged: Delivering sport psychology services to physically disabled athletes. *The Sport Psychologist, 5*, 370–381.

B

Babyak, M., Blumenthal, J. A., Herman, S., Parinda, K., Doraiswamy, M., Moore, K., Craighead, W. E., Baldewicz, T. T., & Krishman, K. R. (1999). Effect of exercise training on older adults with major depression. *Archives of Internal Medicine, 159*, 2349–2356.

Babyak, M., Blumenthal, J. A., Herman, S., Parinda, K., Doraiswamy, M., Moore, K., Craighead, W. E., Baldewicz, T. T., & Krishman, K. R. (2000). Exercise treatment for major depression: Maintenance of therapeutic benefits at 10 months. *Psychosomatic Medicine, 62*, 633–638.

Bach, G. (Fall, 2002). Recommendations for communities comes out of International Youth Sports Congress. *Missouri Parks and Recreation, 10–11*.

Bachman, A. D., Brewer, B. W., & Petitpas, A. J. (1997). Situation specificity of cognitions during running: Replication and extension. *Journal of Applied Sport Psychology, 9*, 204–211.

Baden, D. A., Warwick-Evans, L., & Lakomy, J. (2004). Am I nearly there? The effect of anticipated running distance on perceived exertion and attentional focus. *Journal of Sport and Exercise Psychology, 26*, 215–231.

Baer, L. (1980). Effect of a time-slowing suggestion on performance accuracy on a perceptual motor task. *Perceptual and Motor Skills, 51*, 167–176.

Baer, R. (January 27, 2002). Rock Bridge shocks Hickman. *Columbia Daily Tribune*, B.

Bahrke, M. W., & Morgan, W. P. (1978). Anxiety reduction following exercise and medication. *Cognitive Therapy and Research, 2*, 323–333.

Bahrke, M., Yesalis, C., & Wright, J. (1996). Psychological behavioral effects of endogenous testosterone and anabolic-androgenic steroids: An update. *Sports Medicine, 22*(6), 367–390.

Baker, J., Coté, & Hawes, R. (2000). The relationship between coaching behaviors and sport anxiety in athletes. *Science and Medicine in Sport, 3*, 110–119.

Bandura, A. (1973). *Aggression: A social learning analysis.* Englewood Cliffs, NJ: Prentice-Hall.

Bandura, A. (1977). Self-efficacy: Toward a unifying theory of behavioral change. *Psychological Review, 84*, 191–215.

Bandura, A. (1982). Self-efficacy mechanism in human agency. *American Psychologist, 37*, 122–147.

Bandura, A. (1986). *Social foundations of thought and action: A social cognitive theory.* Englewood Cliffs, NJ: Prentice-Hall.

Bandura, A. (1997). *Self-efficacy: The exercise of control.* San Francisco, CA: Freeman.

Bar-Eli, M., Hartman, I., Levy-Kolker, N. (1994). Using goal setting to improve physical performance of adolescents with behavior disorders: The effect of goal proximity. *Adapted Physical Activity Quarterly, 11*, 86–97.

Bar-Eli, M. B., Tenenbaum, G., Pie, J. S., Kudar, K., Weinberg, R., & Barak, Y. (1997). Aerobic performance under different goal orientations and different goal conditions. *Journal of Sport Behavior, 20*, 3–15.

Barnett, N. P., Smoll, F. L., & Smith, R. E. (1992). Effects of enhancing coach-athlete relationships on youth sport attrition. *The Sport Psychologist, 6*, 111–127.

Barr, K., & Hall, C. (1992). The use of imagery by rowers. *International Journal of Sport Psychology, 23*, 243–261.

Bartholomew, J. B. (1999). The effect of resistance exercise on manipulated preexercise mood states for male exercisers. *Journal of Sport & Exercise Psychology, 21*, 39–51.

Bartholomew, J. B., Moore, J., Todd, J., Todd, T., & Elrod, C. C. (2001). Psychological states following resistant exercise of different workloads. *Journal of Applied Sport Psychology, 13*, 399–410.

Baumeister, R. F., & Steinhilber, A. (1984). Paradoxical effects of supportive audiences on performance under pressure: The home field advantage in sports championships. *Journal of Personality and Psychology, 47*, 85–93.

Beals, K. A. (2000, September). Subclinical eating disorders in female athletes. *Journal of Physical Education, Recreation, and Dance, 71*, 23–29.

Beam, J. W., Serwatka, T. S., & Wilson, W. J. (2004). Preferred leadership of NCAA Division I and II intercollegiate student athletes. *Journal of Sport Behavior, 27*, 3–17.

Beattie, S., Hardy, L., & Woodman, T. (2004). Pre-competition self-confidence: The role of the self. *Journal of Sport & Exercise Psychology, 26*, 427–441.

Beauchamp, M. R., Bray, S. R., Eys, M. A., & Carron, A. V. (2003). The effect of role ambiguity on competitive state anxiety. *Journal of Sport and Exercise Psychology, 25*, 77–92.

Beck, A. T., Ward, C. H., Mendelsohn, M., Mock, J., & Erbaugh, H. (1961). An inventory for measuring depression. *Archives of General Psychiatry, 4*, 561–571.

Beedie, C. J., Terry, P. C., & Lane, A. M. (2000). The profile of mood states and athletic performance: Two meta-analyses. *Journal of Applied Sport Psychology, 12*, 49–68.

Behling, O., & Schriesheim, C. (1976). *Organizational behavior: Theory, research, and application.* Boston: Allyn and Bacon.

Behrendt, T. (October 21, 2004). Yankees' collapse ranks with the worst. FOXSport.com. http://msn.foxsports.com/story?contentID=3096944&print=trus

Beilock, S. L., Afremow, J. A., Rabe, A. L., & Carr, T. H. (2001). "Don't Miss!" The debilitating effects of suppressive imagery on golf putting performance. *Journal of Sport and Exercise Psychology, 23*, 200–221.

Benson, H., Beary, J. F., & Carol, M. P. (1974). The relaxation response. *Psychiatry, 37*, 37–46.

Bergandi, T. A., Shryock, M. G., & Titus, T. G. (1990). The basketball concentration survey: Preliminary development and validation. *The Sport Psychologist, 4*, 119–129.

Berger, B. G., Mott, R. W., Butki, B. D., Martin, D. T., Wilkinson, J. G., & Owen, D. R. (1999). Mood and cycling performance in response to three weeks of high-intensity short duration overtraining. *The Sport Psychologist, 13,* 444–457.

Berglund, B., & Safstrom, H. (1994). Psychological monitoring and modulation of training load of world-class canoeists. *Medicine and Science in Sports and Medicine, 26,* 1036–1040.

Berkowitz, L. (1958). The expression and reduction of hostility. *Psychological Bulletin, 55,* 257–283.

Berkowitz, L. (1993). *Aggression: Its causes, consequences, and control.* Philadelphia: Temple University Press.

Bernstein, L., Henderson, B. E., Hanisch, R., Sullivan-Halley, J., & Ross, R. K. (1994). Physical exercise and reduced risk of breast cancer in young women. *Journal of the National Cancer Institute, 86,* 1403–1408.

Betts, G. H. (1909). *The distribution and functions of mental imagery.* New York: Teachers College, Columbia University.

Beuter, A., & Duda, J. L. (1985). Analysis of the arousal/motor performance relationship in children using movement kinematics. *Journal of Sport Psychology, 7,* 229–243.

Bianco, T. (2001). Social support and recovery from sport injury: Elite skiers share their experiences. *Research Quarterly for Exercise and Sport, 72,* 376–388.

Bianco, T., & Eklund, R. C. (2001). Conceptual considerations for social support research in sport and exercise settings: The case of sport injury. *Journal of Sport and Exercise Psychology, 23,* 85–107.

Bianco, T., Malo, S., & Orlick, T. (1999). Sport injury and illness: Elite skiers describe their experiences. *Research Quarterly for Exercise and Sport, 70,* 157–169.

Biddle, S. J. H. (1995). Exercise and psychosocial health. *Research Quarterly for Exercise and Sport, 66*(4), 292–297.

Biddle, S. J. H., & Hill, A. B. (1992). Relationships between attributions and emotions in a laboratory-based sporting contest. *Journal of Sports Sciences, 10,* 65–75.

Bird, A. M., & Horn, A. (1990). Cognitive anxiety and mental errors in sport. *Journal of Sport & Exercise Psychology, 12,* 211–216.

Bivens, S., & Leonard, W. M. (1994). Race, centrality, and educational attainment: An NFL perspective. *Journal of Sport Behavior, 17,* 24–42.

Bixby, W. R., Spalding, T. W., & Hatfield, B. D. (2000). The temporal dynamics of affect during and following exercise. *Medicine & Science in Sports & Exercise, 32,* Supplement, Abstract 1497, S301.

Black, S. J., & Weiss, M. R. (1992). The relationship among perceived coaching behaviors, perceptions of ability, and motivation in competitive age-group swimmers. *Journal of Sport & Exercise Psychology, 14,* 130–145.

Blake, R. R., & Mouton, J. S. (1985). *The Managerial Grid III.* Houston: Gulf Publishing Company.

Blake, R. R., & Mouton, J. S. (1994). *The Managerial Grid.* Houston: Gulf Publishing Company.

Block, N. (Ed.). (1981). *Imagery.* Cambridge, MA: MIT Press.

Bloom, G. A., Stevens, D. E., & Wickwire, T. L. (2003). Expert coaches' perceptions of team building. *Journal of Applied Sport Psychology, 15,* 129–143.

Blum, R., & Fendrich, H. (2005, Nov. 15). MLB, players strike deal on steroids testing policy. http://USAtoday.com/sports/baseball/2005-11-15-steroids-agreement_x.htm

Blumenstein, B., Bar-Eli, M., & Tenenbaum, G. (1995). The augmenting role of biofeedback: Effects of autogenic, imagery, and music training on physiological indices and athletic performance. *Journal of Sports Sciences, 13,* 343–354.

Bodin, T., & Martinsen, E. W. (2004). Mood and self-efficacy during acute exercise in clinical depression. A randomized, controlled study. *Journal of Sport and Exercise Psychology, 26,* 623–633.

Boixados, M., Cruz, J., Torregrosa, M., & Valiente, L. (2004). Relationships among motivational climate, satisfaction, perceived ability, and fair play attitudes in young soccer players. *Journal of Applied Sport Psychology, 16,* 301–317.

Boone, K. S., Beitel, P., & Kuhlman, J. (1997). The effects of the win/loss record on cohesion. *Journal of Sport Behavior, 20,* 125–134.

Botterill, C. (1983). Goal setting for athletes with examples from hockey. In G. L. Martin & D. Hrycaiko (Eds.), *Behavioral modification and coaching: Principles, procedures, and research* (pp. 67–85). Springfield, IL: Thomas.

Boutcher, S. H., & Rotella, R. J. (1987). A psychological skills education program for closed-skill performance enhancement. *The Sport Psychologist, 1,* 127–137.

Boutcher, S. H., & Trenske, M. (1990). The effects of sensory deprivation and music on perceived exertion and affect during exercise. *Journal of Sport & Exercise Psychology, 12,* 167–176.

Boutcher, S. H., & Zinsser, N. W. (1990). Cardiac deceleration of elite and beginning golfers during putting. *Journal of Sport & Exercise Psychology, 12,* 37–47.

Brawley, L. R. (1993). The practicality of using social psychological theories for exercise and health research and intervention. *Journal of Applied Sport Psychology, 5,* 99–115.

Bray, C. D., & Whaley, D. E. (2001). Team cohesion, effort, and objective individual performance of high school basketball players. *The Sport Psychologist, 15,* 260–275.

Bray, S. R. (1999). The home advantage from an individual team perspective. *Journal of Applied Sport Psychology, 11,* 116–125.

Bray, S. R., & Carron, A. V. (1993). The home advantage in alpine skiing. *The Australian Journal of Science and Medicine in Sport, 25,* 76–81.

Bray, S. R., Law, J., & Foule, J. (2003). Team quality and game location effects in English professional soccer. *Journal of Sport Behavior, 26,* 319–334.

Bray, S. R., & Widmeyer, W. N. (2000). Athletes' perceptions of the home advantage: An investigation of perceived causal factors. *Journal of Sport Behavior, 23,* 1–10.

Bredemeier, B. J. (1978). The assessment of reactive and instrumental athletic aggression. *Proceedings of the International Symposium on Psychological Assessment.* Neyanya, Israel: Wingate Institute for Physical Education and Sport.

Bredemeier, B. J. (1985). Moral reasoning and the perceived legitimacy of intentionally injurious sport acts. *Journal of Sport Psychology, 7,* 110–124.

Bredemeier, B. J. (1994). Children's moral reasoning and their assertive, aggressive, and submissive tendencies in sport and daily life. *Journal of Sport & Exercise Psychology, 16,* 1–14.

Brewer, B. W. (1993). Self-identity and specific vulnerability to depressed mood. *Journal of Personality, 61,* 343–364.

Brewer, B. W. (1998). Adherence to sport injury rehabilitation programs. *Journal of Applied Sport Psychology, 10,* 70–82.

Brewer, B. W., Cornelius, A. E., Van Raalte, J. L., Petitpas, A. J., Sklar, J. H., Pholman, M. H., Krushell, R. J., & Ditmar, T. D. (2003). Protection motivation theory and adherence to sport injury rehabilitation revisited. *The Sport Psychologist, 17,* 95–103.

Brewer, B. W., Van Raalte, J. L., & Linder, D. E. (1993). Athletic identity: Hercules' muscles or achilles' heel? *International Journal of Sport Psychology, 24,* 237–254.

Brewer, B. W., Van Raalte, J. L., & Linder, D. E. (1996). Attentional focus and endurance performance. *Applied Research in Coaching and Athletics Annual, 11,* 1–14.

Brewer, B. W., Van Raalte, J. L., Petitpas, A. J., Sklar, J. H., Pohlman, M. H., Krushell, R. J., Ditmar, T. D., Daily, J. M., & Weinstock,

J. (2000). Preliminary psychometric evaluation of a measure of adherence to clinic based sport injury rehabilitation. *Physical Therapy in Sport, 1,* 68–74.

Broadbent, D. E. (1957). Mechanical model for human attention and immediate memory. *Psychological Review, 64,* 205–215.

Broadbent, D. E. (1958). *Perception and communication.* London: Pergamon Press.

Broucek, M. W., Bartholomew, J. B., Landers, D. M., & Linder, D. E. (1993). The effects of relaxation with a warning cue on pain tolerance. *Journal of Sport Behavior, 16,* 239–254.

Broussard, C. (July 15, 2004). O'Neal trade to Heat shifts balance of power. *The New York Times (NYTimes.com).*

Brown, B. S., & Van Huss, W. D. (1973). Exercise and rat brain catecholamines. *Journal of Applied Physiology, 34,* 664–669.

Brown, C. (July 20, 2004). Parity is par for the course nowadays. *The New York Times,* http://nytimes.com/2004/07/20.

Brown, J. D. (1991). Staying fit and staying well: Physical fitness as a moderator of life stress. *Journal of Personality and Social Psychology, 60*(4), 555–561.

Brown, T. D., VanRaalte, J. L., Brewer, B. W., Winter, C. R., Cornelius, A. E., & Andersen, M. (2002). World Cup soccer home advantage. *Journal of Sport Behavior, 25,* 135–144.

Brunelle, J. P., Janelle, C. M., & Tennant, L. K. (1999). Controlling competitive anger among male soccer players. *Journal of Applied Sport Psychology, 11,* 283–297.

Brustad, R. J. (1996a). Attraction to physical activity in urban school children: Parental socialization and gender influences. *Research Quarterly for Exercise and Sport, 67,* 316–323.

Brustad, R. J. (1996b) Parental and peer influence on children's psychological development through sport. In F. L. Smoll & R. E. Smith (Eds.), *Children and youth in sport: A biopsychosocial perspective* (pp. 112–124). Madison, WI: Brown & Benchmark.

Buck, J. N. (1948, October). The H-T-P technique: A qualitative and quantitative scoring manual. *Journal of Clinical Psychology* (Monog. Suppl. No. 5).

Burke, K., Burke, M., & Joyner, M. (1999). Perceptions of momentum in college and high school basketball: An exploratory, case study investigation. *Journal of Sports Behavior, 22,* 303–309.

Burke, K. L., Edwards, T. C., Weigand, D. A., & Weinber, R. S. (1997). Momentum in sport: A real or illusionary phenomenon for spectators. *International Journal of Sport Psychology, 28,* 79–96.

Burke, K. L., & Houseworth, S. (1995). Structural charting and perceptions of momentum in intercollegiate volleyball. *Journal of Sport Behavior, 18,* 167–182.

Burton, D. (1988). Do anxious swimmers swim slower?: Reexamining the elusive anxiety-performance relationship. *Journal of Sport and Exercise Psychology, 10,* 45–61.

Burton, D., Weinberg, R., Yukelson, D., & Weigand, D. (1998). The goal effectiveness paradox in sport: Examining the goal practices of collegiate athletes. *The Sport Psychologist, 12,* 404–418.

Bushman, B. J., & Anderson, C. A. (2000). Is it time to pull the plug on the hostile versus instrumental aggression dichotomy? *Psychological Review, 108,* 273–279.

Buss, A. H., & Perry, M. (1992). The aggression questionnaire. *Journal of Personality and Social Psychology, 63,* 452–459.

Butcher, J. N., Graham, J. R., Williams, C. L., & Ben-Porath, Y. S. (1990). *Development and use of the MMPI-2 content scales.* Minnesota: University of Minnesota Press.

Butcher, J., Linder, K. J., & Jones, D. P. (2002). Withdrawal from competitive youth sport: A retrospective ten year study. *Journal of Sport Behavior, 25,* 145–163.

Butler, J. L., Baumeister, R. F. (1998). The trouble with friendly faces: Skilled performance with a supportive audience. *Journal of Personality and Social Psychology, 75,* 1213–1230.

Butryn, T. M. (2002). Critically examining white racial identity and privilege in sport psychology consulting. *The Sport Psychologist, 16,* 316–336.

Butt, J., Weinberg, R., & Horn, T. (2003). The intensity and directional interpretation of anxiety: Fluctuations throughout competition and relationship to performance. *The Sport Psychologist, 17,* 35–54.

C

Callow, N., & Hardy, L. (2001). Types of imagery associated with sport confidence in netball players of varying skill levels. *Journal of Applied Sport Psychology, 13,* 1–17.

Callow, N., Hardy, L., & Hall, C. R. (2001). The effects of a motivational general-mastery imagery intervention on the sport confidence of high-level badminton players. *Research Quarterly for Exercise and Sport,* 389–400.

Calmels, C., Berthoumieux, C., & d'Arripe-Longueville, F. (2004). Effects of an imagery training program on selective attention of national softball players. *The Sport Psychologist, 18,* 272–296.

Calmels, C., & Fournier, J. F. (2001). Duration of physical and mental execution of gymnastic routines. *The Sport Psychologist, 15,* 142–150.

Calmels, C., Holmes, P., Berthoumieux, C., & Singer, R. N. (2004). The development of movement imagery vividness through a structured intervention in softball. *Journal of Sport Behavior, 27,* 307–322.

Campbell, P. G., MacAuley, D., McCrum, E., & Evans, A. (2001). Age differences in the motivating factor for exercise. *Journal of Sport and Exercise Psychology, 23,* 191–199.

Campen, C., & Roberts, D. C. (2001). Coping strategies of runners: Perceived effectiveness and match to precompetitive anxiety. *Journal of Sport Behavior, 24,* 144–161.

Cannella, S. (September 4, 2000). Inside baseball. *Sports Illustrated, 93,* 62–63.

Cardinal, B. J. (1995). The stages of exercise scale and stages of exercise behavior in female adults. *Journal of Sports Medicine and Physical Fitness, 35,* 87–92.

Cardinal, B. J. (1997). Predicting exercise behavior using components of the transtheoretical model of behavior change. *Journal of Sport Behavior, 20,* 272–283.

Cardinal, B. J., & Kosma, M. (2004). Self-efficacy and the stages and processes of change associated with adopting and maintaining muscular fitness–promoting behavior. *Research Quarterly for Exercise and Sport, 75,* 186–196.

Cardinal, B. J., Kosma, M., & McCubbin, J. A. (2004). Factors influencing the exercise behavior of adults with physical disabilities. *Medicine & Science in Sport and Exercise, 36,* 868–875.

Cardinal, B. J., Tuominen, K. J., & Rintala, P. (2004). Cross-cultural comparison of American and Finnish college students' exercise behavior using transtheoretical model constructs. *Research Quarterly for Exercise and Sport, 75,* 92–101.

Carey, C. (October 4, 1999). Psych job. *St. Louis Dispatch,* BP12.

Carlson, C. R., & Hoyle, R. H. (1993). Efficacy of abbreviated progressive muscle relaxation training: A quantitative review of behavioral medicine research. *Journal of Consulting and Clinical Psychology, 61,* 1059–1067.

Carpenter, P. J., & Yates, B. (1997). Relationship between achievement goals and the perceived purposes of soccer for semiprofessional and amateur players. *Journal of Sport & Exercise Psychology, 19,* 302–311.

Carr, C. (November 28, 2004). Spectator-sport dynamics can turn frightening. *Indianapolis Star,* http://Indystar.com/2004/11/28

Carr, S., & Weigand, D. A. (2002). The influence of significant others on the goal orientations of youngsters in physical education. *Journal of Sport Behavior, 25,* 19–40.

Carron, A. V. (1980). *Social psychology of sport.* Ithaca, NY: Mouvement Publications.

Carron, A. V. (1982). Cohesiveness in sport groups: Interpretations and considerations. *Journal of Sport Psychology, 4,* 123–138.

Carron, A. V., Burke, S. M., & Prapavessis, H. (2004). Self-presentation and group influence. *Journal of Applied Sport Psychology, 16,* 41–58.

Carron, A. V., Coleman, M. M., Wheeler, J., & Stevens, D. (2002). Cohesion and performance in sport: A meta-analysis. *Journal of Sport and Exercise Psychology, 24,* 168–188.

Carron, A. V., & Dennis, P. W. (1998). The sport team as an effective group. In J. M. Williams (Ed.), *Applied sport psychology: Personal growth to peak performance* (pp. 127–141). Mountain View, CA: Mayfield.

Carron, A. V., Hausenblas, H. A., & Mack, D. (1996). Social influence and exercise: A meta-analysis. *Journal of Sport & Exercise Psychology, 18,* 1–16.

Carron, A. V., Prapavessis, H., & Grove, J. R. (1994). Group effects and self-handicapping. *Journal of Sport & Exercise Psychology, 16,* 246–257.

Carron, A. V., & Spink, K. S. (1992). Internal consistency of the Group Environment Questionnaire modified for an exercise setting. *Perceptual and Motor Skills, 74,* 304–306.

Carron, A. V., Spink, K. S., & Prapavessis, H. (1997). Team building and cohesiveness in the sport and exercise setting: Use of interventions. *Journal of Applied Sport Psychology, 9,* 61–72.

Carver, C. S., Scheier, M. F., & Weintraub, J. K. (1989). Assessing coping strategies: A theoretically based approach. *Journal of Personality and Social Psychology, 56,* 267–283.

Case, B. (1987). Leadership behavior in sport: A field test of the situational leadership theory. *International Journal of Sport Psychology, 18,* 256–268.

Case, R. (1998). Leader member exchange theory and sport: Possible applications. *Journal of Sport Behavior, 21,* 387–395.

Cash, T. F. (1994). *The Multidimensional Body-Self Relations Questionnaire user's manual.* Available from the author, Department of Psychology, Old Dominion University, Norfolk, VA.

Catley, D., & Duda, J. L. (1997). Psychological antecedents of the frequency and intensity of flow in golfers. *International Journal of Sport Psychology, 28,* 309–322.

Cattell, R. B. (1965). *The scientific analysis of personality.* Baltimore: Penguin.

Cattell, R. B. (1973, July). Personality pinned down. *Psychology Today,* 40–46.

Cerin, E. (2003). Anxiety versus fundamental emotions as predictors of perceived functionality of pre-competitive emotional states, threat, and challenge in individual sports. *Journal of Applied Sport Psychology, 15,* 223–238.

Cerin, E., Szabo, A., Hunt, N., & Williams, C. (2000). Temporal patterning of competitive emotions: A critical review. *Journal of Sport Sciences, 18,* 605–626.

Chan, C. S., & Grossman, H. Y. (1988). Psychological effects of running loss on consistent runners. *Perceptual and Motor Skills, 66,* 875–883.

Chapman, C. L., & Castro, J. M. (1990). Running addiction: Measurement and associated psychological characteristics. *The Journal of Sports Medicine and Physical Fitness, 30,* 283–290.

Chartrand, J. M., Jowdy, D. P., & Danish, S. J. (1992). The psychological skills inventory for sports: Psychometric characteristics and applied implications. *Journal of Sport and Exercise Psychology, 14,* 405–413.

Chase, M. A. (2001). Children's self-efficacy, motivational intentions, and attributions in physical education and sport. *Research Quarterly for Sport and Exercise, 72,* 47–54.

Chass, M. (November 9, 1994). Teams look behind plate for managers. *Kansas City Star,* sec. D, 1, 4.

Chelladurai, P. (1978). *A multidimensional model of leadership.* Unpublished doctoral dissertation, University of Waterloo, Waterloo, Ontario.

Chelladurai, P. (1993). Leadership. In R. N. Singer, M. Murphy, & L. K. Tennant (Eds.), *Handbook on research on sport psychology* (p. 447). New York: Macmillan.

Chelladurai, P., & Carron, A. V. (1977). A reanalysis of formal structure in sport. *Canadian Journal of Applied Sport Sciences, 2,* 9–14.

Chelladurai, P., & Saleh, S. D. (1978). Preferred leadership in sport. *Canadian Journal of Applied Sport Sciences, 3,* 85–97.

Chelladurai, P., & Saleh, S. D. (1980). Dimensions of leader behavior in sports: Development of a leadership scale. *Journal of Sport Psychology, 2,* 34–35.

Choma, C. W., Sforzo, G. A., & Keller, B. A. (1998). Impact of rapid weight loss on cognitive function in collegiate wrestlers. *Medicine & Science in Sport & Exercise, 30,* 746–749.

Chosen one (January 22, 2002). Chosen one. *Columbia Daily Tribune,* 4B.

Cinelli, B., Sankaran, G., McConatha, D., & Carson, L. (1992). Knowledge and attitudes of pre-service education majors about AIDS: Implications for curriculum development. *Health Education, 23,* 204–208.

Clark, L. V. (1960). Effect of mental practice on the development of a certain motor skill. *Research Quarterly, 31,* 560–569.

Cleary, T. J., & Zimmerman, B. J. (2001). Self-regulation differences during athletic practice by experts, non-experts, and novices. *Journal of Applied Sport Psychology, 13,* 184–206.

Clingman, J. M., & Hilliard, D. V. (1987). Some personality characteristics of the super-adherer: Following those who go beyond fitness. *Journal of Sport Behavior, 10,* 123–136.

Coakley, J. (1992). Burnout among adolescent athletes: A personal failure or social problem. *Sociology of Sport Journal, 9,* 271–285.

Coen, S. P., & Ogles, B. M. (1993). Psychological characteristics of the obligatory runner: A critical examination of the anorexia analogue hypothesis. *Journal of Sport & Exercise Psychology, 15,* 338–354.

Cofer, C. N., & Johnson, W. R. (1960). Personality dynamics in relation to exercise and sports. In W. R. Johnson (Ed.), *Science and medicine of exercise and sport.* New York: Harper & Row.

Cohen, A., Pargman, D., & Tenenbaum, G. (2003). Critical elaboration and empirical investigation of the Cusp Catastrophe model: A lesson for practitioners. *Journal of Applied Sport Psychology, 15,* 144–159.

Cohen, J. (1992). A power primer. *Psychological Bulletin, 112,* 155–159.

Coleman, T. R. (1976). *A comparative study of certain behavioral, physiological, and phenomenological effects of hypnotic induction and two progressive relaxation procedures.* Ph.D. dissertation, Brigham Young University, Provo, UT.

Conboy, J. K. (1994). The effects of exercise withdrawal on mood states in runners. *Journal of Sport Behavior, 17,* 188–203.

Connelly, S. L. (1991). *Injury and self-esteem: A test of Sonstroem and Morgan's model.* Unpublished master's thesis, South Dakota State University, Brookings.

Connolly, C. T., & Janelle, C. M. (2003). Attentional strategies in rowing: Performance, perceived exertion, and gender considerations. *Journal of Applied Sport Psychology, 15,* 195–212.

Conroy, D. E., & Metzler, J. N. (2004). Patterns of self-talk associated with different forms of competitive anxiety. *Journal of Sport and Exercise Psychology, 26,* 69–89.

Conroy, D. E., Motl, R. W., & Hall, E. G. (1998). Factorial validity of the Self-Presentation in Exercise Questionnaire. *Journal of Applied Sport Psychology, 10,* 270–280.

Conroy, D. E., Motl, R. W., & Hall, E. G. (2000). Progress toward construct validation of the Self-Presentation in Exercise Questionnaire (SPEQ). *Journal of Sport and Exercise Psychology, 23,* 21–38.

Cook, K., & Mravic, M. (May 17, 1999). Scorecard—a purpose pitch. *Sports Illustrated, 90,* 24.

Cooper, L. (1969). Athletics, activity, and personality: A review of the literature. *Research Quarterly, 40,* 17–22.

Corbin, C. B. (1967a). The effects of covert practice on the development of a complex motor skill. *Journal of General Psychology, 76,* 143–150.

Corbin, C. B. (1967b). Effects of mental practice on skill development after controlled practice. *Research Quarterly, 38,* 534–538.

Corbin, C. B. (1977). The reliability and internal consistency of the motivation rating scale and the general trait rating scale. *Medicine and Science in Sports, 9,* 208–211.

Cornelius, A., Silva, J. M., Conroy, D. E., Peterson, G. (1997). The projected performance model: Relating cognitive and performance antecedents of psychological momentum. *Perceptual and Motor Skills, 84,* 475–485.

Costa, A., Bonaccorsi, M., & Scrimali, T. (1984). Biofeedback and control of anxiety preceding athletic competition. *International Journal of Sport Psychology, 15,* 98–109.

Costa, P. T., Jr., & McCrae, R. R. (1992). *Revised NEO Personality Inventory (NEO-PI-R) and NEO Five Factor Inventory (NEO-FFI) professional manual.* Odessa, FL: Psychological Assessment Resources.

Cotman, C. W., & Engesser-Cesar, C. (2002). Exercise enhances and protects brain function. *Exercise and Sport Science Review, 30,* 75–79.

Courneya, K. S. (1995). Perceived severity of the consequences of physical inactivity across the stages of change in older adults. *Journal of Sport & Exercise Psychology, 17,* 447–457.

Courneya, K. S. (2001). Exercise interventions during cancer treatment: Biopsychosocial outcomes. *Exercise and Sport Science Review, 29,* 60–64.

Courneya, K. S., & Carron, A. V. (1991). Effects of travel and length of home stand/road trip on the home advantage. *Journal of Sport & Exercise Psychology, 13,* 42–49.

Courneya, K. S., Mackey, J. R., & Jones, L. W. (May, 2000). Coping with cancer: Can exercise help? *The Physician and Sports Medicine, 28,* 49–73.

Courneya, K. S., & McAuley, E. (1994). Factors affecting the intention–physical activity relationship: Intention versus expectation and scale correspondence. *Research Quarterly for Exercise and Sport, 65,* 280–285.

Couture, R. T., Jerome, W., & Tihanyi, J. (1999). Can associative and dissociative strategies affect the swimming performance of recreational swimmers? *The Sport Psychologist, 13,* 334–343.

Cox, R. H. (1985). *Sport psychology: Concepts and applications.* Dubuque, IA: Wm. C. Brown Publishers.

Cox, R. H. (1987). *Relationship between psychological variables with player position and experience in women's volleyball.* Unpublished manuscript.

Cox, R. H. (1990). *Sport psychology: Concepts and applications.* 2nd ed. Dubuque, IA: Wm. C. Brown Publishers.

Cox, R. H. (1998). *Sport psychology: Concepts and applications.* WCB/McGraw-Hill.

Cox, R. H. (September, 2000). *Confirmatory factor analysis of the Competitive State Anxiety Inventory–2.* Paper presented at the annual meeting of the Association for the Advancement of Applied Sport Psychology, Nashville, TN.

Cox, R. H., & Davis, R. W. (1992, Spring). Psychological skills of elite wheelchair athletes. *Palaestra, 8,* 16–21.

Cox, R. H., Martens, M. P., & Russell, W. D. (2003). Measuring anxiety in athletics: The Revised Competitive State Anxiety Inventory-2. *Journal of Sport and Exercise Psychology, 25,* 519–533.

Cox, R. H., Robb, M., & Russell, W. D. (2000). Concurrent validity of the Revised Anxiety Rating Scale. *Journal of Sport Behavior, 23,* 327–334.

Cox, R. H., Robb, M., & Russell, W. D. (2001). Construct validity of the revised Anxiety Rating Scale (ARS-2). *Journal of Sport Behavior, 24,* 10–18.

Cox, R. H., Thomas, T. R., & Davis, J. E. (2000). Delayed anxiolytic effect associated with an acute bout of aerobic exercise. *Journal of Exercise Physiology Online, 3,* 59–66.

Cox, R. H., Thomas, T. R., Hinton, P. S., & Donahue, O. M. (2004). Effect of acute 60 and 80 percent of VO_2 max bouts of aerobic exercise on state anxiety of women of different age groups across time. *Research Quarterly for Exercise and Sport, 75,* 165–175.

Craft, L. L., & Landers, D. M. (1998). The effect of exercise on clinical depression and depression resulting from mental illness: A meta-analysis. *Journal of Sport & Exercise Psychology, 20,* 339–357.

Craft, L. L., Magyar, T. M., Becker, B. J., & Feltz, D. L. (2003). The relationship between the Competitive State Anxiety Inventory-2 and sport performance: A meta-analysis. *Journal of Sport and Exercise Psychology, 25,* 444–465.

Craighead, D. J., Privette, F. V., & Byrkit, D. (1986). Personality characteristics of basketball players, starters, and nonstarters. *International Journal of Sport Psychology, 17,* 110–119.

Cratty, B. J., & Sage, J. N. (1964). The effects of primary and secondary group interaction upon improvement in a complex movement task. *Research Quarterly, 35,* 164–175.

Crawford, S., & Eklund, R. C. (1994). Social physique anxiety, reasons for exercise, and attitudes toward exercise settings. *Journal of Sport & Exercise Psychology, 16,* 70–82.

Cregg, M., Hall, C. R., & Nederhof, E. (2005). The imagery ability, imagery use, and performance relationship. *The Sport Psychologist, 19,* 93–99.

Crocker, P. R. E. (1989). A follow-up of cognitive-affective stress management training. *Journal of Sport & Exercise Psychology, 11,* 236–242.

Crocker, P. R. E. (1992). Managing stress by competitive athletes: Ways of coping. *International Journal of Sport Psychology, 23,* 161–175.

Crocker, P. R. E., Eklund, R. C., & Graham, T. R. (2002). Evaluating the factorial structure of the Revised Causal Dimension Scale in adolescents. *Research Quarterly for Exercise and Sport, 73,* 211–218.

Crocker, P. R. E., & Graham, T. R. (1995). Coping by competitive athletes with performance stress: Gender differences and relationships with affect. *The Sport Psychologist, 9,* 325–338.

Crocker, P. R. E., & Isaak, K. (1997). Coping during competition and training session: Are youth swimmers consistent? *International Journal of Sport Psychology, 28,* 355–369.

Csikszentimichalyi, M. (1990). *Flow: The psychology of optimal experience.* New York: Harper and Row.

Cullen, J. B., & Cullen, F. T. (1975). The structure and contextual conditions of group norm violations: Some implications from the game of ice hockey. *International Review of Sport Sociology, 10,* 69–77.

Cummings, J., & Hall, R. (2003). Athletes' use of imagery in the off season. *The Sport Psychologist, 16,* 160–172.

Cummings, J. L., & Ste-Marie, D. M. (2001). The cognitive and motivational effects of imagery training: A matter of perspective. *The Sport Psychologist, 21,* 276–288.

Cupal, D. D. (1998). Psychological interventions in sport injury prevention and rehabilitation. *Journal of Applied Sport Psychology, 10,* 103–123.

Czech, D. R., Ploszay, A., & Burke, K. L. (2004). An examination of the maintenance of preshot routines in basketball free throw shooting. *Journal of Sport Behavior, 27,* 323–329.

D

Dabbs, J. M., Jr., Johnson, J. E., & Leventhal, H. (1968). Palmar sweating: A quick and simple measure. *Journal of Experimental Psychology, 78,* 347–350.

Dale, G. A. (2000). Distractions and coping strategies of elite decathletes during their most memorable performances. *The Sport Psychologist, 14,* 17–41.

Daly, J. M., Brewer, B. W., Van Raalte, J. L., Petitpas, A. J., & Sklar, J. H. (1995). Cognitive appraisal, emotional adjustment, and adherence to rehabilitation following knee surgery. *Journal of Sport Rehabilitation, 4,* 22–30.

Danish, S. J., Petitpas, A. J., & Hale, B. D. (1992). A developmental-educational model of sport psychology. *The Sport Psychologist, 6,* 403–415.

Davidson, K. K., Cutting, T. M., & Birch, L. L. (2003). Parents' activity-related parenting practices predict girls' physical activity. *Medicine and Science in Sports and Exercise, 35,* 1589–1595.

Davis, C., & Mogk, J. P. (1994). Some personality correlates of interest and excellence in sport. *International Journal of Sport Psychology, 25,* 131–143.

Davis, C., & Strachan, S. (2001). Elite female athletes with eating disorders: A study of psychopathological characteristics. *Journal of Sport and Exercise Psychology, 23,* 245–253.

Davis, H. (1991). Criterion validity of the athletic motivation inventory: Issues in professional sport. *Journal of Applied Sport Psychology, 3,* 176–182.

Davis, J. E., & Cox, R. H. (2002). Interpreting direction of anxiety within Hanin's individual zone of optimal functioning. *Journal of Applied Sport Psychology, 14,* 43–52.

Davis, M., Eshelman, E. R., & McKay, M. (1995). *The relaxation & stress reduction workbook.* 4th ed. Oakland, CA: New Harbinger Publications, Inc.

Davis, M. H., & Harvey, J. C. (1992). Declines in major league batting performance as a function of game pressure: A drive theory analysis. *Journal of Applied Social Psychology, 22,* 714–735.

Davis, S. F., Huss, M. T., & Becker, A. H. (1995). Norman Triplett and the dawning of sport psychology. *The Sport Psychologist, 9,* 366–375.

DeCharms, R. C., & Carpenter, V. (1968). Measuring motivation in culturally disadvantaged school children. *Journal of Experimental Education, 37,* 31–41.

Deci, E. L., Koestner, R., & Ryan, R. M. (1999). A meta-analytic review of experiments examining the effects of extrinsic rewards on intrinsic motivations. *Psychological Bulletin, 125,* 627–668.

Deci, E. L., & Ryan, R. M. (1985). *Intrinsic motivation and self-determination in human behavior.* New York: Plenum.

Deci, E. L., & Ryan, R. M. (1991). A motivational approach to self: Integration in personality. In R. A. Dienstbier (Ed.), Nebraska Symposium on Motivation 1991: Vol 38. *Perspectives on motivation: Current theory and research in motivation* (pp. 237–288). Lincoln, NE: University of Nebraska Press.

Deci, E. L., Vallerand, R. J., Pelletier, L. G., & Ryan, R. M. (1991). Motivation and education: The self-determination perspective. *The Educational Psychologist, 26,* 325–346.

Deeney, S. P., Hillman, C. H., Janelle, C. M., & Hatfield, B. D. (2003). Cortico-cortical communication and superior performance in skilled marksmen: An EEG coherence analysis. *Journal of Sport and Exercise Psychology, 25,* 188–204.

Deford, F. (May 10, 1999). The ring leader. *Sports Illustrated, 90,* 96–114.

DeFrancesco, C., & Burke, K. L. (1997). Performance enhancement strategies used in a professional tennis tournament. *International Journal of Sport Psychology, 28,* 185–195.

DeMichele, P. E., Gansneder, B., Solomon, G. B. (1998). Success and failure attributions of wrestlers: Further evidence of the self-serving bias. *Journal of Sport Behavior, 21,* 242–255.

Depcik, E., & Williams, L. (2004). Weight training and body satisfaction of body-image-disturbed college women. *Journal of Applied Sport Psychology, 16,* 287–299.

Dess, N. K. (May/June 2000). Killer workout: The dark side of diet and exercise. *Psychology Today, 32,* 26.

Dewey, D., Brawley, L. R., & Allard, F. (1989). Do the TAIS attentional-style scales predict how visual information is processed? *Journal of Sport & Exercise Psychology, 11,* 171–186.

DiBartolo, P. M., & Shaffer, C. (2002). A comparison of female college athletes and nonathletes: Eating disorders symptomatology and psychological well-being. *Journal of Sport and Exercise Psychology, 24,* 33–41.

Dimmock, J. A., & Grove, J. R. (2005). Relationships of fan identification to determinants of aggression. *Journal of Applied Sport Psychology, 17,* 37–47.

Dishman, R. K. (1987). Exercise adherence and habitual physical activity. In W. P. Morgan & S. E. Goldston (Eds.), *Exercise and Mental Health* (pp. 57–83). Washington, DC: Hemisphere Publishing Corporation.

Dishman, R. K. (2001). The problem of exercise adherence: Fighting sloth in nations with market economics. *Quest, 53,* 279–294.

Dishman, R. K., & Buckworth, J. (1996). Increasing physical activity: A quantitative analysis synthesis. *Medicine and Science in Sports and Exercise, 28,* 706–719.

Dohrmann, G. (Dec. 13, 2004). Babo blows up. *Sports Illustrated, 101,* 50–54.

Dollard, J., Miller, N., Doob, I., Mourer, O. H., & Sears, R. R. (1939). *Frustration and aggression.* New Haven, CT: Yale University Press.

Donnelly, P., Carron, A. V., & Chelladurai, P. (1978). *Group cohesion and sport.* Ottawa, Ontario: Canadian Association for Health, Physical Education and Recreation.

DuCharme, K. A., & Brawley, L. R. (1995). Predicting the intentions and behavior of exercise initiatives using two forms of self-efficacy. *Journal of Behavioral Medicine, 18,* 479–497.

Duda, J. L. (1989). Relationship between task and ego orientation and the perceived purpose of sport among high school athletes. *Journal of Sport & Exercise Psychology, 11,* 318–335.

Duffy, E. (1957). The psychological significance of the concept of arousal or activation. *Psychological Review, 64,* 265–275.

Dugdale, J. R., Eklund, R. C., & Gordon, S. (2002). Expected and unexpected stressors in major international competitions: Appraisal, coping, and performance. *The Sport Psychologist, 16,* 20–33.

Duke, M., Johnson, T. C., & Nowicki, S., Jr. (1977). Effects of sports fitness campus experience on locus of control orientation in children, ages 6 to 14. *Research Quarterly, 48*(2), 280–283.

Dunn, A. L., & Blair, S. N. (1997). Exercise prescription. In W. P. Morgan (Ed.), *Physical activity & mental health* (pp. 49–62). Washington, D.C.: Taylor & Francis Publisher.

Dunn, J. G. H. (1999). A theoretical framework for structuring the content of competitive worry in ice hockey. *Journal of Sport & Exercise Psychology, 21,* 259–279.

Dunn, J. G. H., & Dunn, J. C. (1999). Goal orientation, perceptions of aggression, and sportspersonship in elite male youth ice hockey players. *The Sport Psychologist, 13,* 183–200.

Dunn, J. G. H., Dunn, J. D., & Syrotuik, D. G. (2002). Relationship between multidimensional perfectionism and goal orientations in sport. *Journal of Sport and Exercise Psychology, 24,* 376–395.

Dunn, J. G. H., & Holt, N. L. (2003). Collegiate ice hockey players' perceptions of the delivery of an applied sport psychology program. *The Sport Psychologist, 17,* 351–368.

Dunn, J. G. H., & Holt, N. L. (2004). A qualitative investigation of personal-disclosure mutual sharing team building activity. *The Sport Psychologist, 18,* 363–380.

Dunton, G. F., Jamner, M. S., & Cooper, D. M. (2003). Physical self-concept in adolescent girls: Behavioral and physical correlation. *Research Quarterly for Exercise and Sport, 74,* 360–365.

Durand-Bush, N., Salmela, J. H., & Green-Demers, I. (2001). The Ottawa Mental Skills Assessment Tool (OMSAT-3). *The Sport Psychologist, 15,* 1–19.

Durand-Bush, N., & Salmela, J. H. (2002). The development of maintenance of expert athletic performances: Perception of world and Olympic champions. *Journal of Applied Sport Psychology, 14,* 154–171.

Durr, K. R. (1996). *Relationship between state anxiety and performance in high school divers.* Unpublished master's thesis, University of Missouri, Columbia.

D'Urso, V., Petrosso, A., & Robazza, C. (2002). Emotions, perceived qualities, and performance of rugby players. *The Sport Psychologist, 16,* 173–199.

Dweck, C. S. (1975). The role of expectations and attributions in the alleviation of learned helplessness. *Journal of Personality and Social Psychology, 31,* 674–685.

Dweck, C. S. (1980). Learned helplessness in sport. In C. H. Nadeau, W. R. Halliwell, K. M. Newell, & G. C. Roberts (Eds.). *Psychology of motor behavior and sport, 1979.* Champaign, IL: Human Kinetics.

E

Eades, A. (1991). *An investigation of burnout in intercollegiate athletes: The development of the Eades Athletic Burnout Inventory.* Paper presented at the North American Society for the Psychology of Sport and Physical Activity National Conference, Asilomar, CA.

Easterbrook, J. A. (1959). The effect of emotion on cue utilization and the organization of behavior. *Psychological Review, 66,* 183–201.

Ebbeck, V., & Gibbons, S. L. (1998). The effect of a team building program on the self-conceptions of grade 6 and 7 physical education students. *Journal of Sport & Exercise Psychology, 20,* 300–310.

Eccles, D. W., & Tenenbaum, G. (2004). Why an expert team is more than a team of experts: A social-cognitive conceptualization of team coordination and communication in sport. *The Journal of Sport and Exercise Psychology, 26,* 542–560.

Edwards, T., & Hardy, L. (1996). The interactive effects of intensity and direction of cognitive and somatic anxiety and self-confidence upon performance. *Journal of Sport & Exercise Psychology, 18,* 296–312.

Edwards, T., Kington, K., Hardy, L., & Gould, D. (2002). A qualitative analysis of catastrophic performances and the associated thoughts, feelings, and emotions. *The Sport Psychologist, 16,* 1–19.

Eisler, L., & Spink, K. S. (1998). Effects of scoring configuration and task cohesion on the perceptions of psychological momentum. *Journal of Sport & Exercise Psychology, 20,* 311–320.

Ekkekakis, P., Hall, E. E., & Petruzello, S. J. (1999). Measuring state anxiety in the context of acute exercise using the State Anxiety Inventory: An attempt to resolve the brouhaha. *Journal of Sport & Exercise Psychology, 21,* 205–229.

Eklund, R. C., & Crawford, S. (1994). Active women, social physique anxiety, and exercise. *Journal of Sport & Exercise Psychology, 16,* 431–448.

Eklund, R. C., Grove, J. R., & Heard, N. P. (1998). The measurement of slump-related coping: Factorial validity of the COPE and modified-COPE inventories. *Journal of Sport & Exercise Psychology, 20,* 157–175.

Elston, T., & Ginir, K. A. M. (2004). The effects of self-set versus assigned goals on exercises' self-efficacy for an unfamiliar task. *Journal of Sport and Exercise Psychology, 26,* 500–504.

Emery, C. F., & Blumenthal, J. A. (1988). Effects of exercise training on psychological functioning in healthy Type A men. *Psychology and Health, 2,* 367–379.

Endler, N. S. (1978). The interaction model of anxiety: Some possible implications. In D. M. Landers & R. W. Christina (Eds.), *Psychology of motor behavior and sport—1977* (pp. 332–351). Champaign, IL: Human Kinetics.

Endler, N. S. (1983). Interactionism: A personality model but not yet a theory. In M. M. Page (Ed.), *Nebraska Symposium on Motivation (1992): Personality–Current theory and research* (pp. 155–200). Lincoln: University of Nebraska Press.

Endler, N. S., & Parker, J. D. A. (1990). *Coping Inventory for Stressful Situations (CISS): Manual.* Toronto, Ontario: Multihealth Systems, Inc.

Endler, N. S., Parker. J. D. A., Bayby, R. M, & Cox, B. J. (1991). *Journal of Personality and Social Psychology, 60,* 919–926.

Engelhardt, G. M. (1995). Fighting behavior and winning national hockey league games: A paradox. *Perceptual and Motor Skills, 80,* 416–418.

Epstein, J. (1989). Family structures and student motivation: A developmental perspective. In C. Ames & R. Ames (Eds.), *Research on motivation in education* (Vol. 3, pp. 259–295). New York: Academic Press.

Erickson, M. H. (1980). Hypnosis: A general review. In E. L. Rossi (Ed.), *The collected papers of Milton H. Erickson on hypnosis,* Vol. 3 (pp. 13–20). New York: Irvington. (Original work published in 1941.)

Escarti, A., & Guzman, J. F. (1999). Effects of feedback on self-efficacy, performance, and choice in an athletic task. *Journal of Applied Sport Psychology, 11,* 83–96.

Estabrooks, P., & Courneya, K. S. (1997). Relationships among self-schema, intention, and exercise behavior. *Journal of Sport & Exercise Psychology, 19,* 156–168.

Estabrooks, P. A. (2000). Sustaining exercise participation through group cohesion. *Exercise and Sport Science Reviews, 28,* 63–67.

Etnier, J. L., & Landers, D. M. (1996). The influence of procedural variables on the efficacy of mental practice. *The Sport Psychologist, 10,* 48–57.

Etzel, E. F., Watson, J. C., II, & Zizzi, S. (2004). A web-based survey of AAASP members' ethical beliefs and behaviors in the new millennium. *Journal of Applied Sport Psychology, 16,* 236–250.

Eubank, M., Collins, D., & Smith, N. (2000). The influence of anxiety direction on processing bias. *Journal of Sport and Exercise Psychology, 22,* 292–306.

Eubank, M., Collins, D., & Smith, N. (2002). Anxiety and ambiguity: It's all open to interpretation. *Journal of Sport and Exercise Psychology, 24,* 239–253.

Evans, L., & Hardy, L. (2002a). Injury rehabilitation: A goal-setting intervention study. *Research Quarterly for Exercise and Sport, 73,* 310–319.

Evans, L., & Hardy, L. (2002b). Injury rehabilitation: A qualitative follow-up study. *Research Quarterly for Exercise and Sport, 73,* 320–329.

Evans, L., Jones, L., & Mullen, R. (2004). Am imagery intervention during the competitive season with an elite rugby union player. *The Sport Psychologist, 18,* 252–271.

Ewing, M. E., & Seefeldt, V. (1996). Patterns of participation and attrition in American agency-sponsored youth sports. In F. L. Smoll & R. E. Smith (Eds.), *Children and youth in sport: A biopsychosocial perspective* (pp. 31–45). Madison, WI: Brown & Benchmark.

Exner, J. E., Jr. (1986). *The Rorschach: A comprehensive system.* New York, NY. Wiley.

Eys, M. A., Hardy, J., Carron, A. V., & Beauchamp, M. R. (2003). The relationship between task cohesion and competitive state anxiety. *Journal of Sport and Exercise Psychology, 25,* 66–76.

Eysenck, H. J., & Eysenck, S. B. G. (1968). *Eysenck personality inventory manual.* London: University of London Press.

F

Fairall, D. G., & Rodgers, W. M. (1997). The effects of goal-setting method on goal attributes in athletics: A field experiment. *Journal of Sport & Exercise Psychology, 19,* 1–16.

Fallstrom, R. B. (Feb. 7, 1993). Antlers rack up reputation with opponents. *Columbia Daily Tribune* (MO), 5B.

Farrell, P. A., Gustafson, A. B., Garthwaite, T. L., Kalkhoff, R. K., Cowley, A. W., Jr., & Morgan, W. P. (1986). Influence of endogenous opioids on the response of selected hormones to exercise in man. *Journal of Applied Physiology, 61*(3), 1051–1057.

Faulkner, F., & Sparkes, S. (1999). Exercise as therapy for schizophrenia: An ethnographic study. *Journal of Sport & Exercise Psychology, 21,* 52–69.

Fave, A. D., Bassi, M., & Massimini, F. (2003). Quality of experience and risk perception in high-altitude rock climbing. *Journal of Applied Sport Psychology, 15,* 82–98.

Fawcett, J., Mass, J. W., & Dekirmenjiar, H. (1972). Depression and MHPG excretion. *Archives of General Psychiatry, 26,* 246–251.

Fazey, J., & Hardy, L. (1988). *The inverted-U hypothesis: A catastrophe for sport psychology?* British Association of Sports Sciences Monograph No. 1. Leeds: The National Coaching Foundation.

Feinstein, J. (October 21, 2002). The punch. *SportsIllustrated, 97,* 68–75.

Feltz, D. L., Chase, M. A., Moritz, S., & Sullivan, P. (1999). Development of the multidimensional coaching efficacy scale. *Journal of Educational Psychology, 91,* 765–776.

Feltz, D. L., & Landers, D. M. (1983). The effects of mental practice on motor skill learning and performance: A meta-analysis. *Journal of Sport Psychology, 5,* 25–57.

Fender, L. K. (1989). Athlete burnout: Potential for research and intervention strategies. *The Sport Psychologist, 3,* 63–71.

Fenz, W. D. (1975). Coping mechanisms and performance under stress. In D. M. Landers (Ed.), *Psychology of sport and motor behavior, 11* (pp. 3–24). Penn State HPER Series, No. 10. University Park: Pennsylvania State University Press.

FEPSAC (1996). Position statement of the European Federation of Sport Psychology (FEPSAC): I. Definition of sport psychology. *The Sport Psychologist, 10,* 221–223.

Ferrer-Caja, E., & Weiss, M. R. (2000). Predictors of intrinsic motivation among adolescent students in physical education. *Research Quarterly for Exercise and Sport, 71,* 267–279.

Fiedler, F. E. (1967). *A theory of leadership effectiveness.* New York: McGraw-Hill.

Fiedler, F. E., Chemers, M. M., & Mahar, L. (1977). *Improving leadership effectiveness—the leader match concept.* New York: John Wiley and Sons.

Filby, W. C. D., Maynard, I. W., & Graydon, J. K. (1999). The effect of multiple-goal strategies on performance outcomes in training and competition. *Journal of Applied Sport Psychology, 11,* 230–246.

Fimrite, R. (1985, November 4). K. C. had a blast. *Sports Illustrated,* 22–38.

Fisher, A. C. (1976). *Psychology of sport.* Palo Alto, CA: Mayfield.

Fisher, A. C. (1986, April). *Imagery from a sport psychology perspective.* Paper presented at the meeting of the American Alliance for Health, Physical Education, Recreation and Dance, Cincinnati, Ohio.

Fitts, P. M., & Posner, M. I. (1967). *Human performance.* Belmont, CA: Brooks/Cole.

Fleming, J. C., & Ginis, K. A. M. (2004). The effects of commercial exercise video models on women's self-presentational efficacy and exercise task self-efficacy. *Journal of Applied Sport Psychology, 16,* 92–102.

Fletcher, D., & Hanton, S. (2003). Sources of organizational stress in elite sports performances. *The Sport Psychologist, 17,* 175–195.

Flint, F. A. (1991). *The psychological effect of modeling in athletic injury rehabilitation.* Unpublished doctoral dissertation, University of Oregon, Eugene.

Focht, B. C., & Hausenblas, H. A. (2003). State anxiety responses to acute exercise in women with high social physique anxiety. *Journal of Sport and Exercise Psychology, 25,* 123–144.

Focht, B. C., & Hausenblas, H. A. (2004). Perceived evaluations threat and state anxiety during exercise in women with social physique anxiety. *Journal of Applied Sport Psychology, 16,* 361–368.

Focht, B. C., & Koltyn, K. F. (1999). Influence of resistance exercise of different intensities on state anxiety and blood pressure. *Medicine & Science in Sports & Exercise, 31,* 456–463.

Folkman, S., & Lazarus, R. S. (1985). If it changes it must be a process: Study of emotion and coping during three stages of a college examination. *Journal of Personality and Social Psychology, 48,* 150–170.

Fortier, M. S., Vallerand, R. J., Briere, N. M., & Provencher, P. J. (1995). Competitive and recreational sport structures and gender: A test of their relationship with sport motivation. *International Journal of Sport Psychology, 26,* 24–39.

Fox, K. R. (1990). *The physical self-perception profile manual.* DeKalb, IL: Northern Illinois University, Office for Health Promotion.

Fox, K. R., & Corbin, C. B. (1989). The physical self-perception profile: Development and preliminary validation. *Journal of Sport & Exercise Psychology, 11,* 408–430.

Fox, K. R., Goudas, M., Biddle, S., Duda, J., & Armstrong, N. (1994). Children's task and ego goal profiles in sport. *British Journal of Educational Psychology, 64,* 253–261.

Franken, R. E., Hill, R., & Kierstead, J. (1994). Sport interest as predicted by the personality measures of competitiveness, mastery, instrumentality, expressivity, and sensation seeking. *Personality and Individual Differences, 17*(4), 467–476.

Frederick, C. M., & Ryan, R. M. (1995). Self-determination in sport: A review using cognitive evaluation theory. *International Journal of Sport Psychology, 26,* 5–23.

Fredericks, J. A., & Eccles, J. (2004). Parental influences on youth involvement in sports. In M. R. Weiss (Ed.), *Developmental sport and exercise psychology: A lifespan perspective* (pp. 145–164). Morgantown, WV: Fitness Information Technology.

Freedson, P. S., Mihevic, P., Loucks, A., & Girandola, R. (1983). Physique, body composition, and psychological characteristics of competitive female bodybuilders. *The Physician and Sports Medicine, 11,* 85–90, 93.

Freud, S. (1933). *New introductory lectures on psychoanalysis.* New York: Norton.

Freud, S. (1950). Why war? In J. Strachey (Ed.), *Collected papers.* London: Hogarth.

Frey, M., Laguna, P. L., & Ravizza, K. (2003). Collegiate athletes' mental skill use and perception of success: An exploration of the practice and competition settings. *Journal of Applied Sport Psychology, 15,* 115–128.

Frieze, I. H. (1976). Causal attributions and information seeking to explain success and failure. *Journal of Research in Personality, 10,* 293–305.

Frost, R. O., Marten, P., Lahart, C., & Rosenblate, R. (1990). The dimensions of perfectionism. *Cognitive Therapy and Research, 14,* 449–468.

Fry, M. D. (2000). A developmental analysis of children's and adolescents' understanding of luck and ability in the physical domain. *Journal of Sport & Exercise Psychology, 22,* 145–166.

Fry, M. D., & Duda, J. L. (1997). A developmental examination of children's understanding of effort and ability in the physical and academic domains. *Research Quarterly for Exercise and Sport, 68,* 331–444.

Fry, M. D., & Newton, M. (2003). Application of achievement goal theory in an urban youth tennis setting. *Journal of Applied Sport Psychology, 15,* 50–66.

G

Gagne, M., Ryan, R. M., & Bargmann, K. (2003). Autonomy support and need satisfaction in the motivation and well-being of gymnasts. *Journal of Applied Sport Psychology, 15,* 372–390.

Gallimore, R., & Tharp, P. (2004). What a coach can teach a teacher, 1975–2004: Reflections and re-analysis of John Wooden's teaching practices. *The Sport Psychologist, 18,* 119–137.

Galros, N. M., & Janelle, C. M. (2001). Varying the mode of cardiovascular exercise to increase adherence. *Journal of Sport Behavior, 24,* 42–62.

Gammage, K. L., Ginis, K. A. M., & Hall, C. R. (2004). Self-presentational efficacy: Its influence on social anxiety in an exercise context. *Journal of Sport and Exercise Psychology, 26,* 179–190.

Gammage, K. L., Hall, C. R., Prapavessis, H., Maddison, R., Haase, A., & Martin, K. A. (2004). Re-examination of the factor structure and composition of the Self-Presentation in Exercise Questionnaire (SPEQ). *Journal of Applied Sport Psychology, 16,* 82–91.

Gammage, K. L., Hall, C. R., & Rodgers, W. M. (2000). More about exercise imagery. *The Sport Psychologist, 14,* 348–359.

Gano-Overway, L. A., & Ewing, M. E. (2004). A longitudinal perspective of the relationship between perceived motivational climate, goal orientations, and strategy use. *Research Quarterly for Exercise and Sport, 75,* 315–325.

Gardner, F. L., & Moore, Z. E. (2004). The multilevel clarification system for sport psychology(MCS-SP). *The Sport Psychologist, 18,* 89–109.

Garland, D. J., & Barry, J. R. (1990). Personality and leader behaviors in collegiate football: A multidimensional approach to performance. *Journal of Research in Personality, 24,* 355–370.

Garner, D. M., & Olmsted, M. P. (1984). *Eating disorders inventory manual.* Lutz, Florida: Psychological Assessment Resources.

Garrity, J. (June 26, 2000). Open and shut. *Sports Illustrated, 92,* 58–64.

Garza, D. L., & Feltz, D. L. (1998). Effects of selected mental practice on performance, self-efficacy, and competition confidence of figure skaters. *The Sport Psychologist, 12,* 1–15.

Gat, I., & McWhirter, B. (1998). Personality characteristics of competitive and recreational cyclists. *Journal of Sport Behavior, 21,* 408–420.

Gaudreau, P., & Blondin, J.-P. (2002). Development of a questionnaire for the assessment of coping strategies employed by athletes in competitive sport settings. *Psychology of Sport and Exercise, 3,* 1–34.

Gauvin, L., & Rejeski, W. J. (1993). The exercise-induced feeling inventory: Development and initial validation. *Journal of Sport & Exercise Psychology, 15,* 403–423.

Gayton, W. F., Very, M., & Hearns, J. (1993). Psychological momentum in team sports. *Journal of Sport Behavior, 16,* 121–123.

George, T. R., & Feltz, D. L. (1995). Motivation in sport from a collective efficacy perspective. *International Journal of Sport Psychology, 26,* 98–116.

Gernigon, C., d'Arripe-Longueville, F., Delignieres, D., & Ninot, G. (2004). A dynamic systems perspective on goal involvement states in sport. *Journal of Sport & Exercise Psychology, 26,* 572–596.

Gernigon, C., & Delloye, J. B. (2003). Self-efficacy, causal attribution, and track athlete performance following unexpected success or failure among elite sprinters. *The Sport Psychologist, 17,* 55–56.

Giacobbi, P., Jr., Foore, B., & Weinberg, R. S. (2004). Broken clubs and expletives: The sources of stress and coping responses of skilled and moderately skilled golfers. *Journal of Applied Sport Psychology, 16,* 166–182.

Giacobbi, P. R., Hausenblas, H. A., Fallon, E. A., & Hall, C. A. (2003). Even more about exercise imagery: A grounded theory of exercise imagery. *Journal of Applied Sport Psychology, 15,* 160–175.

Giacobbi, P. R., & Weinberg, R. S. (2000). An examination of coping in sport: Individual trait anxiety differences and situational consistency. *The Sport Psychologist, 14,* 42–62.

Gilbourne, D., & Taylor, A. H. (1998). From theory to practice: The integration of goal perspective theory and life development approaches within an injury-specific goal-setting program. *Journal of Applied Sport Psychology, 10,* 124–139.

Gill, D. L. (1980). Success-failure attributions in competitive groups: An exception to egocentrism. *Journal of Sport Psychology, 2,* 106–114.

Gill, D. L. (1993). Competitiveness and competitive orientation in sport. In R. N. Singer, M. Murphey, & L. K. Tennant (Eds.), *Handbook of research on sport psychology* (pp. 314–327). New York: Macmillan.

Gill, D. L. (1995). Women's place in the history of sport psychology. *The Sport Psychologist, 9,* 418–433.

Gill, D. L. (2001). Feminist sport psychology: A guide for our journey. *The Sport Psychologist, 15,* 363–372.

Gill, D. L., & Deeter, T. E. (1988). Development of the SOQ. *Research Quarterly for Exercise and Sport, 59,* 191–202.

Gill, D. L., Gross, J. B., & Huddleston, S. (1983). Participation motivation in youth sports. *International Journal of Sport Psychology, 14,* 1–14.

Ginnis, K. A. M., & Leary, M. R. (2004). Self-presentational processes in health-damaging behavior. *Journal of Applied Sport Psychology, 16,* 59–74.

Gladue, B. A. (1991). Qualitative and quantitative sex differences in self-reported aggressive behavior characteristics. *Psychological Reports, 68,* 675–684.

Gladwell, M. (August 2, 1999). The physical genius. *The New Yorker, 75,* 57–65.

Gladwell, M. (August 21 & 28, 2000). The art of failure: Why some people choke and others panic. *The New Yorker,* 84–92.

Godin, G. (1994). Theories of reasoned action and planned behavior: Usefulness for exercise promotion. *Medicine and Science in Sports and Exercise, 26,* 1391–1394.

Goode, K. T., & Roth, D. L. (1993). Factor analysis of cognitions during running: Association with mood change. *Journal of Sport & Exercise Psychology, 15,* 375–389.

Goodkin, K. (1988). Psychiatric aspects of HIV infection. *Texas Medicine, 84,* 55–61.

Gordon, S. (1990). A mental skills training program for the Western Australia cricket team. *The Sport Psychologist, 4,* 368–399.

Gordon, S., Potter, M., & Ford, I. W. (1998). Toward a psychoeducational curriculum for training sport-injury rehabilitation personnel. *Journal of Applied Sport Psychology, 10,* 140–156.

Gorely, T., & Gordon, S. (1995). An examination of the transtheoretical model and exercise behavior in older adults. *Journal of Sports & Exercise Psychology, 17,* 312–324.

Gotwals, J. K., Dunn, J. G. H., & Wayment, H. A. (2003). An examination of perfectionism and self-esteem in intercollegiate athletes. *Journal of Sport Behavior, 26,* 17–38.

Gould, D. (2002a). Sport psychology in the new millennium: The psychology of athletic excellence and beyond. *Journal of Applied Sport Psychology,* 137–139.

Gould, D. (2002b). Moving beyond the psychology of athletic excellences. *Journal of Applied Sport Psychology, 14,* 247–298.

Gould, D. (2006). Goal setting for peak performance. In J. M. Williams (Ed.), *Applied sport psychology: Personal growth to peak performance* (349–381). McGraw-Hill.

Gould, D., Dieffenbach, K., & Moffett, A. (2002). Psychological characteristics and their development in Olympic champions. *Journal of Applied Sport Psychology, 14,* 172–204.

Gould, D., Eklund, R. C., & Jackson, S. A. (1993). Coping strategies used by U.S. Olympic wrestlers. *Research Quarterly for Exercise and Sport, 64,* 83–93.

Gould, D., Feltz, D., Horn, T., & Weiss, M. (1982). Reasons for attrition in competitive youth swimming. *Journal of Sports Behavior, 5,* 155–165.

Gould, D., Finch, L. M., & Jackson, S. A. (1993). Coping strategies used by national champion figure skaters. *Research Quarterly for Exercise and Sport, 64,* 453–468.

Gould, D., Greenleaf, C., Chung, Y., & Guinan, D. (2002). A survey of U.S. Atlanta and Nagano Olympians: Variables perceived to influence performance. *Research Quarterly for Exercise and Sport, 73,* 175–186.

Gould, D., Greenleaf, C., Guinan, D., & Chung, Y. (2002). A survey of U.S. Olympic coaches: Variables perceived to have influenced athlete performances and coach effectiveness. *The Sport Psychologist, 16,* 229–250.

Gould, D., & Petlichkoff, L. (1988). Participation motivation and attrition in young athletes. In F. Smoll, R. Magill, & M. Ash (Eds.), *Children in sport* (pp. 161–178). Champaign, IL: Human Kinetics.

Gould, D., Petlichkoff, L., Simons, J., & Vevera, M. (1987). Relationship between competitive state anxiety inventory-2 subscales scores and pistol shooting performance. *Journal of Sport Psychology, 9,* 33–42.

Gould, D., & Pick, S. (1995). Sport psychology: The Griffith era. *The Sport Psychologist, 9,* 391–405.

Gould, D., Russell, M., Damarjian, N., & Lauer, L. (1999). A survey of mental skills training knowledge, opinions, and practices of junior tennis coaches. *Journal of Applied Sport Psychology, 11,* 28–50.

Gould, D., Tuffey, S., Udry, E., & Loehr, J. (1996). Burnout in competitive junior tennis players: II. Qualitative analysis. *The Sport Psychologist, 10,* 341–366.

Gould, D., Tuffey, S., Udry, E., & Loehr, J. (1997). Burnout in competitive junior tennis players: III. Individual differences in the burnout experience. *The Sport Psychologist, 11,* 257–276.

Gould, D., Udry, E., Bridges, D., & Beck, L. (1997). Stress sources encountered when rehabilitating from season-ending ski injuries. *The Sport Psychologist, 11,* 361–378.

Gould, D., Udry, E., Tuffy, S., & Loehr, J. (1996). Burnout in competitive junior tennis players: I. A quantitative psychological assessment. *The Sport Psychologist, 10,* 322–340.

Gould, S. J. (June 25, 2000). The brain of brawn. *The New York Times,* CXLIX, (#51, 430), section 4, p. 17.

Granito, V. J. (2002). Excellence is a journey, not a goal: The historical significance of Betty J. Wentz (1934–2001). *The Sport Psychologist, 16,* 291–295.

Gray, S. W., & Fernandez, S. J. (1990). Effects of visuo-motor behavior rehearsal with videotaped modeling on basketball shooting performance. *Psychology: A Journal of Human Behavior, 26,* 41–47.

Green, C. D. (2003). Psychology strikes out: Coleman R. Griffith and the Chicago Cubs. *History of Psychology, 6,* 267–283.

Green, S. L., & Weinberg, R. S. (2001). Relationships among athletic identity, coping skills, social support, and the psychological impact of injury in recreational participants. *Journal of Applied Sport Psychology, 13,* 40–59.

Greenberg, J. S. (1996). *Comprehensive stress management.* 5th ed. Madison, WI: Brown & Benchmark.

Greenleaf, C., Gould, D., & Dieffenbach, K. (2001). Factors influencing Olympic performance: Interviews with Atlanta and Nagano U.S. Olympics. *Journal of Applied Sport Psychology, 13,* 154–184.

Greenspan, M. J., & Feltz, D. L. (1989). Psychological interventions with athletes in competitive situations: A review. *The Sport Psychologist, 3,* 219–236.

Greenwood, C. M., Dzewaltowski, D. A., & French, R. (1990). Self-efficacy and psychological well being of wheelchair tennis participants. *Adapted Physical Activity Quarterly, 7,* 12–21.

Greer, D. L. (1983). Spectator booing and the home advantage: A study of social influence in the basketball arena. *Social Psychology Quarterly, 46,* 252–261.

Gregg, E., & Rejeski, J. (1990). Social psychobiologic dysfunction associated with anabolic steroid abuse: A review. *The Sport Psychologist, 4,* 275–284.

Grieve, F. G., Whelan, J. P., & Meyers, A. W. (2000). An experimental examination of the cohesion-performance relationship in an interactive team. *Journal of Applied Sport Psychology, 12,* 219–235.

Groslambert, A., Candau, R., Groppe, F., Dugue, B., & Rouillon, J. D. (2003). Effects of autogenic and imagery training on the shooting performances in Biathlon. *Research Quarterly for Exercise and Sport, 74,* 337–341.

Grouios, G. (1992). Mental practice: A review. *Journal of Sport Behavior, 15,* 42–59.

Grove, J. R., Fish, M., & Eklund, R. C. (2004). Changes in athletic identity following team selection: Self-protection versus self-enhancement. *Journal of Applied Sport Psychology, 16,* 75–81.

Grove, J. R., & Heard, N. P. (1997). Optimism and sport confidence as correlates of slump related coping among athletes. *The Sport Psychologist, 11,* 400–410.

Grove, J. R., Norton, P. J., Van Raalte, J. L., & Brewer, B. W. (1999). Stages of change as an outcome measure in the evaluation of mental skills training programs. *The Sport Psychologist, 13,* 107–116.

Grove, J. R., & Pargmann, D. (1986). Attributions and performance during competition. *Journal of Sport Psychology, 8,* 129–134.

Grove, J. R., & Prapavessis, H. (1992). Preliminary evidence for the reliability and validity of an abbreviated profile of mood states. *International Journal of Sport Psychology, 23,* 93–109.

Grove, J. R., & Prapavessis, H. (1995). The effect of skill level and sport outcomes on dimensional aspects of causal attributions. *Australian Psychologist, 30,* 92–95.

Gruber, J. J., & Gray, G. R. (1981). Factor patterns of variables influencing cohesiveness at various levels of basketball competition. *Research Quarterly for Exercise and Sport, 52,* 19–30.

Grusky, O. (1963). The effects of formal structure on managerial recruitment: A study of baseball organization. *Sociometry, 26,* 345–353.

Gutkind, S. M. (2004). Using solution-focused brief counseling to provide injury support. *The Sport Psychologist, 18,* 75–88.

Guyton, A. C. (1991). *Basic neuroscience: Anatomy & Physiology.* 2d ed. Philadelphia, PA: W. B. Saunders.

H

Haggar, M. S., Chatzisarantis, N. L. D., & Biddle, S. J. H. (2003). A meta-analytic review of the theories of reasoned action and planned behavior in physical activity: Predictive validity and the contribution of additional variables. *Journal of Sport and Exercise Psychology, 24,* 3–32.

Halberstam, D. (1994). *October 1964.* New York: Villard Books.

Hale, B. D., & Dannish, S. J. (1999). Putting the accreditation cart before the AAASP horse: A reply to Silva, Conroy and Zizzi. *Journal of Applied Sport Psychology, 11,* 321–328.

Hale, B. D., & Whitehouse, A. (1998). The effects of imagery-manipulated appraisal on intensity and direction of competitive anxiety. *The Sport Psychologist, 12,* 40–51.

Hale, B. S., Koch, K. R., & Raglin, J. S. (2000). State anxiety responses to 60-minutes of cross-training. *Medicine & Science in Sports & Exercise, 32,* Supplement, Abstract #497, S124.

Hall, C. R., Mack, D. E., Paivio, A., & Hausenblas, H. A. (1998). Imagery use by athletes: Development of the sport imagery questionnaire. *International Journal of Sport Psychology, 29,* 73–89.

Hall, C. R., & Martin, K. A. (1997). Measuring movement imagery abilities: A revision of the Movement Imagery Questionnaire. *Journal of Mental Imagery, 21,* 143–154.

Hall, C. R., & Pongrac, J. (1983). *Movement imagery questionnaire.* London, Ontario: University of Western Ontario.

Hall, C. R., Rodgers, W. M., & Barr, K. A. (1990). The use of imagery by athletes in selected sports. *The Sport Psychologist, 4,* 1–10.

Hall, E. G., & Hardy, C. J. (1991). Ready, aim, fire . . . relaxation strategies for enhancing pistol marksmanship. *Perceptual and Motor Skills, 72,* 775–786.

Hall, H. K., Kerr, A. W., & Matthews, J. (1998). Precompetitive anxiety in sport: The contribution of achievement goals and perfectionism. *Journal of Sport & Exercise Psychology, 20,* 194–217.

Hall, R. L. (2001). Shaking the foundation: Women of color in sport. *The Sport Psychologist, 15,* 386–400.

Halliburton, A. L., & Weiss, M. R. (2002). Sources of competence information and perceived motivational climate among adolescent female gymnasts varying in skill level. *Journal of Sport & Exercise Psychology, 24,* 396–419.

Hallinan, C. J. (1998). Dimensions of gender differentiation and centrality in the employment of university recreation centers. *Journal of Sport Behavior, 21,* 256–264.

Halpin, A. W. (1966). *Theory and research in administration.* London: Macmillan.

Hamilton, S. A., & Fremouw, W. J. (1985). Cognitive behavioral training for college basketball free-throw performance. *Cognitive Therapy and Research, 9,* 479–483.

Hammereister, J., & Burton, D. (2001). Stress, appraisal, and coping revisited: Examining the antecedents of competitive state anxiety with endurance athletes. *The Sport Psychologist, 15,* 66–90.

Hammereister, J., & Burton, D. (2004). Gender differences in coping with endurance sport stress: Are men from Mars and women from Venus? *Journal of Sport Behavior, 27,* 148–164.

Hanin, Y. L. (1980). A study of anxiety in sports. In W. F. Straub (Ed.), *Sport psychology: An analysis of athlete behavior* (pp. 236–249). New York: Mouvement Publications.

Hanin, Y. L. (1986). State-trait anxiety research on sports in the USSR. In C. D. Speilberger & R. Dias-Guerrero (Eds.), *Cross-cultural anxiety* (pp. 45–64). Washington, DC: Hemisphere.

Hanin, Y. L. (1989). Interpersonal and intragroup anxiety: Conceptual and methodological issues. In D. Hackfort & C. D. Spielberger (Eds.), *Anxiety in sports: An international perspective* (pp. 19–28). Washington, DC: Hemisphere Publishing Corporation.

Hanin, Y. L. (2000). Appendix B. IZOF-based emotions—profiling: Step-wise procedures and forms. In Y. L. Hanin (Ed.), *Emotions in Sport* (pp. 303–313). Champaign, IL: Human Kinetics.

Hanin, Y. L., & Stambulora, N. B. (2002). Metaphoric description of performance states: An application of the IZOF model. *The Sport Psychologist, 16,* 396–415.

Hanin, Y. L., & Syrja, P. (1995). Performance affect in junior ice hockey players: An application of the individual zones of optimal functioning model. *The Sport Psychologist, 9,* 169–187.

Hanlon, T. (1994). *SportParent.* Champaign, IL: Human Kinetics.

Hanson, S. J., McCullagh, P., & Tonymon, P. (1992). The relationship of personality characteristics, life stress, and coping resources to athletic injury. *Journal of Sport and Exercise Psychology, 14*(3), 262–272.

Hanson, T. W., & Gould, D. (1988). Factors affecting the ability of coaches to estimate their athlete's trait and state anxiety levels. *The Sport Psychologist, 2,* 298–313.

Hanton, S., & Connaughton, D. (2002). Perceived control of anxiety and its relationship to self-confidence. *Research Quarterly for Exercise and Sport, 73,* 87–97.

Hanton, S., & Jones, G. (1999a). The acquisition and development of cognitive skills and strategies: I. Making the butterflies fly in formation. *The Sport Psychologist, 13,* 1–21.

Hanton, S., & Jones, G. (1999b). The effects of a multimodal intervention program on performers: II. Training the butterflies to fly in formation. *The Sport Psychologist, 13,* 22–41.

Hardman, K. (1973). A dual approach to the study of personality and performance in sport. In H. T. A. Whiting, K. Hardman, L. B. Hendry, & M. G. Jones (Eds.), *Personality and performance in physical education and sport.* London: Kimpton.

Hardy, J., Gammage, K., & Hall, C. (2001). A descriptive study of athlete self-talk. *The Sport Psychologist 15,* 306–318.

Hardy, J., Hall, C. R., & Hardy, L. (2004). A note on athletes' use of self-talk. *Journal of Applied Sport Psychology, 16,* 251–257.

Hardy, L. (1997). The Coleman Roberts Griffith address: Three myths about applied consulting work. *Journal of Applied Sport Psychology, 9,* 277–284.

Hardy, L., & Callow, N. (1999). Efficacy of external and internal visual imagery perspectives for the enhancement of performance on tasks in which form is important. *Journal of Sport & Exercise Psychology, 21,* 95–112.

Hardy, L., & Parfitt, G. (1991). A catastrophe model of anxiety and performance. *British Journal of Psychology, 82,* 163–178.

Hardy, L., Parfitt, G., & Pates, J. (1994). Performance catastrophes in sport: A test of the hysteresis hypothesis. *Journal of Sport Sciences, 12,* 327–334.

Hardy, L., Woodman, T., & Carrington (2004). Is self-confidence a bias factor in higher–order catastrophe models? *Journal of Sport and Exercise Psychology, 26,* 359–368.

Harger, G. J., & Raglin, J. S. (1994). Correspondence between actual and recalled precompetition anxiety in collegiate track and field athletes. *Journal of Sport & Exercise Psychology, 16,* 206–211.

Harlow, R. G. (1951). Masculine inadequacy and compensatory development of physique. *Journal of Personality, 19,* 312–323.

Harrell, W. A. (1980). Aggression by high school basketball players: An observational study of the effects of opponents' aggression and frustration-inducing factors. *International Journal of Sport Psychology, 11,* 290–298.

Harris, D. V., & Robinson, W. J. (1986). The effects of skill level on EMG activity during internal and external imagery. *Journal of Sport Psychology, 8,* 105–111.

Harrison, J., & MacKinnon, P. C. B. (1966). Physiological role of the adrenal medulla in the palmar anhidrotic response in stress. *Journal of Applied Physiology, 21,* 88–92.

Hart, E. A., Leary, M. R., & Rejeski, W. J. (1989). The measurement of social physique anxiety. *Journal of Sport & Exercise Psychology, 11,* 94–104.

Harte, J. L., & Eifert, G. H. (1995). The effects of running, environment, and attentional focus on athletes' catecholamine and cortisol levels and mood. *Psychophysiology, 32,* 49–54.

Harter, S. (1978). Effectance motivation reconsidered: Towards a developmental model. *Human Development, 21,* 34–64.

Hartung, G. H., & Farge, E. J. (1977). Personality and physiological traits in middle-aged runners and joggers. *Journal of Gerontology, 32,* 541–548.

Harwood, C. (2002). Assessing achievement goals in sport: Caveats for consultants and a case for contextualization. *Journal of Applied Sport Psychology, 14,* 106–119.

Harwood, C., Cummings, J., & Fletcher, D. (2004). Motivational profiles and psychological skills use within elite youth sport. *Journal of Applied Sport Psychology, 16,* 318–332.

Harwood, C., Cummings, J., & Hall, C. R. (2003). Imagery use in elite youth sport participants: Reinforcing the applied significance of achievement goal theory. *Research Quarterly for Exercise and Sport, 74,* 292–300.

Harwood, C., & Hardy, L. (2001). Persistence and effort in moving achievement goal research forward: A response to Treasure and colleagues. *Journal of Sport & Exercise Psychology, 23,* 330–345.

Harwood, C., Hardy, L., & Swain, A. (2000). Achievement goals in sport: A critique of conceptual and measurement issues. *Journal of Sport & Exercise Psychology, 22,* 235–255.

Harwood, C., & Swain, A. (2001). The development and activation of achievement goals in tennis: I. Understanding the underlying factors. *The Sport Psychologist, 15,* 319–341.

Harwood, C., & Swain, A. (2002). The development and activation of achievement goals in tennis: II. A player, parent, and coach intervention. *The Sport Psychologist, 16,* 138–159.

Hathaway, S. R., & McKinley, J. C. (1940). A multiphasic personality schedule (Minnesota): I. Construction of the schedule. *Journal of Psychology, 10,* 249–254.

Hathaway, S. R., & McKinley, J. C. (1967). *Minnesota Multiphasic Personality Inventory manual.* New York: Psychological Corporation.

Hatzigeorgiadis, A., & Biddle, S. (1999). The effect of goal orientation and perceived competence on cognitive interference during tennis and snooker performance. *Journal of Sports Behavior, 22,* 479–501.

Hatzigeorgiadis, A., Theodorakis, Y., & Zourbanos, N. (2004). Self-talk in the swimming pool: The effects of self-talk on thought content and performance on water-polo tasks. *Journal of Applied Sport Psychology, 16,* 138–150.

Hausenblas, H. A., Brewer, B. W., & Van Raalte, J. L. (2004). Self-presentation and exercise. *Journal of Applied Sport Psychology, 16,* 3–18.

Hausenblas, H. A., & Carron, A. V. (1996). Group cohesion and self-handicapping in female and male athletes. *Journal of Sport & Exercise Psychology, 18,* 132–143.

Hausenblas, H. A., & Carron, A. V. (1999). Eating disorder indices and athletes: An integration. *Journal of Sport & Exercise Psychology, 21,* 230–258.

Hausenblas, H. A., & Carron, A. V. (2000). Group influences on eating and dieting behaviors in male and female varsity athletes. *Journal of Sport Behavior, 23,* 33–41.

Hausenblas, H. A., Carron, A. V., & Mack, D. E. (1997). Application of the theories of reasoned action and planned behavior to exercise behavior: A meta-analysis. *Journal of Sport & Exercise Psychology, 19,* 36–51.

Hausenblas, H. A., & Downs, D. S. (2001). Comparison of body image between athletes and nonathletes: A meta-analytic review. *Journal of Applied Sport Psychology, 13,* 323–339.

Hausenblas, H. A., Hall, C. R., Rodgers, W. M., & Munroe, K. J. (1999). Exercise imagery: Its nature and measurement. *Journal of Applied Sport Psychology, 11,* 171–180.

Hausenblas, H. A., & McNally, K. D. (2004). Eating disorder prevalence and symptoms for track and field athletes and nonathletes. *Journal of Applied Sport Psychology, 16,* 274–286.

Hayes, S., Crocker, P., & Kowalski, K. (1999). Gender differences in physical self-perceptions, global self-esteem and physical activity: Evaluation of the physical self-perception profile model. *Journal of Sport Behavior, 22,* 1–14.

Hays, K. F. (2002). The enhancement of performance excellence among performing artists. *Journal of Applied Sport Psychology, 14,* 299–312.

Hecker, J. E., & Kaczor, L. M. (1988). Application of imagery theory to sport psychology: Some preliminary findings. *Journal of Sport & Exercise Psychology, 10,* 363–373.

Heider, F. (1944). Social perception and phenomenal causality. *Psychological Review, 51,* 358–374.

Heider, F. (1958). *The psychology of interpersonal relations.* New York: John Wiley and Sons.

Heil, J. (1993). *Psychology of sport injury.* Champaign, IL: Human Kinetics.

Henry, F. M. (1941). Personality differences in athletes, physical education, and aviation students. *Psychological Bulletin, 38,* 745.

Henschen, K. P., Horvat, M., & French, R. (1984). A visual comparison of psychological profiles between able-bodied and wheelchair athletes. *Adapted Physical Activity Quarterly, 1,* 118–124.

Hersey, P., & Blanchard, K. H. (1977). *Management of organizational behavior.* Englewood Cliffs, NJ: Prentice-Hall.

Heuzé, J.-P., & Fontayne, P. (2002). Questionnaire sur 1, Ambiance du Groupe: A French-language instrument for measuring group cohesion. *Journal of Sport and Exercise Psychology,* 42–67.

Hewitt, P. L., & Flett, G. L. (1991). Perfectionism in the self and social contexts: Conceptualization, assessment, and association with psychopathology. *Journal of Personality and Social Psychology, 60,* 456–470.

Heyman, S. R. (1987). Research and intervention in sport psychology: Issues encountered in working with an amateur boxer. *The Sport Psychologist, 1,* 208–223.

Hilgard, E. R. (1973). A neodissociation interpretation of pain reduction in hypnosis. *Psychological Review, 80,* 396–411.

Hilgard, E. R. (1986). *Divided consciousness: Multiple controls in human thought and action* (expanded edition). New York: Wiley.

Hilgard, E. R. (1994). Neodissociation theory. In S. J. Lynn & J. W. Rhue (Eds.), *Dissociation: Clinical and theoretical perspectives.* New York: Guilford.

Hill, K. L., & Borden, F. (1995). The effect of attentional cueing scripts on competitive bowling performance. *International Journal of Sport Psychology, 26,* 503–512.

Hinshaw, K. E. (1991). The effects of mental practice on motor skill performance: Critical evaluation and meta-analysis. *Imagination, Cognition, and Personality, 11,* 3–35.

Hird, J. S., Landers, D. M., Thomas, J. R., & Horan, J. J. (1991). Physical practice is superior to mental practice in enhancing cognitive and motor task performance. *Journal of Sport & Exercise Performance, 13,* 281–293.

Hodge, K., & Petlichkoff, L. (2000). Goal profiles in sport motivation: A cluster analysis. *Journal of Sport & Exercise Psychology, 22,* 256–272.

Hoffer, R. (April 16, 2001). Four-gone conclusion. *Sports Illustrated, 94,* 34–41.

Hoffman, P. (1997). The endorphin hypothesis. In W. P. Morgan (Ed.), *Physical activity & mental health* (pp. 163–177). Washington, D.C.: Taylor & Francis Publisher.

Hollander, D. B., & Acevedo, E. O. (2000). Successful English Channel swimming: The peak experience. *The Sport Psychologist, 14,* 1–16.

Hollander, E. P. (1976). *Principles and methods of social psychology.* 3rd ed. New York: Oxford University Press.

Holsopple, J. Q., & Miale, F. R. (1954). *Sentence completion.* Springfield, IL: Charles C. Thomas.

Holt, N. L., & Hogg, J. M. (2002). Perceptions of stress and coping during preparations for the 1999 Women's Soccer World Cup finals. *The Sport Psychologist, 16,* 251–271.

Holt, N. L., & Morley, D. (2004). Gender differences in psychosocial factors associated with athletic success during childhood. *The Sport Psychologist, 18,* 138–153.

Holt, N. L., & Sparkes, A. C. (2001). An ethnographic study of cohesiveness in a college soccer team over a season. *The Sport Psychologist,* 237–259.

Hooper, S. L., & MacKinnon, L. T. (1995). Monitoring overtraining in athletes: Recommendations. *Sports Medicine, 20,* 321–327.

Hooper, S. L., MacKinnon, L. T., & Hanzahan, S. (1997). Mood states as an indication of staleness and recovery. *International Journal of Sport Psychology, 28,* 1–12.

Horn, T. S. (1984). Expectancy effects in the interscholastic athletic setting: Methodological considerations. *Journal of Sport Psychology, 6,* 60–76.

Horne, T., & Carron, A. V. (1985). Compatibility in coach-athlete relationships. *Journal of Sport Psychology, 7,* 137–149.

House, R. J., & Mitchell, T. R. (1974, Autumn). Path-goal theory of leadership. *Journal of Contemporary Business, 5,* 81–97.

Huddy, D. C., & Cash, T. F. (1997). Body image attitudes among male marathon runners: A controlled comparative study. *International Journal of Sport Psychology, 28,* 227–236.

Hudson, J., & Bates, M. D. (2000). Factors affecting reversals: A laboratory study. *Perceptual and Motion Skills, 91,* 373–384.

Hudson, J., & Walker, N. C. (2002). Metamotivational state reversals during matchplay golf: An idiographic approach. *The Sport Psychologist, 16,* 200–217.

Hughes, S. L., Case, H. S., Stuempfle, K. J., & Evans, D. S. (2003). Personality profiles of Iditasport Ultra-marathon participants. *Journal of Applied Sport Psychology, 15,* 256–261.

Hull, C. L. (1943). *Principles of behavior.* New York: Appleton-Century-Crofts, Inc.

Hull, C. L. (1951). *Essentials of behavior.* New Haven, CT: Yale University Press.

Husak, W. S., & Hemenway, D. P. (1986). The influence of competition day practice on the activation and performance of collegiate swimmers. *Journal of Sport Behavior, 9,* 95–100.

I

Imlay, G. J., Carda, R. D., Stanbrough, M. E., Dreiling, A. M., & O'-Connor, P. J. (1995). Anxiety and athletic performance: A test of Zone of Optimal Functioning theory. *International Journal of Sport Psychology, 26,* 295–306.

Ironson, G., LaPerriere, A., Antoni, M., Klimas, N., Fletcher, M. A., & Schneiderman, N. (1990). Changes in immunologic and psychological measures as a function of anticipation and reaction to news of HIV–1 antibody status. *Psychosomatic Medicine, 52,* 247–270.

Is it safe. (2000, December 19). Androstenedione (made famous by baseball's Mark McGuire)—Is it safe? *Columbia University's Health Education Fitness Nutrition Web-page* (www.goaskalice .columbia.edu/1385).

Isaac, A., Marks, D. F., & Russell, D. G. (1986). An instrument for assessing imagery of movement: The vividness of movement imagery questionnaire (VMIQ). *Journal of Mental Imagery, 10,* 23–30.

Isaacs, P. (1982). *Hypnotic responsiveness and dimensions of thinking style and imagery.* Unpublished doctoral dissertation, University of Waterloo, Waterloo, Ontario.

Ito, M. (1979). The differential effects of hypnosis and motivational suggestions on muscular strength. *Japanese Journal of Physical Education, 24,* 93–100.

J

Jackson, S. A. (1992). Athletes in flow: A qualitative investigation of flow states in elite figure skaters. *Journal of Applied Sport Psychology, 4,* 161–180.

Jackson, S. A. (1995). Factors influencing the occurrence of flow state in elite athletes. *Journal of Applied Sport Psychology, 7,* 138–166.

Jackson, S. A. (1996). Toward a conceptual understanding of the flow experience in elite athletes. *Research Quarterly for Exercise and Sport, 67,* 76–90.

Jackson, S. A., & Eklund, R. C. (2002). Assessing flow in physical activity: The Flow State Scale-2 and Dispositional Flow Scale-2, *Journal of Sport and Educational Psychology, 24,* 133–150.

Jackson, S. A., & Marsh, H. W. (1996). Development and validation of a scale to measure optimal experience: The flow state scale. *Journal of Sport and Exercise Psychology, 18,* 17–35.

Jackson, S. A., Ford, S. K., Kimiecik, J. G., & Marsh, H. W. (1998). Psychological correlates of flow in sport. *Journal of Sport & Exercise Psychology, 20,* 358–378.

Jackson, S. A., Thomas, P. R., Marsh, H. W., Smethurst, C. J. (2001). Relationship between flow, self-concept, psychological skills, and performance. *Journal of Applied Sport Psychology, 13,* 229–153.

Jacobson, E. (1929). *Progressive relaxation.* 1st ed. Chicago: University of Chicago Press.

Jacobson, E. (1938). *Progressive relaxation.* 2d ed. Chicago: University of Chicago Press.

Jakicic, J. M., Winters, C., Lang, W., & Wing, R. R. (1999, October 27). Effects of intermittent exercise and use of home exercise equipment on adherence, weight loss, and fitness in overweight women. *Journal of American Medical Association, 282,* 1554–1560.

Jambor, E. A., & Rudisill, M. E. (1992). The relationship between children's locus of control and sport choices. *Journal of Human Movement Studies, 22,* 35–48.

Jambor, E. A., & Zhang, J. J. (1997). Investigating leadership, gender and coaching level using the revised leadership for sport scale. *Journal of Sport Behavior, 20,* 313–321.

James, W. (1890). *The principles of psychology* (Vol. 1). New York: Henry Holt and Company.

Janelle, C. M., Singer, R. N., & Williams, A. M. (1999). External distraction and attentional narrowing: Visual search evidence. *Journal of Sport & Exercise Psychology, 21,* 70–91.

Janssen, J. J., & Sheikh, A. A. (1994). Enhancing athletic performance through imagery: An overview. In A. A. Sheikh & E. R. Korn (Eds.), *Imagery in sports and physical performance.* Amityville, NY: Baywood.

Jenkins, L. (December 27, 2004). Peyton Manning breaks Marino's record. *The New York Times* (*NYTimes.com*). http://www.nytimes.com/2004/ 12/27/sports/football

Jerome, G. J., & Williams, J. M. (2000). Intensity and interpretation of competitive state anxiety: Relationship to performance and repressive coping. *Journal of Applied Sport Psychology, 12,* 236–250.

John, O. P., & Srivastava, S. (1999). The big five trait taxonomy: History, measurement, and theoretical perspectives. In L. A. Pervin & O. P. John (Eds.), *Handbook of personality: Theory and research* (pp. 102–138). New York: The Guilford Press.

Johnson, J. E., & Dabbs, J. M., Jr. (1967). Enumeration of active sweat glands: A sample physiological indicator of psychological changes. *Nursing Research, 16,* 273–276.

Johnson, J. J. M., Hrycaiko, D. W., Johnson, G. V., & Halas, J. M. (2004). Self-talk and female youth soccer performance. *The Sport Psychologist, 18,* 44–59.

Johnson, S. R., Ostrow, A. C., Perna, F. M., & Etzel, E. F. (1997). The effects of group versus individual goal setting on bowling performance. *The Sport Psychologist, 11,* 190–200.

Johnson, W. O., & Moore, K. (Oct. 3, 1988). The loser. *Sports Illustrated, 69,* 20–27.

Johnson, W. R. (1961). Hypnosis and muscular performance. *Journal of Sports Medicine and Physical Fitness, 1,* 71–79.

Jones, E. E., & Rhodewalt, F. (1982). *The Self-handicapping scale.* Unpublished manuscript, Department of Psychology, Princeton Press.

Jones, G. (1991). Recent developments and current issues in competitive state anxiety research. *The Psychologist: Bulletin of the British Psychological Society, 4,* 152–155.

Jones, G. (2002). Performance excellence: A personal perspective on the link between sport and business. *Journal of Applied Sport Psychology, 14,* 268–281.

Jones, G., & Hanton, S. (1996). Interpretation of competitive anxiety symptoms and goal attainment expectancies. *Journal of Sport & Exercise Psy-chology, 18,* 144–157.

Jones, G., Hanton, S., & Connaughton, D. (2002). What is this thing called mental toughness? An investigation of elite sport performers. *Journal of Applied Sport Psychology, 14,* 205–218.

Jones, G., Hanton, S., & Swain, A. (1994). Intensity and interpretation of anxiety symptoms in elite and non-elite sports performers. *Personality & Individual Differences, 17,* 657–663.

Jones, G., & Swain, A. (1995). Predispositions to experience debilitative and facilitative anxiety in elite and nonelite performers. *The Sport Psychologist, 9,* 201–211.

Jones, J. G., & Cale, A. (1989). Precompetition temporal patterning of anxiety and self-confidence in males and females. *Journal of Sport Behavior, 12,* 183–195

Jones J. G., Swain, A., & Cale, A. (1991). Gender differences in precompetition temporal patterning and antecedents of anxiety and self-confidence. *Journal of Sport & Exercise Psychology, 13,* 1–15.

Jones, M. V. (2003). Controlling emotions in sport. *The Sport Psychologist, 17,* 471–486.

Jones, M. V., Mace, R. D., Bray, S. R., MacRae, A. W., & Stockbridge, C. (2002). The impact of motivational imagery on the emotional state and self-efficacy levels of novice climbers. *Journal of Sport Behavior, 25,* 57–73.

Jordan, M. (1994). *I can't accept not trying.* New York: Harper Collins Publishers.

Jowdy, D. P., & Harris, D. V. (1990). Muscular responses during mental imagery as a function of motor skill level. *Journal of Sport & Exercise Psychology, 12,* 191–201.

Jowett, S. (2003). When the "honeymoon" is over: A case study of a coach-athlete dyad in crisis. *The Sport Psychologist, 17,* 444–460.

Jowett, S., & Meek, G. A. (2000). The coach-athlete relationship in married couples: An exploratory content analysis. *The Sport Psychologist, 14,* 157–175.

K

Kahn, R. I., & Katz, D. (1960). Leadership practices in relation to productivity and morale. In D. Cartwright & A.T. Zander (Eds.), *Group dynamics.* Evanston, IL: Row, Peterson and Company.

Kalat, J. W. (1999). *Introduction to psychology.* Pacific Grove, CA: Brooks/Cole Wadsworth.

Kamata, A., Tenenbaum, G., & Hanin, Y. L. (2002). Individual zone of optional functioning (IZOF): A probabilistic estimation. *Journal of Sport and Exercise Psychology, 24,* 189–208.

Kane, J. E. (1970). Personality and physical abilities. In G. S. Kenyon (Ed.), *Contemporary psychology of sport: Second International Congress of Sports Psychology.* Chicago: The Athletic Institute.

Karteroliotis, C., & Gill, D. L. (1987). Temporal changes in psychological and physiological components of state anxiety. *Journal of Sport Psychology, 9,* 261–274.

Kavussanu, M., Crews, D. J., & Gill, D. L. (1998). The effects of single versus multiple measures of biofeedback on basketball free throw shooting performance. *International Journal of Sport Psychology, 29,* 132–144.

Kavussanu, M., & Ntoumanis, N. (2003). Participation in sport and moral functioning: Does ego orientation mediate their relationship? *Journal of Sport & Exercise Psychology, 25,* 501–518.

Kavussanu, M., & Roberts, G. C. (2001). Moral functioning in sport: An achievement goal perspective. *Journal of Sport & Exercise Psychology, 23,* 37–54.

Kavussanu, M., Roberts, G. C., & Ntoumanis, N. (2002). Contextual influences on moral functioning of college basketball players. *The Sport Psychologist, 16,* 347–367.

Kay, J. (1988, June 30). Trouble in river city: Players can't cite reason for Red's poor play. *Muncie Evening Press,* 15.

Keele, S. W. (1973). *Attention and human performance.* Pacific Palisades, CA: Goodyear Publishing Company.

Keele, S. W., & Hawkins, H. (1982). Exploration of individual differences relevant to high level skill. *Journal of Motor Behavior, 14,* 3–23.

Kellman, M., Attenburg, D., Lormes, W., & Steinacker, J. M. (2001). Assessing stress and recovery during preparation for the world championships in rowing. *The Sport Psychologist. 15,* 151–167.

Kellman, M., & Kallus, K. W. (2001). *The Recovery-Stress Questionnaire for Athletes: User Manual.* Champaign, IL: Human Kinetics.

Kendzierski, D. (1988). Self-schemata and exercise. *Basic and Applied Social Psychology, 9,* 45–61.

Kendzierski, D. (1990). Exercise self-schemata: Cognitive and behavioral correlates. *Health Psychology, 9,* 69–82.

Kendzierski, D. (October 2004). *Physical activity self-definitions: Research, issues, and implications.* Keynote address presented at the annual convention of the Association for the Advancement of Applied Sport Psychology, Minneapolis, Minnesota, October, 2004.

Kendzierski, D., Furr, R. M., Jr., & Schiavoni, J. (1998). Physical activity self-definitions: Correlates and perceived criteria. *Journal of Sport and Exercise Psychology, 20,* 176–193.

Kendzierski, D., & Sheffield, A. (2000). Self-schema and attributions for an exercise laps. *Basic and Applied Social Psychology, 22,* 1–8.

Kendzierski, D., Sheffield, A., & Morganstein, M. S. (2002). The role of self-schema in attributions for own versus other's exercise laps. *Basic and Applied Social Psychology, 24,* 251–260.

Kendzierski, D., & Whitaker, D. (1997). The role of self-schema in linking intentions with behavior. *Personality and Social Psychology Bulletin, 23,* 139–147.

Kenow, L. J., & Williams, J. M. (1992). Relationship between anxiety, self-confidence, and the evaluation of coaching behaviors. *The Sport Psychologist, 6,* 344–357.

Kenow, L. J., & Williams, J. M. (1999). Coach-athlete compatibility and athlete's perception of coaching behaviors. *Journal of Sport Behavior, 22,* 251–259.

Kepner, T. (2003, October 7). If pitching is the key Yankees like chances. *The New York Times,* http://www.nytimes.com/2003/10/7

Kepner, T. (2004, October 19). Even longer: Red Sox win game 5 in 14 innings. *The New York Times,* http://www.nytimes.com/2004/10/19/sports/baseball/19yankees.html?

Kepner, T. (2005, January 14). Baseball players and owners set though policy on steroid use. *The New York Times,* http://www.nytimes.com/2005/1/14/ sports/baseball

Kerick, S. E., Iso-Ahola, S. E., & Hatfield, B. D. (2000). Psychological momentum in target shooting: Cortical, cognitive-affective, and behavioral responses. *Journal of Sport & Exercise Psychology, 22,* 1–20.

Kerr, G., & Goss, J. (1996). The effects of a stress management program on injuries and stress levels. *Journal of Applied Sport Psychology, 8,* 109–117.

Kerr, G., & Leith, L. (1993). Stress management and athletic performance. *The Sport Psychologist, 7,* 221–231.

Kerr, J. H. (1997). *Motivation and emotion in sport: Reversal theory.* East Sussex, United Kingdom: Psychology Press Ltd.

Kerr, J. H., & Vlaswinkel, E. H. (1995). Sports participation at work: An aid to stress management. *International Journal of Stress Management, 2,* 87–96.

Keys, S., Tyminski, M., Davis, J., Bacon, C., Bengiovanni, J., & Hossain, A. (2001, May). The effects of long-term creatine supplementation on liver architecture in mice. *Medicine & Science in Sports & Exercise, 33,* S206, Abstract 1162.

Kilpatrick, M., Bartholomew, J., & Reimer, H. (2003). The measurement of goal orientations in exercise. *Journal of Sport Behavior, 26,* 121–136.

Kim, M. S., & Duda, J. L. (2003). The coping process: Cognitive appraisals of stress, coping strategies, and coping effectiveness. *The Sport Psychologist, 17,* 406–425.

Kim, M. Y., & Sugiyama, Y. (1992). The relation of performance norms and cohesiveness for Japanese school athletic teams. *Perceptual and Motor Skills, 74,* 1096–1098.

Kimiecik, J. C., & Horn, T. S. (1998). Parental beliefs and children's moderate-to-vigorous physical activity. *Research Quarterly for Exercise and Sport, 69,* 163–175.

Kimiecik, J. C., Horn, T. S., & Shurin, C. S. (1996). Relationships among children's beliefs, perceptions of their parent's beliefs and their moderate-to-vigorous physical activity. *Research Quarterly for Exercise and Sport, 67,* 324–336.

Kimiecik, J. C., & Stein, G. L. (1992). Examining flow experiences in sports contexts: Conceptual issues and methodological concerns. *Journal of Applied Sport Psychology, 4,* 144–160.

King, L. A., & Williams, T. A. (1997). Goal orientation and performance in martial arts. *Journal of Sport Behavior, 20,* 297–411.

King, P. (August 5, 2002). Inside the NFL. *Sports Illustrated, 97,* 68–69.

Kingston, K. M., & Hardy, L. (1997). Effects of different types of goals on processes that support performance. *The Sport Psychologist, 11,* 277–293.

Kirker, B., Tenenbaum, G., & Mattson, J. (2000). An investigation of the dynamics of aggression: Direct observation in ice hockey and basketball. *Research Quarterly for Exercise and Sport, 71,* 373–386.

Kirsch, I., & Lynn, S. J. (1995). The altered state of hypnosis. *American Psychologist, 50,* 846–858.

Kirsch, I., & Lynn, S. J. (1998). Dissociation theories of hypnosis. *Psychological Bulletin, 123,* 100–115.

Kitsantas, A., & Zimmerman, B. J. (2002). Comparing self-regulatory processes among novice, non-expert, and expert volleyball players: A microanalytic study. *Journal of Applied Sport Psychology, 14,* 91–105.

Klavora, P. (1978). An attempt to derive inverted-U curves based on the relationship between anxiety and athletic performance. In D. M. Landers & R. W. Christina (Eds.), *Psychology of motor behavior and sport—1977* (pp. 369–377). Champaign, IL: Human Kinetics Publishers.

Kleiber, D., & Brock, S. (1992). The effect of career-ending injuries on the subsequent well-being of elite college athletes. *Sociology of Sport Journal, 9,* 70–75.

Knight, J. L., & Giuliano, T. A. (2003). Blood, sweat and jeers: The impact of the media's heterosexist portrayals on perceptions of male and female athletes. *Journal of Sport Behavior, 26,* 272–384.

Knight under review. (February 3, 2004). Knight is under review after incident at market. *The New York Times,* http://www.nytimes.com/2004/2/3

Knott, P. D., & Drost, B. A. (1972). Effects of varying intensity of attack and fear arousal on the intensity of counteraggression. *Journal of Personality, 4,* 27–37.

Koehler, J. J., & Conley, C. A. (2003). The "hot hand" myth in professional basketball. *Journal of Sport & Exercise Psychology, 25,* 253–259.

Kolonay, B. J. (1977). *The effects of visuo-motor behavior rehearsal on athletic performance.* Unpublished master's thesis, Hunter College, New York.

Koltyn, K. F., Lynch, N. A., & Hill, D. W. (1998). Psychological responses to brief exhaustive cycling exercise in the morning and the evening. *International Journal of Sport Psychology, 29,* 145–156.

Kontos, A. P., & Breland-Noble, A. M. (2002). Racial/ethnic diversity in applied sport psychology: A multicultural introduction to working with athletes of color. *The Sport Psychologist, 16,* 296–315.

Kowal, J., & Fortier, M. S. (2000). Testing relationships from the hierarchical model of intrinsic and extrinsic motivation using flow as a motivational consequence. *Research Quarterly for Exercise and Sport, 71,* 171–181.

Kowalski, K. C., & Crocker, P. R. E. (2001). Development and validation of the coping function questionnaire for adolescents in sport. *Journal of Sport and Exercise Psychology, 23,* 136–155.

Kowalski, N. P., Crocker, P. R. E., & Kowalski, K. C. (2001). Physical self and physical activity relationships in college women: Does social physique anxiety moderate effects? *Research Quarterly for Exercise and Sport, 72,* 55–62.

Kozub, S. A., & Button, C. J. (2000). The influence of a competitive outcome on perceptions of cohesion in rugby and swimming teams. *International Journal of Sport Psychology, 31,* 82–95.

Kozub, S. B., & McDonnell, J. F. (2000). Exploring the relationship between cohesion and collective efficacy in rugby teams. *Journal of Sport Behavior, 23,* 120–129.

Kraemer, R. R., Dzewaltowski, D. A., Blair, M. S., Rinehardt, K. F., & Castracane, V. D. (1990). Mood alteration from treadmill running and its relationship to beta-endorphine, corticotrophine, and growth hormone. *The Journal of Sports Medicine and Physical Fitness, 30*(3), 241–246.

Kramer, J. (1970). *Lombardi: Winning is the only thing.* New York: The World Publishing Company.

Krane, T. D., Marks, M. A., Zaccaro, S. J., & Blair, V. (1996). Self-efficacy, personal goals, and wrestlers' self-regulation. *Journal of Sport & Exercise Psychology, 18,* 36–48.

Krane, V. (2001). One lesbian feminist epistemology: Integrating feminist standpoint, queer theory, and feminist cultural studies. *The Sport Psychologist, 15,* 401–411.

Krane, V., & Barber, H. (2005). Identity tensions in lesbian intercollegiate coaches. *Research Quarterly for Exercise and Sport, 76,* 67–81.

Krane, V., Joyce, D., & Rafeld, J. (1994). Competitive anxiety, situation criticality, and softball performance. *The Sport Psychologist, 8,* 58–72.

Kreider, R., Melton, C., Rasmussen, C., Greenwood, M., Cantler, E., Milnor, P., & Almanda, A. (2001, May). Effects of long-term creatine supplementation on renal function and muscle liver enzyme efflux. *Medicine & Science in Sports & Exercise, 33,* S207, Abstract 1163.

Kroll, W. (1967) Sixteen personality factor profiles of collegiate wrestlers. *Research Quarterly, 38,* 49–57.

Kroll, W., & Carlson, R. B. (1967). Discriminant function and hierarchical grouping analysis of karate participants' personality profiles. *Research Quarterly, 38,* 405–411.

Kroll, W., & Crenshaw, W. (1970). Multivariate personality profile analysis of four athletic groups. In G. S. Kenyon (Ed.), *Contemporary psychology of sport: Second International Congress of Sport Psychology* (pp. 97–106). Chicago: The Athletic Institute.

Kruisselbrink, L. D., Dodge, A. M., Swanburg, S. L., & MacLeod, A. L. (2004). Influence of same-sex and mixed sex exercise settings on the social physique anxiety and exercise intentions of males and females. *Journal of Sport and Exercise Psychology, 26,* 616–622.

Kubitz, K. A., & Landers, D. M. (1993). The effects of aerobic training on cardiovascular responses to mental stress: An examination of underlying mechanisms. *Journal of Sport & Exercise Psychology, 15,* 326–337.

Kyllo, L. B., & Landers, D. M. (1995). Goal setting in sport and exercise: A research synthesis to resolve the controversy. *Journal of Sport & Excerise Psychology, 17,* 117–137.

L

Lacy, A. C., & Darst, P. W. (1984). Evolution of systematic observation instrument: The ASU observation instrument. *Journal of Teaching Physical Education, 3,* 59–66.

LaFontaine, T. P., DiLorenzo, T. M., Frensch, P. A., Stucky-Ropp, R. C., Bargman, E. P., & McDonald, D. G. (1992). Aerobic exercise and mood: A brief review, 1985–1990. *Sports Medicine, 13*(3), 160–170.

Lambert, S. M., Moore, D. W., & Dixon, R. S. (1999). Gymnasts in training: The differential effects of self- and coach-set goals as a function of locus of control. *Journal of Applied Sport Psychology, 11,* 72–82.

LaMott, E. E. (1994). *The anterior cruciate ligament injured athlete: The psychological process.* Unpublished doctoral dissertation, University of Minnesota, Minneapolis.

Lampinen, P., Heikkinen, R. L., & Ruoppila, I. (2000). Changes in intensity of physical exercise as predictors of depressive symptoms among older adults: An eight-year follow-up. *Preventive Medicine, 30,* 371–380.

Landers, D. M. (1980). The arousal-performance relationship revisited. *Research Quarterly for Exercise and Sport, 51,* 77–90.

Landers, D. M. (1982). Arousal, attention, and skilled performance: Further considerations. *Quest, 33,* 271–283.

Landers, D. M. (1988, April). *Cognitive states of elite performers: Psychological studies of attention.* Paper presented at the meeting of the American Alliance for Health, Physical Education, Recreation and Dance (Research Consortium Scholar Lecture). Kansas City, MO.

Landers, D. M. (1991). Optimizing individual performance. In D. Druckman & R. A. Bjork (Eds.), *In the mind's eye: Enhancing human performance* (pp. 193–246). Washington, DC: National Academy Press.

Landers, D. M. (1995). Sport psychology: The formative years, 1950–1980. *The Sport Psychologist, 9,* 406–417.

Landers, D. M., & Arent, S. M. (2006). Arousal-performance relationships. In J. M. Williams (Ed.), *Applied sport psyhcology: Personal growth to peak performance, 5th ed.* (pp. 206–228). St. Louis, MO: McGraw-Hill.

Landers, D. M., Arent, S. M., Lutz, R. S. (2001). Affect and cognitive performances in high school wrestlers undergoing rapid weight loss. *Journal of Sport and Exercise Psychology, 23,* 307–316.

Landin, D., & Herbert, E. P. (1999). The influence of self-talk on the performance of skilled female tennis players. *Journal of Applied Sport Psychology, 11,* 263–282.

Landry, J. B., & Solmon, M. A. (2004). African American women's self-determination across the changes of change for exercise. *Journal of Sport and Exercise Psychology, 26,* 457–469.

Lane, A. M., & Terry, P. C. (2000). The nature of mood: Development of a conceptual model with a focus on depression. *Journal of Applied Sport Psychology, 12,* 16–33.

Lane, A. M., Sewell, D. F., Terry, P. C., Bertram, D., & Nesti, M. S. (1999). Confirmatory factor analysis of the Competitive State Anxiety Inventory-2. *Journal of Sport Sciences, 17,* 505–512.

Lane, A. M., Terry, P. C., Beedie, C. J., Curry, D. A., & Clark, N. (2002). Mood and performance: Test of a conceptual model with focus on depressed mood. *Psychology of Sport & Exercise, 2,* 157–172.

Lansing, R. W., Schwartz, E., & Lindsley, D. B. (1956). Reaction time and EEG activation. *American Psychologist, 11,* 433.

Lantz, C. D., Hardy, C. J., & Ainsworth, B. E. (1997). Social physique anxiety and perceived exercise behavior. *Journal of Sport Behavior, 20,* 83–93.

Law, J., Masters, R., Bray, S. R., Eves, F., & Bardswell, I. (2003). Motor performance as a function of audience affability and metaknowledge. *Journal of Sport and Exercise Psychology, 25,* 484–500.

Lawther, J. D. (1951). *Psychology of coaching.* Englewood Cliffs, NJ: Prentice Hall.

Lazarus, R. S. (1984). *Stress, appraisal and coping.* New York: Springer-Verlag.

Lazarus, R. S. (2000a). How emotions influence performance in competitive sports. *The Sport Psychologist, 14,* 229–252.

Lazarus, R. S. (2000b). Cognitive-motivational-relational theory of emotion. In Y. L. Hanin (Ed.), *Emotions in sport* (39–63). Champaign, IL: Human Kinetics.

Lazarus, R. S., & Folkman, S. (1984). *Stress appraisal and coping.* New York: Springer.

Leary, M. R., & Kowalski, R. M. (1990). Impression management: A literature review and two-component model. *Psychological Bulletin, 107,* 34–47.

Leary, M. R. (1992). Self-presentation processes in exercise and sport. *Journal of Sport and Exercise Psychology, 14,* 339–351.

Lee, I. (1995). Exercise and physical health: Cancer and immune function. *Research Quarterly for Exercise and Sport, 66,* 286–291.

Lee, M. J., Whitehead, J., & Balchin, N. (2000). The measurement of values in youth sport: Development of the Youth Sport Values Questionnaire. *Journal of Sport & Exercise Psychology, 22,* 307–326.

Lee, R. E., Nigg, C. R., DiClemente, C. C., & Courneya, K. S. (2001). Validating motivational readiness for exercise behavior with adolescents. *Research Quarterly for Exercise and Sport, 72,* 401–410.

Lefebvre, L. M., & Passer, M. W. (1974). The effects of game location and importance on aggression in team sport. *International Journal of Sport Psychology, 5*(2), 102–110.

Leffingwell, T. R., Rider, S. P., & Williams, J. M. (2001). Application of the transtheoretical model to psychological skills training. *The Sport Psychologist, 15,* 168–187.

Lehmann, M. J., Lormes, W., Optiz-Gress, A., Steinacker, J. M., Netzer, N., Foster, C., & Gastmann, U. (1997). Training and overtraining: An overview and experimental results in en-durance sports. *Journal of Sports Medicine and Physical Fitness, 37,* 7–17.

Leith, L. M., & Taylor, A. H. (1990). Psychological aspects of exercise: A decade literature review. *Journal of Sport Behavior, 13*(4), 219–239.

Lemieux, P., McKelvie, S. J., & Stout, D. (2002). Self-reported hostile aggression in contact athletes, no contact athletes and non-athletes. *Athletic Insight* (online *Journal of Sport Psychology*), http://www.athleticinsight.com/vol4Iss3

Lemyre, P. N., Roberts, G. C., & Ommundsen, Y. (2002). Achievement goal orientations, perceived ability, and sportspersonship in youth soccer. *Journal of Applied Sport Psychology, 14,* 120–136.

Lenney, E. (1977). Women's self-confidence in achievement situations. *Psychological Bulletin, 84,* 1–13.

Leonard, W. M. III (1989). The "home advantage": The case of the modern Olympics. *Journal of Sport Behavior, 12,* 227–241.

Lepper, M. R., & Greene, D. (1975). Turning play into work: Effects of adult surveillance and extrinsic rewards on children's intrinsic motivation. *Journal of Personality and Social Psychology, 31,* 479–486.

Lepper, M. R., & Greene, D. (1976). On understanding overjustification: A reply to Reiss and Sushinsky. *Journal of Personality and Social Psychology, 33,* 25–35.

LeScanff, C., & Taugis, J. (2002). Stress management for police special forces. *Journal of Applied Sport Psychology, 14,* 330–343.

Leslie-Toogood, A., & Martin, G. L., (2003). Do coaches know the mental skills of their athletes? Assessments for volleyball and track. *Journal of Sport Behavior, 26,* 56–68.

LeUnes, A., & Burger, J. (1998). Bibliography of the Profile of Mood States in sport and exercise research, 1971–1998. *Journal of Sport Behavior, 21,* 53–70.

LeUnes, A., & Burger, J. (2000). Profile of mood states research in sport and exercise psychology: Past, present, and future. *Journal of Applied Sport Psychology, 12,* 5–15.

LeUnes, A. D. (2002). *Bibliography on psychological tests used in research and practice in sport and exercise psychology.* Lewiston, NY: The Edwin Mellen Press.

Levenson, H. (1981). Differentiating among internality, powerful others, and chance. In H. M. Lefcourt (Ed.), *Research with the locus of control construct: Assessment methods* (Vol. 1, pp. 15–63). New York: Academic Press.

Li, F., & Harmer, P. (1996). Confirmatory factor analysis to the Group Environment Questionnaire with an intercollegiate sample. *Journal of Sport & Exercise Psychology, 18,* 49–63.

Lidor, R., & Singer, R. N. (September, 2000). Teaching performance routines to beginners. *Journal of Physical Education, Recreation & Dance, 71,* 34–36, 52.

Lieber, J. (1991, July 29). Deep scars. *Sports Illustrated, 75*(5), 36–44.

Lirgg, C. D. (1991). Gender differences in self-confidence in physical activity: A meta-analysis of recent studies. *Journal of Sport & Exercise Psychology, 13,* 294–310.

Lirgg, C. D., George, T. R., Chase, M. A., & Ferguson, R. H. (1996). Impact of conception of ability and sex-type of task on male and female self-efficacy. *Journal of Sport & Exercise Psychology, 18,* 426–434.

Llobet, J. M. (1999). *Correlation between WPAI scores and coaches' ratings.* Unpublished manuscript. PsyMetrics, Inc., Ft. Lauderdale, FL.

Lochbaum, M. R., Karoly, P., & Landers, D. M. (2004). Affect responses to acute bouts of aerobic exercise: A test of opponent-process theory. *Journal of Sport Behavior, 27,* 330–348.

Locke, E. A. (1991). Problems with goal-setting research in sports—and their solution. *Journal of Sport & Exercise Psychology, 8,* 311–316.

Locke, E. A., & Latham, G. P. (1985). The application of goal setting to sports. *Journal of Sports Psychology, 7,* 205–222.

Locke, E. A., & Latham, G. P. (1990). *A theory of goal setting and task performance.* Englewood Cliffs, NJ: Prentice-Hall.

Locke, E. A., Shaw, K. M., Saari, L. M., & Latham, G. P. (1981). Goal setting and task performance: 1969–1980. *Psychological Bulletin, 90,* 125–152.

Loland, N. W. (1998). Body image and physical activity: A survey among Norwegian men and women. *International Journal of Sport Psychology, 29,* 339–365.

Long, B. C., & Van Stavel, R. (1995). Effects of exercise training on anxiety: A meta-analysis. *Journal of Applied Sport Psychology, 7,* 167–189.

Longman, J. (November 18, 2003). Drugs in sports creating games of illusion. *New York Times,* http://www.nytimes.com/2003/11/18

Longman, J. (2004a, January 26). East German steroids toll: They killed Heidi. *The New York Times,* http://www.nytimes.com

Longman, J. (2004b, December 8). Like Jordan and Ruth, Hamm has a home in sports lore. *The New York Times,* C11, C14.

Lorr, M., & McNair, D. M. (1988). *Manual for the Profile of Mood States—Bipolar form.* San Diego, CA: Educational and Industrial Testing Service.

Lowe, R. (1973). *Stress, arousal, and task performance of Little League baseball players.* Unpublished doctoral dissertation, University of Illinois, Urbana-Champaign.

Lowther, J., & Lane, A. (2002). Relationship between mood, cohesion and satisfaction with performance among soccer players. *Athletic Insight* (online *Journal of Sport Psychology*), *4,* http://www.athleticinsight.com.vol4Iss3.

Lox, C. L., McAuley, E., & Tucker, R. S. (1995). Exercise as an intervention for enhancing subjective well-being in an HIV-1 population. *Journal of Sport & Exercise Psychology, 17,* 345–362.

Loy, J. W., & Sage, J. N. (1970). The effects of formal structure on organizational leadership: An investigation of interscholastic baseball teams. In G. S. Kenyon (Ed.), *Contemporary psychology of sport.* Chicago: The Athletic Institute.

M

Macchi, R., & Crossman, J. (1996). After the fall: Reflections of injured classical ballet dancers. *Journal of Sport Behavior, 19,* 222–234.

Mace, R. D., & Carroll, D. (1985). The control of anxiety in sport: Stress inoculation training prior to abseiling. *International Journal of Sport Psychology, 16,* 165–175.

Mace, R. D., & Carroll, D. (1986). Stress inoculation training to control anxiety in sport: Two case studies in squash. *British Journal of Sports Medicine, 16,* 115–117.

Mack, M. G., & Stephens, D. E. (2000). An empirical test of Taylor and Demick's multidimensional model of momentum in sport. *Journal of Sport Behavior, 23,* 349–363.

Mackinnon, L. T. (1994). Current challenges and future expectations in exercise immunology: Back to the future. *Medicine and Science in Sports and Exercise, 26,* 191–194.

Mackinnon, L. T. (2000, July). Chronic exercise training effects on immune function. *Medicine & Science in Sports & Exercise, 32,* S369–S376.

MacMullan, J. (January 17, 2000). Inside the NBA: Gugliotta returns. *Sports Illustrated, 92,* 70–73.

Maddison, R., & Prapavessis, H. (2004). Using self-efficacy and intention to predict exercise compliance among patients with ischemic heart disease. *Journal of Sport and Exercise Psychology, 26,* 511–524.

Maddux, J. E., & Rogers, R. W. (1983). Protection motivation and self-efficacy: A revised theory of fear appeals and attitude change. *Journal of Experimental Social Psychology, 19,* 469–479.

Madison, J. K., Ruma, S. L. (2003). Exercise and athletic involvement as moderators of severity in adolescents with eating disorders. *Journal of Applied Sport Psychology, 15,* 213–222.

Madrigal, R., & James, J. (1999). Team quality and the home advantage. *Journal of Sport Behavior, 22,* 381–398.

Maehr, M., & Braskamp, L. (1986). *The motivational factor: A theory of personal investment.* Lexington, MA: Lexington Books.

Maganaris, C. N., Collins, D., & Sharp, M. (2000). Expectancy effects and strength training: Do steroids make a difference? *The Sport Psychologist, 14,* 272–278.

Magyar, T. M., & Duda, J. L. (2000). Confidence restoration following athletic injury. *The Sport Psychologist, 14,* 372–390.

Mahoney, M. J., Gabriel, T. J., & Perkins, T. S. (1987). Psychological skills and exceptional athletic performance. *The Sport Psychologist, 1,* 181–199.

Males, J. R., & Kerr, J. H. (1996). Stress, emotion, and performance in elite slalom canoeists. *The Sport Psychologist, 10,* 17–36.

Males, J. R., Kerr, J. H., & Gerkovich, M. M. (1998). Metamotivational states during canoe slalom competition: A qualitative analysis using reversal theory. *Journal of Applied Sport Psychology, 10,* 185–200.

Malete, L., & Feltz, D. L. (2000). The effect of a coaching education program on coaching efficacy. *The Sport Psychologist, 14,* 410–417.

Malmo, R. B. (1959). Activation: A neuropsychological dimension. *Psychological Review, 66,* 367–386.

Mamassis, G., & Doganis, G. (2004). The effects of mental training program on juniors' pre-competitive anxiety, self-confidence, and tennis performance. *Journal of Applied Sport Psychology, 16,* 118–137.

Mann, L. (1974). On being a sore loser: How fans react to their team's failure. *Australian Journal of Psychology, 26,* 37–47.

Maniar, S. D., Curry, L. A., Sommers-Flanagan, J., Walsh, J. A. (2001). Student-athlete performances in seeking help when confronted with sport performance problems. *The Sport Psychologist, 15,* 205–223.

Maraniss, D. (September/October, 2001). An elephant ate my baseball. *Modern Maturity, 44W,* 86.

Marchant, D. B., Morris, T., & Anderson, M. B. (1998). Perceived importance of outcome as a contributing factor in competitive state anxiety. *Journal of Sport Behavior, 21,* 71–91.

Marcus, B. H., Eaton, C. A., Rossi, J. S., & Harlow, L. L. (1994). Self-efficacy, decision making, and stages of change: An integrative model of physical exercise. *Journal of Applied Social Psychology, 24,* 489–508.

Marcus, B. H., Rossi, J. S., Selby, V. C., Niaura, R. S., & Abrams, D. B. (1992). The stages and processes of exercise adoption and maintenance in a worksite sample. *Health Psychology, 11,* 386–395.

Marcus, B. H., & Simkin, L. R. (1994). The transtheoretical model: Applications to exercise behavior. *Medicine and Science in Sports and Exercise, 26,* 1400–1404.

Marcus, H. (1977). Self-schemata and processing information about the self. *Journal of Personality and Social Psychology, 35,* 63–78.

Markland, D. (1999). Self-determination moderates the effects of perceived competence on intrinsic motivation in an exercise setting. *Journal of Sport & Exercise Psychology, 21,* 351–361.

Marks, D. F. (1973). Visual imagery differences in recall of pictures. *British Journal of Psychology, 64,* 17–24.

Marsh, H. W. (1994). Sport motivation orientations: Beware of jingle-jangle fallacies. *Journal of Sport & Exercise Psychology, 16,* 365–380.

Marsh, H. W., Asci, F. S., Tomas, I. M. (2002). Multitrait-multimethod analyses of two physical self-concept instruments: A cross-cultural perspective. *Journal of Sport and Exercise Psychology, 24,* 99–119.

Marsh, H. W., Richards, G. E., Johnson, S., Roche, L., & Tremayne, P. (1994). Physical Self-Description Questionnaire: Psychometric properties and a multitrait–multimethod analysis of relations to existing instruments. *Journal of Sport and Exercise Psychology, 16,* 270–305.

Martens, M. P., Mobley, M., & Zizzi, S. J. (2000). Multicultural training in applied sport psychology. *The Sport Psychologist, 14,* 81–97.

Martens, M. P., & Webber, S. N. (2002). Psychometric properties of the Sport Motivation Scale: An evaluation with college varsity athletes from the U.S. *Journal of Sport & Exercise Psychology, 24,* 254–270.

Martens, R. (1975). *Social psychology and physical activity.* New York: Harper & Row.

Martens, R. (1977). *Sport competition anxiety test.* Champaign, IL: Human Kinetics.

Martens, R. (1982). *Sport competition anxiety test.* Champaign, IL: Human Kinetics.

Martens, R. (1987). *American coaching effectiveness program: Level 1 instructor's guide.* Champaign, IL: Human Kinetics.

Martens, R., Burton, D., Vealey, R. S., Bump, L. A., & Smith, D. (1990). Development and validation of the competitive state anxiety inventory—2. In R. Martens, R. S. Vealey, & D. Burton (Eds.), *Competitive anxiety in sport* (pp. 117–190). Champaign, IL: Human Kinetics Books.

Martens, R., & Landers, D. M. (1970). Motor performance under stress: A test of the inverted-U hypothesis, *Journal of Personality and Social Research, 16,* 29–37.

Martens, R., & Peterson, J. A. (1971). Group cohesiveness as a determinant of success and member satisfaction in team performance. *International Review of Sport Sociology, 6,* 49–61.

Martens, R., Vealey, R. S., & Burton, D. (1990). *Competitive anxiety in sport.* Champaign, IL: Human Kinetics.

Martin, D. T., Andersen, M. B., & Gates, W. (2000). Using Profile of Mood States (POMS) to monitor high-intensity training in cyclists: Group versus case studies. *The Sport Psychologist, 14,* 138–156.

Martin, J. E., & Calfas, K. J. (1989). Is it possible to lower blood pressure with exercise? Efficacy and adherence issues. *Journal of Applied Sport Psychology, 1*(2), 109–131.

Martin, J. J. (2002). Training and performance self-efficacy, affect, and performance in wheelchair road races. *The Sport Psychologist, 16,* 384–395.

Martin, J. J., & Cutter, K. (2002). An exploratory study of flow and motivation in theater actors. *Journal of Applied Sport Psychology, 14,* 344–352.

Martin, K. A., & Hausenblas, H. A. (1998). Psychological commitment to exercise and eating disorder symptomatology among female aerobic instructors. *The Sport Psychologist, 12,* 180–190.

Martin, K. A., & Mack, D. (1996). Relationship between physical self-presentation and sport competition trait anxiety: A preliminary study. *Journal of Sport & Exercise Psychology, 18,* 75–82.

Martin, K. A., Moritz, S. E., & Hall, C. R. (1999). Imagery use in sport: A literature review and applied model. *The Sport Psychologist, 13,* 245–268.

Martin, K. A., Rejeski, W. J., Leary, M. R., McAuley, E., & Bane, S. (1997). Is the Social Physique Anxiety Scale really multidimensional? Conceptual and statistical arguments for a unidimensional model. *Journal of Sport and Exercise Psychology, 19,* 359–367.

Martin, L. A. (1976). Effects of competition upon the aggressive responses of college basketball players and wrestlers. *Research Quarterly, 47,* 388–393.

Martin, S. B., Jackson, A. W., Richardson, P. A., & Weiller, K. H. (1999). Coaching preferences of adolescent youths and their parents. *Journal of Applied Sport Psychology, 11,* 247–262.

Martin, S. B., Thompson, C. L., & McKnight, J. (1998). An integrative psychoeducational approach to sport psychology consulting: A case study. *International Journal of Sport Psychology, 29,* 170–186.

Martinsen, E. W., Raglin, J. S., Hoffart, A., & Friis, S. (1998). Tolerance to intensive exercise and high levels of lactate in panic disorder. *Journal of Anxiety Disorders, 12,* 333–342.

Maslach, C., & Jackson, S. (1986). *Maslach Burnout Inventory.* 2nd ed. Palo Alto, CA: Consulting Psychologists Press.

Maslow, A. H. (1970). *Motivation and personality.* New York: Harper & Row.

Maslow, A. H. (1987). *Motivation and personality.* 3rd ed. New York, NY: Harper & Row, Publishers, Inc.

Masters, K. S., & Ogles, B. M. (1998a). Associative and dissociative cognitive strategies in exercise and running: 20 years later, what do we know? *The Sport Psychologist, 12,* 253–270.

Masters, K. S., & Ogles, B. M. (1998b). The relations of cognitive strategies with injury, motivation, and performance among marathon runners: Results from two studies. *Journal of Applied Sport Psychology, 10,* 281–296.

Mastro, J. V., Canabal, M. Y., & French, R. (1988). Psychological mood profiles of sighted and unsighted beep baseball players. *Research Quarterly for Exercise and Sport, 59,* 262–264.

Mastro, J. V., Sherill, C., Gench, B., & French, R. (1987). Psychological characterstics of elite visually impaired athletes: The ice-berg profile. *Journal of Sport Behavior, 10,* 39–46.

Matherson, H., & Crawford-Wright, A. (2000). An examination of eating disorder profiles in student obligatory and non-obligatory exercisers. *Journal of Sport Behavior, 23,* 42–50.

Matheson, H., Mathes, S., & Murray, M. (1997). The effect of winning and losing on female interactive and coactive team cohesion. *Journal of Sport Behavior, 20,* 284–298.

Matter, D. (December 17, 2000). Sold on Pinkel. *Columbia Daily Tribune,* B1.

May, J. R. (1986, Summer). Sport psychology: Should psychologists become involved? *The Clinical Psychologist, 39,* 77–81.

May, J. R., & Brown, L. (1989). Delivery of psychological services to the U. S. alpine ski team prior to and during the Olympics in Calgary. *The Sport Psychologist, 3,* 320–329.

Maynard, I. W., Hemmings, B., & Warwick-Evans, L. (1995). The effects of a somatic intervention strategy on competitive state anxiety and performance in semiprofessional soccer players. *The Sport Psychologist, 9,* 51–64.

Maynard, I. W., Smith, M. J., & Warwick-Evans, L. (1995). The effects of a cognitive intervention strategy on competitive state anxiety and performance in semiprofessional soccer players. *Journal of Sport & Exercise Psychology, 17,* 4228–446.

McAuley, E., & Blissmer, B. (2000). Self-efficacy determinants and consequences of physical activity. *Exercise and Sport Sciences Review, 28,* 85–88.

McAuley, E., Blissmer, B., Katula, J., Duncan, T. E., & Mihalko, S. L. (2000). Physical activity, self-esteem, and self-efficacy relationships in older adults: A randomized controlled trial. *Annals of Behavioral Medicine, 22,* 131–139.

McAuley, E., Blissmer, B., Marquez, D. X., Jerome, G. J., Kramer, A. F., & Katula, J. (2000). Social relations, physical activity, and well being in older adults. *Preventive Medicine, 31,* 608–617.

McAuley, E., & Courneya, K. S. (1994). The subjective exercise experiences scale (SEES): Development and preliminary validation. *Journal of Sport & Exercise Psychology, 16,* 163–177.

McAuley, E., Duncan, T. E., & Russell, D. W. (1992). Measuring causal attributions: The revised causal dimension scale (CDSII). *Personality and Social Psychology Bulletin, 18,* 566–573.

McAuley, E., Duncan, T., & Tammen, V. (1989). Psychometric properties of the Instrinsic Motivation Inventory in a competitive sport setting: A confirmatory factor analysis. *Research Quarterly for Exercise and Sport, 60,* 48–58.

McCafferty, D. (August 12, 2000). The Joe Gibbs way. *USA Weekend,* 6–7.

McCallum, J. (1991, Nov. 11). For whom the Bulls toil. *Sports Illustrated, 75,* 106–118.

McCallum, J. (1994, March 28). Radical stupidity. *Sports Illustrated, 80,* 8.

McClelland, D. C., Atkinson, J. W., Clark, R. W., & Lowell, E. L. (1953). *The achievement motive.* New York: Appleton-Century-Crofts.

McGhie, A., & Chapman, J. (1961). Disorders of attention and perception in early schizophrenia. *British Journal of Medical Psychology, 34,* 103–116.

McGill, J. C., Hall, J. R., Ratliff, W. R., & Moss, R. F. (1986). Personality characteristics of professional rodeo cowboys. *Journal of Sport Behavior, 9,* 143–151.

McGowan, R. W., Pierce, E. F., Williams, M., & Eastman, N. W. (1994). Athletic injury and self-diminution. *The Journal of Sports Medicine and Physical Fitness, 34,* 299–304.

McInman, A. D., & Grove, J. R. (1991). Peak moments in sport: A literature review. *Quest, 43,* 333–351.

McLafferty, C. L., Jr., Hunter, G. R., Wetzstein, C. J., & Bamman, M. M. (2000). Does resistance exercise relate to mood in older adults? *Medicine & Science in Sport & Exercise, 32,* Supplement, Abstract #494, S124.

McNair, D. M., Lorr, M., & Droppleman, L. F. (1971, 1981, 1992). *Profile of Mood States manual.* San Diego: Education and Industrial Testing Service.

Meehan, H. L., Bull, S. J., Wood, D. M., & James, D. V. B. (2004). The overtraining syndrome: A multicontexual assessment. *The Sport Psychologist, 18,* 154–171.

Meichenbaum, D. (1977). *Cognitive behavior modification.* New York: Plenum Press.

Meichenbaum, D. (1985). *Stress inoculation training.* New York: Pergamon Press.

Mellalieu, S. D. (2003). Mood matters: But how much? A comment on Lane and Terry (2000). *Journal of Applied Sport Psychology, 15,* 99–114.

Mellalieu, S. D., Hanton, S., & Jones, G. (2003). Emotional labeling and competitive anxiety in preparation and competition. *The Sport Psychologist, 17,* 157–174.

Menez, G. (October 6, 2003). Special report: The American athlete age 10. *Sports Illustrated, 99,* 59–75.

Metcalf, H. C., & Urwick, L. (Eds.). (1963). *Dynamic administration: The collected papers of Mary Parker Follett,* (p. 277). London: Harper & Brothers.

Miller, A., & Donohue, B. (2003). The development and controlled evaluation of athletic mental preparation strategies in high school distance runners. *Journal of Applied Sport Psychology, 15,* 321–334.

Miller, D. T., & Ross, M. (1975). Self-serving biases in the attribution of causality: Fiction or fact? *Psy-chological Bulletin, 82,* 213–225.

Miller, N. E. (1941). The frustration-aggression hypothesis. *Psychological Review, 48,* 337–342.

Miller, P. S., & Kerr, G. A. (2002). Conceptualizing excellence: Past, present, and future. *Journal of Applied Sport Psychology, 14,* 140–153.

Miller, T. A. (2000). The effect of physical activity on the academic performance and classroom behavior of fourth grade students. Unpublished doctoral dissertation, University of Missouri–Columbia.

Miller, T. W. (1982). Assertiveness training for coaches: The issue of healthy communication between coaches and players. *Journal of Sport Psychology, 4,* 107–114.

Milner, P. M. (1970). *Physiological psychology.* New York: Holt, Rinehart and Winston.

Mintz, L. B., O'Halloran, M. S., Mulholland, A. M., & Schneider, P. A. (1997). Questionnaire for eating disorders: Reliability and validity of operationalizing DSM-IV into a self-report format. *Journal of Counseling Psychology, 44,* 63–79.

Mischel, W. (1986). *Introduction to personality.* New York: Holt, Rinehart and Winston.

Miserandino, M. (1998). Attributional retraining as a method of improving athletic performance. *Journal of Sport Behavior, 21,* 286–297.

Morrow, R. G., & Gill, D. L. (2003). Perceptions of homophobia and heterosexism in physical education. *Research Quarterly for Exercise and Sport, 74,* 205–214.

Monroe-Chandler, K. J., Hall, C. R., & Weinberg, R. S. (2004). A qualitative analysis of the types of goals athletes set in training and competition. *Journal of Sport Behavior, 27,* 58–74.

Montville, L. (August 21, 2000). Stroke of luck. *Sports Illustrated, 93,* 44–48.

Moore, D. L. (May 17, 2000). All eyes on Tom at volleyball tryouts. *USA Today,* 8C.

Moore, J. C., & Brylinski, J. (1995). Facility familiarity and the home advantage. *Journal of Sport Behavior, 18,* 302–310.

Morgan, L. K., Griffin, J., & Heyward, V. H. (1996). Ethnicity, gender, and experience effects on attributional dimensions. *The Sport Psychologist, 10,* 4–16.

Morgan, W. P. (1969). Physical fitness and emotional health: A review. *American Corrective Therapy Journal, 23,* 124–127.

Morgan, W. P. (1972). Hypnosis and muscular performance. In W. P. Morgan (Ed.), *Ergogenic aids in muscular performance* (pp. 193–233). New York: Academic Press.

Morgan, W. P. (1974). Selected psychological considerations in sport. *Research Quarterly, 45,* 324–339.

Morgan, W. P. (1978, April). The mind of the marathoner. *Psychology Today,* 38–49.

Morgan, W. P. (1979). Prediction of performance in athletics. In P. Klavora & J. V. Daniel (Eds.), *Coach, athlete, and the sport psychologist* (pp. 172–186). Champaign, IL: Human Kinetics Publishers.

Morgan, W. P. (1980a). Sport personology: The credulous-skeptical argument in perspective. In W. F. Straub (Ed.), *Sport psychology: An analysis of athlete behavior,* 2nd ed. (pp. 330–339). Ithaca, NY: Mouvement Publications.

Morgan, W. P. (1980b). The trait psychology controversy. *Research Quarterly for Exercise and Sport, 51,* 50–76.

Morgan, W. P. (1985). Affective beneficence of vigorous physical activity. *Medicine and Science in Sports and Exercise, 17,* 94–100.

Morgan, W. P. (2000, June). *A simple solution to the exercise adherence problem.* Paper presented at the annual meeting of the American College of Sports Medicine, Indianapolis, IN.

Morgan, W. P., & Brown, D. R. (1983). Hypnosis. In M. H. Williams (Ed.), *Ergogenic aids in sport* (pp. 223–252). Champaign, IL: Human Kinetics Publishers.

Moritz, S. E., Feltz, D. L., Fahrbach, K. R., & Mack, D. E. (2000). The relation of self-efficacy measures to sports performance: A meta-analytic review. *Research Quarterly for Exercise and Sport, 71,* 280–294.

Morrey, M. A. (1997). *A longitudinal examination of emotional response, cognitive coping, and physical recovery among athletes undergoing anterior cruciate ligament reconstructive surgery.* Unpublished doctoral dissertation, University of Minnesota, Minneapolis.

Moyna, N. M., Robertson, R. J., Meckes, G. L., Peoples, J. A., Millich, N. B., & Thompson, P. D. (2001). Intermodal comparisons of energy expenditure and exercise intensities corresponding to the perceptual preferences range. *Medicine and Science in Sport and Exercise, 33,* 1404–1410.

Mullan, E., Markland, D., & Ingledwe, D. K. (1997). A graded conceptualization of self-determination in the regulation of exercise behavior: Development of a measure using confirmatory factor analytic procedures. *Personality and Individual Differences, 23,* 745–752.

Mullen, B., & Cooper, C. (1994). The relationship between group cohesiveness and performance: An integration. *Psychological Bulletin, 115,* 210–227.

Mummery, P. W. K., & Wankel, L. M. (1999). Training adherence in adolescent competitive swimmers: An application of the theory of planned behavior. *Journal of Sport & Exercise Psychology, 21,* 313–328.

Munroe, K. J., Giacobbi, P. R., Jr., Hall, C. R., & Weinberg, R. (2000). The four Ws of imagery use: Where, when, why, and what. *The Sport Psychologist, 14,* 119–137.

Murphy, A. (August 2, 2004). The joy of six. *Sports Illustrated, 101,* 40–46.

Nack, W. (May 7, 2001). The wrecking yard. *Sport Journal, 94,* 60–75.

Murphy, S. M., Greenspan, M., Jowdy, D., & Tammen, V. (1989, October). *Development of a brief rating instrument of competitive anxiety. Comparisons with the CSAI-2.* Paper presented at the meeting of the Association for the Advancement of Applied Sport Psychology, Seattle, WA.

Murphy, S. M., & Jowdy, D. P. (1992). Imagery and mental practice. In T. S. Horn (Ed.), *Advances in sport psychology* (pp. 221–250). Champaign, IL: Human Kinetics Publishers.

N

Nack, W., & Munson, L. (July 24, 2000). Out of control. *Sports Illustrated, 93,* 86–95.

Nack, W. (May 7, 2001). The wrecking yard. *Sport Journal, 94,* 60–75.

Neff, C. (1990, January). Scorecard: They said it. *Sports Illustrated, 71*(27), 21–24.

Newberg, D., Kimiecik, J., Durand-Bush, N., & Doell, K. (2002). The role of resonance in performance excellence and life engagement. *Journal of Applied Sport Psychology, 14,* 249–267.

Newman, B. (1984). Expediency as a benefactor: How team building saves time and gets the job done. *Training and Development Journal, 38,* 26–30.

Newton, M. (1994, October). *The relationship between perceived motivational climate and dispositional goal orientation on selected indices of intrinsic motivation.* Paper presented at the Association for the Advancement of Applied Sport Psychology, Tahoe, NV.

Newton, M., & Duda, J. L. (1999). The interaction of motivational climate, dispositional goal orientation, and perceived ability in predicting indices of motivation. *International Journal of Sport Psychology, 30,* 63–82.

Newton, M., Duda, J. L., & Yin, Z. (2000). Examination of the psychometric properties of the Perceived Motivational Climate in Sport Questionnaire-2 in a sample of female athletes. *Journal of Sports Sciences, 18,* 275–290.

Nicholls, J. G. (1984). Conceptions of ability and achievement motivation. In R. Ames & C. Ames (Eds.), *Research on motivation in education: Student motivation* (Vol. I). New York: Academic Press.

Nicholls, J. G. (1989). *The competitive ethos and democratic education.* Cambridge, MA: Harvard University Press.

Nicklaus, J. (1974). *Golf my way.* New York: Simon & Schuster.

Nicoloff, G., & Schwenk, T. L. (1995). Using exercise to ward off depression. *The Physician and Sportsmedicine, 23,* 44–56.

Nideffer, R. M. (1976). Test of attentional and interpersonal style. *Journal of Personality and Social Psychology, 34,* 394–404.

Nideffer, R. M. (1985). *Athlete's guide to mental training.* Champaign, IL: Human Kinetics Publishers.

Nideffer, R. M. (1992). *Psyched to win.* Champaign, IL: Leisure Press.

Nideffer, R. M., & Sagal, M. S. (2006). Concentration and attention control training. In J. M. Williams (Ed.), *Applied sport psychology: Personal growth to peak performance* (pp. 382–403). St. Louis, MO: McGraw-Hill.

Nieman, D. C. (2000, July). Is infection risk linked to exercise workload? *Medicine & Science in Sport & Exercise, 32,* S406–S411.

Nieman, D. C. (2001, June). Cold facts on exercise and immunity. Paper present at the annual convention of the American College of Sports Medicine, Baltimore, Maryland.

Nieman, D. C., Kernodle, M. W., Henson, D. R., Sonnenfeld, G., & Morton, D. S. (2000). The acute response of the immune system to tennis drills in adolescent athletes. *Research Quarterly for Exercise and Sport, 71,* 403–408.

Nietfeld, J. L. (2003). An examination of metacognitive strategy use and monitoring skills by competitive middle distance runners. *Journal of Applied Sport Psychology, 15,* 307–320.

Noblett, A. J., & Gifford, S. M. (2002). The sources of stress experienced by professional Australian footballers. *Journal of Applied Sport Psychology, 14,* 1–13.

Noel, R. C. (1980). The effect of visuo-motor behavior rehearsal on tennis performance. *Journal of Sport Psychology, 2,* 221–226.

Nordin, S. M., & Cummings, J. (2005). More than meets the eye: Investigating imagery type, direction, and outcome. *The Sport Psychologist, 19,* 1–17.

Norman, D. A. (1968). Toward a theory of memory and attention. *Psychological Review, 75,* 522–536.

Norris, J., & Jones, R. L. (1998). Towards a clearer definition and application of the centrality hypothesis in English Professional Association Football. *Journal of Sport Behavior, 21,* 181–195.

North, T. C., McCullagh, P., & Tran, Z. V. (1990). Effect of exercise on depression. In K. B. Pandolf & J. O. Holloszy (Eds.), *Exercise and sport science reviews, 18,* 379–415. Baltimore: William & Wilkins.

Nowlis, V. (1965). Research with the Mood Adjective Check List. In S. S. Tomkins & C. E. Izard (Eds.), *Affect, cognition and personality* (pp. 352–389). New York: Springer.

NSCA (1993). Position statement: Anabolic-androgenic steroid use by athletes. *National Strength and Conditioning Association Journal, 15,* 9.

Ntoumanis, N., & Biddle, S. J. H. (2000). Relationship of intensity and direction of competitive anxiety with coping strategies. *The Sport Psychologist, 14,* 360–371.

Ntoumanis, N., & Jones, G. (1998). Interpretation of competitive trait anxiety symptoms as a function of locus of control beliefs. *International Journal of Sport Psychology, 29,* 99–114.

Ntoumanis, N., Pensgaard, A. M., Martin, C., & Pipe, K. (2004). An idiographic analysis of amotivation in compulsory school physical education. *Journal of Sport & Exercise Psychology, 26,* 197–214.

O

O'Brian, D., & Sloan, R. (1999, September). *Physical and mental preparation of the world's greatest athlete.* Paper presented at the meeting of the Association for the Advancement of Applied Sport Psychology, Banff, Alberta, Canada.

O'Connell, B. (1998). *Solution-focused therapy.* London: Sage Publications.

O'Connor, E. A., Jr. (2004). Which questionnaire? Assessment practices of sport psychology consultants. *The Sport Psychologist, 18,* 464–468.

O'Connor, P. J., & Davis, J. C. (1992). Psychobiologic responses to exercise at different times of day. *Medicine and Science in Sports and Exercise, 24,* 714–719.

Ogilvie, B., Taylor, J. (1993). Career termination issues among elite athletes. In R. N. Singer, M. Murphy, and L. K. Tennant (Eds.), *Handbook of Research on Sport Psychology* (pp. 761–778). New York: Macmillan.

Ogilvie, B. C. (1968). Psychological consistencies within the personality of high-level competitors. *Journal of the American Medical Association, 205,* 780–786.

Ogilvie, B. C. (1976). Psychological consistencies within the personality of high-level competitors. In A. C. Fisher (Ed.), *Psychology of sport.* Palo Alto, CA: Mayfield Publishing Company.

Ogilvie, B. C. (1985). Sports psychologist and the disabled athlete. *Palaestra, 1,* 36–40, 43.

Ogilvie, B. C., Johnsgard, K., & Tutko, T. A. (1971). Personality: Effects of activity. In L. A. Larson (Ed.), *Encyclopedia of sport sciences and medicine.* New York: Macmillan.

Ogilvie, B. C., & Tutko, T. A. (1966). *Problem athletes and how to handle them.* London: Palham Books.

Ogles, B. M., Masters, K. S., & Richardson, S. A. (1995). Obligatory running and gender: An analysis of participative motives and training habits. *International Journal of Sport Psychology, 26,* 233–248.

Oglesby, C. A. (2001). To unearth the legacy. *The Sport Psychologist, 15,* 373–385.

Olivardia, R., & Pope, H. G. (2000). Muscle dysmorphia in male weightlifters: A case-control study. *American Journal of Psychiatry, 157,* 1291–1296.

Olney, B. (February 19, 2003). Players seek every edge in modern training culture. *The New York Times,* http://www.nytimes.com/2001/2/19

Olrich, T. W., & Ewing, M. E. (1999). Life on steroids: Bodybuilders describe their perceptions of the anabolic-androgenic steroid use period. *The Sport Psychologist, 13,* 299–312.

Oman, R. F., & King, A. C. (2000). The effect of life events and exercise program format on the adoption and maintenance of exercise behavior. *Health Psychology, 19,* 605–612.

Ommundsen, Y. (2001). Self-handicapping strategies in physical education classes. The ability and achievement goal orientation. *Psychology of Sport and Exercise, 2,* 139–156.

Ommundsen, Y. (2004). Self-handicapping related to task and performance-approach and avoidance goals in physical education. *Journal of Applied Sport Psychology, 16,* 183–197.

Orbach, I., Singer, R. N., & Murphey, M. (1997). Changing attributions with an attribution training technique related to basketball dribbling. *The Sport Psychologist, 11,* 294–304.

Orbach, I., Singer, R., & Price, S. (1999). An attribution training program and achievement in sport. *The Sport Psychologist, 13,* 69–82.

Orlick, T. (1986). *Psyching for sport: Mental training for athletes.* Champaign, IL: Leisure Press.

Orlick, T. (1990). *In pursuit of excellence.* 2nd ed. Champaign, IL: Human Kinetics.

Orlick, T., & Partington, J. (1988). Mental links to excellence. *The Sport Psychologist, 2,* 105–130.

Orlick, T., & Zitzelsberger, L. (1996). Enhancing children's sport experiences. In F. L. Smoll & R. E. Smith (Eds.), *Children and youth in sport: A biopsychosocial perspective* (pp. 330–337). Human Kinetics. Champaign, IL:

Osborn, R. N., & Hunt, J. G. (1975). An adaptive-reactive theory of leadership: The role of macro variables in leadership research. In J. G. Hunt & L. L. Larson (Eds.), *Leadership frontiers.* Kent, OH: Kent State University Press.

Ostrow, A. C. (Ed.). (1996). *Directory of psychological tests in the sport and exercise sciences.* 2nd ed. Morgantown, WV: Fitness Information Technology, Inc.

Oxendine, J. B. (1968). *Psychology of motor learning.* New York: Appleton-Century-Crofts.

Oxendine, J. B. (1970). Emotional arousal and motor performance. *Quest, 13,* 23–30.

P

Paa, H. K., Sime, W. E., & Llobet, J. (September, 1999). *An examination of sport-specific psychological characteristics among high school, collegiate, and professional athletes.* Poster session presented at the annual meeting of the Association for the Advancement of Applied Sport Psychology, Banff, Alberta, Canada.

Paffenbarger, R. S. (1994). 40 years of progress: Physical activity, health and fitness. In *40th anniversary lectures* (pp. 93–109). Indianapolis, IN: American College of Sports Medicine.

Page, S. J., Sime, W., & Nordell, K. (1999). The effects of imagery on female college swimmers' perceptions of anxiety. *The Sport Psychologist, 13,* 458–469.

Paivio, A. (1971). *Imagery and verbal processes.* New York: Holt, Rinehart and Winston.

Paivio, A. (1985). Cognitive and motivational functions of imagery in human performance. *Canadian Journal of Applied Sport Sciences, 10,* 225–285.

Parfitt, G., Hardy, L., & Pates, J. (1995). Somatic anxiety and physiological arousal: Their effects upon a high anaerobic, low memory demand task. *International Journal of Sport Psychology, 26,* 196–213.

Park, J. K. (2000). Coping strategies used by Korean national athletes. *The Sport Psychologist, 14,* 63–80.

Parker, R. M., Lambert, M. J., & Burlington, G. M. (1994). Psychological features of female runners presenting with pathological weight control behaviors. *Journal of Sport & Exercise Psychology, 16,* 119–134.

Partington, J. T., & Shangi, G. M. (1992). Developing an understanding of team psychology. *International Journal of Sport Psychology, 23,* 28–47.

Passer, M. W. (1996). At what age are children ready to compete? Some psychological considerations. In F. L. Smoll & R. E. Smith (Eds.), *Children and youth in sport: A biopsychosocial perspective* (pp. 73–86). Madison, WI: Brown & Benchmark.

Pate, R. R., et al. (1995). Physical activity and public health. *Journal of the American Medical Association, 273,* 402–407.

Pate, R. R., Trost, S. G., Levin, S., & Dowda, M. (September 2000). Sports participation and health-related behaviors among US youth. *Archives of Pediatrics & Adolescent Medicine, 154,* 904–911.

Paternoster, R. (1987). The deterrent effect of the perceived certainty and severity of punishment: A review of the evidence and issues. *Justice Quarterly, 4,* 173–217.

Pates, J., Cummings, A., & Maynard, I. (2002). The effects of hypnosis on flow states and three-point shooting performance in basketball players. *The Sport Psychologist, 16,* 34–45.

Pates, J., Maynard, I., & Westbury, T. (2001). An investigation into the effects of hypnosis on basketball performance. *Journal of Applied Sport Psychology, 13,* 84–102.

Pates, J., Oliver, R., & Maynard, I. (2001). The effects of hypnosis on flow states and golf-putting performance. *Journal of Applied Sport Psychology, 13,* 341–354.

Patterson, E. L., Smith, R. E., Everett, J. J., & Ptacek, J. T. (1998). Psychosocial factors as predictors of ballet injuries. *Journal of Sport Behavior, 21,* 101–112.

Pelletier, L. G., Fortier, M. S., Vallerand, R. J., Tuson, K. M., Briere, N. M., & Blais, M. R. (1995). Toward a new measure of intrinsic motivation, extrinsic motivation, and amotivation in sports: The sport motivation scale (SMS). *Journal of Sport & Exercise Psychology, 17,* 35–53.

Pennington, B. (November 12, 2003). As team sports conflict, some parents rebel. *The New York Times,* http://www.nytimes.com/2003/11/12

Pensgaard, A. M., & Duda, J. L. (2002). "If we work hard, we can do it": A tale from an Olympic medalist. *Journal of Applied Sport Psychology, 14,* 219–236.

Pensgaard, A. M., & Duda, J. L. (2003). Sydney 2000: The interplay between emotions, coping, and the performance of Olympic-level athletes. *The Sport Psychologist, 17,* 253–267.

Perkins, D., Wilson, G. V., & Kerr, J. H. (2001). The effects of elevated arousal and mood on maximal strength performance in athletes. *Journal of Applied Sport Psychology, 13,* 239–259.

Perkins-Ceccato, N., Passmore, S. R., & Lee, T. D. (2003). Effects of focus of attention depend on golfer's skill. *Journal of Sports Sciences, 21,* 593–600.

Perkos, S., Theodorakis, Y., & Chroni, S. (2002). Enhancing performance and skill acquisition in novice basketball players with instructional self-talk. *The Sport Psychologist, 16,* 368–383.

Perreault, S., Vallerand, R. J., Montgomery, D., & Provencher, P. (1998). Coming from behind: On the effect of psychological momentum on sport performance. *Journal of Sport & Exercise Psychology, 20,* 421–436.

Perri, M. G., Anton, S. D., Durning, P. E., Ketterson, T. W., Sydeman, S. J., Berlant, N. E., Kanasky, Jr., W. F., Newton, Jr., R. L., Limacher, M. C., & Martin, A. D. (2002). Adherence to exercise prescriptions: Effects of prescribing moderate versus higher levels of intensity and frequency. *Health Psychology, 21,* 452–458.

Perry, J. D., & Williams, J. M. (1998). Relationship of intensity and direction of competitive trait anxiety to skill level and gender in tennis. *The Sport Psychologist, 12,* 169–179.

Petitpas, A. J. (1998). Practical considerations in providing psychological services to sports medicine clinic patients. *Journal of Applied Sport Psychology, 10,* 157–167.

Petrie, T. A. (1993). Coping skills, competitive trait anxiety, and playing status: Moderating effects on the life stress-injury relationship. *Journal of Sport & Exercise Psychology, 15,* 261–274.

Petrie, T. A. (1996). Differences between male and female college lean sport athletes, nonlean sport athletes, and nonathletes on behavioral and psychological indices of eating disorders. *Journal of Applied Sport Psychology, 8,* 218–230.

Petrie, T. A., & Stoever, S. (1993). The incidence of bulimia nervosa and pathogenic weight control behaviors in female collegiate gymnasts. *Research Quarterly for Exercise and Sport, 64,* 238–241.

Petruzzello, S. J., Landers, D. M., Hatfield, B. D., Kubitz, K. A., & Salazar, W. (1991). A meta-analysis on the anxiety reducing effects of acute and chronic exercise. *Sports Medicine, 11*(3), 143–182.

Pierce, B. E., & Burton, D. (1998). Scoring the perfect 10: Investigating the impact of goal-setting styles on a goal setting program for female gymnasts. *The Sport Psychologist, 12,* 156–168.

Plotnikoff, R. C., Hotz, S. B., Birkett, N. J., & Courneya, K. S. (2001). Exercise and the transtheoretical model: A longitudinal test of a population sample. *Preventive Medicine, 33,* 441–452.

Poczwardowski, A., & Conroy, D. E. (2002). Coping responses to failure and success among elite athletes and performing artists. *Journal of Applied Sport Psychology, 14,* 313–329.

Poczwardowski, A., Sherman, C. P., & Ravizza, K. (2004). Professional philosophy in the sport psychology service delivery: Building on theory and practice. *The Sport Psychologist, 18,* 445–463.

Posnanski, J. (January 9, 1998). Seconds can tick so loudly. *The Kansas City Star,* D1, D9.

Posner, M. I., & Raichle, M. E. (1997). *Images of mind.* New York: NY: Scientific American Library.

Prapavessis, H. (2000). The POMS and sports performance: A review. *Journal of Applied Sport Psychology, 12,* 34–48.

Prapavessis, H., & Carron, A. V. (1988). Learned helplessness in sport. *The Sport Psychologist, 2,* 189–201.

Prapavessis, H., & Carron, A. V. (1996). The effect of group cohesion on competitive state anxiety. *Journal of Sport & Excerise Psychology, 18,* 64–74.

Prapavessis, H., & Grove, J. R. (1991). Precompetitive emotions and shooting performance: The mental health and zone of optimal function models. *The Sport Psychologist, 5,* 223–234.

Prapavessis, H., & Grove, R. (1994a). Personality variables as antecedents of precompetitive mood states. *International Journal of Sport Psychology, 25,* 81–99.

Prapavessis, H., & Grove, R. (1994b). Personality variables as antecedents of precompetitive mood state temporal patterning. *International Journal of Sport Psychology, 25,* 347–365.

Prapavessis, H., Grove, J. R., & Eklund, R. C. (2004). Self-presentational issues in competition and sport. *Journal of Applied Sport Psychology, 16,* 19–40.

President's Council on Physical Fitness and Sports (June 2001). Does exercise alter minimum function and respiratory infections? *Research Digest,* series 3, no. 13.

Prezuhy, A. M., & Etnier, J. L. (2001). Attentional patterns of horseshoe pitchers at two levels of task difficulty. *Research Quarterly for Exercise and Sport, 72,* 293–298.

Price, M. S., & Weiss, M. R. (2000). Relationships among coach burnout, coach behaviors, and athletes' psychological responses. *The Sport Psychologist, 14,* 391–409.

Price, S. L. (2003, April 28). When fans attack. *Sports Illustrated, 98,* 48–53.

Price, S. L. (2004, June 28). Lance in France (part 6). *Sports Illustrated, 100,* 46–53.

Prince, M. (1929). *Clinical and experimental studies in personality.* Cambridge, MA: Harvard University Press.

Prochaska, J. O., & DiClemente, C. C. (1986). Toward a comprehensive model of change. In W. E. Miller & N. Heather (Eds.), *Treating addictive behaviors* (pp. 3–27). London: Plenum Press.

Prochaska, J. O., & Marcus, B. H. (1994). The transtheoretical model: The applications to exercise. In R. K. Dishman (Ed.), *Advances in exercise adherence* (pp. 161–180). Champaign, IL: Human Kinetics Books.

Prochaska, J. O., & Velicer, W. F. (1997). The transtheoretical model of behavioral change. *American Journal of Health Promotion, 12,* 38–48.

Psychological profiles help in making picks. (April 20, 1997). *The New York Times,* CXL VI (#50,768), p. 26.

Puffer, J. C., & McShane, J. M. (1992). Depression and chronic fatigue in athletes. *Clinics in Sports Medicine, 11,* 327–338.

Purcell, I. (1999). Verbal protocols and structured interviews for motives, plans, and decisions in golf. In J. H. Kerr (Ed.), *Experiencing sport: Revised Theory* (pp. 69–100). Chickester: Wiley & Sons.

Q

Quinn, A. M., & Fallon, B. J. (1999). The changes in psychological characteristics and reactions of elite athletes from injury onset until full recovery. *Journal of Applied Sport Psychology, 11,* 194–209.

Quitmeir, L. (November 16, 2000). Olympic trial and error. *Columbia Missourian,* B1, B3.

R

Raedeke, T. D. (1997). Is athlete burnout more than just stress? A sport commitment perspective. *Journal of Sport & Exercise Psychology, 19,* 396–417.

Raedeke, T. D. (2004). Coach commitment and burnout: A one-year follow-up. *Journal of Applied Sport Psychology, 16,* 333–349.

Raedeke, T. D., Granzyk, T. L., & Warren, A. (2000). Why coaches experience burnout: A commitment perspective. *Journal of Sport & Exercise Psychology, 22,* 85–105.

Raedeke, T. D., Lunney, K., & Venables, K. (2002). Understanding athlete burnout: Coach perspectives. *Journal of Sport Behavior, 25,* 181–206.

Raedeke, T. D., & Smith, A. L. (2001). Development and preliminary validation of an athlete burnout measure. *Journal of Sport and Exercise Psychology, 23,* 281–306.

Raedeke, T. D., & Smith, A. (2004). Coping resources and athlete burnout: An examination of stress mediated and moderation hypotheses. *Journal of Sport and Exercise Psychology, 26,* 525–543.

Raedeke, T. D., & Stein, G. L. (1994). Felt arousal, thoughts/feelings, and ski performance. *The Sport Psychologist, 8,* 360–375.

Raedeke, T. D., Warren, A. H., Granzyk, T. L. (2002). Coaching commitment and turnovers: A comparison of current and former coaches. *Research Quarterly for Exercise and Sport, 73,* 73–86.

Raglin, J. S., Eksten, F., & Garl, T. (1995). Mood state responses to a pre-season conditioning program in male collegiate basketball players. *International Journal of Sport Psychology, 26,* 214–225.

Raglin, J. S., & Hanin, Y. L. (2000). Competitive anxiety. In Y. L. Hanin (Ed.), *Emotions in sport* (93–112). Champaign, IL: Human Kinetics.

Raglin, J. S., Koceja, D. M., Stager, J. M., & Harms, C. A. (1996). Mood, neuromuscular function, and performance during training in female swimmers. *Medicine and Science in Sports and Exercise, 28,* 372–375.

Raglin, J. S., & Morris, M. J. (1994). Precompetition anxiety in women volleyball players: A test of ZOF theory in a team sport. *British Journal of Sports Medicine, 28,* 47–51.

Raglin, J. S., & Turner, P. E. (1993). Anxiety and performance in track and field athletes: A comparison of the inverted-U hypothesis with zone of optimal functioning theory. *Personality and Individual Differences, 14,* 163–171.

Ram, N., & McCullagh, P. (2003). Self-modeling: Influence on psychological responses and physical performance. *The Sport Psychologist, 17,* 220–241.

Ram, N., Stareck, J., & Johnson, J. (2004). Race, ethnicity, and sexual orientation: Still a void in sport and exercise psychology? *Journal of Sport & Exercise Psychology, 26,* 250–268.

Rand, J. (February 27, 2000). The profiler. *The Kansas City Star,* C4.

Randle, S., & Weinberg, R. (1997). Multidimensional anxiety and performance: An exploratory examination of the zone of optimal functioning hypothesis. *The Sport Psychologist, 11,* 160–174.

Rascle, O., Coulomb-Cabagno, G., & Delsarte, A. (2005). Perceived motivational climate and observed aggression as a function of competitive level in youth male French handball. *Journal of Sport Behavior, 28,* 51–67.

Raudenbush, B., Corley, N., & Eppich, W. (2001). Enhancing athletic performances through the administration of peppermint odor. *Journal of Sport and Exercise Psychology, 23,* 156–160.

Raudenbush, B., & Meyer, B. (2003). Muscular dissatisfaction and supplement use among male intercollegiate athletes. *Journal of Sport and Exercise Psychology, 25,* 161–170.

Raynor, D. A., Coleman, K. J., & Epstein, L. H. (1998). Effects of proximity on the choice to be physically active or sedentary. *Research Quarterly for Exercise and Sport, 69,* 99–103.

Reddy, J. K., Bai, A. J. L., & Rao, V. R. (1976). The effects of the transcendental meditation program on athletic performance. In D. J. Orme-Johnson & I. Farrow (Eds.), *Scientific research on the transcendental meditation program* (Collected papers, Vol. 1). Weggis, Switzerland: MERU Press.

Reifman, A. S., Larrick, R. P., & Fein, S. (1991). Temper and temperature on the diamond: The heat–aggression relationship in major league baseball. *Personality and Social Psychology Bulletin, 17,* 580–585.

Reilly, R. (1996, April 22). Master strokes. *Sports Illustrated, 84,* 24–31.

Reilly, R. (2000, February 28). Bringing parents up to code. *Sports Illustrated, 92,* 88.

Rejeski, W. J., Brawley, L. R., & Schumaker, S. A. (1996). Physical activity and health-related quality of life. In J. O. Holloszy (Ed.), *Exercise and Sport Science Reviews, 24,* 71–108.

Reynolds, J. (Fall 2003). From dead last to National Champions. *BYU Magazine, 7.*

Reynolds, W. M. (1982). Development of reliable and valid short forms of the Marlowe-Crowne Social Desirability Scale. *Journal of Clinical Psychology, 38,* 119–125.

Rhodes, R. E., Courneya, K. S., & Hayduk, I. A. (2001). Does personality moderate the theory of planned behavior in the exercise domain? *Journal of Sport and Exercise Psychology, 24,* 120–132.

Rhodes, R. E., Jones, L. W., & Courneya, K. S. (2002). Extending the theory of planned behavior in the exercise domain: A comparison of social support and subjective norm. *Research Quarterly for Exercise and Sport, 73,* 193–199.

Richardson, A. (1969). *Mental imagery.* New York: Springer.

Riemer, B. A., & Visio, M. E. (2003). Gender typing of sports: An investigation of Metheny's classification. *Research Quarterly for Exercise and Sport, 74,* 193–205.

Riemer, H. A., & Chelladurai, P. (1995). Leadership and satisfaction in athletics. *Journal of Sport & Exercise Psychology, 17,* 276–293.

Riemer, H. A., & Chelladurai, P. (1998). Development of the Athlete Satisfaction Questionnaire (ASQ). *Journal of Sport and Exercise Psychology, 20,* 127–156.

Riemer, H. A., & Toon, K. (2001). Leadership and satisfaction in tennis: Examination of congruence, gender, and ability. *Research Quarterly for Exercise and Sport, 72,* 243–256.

Reinboth, M., & Duda, J. L. (2004). The motivational climate, perceived ability, and athletes' psychological and physical well being. *The Sport Psychologist, 18,* 237–251.

Rigsby, L. W., Dishman, R. K., Jackson, A. W., MaClean, G. S., & Raven, P. B. (1992). Effects of exercise training on men seropositive for human immunodeficiency virus-1. *Medicine and Science in Sports and Exercise, 24*(1), 6–12.

Robazza, C., & Bartoli, L. (2003). Intensity, idiosyncratic content and functional impact of performance-related emotions in athletes. *Journal of Sport Sciences, 21,* 171–189.

Robazza, C., Bartoli, L., & Hanin, Y. (2004). Pre-competition emotions, bodily symptoms, and task specific qualities as predictors of performance in high-level karate athletes. *Journal of Applied Sport Psychology, 16,* 151–165.

Roberts, G. C. (1982). Achievement motivation in sport. In R. Terjung (Ed.), *Exercise and sport science reviews* (Vol. 10). Philadelphia: Franklin Institute Press.

Roberts, G. C. (1993). Motivation in sport: Understanding and enhancing the motivation and achievement of children. In R. N. Singer, M. Murphey, & L. K. Tennant (Eds.), *Handbook of research on sport psychology* (pp. 405–420). New York: Macmillan.

Roberts, G. C., & Pascuzzi, D. (1979). Causal attributions in sport: Some theoretical implications. *Journal of Sport Psychology, 1,* 203–211.

Roberts, G. C., & Treasure, D. C. (1995). Achievement goals, motivation climate and achievement strategies and behaviors in sport. *International Journal of Sport Psychology, 26,* 64–80.

Robertson, O. (December 19, 2004). From the past, a new game emerges. *The New York Times,* http//www.nytimes.com/2004/12/19/sports/basketball.

Robinson, D. W. (1985). Stress seeking: Selected behavioral characteristics of elite rock climbers. *Journal of Sport Psychology, 7,* 400–404.

Roeder, L. K., & Aufsesser, P. M. (1986, Winter). Se-lected attentional and interpersonal characteristics of wheelchair athletes. *Palaestra, 2,* 28–32, 43–44.

Roemmich, J. N., Gurgol, C. M., & Epstein, L. H. (2004). Open-loop feedback increases physical activity of youth. *Medicine and Science in Sports and Exercise, 36,* 668–673.

Rogerson, L. J., & Hrycaiko, D. W. (2002). Enhancing competitive performance of ice hockey goaltenders using centering and self-talk. *Journal of Applied Sport Psychology, 14,* 14–26.

Rojas, R., Schlicht, W., & Hautzinger, M. (2003). Effects of exercise training on quality of life, psychological well-being, immune status, and cardiopulmonary fitness in HIV-1 positive populations. *Journal of Sport and Exercise Psychology, 25,* 440–455.

Roper, E. A. (2002). Women working in the applied domain: Examining the gender bias in applied sport psychology. *Journal of Applied Sport Psychology, 14,* 53–66.

Rose, J., & Jevne, R. F. J. (1993). Psychosocial processes associated with athletic injuries. *The Sport Psychologist, 7,* 309–328.

Rotella, R. (October 9, 2003). *Lessons learned in applied sport psychology consulting.* Keynote address, Annual Convention of the Association of the Advancement of Applied Sport Psychology, Philadelphia, PA.

Rotter, J. B. (1966). Generalized expectancies for internal versus external control of reinforcement. *Psychological Monographs: General and Applied, 80*(1, Whole No. 609).

Rotter, J. B. (1971, June). External control and internal control. *Psychology Today, 5*(1), 37–42, 58–59.

Rowbottom, D. G., & Green, K. J. (2000, July). Acute exercise effects on the immune system. *Medicine & Science in Sport & Exercise, 32,* S396–S405.

Rowley, A., Landers, D. M., Kyllo, L., & Etnier, J. (1995). Does the iceberg profile discriminate between successful and less successful athletes? A meta-analysis. *Journal of Sport & Exercise Psychology, 17,* 185–199.

Rudisill, M. E. (1998). The influences of causal dimension orientations and perceived competence on adults' expectations, persistence, performance and the selection of causal dimensions. *International Journal of Sport Psychology, 19,* 184–198.

Ruffer, W. A. (1975). Personality traits of athletes. *The Physical Educator, 32*(1), 105–109.

Ruffer, W. A. (1976a). Personality traits of athletes. *The Physical Educator, 33*(1), 50–55.

Ruffer, W. A. (1976b). Personality traits of athletes. *The Physical Educator, 33*(4), 211–214.

Ruiz, M. C., & Hanin, Y. L. (2004). Metaphoric description and individualized emotion profiling of performance states in top karate athletes. *Journal of Applied Sport Psychology, 26,* 258–273.

Rushall, B. S. (1970). An evaluation of the relationship between personality and physical performance categories. In G. S. Kenyon (Ed.), *Contemporary psychology of sport: Second International Congress of Sports Psychology.* Chicago: The Athletic Institute.

Rushall, B. S. (1972). Three studies relating personality variables to football performance. *International Journal of Sport Psychology, 3,* 12–24.

Rushall, B. S. (1973). The status of personality research and application in sports and physical education. *Journal of Sports Medicine and Physical Fitness, 13,* 281–290.

Rushall, B. S., & Lippman, L. G. (1998). The role of imagery in physical performance. *International Journal of Sport Psychology, 29,* 57–72.

Rushin, S. (July 31, 2000). Grand stand. *Sports Illustrated, 93,* 52–61.

Russell, D. (1982). The causal dimension scale: A measure of how individuals perceive causes. *Journal of Personality and Social Psychology, 42,* 1137–1145.

Russell, D., McAuley, E., & Tarico, V. (1987). Measuring causal attributions for success and failure: A comparison of methodologies for assessing causal dimensions. *Journal of Personality and Social Psychology, 52,* 1248–1257.

Russell, G. W. (1995). Personalities in the crowd: Those who would escalate a sports riot. *Aggressive Behavior, 21,* 91–100.

Russell, G. W. (1999). Spectators, hostility, and riots. In G. G. Brannigan (Ed.), *The sport scientists: Research interests.* New York: Longman.

Russell, G. W., & Arms, R. L. (1995). False consensus effect, physical aggression, anger, and a willingness to escalate a disturbance. *Aggressive Behavior, 21,* 381–386.

Russell, G. W., & Arms, R. L. (1998). Toward a social psychological profile of would-be rioters. *Aggressive Behavior, 24,* 219–226.

Russell, G. W., & Drewery, B. P. (1976). Crowd size and competitive aspects of aggression in ice hockey: An archival study. *Human Relations, 29,* 723–735.

Russell, G. W., & Mustonen, A. (1998). Peacemakers: Those who would intervene to quell a sports riot. *Personality and Individual Differences, 24,* 335–339.

Russell, M. T., & Karol, D. L. (1994). *The 16 PF fifth edition administrator's manual.* Champaign, IL: Institute for Personality and Ability Testing.

Russell, W. D. (2000, September). Coping with injuries in scholastic athletics. *Journal of Physical Education, Recreation, and Dance, 71,* 41–46.

Russell, W. D., & Cox, R. H. (2000). A laboratory investigation of positive and negative affect within individual zones of optimal functioning theory. *Journal of Sport Behavior, 23,* 164–180.

Russell, W. D. (2002). Comparison of self-esteem, body satisfaction, and social physique anxiety across males of different exercise frequency and racial background. *Journal of Sport Behavior, 25,* 74–90.

Russell, W. D., & Cox, R. H. (2003). Social physique anxiety, body dissatisfaction, and self-esteem in college females differing in exercise frequency, perceived weight discrepancy and race. *Journal of Sport Behavior, 26,* 298–318.

Ryan, E. D. (1977). Attribution, intrinsic motivation, and athletics. In L. I. Gedvilas & M. E., Kneer (Eds.), *Proceedings of the NCPEAM/NAPECW National Conference, 1977.* Chicago, IL: University of Illinois at Chicago Circle.

Ryan, E. D. (1980). Attribution, intrinsic motivation and athletics: A replication and extension. In C. H. Nadeau (Ed.), *Psychology of motor behavior and sport, 1979.* Champaign, IL: Human Kinetics Publishers.

Ryan, E. D., & Simons, J. (1981). Cognitive demand, imagery, and frequency of mental rehearsal as factors influencing acquisition of motor skills. *Journal of Sport Psychology, 1,* 35–45.

Ryan, R. M. (2000, October). *Vital research: Intrinsic and extrinsic motivation for sport, exercise, and other health-related behaviors.* Paper presented at the meeting of the Association for the Advancement of Applied Sport Psychology, Nashville, TN.

Ryan, R. M., Frederick, C. M., Lepes, D., Rubio, N., & Sheldon, K. M. (1997). Intrinsic motivation and exercise adherence. *International Journal of Sport Psychology, 28,* 335–354.

Ryska, T., Zenong, Y., & Boyd, M. (1999). The role of dispositional and goal orientation and team climate on situational self-handicapping among young athletes. *Journal of Sport Behavior, 22,* 410–425.

S

Sabiston, C. M., Crocker, P. R. E., & Munroe-Chanceller, K. J. (2005). Examining current discrepancy scores and exercise motivation as predictors of social physique anxiety in exercising females. *Journal of Sport Behavior, 28,* 68–85.

Sage, G. H. (1975). An occupational analysis of the college coach. In D. W. Ball & J. W. Loy (Eds.), *Sport and social order* (pp. 408–455). Reading, MA: Addison-Wesley.

Salili, F., Maehr, M. L., & Gillmore, G. (1976). Achievement and morality: A cross-cultural analysis of causal attribution and evaluation. *Journal of Personality and Social Psychology, 33,* 327–337.

Sallis, J. F., Haskell, W. L., Fortmann, S. P., Vranizan, K. M., Taylor, C. B., & Solomon, D. S. (1986). Predictors of adoption and maintenance of physical activity in a community sample. *Preventive Medicine, 15,* 331–341.

Sallis, J. F., & Hovell, M. F. (1990). Determinants of exercise behavior. In K. B. Pandolf & J. O. Holloszy (Eds.), *Exercise and sport science reviews,* Vol. 18 (pp. 307–330). Baltimore: Williams & Wilkins.

Sallis, J. F., Johnson, M. F., Calfas, K. J., Caparosa, S., & Nichols, J. F. (1997). Assessing perceived environmental variables that may influence physical activity. *Research Quarterly for Exercise and Sport, 68,* 345–351.

Salmon, J., Hall, C. R., & Haslam, I. (1994). The use of imagery by soccer players. *Journal of Applied Sport Psychology, 6,* 116–133.

Salmon, J., Owen, N., Crawford, B. Bauman, A., & Sallis, J. F. (2003). Physical activity and sedentary behavior: A population-based study of barriers, enjoyment, and preference. *Health Psychology, 22,* 178–188.

Sanford-Martens, T. C., Davidson, M. M., Yakushko, O. F., Martens, M. P., Hinton, P., & Beck, N. (2005). Chemical and subchemical eating disorders: An examination of collegiate athletes. *Journal of Applied Sport Psychology, 17,* 79–86.

Sarason, S. B. (1954). *The clinical interaction with special reference to Rorschach.* New York: Harper.

Sarbin, T. R. (1989). The constructions and reconstruction of hypnosis. In N. P. Spanos & J. F. Chames (Eds.), *Hypnosis: The cognitive-behavioral perspective* (pp. 400–416). Buffalo, NY: Prometheus Books.

Sarrazin, P., Roberts, G., Cury, F., Biddle, S., & Famose, J. P. (2002). Exerted effort and performance in climbing among boys: The influence of achievement goals, perceived ability, and task difficulty. *Research Quarterly for Exercise and Sport, 73,* 425–436.

Schacham, S. (1983). A shortened version of the Profile of Mood States. *Journal of Personality Assessment, 47,* 305–306.

Schedlowski, M., & Tewes, U. (1992). Physiological arousal and perception of bodily state during parachute jumping. *Psychophysiology, 29,* 95–103.

Scheer, J. K., & Ansorge, C. J. (1979). Influence due to expectations of judges: A function of internal-external locus of control. *Journal of Sport Psychology, 1,* 53–58.

Schilling, T. A., & Hayashi, C. T. (2001). Achievement motivation among high school basketball and cross-country athletes: A personal investment perspective. *Journal of Applied Sport Psychology, 13,* 103–127.

Schmid, A., & Peper, E. (1998). Training strategies for concentration. In J. M. Williams (Ed.), *Applied sport psychology: Personal growth to peak performance* (pp. 316–328). Mountain View, CA: Mayfield Publishing Company.

Schmidt, G. W., & Stein, G. L. (1991). Sport commitment: A model integrating enjoyment, dropout, and burnout. *Journal of Sport and Exercise Psychology, 13,* 254–265.

Schnurr, P. P., Vaillant, C. O., & Vaillant, G. E. (1990). Predicting exercise in later midlife from young adult personality characteristics. *International Journal of Aging and Human Development, 30,* 153–160.

Schomer, H. H. (1990). A cognitive strategy training programme for marathon runners: Ten case studies. *South African Journal for Research in Sport, Physical Education and Recreation, 13,* 47–78.

Schultz, J. H., & Luthe, W. (1959). *Autogenic training: A psychophysiological approach to psychotherapy.* New York: Grune and Stratton.

Schunk, D. H. (1995). Self-efficacy, motivation, and performance. *Journal of Applied Sport Psychology, 7,* 112–137.

Schurr, K. T., Ashley, M. A., & Joy, K. L. (1977). A multivariate analysis of male athlete characteristics: Sport type and success. *Multivariate Exper-imental Clinical Research, 3,* 53–68.

Schurr, K. T., Ruble, V. E., Nisbet, J., & Wallace, D. (1984). Myers-Briggs type inventory characteristics of more and less successful players on an American football team. *Journal of Sport Be-havior, 7,* 47–57.

Schutte, N. S., Malouff, J. M., Hall, L. E., Haggerty, D. J., Cooper, J. T., Golden, C. J., et al. (1998). Development and validation of a measure of emotional intelligence. *Personality and Individual Differences, 25,* 167–177.

Schutz, R. W., Eom, H. J., Smoll, F. L., & Smith, R. E. (1994). Examination of the factorial validity of the Group Environment Questionnaire. *Research Quarterly for Exercise and Sport, 65,* 226–236.

Schutz, W. C. (1966). *The interpersonal underworld.* Palo Alto, CA: Science and Behavior Books.

Schwartz, B., & Barsky, S. F. (1977). The home advantage. *Social Forces, 55,* 641–661.

Schwartz, G. E., Davidson, R. J., & Goleman, D. J. (1978). Patterning of cognitive and somatic processes in the self-regulation of anxiety: Effects of meditation vs. exercise. *Psychosomatic Medicine, 40,* 321–328.

Scott, L. M., Scott, D., Bedic, S. P., & Dowd, J. (1999). The effect of associative and dissociative strategies on rowing ergometer performance. *The Sport Psychologist, 13,* 57–68.

Seabourne, T. G., Weinberg, R. S., & Jackson, A. (1984). The effect of individualized practice and training of visuo-motor behavior rehearsal in enhancing karate performance. *Journal of Sport Behavior, 7,* 58–67.

Seefeldt, V., & Brown, E. W. (Eds.). (1992). *Program for athletic coaches' education.* Dubuque, IA: Brown & Benchmark.

Seifriz, J. J., Duda, J. L., & Chi, L. (1992). The relationship of perceived motivational climate to intrinsic motivation and beliefs about success in basketball. *Journal of Sport & Exercise Psychology, 14,* 375–391.

Seldman, R. (October 2004). *Letting go to win: A person-centered approach to sports enhancement.* Keynote address at the annual convention of the Association for the Advancement of Applied Sport Psychology, Minneapolis, MN.

Seligman, M. E. P. (1995). *The optimistic child.* New York: Houghton Mifflin Company.

Seligman, M. E. P., & Csikszentmihalyi, M. (2000). Positive psychology: An introduction. *American Psychologist, 55,* 5–14.

Selye, H. (1983). The stress concept: Past, present, and future. In C. L. Cooper (Ed.), *Stress research* (pp. 1–20). New York: John Wiley & Sons.

Sharp, M., & Collins, D. (1998). Exploring the "inevitability" of the relationship between anabolic- androgenic steroid use and aggression in human males. *Journal of Sport & Exercise Psychology, 20,* 379–394.

Shaw, J. M., Dzewaltowski, D. A., & McElroy, M. (1992). Self-efficacy and causal attributions as mediators of perceptions of psychological momentum. *Journal of Sport & Exercise Psychology, 14,* 134–147.

Shay, K. A., & Roth, D. L. (1992). Association between aerobic fitness and visuospatial performance in healthy older adults. *Psychology of Aging, 7,* 15–24.

Sheehan, P. W. (1967). A shortened version of Betts' questionnaire on mental imagery. *Journal of Clinical Psychology, 23,* 386–389.

Sheldon, J. P., & Aimor, C. M. (2001). The role aggression plays in successful and unsuccessful ice hockey behavior. *Research Quarterly for Exercise and Sport, 72,* 304–309.

Shephard, R. J. (1990). *Fitness in special populations.* Champaign, IL: Human Kinetics Books.

Shephard, R. J., & Shek, P. N. (1994). Potential impact of physical activity and sport on the immune system—a brief review. *British Journal of Sports Medicine, 28,* 247–255.

Shephard, R. J., Rhind, S., & Shek, P. N. (1995). The impact of exercise on the immune system: NK cells, interleukins 1 and 2, and related responses. *Exercises and Sport Science Reviews, 23,* 215–241.

Short, S. E., Bruggeman, J. M., Enel, S. G., Marback, T. L., Wang, L. J., Willadsen, A., & Short, M. W. (2002). The effect of imagery function and imagery direction on self-efficacy and performance on a golf putting task. *The Sport Psychologist, 16,* 48–67.

Short, S. E., Monsma, E. V., & Short, M. W. (2004). Is what you see really what you get? Athletes' perceptions of imagery's functions. *The Sport Psychologist, 18,* 341–349.

Sibley, B. A., & Etnier, J. L. (2004). Time course of attention and decision making during a volleyball set. *Research Quarterly for Exercise and Sport, 75* 102–106.

Siedentop, D., & Ramey, G. (1977). Extrinsic rewards and intrinsic motivation. *Motor Skills: Theory into Practice, 2,* 49–62.

Silva, J. M., III. (1989). The evolution of AAASP and JASP. *Journal of Applied Sport Psychology, 1,* 1–3.

Silva, J. M., III. (1990). An analysis of the training stress syndrome in competitive athletics. *Journal of Applied Sport Psychology, 2,* 5–20.

Silva, J. M., III, & Andrew, J. A. (1987). An analysis of game location and basketball performance in the Atlantic coast conference. *International Journal of Sport Psychology, 18,* 188–204.

Silva, J. M., III., & Appelbaum, M. I. (1989). Association-dissociation patterns of United States Olympic Marathon Trial contestants. *Cognitive Therapy and Research, 13,* 185–192.

Silva, J. M., III, Conroy, D. E., & Zizzi, S. J. (1999). Critical issues confronting the advancement of applied sport psychology. *Journal of Applied Sport Psychology, 11,* 298–320.

Silva, J. M., III, Hardy, C. J., & Grace, R. K. (1998). Analysis of psychological momentum in intercollegiate tennis. *Journal of Sport & Excercise Psychology, 10,* 346–354.

Silva, J. M., III, Shultz, B. B., Haslam, R. W., Martin, T. P., & Murray, D. F. (1985). Discriminating characteristics of contestants at the United States Olympic wrestling trials. *International Journal of Sport Psychology, 16,* 79–102.

Silva, J. M., III, Shultz, B. B., Haslam, R. W., & Murray, D. (1981). A psychological assessment of elite wrestlers. *Research Quarterly for Exercise and Sport, 52,* 348–358.

Silverman, J. (1964). The problem of attention in research and theory in schizophrenia. *Psychological Review, 71,* 352–379.

Simons, A. D., Epstein, L. H., McGowan, C. R., Kupfer, D. J., & Robertson, R. J. (1985). Exercise as a treatment for depression: An update. *Clinical Psychology Review, 5,* 553–568.

Singer, R. N. (1968). *Motor learning and human performance: An application to motor skills and movement behaviors.* New York: Macmillan.

Singer, R. N. (1969). Personality differences between and within baseball and tennis players. *Research Quarterly, 40,* 582–587.

Singer, R. N. (2002). Preperformance state, routines, and automaticity: What does it take to realize expertise in self-paced events? *Journal of Sport & Exercise Psychology, 24,* 359–375.

Skinner, B. F. (1938). *The behavior of organisms: An experimental analysis.* New York: Appleton-Century-Crofts.

Skinner, B. F. (1953). *Science and human behavior.* New York: Macmillan.

Skinner, N., & Brewer, N. (2004). Adaptive approaches to competition: Challenge appraisals and positive emotion. *Journal of Sport and Exercise Psychology, 26,* 283–305.

Skinner, S. (June 8, 2000). Striving for perfection. *Columbia Missourian Voxmagazine,* 8–13.

Slade, J. M., Landers, D. M., & Martin, P. E. (2002). Muscular activity during real and imagined movements: A test of inflow explanations. *Journal of Sport and Exercise Psychology,* 151–167.

Smith, A. L. (1999). Perceptions of peer relationships and physical activity participation in early adolescence. *Journal of Sport & Exercise Psychology, 21,* 329–350.

Smith, A. M. (1996). Psychological impact of injuries in athletes. *Sports Medicine, 22,* 391–405.

Smith, A. M., & Milliner, E. K. (1994). The risk of suicide in athletes. *Journal of Athletic Training, 29,* 337–341.

Smith, A. M., Scott, S. G., Wiese, D. M. (1990). The psychological effects of sports injuries: Coping. *Sports Medicine, 9,* 352–369.

Smith, D. (1992). The coach as sport psychologist: An alternate view. *Journal of Applied Sport Psychology, 4,* 56–62.

Smith, D. (Winter 2005). Golden rules. *Mizzou, 93,* 32–37.

Smith, D., & Stewart, S. (2003). Sexual aggression and sports participation. *Journal of Sport Behavior, 26,* 384–395.

Smith, D., & Collins, D. (2004). Mental practice, motor performance, and the late CNV. *Journal of Sport and Exercise Psychology, 26,* 412–426.

Smith, D., & Holmes, P. (2004). The effect of imagery modality on golf putting performance. *Journal of Sport and Exercise Psychology, 26*(3), 385–395.

Smith, G. (2004, May 3). Pat Tillman 1976–2004: Code of honor. *Sports Illustrated, 100,* 40–46.

Smith, G. (2005, March 28). Steroids and baseball: What do we do now? *Sports Illustrated, 102,* 40–50.

Smith, M. D. (1980). Hockey violence: Interring some myths. In W. F. Straub (Ed.), *Sport psychology: An analysis of athlete behavior.* 2nd ed. Ithaca, NY: Mouvement Publications.

Smith, R. E. (1980). A cognitive-affective approach to stress management training for athletes. In C. H. Nadeau (Ed.), *Psychology of motor behavior and sport, 1979.* Champaign, IL: Human Kinetics Publishers.

Smith, R. E. (1986). Toward a cognitive-affective model of athletic burnout. *Journal of Sport Psychology, 8,* 36–50.

Smith, R. E. (1996). Performance anxiety, cognitive interference, and concentration enhancement strategies in sports. In I. G. Sarason, G. R. Pierce, & B. R. Sarason (Eds.), *Cognitive interference: Theories, methods, and findings* (pp. 261–283). Mahwah, NJ: Erlbaum.

Smith, R. E. (1999). Generalization effects in coping skills training. *Journal of Sport & Exercise Psychology, 21,* 189–204.

Smith, R. E., & Christensen, D. S. (1995). Psychological skills as predictors of performance and survival in professional baseball. *Journal of Sport & Exercise Psychology, 17,* 399–415.

Smith, R. E., & Johnson, J. (1990). An organizational empowerment approach to consultation in professional baseball. *The Sport Psychologist, 4,* 347–357.

Smith, R. E., Schutz, R. W., Smoll, F. L., & Ptacek, J. T. (1995). Development and validation of a multidimensional measure of sport specific psychological skills: The athletic coping skills inventory-28. *Journal of Sport & Exercise Psychology, 17,* 379–398.

Smith, R. E., & Smoll, F. L. (1997a). Coach-mediated team building in youth sports. *Journal of Applied Sport Psychology, 9,* 114–132.

Smith, R. E., & Smoll, F. L. (1997b, February). Coaching the coaches: Youth sports as a scientific and applied behaviorial setting. *Current Directions in Psychological Science, 6,* 16–21.

Smith, R. E., Smoll, F. L., & Barnett, N. P. (1995). Reduction of children's sport performance anxiety through social support and stress-reduction training for coaches. *Journal of Applied Developmental Psychology, 16,* 125–142.

Smith, R. E., Smoll, F. L., & Curtis, B. (1979). Coach effectiveness training: A cognitive-behavioral ap-proach to enhancing relationship skills in youth sport coaches. *Journal of Sport Psychology, 1,* 59–75.

Smith, R. E., Smoll, F. L., & Hunt, E. (1977). A system for the behavioral assessment of athletic coaches. *Research Quarterly, 48,* 401–407.

Smith, R. E., Smoll, F. L., & Ptacek, J. T. (1990). Conjunctive moderatory variables in vulnerability and resiliency research: Life stress, social support and coping skills, and adolescent sport injuries. *Journal of Personality and Social Psychology, 58*(2), 560–570.

Smith, R. E., Smoll, F. L., & Schutz, R. W. (1990). Measurement correlates of sport specific cognitive and somatic trait anxiety: The sport anxiety scale. *Anxiety Research, 2,* 263–280.

Smoll, F. L. (1998). Improving the quality of coach-parent relationships in youth sports. In J. M. Williams (Ed.), *Applied sport psychology: Personal growth to peak performance* (pp. 63–73).

Smoll, F. L. (2001). Coach-parent relationships in youth sports: Increasing harmony and minimizing hassle. In J. M. Williams (Ed.), *Applied sport psychology: Personal growth to peak performance* (pp. 150–161). Mountain View, CA: Mayfield Publishing Company.

Smoll, F. L., & Cumming, S. P. (192–204). Enhancing coach-parent relationships in youth sports: Increasing harmony and minimizing hassle. In J. M. Williams (Ed.), *Applied sport psychology: Personal growth to peak performance* (pp. 192–204). McGraw-Hill.

Smoll, F. L., & Smith, R. E. (1989). Leadership behaviors in sport: A theoretical model and research paradigm. *Journal of Applied Social Psychology, 19,* 1522–1551.

Smoll, F. L., & Smith, R. E. (1998). Conducting psychologically oriented coach-training programs: Cognitive-behavioral principles and techniques. In J. M. Williams (Ed.), *Applied sport psychology: Personal growth to peak performance* (pp. 41–62). Mountain View, CA: Mayfield Publishing Company.

Smoll, F. L., & Smith, R. E. (1999). Coaching behavior research in youth sports: Sport psychology goes to the ballpark. In G. G. Brannigan (Ed.), *The sport scientists: Research interests* (pp. 113–132). New York: Longman.

Smoll, F. L., Smith, R. E., Curtis, B., & Hunt, E. (1978). Toward a mediational model of coach-player relationships. *Research Quarterly, 49,* 528–541.

Sonstroem, R. J., & Bermardo, P. (1982). Intraindividual pregame state anxiety and basketball performance: A reexamination of the inverted-U curve. *Journal of Sport Psychology, 4,* 235–245.

Spanos, N. P. (1991). A sociocognitive approach to hypnosis. In S. J. Lynn & J. W. Rhue (Eds.), *Theories of hypnosis: Current models and perspectives* (pp. 324–361). New York: Guilford Press.

Spence, K. W. (1956). *Behavior theory and conditioning.* New Haven, CT: Yale University Press.

Spielberger, C. D. (1971). Trait-state anxiety and motor behavior. *Journal of Motor Behavior, 3,* 265–279.

Spielberger, C. D. (1983). *Manual for the state-trait anxiety inventory* (Form Y). Palo Alto, CA: Consulting Psychologists Press.

Spigolon, L., & Annalisa, D. (1985). Autogenic training in frogmen. *International Journal of Sport Psychology, 16,* 312–320.

Spink, K. S. (1992). Group cohesion and starting status in successful and less successful elite volleyball teams. *Journal of Sport Sciences, 10,* 379–388.

Spink, K. S. (1995). Cohesion and intention to participate of female sport team athletes. *Journal of Sport & Exercise Psychology, 17,* 416–427.

Stadulis, R. E., Eidson, T. A., & MacCracken, M. J. (1994). A children's form of the competitive state anxiety inventory (CSAI-2C). *Journal of Sport & Exercise Psychology, 16,* S109.

Staff. (1992, September/October). AHA declares regular exercise to be a major factor in cardiovascular health. *President's Council on Physical Fitness and Sports Newsletter, 92*(5), 1, 5.

Steers, D. (1982, November). Trapped in Peru, U.S. women shouted down. *Volleyball Monthly,* 15–21.

Stein, G. L., Kimiecik, J. C., Daniels, J., & Jackson, S. A. (1995). Psychological antecedents of flow in recreational sport. *Personality and Social Psychology Bulletin, 21,* 125–135.

Stein, J. (October 4, 1999). The oldest rookie. *Time, 154,* 6.

Steinberg, G. M. B., Singer, R. N., & Murphy, M. (2000). The benefits to sport achievement when a multiple goal orientation is emphasized. *Journal of Sport Behavior, 23,* 407–422.

Stennet, R. C. (1957). The relationship of performance level to level of arousal. *Journal of Experimental Psychology, 54,* 54–61.

Stephen, D. E., & Bredemeier, B. J. L. (1996). Moral atmosphere and judgments about aggression in girls' soccer: Relationships among moral and motivational variables. *Journal of Sport & Exercise Psychology, 18,* 158–173.

Stephens, D. E. (2000). Predictors of likelihood to aggress in youth soccer: An examination of coed and all-girls teams. *Journal of Sport Behavior, 23,* 311–325.

Stephens, D. E. (2001). Predictors of aggressive tendencies in girls' basketball: An examination of beginning and advanced participants in a summer skills camp. *Research Quarterly for Exercise Sport, 72,* 257–266.

Sternfeld, B. (1992). Cancer and the protective effect of physical activity: The epidemiological evidence. *Medicine and Science in Sports and Exercise, 24,* 1195–1209.

Steroids made baseball career possible (February 13, 2005). Canseco: Steroids made baseball career possible, http://www.USAtoday.com/2005/2/13/

Stevinson, C. D., & Biddle, S. J. H. (1999). Cognitive strategies in running: A response to Masters and Ogles (1998). *The Sport Psychologist, 13,* 234–236.

Stogdill, R. M. (1948). Personal factors associated with leadership: Survey of literature. *Journal of Psychology, 25,* 35–71.

Stone, M. H. (1993). Literature review: Anabolic-androgenic steroid use by athletes. *National Strength and Conditioning Association Journal, 15,* 10–28.

Storch, E. A., Storch, J. B., Kovacs, A. H., Okum, A., & Welsh, E. (2003). Intrinsic religiosity and substance use in intercollegiate athletes. *Journal of Sports and Exercise Psychology, 25,* 248–252.

Storch, E. A., Werner, N. E., & Storch, J. B. (2003). Relational aggression and psychosocial adjustment in intercollegiate athletes. *Journal of Sport Behavior, 26,* 155–167.

Strelan, P., & Boeckmann, R. J. (2003). A new model for understanding performance-enhancing drug use by elite athletes. *Journal of Applied Sport Psychology, 15,* 176–183.

Stringer, W. W., Berezovskaya, M., O'Brian, W. A., Beck, C. K., & Casaburi, R. (1998). The effect of exercise training on aerobic fitness, immune indices, and quality of life in HIV-positive patients. *Medicine & Science in Sports & Exercise, 30,* 11–16.

Stuntz, C. P., & Weiss, M. R. (2003). Influence of social goal orientation and peers on unsportsman-like play. *Research Quarterly for Exercise and Sport, 74,* 421–435.

Sturman, J. S., & Thibodeau, R. (2001). Performance-undermining effects of baseball free agent contracts. *Journal of Sport & Exercise Psychology,* 23–34.

Sue, D., & Sue, D. W. (1999). *Counseling the culturally different: Theory and practice.* 3rd ed. New York: Wiley.

Suedfeld, P., & Bruno, T. (1990). Flotation REST and imagery in the improvement of athletic performance. *Journal of Sport & Exercise Psychology, 12,* 82–85.

Suinn, R. (2000, October). *Psychological interventions with heart disease, cancer, and pain management.* Paper presented at the meeting of the Association for the Advancement of Applied Sport Psychology, Nashville, TN.

Suinn, R. M. (1972). Removing emotional obstacles to learning and performance by visuo-motor behavior rehearsal. *Behavioral Therapy, 31,* 308–310.

Suinn, R. M. (1994). Visualization in sports. In A. A. Sheikh & E. R. Korn (Eds.), *Imagery in sports and physical performance* (pp. 23–42). Amityville, NY: Baywood.

Sullivan, M. I. L., Bishop, S., & Pivik, J. (1995). The Pain Catastrophizing Scale: Development and validation. *Psychological Assessment, 7,* 524–532.

Sullivan, M. I. L., Tripp, D. A., Rodgers, W. M., & Stanish, W. (2000). Catastrophizing and pain perception in sport participants. *Journal of Applied Sport Psychology, 12,* 151–167.

Sullivan, P. J., & Kent, A. (2003). Coaching efficacy as a predictor of leadership style in intercollegiate athletics. *Journal of Applied Sport Psychology, 15,* 1–11.

Sutarman & Thompson, H. L. (1952). A new technique for enumerating active sweat glands in man. *Journal of Physiology, 117,* 51.

Swain, A. & Jones, G. (1992). Relationship between sport achievement orientation and competitive state anxiety. *The Sport Psychologist, 6,* 42–54.

Swift, E. M. (August 30, 2004). How the fallen was mighty. *Sports Illustrated, 101,* 44–47.

T

Tammen, V. V. (1996). Elite middle and long distance runners associative/dissociative coping. *Journal of Applied Sport Psychology, 8,* 1–8.

Tattersfield, C. R. (1971). *Competitive sport and personality development.* Unpublished doctoral dissertation, University of Durham, NC.

Taylor, A. J., & May, S. (1996). Threat and coping appraisal as determinants of compliance to sports injury rehabilitation: An application of protection motivation theory. *Journal of Sports Sciences, 14,* 471–482.

Taylor, J. (1994). Examining the boundaries of sport science and psychology trained practitioners in applied sport psychology: Title usage and area of competence. *The Sport Psychologist, 6,* 185–195.

Taylor, J., & Demick, A. (1994). A multidimensional model of momentum in sports. *Journal of Applied Sport Psychology, 6,* 51–70.

Taylor, J., & Ogilvie, B. (1994). A conceptual model of adaptation to retirement among athletes. *Journal of Applied Sport Psychology, 6,* 1–20.

Taylor, J., & Ogilvie, B. C. (2001). Career termination among athletes. In R. N. Singer, H. A. Hausenblas, & M. C. M. Janelle (Eds.), *Handbook of Sport Psychology* (pp. 672–694). New York: John Wiley & Sons, Inc.

Taylor, J., & Taylor, S. (1998). Pain education and management in the rehabilitation from sports injury. *The Sport Psychologist, 12,* 68–88.

Taylor, J., Horevitz, R., & Balague, G. (1993). The use of hypnosis in applied sport psychology. *The Sport Psychologist, 7,* 58–78.

Taylor, P. (December 15, 1997). Center of the storm. *Sports Illustrated, 87,* 60–67.

Tenenbaum, G. (1984). A note on the measurement and relationships of physiological and psychological components of anxiety. *International Journal of Sport Psychology, 15,* 88–97.

Tenenbaum, G., Bar-Eli, M., & Yaaron, M. (1999). The dynamics of goal setting: Interactive effects of goal difficulty, goal specificity and duration of practice time intervals. *International Journal of Sport Psychology, 30,* 325–338.

Tenenbaum, G., Corbett, M., & Kitsantas, A. (2002). Biofeedback: Applications and methodological concerns. In B. Blumenstein, M. Bar-Eli, & G. Tenenbaum (Eds.). *Brain and body in sport and exercise: Biofeedback applications in performance enhancement* (pp. 101–122). John Wiley & Sons, Ltd.

Tenenbaum, G., & Elran, E. (2003). Congruence between actual and retrospective reports of emotions for pre- and postcompetition states. *Journal of Sport and Exercise Psychology, 25,* 323–340.

Tenenbaum, G., Lloyd, M., Pretty, G., & Hanin, Y. L. (2002). Congruence of actual and retrospective reports of pre-competition emotions in equestrians. *Journal of Sport and Exercise Psychology, 24,* 271–288.

Tenenbaum, G., Stewart, E., Singer, R. N., & Duda, J. (1997). Aggression and violence in sport: An ISSP position stand. *The Sport Psychologist, 11,* 1–7.

Terry, P. C. (1995). The efficacy of mood state profiling with elite performers: A review and synthesis. *The Sport Psychologist, 9,* 309–324.

Terry, P. C., Keohane, L., & Lane, H. (1996). Development and validation of a shortened version of the profile of mood states suitable for use with young athletes. *Journal of Sports Sciences, 14,* 49.

Terry, P. C., & Lane, A. M. (2000). Normative values for the profile of mood states for use with athletic samples. *Journal of Applied Sport Psychology, 12,* 93–109.

Terry, P. C., Mayer, J. L., & Howe, B. L. (1998). Effectiveness of a mental training program for novice scuba divers. *Journal of Applied Sport Psychology, 10,* 251–267.

Thamel, P. (2003, May 5). Mavericks avoid meltdown. *The New York Times,* http://www.nytimes.com/2003/5/5/sports/basketball/

Thamel, P. (2004, October 27). At Oklahoma, dealing with the invisible injuries. *The New York Times,* http://www.nytimes.com

Tharp, R. G., & Gallimore, R. (1976). Basketball's John Wooden: What a coach can teach a teacher. *Psychology Today, 9,* 74–78.

Thayer, R. E. (1986). Activation-Deactivation Check List: Current overview and structural analysis. *Psychological Reports, 58,* 607–614.

Thelwell, R. C., & Greenless, I. A. (2001). The effects of a mental skills training package on gymnasium triathlon performances. *The Sport Psychologist, 15,* 127–141.

Thelwell, R. C., & Greenless, I. A. (2003). Developing competitive endurance performance using mental skills training. *The Sport Psychologist, 17,* 318–337.

Theodorakis, Y. (1996). The influence of goals, commitment, self-efficacy and self-satisfaction on motor performance. *Journal of Applied Sport Psychology, 8,* 171–182.

Theodorakis, Y., Chroni, S., & Laparidis, K., Bebetos, V., & Duoma, I. (2001). Self-talk in a basketball shooting task. *Perceptual and Motor Skills, 92,* 309–315.

Theodorakis, Y., Weinberg, R., Natsis, P., Douma, I., & Kazakas, P. (2000). The effects of motivational versus instructional self-talk on improving motor performance. *The Sport Psychologist, 14,* 253–271.

Thirer, J., & Greer, D. L. (1981). Personality characteristics associated with beginning, intermediate, and competitive bodybuilders. *Journal of Sport Behavior, 4,* 3–11.

Thomas, O., Hanton, S., & Jones, G. (2002). An alternative approach to short-form self-report assessment of competitive anxiety: A research note. *International Journal of Sport Psychology, 33,* 325–336.

Thomas, O., Maynard, I., & Hanton, S. (2004). Temporal aspects of competitive anxiety and self-confidence as a function of anxiety perception. *The Sport Psychologist, 18,* 172–187.

Thomas, P. R., Murphey, S. M., & Hardy, L. (1999). Test of performance strategies: Development and preliminary validation of a comprehensive measure of athletes' psychological skills. *Journal of Sport Sciences, 17,* 697–713.

Thompson, B. (March 20, 2002). Homecoming kings. *Columbia Daily Tribune,* B.

Thorn, B. E., & Williams, G. A. (1989). Goal specifications alters perceived pain intensity and tolerance latency. *Cognitive Therapy and Research, 2,* 171–183.

Thune, A. R. (1949). Personality of weight lifters. *Research Quarterly, 20,* 296–306.

Thuot, S., Kavouras, S., & Kenefick, R. (1998). Effect of perceived ability, game location, and state anxiety on basketball performance. *Journal of Sport Behavior, 21,* 311–321.

Tolson, J. (July 3, 2000). Into the zone. *U.S. News & World Report, 129,* 38–45.

Tompkins, S. S. (1947). *The Thematic Apperception Test: The theory and technique of interpretation.* New York: Grune and Stratton.

Tomorowski, P. D., Ellis, N. R. (1986). Effects of exercise on cognitive processes: A review. *Psychological Bulletin, 99,* 338–346.

Tomson, L. M., Pangrazi, R. P., Friedman, G., & Hutchison, N. (2003). Childhood depression symptoms, physical activity and health related fitness, *Journal of Sport and Exercise Psychology, 25,* 419–439.

Tracey, J. (2003). The emotional response to the injury and rehabilitation process. *Journal of Applied Sport Psychology, 15,* 279–293.

Treasure, D. C. (1997). Perceptions of the motivational climate and elementary school children's cognitive and affective response. *Journal of Sport & Exercise Psychology, 19,* 278–290.

Treasure, D. C., Duda, J. L., Hall, H. K., Roberts, G. C., Ames, C., & Maehr, M. L. (2001). Clarifying misconceptions and misrepresentations in achievement goal research in sport: A response to Haywood, Hardy, and Swain. *Journal of Sport & Exercise Psychology, 23,* 317–329.

Treasure, D. C., Lox, C. L., & Lawton, B. R. (1998). Determinants of physical activity in a sedentary obese female population. *Journal of Sport & Exercise Psychology, 20,* 218–224.

Treasure, D. C., Monson, J., & Lox, C. L. (1996). Relationship between self-efficacy, wrestling performance, and affect prior to competition. *The Sport Psychologist, 10,* 73–83.

Treasure, D. C., & Roberts, G. C. (1995). Application of achievement goal theory to physical education: Implications for enhancing motivation. *Quest, 47,* 475–489.

Treasure, D. C., & Roberts, G. C. (1998). Relationship between female adolescents' achievement goal orientations, perceptions of the motivational climate, belief about success and sources of satisfaction in basketball. *International Journal of Sport Psychology, 29,* 211–230.

Treisman, A. M. (1965). Our limited attention. *The Advancement of Science, 22,* 600–611.

Triplett, N. (1897). The dynamogenic factors in pacemaking and competition. *American Journal of Psychology, 9,* 507–553.

Tucker, L. W., & Parks, J. B. (2001). Effects of gender and sport type on intercollegiate athletes' perceptions of the legitimacy of aggressive behavior in sport. *Sociology of Sport Journal, 18,* 403–413.

Tuckman, B. W. (1965). Developmental sequences in small groups. *Psychological Bulletin, 63,* 384–399.

Turatto, M., Benso, F., & Umilta, C. (1999). Focusing of attention in professional women skiers. *International Journal of Sport Psychology, 30,* 339–349.

Turner, E. E., Rejeski, W. J., & Brawley, L. R. (1997). Psychological benefits of physical activity are influenced by the social environment. *Journal of Sport & Exercise Psychology, 19,* 119–130.

Turner, P. E., & Raglin, J. S. (1996). Variability in precompetition anxiety and performance in college track and field athletes. *Medicine and Science in Sports and Exercise, 28,* 378–385.

Tutko, T. A., & Richards, J. W. (1971). *Psychology of coaching.* Boston: Allyn and Bacon.

Tutko, T. A., & Richards, J. W. (1972). *Coaches' practical guide to athletic motivation.* Boston: Allyn and Bacon.

U

Udry, E. (1997). Coping and social support among injured athletes following surgery. *Journal of Sport & Exercise Psychology, 19,* 71–90.

Udry, E., Gould, D., Bridges, D., & Beck, L. (1997a). Down but not out: Athlete responses to season-ending injuries. *Journal of Sport & Exercise Psychology, 19,* 229–248.

Udry, E., Gould, D., Bridges, D., & Tuffey, S. (1997b). People helping people? Examining the social ties of athletes coping with burnout and injury stress. *Journal of Sport & Exercise Psychology, 19,* 368–395.

Ulett, G. A., & Peterson, D. B. (1965). *Applied hypnosis and positive suggestion.* St. Louis: C. V. Mosby.

Ulrich, R. P. (1973). *The effect of hypnotic and non-hypnotic suggestions on archery performance.* Unpublished doctoral dissertation, University of Utah, Salt Lake City.

United States Olympic Committee (1983). US Olympic Committee establishes guidelines for sport psychology services. *Journal of Sport Psychology, 5,* 4–7

V

Vallerand, R. J. (1997). Toward a hierarchical model of intrinsic and extrinsic motivation. In M. P. Zanna (Ed.), *Advances in experimental and social psychology,* Vol. 29 (pp. 271–360). New York: Academic Press.

Vallerand, R. J., & Blanchard, C. M. (2000). The study of emotion in sport and exercise. In Y. L. Hanin (Ed.), *Emotions in sport* (pp. 3–38). Champaign, IL: Human Kinetics.

Vallerand, R. J., Colavecchio, P. G., & Pelletier, L. G. (1988). Psychological momentum and performance: A preliminary test of the antecedents-consequences psychological momentum model. *Journal of Sport and Exercise Psychology, 10,* 92–108.

Vallerand, R. J., & Losier, G. F. (1999). An integrative analysis of intrinsic and extrinsic motivation in sport. *Journal of Applied Sport Psychology, 11,* 142–169.

Van Landuyt, L. M., Ekkekakis, P., Hall, E. E., & Petruzzello, S. J. (2000). Throwing the mountains into the lakes: On the perils of nomothetic conceptions of the exercise-affect relationship. *Journal of Sport & Exercise Psychology, 22,* 208–234.

Van Raalte, J. L., Brewer, B. W., Rivera, P. M., & Petitpas, A. S. (1994). The relationship between observable self-talk and competitive junior tennis players' match performances. *Journal of Sport and Exercise Psychology, 16,* 400–415.

Van Raalte, J. L., Cornelius, A. E., Brewer, B. W., & Hatten, S. J. (2000). The antecedents and consequences of self-talk in competitive tennis. *Journal of Sport and Exercise Psychology, 22,* 345–356.

Van Raalte, J. L., et al. (2000). An on-line survey of graduate course offerings satisfying AAASP certification criteria. *The Sport Psychologist, 14,* 98–104.

Van Schoyck, S. R., & Grasha, A. F. (1981). Attentional style variations and athletic ability: The advantages of the sports specific test. *Journal of Sport Psychology, 3,* 149–165.

Vansteenkiste, M., Simons, J., Soenens, B., & Lens, W. (2004). How to become a persevering exerciser? Providing a clear future intrinsic goal in an autonomy-supportive way. *Journal of Sport & Exercise Psychology, 26,* 232–249.

VanVorst, J. G., Buckworth, J., & Mattern, C. (2002). Physical self-concept and strength changes in college weight training classes. *Research Quarterly for Exercise and Sport, 73,* 113–117.

Van Yperen, N. W. (1997). Inequity and vulnerability to dropout symptoms: An exploratory causal analysis among highly skilled youth soccer players. *The Sport Psychologist, 11,* 318–325.

Vandenberg, S., & Kuse, A. R. (1978). Mental rotations: A group of three-dimensional spatial visualization. *Perceptual and Motor Skills, 47,* 599–604.

Vanek, M., & Cratty, B. J. (1970). *Psychology and the superior athlete.* London: Macmillan.

Varca, P. E. (1980). An analysis of home and away game performance of male college basketball teams. *Journal of Sport Psychology, 2,* 245–257.

Vargas-Tunsing, T. M., Myers, N. D., & Feltz, D. L. (2004). Coaches' and athletes' perceptions of efficacy-enhancing techniques. *The Sport Psychologist, 18,* 397–414.

Vealey, R. S. (1986). Conceptualization of sport-confidence and competitive orientation: Preliminary investigation and instrument development. *Journal of Sport Psychology, 8,* 221–246.

Vealey, R. S. (1988a). Future directions in psychological skills training. *The Sport Psychologist, 2,* 318–336.

Vealey, R. S. (1988b). Sport-confidence and competitive orientation: An addendum on scoring procedures and gender differences. *Journal of Sport & Exercise Psychology, 10,* 471–478.

Vealey, R. S. (1994). Current status and prominent issues in sport psychology interventions. *Medicine and Science in Sport and Exercise, 26,* 495–502.

Vealey, R. S., Armstrong, L., Comar, W., & Greenleaf, C. A. (1998). Influence of perceived coaching behaviors on burnout and competitive anxiety in female collegiate athletes. *Journal of Applied Sport Psychology, 10,* 297–318.

Vealey, R. S., & Greenleaf, C. A. (2001). Seeing is believing: Understanding and using imagery in sport. In J. M. Williams (Ed.), *Applied sport psychology: Personal growth to peak perfomance* (pp. 247–272). Mountain View, CA: Mayfield Publishing Comapny.

Vealey, R. S., Hayashi, S. W., Garner-Holman, M., & Giacobbi, P. (1998). Sources of sports confidence: Conceptualization and instrument development. *Journal of Sport & Exercise Psychology, 20,* 54–80.

Vealey, R. S., Knight, B. J., & Pappas, G. (November 2, 2002). *Self-confidence in sport: Conceptual and psychological advancement.* Paper presented at the annual convention of the Association for the Advancement of Applied Sport Psychology, Tucson, AZ.

Vecsey, G. (March 11, 2004). Must crack down on threats. *The New York Times,* http://www.nytimes.com/2004/3/11/sports

Verducci, T. (2001, June 18). High-wire act. *Sports Illustrated, 94,* 82–96.

Verducci, T. (2003a, March 31). The ultimate gamer. *Sports Illustrated, 98,* 70–81.

Verducci, T. (2003b, July 7). Blackout: The African American baseball player is vanishing. Does he have a future? *Sports Illustrated, 99,* 56–66.

Vlachopoulos, S., & Biddle, S. J. H. (1999). Modeling the relation of goal orientation to achievement-related affect in physical education: Does perceived ability matter? *Journal of Sport & Exercise Psychology, 19,* 169–187.

Volek, J. S. (1999, May/June). What we now know about creatine. *American College of Sport Medicine Health & Fitness Journal, 3,* 27–33.

Volkamer, N. (1972). Investigations into the aggressiveness in competitive social systems. *Sportwissenschaft, 1,* 33–64.

Von Rein, Patricia (November 22, 2001). Weighing the issue. *Voc-magazine,* p. 4.

Vroom, V. H., & Yetton, P. W. (1973). *Leadership and decision making.* Pittsburgh: University of Pittsburgh Press.

W

Wachtel, P. (1967). Conceptions of broad and narrow attention. *Psychological Bulletin, 68,* 417–429.

Wagman, D., & Khelifa, M. (1996). Psychological issues in sport injury rehabilitation: Current knowledge and practice. *Journal of Athletic Training, 13,* 257–261.

Wagner, G., Rabkin, J., & Rabkin, R. (1998). Exercise as a mediator of psychological and nutritional effects of testosterone therapy in HIV-positive men. *Medicine & Science in Sports & Exercise, 30,* 811–817.

Wahl, G., Wertheim, L. J., & Dohrmann, G. (September 10, 2001). Special report: Passion. *Sports Illustrated, 95,* 59–68.

Walker, B. (1996, October 23). Yanks win on road. Columbia Missourian, p. B1.

Walling, M. D., Duda, J. L., & Chi, L. (1993). The perceived motivational climate in sport questionnaire: Construct and predictive validity. *Journal of Sport & Exercise Psychology, 15,* 172–183.

Walton, B. (May 29, 2000). Basketball's tarnished Knight. *Time, 155* (22), 96.

Wang, C. K. J., & Biddle, S. J. H. (2001). Young people's motivational profiles in physical activity: A cluster analysis. *Journal of Sport & Exercise Psychology, 23,* 1–22.

Wankel, L. M. (1972). An examination of illegal aggression in intercollegiate hockey. In I. D. Williams & L. M. Wankel (Eds.), *Proceedings of the Fourth Canadian Psychomotor Learning and Sport Psychology Symposium* (pp. 531–542). Waterloo, Ontario: University of Waterloo.

Wankel, L. M., & Kreisel, S. J. P. (1985). Factors underlying enjoyment of youth sports: Sport and age group comparisons. *Journal of Sport Psychology, 7,* 51–64.

Wankel, L. M., & Mummery, W. K. (1993). Using national survey data incorporating the theory of planned behavior: Implications for social marketing strategies in physical activity. *Journal of Applied Sport Psychology, 5,* 158–177.

Wanlin, C. M., Hrycaiko, D. W., Martin, G. L., & Mahan, M. (1997). The effects of a goal setting package on the performance of speed skaters. *Journal of Applied Sport Psychology, 9,* 212–228.

Ward, D. G., & Cox, R. H. (2004). The Sport Grid–Revised as a measure of felt arousal and cognitive anxiety. *Journal of Sport Behavior, 27,* 93–113.

Watson, D., Clark, L. A., & Tellegen, A. (1988). Development and validation of brief measures of positive and negative affect: The PANAS scales. *Journal of Personality and Social Psychology, 54,* 1063–1070.

Webb, W., Nasco, S., Riley, S., & Headrick, B. (1998). Athlete identity and reactions to retirement from sports. *Journal of Sport Behavior, 21,* 338–362.

Wegner, D. M. (1997). When the antidote is the poison: Ironic mental control processes. *Psychological Science, 8,* 148–150.

Weigand, D. A., & Broadhurst, C. J. (1998). The relationship among perceived competence, intrinsic motivation, and control perceptions in youth soccer. *International Journal of Sport Psychology, 29,* 324–338.

Weigand, D. A., & Burton, S. (2002). Manipulating achievement motivation in physical education by manipulating the motivational climate. *European Journal of Sport Science, 2*(1), 1–14.

Weinberg, R. S., Burke, K., & Jackson, A. (1997). Coaches and players' perceptions of goal setting in junior tennis: An exploratory investigation. *The Sport Psychologist, 11,* 426–439.

Weinberg, R. S., Burton, D., Yukelson, D., & Weigand, D. (1993). Goal setting in competitive sport: An exploratory investigation of practices of collegiate athletes. *The Sport Psychologist, 7,* 275–289.

Weinberg, R. S., Burton, D., Yukelson, D., & Weigand, D. (2000). Perceived goal setting practices of Olympic athletes: An exploratory investigation. *The Sport Psychologist, 14,* 279–295.

Weinberg, R. S., Butt, J., & Knight, B. (2001). High school coaches' perceptions of the process of goal setting. *The Sport Psychologist, 15,* 20–47.

Weinberg, R. S., Butt, J., Knight, B., & Perritt, N. (2001). Collegiate coaches' perceptions of their goal-setting practices: A qualitative investigation. *Journal of Applied Sport Psychology, 13,* 374–398.

Weinberg, R. S., & Comar, W. (1994). The effectiveness of psychological interventions in competitive sport. *Sports Medicine Journal, 18,* 406–418.

Weinberg, R. S., & Gould, D. (1999). *Foundations of sport and exercise psychology.* Champaign, IL: Human Kinetics.

Weinberg, R. S., & McDermott, M. (2002). A comparative analysis of sport and business organizations: Factors perceived critical for organizational stress. *Journal of Applied Sport Psychology, 14,* 282–298.

Weinberg, R. S., Butt, J., Knight, B., Burke, K. L., & Jackson, A. (2003). The relationship between the use and effectiveness of imagery: An exploratory investigation. *Journal of Applied Sport Psychology, 15,* 26–40.

Weinberg, R. S., & Williams, J. M. (1998). Integrating and implementing a psychological skills training program. In J. M. Williams (Ed.), *Applied sport psychology: Personal growth to peak performance* (pp. 329–358). Mountain View, CA: Mayfield Publishing Company.

Weinberg, R. S., & Williams, J. M. (2006). Intergrating and implementing a psychological skills training program. In J. M. Williams (Ed.), *Applied sport psychology: Personal growth to peak performance,* 5th ed. (pp. 425–457). St. Louis, MO: McGraw-Hill.

Weiner, B. (1972). *Theories of motivation: From mechanism to cognition.* Chicago: Rand McNally.

Weiner, B. (1979). A theory of motivation for some classroom experiences. *Journal of Educational Psychology, 71,* 3–25.

Weiner, B. (1985). An attributional theory of achievement motivation and emotion. *Psychological Review, 92,* 548–573.

Weiner, I. B. (1994). Rorschach assessment. In M. E. Maruish (Ed.), *The use of psychological testing for treatment planning and outcome assessment* (pp. 249–278). Hillsdale, NJ: Erlbaum.

Weiss, M. R. & Chaumeton, N. (1992). Motivational orientations in sport. In T. S. Horn (Ed.), *Advances in sport psychology* (pp. 61–99). Champaign, IL: Human Kinetics.

Weiss, M. R., & Horn, T. S. (1990). The relationship between children's accuracy estimates of their physical competence and achievement-related characteristics. *Research Quarterly for Exercise and Sport, 61,* 250–258.

Weiss, W. M., & Weiss, M. R. (2003). Attraction- and entrapment-based commitment among competitive female gymnasts. *Journal of Sport and Exercise Psychology, 25,* 229–247.

Weitzenhoffer, A. M. (2000). *The practice of hypnotism.* New York: John Wiley & Sons.

Welford, A. T. (1962). Arousal, channel-capacity, and decision. *Nature, 194,* 365–366.

Welford, A. T. (1965). Stress and achievement. *Australian Journal of Psychology, 17,* 1–9.

Welford, A. T. (1973). Stress and performance. *Ergonomics, 16,* 567–580.

Wertheim, L. J. (April 7, 2003). Jolt of reality. *Sports Illustrated, 98,* 68–78.

Whelan, J. P., & Meyers, A. W. (1998). An efficient measure of immediate mood state: The brief assessment of mood. Unpublished manuscript, University of Memphis.

White, R. (1959). Motivation reconsidered. The concept of competence. *Psychological Review, 66,* 297–323.

White, S., Duda, J., & Keller, M. (1998). The relationship between goal orientation and perceived purposes of sport among youth sport participants. *Journal of Sport Behavior, 21,* 474–483.

White, S. A., & Duda, J. L. (1994). The relationship of gender, level of sport involvement, and participation motivation to task and ego orientation. *International Journal of Sport Psychology, 25,* 4–18.

Whitmarsh, B. G., & Alderman, R. B. (1993). Role of psychological skills training in increasing pain tolerance. *The Sport Psychologist, 7,* 388–399.

Wickwire, T. L., Bloom, G. A., & Loughead, T. M. (2004). The environmental structure, and interaction process of elite same-sex dyadic sport teams. *The Sport Psychologist, 18,* 381–396.

Widman, G. (February 25, 2005). Temple coach Cheney to take seat for rest of regular season. http://www.usatoday.com/2005/2/25

Widmeyer, W. N., Brawley, L. R., & Carron, A. V. (1985). *The measurement of cohesion in sport teams: The group environment questionnaire.* London, Ontario: Sports Dynamics.

Widmeyer, W. N., Brawley, L. R., & Carron, A. V. (1990). The effects of group size in sport. *Journal of Sport & Exercise Psychology, 12,* 177–190.

Widmeyer, W. N., Carron, A. V., & Brawley, L. R. (1993). Group cohesion in sport and exercise. In J. M. Williams (Ed.), *Applied sport psychology: Personal growth to peak performance* (pp. 672–692). Mountain View, CA: Mayfield.

Widmeyer, W. N., & McGuire, E. J. (1997). Frequency of competion and aggression in professional ice hockey. *International Journal of Sport Psychology, 28,* 57–66.

Widmeyer, W. N., & Williams, J. M. (1991). Predicting cohesion in coaching sport. *Small Group Research, 22,* 548–570.

Wiebush, J. (1971). *Lombardi.* Chicago: Follett Publishing Company, A National Football League Book.

Wiechman, S. A., Smith, R. E., Small, F. L., & Ptacek, J. T. (2000). Masking effects of social desirability response set on relations between psychosocial factors and sport injuries: A methodological note: *Journal of Science and Medicine in Sport, 3,* 194–202.

Wiese-Bjornstal, D. M., Smith, A. M., & LaMott, E. E. (1995). A model of psychologic response to athletic injury and rehabilitation. *Athletic Training: Sports Health Care Perspectives, 1,* 17–30.

Wiese-Bjornstal, D. M., Smith, A. M., Shaffer, S. M., & Morrey, M. A. (1998). An integrated model of response to sport injury: Psychological and sociological dynamics. *Journal of Applied Sports Psychology, 10,* 46–70.

Wiggins, D. K. (1996). A history of highly competitive sport for American children. In F. L. Smoll & R. E. Smith (Eds.), *Children and youth in sport: A biopsychosocial perspective* (pp. 15–30). Madison, WI: Brown & Benchmark.

Wiggins, M. S. (1998). Anxiety intensity and direction: Preperformance temporal patterns and expectations in athletes. *Journal of Applied Sport Psychology, 10,* 201–211.

Williams, A. M., & Elliot, D. (1999). Anxiety, expertise, and visual search strategy in karate. *Journal of Sport & Exercise Psychology, 21,* 362–375.

Williams, D. M., Anderson, E. S., & Winett, R. (2004). Social cognitive predictors of creative use versus non-use among male, undergraduate, recreational resistance trainers. *Journal of Sport Behavior, 27,* 170–183.

Williams, J. M. (1980). Personality characteristics of the successful female athlete. In W. F. Straub (Ed.), *Sport psychology: An analysis of athlete behavior.* 2nd ed. (pp. 353–359). Ithaca, NY: Mouvement Publications.

Williams, J. M., & Andersen, M. B. (1998). Psychosocial antecedents of sport injury: Review and critique of the stress and injury model. *Journal of Applied Sport Psychology, 10,* 5–25.

Williams, J. M., Hogan, T., & Andersen, M. (1993). Positive states of mind and athletic injury risk. *Psychosomatic Medicine, 55,* 468–472.

Williams, J. M., Jerome, G. J., Kenow, L. J., Rogers, T. Sartain, T. A., & Darland, G. (2003). Factor structure of the Coaching Behavior Questionnaire and its relationship to athlete variables. *The Sport Psychologist, 17,* 16–34.

Williams, J. M., & Scherzer, C. B. (2003). Tracking the training and careers of graduates of advanced degree programs in sport psychology, 1994 to 1999. *Journal of Applied Sport Psychology, 15,* 335–353.

Williams, J. M., Tonymon, P., & Andersen, M. B. (1991). The effects of stressors and coping resources on anxiety and peripheral narrowing. *Journal of Applied Sport Psychology, 3*(2), 126–141.

Williams, L. (1998). Contextual influences and goal perspectives among female youth sport participants. *Research Quarterly for Sport and Exercise, 69,* 47–57.

Williams, L. R. T., & Parkin, W. A. (1980). Personality profiles of three hockey groups. *International Journal of Sport Psychology, 11,* 113–120.

Williams, M. H., (1998). *The ergogenics edge: Pushing the limits of sports performance.* Champaign, IL: Human Kinetics.

Wilson, G. S., & Steinke, J. S. (2002). Cognitive orientation, precompetition, and actual competition anxiety. *Research Quarterly for Exercise and Sport, 73,* 335–339.

Wilson, P. M., Rodgers, W. M., Fraser, S. N., & Murray, T. C. (2004). Relationships between exercise regulations and motivational consequences in university students. *Research Quarterly for Exercise and Sport, 75,* 81–91.

Wilson, P. M., Rodgers, W. M., Hall, C. R., & Gammage, K. L. (2003). Do autonomous exercise regulations underpin different types of exercise imagery? *Journal of Applied Sport Psychology, 15,* 294–306.

Wilstein, S. (November 21, 2004). Ugly sign of violent times. *Columbia Daily Tribune,* 10B.

Wines, M. (June 10, 2002). Soccer loss causes brawl in Moscow. *The New York Times,* http://www.nytimes.com/2002/6/10/

Wolpe, J. (1958). *Psychotherapy by reciprocal inhibition.* Stanford, CA: Stanford University Press.

Woodman, T., Albinson, J. G., & Hardy, L. (1997). An investigation of the zones of optimal functioning hypothesis within a multidimensional framework. *Journal of Sport & Exercise Psychology, 19,* 131–141.

Woodman, T., & Hardy, L. (2001). A case study of organizational stress in elite sport. *Journal of Applied Sport Psychology, 13,* 207–238.

Woodman, T., & Hardy, L. (2003). The relative impact of cognitive anxiety and self-confidence upon sport performances: A meta-analysis. *Journal of Sport Sciences, 21,* 443–457.

Woodworth, R. S., & Schlosberg, H. (1954). *Experimental psychology.* Revised ed. New York: Holt, Rinehart and Winston.

Wright, A., & Côté, J. (2003). A retrospective analysis of leadership development. *The Sport Psychologist, 17,* 268–291.

Wright, E. F., Voyer, D., Wright, R. D., & Roney, C. (1995). Supporting audiences and performance under pressure: The home-ice disadvantage in hockey championships. *Journal of Sport Behavior, 18,* 21–28.

Wrisberg, C. A. (1990). An interview with Pat Head Summitt. *The Sport Psychologist, 4,* 180–191.

Wrisberg, C. A., & Anshel, M. H. (1989). The effect of cognitive strategies on the free throw shooting performance of young athletes. *The Sport Psychologist, 3,* 95–104.

Wrisberg, C. A., & Pein, R. L. (1992). The preshot interval and free throw shooting accuracy: An exploratory investigation. *The Sport Psychologist, 6,* 14–23.

Wrisberg, C. A., & Shea, C. H. (1978). Shifts in attention demands and motor program utilization during motor learning. *Journal of Motor Behavior, 10,* 149–158.

Y

Yanada, H., & Hirata, H. (1970). Personality traits of students who dropped out of athletic clubs. *Proceedings of the College of Physical Education,* (5), University of Tokyo.

Yancey, D. (1999). *Eating disorders.* Brookfield, CT: Twenty-First Century Books.

Yannis, T. (1994). Planned behavior, attitude strength, role identity, and the prediction of exercise behavior. *The Sport Psychologist, 8,* 149–165.

Yates, A. (1987). Eating disorders and long distance running: The ascetic condition. *Integrated Psychiatry, 5,* 201–204.

Yates, A. (1991). *Compulsive exercise and eating disorders: Toward an integrated theory of activity.* New York: Brunner/Mazel.

Yerkes, R. M., & Dodson, J. D. (1908). The relationship of strength of stimulus to rapidity of habit formation. *Journal of Comparative Neurology and Psychology, 18,* 459–482.

Youth sport parent convicted (January 12, 2002). AP news item on Thomas Junta conviction. *New York Times,* http://www.nytimes.com/2000/1/12/

Yukelson, D. (1997). Principles of effective team building interventions in sport: A direct services approach at Penn State University. *Journal of Applied Sport Psychology, 9,* 73–96.

Yukelson, D., Weinberg, R., & Jackson, A. (1984). A multidimenisional group cohesion instrument for intercollegiate basketball teams. *Journal of Sport Psychology, 6,* 103–117.

Yukelson, D. P. (2001). Communicating effectively. In J. M. Williams (Ed.), *Applied sport psychology personal growth to peak performance* (pp. 135–149). Mountain View, CA: Mayfield publishing Company.

Yukelson, D. P. (2006). Communicating effectively. In J. M. Williams (Ed.), *Applied sport psychology-Personal growth to peak performance* (pp. 174–191). McGraw-Hill.

Z

Zaichkowsky, L. D, & Fuchs, C. (1988). Biofeedback applications in exercise and athletic performance. *Exercise and Sport Science Reviews, 16,* 381–421.

Zajonc, R. B. (1965). Social facilitation. *Science, 149,* 269–274.

Zervas, Y., & Kakkos, V. (1995). The effect of visuomotor behavior rehearsal on shooting performance of beginning archers. *International Journal of Sport Psychology, 26,* 337–347.

Zhang, J., Jensen, B. E., & Mann, B. L. (1997). Modification and revision of the leadership scale for sport. *Journal of Sport Behavior, 20,* 105–122.

Ziegler, S. G., Klinzing, J., & Williamson, K. (1982). The effects of two stress management training programs on cardiorespiratory efficiency. *Journal of Sport Psychology, 4,* 280–289.

Zientek, C. E. C., & Breakwell, G. M. (1991). Attributional schema of players before and after knowledge of game outcome. *Journal of Sport Behavior, 14,* 211–222.

Zinsser, N., Bunker, L., & Williams, J. M. (1998). Cognitive techniques for building confidence and enhancing performance. In J. M. Williams (Ed.), *Applied sport psychology: Personal growth to peak performance* (pp. 270–295). Mountain View, CA: Mayfield Publishing Company.

Zinsser, N., Bunker, L., & Williams, J. M. (2001). Cognitive techniques for building confidence and enhancing performance. In J. M. Williams (Ed.), *Applied sport psychology: Personal growth to peak performance* (pp. 284–311). Mountain View, CA: Mayfield Publishing Company.

Zinsser, N. Bunker, L., & Williams, J. M. (2006). Cognitive techniques for building confidence and enhancing performance. In J. M. Williams (Ed.), *Applied sport psychology: Personal growth to peak performance* (349–381). McGraw-Hill.

Zizzi, S. J., Deaner, H. R., & Hirschhorn, D. K. (2003). The relationship between emotional intelligence and performance. *Journal of Applied Sport Psychology, 15,* 262–269.

Name Index